BLAIR'S BRITAIN,
1997–2007

Tony Blair has dominated British political life for more than a decade. Like Margaret Thatcher before him, he has changed the terms of political debate and provoked as much condemnation as admiration. At the end of his era in power, this book presents a wide-ranging overview of the achievements and failures of the Blair governments. Bringing together Britain's most eminent academics and commentators on British politics and society, it examines the effect of the Prime Minister and his administration on the machinery of government, economic and social policy and foreign relations. Combining serious scholarship with clarity and accessibility, this book represents the authoritative verdict on the impact of the Blair years on British politics and society.

ANTHONY SELDON is Master of Wellington College and the co-founder of the Institute of Contemporary British History. He is a prominent commentator on British political leadership and the leading author on Tony Blair, having written or edited five books on him including *The Blair Effect 2001–5* (with Dennis Kavanagh, Cambridge, 2005).

BLAIR'S BRITAIN,
1997–2007

EDITED BY
ANTHONY SELDON

CAMBRIDGE
UNIVERSITY PRESS

CAMBRIDGE UNIVERSITY PRESS
Cambridge, New York, Melbourne, Madrid, Cape Town, Singapore, São Paulo, Delhi

Cambridge University Press
The Edinburgh Building, Cambridge CB2 8RU, UK

Published in the United States of America by Cambridge University Press, New York

www.cambridge.org
Information on this title: www.cambridge.org/9780521709460

© Cambridge University Press 2007

First published 2007
Reprinted 2007

Printed in the United Kingdom at the University Press, Cambridge

A catalogue record for this publication is available from the British Library

ISBN 978-0-521-88293-4 hardback
ISBN 978-0-521-70946-0 paperback

DEDICATION

This book is dedicated to
Dennis Kavanagh for twenty years'
partnership, inspiration and friendship

CONTENTS

CONTRIBUTORS

Ian Bache is Reader in Politics at the University of Sheffield. His publications include: *The Europeanization of British Politics* (co-editor, Palgrave 2006), *Politics in the European Union*, 2nd edn (co-author, Oxford University Press, 2006) and *Europeanization and Multi-level Governance: Cohesion Policy in the European Union and Britain* (forthcoming, Rowman and Littlefield).

Michael Beloff, QC, is a Master of the Bench and Treasurer-Elect of Gray's Inn. He is Senior Ordinary Appeals Judge of the Courts of Appeal of Jersey and Guernsey, and was previously a Deputy High Court Judge and Recorder of the Crown Court. He was the first Chairman of the Administrative Law Bar Association and is President of the British Association of Sport and Law. Between 1996 and 2006 he was President of Trinity College, Oxford.

Vernon Bogdanor is Professor of Government at Oxford University, Gresham Professor of Law, a Fellow of the British Academy and Honorary Fellow of the Institute for Advanced Legal Studies. He has been an adviser to a number of governments, including the Czech Republic, Hungary, Kosovo, Israel and Slovakia. His books include, *The People and the Party System: The Referendum and Electoral Reform in British Politics*, *Multi-Party Politics and the Constitution*, *Power and the People: A Guide to Constitutional Reform* and *Devolution in the United Kingdom*. He is editor of, amongst other books, *The British Constitution in the 20th Century* and *Joined-Up Government*. He is at present completing an interpretation of what he regards as our new British Constitution. He is a frequent contributor to TV, radio and the press.

Nick Bosanquet is a health economist Professor of Health Policy at Imperial College. He is consultant director of the non-party think-tank REFORM and recently acted as independent chairman of a review of health services in Cornwall. Publications include (with Professor K. Sikora) *The Economics of Cancer Care* (Cambridge University Press, 2006).

In 2007 he served on the Government Advisory Committee on a reform-cancer strategy.

Michael Clarke is the Director of the Royal United Services Institute, having formerly been, since 1995, the Professor of Defence Studies at King's College London and the founding Director of both the Centre for Defence Studies and the International Policy Institute at King's. He is an adviser to the House of Commons Defence Committee.

Philip Cowley is Professor of Parliamentary Government at the University of Nottingham. He is author of *The Rebels: How Blair Mislaid His Majority* (Politico's) and joint editor of the *Developments in British Politics* series (Palgrave).

Nicholas Crafts is Professor of Economic History at Warwick University. He previously taught at several other institutions including LSE and Oxford. His research has focused on long-run economic performance in the UK from the industrial revolution to the present day and the international historical experience of economic growth.

John Curtice is Professor of Politics at Strathclyde University. He was co-director of the British Election Study from 1983 to 1992 and has been a co-editor of the British Social Attitudes series since 1994. His previous writing includes (as co-editor) *Labour's Last Chance?* and (as co-author) *The Rise of New Labour*.

Paul Fawcett is a Doctoral Candidate at the Department of Political Science and International Studies, University of Birmingham, and a Visiting Student at the Political Science Program, Research School of Social Sciences, Australian National University.

Lawrence Freedman is Professor of War Studies and Vice-Principal (Research) at King's College London. Among his recent books are the *Official History of the Falklands Campaign, Deterrence* and *The Transformation of Strategic Affairs*.

Timothy Garton Ash is Professor of European Studies in the University of Oxford, Isaiah Berlin Professorial Fellow at St Antony's College, Oxford, and a Senior Fellow at the Hoover Institution, Stanford University. He is a columnist in *The Guardian*, a regular contributor to the *New York Review of Books*, and the author of eight books of contemporary history and political writing including, most recently, *Free World: Why a Crisis of the West Reveals the Opportunity of our Time* (Penguin, 2004).

Stephen Glaister, CBE, FICE, FTRF, FCGI, is Professor of Transport and Infrastructure at Imperial College London. He has been a member of the Board of Transport for London since July 2000. He has been adviser to the Rail Regulator, various government bodies and an adviser to Sir Rod Eddington on his Transport Study, 2006. He has published widely on transport policy and also on utilities regulation.

Richard Heffernan is a Reader in Government at the Open University and presently a Visiting Professor at the University of Notre Dame. He is the author of *New Labour and Thatcherism: Political Change in Britain* (Palgrave Macmillan) and lead editor of the Developments in British Politics series (Palgrave Macmillan).

Dennis Kavanagh is Emeritus Professor of Politics and Communications at Liverpool University. He has co-authored and co-edited a number of books with Anthony Seldon, and his most recent books are *The British General Election of 2005* (2005) and *British Politics*, 5th edn (2006).

Kunal Khatri is a graduate of the University of Oxford and LSE. He has since worked in the House of Lords as a researcher on climate change and energy policy, and is currently working as a senior researcher to Anthony Seldon on his forthcoming biography of Tony Blair, *Blair Unbound*.

Raymond Kuhn is Professor of Politics at Queen Mary, University of London. He has published widely on the politics of the British and French media, including the single-authored works *Politics and the Media in Britain* (2007) and *The Media in France* (1995). He is currently working on a new book on media policy in France in the digital age.

Iain McLean is Professor of Politics at Oxford University. He has previously worked at Warwick and Newcastle upon Tyne, and has held visiting appointments at Stanford and Yale. Born and brought up in Edinburgh, his recent work has touched on the Scottish Enlightenment (*Adam Smith, Radical and Egalitarian*, 2006) and Unionism in the United Kingdom (*State of the Union*, with Alistair McMillan, 2005).

Richard Manning has been Chair of the Development Assistance Committee of the OECD since June 2003. Before that, he spent his career in the Department for International Development and its predecessor agencies, and served as one of its Directors-General from 1996.

Frank Millar was appointed London Editor of the *Irish Times* in December 1990. The author of *David Trimble: The Price of Peace* (Liffey

Press, 2004), he was named Irish Print Journalist of the Year for his coverage of the negotiation of the Belfast Agreement in 1998.

Tim Newburn is Professor of Criminology and Social Policy, and Director of the Mannheim Centre of Criminology, at the London School of Economics. He is the author of numerous books, the most recent of which are *Plural Policing* (edited with Trevor Jones, Routledge, 2006); *The Politics of Crime Control* (edited with Paul Rock, Oxford University Press, 2006); *Policy Transfer and Criminal Justice* (with Trevor Jones, Open University Press, 2007); and *The Handbook of Criminal Investigation* (edited with Tom Williamson and Alan Wright, Willan, 2007). He is currently President of the British Society of Criminology.

Philip Norton (Lord Norton of Louth) is Professor of Government and Director of the Centre for Legislative Studies at the University of Hull. His publications include twenty-six books and over a hundred book chapters and journal articles. He is President of the Politics Association and Vice-President of the Political Studies Association.

Neill Nugent is Professor of Politics and Jean Monnet Professor of European Integration at Manchester Metropolitan University. Amongst his recent publications are *The Government and Politics of the European Union*, 6th edn, (Palgrave Macmillan, 2006) and *European Union Enlargement* (editor, Palgrave Macmillan, 2004). He is Visiting Professor at the Centre of European Integration at the University of Bonn and also at the College of Europe in Bruges.

John O'Leary is a freelance journalist and education consultant. He edited the *Times Higher Education Supplement* from June 2002 until March 2007 and was previously Education Editor of *The Times*, having joined the paper in 1990 as Higher Education Correspondent. He edits *The Times Good University Guide*, which has been published annually since 1993, and the *Guide to the World's Top Universities*, first published in 2006.

Ben Page was named one of the '100 most influential people in the public sector' by *The Guardian* newspaper. He is Chairman of the Ipsos MORI Social Research Institute. He joined MORI in 1987 after graduating in Modern History from St John's College Oxford in 1986. He has worked closely with ministers and senior policymakers across government since 1992, working with Downing Street, the Cabinet Office and many departments and local public services.

Robert Reiner is Professor of Criminology in the Law Department, London School of Economics. His most recent books are: *The Politics of the Police*, 3rd edn (Oxford University Press 2000); (ed. with M. Maguire and R. Morgan) *The Oxford Handbook of Criminology*, 4th edn (Oxford University Press, 2007); *Law and Order: An Honest Citizen's Guide to Crime and Control* (Polity, 2007). He was President of the British Society of Criminology from 1993 to 1996.

Rob Rhodes is Director of the Research School of Social Sciences and Distinguished Professor of Political Science at the Australian National University. His recent books include *The Oxford Handbook of Political Institutions* (joint editor, 2006), and *Governance Stories* (with Mark Bevir, 2006).

Anthony Seldon is Master at Wellington College. He edits and writes in his spare time.

Peter Sinclair is Professor of Economics at the University of Birmingham. He has held visiting professorships at the University of British Columbia , Queen's (Ontario) and Witwatersrand. His previous posts include Director of the Centre for Central Banking Studies at the Bank of England, and Fellow and Tutor in Economics at Brasenose College, Oxford. Much of his research is devoted to policy issues in international, monetary and taxation economics.

Alan Smithers is the Professor of Education and Director of the Centre for Education and Employment Research at the University of Buckingham. He has previously held chairs at the University of Liverpool, Brunel University and the University of Manchester. Throughout Blair's tenure he has been special adviser to the Commons Education Select Committee.

Sarah Spencer, CBE, is Associate Director of the Centre on Migration, Policy and Society at the University of Oxford and a Visiting Professor at the Human Rights Centre, University of Essex. She is Chair of the Equality and Diversity Forum and a former Deputy Chair of the Commission for Racial Equality. Her books include *The Politics of Migration: Managing Opportunity, Conflict and Change* (2003).

Philip Stephens is Associate Editor of the *Financial Times* and a senior political and international affairs commentator. He is a well-known author, commentator and broadcaster. He is the author of *Politics and the Pound* (Macmillan), a study of the British government's exchange rate management and its relations with Europe since 1979, and of *Tony Blair*

(Viking/Politico's), a biography of the British Prime Minister. He is a Fulbright Fellow and winner of the 2002 David Watt Prize for outstanding political journalism. He was named in 2005 as Political Journalist of the Year by the Political Studies Association. He is a governor of the Ditchley Foundation and Treasurer of the Franco-British Colloque.

Kitty Stewart is Research Fellow at the Centre for Analysis of Social Exclusion (CASE) at the London School of Economics and Political Science. Her current research interests include child poverty, international comparisons of policy and outcomes relating to poverty and inequality, and employment trajectories for low-skilled workers. She is the co-editor, with John Hills, of *A More Equal Society? New Labour, Poverty, Inequality and Exclusion* (2005).

Robert Taylor is a research associate at the Centre for Economic Performance at the London School of Economics and Political Science and Associate Visitor at Nuffield College, Oxford. Former employment editor of the *Financial Times* and labour editor of *The Observer*, he has written four books on trade unions and labour markets. He is writing a history of the parliamentary Labour Party.

Tony Travers is Director of LSE London at the London School of Economics. He is Expenditure Adviser to the House of Commons Education and Skills Committee and has also advised other parliamentary committees. He was a member of the Audit Commission from 1992 to 1997 and an Associate of the Kings Fund. He has published a number of books and articles about local government and cities, including *The Politics of London: Governing an Ungovernable City*.

This is the fifth volume in the series which analyses the impact of British contemporary government. The earlier volumes, often co-edited with Dennis Kavanagh, *The Thatcher Effect*, *The Major Effect*, *The Blair Effect 1997–2001* and *The Blair Effect 2001–05*, were published in 1989, 1994, 2001 and 2005, respectively. The focus of enquiry has remained always the same. What difference does a prime minister make across the water-front of policy and government? The books were inspired by the Institute (now Centre) of Contemporary British History, founded in 1986.

The formula in all five volumes has not changed. Leading authorities from academe and the commentariat were asked to address common themes in their own specialist area:

- What was the state of your area when Labour took office in May 1997?
- What was the state of the area in June 2007, when Tony Blair left office?
- What changed and why?
- How successful or effective have the changes been?
- Where relevant, why was more not achieved?
- To what extent was change driven by the Prime Minister himself, by No. 10 in general, by Gordon Brown, by other ministers, departments, think-tanks, or by any other factors?
- What has been the net 'Blair effect' in your area between 1994/7 and 2007?
- To what extent did policy mark a departure from traditional Labour (and Thatcher/Major) policy?
- Finally, how enduring might those changes prove?

Authors were presented with these questions and asked to address them, while also being encouraged to develop distinctive approaches of their own. With such a diverse team of individuals, it is unsurprising that some interpreted their brief more loosely, while others saw the questions almost as a series of short essay titles to be addressed sequentially. The timeframe was the bookends of Blair's government, since his election in

May 1997 until his departure in June 2007, while also taking heed of what he had done as party leader from July 1994 onwards. Several new chapter subjects were added to this volume, including development (covering international poverty and Africa) and climate change, neither of which featured prominently for Blair in his first two terms. Two authors, Tim Garton Ash and Philip Stephens, offer short commentaries at the end of the book, and I write a brief concluding essay looking at Blair's personal achievement and why it came so late in his premiership.

Books in this series aim to be scrupulously non-party political. Where individual authors have particular political persuasions, I sought to balance them by others with alternative outlooks. It is hard to achieve a clear perspective on governments on the cusp of their ending. The challenge is heightened, but made much more rewarding, if they were unpopular and controversial, as was the case with the Blair government, above all for taking Britain into a highly unpopular and contentious war. The task was all the more fascinating, and necessary, when the principal political resistance came not from the opposition parties, but from the Prime Minister's own party.

This book aims to achieve a balanced perspective not only on the man but also his government. As such, the hope is that it will not only be interesting in 2007 and 2008, but also in 2017 and 2032, on the twenty-fifth anniversary of Blair's departure. Experience shows that judgements of contemporary history can be of enduring value, not only for describing how a government looked at the time, but also long after. All history is contemporary history, because every new generation judges the past afresh.

Finally, I would like to thank the authors for being so punctilious and pleasant to work with, to Julia Harris for being such an outstanding editor's assistant, for John Haslam, Liz Davey and the team at Cambridge University Press for making the book's production a pleasure, to my Blair biography team, Peter Snowdon, Daniel Collings, Rob McNamara, and Susanna Sharpe for excellent back-up and particularly to Kunal Khatri for bringing the book together in the final stages, to Tom Lowe for final checking, to Dennis Kavanagh to whom I dedicate this book, and finally to my colleagues and governors at Wellington College for being so understanding and stimulating throughout.

PART I

Politics and government

1

The Blair premiership

DENNIS KAVANAGH

There is no doubt that Tony Blair has been a considerable figure in British and Labour party politics. He led Labour to three successive general election victories and is the party's greatest election winner. His governments form one of three successful progressive administrations since 1906. He has been a successful Prime Minster, who has set a new path for the public services and leaves Britain a better place than he found it in 1997.

But beyond those accomplishments, how considerable a figure he was and whether he could have left a larger mark are still unresolved questions, and this after more than a dozen biographies and hundreds of essays and articles. The interest has been and continues to be remarkable. Of prime ministers over the last century only Lloyd George, Churchill and Thatcher have commanded such attention. In that respect at least Blair is in the top rank.

To disappoint was probably always going to be Blair's fate, no matter how successful he was. In 1997 the opportunities seemed so immense. Of all the post-war new governments (1945, 1951, 1964, 1970, 1974 and 1979) none was as fortunate as Labour in 1997. Virtually all were hampered from the outset by a weak economy and/or a narrow or non-existent majority in parliament. But in 1997 Tony Blair was blessed with a strong economy and a large majority in the House of Commons. The Labour Party and the cabinet were gratified that their hunger for office had at long last been satisfied and many attributed it to Blair's strong leadership. Brussels and the EU capitals looked forward to the young dynamic Prime Minister who would at long last positively engage with the EU. Blair also had good relations with the US President. For the first time in a general election Labour had been backed by a majority of the national newspapers. And the Conservative opposition was exhausted, divided and discredited. The bar for evaluation was set high.

A second reason for inevitable disappointment was the exaggerated sense of excitement and expectation in May 1997. Some of this was whipped up by the incontinent rhetoric of Blair and his colleagues and some by an uncritical media. But none of the advantages mentioned above render such challenges as, say, family breakdown, declining economic competitiveness or climate change, any easier to tackle.

Harold Wilson in 1964 was the last Prime Minister to enter office after his party had been out of power for thirteen years and amid great expectations. He had also promised to build a 'new Britain', spoke of 'modernisation', and planned to make No. 10 'a powerhouse'. It was not a comforting precedent.

I

What did Blair find when he entered office? First, the reputation of the premiership was at one of its low periods. John Major, beset by a tiny and unreliable majority, and badly damaged by the experience of British membership of the ERM and attacks by his predecessor and much of the Conservative press, lacked authority. Blair taunted him at the despatch box in 1995: 'I lead my party – he follows his.' Much of his electoral appeal lay in his promise of strong leadership and willingness to challenge his party. Major was very much a negative model for Blair.

But from 1994 when he became party leader he was also reacting to previous Labour prime ministers. He noted (or was told) that Harold Wilson and James Callaghan had to balance cabinet appointments between left and right in the interest of party unity, that they were forced to negotiate with the NEC and the trades unions over key policies and that a new Labour prime minister had to appoint to cabinet members of the shadow cabinet elected by MPs. Labour leaders were constrained by the party's constitution and ethos, both shaped when Labour was a minor party with little prospect of ever forming a government. There was a certain immobilism about Labour in the 1970s (Blair joined the party in 1975) and 1980s. A number of policies were simply 'unthinkable' for a Labour leader, including rewriting Clause 4 of the party constitution, which committed the party to widespread public ownership.

Labour rode the public mood for change on many fronts in 1997. There was widespread agreement on the need for constitutional reform, more investment in and reform of the core public services and investment in the country's infrastructure, improving Britain's poor relations with Europe (although this did not involve a wish for more integration) and ending the sleaze associated with the outgoing Conservative government. But, in other respects, notably economic management, there was no great call for change. Overall, voters concluded that the Conservatives after eighteen years in office had outstayed their welcome and thought it was time to give Labour a chance. Blair offered change but with reassurance. Other chapters in the book examine the extent to which Blair ended in credit on the above.

Not everything started with Blair. He inherited most of his constitutional programme from the previous Labour leader John Smith. Indeed, Andrew Gamble has argued that the programme was less a new agenda than the completion of an agenda dating back a hundred years. His achievement in bringing peace and a semblance of 'normal politics' to Northern Ireland built on the work begun by John Major. Gordon Brown's successful low-inflation policies continued the approach of the previous government; Peter Riddell suggested that an economist from Mars 'would conclude that the same government had been in charge throughout the second half of the 1990s'.

There is a certain shape and character to Blair's three terms of office. He has expressed disappointment with the first 1997–2001 term. This was when his political capital was at his highest but by 2001 he had little to show for it, beyond preparing for and winning a second term. The public service reform agenda hardly existed, certainly in the form of increasing choice and diversity. The Conservatives' health service internal market and city technology colleges were scrapped, before being effectively re-created in the second and third terms with different names – adversary politics at its worst. There were many 'headline- catching initiatives' and No. 10 and ministers acquired a reputation for putting presentation before substance. In the first twelve months ministers created nearly 200 task forces, inquiries and Royal Commissions; most proved to be substitutes for action.

Blair planned for the second term to be about 'delivery' of the reforms and improvements in public services. Instead he was thrown off course by the 9/11 attack on the Twin Towers and the consequent war on terror, Iraq, and a running battle with Gordon Brown over the succession and policy. He reached a stage when he thought about standing down in 2002 and eventually promised in September 2004 that, if elected again at the 2005 general election, he would not serve beyond a third term. Lack of progress in Iraq and controversy over whether Blair had lied or misused the intelligence to make the case for war was deeply damaging to him personally and politically. He continued to struggle with reform but with depleted political capital and facing increasingly rebellious Labour MPs.

In the third term an attempted coup by Labour MPs in September 2006 confirmed in his own mind a decision he had already made in May of that year to go in the summer of 2007. But he pressed on with reforms of pensions, energy, disability benefits, criminal justice, and trust schools (relying on the support of Conservative MPs). At the end there was a smooth and orderly handover to Gordon Brown and the Labour left had been so marginalised in parliament that it could not raise the forty-two MPs necessary to nominate a candidate to force a leadership election.

Blair speaks with pride of his record over ten years in office and expresses confidence that the ideas of New Labour are now accepted across the main political parties. But he might reflect that he could have done more if: (a) his relationship with his Chancellor had been more harmonious or if the latter had been willing to defer to his authority; (b) if he (alone among leaders of social democratic parties) had not allied himself so closely over the war on terror and Iraq with President Bush and his neo-conservative team; and (c) been bolder in his reform of public services much earlier.

II

Blair's ideas about the premiership were shaped more positively by his experience as Leader of the Opposition. His leadership as Prime Minister was marked by:

a. a stronger political direction from No. 10, substantially increasing the size and influence of the political office, policy unit and press office. The number of political appointees in No. 10 grew from 8 to 28.

b. new units, focusing on policy innovation and implementation, such as the delivery unit and strategy unit, and an expanded Cabinet Office. The Cabinet Office focused more on driving through No. 10's agenda and less on acting as a broker between departments and overseeing the smooth working of the cabinet system. A senior No. 10 figure said to the author in 1998: 'We want the Cabinet Secretary [then Sir Richard Wilson] to be our chief whip in Whitehall.'

c. a larger and much stronger media apparatus, eventually leading to the creation of a Strategic Communications Unit and Research and Intelligence Unit to complement the Press Office. To cope with the 24/7 media, the communications team was more political and proactive than hitherto. Blair attributed New Labour's success as a campaigning operation in large part to the effectiveness of its communications arm.

d. listening to voters rather than the party. As in opposition he relied on the views of the median voter (obviously to the political right of Labour trade union activists and the annual party conference). He used focus groups and opinion polls, rather than party institutions, to keep him in touch with the 'centre ground'.

As leader Blair in part built on existing trends and in part responded to changing circumstances, a mix of pressures and opportunities. Richard Rose[1] argues that he has fashioned a new-style premiership. The features include: working with circles of confidants and advisers in No. 10, regarding cabinet and formal meetings as often unproductive; spending less time in the House of Commons; taking more time to manage the media and appear live on television. Blair's scant regard for cabinet in the first term was shown by the brevity of meetings. The importance he attached to parliament is reflected in how little time he spent there, although that continued a trend among prime ministers over recent decades.

Over time Blair has learnt the limits of prime ministerial leadership. Academic analysis now shares with business models less interest in zero-sum ideas of power and more in models in which the leader and his team share power with other key actors (such as ministers, senior officials, the Treasury, the Cabinet Office, etc.) in a core executive; resources are traded and the relative power of the Prime Minister and other actors depends on the particular issue and circumstances.

For such a so-called presidential figure Blair was blocked in key areas. The Chancellor carved out a measure of autonomy hardly ever achieved by a minister. Certain departments were regarded as Brown preserves, certain ministers regarded as Brownites, and No. 10 staff complained that on occasions there was almost a separate whipping operation. Across much domestic policy Blair shared power with Gordon Brown. Brown unilaterally took control of entry to the euro ('our destiny', according to Blair) by announcing that it would be an economic decision. The Treasury decided on the five tests that had to be satisfied for entry and conducted the studies. Blair found Brown as niggardly in providing information on the work as he was in giving advance details of his Budgets. According to well-placed sources Blair was so committed to entry that he offered to surrender the premiership in return for Brown's support for membership. He failed to achieve entry, a policy central to his goal of putting Britain at the heart of EU decision-making.

---

[1] Richard Rose, *The Prime Minister in a Shrinking World* (Cambridge: Polity, 2001).

In domestic policy the Treasury and No. 10 were often at odds after 2001. Brown's opposition to foundation hospitals (involving a letter circulated to the cabinet outlining his disagreement with the Prime Minister's policy) and academy schools meant that the final schemes were severely watered down. In both health and education Treasury opposition to Blair's agenda of diversity of suppliers and choice for consumers was supported by a number of Labour MPs. Not until 2006 and 2007 was Blair able to curb Brown's passion for means testing and tax credits and effect compromises on pensions and disability benefits.

Not surprisingly, Blair was pressed by many of his entourage to demonstrate his authority and sack or move Brown from the Treasury. Some of his staff in late 2004 and early 2005 argued that this would be necessary if he was to rescue or further his domestic reform agenda. Blair and his staff held discussions about moving Brown and plans were prepared to split the Treasury after the 2005 general election. Blair did not act, regarding both as politically impossible after the 2005 general election: one reason for his feeling deflated for a time after the election result was that it had not given him the mandate to move against the Chancellor. His unwillingness to move was remarkable testimony to Brown's power. Only the Wilson–Callaghan government (1974–9) and Churchill's administration (1951–5) had a single Chancellor. Margaret Thatcher had three and Major two Chancellors. What was sometimes called a dual premiership was inherently destabilising; the tensions between the rival tribes of No. 10 and No. 11 wasted so much energy. A senior official who worked closely for both men reflected sadly; 'When you think of everything they could have done together the conflict preventing them is just the most extraordinary waste.'

Despite the continued attempts to resource No. 10 so that it could drive departments and draw up public service targets, impose reviews of policy under Lord Birt, and hold bimonthly bilaterals with ministers in key departments to monitor progress, Blair was often frustrated. Senior officials sometimes commented that Blair (who had no prior departmental experience) and his staff seemed to have little idea of how departments worked. The departments are better resourced in staff, budgets and expertise than No. 10 and after the departure of Derek Scott from No. 10 in 2003 Blair had no economic adviser. He had become aware of the limits of central control. Charles Leadbeater and Peter Hyman, both of whom had worked for Blair, reported after they left Downing Street on how the great expectations of No. 10 are often wrecked on the front line. Appearing before the Liaison Committee in 2002 Blair admitted: 'After five years in government. I know only too well that passing legislation or making speeches will not solve vandalism on estates, raise standards in secondary schools, look after the elderly at risk. Indeed the state can sometimes become part of the problem.' He could echo Hotspur's rejoinder to Glendower's 'I can call spirits from the very deep', 'But will they come when you do call for them?'

Over twenty years ago Sir John Hoskyns, the first head of Margaret Thatcher's Policy Unit, challenged the belief that the gene pool of the majority party in the House of Commons was large enough to find the staff to run a modern government. Blair may have had less ministerial talent at his disposal than Attlee (with Bevin, Bevan, Cripps, Morrison and Gaitskell) or Thatcher (with Howe, Hurd, Lawson, Clarke, Patten and Heseltine). He had Brown and for a time Blunkett, but after that it is hard to make a positive case for the rest.

The drive for public service reform came almost entirely from No. 10. He was aided by a few ministers and relied heavily on his principal private secretaries, Jeremy Heywood and Ivan Rodgers, on Policy Unit heads Andrew (now Lord) Adonis and David Bennett, and on advisers Simon Stevens and Paul Corrigan for health. In forming his new government in 2001 he was determined to tackle the reform of public services, and he promised ministers in four key departments that they would remain in post for the duration of the parliament. Within two years three had, for various reasons, left and the fourth did not stay the course.

Blair, the greatest election winner in the party's history, has been an outstanding coalition-builder. Successful electoral leaders bring 'added value' to the party's normal vote. Since Margaret Thatcher and John Major in 1992 Conservative leaders have been unable to reach beyond the party's core vote. Until 1997 this was also a challenge for Labour, as the size of its base in the working class, trade unions and council estates was shrinking. Blair and the creators of New Labour knew that the party had to attract not only those who had left the party but those who had never voted for it. The target voters (those the party needed to win over) were female, in the south-east, homeowners, and among the aspirational working class who had switched to Margaret Thatcher. Blair has always courted the median voter. Even after ten years in office surveys report that voters still place Blair at the mid-point of the political spectrum, which is where most voters place themselves; they locate Brown and the Labour Party to the left of the centre. In the 2005 election Labour's share of the working-class vote was the same as in 1992 but was 11% higher among middle-class professionals.

Blair broke new ground for the party; his big tent could include everybody. He appealed to business and the City and cultivated the Murdoch press. Lance Price, a No. 10 press secretary, claimed that Rupert Murdoch's influence on the government at times seemed to be second only to that of Blair and Brown. Blair dispensed with ideology, proudly proclaiming that he was in favour of what works. He shamelessly borrowed from the centre-right parties to call Labour the people's party or a one-nation party.

Like a number of former premiers, he has said that he wished he had been bolder. Yet he took risks with his party over top-up tuition fees, foundation hospitals, academies, public private partnerships and of course allying Britain with such a right-wing US President. He took the party beyond its comfort zone and this was reflected in the rise of dissent among Labour MPs, as Philip Cowley shows in chapter 2.

In 1997 New Labour transformed British election campaigning. It was so successful that the Conservatives have been trying to copy it. William Hague gave each member of his shadow cabinet a copy of Philip Gould's *The Unfinished Revolution. How The Modernisers Saved the Labour Party*,[2] with the inscription, 'Know Thine Enemy'. The book became a campaign manual for the party. But it was soon clear that if Labour's support was wide it was not deep. A consequence of the decline in party loyalty is that voting ties are often conditional and held lightly; the electorate is more volatile; and more voters are inclined not to vote at all. A downside of the big tent approach has been, as his former strategy chief Geoff Mulgan points out, that the government was reluctant to tackle a number of vested interests in the media, business and the City.

Tony Blair, like Attlee and Gaitskell, also public school-educated, was not born to the Labour Party; he chose it. But his determination not to be constrained by it and his impatience with the party's democratic procedures – again (like Whitehall) he dismissed as 'process' – have helped to de-energise the party. One needs to be careful here. Mass political parties have been in decline for some years across Europe and a spell in government often results in the weakening of the party, as Labour found in 1970 and 1979 and the Conservatives by 1997. Blair's approach to election campaigning, fund-raising and policy-making has allowed little influence to the party. His tendency to 'triangulate' policy positions between Labour traditions and the opposition encouraged him to stand apart from his

---

[2] Philip Gould, *The Unfinished Revolution. How The Modernisers Saved the Labour* Party (London: Little, Brown, 1997).

party. The 'third way' was a good example of finding a way between state socialism and free market conservatism.

Cabinet government rarely thrived under Blair. Compared with his predecessors, his cabinets met less frequently, were shorter and had fewer papers before them. Starting with the Bank of England decision ('They'll back it', he told the Cabinet Secretary when explaining why there was no need to discuss the important change of policy) and the perfunctory cabinet discussion to proceed with the Dome ('Let's back Tony', said John Prescott, the Deputy Prime Minister), Blair has preferred informal discussion, often un-minuted, in what has been called 'sofa government'. He has been impatient with Whitehall commitment to what he referred dismissively as 'process'. Lord Butler's report in 2004 on the quality of the intelligence before the Iraq War complained that Blair's approach suffered from 'a lack of reasoned deliberation', too much preoccupation with presentation, and 'too much central control'. The report also noted that although there were several cabinet meetings to discuss the decision to go to war ministers rarely saw the high-quality papers written by officials. Perhaps because he realised that his influence was waning, he did use the cabinet more during 2004 for the five-year plans, and again during his last six months in working on six policy commissions.

The number of policy failures would provide ample material for an updated version of Paul Ormerod's *Why Most Things Fail*.[3] Over the Blair decade the Audit Commission and the House of Commons Public Accounts Committee have gathered a rich harvest of failed initiatives. Just a sample would include: expensive IT disasters; hardship caused for poor families by errors in the working families tax credit system; several costly reorganisations in the health service, schools and examination systems and the Home Office; failure to build more prisons to accommodate the rising number of offenders consequent on the scores of offences created by over fifty law-and-order measures; and the chaos caused by the introduction of the online schemes of application for training places for junior doctors.

Promising to be purer than pure in the wake of the damage that allegations of sleaze had done for the Major government, Blair made a good start with a reform of party finance. But the Ecclestone donation to party funds and the exemption of his Formula One from the ban on cigarette advertising, down to the Labour loans scandal (and keeping them secret from the party treasurer) destroyed Blair's reputation for transparency.

---

[3] Paul Ormerod, *Why Most Things Fail* (London: Faber and Faber, 2005).

Of course, Blair's government was only the latest to reward donors and lenders of funds with favours and political honours, but no previous prime minister had been so outspoken about transparency and 'cleaning up' party finance.

The degeneration of the commitment to good communications to the worst types of political 'spin' and economy with the truth has often been described by journalists and disillusioned Labour colleagues. Promises of future action and boasts of achievements were never understated. It is embarrassing to recall the double and triple counting of spending, or the '48 hours to save the NHS', Britain as 'a beacon to the world', and 'world-class services'. Ultimately it was self-defeating. The misuse of the intelligence to justify war with Iraq only further dented public confidence in the honesty of the Prime Minister. There has been a steady decline in the public's willingness to believe in either what ministers say or their integrity. Not surprisingly, in 2007 Gordon Brown, the Prime Minister-designate, and candidates for the party's deputy leadership spoke of the need to restore trust in government. It was a sad epitaph to the ten years in office.

III

Blair came to office with no experience of foreign affairs. His goals were to put Britain at the heart of the EU, including British entry to the single currency, and act as a bridge between Europe and the United States. He failed on all counts.

The decision to go to war with Iraq dominated the second half of his premiership and on his watch Britain was involved in more wars than under any other leader. Neither could have been anticipated in 1997. All prime ministers over time become more involved in what is happening abroad: it is a consequence of increasing globalisation and interdependence and the growth of so many inter-governmental institutions and summits of political heads of state and leaders. Richard Rose argues that the increasing mix of domestic and international politics has given rise to an 'intermestic premiership'. Abroad, prime ministers often play before less critical audiences than at home; there is no Leader of the Opposition and no adversarial party system. The list of prime ministers who have fallen from office because of failures in war and foreign policy is a long one: Asquith, Lloyd George, Chamberlain and Eden were direct casualties. Power was slipping away from Callaghan while he was sunning himself in Guadaloupe and the rest of the country was shivering in the winter of discontent, and power-dressed Margaret Thatcher was being feted in Paris when she learnt that she had failed to achieve a decisive winning margin in her party's leadership contest. History, as Blair often says, will decide, but it has not been kinder to Chamberlain and appeasement or to Eden and Suez.

For many commentators, voters and members of the Labour Party Iraq has been a disaster and blighted Blair's premiership. Indeed harsher critics see it as emblematic of his entire premiership. The decision to go to war met significant opposition from the public and Labour MPs but was backed by the cabinet – except for Robin Cook – and parliament. Yet it was very much Blair's personal decision and he has never apologised for it. He still believes that at the time it was the right thing to do. Iraq is discussed in many of the following chapters but what is remarkable is how Blair was able to compartmentalise the war and its fall-out. In spite of the damage it continued to do to him and his policies he remained throughout committed to his reform programme. Down to the final months there was no slackening of his energy or his impatience with departments (notably the Home Office) that he thought were not performing.

But many of the causes he held dear and even hoped that Iraq might advance have actually been harmed. He has ended up with a huge deficit. Many of his party and much of the public have become negative about Britain's relationship with the US. Blair has been criticised for being too supine towards President Bush, not offering a more independent voice and not exercising more leverage, particularly over the Middle East and post-war planning for Iraq. The war has set back his case for liberal interventionism against 'rogue' states (advanced in his Chicago speech in 1999). It is now harder for the US or Britain, even if they were so inclined, to intervene or try to mobilise the international community to do so. The war has further radicalised Muslims across the world and probably increased the threat of terrorism. In his closeness to Bush, Blair damaged Britain's relations with Germany and France and ruined his hopes of acting as a bridge between the EU and US. In future, the British public, parliament and cabinet are more likely to be more sceptical about the intelligence a prime minister presents when making the case for war. And, as Andrew Gamble has argued,[4] Britain is no nearer to resolving its international role between the poles of Europe and the United States. And of course Blair had lost so much of the political capital he needed when he turned his attention to radical public service reform.

---

[4] Andrew Gamble, *Between Europe and America. The Future of British Politics* (London: Palgrave Macmillan, 2003).

Conclusion

The two agenda-setting premierships of the last sixty years have been those of Clement Attlee and Margaret Thatcher. Neither scored highly on charisma and media skills, the qualities associated with Blair. But their records have provided the bookends of modern British politics. The agenda-shaper's success is best measured by the extent to which the opposition party accepts his/her policies. The 1945 Labour government's success was seen in the Conservative acceptance of full employment, the NHS and the welfare state, and public ownership of the main utilities. The Thatcher influence was seen in Labour's gradual acceptance of so many policies they had once opposed – privatisation, levels of direct taxation, the use of the free market in public services and changes in industrial relations laws. Indeed the consolidation of the reforms led Simon Jenkins to call Blair and Brown 'Sons of Thatcher'.

This is hardly fair. Would Thatcher or Major have brought in devolution and proportional representation for non-Westminster elections, the minimum wage, the social chapter, the redistributive budgets of Gordon Brown, sought to enter the single currency or repealed Section 28? Although he accepted much of the Thatcher settlement Blair willingly presided over rises in taxation, public spending and public sector employment.

The comparison with Thatcher can be pushed further. They are the two dominant post-war premiers; they were the greatest election winners in their parties' histories, who created distinctive approaches – Thatcherism and New Labour; they were figures who stood apart from their parties but for many voters came to personify the party; and both were helped greatly by the ineptitude and internal divisions of their opponents. Thatcherism was in large part a reaction to the post-1945 Attlee settlement and the country's decline she associated with it. New Labour was, obviously, a reaction to the party's decline but also to Thatcherism.

The New Labour agenda of economic efficiency and social justice is hardly distinctive – most administrations have at least paid lip service to the goals, while differing about the means. But Blair has done much to define the common ground between the main parties. David Cameron's Conservatives, on the back of three election defeats, have explicitly accepted the mantra. By 2007 they had accepted the post-1997 constitutional changes, the minimum wage, repeal of Section 28, tuition fees in higher education, and accorded spending on public services a greater priority than tax cuts. They largely agree with the framework of the health service and secondary schools by abandoning the 2005 promises of extending grammar schools and introducing passports in health care and schooling. Blair has made the opposition party uncomfortable by taking over traditional Conservative ground on such issues as schools, anti-social behaviour orders and security. He has been willing to tackle complex and emerging issues like immigration and asylum, energy and climate change, terrorism and security, and breaking up the one-size-fits-all public services.

Politicians who retire under a cloud often say that it is for history to judge their record. Blair has said this, rather forlornly, about Iraq. They then usually give the lie to the disclaimer with their memoirs, interviews and, where possible, farewell tours. Displaying little willingness to wait for the verdict of history they try to write the first draft themselves. Winston Churchill said that history would be kind to him for he intended to write it. Judgements may change over time but it is worth noting that the reputations of most British premiers have not changed much over the years. Time has not done much to alter verdicts on, for example, Baldwin, Chamberlain, Eden, Wilson or Thatcher. Perhaps only Attlee's reputation has risen over time. Although Iraq is a huge minus my guess is that shares in Blair will also rise, albeit modestly.

2

Parliament

PHILIP COWLEY

The case for the prosecution goes something like this. Tony Blair himself was not a 'House of Commons man'. He was rarely seen there during his premiership, participating in just 8% of parliamentary votes between 1997 and 2007, a record low for any Prime Minister. He also had little understanding of, or respect for, the traditions of parliament – and would blithely demolish those practices he found inconvenient. One of his first acts as Prime Minister was to change, without any consultation, Prime Minister's Questions from two sessions a week to just a single session, thus reducing the ability of the Commons to hold him to account.

The government then carried out a string of other reforms, under the guise of 'modernisation', which yet further limited parliamentary scrutiny. Driven through by the newly established Committee on Modernisation – a committee which was, extraordinarily, chaired by a member of the cabinet – these reforms included restricting debate through the use of programming motions (effectively a regularised use of the guillotine) and a series of other procedural changes which made it harder for MPs to challenge the executive.

Matters were made worse by the behaviour of Labour MPs, who were especially acquiescent, failing in their duty to challenge the government. As well as sheep (a routine comparison), they were frequently compared to poodles, clones, robots and – most bizarrely of all – daleks. Singled out for especially acidic criticism were many of the women MPs – particularly those elected in 1997. Dismissed as 'Blair's babes', they were frequently compared to the Stepford Wives – although the Conservative MP Ann Widdecombe complained that the comparison was unfair to the Stepford Wives.

The government's damaging reforms included the upper chamber, where the House of Lords Act 1999 removed most of the hereditary peers – those who would defeat the government. These were replaced by life peers more beholden to the Prime Minister, the so-called 'Tony's cronies'. Despite their initial claims that this was just the first stage of an ongoing process of Lords reform, the government then blocked any further attempts to seriously reform the House of Lords, for fear of creating a stronger and more assertive upper House.

In short, parliament was systematically weakened under Tony Blair. The modish Power Inquiry, which reported on the state of British democracy in 2006, argued that 'the Executive in Britain is now more powerful in relation to parliament than it has been probably since the time of Walpole'.[1] Writing in *The Observer* in 2007, the journalist Henry Porter claimed that it was 'one of the assured parts of [Tony Blair's] legacy that he leaves the House of Commons in a far worse state than he found it'.[2]

This case for the prosecution is heard with such frequency that it has achieved the status of received wisdom. It would be possible to produce dozens, maybe hundreds, of examples of claims akin to those listed above, from the pages of newspapers and magazines, from within parliament itself, or from general political discourse. Yet the true picture of parliament during the Blair era was more complicated than this. *Pace* Henry Porter *et al.*, it is certainly not one of the assured parts of the Blair legacy that he left the Commons – or parliament as a whole – in a worse state than when he became Prime Minister. The true picture was messier, and more balanced, than this melancholy caricature. The process of Commons reform was more positive than many critics acknowledged. That reform was accompanied by a growing activism and rebelliousness amongst backbench Labour MPs, who became increasingly willing to defy the leadership. Labour's much maligned women MPs were also able to point to a string of achievements. Similarly, the process of Lords reform, whilst cack-handed and mismanaged, resulted in a much more active and assertive second chamber: one which was prepared to defy the government with increasing frequency and effect.

This chapter outlines the changes that occurred in parliament during the Blair decade. The combined result of these developments was that for most of its time in office the Blair government faced a partly reformed but much more assertive House of Commons and a partly reformed but much more assertive House of Lords. This was not really what it intended nor what the Prime Minister desired, but it is also a more positive picture than the government's many critics appreciated.

---

[1] *Power to the People* (London: The Power Inquiry, 2006), p. 128. You will, however, search the list of experts who gave evidence to the Inquiry in vain for anyone who actually knew anything about parliament at the time of Walpole.

[2] Henry Porter, 'Less a Servant of the People, more a Hammer of Parliament', *The Observer*, 25 February 2007.

Modernisation

Labour came to power in 1997 pledging to reform both the House of Commons and the House of Lords. Its 1997 manifesto contained a section entitled 'An effective House of Commons', which declared that the Commons was 'in need of modernisation'.[3] This had been preceded, in 1996, by a speech from Ann Taylor, then Shadow Leader of the House, in which she had claimed that 'Labour's true project for parliament' would be both to produce better legislation and to make MPs more effective at holding the executive to account. 'Awkward though it may appear to a few on our side', she argued, 'a more accountable government is a better government.'[4] A commitment to Commons reform was also part of the pre-1997 Cook–Maclennan agreement between Labour and the Liberal Democrats on the future direction of constitutional reform.

The majority of the Blair government's reforms came through the Select Committee on the Modernisation of the House of Commons, a cross-party committee of the Commons, which was established in June 1997. The Committee was established 'to consider how the practices and procedures of the House should be modernised, and to make recommendations thereon'. It proposed (and in most cases implemented) reforms encompassing changes to the timetable, to the legislative process, to select committees, to debates, to questions, and to public access. If nothing else, the activities of the Modernisation Committee showed that it *was* possible to reform the House of Commons. The Commons of 2007 was procedurally significantly different to that of 1997. As a Hansard Society study into modernisation noted: 'The changes that have been implemented stand as a tangible correction to those who assert, wrongly, that Westminster is a fossilised institution, unable or unwilling to adapt itself to changed circumstances.'[5]

More debatable though was the nature of that change. Part of the problem was that the word modernisation was itself largely meaningless. As Richard Rose pointed out in 2001, the term 'shows a preference for what is new rather than what is old, and for change against the status quo. But it did not identify what direction change should take.'[6] As a result,

[3] *Because Britain Deserves Better* (London: Labour Party, 1997), p. 33.
[4] Speech to Charter 88, 14 May 1996.
[5] Alex Brazier, Matthew Flinders and Declan McHugh, *New Politics, New Parliament? A Review of Parliamentary Modernisation since 1997* (London: Hansard Society, 2005).
[6] Richard Rose, *The Prime Minister in a Shrinking World* (London: Polity, 2001), p. 228.

modernisation meant different things to different people.[7] For some, it was about making the Commons appear more modern, stripping away some of the more antiquated procedures and practices. Others wanted to make the Commons more efficient, changing the hours and making the passage of legislation more predictable. Others wanted to make the Commons more accessible to the public. Yet others wanted to make it stronger, 'shifting the balance' – a much used phrase – between the Commons and the executive.

Partly because of the vagaries of the terminology, the record of Commons modernisation during the Blair government was decidedly mixed. The process was variously criticised for reducing the ability of the Commons to hold the government to account, for being too piecemeal, and for lacking coherence. Some of the Modernisation Committee's early proposals – such as removing the requirement for MPs to wear a top hat when making a point of order during a division – had been useful and sensible. Others – such as the introduction of the Westminster Hall debating chamber – usefully enabled greater discussion.[8] But few of the early proposals had the potential to enhance the scrutinising role of the Commons. Of the substantive reports published by the Modernisation Committee between 1997 and 2001, only two contained proposals to help enhance the power of the Commons in relation to the executive. The others were designed for cosmetic or tidying-up purposes, or for the convenience of members. As one Labour MP complained: 'I was sent here to do a job, and it has been put to me that in many ways, the proposals will make my job easier. But I was not elected to have an easy job; I was elected to scrutinise legislation.'[9] Writing at the end of the first Blair term, Philip Norton was to argue that the unfocused nature of the reforms advocated by the Modernisation Committee meant that 'the "Blair effect" on parliament appeared to be to weaken rather than strengthen it'.[10]

The direction and extent of modernisation largely depended on the agenda pursued by the Leader of the House.[11] Their stance was especially

---

[7] Tony Wright, 'Prospects for Parliamentary Reform', *Parliamentary Affairs*, 57, 2004: 867–76.

[8] Even many of the initial Conservative opponents of the scheme came around to Westminster Hall – although not the one who memorably described it as 'the Bongo Bongo parish council room above the policemen's caff' – once they saw it as constituting an improvement in the avenues open to backbenchers to debate policy.

[9] House of Commons Debates, 7 November 2000, c. 176.

[10] Philip Norton, 'Parliament', in A. Seldon (ed.), *The Blair Effect* (London: Little, Brown, 2001), p. 49.

[11] Alexandra Kelso, 'The House of Commons Modernisation Committee: Who Needs It?', *British Journal of Politics and International Relations*, 9, 2007: 139–43.

important since they chaired the Modernisation Committee. The post of Leader of the House has a dual role, being both the government's voice in the Commons but also the Commons' voice in the cabinet. Some occupants of the post gave precedence to the former, others to the latter. Ann Taylor (1997–8) began with the good intentions signalled in her Charter 88 speech, but soon failed to deliver on these early promises. Margaret Beckett (1998–2001) was even more executive-minded, and unwilling to do anything that might cause the Commons to become increasingly assertive. John Reid (2003) was only in post for a couple of months, whilst Peter Hain (2003–5) and Geoff Hoon (2005–6) both pursued reforms but not those that would have had the effect of rebalancing the Commons against the government.

The high points of modernisation came, after 2001, under two ex-Foreign Secretaries: Robin Cook who was Leader of the House between 2001 and 2003, and Jack Straw who was appointed in 2006, and who stayed in post until the end of the Blair era. Both successfully managed to pilot through significant reforms of Commons procedure and practice. Cook's reform package was the most ambitious, and he struggled to enact it in its entirety, facing opposition not least from the government whips' office.[12] His attempt to reform the way that select committee members were chosen, for example, narrowly failed, after allegations that the whips had been working behind the scenes to undermine support for them.[13] The resistance of the whips, who were afraid of losing too much control of the legislative agenda, had begun in 1997 (Blair's first Chief Whip Nick Brown was very resistant to some of Ann Taylor's suggested reforms) and ran throughout most of the Blair decade. In itself, resistance from the whips is useful evidence that not all of the proposed changes were being advanced through a desire to strengthen the executive.

Yet despite resistance, in 2002 Cook still managed to enact a more comprehensive set of reforms than would have seemed possible a year before – and far more than had been achieved in the preceding parliament. These included: more resources for select committees; payment for select committee chairs (to try to develop a parliamentary career path as an alternative to becoming a minister); more topical Parliamentary

---

[12] *Modernisation of the House of Commons: A Reform Programme for Consultation*, memorandum submitted by the Leader of the House of Commons, HC 440 (2001–2).

[13] See, for example, Alexandra Kelso, ' "Where Were the Massed Ranks of Parliamentary Reformers?" ' – "Attitudinal" and "Contextual" Approaches to Parliamentary Reform', *Journal of Legislative Studies*, 9, 2003: 57–76, or Cook's own account of his battles, in *Point of Departure* (London: Simon and Schuster, 2003).

Questions; and changes to the parliamentary timetable.[14] The reforms generated a letter to *The Times* from Michael Ryle, a former Parliamentary Clerk and one of the founders of the academic Study of Parliament Group, who argued that they brought 'almost to completion the most systematic package of parliamentary reforms for 100 years'. His letter ended: 'As a campaigner for parliamentary reform for more than 40 years, I can now retire happy.'[15]

With the benefit of hindsight, though, it is possible to be slightly more sceptical. Not all of the reforms bedded in – or achieved what had been expected. As a result of some MPs' complaints about the revised timetable (especially those involving a late ending on Mondays, followed up by an early start for committees on Tuesday mornings), the hours were partially reformed again in January 2005, with the hours of business on Tuesday reverting to those that had existed prior to October 2002.[16] The early September sittings were also practically stillborn.[17] The new carry-over facility – allowing a Bill to continue for more than one session – was restricted to a very small number of Bills. The innovation of pre-legislative scrutiny (another favourite of parliamentary reformers for years) also proved less than entirely satisfactory, remaining very much the exception rather than the rule.[18] Yet Cook's period as Leader of the House can still be characterised fairly as delivering significant changes to Commons procedure.

Jack Straw's period as Leader was noticeable for the reforms to the standing committee process. This had long been identified as one of the weak points – if not *the* weak point – in the legislative process. Standing committees were seen as overly partisan, frequently ill-informed, and almost always adding very little to the scrutiny a Bill was receiving. Straw piloted through both a change in nomenclature (from the confusing 'standing committee' to the somewhat more straightforward 'public Bill committee') and, much more importantly, in procedure, by allowing committees to receive both oral and written evidence before they began the process of scrutinising a Bill. Straw's reforms were still in their infancy

---

[14] See Philip Cowley and Mark Stuart, 'Parliament', in A. Seldon and D. Kavanagh (eds.), *The Blair Effect 2001–5* (Cambridge: Cambridge University Press, 2005).

[15] *The Times*, 5 November 2002.   [16] That is, 2.30 p.m. to 10 p.m.

[17] The Commons met for two weeks in 2003 and 2004 but conducted relatively little important business, and an attempt in 2006 to try to reintroduce regular September sittings failed by 122 votes to 354, a wide margin of 232.

[18] Jennifer Smookler, 'Making a Difference? The Effectiveness of Pre-Legislative Scrutiny', *Parliamentary Affairs*, 59, 2006: 522–35.

when Blair left office, making it difficult to assess their full impact, but they had at least the potential to do more to improve the quality of the parliamentary scrutiny of Bills than any other Commons reform in the last twenty (or more) years.[19] If the Blair effect in the first term was negative overall, the effects in the second and third terms therefore were more mixed – and contained some real advances.

It was, however, unfortunate that the process of modernisation ceased to be a cross-party initiative in any meaningful way. Many of the reforms in the 2001 parliament and after were driven through the Commons using the bulk vote of the Parliamentary Labour Party (PLP), albeit on free votes, supported by very few opposition party MPs. One of the most important in terms of its impact on the legislative process was the automatic timetabling ('programming') of legislation, which meant that each Bill went through a pre-arranged timetable of debates. Of all the reforms during the Blair era, it was the one most often cited as strengthening the executive. Ironically, the idea had come initially from those who wished to strengthen the Commons – programming was, for example, proposed by the Procedure Committee in 1985 and in two separate reports published in 1992 – when the complaint was that parliament's scrutiny of legislation was far too unstructured. But although programming began as a voluntary agreement between the usual channels, it was soon being imposed on the Commons by the bulk vote of government MPs, provoking complaints that the government was using it to stifle debate. The vote to make programming of government Bills a permanent reform saw not a single Liberal Democrat or Conservative MP vote in its favour.[20] This did little to weaken the suspicion that reforms were not aimed at improving the scrutiny of government.

Labour's modernisation reforms, therefore, were not the full-blown and enthusiastic reforms initially promised by Ann Taylor in 1996. They were half-hearted and patchy, and many did not facilitate better scrutiny of the executive. Indeed, some had the opposite effect. The Commons has certainly become more efficient in what it does, but it has not necessarily become much stronger or more effective as a result. Yet equally, it is not clear that taken overall the reforms have made the Commons weaker. Several of the modernisation reforms, especially some of those introduced since 2001, have served to enhance the role of the House of Commons.

[19] The key word here is 'potential'; it will be possible for the reforms to be fatally undermined, should they lack support in the early years of a Brown government.
[20] Votes in 2006 to introduce a communications allowance and to alter the procedures for amendments to legislation were similarly also supported by the bulk of the PLP but a mere handful of opposition MPs.

Other reforms and the rise of the constituency role

There were three other reforms in the Commons, none of which was part of the process of modernisation per se, but all of which will have longer-lasting importance than some of the more esoteric procedural reforms.

Labour's first reform was announced on 9 May 1997, and involved a change to Prime Minister's Questions, moving from two fifteen-minute slots on Tuesday and Thursday, to one half-hour slot on a Wednesday.[21] This was not explicitly outlined in the 1997 manifesto, although there had been a vague commitment to make PMQs 'more effective'. In opposition, Blair had thought the amount of preparation required twice a week a 'ridiculous use of a Prime Minister's time'.[22] The reform had the effect of narrowing the focus of the parliamentary week as well as occasionally making PMQs less topical; some MPs also felt it contributed to a lessening of televised coverage of the Commons. However, although this was not the rationale of the reform, the new half-hour sessions also allowed greater persistence in questioning, something skilled parliamentary performers, most notably William Hague between 1997 and 2001, were able to use to their advantage. As a result Tony Blair endured some difficult sessions in the 'more effective' PMQs.

The second reform was Tony Blair's decision to appear before the Liaison Committee – the committee consisting of the chairs of the other select committees – twice a year. The first meeting took place in July 2002, and his appearances lasted for two and a half hours at a time, during which he was quizzed by the MPs in depth. Each session covered a different theme or set of themes, with the Prime Minister knowing in advance the subjects to be covered but not the exact questions. These sessions did not attract the attention that they deserved, partly because Tony Blair proved rather good at answering or deflecting the MPs' questions, and so the committee rarely landed any heavy blows. But the innovation remained considerable. It represented a significant advance in the scrutiny of the Prime Minister: it was the first time for sixty-five years that a Prime Minister had been before a select committee – and it will now be very difficult for any future Prime Minister to refuse to attend such meetings. It is also difficult to think of any other world leader who would appear, alone and unaided, before their senior parliamentarians for two and a half hours.

---

[21] In 2002 PMQs moved to noon on a Wednesday, instead of the traditional 3 p.m., in a bid to generate better media coverage.

[22] Derek Draper, *Blair's Hundred Days* (London: Faber and Faber, 1997), p. 36.

The third significant reform occurred in late 2004, and was effectively forced onto the Commons as a result of other government legislation. Anticipating the coming into force of the Freedom of Information Act in January 2005, the House of Commons authorities published details of the expenditure claims made by each MP. A further reform in 2007 published more detailed breakdowns of the data, indicating how much MPs spent on various types of travel. The first batch of figures revealed that MPs claimed a total of just over £78 million in allowances and expenses between April 2003 and March 2004. By October 2006, the figure for 2005–6 had risen to 86.8 million, an average of £131,000 per MP.

Press coverage was not positive, with newspapers depicting MPs as a 'bunch of thieving, fiddling, wasteful, good for nothing, feather-bedded spongers', languishing in the Palace of 'Wasteminster'. Most headlines talked of MPs getting an extra £100,000-plus on top of their salary. Press coverage was even more hostile in 2007 when there was an attempt to exempt parliament from the Freedom of Information Act. But anyone giving the figures even a cursory glance could see that most of the expenditure did not consist of 'expenses' in the way that the phrase was normally understood. The bulk of the money went on staff costs, office space, and stationery and travel expenses – along with allowances for second homes if the MP lived outside London. Rather than seeing them as an example of MPs corruptly trousering taxpayers' money, the expenses are better seen as evidence of the continuing development of the constituency role of British MPs.

This development predates the Blair era, but the amount of time and money spent by MPs engaging with the constituency grew during the Blair years. The large influx of (mostly Labour) MPs elected in both 1997 and 2001 were especially constituency focused, not least as a result of Labour's key seat strategy which emphasised local campaigning.[23] A survey of the 1997 intake found that 86% ranked 'being a good constituency member' as the most important role of an MP, compared to just 13% who thought 'checking the executive' was the most important task. By 2005 this constituency focus had also spread to the large Conservative intake elected in that year's election. One study into the 2005 intake discovered that they

---

[23] This tendency was enhanced during the early years of the Blair government by the practice of allowing MPs – especially those in marginal seats – to spend extended periods away from Westminster, 'digging in' to the constituency. See Ron Johnston, Philip Cowley, Charles Pattie and Mark Stuart, 'Voting in the House or Wooing the Voters at Home: Labour MPs and the 2001 General Election Campaign', *Journal of Legislative Studies*, 8, 2002: 9–22.

reported spending a full 49% of their time on constituency work.[24] Factor in some of the time the research allocated to 'other' tasks – which included constituency-facing work – and the most recently elected batch of MPs spend more than half of their time and energy looking away from Westminster and to their constituencies. It is possible simultaneously to value the constituency link (and it is valued by both MPs and constituents) and still think that it is now in danger of growing out of all proportion. A modernisation committee investigation into the role of the backbencher in 2006 noted that the 'primary' role of the MP was at Westminster. But this was by then more an aspiration, and a call for a refocusing of priorities, than it was a statement of fact.

Backbench behaviour

A key part of the thesis of parliamentary decline under Tony Blair was the belief that there was an increasing lack of independence amongst backbench MPs – from Roy Hattersley's claim that Labour MPs were 'the most supine Members of Parliament in British history' to the belief of the Power Inquiry that the whips 'have enforced party discipline more forcefully and fully than they did in the past'.[25] Yet there is simply no evidence that party cohesion today is higher than it was in the past. Rather the opposite: there is plenty of evidence that MPs today are more independent-minded and willing to defy their whips than they used to be. In the sixty-plus years of the post-war era – the period for which we have the most reliable data – cohesion was at its highest at Westminster in the 1950s.[26] There were two whole sessions in the 1950s during which not a single Conservative MP voted against their whip. Tony Blair's whips would have sold their souls for that sort of discipline.

It is certainly true that Tony Blair wanted his MPs to behave in a cohesive and disciplined way. Unity was supposed to be one of the defining characteristics of New Labour – it was supposed to be what distinguished it both from Old Labour and from John Major's Conservatives. In his first speech to the Parliamentary Labour Party after the 1997 election (which had to be held in Church House as there was no room at Westminster large enough to hold the massed ranks of Labour MPs), Tony Blair

---

[24] Gemma Rosenblatt, *A Year in the Life: From Member of Public to Member of Parliament* (London: Hansard Society, 2006), pp. 31–2.

[25] *The Times*, 3 November 2005; *Power to the People*, p. 133.

[26] See Philip Norton, *Dissension in the House of Commons, 1945–1974* (London: Macmillan, 1975).

emphasised the need for party discipline. Look at the Tories, he said, and
see what happened to them. 'They were all swept away, rebels and loyalists alike. Of course, speak your minds. But realise why you are here: you
are here because of the Labour Party under which you fought.' And for a
short while, it appeared the Prime Minister had got his wish, as Labour
MPs acquired a widespread reputation for levels of discipline that would
have stunned previous Labour leaders.[27]

But any initial self-discipline soon wore off, and the decade following
Blair's Church House speech saw the PLP break a series of historical
records for dissent. The 2001 parliament, for example, can lay claim to
being the most rebellious parliament in the post-war era – seeing a rebellion by Labour MPs in 21% of divisions.[28] The enormous rebellion in
March 2003, when 139 Labour MPs voted against the Iraq War, was the
largest rebellion against the party whip seen under *any* party on *any* issue
for 150 years. To find a larger backbench revolt than Iraq, you have to go
back to the revolt over the Corn Laws in the middle of the nineteenth
century, when the franchise was enjoyed by just 5% of the population, and
before anything that resembled modern political parties had been formed.
In addition, the Blair era witnessed the largest Labour rebellion ever in
government over education policy (top-up fees), heath policy (foundation hospitals), and defence policy (Trident).[29] One of the Conservatives'
'New Labour, New Danger' ads prior to 1997 had tried to imagine what life
would be like under Labour – and included a sentence about a rebellion
involving 'fifty Labour MPs'. There were plenty of occasions during the
Blair era when a mere fifty would have been a relief for the whips.

In part, the rise in backbench dissent was merely the inevitable
product of being in office continually for ten years – a phenomenon that
would be recognised by most previous Prime Ministers. Just four years
into the Blair governments, one senior whip noted that the government
were already getting trouble from what he termed the three dis's: the dissidents, the dismissed, and the disgruntled. Of these three groups, the last
two inevitably grew over time, as MPs left government or failed to achieve
what they felt they deserved. Ironically, given what was to come, the

---

[27] Even in the first Blair term, though, when the PLP was acquiring this reputation for bovine
loyalty, the reality was more complicated, with the PLP being more rebellious than was
widely realised. See Philip Cowley, *Revolts and Rebellions: Parliamentary Voting under
Blair* (London: Politico's, 2002).
[28] See Philip Cowley, *The Rebels: How Blair Mislaid his Majority* (London: Politico's, 2005).
[29] The revolts included the (joint-)largest rebellion at second reading since 1945 (top-up
fees) and the largest rebellion at third reading ever against a Labour government (schools
reform).

whips attempted an ambitious long-term strategy, trying to look ahead to the third term: the goal of the second term was supposed to be to nurture good relationships with backbenchers and to prevent the habit of rebellion from becoming too widespread, so that once the majority fell in the third term (as they assumed it would), the government would have credit to fall back on with their backbenchers. Yet the range of controversial policies presented to the Commons during the second term blew this strategy out of the water. Instead of being able to build up goodwill for the third term, the whips frequently found themselves using it up as they struggled to get legislation through the Commons. The rise in backbench dissent was therefore at least as much a consequence of the Blair style of government – with Labour MPs growing increasingly irritated by his habit of dropping fully formed policies on them and expecting their automatic wholehearted support – as it was an inevitable consequence of the government's longevity.

Predictions from within the leadership that the smaller majority after 2005 would reduce dissent ('concentrate the minds') proved an example of wishful thinking.[30] The first session of the 2005 parliament saw Labour MPs rebel in 28% of divisions, easily eclipsing what had until recently been the most rebellious first session of the post-war era, the 1992–3 session (a revolt in 23% of divisions) when John Major had struggled so terribly with the Maastricht legislation. The government went down to four Commons defeats in one session – two on anti-terrorism legislation, two on racial and religious hatred.[31] John Major's much-derided Tories had suffered just four defeats as a result of backbench dissent on whipped votes in the five years between 1992 and 1997. The third Blair term thus managed to achieve in its first year what it took Major five years to do, despite having a majority three times the size. It also scraped past other votes with minuscule majorities; won other votes thanks to a series of retreats and deals; and won yet others only thanks to the support of the Conservatives. Three key policies of the Blair era only passed the Commons thanks to Conservative support: encompassing foreign policy (Iraq), domestic policy (schools reform) and defence (Trident).

[30] Philip Cowley and Mark Stuart, *Dissension Amongst the Parliamentary Labour Party, 2005–2006: A Data Handbook, 2006* (available from www.revolts.co.uk).

[31] The defeats are explained in Richard Kelly, Oonagh Gay and Philip Cowley, 'Parliament: The House of Commons', in M. Rush and P. Giddings (eds.), *The Palgrave Review of British Politics 2005* (London, Palgrave, 2006), esp. pp. 106–8; and Richard Kelly, Oonagh Gay and Philip Cowley, 'Parliament: The House of Commons', in M. Rush and P. Giddings (eds.), *The Palgrave Review of British Politics 2006* (London, Palgrave, 2007), esp. pp. 102–3.

Not that he could have done much about it, but it is now clear that Tony Blair would have been better off had he been able to have his parliamentary majorities in a different order. Margaret Thatcher had a small but workable majority in her first parliament – when MPs' self-discipline is at its tightest – followed by two landslide majorities to cushion her against any tendency to increased rebellion. Tony Blair had his largest majorities first, during which rebellions became commonplace, and he then saw the cushion removed, with a majority of just sixty-six after 2005. By the end of his premiership, what one whip described as the 'threshold of rebellion' had been crossed by most Labour MPs.

Women MPs

Labour's 1997 manifesto had noted that it was 'proud to be making major strides to rectify the under-representation of women in public life'. Largely as a result of its policy of All-Women Shortlists (AWS), the 1997 election saw a dramatic increase in the number of women MPs – up to 120, 18% of the House of Commons – with all but nineteen of them on the Labour benches. The lack of AWS at the subsequent election (the policy had been declared illegal) then led to a slight drop in the number of women MPs in 2001 – the first time female representation in the Commons had declined since 1979 – and prompted legislative action following the election.[32] The Sexual Discrimination (Election Candidates) Act 2002 allowed parties to employ measures to increase female representation. As a result, there was another increase in 2005 – with a total of 128 women MPs elected.

In a purely descriptive sense, this has been a major change in parliament during the Blair era – and perhaps the most visible. After the 1992 election, women constituted roughly 4% of the House of Commons; after the 2005 election, the figure was 20%, a fivefold increase. Moreover, because of the asymmetric nature of this transformation – being entirely a result of a change in the Labour Party – the increase in government was even more dramatic, with almost every department of state having women ministers, many for the first time. When the Prime Minister set out his own record of achievements, shortly before his departure from No. 10, he did not mention any of the modernisation reforms – indeed, it was noticeable that he hardly mentioned parliament at all – but he did

[32] After abandoning AWS, Labour moved onto 50:50 shortlists, and out of forty seats where Labour MPs were retiring, just four constituencies selected women replacements. Byron Criddle, 'MPs and Candidates', in D. Butler and D. Kavanagh, *The British General Election of 2001* (London: Palgrave, 2002), p. 195.

single out the increase in women MPs and ministers as one of the government's achievements.

As with modernisation, however, it is one thing to note the development, another to judge it. Labour's women MPs, especially those elected in 1997, became possibly the most criticised of all Labour's MPs. Criticisms began with their appearance, moved on to their devotion to the party line, and then ended up with their supposed overall lack of achievements.[33] These complaints did not just come from those who always wanted the women to fail, but also from those who felt let down by them. As Anne Perkins wrote in *The Guardian*, two years into the Blair era: 'It was their failure to fight collectively, in particular to unite against the lone parent benefit cut that caused such a rumpus in late 1997, that earned them the reputation of betraying women who needed them for the sake of their own political futures. Most damaging, it was a view shared by more experienced women colleagues.'[34]

Yet later assessments of the effects of the influx of women MPs, particularly those from the academic community based on evidence rather than assertion, were more positive. Lovenduski noted that although it was 'notoriously difficult' to identify cause and effect, there was now a 'substantial amount of circumstantial evidence' connecting the increased women's presence to policies which address women's concerns.[35] Examples would include the enhanced priority given to policies such as childcare, maternity and paternity rights, equal pay and domestic violence.[36] Research, for example, showed differences in the type of issues raised by women MPs – providing clear evidence that the Labour women MPs performed an agenda-setting function, pushing issues up the agenda that might otherwise have been downplayed or ignored altogether.[37] This was often achieved despite obstructive (and sometimes downright offensive) behaviour from some male MPs.[38] And whilst there were

---

[33] Sarah Childs, *New Labour's Women MPs: Women Representing Women* (London: Routledge, 2004), esp. ch. 1.

[34] *The Guardian*, 29 April 1999.

[35] Joni Lovenduski, *Feminizing Politics* (Cambridge: Polity, 2005), p. 180.

[36] See Sarah Childs, Joni Lovenduski and Rosie Campbell, *Women at the Top 2005: Changing Numbers, Changing Politics* (London: Hansard Society, 2005), section 2.

[37] See, for example, Karen Bird, 'Gendering Parliamentary Questions', *British Journal of Politics and International Relations*, 7, 2005: 353–70; or Sarah Childs and Julie Withey, 'Do Women Sign for Women? Sex and the Signing of Early Day Motions in the 1997 Parliament', *Political Studies*, 52, 2004: 552–64.

[38] For a series of examples, see Bonnie Sones, Margaret Moran and Joni Lovenduski, *Women in Parliament: The New Suffragettes* (London, Politico's, 2005).

differences in the way the women MPs voted from their male counterparts, these differences were less dramatic than much of the coverage
implied.[39]

Overall, the effect of the increased numbers of women in the
Commons was probably not as great as many of the proponents of AWS
would have originally hoped. But it was greater than many of their critics
acknowledged.

The House of Lords

The process of House of Lords reform – discussed by Philip Norton in
chapter 6 – was not Labour's finest hour in government. It consisted of a
compromise followed by a hapless White Paper followed by a U-turn followed by a farce followed by another U-turn.[40] By the time Tony Blair left
office Labour had still not fully implemented its manifesto pledges to
make the House of Lords more 'democratic and representative' (1997) or
'representative and democratic' (2001).

Yet the understandable focus on the botched debate on Lords reform
has tended to obscure the way the Lords is now actually functioning. As
with so much of the Blair legacy in parliament, the reality is more complicated than the government's critics allow. When the government
brought forward the House of Lords Bill in 1999, the accusation was that
this was an attempt to weaken the second chamber. By removing most of
the hereditary peers, critics argued that the government was emasculat-
ing one of the remaining checks on its dominance of parliament. For
example, of the first fifty-three defeats the government suffered in the
Lords after 1997, all but six occurred as a result of the votes of the hereditary peers. And so, the argument went, remove the hereditary peers and
you remove any effective opposition.

Yet, as was clear within a year or two of the House of Lords Act 1999
coming into effect, the exact opposite occurred. The pre-reform House of
Lords, conscious that its legitimacy was limited by the presence of so many
hereditary peers, frequently practised a self-denying ordinance, pulling
back from many confrontations with the government. But once the hered-
itaries had largely gone, those peers that remained saw themselves as more

---

[39] Philip Cowley and Sarah Childs, 'Too Spineless to Rebel? New Labour's Women MPs',
    British Journal of Political Science, 33, 2003: 345–65.
[40] There were also other much less glamorous but important changes to the internal pro-
    ceedings of the Lords, including a compulsory register of interests and the introduction of
    a Lords Speaker.

PARLIAMENT 31

legitimate and became more assertive than before. If the government hoped it had created a poodle of an upper chamber, then it was very much mistaken.

The full consequences of reform became increasingly clear during the second Blair term. The 2001–5 parliament saw the government defeated on 245 separate occasions, more than double the number of defeats in the first Blair term (108). The first session of the 2005 parliament brought another sixty-two defeats, with more than thirty in the second session. The comparison with the preceding Conservative governments was particularly stark. The (mean) average number of Lords defeats per session during the extended period of Conservative government between 1979 and 1997 was just over thirteen. The (mean) average for the 2001 parliament was just over sixty-one. In other words, the Lords were defeating the Labour government of 2001–5 more than four times as often as they defeated the Thatcher and Major governments.

These defeats ranged across almost every major piece of government legislation, and as the Blair era went on, and the partly-reformed Lords became more confident, so they became more intransigent and less willing to give way, with the result that the sight of a Bill pinging back and forth between Commons and Lords became commonplace at the end of a parliamentary session.[41] This was most obvious during the passage of the Prevention of Terrorism Bill, just before the 2005 election, when the Lords resisted several clauses in the Bill, and it shuttled back and forth between the Lords and the Commons for almost twenty-nine hours before a compromise was worked out between the two Houses.[42] This, however, was merely the most high-profile of a number of stand-offs throughout the parliament, such as over foundation hospitals, jury trials and the Pensions Bill. As research from the Constitution Unit at University College London showed, these defeats were not just on minor matters, nor were they all simply overturned. In around 40% of defeats, the Lords had a significant impact on the final policy outcome.[43]

Of the two Houses of parliament, therefore, it was the Lords that was more of a block on the government throughout the Blair era. Government

[41] Richard Whitaker, 'Ping-Pong and Policy Influence: Relations Between the Lords and Commons, 2005–06', *Parliamentary Affairs*, 59, 2006: 536–45.

[42] Meg Russell and Maria Sciara, 'Parliament: The House of Lords – A More Representative and Assertive Chamber?', in Rush and Giddings, *Palgrave Review of British Politics 2005*, pp. 128 –30.

[43] See, for example, Meg Russell and Maria Sciara, 'The Policy Impact of Defeats in the House of Lords', paper presented to the Political Studies Association Conference, University of Bath, April 2007.

ministers preparing legislation for its passage through parliament knew that they faced a more serious test in the Lords than they did in the Commons, and ministers routinely resisted giving too many compromises whilst a Bill was passing through the Commons in order to be able to offer placatory gestures to their Lordships.

The extra problems which the government faced in the Lords were sometimes ascribed to the greater sagacity of peers, their great wisdom, and their increased independence of thought. In fact, the parliamentary parties in the Lords are no less cohesive than those in the Commons.[44] The difference – and it is a crucial one – is that after the reform of 1999 no one party held a majority in the Lords. Despite Labour increasing its membership in the Lords throughout the Blair years (its supposed 'packing' of the Lords with 'cronies') the government remained permanently in a minority position, with fewer than one-third of the votes of peers. It was sometimes erroneously reported as being the majority party; it was, in fact, merely the plurality party. In order to win votes in such a 'hung' chamber, the government needed to persuade at least one of the other party groupings to support them. Indeed, in an irony not lost on members of the upper chamber, after the 2005 election, the composition of the Lords better reflected the pattern of votes cast than did the Commons.[45] The process of Lords reform since 1999 thus created a more representative second chamber, one which was permanently hung, and one which was willing to stand up to, and regularly defeat, the government of the day.

The real significance of this will become clear when the Conservatives next enjoy a majority in the Commons; it too will face this permanently hung, and increasingly assertive, second chamber. No future Conservative government will inherit the overwhelmingly Conservative upper chamber of the past. Shortly after the 2005 election, the Liberal Democrats announced that they would no longer be abiding by the Salisbury Convention, the convention dating back to 1947 which guaranteed that the Lords would not block legislation promised in a government's election manifesto. The Liberal Democrats argued that when the Lords better represented the electorate than did the Commons, there was no longer any justification for the Commons automatically getting its way; Lord McNally, the Liberal Democrat leader in the Lords described

---

[44] See for example, Philip Norton, 'Cohesion Without Discipline: Party Voting in the House of Lords', *Journal of Legislative Studies*, 9, 2003: 57–72.

[45] Russell and Sciara, 'Parliament: The House of Lords', pp. 125–7.

the 'continual plea to the Salisbury convention' as 'the last refuge of leg-islative scoundrels'. Given that the Liberal Democrats frequently act as the swing voters in the Lords, determining government victory or defeat, this means that any government will face even more difficulties getting its legislation through the Lords in future.

There is still a legitimate debate about the extent to which the Lords should be elected, and whether (as a result) the Lords should be yet more powerful. That debate should not obscure the fact that the Lords in recent years has become increasingly powerful and assertive, not less.

Conclusion

One of the most misunderstood parts of the Blair premiership was its effect on parliament. Whilst many of the criticisms made of the Blair gov-ernment's actions and intentions are valid, critics often misunderstand their effect on parliament. Rather than simply being a period of increased marginalisation, in several areas the Blair era saw at least a partial revital-isation of the institution.

Almost none of this was intentional on the part of Blair or his immedi-ate circle. Blair can take credit for his decision to appear before the Liaison Committee, but his involvement in most other areas of parlia-mentary reform was marginal at best. The government's record in terms of reform of the House of Commons was extremely patchy – and, for the most part, compared poorly with Labour's stated intentions before 1997. Although there was a significant amount of parliamentary reform between 1997 and 2007, too little of it helped strengthen the House of Commons. It was not that the Blair government invented the executive's dominance of the legislature – and certainly too much of the criticism of parliament under New Labour harked back to a golden age that had never existed – but not enough of the reform helped limit or reverse that domi-nance. Some of it – most notably the over-use of programming motions – almost certainly had a deleterious effect on parliamentary scrutiny of legislation. The positive reforms – such as the changes to both select and standing committees – were reliant on reform-minded Leaders of the House driving them through, often against resistance from others within government.

Other positives from the Blair era were merely fortuitous accidents. The House of Lords Act 1999, for example, was not intended to result in the far more assertive body that it created – but it did. Similarly, it was not the wish of the government that its backbenchers, routinely dismissed as weak and feeble when they were first elected to government, should became increasingly rebellious during the second Blair term and after – but they did, with real consequences for the government's programme.

The verdict on parliament under Blair may be more positive than most people realise, but Tony Blair himself gets very little of the credit.

3

Elections and public opinion

JOHN CURTICE

Tony Blair is guaranteed a favourable place in the history books so far as his electoral record is concerned. He was the first Labour leader to lead his party to three electoral victories in a row. On the first occasion, in 1997, he secured an overall majority of 179, the biggest Labour majority ever. If the twentieth century had been predominantly a Conservative one, Blair apparently gave his party a head start in making the twenty-first century a period of Labour dominance.

This success was achieved following a transformation of the party that was instigated by Blair in the early years of his leadership. Ideologically, the party moved to the right, symbolised by the abolition in 1995 of Clause 4 of its constitution, which committed the party to 'the common ownership of the means of production, distribution and exchange'. The party rejected the 'socialist' position that the state should own and run the country's major industries and instead embraced the market. As well as being repositioned ideologically, the party was 'rebranded' as 'New Labour', a description that was designed to symbolise the degree to which it had cast off its ideological past.[1]

For many of Blair's followers the two events are not unconnected. Labour's unprecedented success in 1997 and thereafter only came about, they believe, because the repositioning and rebranding of the party enabled it to reach parts of the electorate amongst whom hitherto it had been relatively weak. Equally, as Blair's tenure in office gradually came to an end in 2006–7, 'Blairites' argued that it would be electorally disastrous if the party were to abandon the programme of 'reform' undertaken during Blair's tenure. In short, Blairites believe that Labour would never have won power but for its reformulation as 'New Labour', and that it is bound to lose power should the New Labour 'project' ever be abandoned.

---

[1] P. Gould, *The Unfinished Revolution: How the Modernisers Saved the Labour Party*, (London: Little, Brown, 1998).

This chapter examines these claims. First, we consider Labour's electoral record under Tony Blair's leadership. How well does the argument that Blair's New Labour project turned his party's fortunes around stand up to scrutiny? And how impressive in fact is Blair's electoral record? Second, we ask how far people's perceptions of the Labour Party changed under Blair's leadership and assess whether the rebranding of the party did help to change the kind of person who was willing to vote for it. Third, we examine what impact the repositioning of the Labour Party had on public opinion. While Blair's principal aim might have been to ensure that his party stood on the centre ground of public opinion, perhaps in practice it simply changed where the centre ground was located – and in a manner that may not be to the party's advantage in future.

The electoral record

In 1983 the Labour Party hit rock bottom. It won just 28% of the vote, its lowest share since 1918. This disaster occurred in the wake of a distinct movement to the left in reaction to an unhappy period in office that ended in defeat in 1979. But the road back to recovery proved to be a slow and rocky one. In 1987 the party only achieved a modest increase in its support to just over 31%. Then, in 1992, high hopes that the party would at least deny the Conservatives an overall majority were dashed when the opinion polls proved to be erroneous. Instead Labour still trailed the Conservatives by as many as eight percentage points. It is perhaps little wonder that after this fourth crushing defeat in a row many people in the party felt that it was in need of root-and-branch reform.

Yet the party had not stood still since 1983. Although once regarded as being on the left of the party, on becoming leader following the 1983 debacle, Neil Kinnock steered it back towards the centre, and especially so after the 1987 defeat. Two totemic policies of the left, unilateral nuclear disarmament and withdrawal from the European Union, were jettisoned as part of a systematic review of party policy in the late 1980s. By 1990 the party appeared competitive once more. Nevertheless it had fought the 1992 election on a platform of higher taxation for the better-off, a platform that enabled the Conservatives to claim that taxes in general would go up under Labour and one that rightly or wrongly many in the party blamed for its unexpected defeat in that election.

Meanwhile, after the 1992 election events did not stand still either. In 1990 the then Chancellor, John Major, finally persuaded his deeply reluctant Prime Minister, Margaret Thatcher, that the pound should join the European Exchange Rate Mechanism (ERM). Under this mechanism the values of the member currencies only varied within relatively narrow bands, a move made in anticipation of the creation of a single European currency. However, thanks to its delayed entry the pound joined at a relatively high value. And on 'Black Wednesday' in September 1992, just months after its election victory, the Conservative government, now headed by Prime Minister Major, proved unable to defend this value on the foreign exchange markets, despite at one stage raising interest rates to as high as 15%. It was compelled to withdraw the pound from the ERM. In effect the government was forced by a 'currency crisis' to 'devalue' the pound.

This was a novel experience for a Conservative government. But it had been an all too familiar one for Labour administrations. Every previous post-war Labour government had suffered a similar 'currency crisis' – and had lost popularity immediately thereafter. 'Black Wednesday' had an equally corrosive impact on the reputation of the Conservative Party as an effective manager of the economy. By Christmas 1992 Labour already enjoyed a double-digit lead in the polls. Neil Kinnock's successor as Labour leader, John Smith, whose taxation policy (as Shadow Chancellor) it was that had been targeted by the Conservatives in the 1992 election earlier, appeared to calculate that his party did not need further radical reform. All that it needed to do was to ensure that it profited from the Conservatives' misfortunes.

And profit it did. In May 1994, the month that John Smith suddenly died, the party was no fewer than twenty-three points ahead of the Conservatives in the opinion polls. In the local elections that month the party put in its best performance since 1979. Meanwhile in the European elections in June, the party secured 44% of the vote, its best performance yet in a European election and putting it as many as sixteen points ahead of the Conservatives. There was no doubt that the party's position was now far stronger than it had been during the mid-term of any of the previous three parliaments.

In short, although Labour may still have been bearing the psychological scars of electoral defeat, by the time Blair became leader in July 2004 the party was already enjoying considerable electoral success. Not only was Labour enjoying unprecedented opinion poll leads, it was also securing victories at the ballot box. Tony Blair's task was to maintain the favourable legacy he had inherited. He did not need to create his own fortune.

He certainly achieved that task. In 1997 Labour inflicted on the Conservatives their worst-ever defeat. In a result that in some respects uncannily resembled that of the 1994 European elections, the party won 44% of the nationwide vote, leaving it thirteen points ahead of the Conservatives, a lead that proved sufficient to generate that record parliamentary majority of 179. The swing since 1992 of 10.3% from Labour to Conservative was the biggest electoral turnaround in post-war British history. Even so, Labour's 44% share of the vote was still less than what the party had achieved at any election between 1945 and 1966, including the three it had lost between 1951 and 1959.

Meanwhile Blair managed to maintain his party's popularity throughout its first term in office. Apart from one short period in September 2000 when the government was faced with a blockade of petrol depots by lorry drivers unhappy at the increasing costs of running their businesses, Labour continued to enjoy double-digit poll leads throughout. It avoided the mid-term blues that had been suffered by every previous government since the 1950s. Meanwhile, in 2001, the party almost managed to replicate its success four years earlier, with an overall majority of 167. However, the party's vote fell by as much as 2.4 percentage points, a bigger drop than that suffered by the Conservatives at any time between 1979 and 1992, or by Clement Attlee in 1950, and matching the fall suffered by Labour under Jim Callaghan in 1979. The only two previous post-war administrations to have secured office with a lower share of the vote were the two Labour governments that came to power after the elections of February and October 1974, both of which were only minority administrations for at least part of their lives.

Even so, Blair's second administration still managed to maintain a lead in the opinion polls, albeit one that had begun to fall even before the invasion of Iraq in 2003. But its performance at the ballot box was rather more disturbing. In September 2003 it unexpectedly lost a parliamentary by-election in Brent East to the Liberal Democrats. This was the first time in post-war British politics that the party had lost a by-election to the Liberal Democrats other than in a seat where there was a prior history of local Liberal activity. A constituency with a substantial Muslim population, it was the first sign that the invasion of Iraq had cost Labour votes amongst that community at least, a pattern that was to be repeated in a number of other by-elections in the ensuing eighteen months.

Equally dramatic – and damaging – was the party's performance in local and European elections held on the same day in June 2004. Labour won just 23% of the European election vote, easily its worst-ever performance since such elections were first held in 1979. In the local elections, where the parties' performances are regularly extrapolated into a projected share of the national vote, the party was estimated to have secured the equivalent of 26% of the vote – easily its worst-ever local election performance since such contests became predominantly party political affairs in the post-war era.

Nevertheless Blair still pulled off his record-breaking third electoral victory in a row in 2005. While at sixty-six his overall parliamentary majority was well below those secured in 1997 and 2001, it was still more than enough for the party to enjoy another four or five years of secure majority government. However, looked at in terms of votes, the performance was even less impressive than it had been in 2001. The party secured just a 36% share, less than that won by any previous majority government. That performance represented a drop of no fewer than eight points in the party's support since 1997, easily the biggest loss of support suffered by any Labour government. The party was almost back to the 35% that had proved such a disappointment in 1992.

Blair's remaining two years brought little better cheer. Towards the end of April 2006 the party fell behind the Conservatives in the polls for the first time (consistently) since Black Wednesday in September 1992. The party's performance in local elections in 2006 and 2007 was little better than the record-breaking low suffered in 2004. Meanwhile just before Blair announced his resignation in May 2007, Labour lost a Scottish Parliament election to the Scottish National Party (SNP), the party's first defeat in a major election in Scotland for fifty years, while it was left in a highly precarious position in the Welsh Assembly after winning less than a third of the vote for the first time in the principality since 1918.

In short Blair's electoral record combines record-breaking success with dramatic decline. His ability to secure such success depended on two crucial pieces of good fortune – a Conservative party in disarray and an electoral system for the House of Commons that was unprecedentedly biased in Labour's favour. The first condition he inherited when he became leader in 1994.[2] The second was the product of circumstances for which he can claim little credit – smaller electorates in Labour seats, lower turnout in such seats, and the fact that when the Conservative vote

---

[2] It was of course a fortune that was maintained when the Conservatives voted with the government in support of the invasion of Iraq, thereby making it difficult for the party to profit from the public's unease about that invasion. Although, as discussed further below, the Liberal Democrats, who voted against the invasion, did secure the support of the invasion's opponents, they were less able to turn votes gained from Labour into seats.

collapsed in 1997 it did so largely in those areas where the party had previously been strongest.[3] Without those two pieces of good fortune Blair
would certainly never have secured his historic third victory in a row in
2005. Moreover by 2007 Tony Blair's legacy to his successor, Gordon
Brown, looked more like the weak electoral position that Neil Kinnock
inherited in 1983 from his predecessor, Michael Foot, than the strong one
left for Blair by John Smith.

New Labour, new voters?

Still, however strong a position Blair inherited in 1994, and however weak
Labour looked by 2007, this does not necessarily mean that Blair did not
leave his mark on the character of Labour's vote. The repositioning and
rebranding of the party that he instigated may well have changed people's
image of the party and the kind of person who was willing to vote for it
even if did not necessarily deliver much long-term benefit in terms of the
party's overall level of support.

The 'New Labour' project was founded on two key assumptions. The
first was that Labour's traditional working-class base had become too
small to provide an adequate foundation for electoral success. The
decline of manufacturing and the rise of the service sector meant that
increasingly fewer people were employed in manual jobs, while more
earned their living in white-collar middle-class occupations.[4] The party
thus needed to strike a stance that made it more attractive to those who
worked in white-collar jobs. The second assumption was that what was
left of the working class had changed in character. Many now owned their
own homes and their own cars and hoped their children would rise up
the occupational ladder by securing white-collar employment. Many in
the working class were now individualistic, materialistic and aspirational

---

[3] J. Curtice and M. Steed, 'Appendix 2: The Results Analysed', in D. Butler and D. Kavanagh,
   The British General Election of 1997 (Basingstoke: Macmillan, 1997), pp. 295–325; J.
   Curtice, 'The Electoral System: Biased to Blair?', *Parliamentary Affairs*, 54, 2001: 803–14; J.
   Curtice, S. Fisher and M. Steed, 'Appendix 2: The Results Analysed', in D. Kavanagh and D.
   Butler, *The British General Election of 2005* (Basingstoke: Palgrave, 2005), pp. 235–59; R.
   Johnston, C. Pattie, D. Dorling and D. Rossiter, *From Votes to Seats: The Operation of the
   UK Electoral System since 1945* (Manchester: Manchester University Press, 2001). Note
   that if the overall levels of support for Labour and the Conservatives in 2005 had been
   reversed, and the Conservatives had been three points ahead with 36% of the vote, the
   party would not have secured an overall majority. Indeed, it is highly unlikely that the
   Conservatives would have even been the largest party.
[4] A. Heath and S.-K. McDonald, 'Social Change and the Future of the Left', *Political
   Quarterly*, 58, 1987: 364–77.

in their outlook rather than solidaristic and collectivist. Nowhere was this more evident than in the south of England where so-called 'Essex man' had fallen for the attractions of Thatcherism in the 1980s. Unless Labour could fashion a message that was more in tune with the philosophy of 'Essex man', the party would continue to suffer 'southern discomfort'.[5]

So the party that was originally founded in 1900 to promote 'the direct interests of labour' now attempted to shed its traditional working-class image. As table 3.1 overleaf shows, it succeeded spectacularly. In 1987 nearly half the public thought that Labour looked after the interests of working-class people 'very closely', while little more than one in twenty reckoned it did the same for middle-class people. By 1997 the picture was rather different. Only a third now thought Labour looked after the interests of working-class people very closely. True, still only one in ten thought the same about the middle class, but the proportion who thought that it did not look after middle-class interests very closely, or even not at all, now stood at only 14% compared with 38% ten years earlier. Certainly by the time Blair first became Prime Minister Labour was no longer widely regarded as being antipathetic to the middle class.

But after four years of Blair in power Labour had lost its distinctive class image entirely. By 2001 if anything slightly more people thought that Labour looked very or fairly closely after the interests of middle-class people than thought it did those of working-class people. The position was little different in 2005. This transformation of the class image of the Labour Party was one of the major achievements of the New Labour project instigated by Blair. Labour was truly 'rebranded' under his leadership. However, we should note that much of the change in the party's image occurred after the party came to power rather than beforehand; it was as much a consequence of the style of the Blair government as it was a strategy that enabled the party to secure power in the first place.

What, however, of the repositioning of the party that Blair also promoted? Was this part of the party's attempt to reach out to what came to be dubbed 'middle England' also noticed by the public? To assess this we can examine what people said when they were asked by the British Election Study to indicate where they thought the Labour Party stood on four scales, each of which described polar opposites. Thus, for example, on a scale on taxes and spending, one end was labelled, 'government

---

[5] G. Radice, *Southern Discomfort*, Fabian Pamphlet 555 (London: Fabian Society, 1992); G. Radice and S. Pollard, *More Southern Discomfort: A Year On – Taxing and Spending*, Fabian Pamphlet 560 (London: Fabian Society, 1993).

Table 3.1. Class image of the Labour Party

	1987	1997	2001	2005
Percentage saying Labour looks after interests of working-class people				
Very closely	46	33	11	10
Fairly closely	43	58	54	54
Not very closely	8	6	28	30
Not at all closely	1	1	7	7
Percentage saying Labour looks after interests of middle-class people				
Very closely	6	10	14	7
Fairly closely	52	71	60	56
Not very closely	35	13	20	28
Not at all closely	5	1	6	9

Notes:
(1) Columns do not add up to 100% because those saying 'Don't know', etc. are not shown.
(2) In 2001 and 2005 the question asked how 'well' Labour looked after the interests of working- and middle-class people. For those years the table shows in the 'Very closely' row the proportion saying. 'Very well', etc.[6]

should put up taxes a lot and spend much more on health and social services', while the other was headed, 'government should cut taxes a lot and spend much less on health and social services'. Respondents could place Labour at one of these two ends or at any one of nine points in between. The position they chose was then given a score between one and eleven, such that the lower the score the more Labour was thought to be in favour of more taxation and spending. Meanwhile, the three other scales were:

> Government should nationalise many more private companies
> vs.
> Government should sell off many more nationalised industries

[6] This change of wording does not appear to have made a material difference to the pattern of responses. An ICM poll that was conducted for the BBC immediately prior to the 2001 election, and which used the same wording as the 1987 and 1997 surveys, found 9% saying that the Labour Party looked after the interests of working-class people 'very closely', 48% fairly closely, 26% not very closely and 12% not at all closely. The equivalent figures for the middle class were 12%, 56%, 16% and 9% respectively.

Getting people back to work should be the government's top priority
vs.
Keeping prices down should be the government's top priority

and

*Government should make much greater efforts to make people's incomes more
equal*
vs.
*Government should be much less concerned about how equal people's
incomes are*

The average position at which Labour was placed on these scales is
shown in table 3.2 overleaf. We can see that even before Tony Blair
became leader the repositioning of the party under Neil Kinnock had
already had some impact on public perceptions. By 1992 Labour was
thought to be somewhat less keen on nationalisation and more concerned to keep inflation down rather than cut unemployment than it had
been five years earlier. On the other hand, the party was thought to have
become yet keener on more taxation and more spending, an indication
no doubt of the impact of the Conservatives' attacks on Labour on this
score during the 1992 election campaign.

This last trend was reversed under John Smith's leadership as the party
recoiled from the policy stance that it thought had lost it the election.[7]
Otherwise it appears that Labour's image stood still between 1992 and
1994. But by 1997, by which time Blair had persuaded his party to jettison
Clause 4, far fewer people thought that Labour was committed to nationalisation. Perceptions of the party also drifted somewhat further to the
right on the other scales, most notably on the degree to which the party
was thought to be concerned to produce greater equality.

But as in the case of the party's class image, the experience of Labour in
office under Blair's leadership did yet more to change people's perceptions of the party. By 2005 equality was no longer widely thought to be as
central a feature of Labour's agenda as it had been just a few years earlier.
People were now almost as likely to put the party to the right of centre on
nationalisation as they were to put it to the left of centre. Although two
years of keeping to the Conservatives' overall tax and spending plans
between 1997 and 1999 had subsequently been followed by an emphasis
on improving public services (and increasing expenditure thereon),
Labour was still thought to have moved yet further away from wanting

[7] Butler and Kavanagh, *The British General Election of 1997*.

Table 3.2. Perceptions of what Labour stood for 1992–2001

	1987	1992	1994	1997	2001
Tax and spend	3.0	2.8	3.5	3.6	4.1
Nationalisation	2.9	3.6	3.5	4.7	5.5
Reduce unemployment vs. inflation	2.3	3.0	2.9	3.2	3.8
Equalise incomes	2.9	3.0	n/a	3.5	4.7

Notes:
(1) Scores show the average position on which the Labour was placed on an eleven-point scale as described in the main text. The lower the score the more to the 'left' Labour was thought to be.
(2) n/a = not asked
Source: British Election Study 1987; British Election Panel Study 1992–97; British Election Panel Study 1997–2001.

more taxes and spending. Meanwhile, four years of low inflation also seem to have helped change perceptions of Labour's economic priorities somewhat.

So the repositioning of Labour under Blair's leadership was noticed by the public – although, as in the case of the party's rebranding, much of the impact only registered itself *after* Labour had secured office rather than before. Evidently it was as much a consequence of the strategy that Labour deployed after it had secured electoral success as it was a precursor of that success. Nevertheless we should still examine whether the rebranding and repositioning of New Labour helped to strengthen the party's support amongst its key intended targets – the middle class and the south of England.

Table 3.3 shows the propensity of those in each social grade as measured by market researchers to vote Labour at each election between 1992 and 2005. Those in social grade AB consist primarily of those in professional and managerial occupations, those in C1 those in more junior white-collar occupations, while the C2s comprise foremen and skilled manual workers and the DEs unskilled manual workers, together with those wholly reliant on a state pension. The table shows that even after a decade of New Labour the party was still far more popular amongst those in working-class occupations than it was amongst those in middle-class ones. Nevertheless, relatively speaking at least, the party was more popular amongst middle-class voters in 2005 than it had been in 1992

Table 3.3. Labour support by social grade, 1992–2005

	Social grade			
	AB	C1	C2	DE
% voted Labour				
1992	19	25	40	49
1997	31	37	50	59
2001	30	38	49	55
2005	28	32	40	48
Change 92–05	+11	+7	0	−1

Table based only on those voting.
Source: MORI.

before Blair became leader. Indeed, according to MORI's data the key difference between 1992 and 2005 was that amongst middle-class voters the party was still more popular than it had been in 1992, whereas amongst those in the working class it was no more popular in 2005 than it had been thirteen years earlier.

Again, however, we should note that some of the change only occurred after Labour came to power.[8] In particular we might note that much of the narrowing of the class gap in Labour support apparently occurred between 2001 and 2005 and did so because the party suffered particularly heavy losses amongst working-class voters during this period. One of the risks of Tony Blair's New Labour strategy was that in attempting to secure the support of middle-class voters he might undermine the party's support amongst more traditional working-class ones. By 2005 at least that risk may have become a reality.[9]

But what of the geography of Labour support? Did the party achieve its objective of easing its 'southern discomfort'? Table 3.4 shows the change in Labour's support in three broad regions of England together with

[8] Though for further evidence that Labour did gain relatively strongly amongst middle-class voters between 1992 and 1997 see G. Evans, A. Heath and C. Payne, 'Labour as a Catch-All Party?', in G. Evans and P. Norris (eds.), *Critical Election: British Parties and Voters in Long-Term Perspective* (London: Sage, 1999), pp. 87–101; A. Heath, R. Jowell and J. Curtice, *The Rise of New Labour: Party Policies and Voter Choices* (Oxford: Oxford University Press, 2001).

[9] We should, however, note that the relative decline in Labour support between 2001 and 2005 amongst the working class is not so immediately apparent in the British Election Study data.

Table 3.4. The changing geography of Labour support 1992–2005

% share of vote in constituencies in	Average change in Labour		
	1992–97	1997–2001	2001–05
England			
South	+ 10.9	− 0.6	− 6.2
Midlands	+ 10.1	− 2.2	− 6.3
North	+ 9.5	− 3.0	− 5.7
Wales	+ 5.6	− 5.8	− 5.7
Scotland	+ 6.9	− 1.5	− 4.2

South = constituencies in Greater London and the former South-East and South-West standard regions.
Midlands = East Anglia, East and West Midlands standard regions.
North = Yorkshire and Humberside, the North-West and Northern standard regions.
Source: Author's calculations.

Scotland and Wales. Labour's progress between 1992 and 1997 was clearly stronger in the south of England than elsewhere, and particularly stronger than in Scotland or Wales. Moreover, in part at least this seems to have happened because voters in the southern half of the country were particularly likely to think that Labour had moved ideologically between 1992 and 1997 towards the centre ground.[10] But again we discover that only part of Labour's success in achieving its objective occurred before it secured office. Further progress was made after it took office, for between 1997 and 2001 it lost less ground in the south of England than elsewhere. By 2001 the party's support was more than ten points higher in the average constituency in the south of England than it had been in 1992, whereas the equivalent figure in the North was only somewhat over six points. Meanwhile in Wales Labour was actually no stronger at all. However, the party was unable to repeat its relatively strong performance in the southern half of the country in 2005; during Blair's second term the party's support actually fell slightly more in the south of England and in the Midlands than it did elsewhere.

So Tony Blair's rebranding and repositioning of his party does appear to have changed somewhat the kind of person who voted Labour. He left

[10] J. Curtice and A. Park, 'Region: New Labour, New Geography?', in Evans and Norris, *Critical Election*, pp. 124–47.

the party relatively better able to appeal to middle-class voters and those living in the south of England. However this change did not simply occur before 1997; much of it happened after Labour had secured power. As a result, the degree to which its rebranding and repositioning enabled the party to secure power should not be exaggerated. Moreover, as we have already seen, it certainly did not ensure the party could maintain its overall level of support once it had secured office.

In truth Blairites have always been inclined to exaggerate the importance of a party's ideological position in determining its level of electoral success.[11] So long as a party is not beyond the pale ideologically (as indeed Labour may well have been in the 1980s but not necessarily by 1994), what matters most in determining whether its fortunes wax or wane are not perceptions of its ideology but its competence. It was perceived incompetence in the wake of Black Wednesday that undid the Conservatives in 1992 and ensured that Blair inherited such a strong position in 1994. And it was perceived incompetence that damaged Labour's electoral credibility during Blair's tenure as leader, thereby creating an ebb tide that no amount of ideological positioning or rebranding could stop.

This can be seen quite clearly in the pattern of losses that Labour suffered in 2005.[12] According to data from the British Election Study, those who voted for Labour in 2001 and put themselves on the right of the ideological spectrum were just as likely to defect from Labour as those on the left. Equally, those 2001 Labour voters who wanted higher taxes and higher spending were just as likely to defect as those who wanted lower taxes and lower spending. What did distinguish those who remained loyal to Labour and those who did not were perceptions of the government's record in office. As many as 83% of those 2001 Labour voters who thought that the NHS had got better in recent years voted for the party again in 2005 – but only 58% of those who thought it had got worse. Meanwhile, although most of those 2001 Labour voters who approved of Britain's involvement in Iraq were willing to vote for the party again in 2005, only just over half of those who strongly disapproved – a group comprising no less than one in four of all former Labour voters – were willing to back the party again. Over one in four of this latter group opted for the Liberal Democrats instead.

---

[11] See also Heath *et al.*, *Rise of New Labour*, ch. 9.
[12] J. Curtice, 'New Labour, New Protest? How the Liberal Democrats Profited from Blair's Mistakes', *Political Quarterly*, 78, 2007: 117–27.

Moving the centre?

In moving his party towards the centre, Blair assumed that he was taking his party closer to where the electorate already were ideologically. But if a party changes what it stands for, it may not simply change people's perceptions of that party, it may also mean that people change their own beliefs too. After all, if as a result of a party changing its stance there is no longer a mainstream party advocating, say, greater equality or more nationalisation, then it is not unreasonable to anticipate that increasingly fewer people will be persuaded of the value of such policies. Moreover, it is often argued that people take their cues about what they believe from the party to which they feel a sense of emotional attachment.[13] So if the Labour Party moves to the centre, as it did under Tony Blair, there is good reason to believe that many of its supporters will change their own views in sympathy.

This potentially raises two problems for a party that moves towards the centre. First, it means that in reaching for the centre ground it is in part chasing a moving target. The more it moves towards the centre, the more the centre itself moves. Second, it raises questions about the ability of the party to generate and maintain long-term support for itself. At any one point in time those on the 'left' on any issue are more likely to support Labour than are those on the 'right'.[14] So if the proportion of the electorate on the left declines, then Labour's ability to win votes – whatever its perceived level of competence – is likely to suffer.

So we now look to see what has happened to public opinion while Blair has been leader of the Labour Party. Did he not only change what people believed about the Labour Party but also what they themselves believed? In particular did the Blair era see a decline in support for greater equality and for government intervention in the economy – that is, in the values that have traditionally been associated with the 'left' in Britain?

We can best answer these questions by looking at data from the British Social Attitudes survey which over the last twenty years has regularly asked a number of questions that tap support for 'left-wing' and 'right-wing' attitudes. The first of these questions is about unemployment benefit. It asks:

[13] D. Butler and D. Stokes, *Political Change in Britain: The Electoral Choice*, 2nd edn (Basingstoke: Macmillan, 1974).
[14] A. Heath, R. Jowell and J. Curtice, *How Britain Votes* (Oxford: Pergamon Press, 1985); Heath *et al.*, *Rise of New Labour*.

Opinions differ about the level of benefits for unemployed people. Which of these two statements comes closest to your own view . . .

. . . benefits for unemployed people are too low and cause hardship,

or, benefits for unemployed people are too high and discourage them from finding jobs?

Unemployment is of course an important source of income inequality while unemployment benefit is one of the mechanisms that government can use to counteract its effects. Meanwhile a second question asks more directly about inequality and what the government should do to counteract its incidence. Respondents to the survey are asked whether they agree or disagree (on a five-point scale from 'strongly agree' to 'strongly disagree' that:

Government should redistribute income from the better off to those who are less well off.

This question is in fact part of a suite of five questions that between them are designed to tap how far people value equality and how much of a role they think government should have in trying to make society more equal.[15] The four additional questions, each of them again comprising a proposition to which people are invited to indicate agreement or disagreement, are as follows:

Big business benefits owners at the expense of workers.

Ordinary people do not get their fair share of the nation's wealth.

There is one law for the rich and one for the poor.

Management will always try to get the better of employees if it gets the chance.

By aggregating responses to all five questions (each of which can be scored from one to five and each of which is worded in a 'left-wing' direction) we can identify how many people on average are inclined to give 'left of centre' rather than 'right of centre' responses.

Table 3.5 overleaf shows how the pattern of answers to our two individual questions plus the broader left–right scale changed between 1983 and 2005. It shows in each case the proportion giving a left-wing response.

---

[15] G. Evans and A. Heath, 'The Measurement of Left–Right and Libertarian–Authoritarian Scales: Comparing Balanced and Unbalanced Scales', *Quality and Quantity*, 29, 1995: 191–206; A. Park, J. Curtice, K. Thomson, M. Phillips and M. Johnson (eds.), *British Social Attitudes: The 23rd Report: Perspectives on a Changing Society* (London: Sage, 2007).

Table 3.5. Incidence of 'left-wing' attitudes 1983–2005

	Unemployment benefits are too low (%)	Government should redistribute from better off to less well off (%)	Left of centre (%)
1983	46	n/a	n/a
1984	49	n/a	n/a
1985	44	n/a	n/a
1986	44	43	52
1987	51	45	55
1989	53	51	58
1990	52	51	59
1991	54	50	54
1993	58	48	59
1994	53	51	64
1995	51	47	61
1996	48	44	58
1997	46	n/a	n/a
1998	29	39	52
1999	33	36	50
2000	40	39	52
2001	37	38	49
2002	29	39	53
2003	34	42	51
2004	23	32	42
2005	26	32	44

n/a = not asked.
Source: British Social Attitudes survey.

First we might note that despite her stated ambition and her best efforts, Margaret Thatcher failed to shift Britain to the right. If anything by 1990, the year that Thatcher resigned as Prime Minister, people were slightly more inclined to give a left-wing response than they had been the first time each of our questions was included on the Social Attitudes survey. Meanwhile little changed in the period between Thatcher's demise and Blair's accession to the Labour leadership.

But thereafter there was a marked change. On all three of our measures people were somewhat less likely to offer a left-wing response by 1997 than they had been three years earlier. The perception that unemployment benefits were too low had fallen by seven points, as had (by 1996) the proportion who thought the government should redistribute income, while (again by 1996) the proportion classified as 'left of centre' had dropped by six points. But it was in the period after Tony Blair became Prime Minister that attitudes changed most sharply. In just the first year of his premiership there was no less than a seventeen-point drop – from 46% to 29% – in the proportion thinking that unemployment was too low. At the same time there were also further drops in support for greater income equality, as well as in the proportion giving 'left of centre' responses on our scale. Thereafter, despite some fluctuation in both directions, overall the country moved yet further to the right. Thus by 2005 support for income redistribution had fallen by twelve points since 1996, while the proportion who could be called 'left of centre' had dropped by fourteen points. Indeed according to the latter measure it appears that during Blair's tenure in office Britain changed from being a predominantly left-of-centre country to a majority right-of-centre one.

Of course we might still wonder how much responsibility for this rightward drift lies at Blair's door. As we remarked earlier, we would anticipate that if indeed Labour's move to the right influenced attitudes, then it is Labour supporters whose attitudes should have been influenced the most. Table 3.6 overleaf suggests that this is indeed what happened.[16] The decline in support for redistribution and the decline in the proportion who overall could be classified as 'left of centre' was considerably greater amongst Labour supporters than Conservative adherents, both over the whole period of Blair's Labour leadership and during his tenure as Prime Minister. As a result, by the time Blair's premiership was drawing to a close only a bare majority of Labour supporters could be classified as 'left of centre'.[17]

So it seems that in moving his party to the centre Blair did not simply change people's perceptions of the Labour Party – he also discouraged them from supporting the values with which the party had traditionally been associated. As a result, the ideological terrain on which Gordon Brown will have to fight his party's cause is more rugged than the one that

[16] For further evidence using panel data that takes into account the possible impact of changes in the kind of person that supports the Labour Party, see J. Curtice and S. Fisher, 'The Power to Persuade? A Tale of Two Prime Ministers', in A. Park, J. Curtice, K. Thomson, L. Jarvis and C. Bromley (eds.), British Social Attitudes: The 20th Report: Continuity and Change over Two Decades (London: Sage, 2003), pp. 233–53.

[17] Much the same is also true of attitudes to unemployment benefit. In 1994, 67% of Labour identifiers thought this benefit was too low, as did 58% in 1997. By 2005 the figure had fallen to 32%. The equivalent figures for Conservative identifiers were 34%, 30% and 13% respectively.

Table 3.6. Left–right attitudes by party identification 1986–2005

	Support redistribution (%)		Left of centre (%)	
	Conservative identifiers	Labour identifiers	Conservative identifiers	Labour identifiers
1986	22	64	29	76
1994	26	68	37	81
1996	22	58	33	75
1998	23	48	34	63
2001	22	46	31	58
2005	16	39	26	51

Source: British Social Attitudes survey.

Tony Blair inherited. Fewer voters now believe in the things that Labour (once) believe(d). While, as we have seen, ideology is far from being all in the battle for electoral supremacy, in having encouraged the nation's values to move in a more conservative direction Blair has certainly not made it any easier for his party to achieve electoral success over the long term.

Conclusion

History is usually written by the victors. Thus, because Labour won the 1997 election so decisively, supporters of Blair were able to claim that it was thanks to his repositioning and rebranding of the party that Labour secured its decisive victory. Equally when Blair became the first Labour leader to win three general elections in a row, they have been able to argue that it was his leadership that enabled the party to achieve unprecedented electoral success.

Our critical scrutiny has, however, painted a far more prosaic picture. Blair inherited a party that was already heading for victory thanks to the Conservatives' misfortunes on 'Black Wednesday' in 1992. He benefited crucially from a biased electoral system that ensured that the heaviest loss of electoral support ever suffered by a Labour government did not stand between him and his third electoral victory. True, his rebranding and repositioning of his party did change people's perceptions of the Labour Party and appears to have hit its target in that it encouraged middle-class voters and those living in the south of England to vote for the party. But much of this change happened *after* Blair secured power, not before. In any event it proved no barrier to a severe loss of electoral support at the ballot box, a loss that in the local and devolved elections held towards the end of his leadership was not masked by the electoral system. Moreover, Blair's strategy seems to have dissuaded people from wanting a more equal society, and government action to secure that aim, a change that will certainly not make it any easier for his party to win elections in future.

The crucial piece of the electoral jigsaw that was persistently ignored in the claims made by advocates of the New Labour project was competence. Image and ideology may provide the foundations on which victory may be built. But they are worth little if a party is thought incapable of delivering on its promises. After his second victory in 2001 at least – and especially so after the Iraq invasion in 2003 – the longer that Blair governed, the more his own and his party's competence was questioned, leading to a serious erosion of his party's electoral support. The key electoral task facing his successor, Gordon Brown, is to try to find a way of reversing this 'Blair effect'.

4

Local government

TONY TRAVERS

Before 1997

Local government had long played a key role in the Labour Party's organisation and activist base. Several parts of the country, notably South Wales, Tyneside and parts of east London have been dominated by Labour ever since the party developed. During the eighteen years of Conservative rule from 1979 to 1997, Labour had developed huge strength in town halls. However, during Labour's long years in opposition the party had often been embarrassed by so-called 'loony left' councillors in places such as Liverpool, Sheffield and Lambeth. Margaret Thatcher's government had abolished the Greater London Council and metropolitan county authorities, introduced the poll tax and 'rate capping', and more generally conducted a prolonged war against town halls. Although John Major's ministers were more emollient, the central–local relationship in 1997 was still fragile.

Many senior New Labour politicians were wary of local government. The behaviour of radical Labour councils in the 1980s and early 1990s was widely believed to have cost the party votes in general elections. Tony Blair had never been a councillor and showed no particular concern for the subject. Moreover, his 1997 government wished to project an image of modernity and prudence. There was no room for outdated practices within government, including at the local level. However, despite this challenging background, many senior figures within local government hoped the new Labour government would improve and strengthen local democracy.

1997–2001

Labour's first term

Labour's 1997 manifesto[1] was a predictor of the fundamentally cautious approach adopted by the party once it had won power. The main points of the party's plans were: to remove expenditure capping; to give councils powers to promote economic, social and environmental well-being; annual elections for all councils; experiments with elected mayors; the introduction of a 'Best Value' regime; the abolition of compulsory competitive tendering; a 'fair' grant distribution; a directly elected mayor and Assembly for London; a Scottish Parliament and Welsh Assembly; and Regional Development Agencies for England.

Soon after taking office, Labour decided to merge the Department of the Environment (local government's sponsor) with the Department of Transport. This returned the Whitehall arrangements to those that had existed during the Heath government of 1970–4. The new Department of the Environment, Transport and the Regions was to be headed by John Prescott (also Deputy Prime Minister), with Hilary Armstrong as Minister of State for Local Government. Nick Raynsford was given specific responsibility for the creation of a new local government structure in London.

The Blair government signalled its intention to reform councils by the publication of a series of consultative papers, under the title 'Modernising Local Government'. The notion of 'modernisation' was to become key to the Blair government's approach to local authorities. Senior Labour figures believed the existing system of local authorities – and, indeed, many councillors – were antiquated and conservative. Wholesale modernisation was required.

Six consultative papers were produced during 1997. Three were about management, probity and effectiveness: 'Local Democracy and Community Leadership', 'Improving Local Services Through Best Value', and 'A New Ethical Framework'. The remaining three tackled the perennial issue of finance: 'Improving Local Financial Accountability', 'Capital Finance' and 'Business Rates'. These documents implied government radicalism in its approach to the internal management of local authorities and deep conservatism about finance.

The papers on internal management and processes suggested that local government should move away from its traditional reliance on the

[1] Labour Party, *New Labour Because Britain Deserves Better* (London: Labour Party, 1997), pp. 34 and 35.

committee system and instead split the 'executive' and 'non-executive' roles of councillors within each local authority. In particular, the possibility of introducing an executive mayor or a cabinet system was outlined.[2] The government argued that councils should provide more effective civic leadership. Concern was expressed at low electoral turnouts in local government. Potential reforms such as annual elections for all councils and ways of easing access to voting were put forward.

The proposed Best Value regime provided clear evidence of New Labour's approach. The government was determined to keep pressure on councils to deliver the kind of public service efficiencies and effectiveness that the previous Conservative governments had – with some success – striven for. However, ministers wanted to differentiate themselves from the Tories' preoccupation with 'value for money', also delivering effectiveness and quality in local services, backed up by targets and performance indicators.[3]

Best Value was to involve each authority in producing a performance plan that would then be independently audited. It was a highly technical solution to the government's problem of how to ensure that (often Labour) authorities did not revert to the kind of behaviour and inefficiency commonplace in the bad old days before Margaret Thatcher's government had tamed them. But although the Blair government's motives were obvious, there was less certainty about how Best Value would actually operate.

Blair's government showed no desire to unravel the system of local government finance. Margaret Thatcher had, in part, been brought down by a new, disliked, local government tax. The best John Prescott could offer was the removal of 'crude and universal' expenditure capping, the possibility of a small local supplement to the national non-domestic rate (which the Tories had nationalised in 1990) and some delegation of control over capital spending.

The final key element in Labour's approach was the proposal that all councils should adopt a 'new ethical framework', which would involve the adoption of a new code of conduct for councillors and officers, the creation of a 'standards committee' for each authority and an appeal mechanism involving independent members. Many decisions about possible standards breaches would be made by a nationally appointed

[2] Department of the Environment, Transport and the Regions, *Modernising Local Government. Local Democracy and Community Leadership* (London: TSO, 1998), p. 33.
[3] Department of the Environment, Transport and the Regions, *Modernising Local Government. Improving Local Services Through Best Value* (London: TSO, 1998), p. 9.

regional board. The perceived need for such reforms arose from the recommendations of the Nolan Report.[4]

Local authorities saw the new government's approach as a mixture of
carrots and sticks. While the Local Government Association was happy
enough with the abolition of capping and compulsory competitive tendering, it was less content with the performance-driven threat of Best
Value, which it viewed as centralisation. There was virtually no support
for the idea of elected mayors. From local government's point of view the
Blair administration was planning to be radical where councillors wanted
no change (i.e. the internal workings of local government) and cautious
where local authorities wanted reform (i.e. finance).

In one area of policy there was little or no opposition to Blair's
approach to local government. The manifesto had promised a new city-
wide government for the capital, to replace the Greater London Council
(GLC), which had been abolished by the Conservatives in 1986. A Green
Paper on London government was published in July 1997,[5] followed by
the legislation required to test public opinion in a referendum to be held
in May 1998. While the overall proposals for the capital were widely welcomed, there was some opposition to the idea of an American-style
directly elected mayor.

The introduction of a mayor for London was a radical proposal. The
United Kingdom had no previous experience of such an elected executive. The proposed Scottish Parliament and Welsh Assembly were conventional administrations which involved the election of a number of
members who would, between them, create an executive and elect a First
Minister. But the London reform created an elected single-person executive, subject only to scrutiny by a small assembly, and who could not be
removed between elections.

What was the Blair government seeking to do?

The single word most used by ministers within the Blair government to
describe their approach to local authorities was 'modernisation'. It
appeared again and again in Green and White Papers. It was used by supporters of the government and (as a term of abuse) by its opponents.
Different parts of the government were more committed to this process

---

[4] Committee on Standards in Public Life, *Standards of Conduct in Local Government in England, Scotland and Wales*, Third Report, Cm. 3702 (London: TSO, 1997).
[5] Department of the Environment, Transport and the Regions, *New Leadership for London* Cm. 3724 (London: TSO, 1997).

of modernisation than others. Downing Street and the Treasury were strongly in favour of changing the culture of local councils and councillors, whereas the Department of the Environment, Transport and the Regions was more modest in its aspirations. Many Labour supporters in local authorities and constituency parties were amongst the most bitter opponents of modernisation.

Tony Blair explained his own vision for local government in an Institute for Public Policy Research pamphlet published in 1998.[6] In it, Blair claimed change was needed because: (i) localities lacked a clear sense of direction; (ii) there was a lack of coherence and cohesion in delivering local services; and (iii) the quality of local services was too variable.

He went on to criticise local authorities for a number of failings before offering an olive branch. First: 'Britain comes bottom of the European league table for turnout in local elections'. Second: 'most people do not know the name of the leader of their council'. Third: 'the committee system takes up an enormous amount of time . . . A radical reform is needed'. Fourth: 'the government will intervene if authorities are incapable of improving their performance', and finally 'councils that are performing well could be given more freedom and powers'.

Labour's modest proposals for local government were backed up by the kind of public rhetoric and private ministerial comment that amounted to a powerful critique of local government. Although the Prime Minister and his advisers believed in the constitutional importance of elected local authorities, they did not much like its existing manifestations.

The Blair view of local government went well beyond the distaste felt by senior Labour politicians such as Neil Kinnock and John Cunningham as they had battled with the left during the 1980s.[7] By 1997 virtually the whole of local government – including former hot-spots of militancy such as Liverpool and Lambeth – was under the control of conventional politicians, whether Labour, Conservative, Liberal Democrat or others. Downing Street was concerned with the 'complacent average' authorities that appeared to coast along with outdated and inefficient political leadership and which were gradually, it was believed, losing public support.

The new Best Value policy was resented within local councils as a technocratic, top-down incursion into local democracy. The policy required

---

[6] Tony Blair, *Leading the Way: A New Vision for Local Government* (London: IPPR, 1998).
[7] David Butler, Andrew Adonis and Tony Travers, *Failure in British Government. The Politics of the Poll Tax* (Oxford: Oxford University Press, 1994), pp 256–7.

detailed service-by-service performance plans, including dozens of targets and key indicators. It was viewed within local government as bureaucratic and intrusive. After it started operating in the spring of 2000 many councillors found it difficult fully to understand how Best Value worked.

Local government appeared more comfortable with the Local Public Service Agreements (PSAs) that were invented in 2000.[8] Local PSAs were designed to sign local authorities up to a national pattern of improved public service provision: the Treasury could negotiate with the Local Government Association about outputs and outcomes to be derived as a result of public spending increases.

A further Blair government initiative designed to drive up quality was the beacon council scheme.[9] An independent panel was appointed by DETR ministers to select councils that excelled in particular services. Such authorities were awarded beacon council status for a fixed period of years. A council that qualified as a beacon authority in a number of services could apply for overall beacon status. Such authorities were in future to be given wider discretion over service provision.

The policy of introducing elected mayors stirred up a determined response from councillors of all parties. Most council members believed their existing pattern of committees, departments and service provision was reasonably effective. The idea that every council would be forced to choose between a cabinet, directly elected mayor or mayor-plus-council-manager model, eventually outlined by Labour in 1998,[10] proved hugely unpopular within local government.[11] It appeared that only a handful of councils appeared likely to opt for holding the referendum that might lead to the election of a mayor.

Local authorities also supported the government's decision to give them a power to promote the 'social, environmental and economic well-being' of their populations. This change was partly real, in that it gave councils greater freedom to use resources for certain purposes, and partly symbolic, because it suggested that local government could be trusted with (limited) additional freedoms.

[8] HM Treasury, *2000 Spending Review: New Public Spending Plans for 2001–2004*, Cm. 4807 (London: TSO, 2000), para. 33.3.
[9] Department of the Environment, Transport and the Regions, *Modern Local Government in Touch with the People*, Cm. 4114 (London: TSO, 1998), p. 21.
[10] *Ibid.*, pp. 26–30.
[11] Local Government Association, *Modern Local Government: Taking the Initiative. An LGA Survey of Local Authorities* (London: LGA, 1999), p. 21.

Financing local government

Few issues had taxed successive British governments more than the country's Byzantine local government finance system. The Thatcher and Major governments had undertaken three separate reviews of the subject. The introduction of the 'community charge', popularly known as the poll tax, in 1990 (1989 in Scotland) and its replacement – by council tax – in 1993 lived on in the memories of politicians as a terrible warning about the dangers of over-ambitious reforms of local taxation. Moreover, New Labour fought the 1997 election on a platform of fiscal rectitude. Every effort was made to convince the electorate that the election of a Labour government would not lead to a return to the bad old days of the late 1970s.

Local authorities, on the other hand, had long imagined that if the Conservatives were vanquished from national government it would be possible to move to a world of greater funding autonomy. In particular, they wanted three financial reforms: the abolition of tax capping (Labour had long been committed this); the return of local control over the non-domestic rate; and a fairer system of distributing government grants to councils. Many Labour and Liberal Democrat councillors (and national-ists in Scotland and Wales) also hoped that council tax would be reformed so as to make it less regressive.

Labour abandoned 'crude and universal' capping soon after taking office. However, in a sign of how far the Treasury intended to keep a grip over council finances, two conditions were set. First, the threat of selective capping would remain. Second, a scheme was introduced to penalise coun-cils that increased their council tax by more than a Whitehall-set figure.

In committing itself to making the Revenue Support Grant (RSG) fairer, Labour had made a promise that was to prove hard to keep. A major review of the grant system was undertaken during 1999 and 2000. International experience was researched. Other ways of allocating grants were considered, notably bid-based or performance-based systems. The Department for Education and Employment fought for ring-fenced edu-cation grants. There was even discussion in the press about removing education from local government altogether. However, councils success-fully defended education as a core local government service.

The conclusions of the government's review of finance were published in a Green Paper during the autumn of 2000.[12] None of the options for

---

[12] Department of the Environment, Transport and the Regions, *Modernising Local Government Finance: A Green Paper* (London: TSO, 2000).

reforming the grant system was ruled out, though none was signalled as a particular priority. A future government might continue with formula-based general grants or, alternatively move to bid-, performance- or plan-based specific grants. No full reform of the system could, it was argued, take place before 2003–4.

London

Ever since the Thatcher government abolished the Greater London Council in 1986, Labour had been committed to re-create a system of London-wide government. In the 1987 and 1992 general election mani-festos it was clear that any new authority for the capital would be a slim-line ('strategic') version of a conventional British local council.

The death of John Smith and the election of Tony Blair as leader of the Labour Party led to a change in policy towards London government. Blair became convinced that the capital should have Britain's first directly elected executive mayor. Immediately after Labour's 1997 victory a Green Paper[13] was published to flesh out the details of the London policy. There was to be a Greater London Authority, consisting of a directly elected mayor, who would be held to account by an elected Assembly. Elections would be by a form of proportional representation (the 'additional member' system). Services would be delivered by four 'functional bodies', whose boards would be appointed by the mayor. The Authority would be able to set a council tax precept.

Following consultation on the outline scheme in the Green Paper, a White Paper was published during the spring of 1998.[14] Immediately afterwards a referendum was held to test public opinion. Although the turnout was low (34%), the result strongly endorsed the White Paper proposals for a mayor and an Assembly (by 72% to 38%).

After a long and difficult parliamentary process (during which the government decided to amend the legislation so as to introduce a complex public–private partnership to finance the reconstruction of London Underground's infrastructure), the Greater London Authority was elected for the first time in May 2000. Although the legislation created a strong mayor (and a correspondingly weak Assembly), it also left ministers a number of fall-back powers of intervention just in case a

---

[13] Department of the Environment, Transport and the Regions, *New Leadership for London*, Cm. 3724 (London: TSO, 1997).
[14] Department of the Environment, Transport and the Regions, *A Mayor and Assembly for London*, Cm. 3897 (London: TSO, 1998).

mayor indulged in too many policies that proved unacceptable to central government.

The process of electing the capital's first directly elected chief executive was sufficiently exotic to have generated a separate book in its own right.[15] Both the Conservative and Labour parties became involved in highly publicised and chaotic efforts to choose a candidate. In a country with no history of primary elections of the kind commonplace in the United States, both parties had to invent processes to select their candidates.

The Tories first chose Lord (Jeffrey) Archer, who later had to resign because of a newspaper allegation about perjury in a previous court case. A second attempt to find a mayoral candidate was thrown into disarray when the favourite – Steven Norris, who had been defeated by Archer first time round – was ruled out of the contest by the party selection committee. Eventually Norris was reinstated and went on to become the candidate.

However, the Conservatives' efforts were positively well choreographed compared with the Labour Party's. Ever since the 1997 election victory and the certainty that London would soon have a directly elected mayor, there had been speculation that the final leader of the Greater London Council, Ken Livingstone, would stand as Labour candidate for the new role. However, to Blair and the New Labour machine, Livingstone embodied everything that was wrong with the party's previous image with the electorate. He was seen as extremist, oppositional and dangerous.[16]

Blair and his New Labour colleagues were determined to stop the ex-GLC leader. A complex electoral college was set up to select a candidate. Tony Blair and Gordon Brown made speeches denouncing Livingstone. The process resulted in Frank Dobson, previously Health Secretary, being chosen as Labour's candidate. Livingstone then decided to stand as an independent.

Blair's apparent efforts to martyr Livingstone, like those of Margaret Thatcher when she abolished the GLC in the mid-1980s, proved wholly counter-productive. 'Ken', as he was universally known, was seen as an underdog and a London populist. He was also strangely glamorous. It was small wonder that, on 5 May 2000, Livingstone became London's first-ever directly elected Mayor.

In office Ken Livingstone adopted a number of Blairite characteristics. Efforts were made to be consensual and to adopt more moderate policies, particularly towards big business. What became known by some as the

---

[15] Mark Darcy and Rory Mclean, *Nightmayor* (London: Politico's, 2000).
[16] John Carvel, *Citizen Ken* (London: Chatto and Windus, 1984).

'Kenocracy' proved, in many ways, to be the least-worst version of a Livingstone regime imaginable from Tony Blair's point of view.[17] However, when efforts were made by Livingstone supporters to seek the Mayor's re-admission to the Labour Party, the view within the party leadership remained one of 'wait and see'.

The English regions

Labour's approach to regional government in England outside London was muddled. Progress was made by the introduction in 1998 of Regional Development Agencies (RDAs), though these were appointed, not elected, institutions. RDAs were charged with improving the economic competitiveness and success of their areas. At the same time that RDAs were created, regional 'chambers' (which generally became known as 'assemblies') were set up to oversee them. These chambers or assemblies, which were intended to secure some form of local political accountability, were indirectly elected, with members drawn from local authorities within their areas plus a minority of individuals from other representative organisations.

The Blair government made no move towards fully fledged regional government in England. Despite a genuine shift of power to Scotland, Wales, Northern Ireland, devolution in England (apart from the capital) proved a reform too far for New Labour's constitutional modernisers. Press reports between 1997 and 2001 suggested the cabinet remained split about the issue.

By 2001, devolved government had arrived in three parts of Britain and, haltingly, in Northern Ireland, but it remained a shadow or compromise in England outside London. Possibly the consequences of a transfer of powers to Bristol, Birmingham, Manchester, Leeds and Newcastle was, at least during a first term of office, seen as providing Westminster with too great a threat to its power.

2001–2005

Labour in office

The second Blair government continued to evolve policies that created new service-delivery units for education, health, regeneration, housing

---

[17] See Tony Travers, *The Politics of London Governing an Ungovernable City* (Basingstoke: Palgrave Macmillan, 2004); and Ben Pimlott and Nirmala Rao, *Governing London* (Oxford: Oxford University Press, 2002).

and policing. It also sought to create consistency between different providers and to reduce the extent to which Whitehall departments handed
down policies that were disconnected from those in other parts of government. Local government became 'governance', embracing a number
of different organisations and requiring councils to lead coalitions of
local service providers. By 2005, the emphasis had shifted towards 'neighbourhood' and 'community' governance.

The programme of devolution that had started between 1997 and
2001 was to continue in 2004 with a referendum on whether or not to set
up an elected regional government for the North-East of England. The
voters rejected the idea, though the possibility of 'city region' government
was then proposed. There was no obvious end point to the programme of
continuing reform to neighbourhood, local and regional government. It
simply continued.

The development of 'new localism'

The second Blair government undertook a number of reforms that came
to be described as 'new localism'. As different ministers pursued departmental policies, a number of them evolved policies that could be seen as
being 'local', though they moved beyond traditional concepts of elected
local democracy. Thus, the evolution of autonomous schools, hospitals,
urban renewal partnerships, social housing providers and crime reduction partnerships made it possible for ministers to argue that a new kind
of 'governance' was being developed.

The New Local Government Network (NLGN), a think-tank, applied a
degree of intellectual coherence to a number of separately evolved policies that had bubbled up from the Blair government. In 2000, NLGN
published a document entitled *Towards New Localism: A Discussion Paper*
and in so doing kick-started the wider use of the term 'new localism'.[18]
The purposes of the new policy were outlined:

> Councils would develop a Partnership Contract proposal with their local
> communities setting out how they intend to address the social, environ-
> mental and economic needs of their localities, supported by stakeholders
> to deliver major improvements over a five-year period. As part of this, local
> government would show how they would deliver on central government

---

[18] New Local Government Network, *Towards a New Localism: A Discussion Paper*, by Lord
Filkin, Professor Gerry Stoker, Cllr Greg Wilkinson and John Williams (London: NLGN,
2000).

targets, as in Local PSAs. Central government would then enter into a Partnership Contract with the council to support the delivery of local objectives and national targets.

New localism would require the council to work with other local institutions to address a wide range of public policy questions, though they would have to do so in such a way as to hit government targets. Whitehall would agree to behave in a way that was consistent with this objective. Local authorities would be the leader of this process, but not the sole provider. Moreover, there was an acceptance of the legitimacy of a significant degree of central intervention.

Such pragmatism was reasonable. Local government, in common with health authorities, the police, regeneration partnerships and housing providers was expected to hit dozens of targets that were set for it. Councils and other providers found themselves required to achieve a number of – often inconsistent – objectives set by different parts of Whitehall.[19] One of the purposes of the new localism was to square this particular circle.

Between 2001 and 2005, different departments of state moved to strengthen or create new local institutions as the delivery vehicle for public services. By far the most important of these new 'micro' institutions were NHS Foundation Trusts,[20] announced in early 2002, and which were intended to be independent local health service agencies. Schools were to be given greater freedom to determine their own affairs. New kinds of partly privately funded schools ('academies') were created alongside many new 'specialist' institutions. From 2006–7, schools' funding would come not as the result of local authority funding decisions but through a nationally determined ring-fenced funding arrangement.[21]

In housing, social provision had for many years been gradually transferred away from local government control. Registered social landlords (RSLs) (not-for-profit companies and trusts) had taken the role that up to the 1980s had been the responsibility of local government. Much council housing had been block-transferred to RSL control. Where this had not happened, the Blair government had required the creation of Arms-Length Management Organisations (ALMOs) or had insisted that

---

[19] Public Administration Committee, *On Target? Government by Measurement*, Fifth Report, vol. I: HC 62-I, Session 2002–3 (London: TSO, 2003).

[20] Annabel Ferriman, 'Milburn Announces Setting up of "Foundation" Hospitals', *British Medical Journal*, 19 January 2002.

[21] Department for Education and Skills, *Consultation on New School Funding: Arrangements from 2006–07* (London: DfES, 2005).

authorities redeveloped their housing stock by means of Private Finance Initiative (PFI) deals.[22] Social housing was, therefore, in the hands of a bewildering array of RSLs, ALMOs and, in some cases, local authorities. Private developers were also involved because of planning deals that required them to finance a proportion of 'affordable' housing as a condition of receiving planning permission. Regeneration partnerships, which were generally funded either by Whitehall or by regional development agencies, usually had developers, housing providers, local authorities and several other key local players in membership.

Regeneration bodies, along with the police, health authorities, transport providers and a number of regional agencies, were by no means the only other players involved in 'new localism'. 'Faith communities', non-governmental organisations, business leaders, utilities providers and innumerable government agencies were often drawn in. Taken together, these bodies came increasingly to be known as 'governance'. Each 'stakeholder' had a role to play in the achievement of goals for an area.

After a short period at the start of Blair's second government, during which different micro-units of provision had evolved, efforts were initiated to encourage councils and other local institutions to work together.[23] Ministers realised there were difficulties in having innumerable single-service providers operating alongside local government.

A number of policy developments occurred between 2001 and 2005, including Best Value plans, Local Public Service Agreements (LPSAs), Local Area Agreements (LAAs) and, predictably, a raft of further consultation papers. LPSAs were agreements between the Treasury and individual councils about the achievement of particular public service objectives.[24] Additional resources were provided both to fund new initiatives and as a reward if improvements were delivered. LAAs, which evolved in 2004 and 2005, involved replacing a number of different funding streams with a single one that would generally be paid to an area's Local Strategic Partnership (LSP).[25] Such partnerships, which were a further manifestation of new localism, brought together the council,

[22] Office of the Deputy Prime Minister, *The Decent Homes Target Implementation Plan* (London: ODPM, 2003).
[23] Office of the Deputy Prime Minister, *Supporting Strategic Service Delivery Partnerships in Local Government: A Research and Development Programme* (London: ODPM, 2001).
[24] See, for example, Local Government Association, *Improving Local Services Local Public Service Agreements* (London: LGA, 2001).
[25] Office of the Deputy Prime Minister, *Local Area Agreements: A Prospectus* (London: ODPM, 2004).

health authority, police, business, the voluntary sector and others into another new local institution.

The Local Government Association and its leadership were suspicious of new localism,[26] fearing it would damage traditional local government by encouraging new single-service micro-units of government and/or by accepting the supremacy of the centre in requiring councils to hit targets. By 2005, new localism had started to evolve into something rather different from the ideas outlined in the period from 2000 to 2003.

New localism did not demonstrably improve either the quality of public services or the strength of local democracy in the way its proponents had hoped. For example, the interest shown in elections for membership of Foundation Hospital boards proved minimal. Partnerships often proved complex to administer and, in the case of some regeneration projects, could actually inhibit effective delivery.[27] The very term 'joined-up' government had become a cliché. The time had arrived for new localism to move on.

From new localism to community governance

In the summer of 2004, the government published a document[28] entitled *The Future of Local Government.* The government accepted there had been too many central controls, targets and random initiatives. There should be more citizen engagement, better local leadership and improved service delivery. The government believed greater citizen engagement was an essential element in improving the quality of provision while simultaneously 're-engaging citizens in civic life and building social capital'. 'Alongside local elections, as well as voter turnouts, there need to be more and better opportunities to participate and exert influence on local issues and decisions. Devolution should not stop at the town hall.'

In a document entitled *Sustainable Communities: People, Places and Prosperity,* published early in 2005, the government expanded on its new, community-based, policy.[29] The government's 'programme of action' for

[26] See, for example, Jeremy Beecham, 'Heading Back to the Silo', *Public Finance,* 21–27 March (London: CIPFA, 2003).
[27] Audit Commission, *Governing Partnerships Bridging the Accountability Gap* (London: Audit Commission, 2005).
[28] Office of the Deputy Prime Minister, *The Future of Local Government Developing a 10 Year Vision* (London: ODPM, 2004).
[29] Office of the Deputy Prime Minister, *Sustainable Communities: People, Places and Prosperity* (London: ODPM, 2005).

communities would provide 'opportunities for all communities to have more control over their own neighbourhoods'. There would be a 'Neighbourhoods Charter' which would allow communities to own local assets (for example, playgrounds or community centres), to trigger action by public authorities, to have devolved budgets and to use bye-laws. Schools, health services and the police would be required to be 'more responsive'. Local councillors would provide democratically legitimate leadership for any new neighbourhood arrangements.

Yet another document,[30] published at the same time as the *Sustainable Communities* paper cited above, explained that the government wanted to use new forms of community and neighbourhood governance to change the very nature of British democracy.

> Western democracies are all facing a decline in interest in conventional forms of politics. Voter turnout at elections in England has generally declined. The gap between local and national turnout remains high . . . Fewer people are willing to participate in political parties and traditional democratic processes. All this has serious implications for the legitimacy of existing political institutions and the priorities they set for public services.

It would be possible for new neighbourhood or parish bodies to write contracts with local authorities and other service providers (presumably including the NHS, police or social landlords). Local councils would be allowed to pass new bye-laws to allow neighbourhoods to control particular activities within their areas. The costs of the new neighbourhood governance would be limited, but not zero. Arrangements were 'principally about using existing resources more effectively, not about increasing expenditure overall'.

Thus, by the end of the second Blair government, new localism had evolved into a new, neighbourhood-oriented (as yet theoretical) variant of itself. This new type of institutional mechanism would have to operate in a way that allowed choice and which was responsive. It had to take account of the needs of a wide variety of groups, including faith communities, pensioners, patients, the young, those concerned with transport, and of course local residents within a geographical area. But in operating successfully, these new bodies also had to adhere to public service requirements for equity, fairness and accountability.

[30] Office of the Deputy Prime Minister and the Home Office, *Citizen Engagement and Public Services: Why Neighbourhoods Matter* (London: ODPM, 2005).

The 'balance of funding' issue

The second Blair term of office inherited the unfinished business of the first. Local government continued to complain about the 'balance of funding' between central and local government. Three-quarters of council revenue income derived from Whitehall grants, with only a quarter coming from council tax. This balance meant that, at the margin, if a council added 1% to its spending, there would be a 4% increase in local taxation. Within government, this phenomenon was referred to as 'the gearing effect'.

By the end of 2002, the government could no longer put off the reform of grants. The Revenue Support Grant for 2003–4 would be based on new 'Formula Spending Shares', a somewhat reformed version of the previous measures. Then, in January 2003, a review was set up under the chairmanship of Nick Raynsford to consider the balance of central and local resources for councils.

Just as the 'balance of funding' review was getting under way in the early months of 2003, the impact of the grant reforms introduced in the RSG settlement began to bite. Because grant was redistributed – albeit modestly – the heavily geared impact of these reforms led to an average rise in council tax of 13% over England as a whole. More awkwardly for the government, many schools found they were receiving far less additional cash than ministers had suggested they would from a settlement that was, overall, intended to raise education expenditure at a rate well above inflation.

Later in 2003, the Audit Commission published a report[31] that, in effect, blamed the government for the 2003–4 council tax hike. A second report from the Commission suggested that, in fact, councils had allocated more money to schools than the government had originally projected.[32] There had never really been a significant funding 'crisis', though some schools had fared less well than they expected because of the redistribution of government grant between authorities and because a number of specific-purpose grants had been abolished.

As a result of the difficulties that had faced school funding in 2003, the Department for Education and Skills announced that, from 2004–5, there would be a 'minimum funding guarantee' for each school. Starting in

---

[31] Audit Commission, *Council Tax Increases 2003/04: Why Were They So High?* (London: TSO, 2003).
[32] Audit Commission, *Education Funding: The Impact and Effectiveness of Measures to Stabilise School Funding* (London: TSO, 2004).

2006–7, school funding would be ring-fenced and, in effect, removed from the general resources provided to local government.

The 13% jump in council tax in 2003 led the government to decide to threaten to reuse their briefly dormant capping powers. Having scrapped the universal capping of local tax they had inherited from the Major government, Labour now found themselves under intense pressure – particularly from pensioners – to limit or abolish council tax.

The Raynsford review published its final report in July 2004, addressing the central issue of whether the existing balance of funding between councils' central and local resource-raising was, in fact, a problem. In paragraph 1.33, it concluded 'there are strong arguments in favour of a shift in the balance of funding, but the case for any shift depends on the feasibility and desirability of any measures which might be used to achieve it'. Gearing 'can cloud the accountability and transparency of local spending decisions and can contribute to unsustainable council tax increases'.[33]

The acceptance that there were arguments in favour of a change in the balance of funding was heavily tempered by the idea that 'the feasibility and desirability of any measures which might be used to achieve it' should be a constraint on reform. It was easy to read the latter words as an effective bar on reform.

Raynsford went on to consider a number of possible reforms to council tax, and accepted a clear case for reviewing the number of tax bands and the ratios between them – at the time of the next revaluation. Council tax benefit take-up should be improved. Business rates could be re-localised, with safeguards for business. A local income tax was examined, including issues such as administration costs, implications for business and the treatment of particular categories of income. But the overall conclusion, as with other parts of the review, was that 'considerable further work would be required' to address technical, administrative and distributional impacts.

Smaller taxes and charges, e.g. a local tourist bed tax, a localised vehicle excise duty or green taxes, could not, the review stated, have achieved a significant shift in the balance of funding. 'The case for and against each of these options should be judged on its own merits.' The review itself did not, however, offer views on such merits.

On the day Raynsford reported, the government announced that Sir Michael Lyons would head a follow-up inquiry to complete the work

---

[33] Office of the Deputy Prime Minister, *Balance of Funding Review – Report* (London: ODPM, 2004).

undertaken by Raynsford. Lyons' report would be published in December 2005 and was expected to produce detailed exemplifications of some of the possible changes touched on by Raynsford. The government's decision to implement a revaluation of the council tax base in England in 2007 (a revaluation took place in April 2005 in Wales) was expected to create an additional dimension to Lyons' work. However, the revaluation was abandoned in the autumn of 2005.

If the future of revenue funding remained in the 'pending' tray throughout Labour's first eight years in office, capital finance was reformed in a way that was, at least in intent, expected to decentralise political control. A system of 'prudential rules' was introduced to replace the belt-and-braces controls that had previously been used to limit councils' freedom to spend on major capital projects. The new arrangements made it possible for authorities to incur new capital spending so long as they adhered to a number of common-sense rules concerning their capacity to make repayments and the total of their outstanding debts. Unfortunately, the freedoms offered were not widely taken up because councils were concerned about the long-term impacts of new borrowing on their revenue expenditure. That is, they feared that extra debt charges would lead to future capping.

Regional government for England

The four forms of devolved government – Scotland, Wales, London and Northern Ireland – operating within the United Kingdom in 2001 were each, predictably, significantly different from the others. In May 2002 the Office of the Deputy Prime Minister published a consultative document on the creation of regional governments within England.[34] The next stage of devolution was under way.

The government outlined a model of regional government for England that was substantially different from those already adopted for other parts of the UK. English regions were to be given a weaker form of assembly than that operating in London. However, unlike the London system, those for other parts of England would not have a 'mayor' but would instead (like Scotland and Wales) select a leader from among assembly members. Thus, the rest of the English regions were to use a form of government based on the traditional British parliamentary or local

---

[34] Department for Transport, Local Government and the Regions, *Your Region, Your Choice Revitalising the English Regions* (London: TSO, 2002).

government model. Only the capital's regional arrangements would feature a directly elected executive.

The powers to be devolved to the new English regions would include the economic regeneration responsibilities already given to Regional Development Agencies, plus strategic planning, the allocation of social housing resources to local authorities and a requirement to publish a number of strategies. These strategies would, separately, allow the region influence over skills and employment, transport, waste, health improvement, culture and biodiversity.

The capacity of the regions to raise their own resources was also heavily circumscribed. English assemblies were to be given the same power to set a council tax precept that had been given to the Greater London Authority (though not, oddly, to the Welsh Assembly). However the government proposed 'initially to limit assembly precepts through arrangements comparable to the existing local authority capping regime' (paragraph 5.9). The new English assemblies were to be capped before they had even been created.

The new authorities would be elected using the Additional Member System, a form of proportional representation that had been used in Scotland, Wales and for the London Assembly. Where a region voted to introduce regional government, any areas with two-tier local government (i.e. non-metropolitan counties and districts) would be required to move to a single tier of unitary councils. The government did not believe the electorate would be prepared to accept three levels of government below Westminster.

A Regional Assemblies (Preparations) Act received royal assent in May 2003, allowing the government to move ahead with referendums and other preparatory work, such as the need to review local government boundaries within regions where regional assemblies were to be created. Also during 2003, the government undertook a 'soundings' exercise – including opinion polling – to see which regions were likely to show the greatest interest in holding a referendum. As a result, Local and Regional Government Minister Nick Raynsford announced in July 2004 that people in three northern regions would be allowed to vote later that year on whether or not to set up regional governments in their areas.

Later, in July 2004, the government published a Draft Regional Assemblies Bill. On the same day, ministers made it clear that they were to postpone the referendums planned for the North-West and Yorkshire and Humberside: only the North-East of England would vote in November that year.

In the run-up to the referendum, it became clear that opinion was running against the proposed regional authority. While the 'Yes' campaign received the support of a wide range of regional Establishment and media figures, the 'No' campaign publicised their message using an inflatable white elephant which, they believed, symbolised the bureaucratic and feeble nature of the proposed new government. On 4 November 2004, in an all-postal ballot, the voters of the North-East rejected an elected regional assembly by 78% to 22%. The turnout was 48%. Electors in every district in the whole region voted 'No'. It is hard to exaggerate the scale of the rejection.

Deputy Prime Minister John Prescott conceded on 8 November 2004 that devolution to the English regions was to be abandoned for the foreseeable future. There would be no referendum in either the North-West or Yorkshire and Humberside. The voters of the North-East had, in the event, spoken for the whole of England.

2005–2007

Steady as she goes

A number of issues that had emerged during the first two governments continued to have an impact on Labour in Blair's third term. The funding of local government was subject to a review that was due to report in December 2005. In the event, the Lyons Inquiry was delayed until December 2006, then March 2007. A revaluation of homes for council tax, planned for April 2007, had been abandoned by the government during the autumn of 2005. Other official inquiries, into the planning system, skills and transport provision were initiated by the Chancellor and reported in 2006 and 2007.

A gradual process, which had started under John Major, of encouraging councils to propose a single tier of 'unitary' authorities continued in areas where there were county and districts. By early 2007 it was clear that the Treasury was attempting to slow down even the limited progress that was being made.

Local government's sponsoring department, the Office of the Deputy Prime Minister (ODPM), was radically reconfigured in May 2006. A new Department for Communities and Local Government was created with a brief that added 'equalities' and 'community cohesion' to the traditional grouping of housing, planning and local government. This was a long way from the megalithic Department of Environment, Transport and the

Regions that had included transport and the regions, created back in 1997.

But, from 2005 onwards, there were few expectations of radicalism from the Blair government. There were, however, a number of carry-over issues that will be considered below.

The Northern Way, regions, city regions and cities

Following the rejection of the proposed regional assembly in the North-East in 2004, the post-2005 government sought new ways to advance the governance of areas larger than existing units of local government. David Miliband, who was appointed as a cabinet minister within the ODPM after the 2005 election, spent a year examining local government and became an exponent of 'city regional' arrangements.

The 1997–2001 and 2001–5 governments had already created a significant number of 'regional' institutions. In addition to the Regional Development Agencies and indirectly elected 'assemblies' considered above, the three northern regions (the North-East, the North-West and Yorkshire and Humberside) were grouped together in the supra-regional Northern Way, a grouping that had its own officials and governing body. Below the regional level, the eight 'core cities' (Birmingham, Bristol, Leeds, Liverpool, Manchester, Newcastle, Nottingham and Sheffield) had developed a strong case for these major centres to be seen as the drivers of economic and social change across their regions.

David Miliband advanced the case for a level of governance between the city and the region.[35] He argued that there would possibly be advantages to a city-regional level of government, coupled with a directly elected mayor. The Centre for Cities, an urban think-tank, provided intellectual support for the idea.[36] Such an arrangement would broadly replicate the Greater London Authority, which had been created for the capital in 2000 and which ministers judged a success. Metropolitan authority leaders and authorities were not convinced by the Miliband plan, though they were prepared to create voluntary joint boards across city regional areas.

They need not have worried. In May 2006, Miliband was moved on and his successor, Ruth Kelly, appeared less convinced by city regions. Moreover, a pamphlet published in July 2006 by the New Local

[35] See, for example, ODPM, *A Framework for City Regions* (London: TSO, 2006), which explored the subject in the light of Miliband's concerns.
[36] Adam Marshall and Dermot Finch, *City Leadership Giving City-Regions the Power to Grow*, Centre for Cities (London: IPPR, 2006).

Government Network and, crucially, authored by Treasury ministers Ed Balls and John Healey, argued that regions, not city regions, were the way ahead.[37] The apparent stand-off between regionalists and city-regionalists was to be informed further by the completion of a 'sub-national review' of economic development and government, which fed into the autumn 2007 Comprehensive Spending Review.

In the last days of the Blair premiership, the Department for Transport (DfT) published its own proposals to strengthen the governance of transport at the level above the core cities, but below the region.[38] There had been a number of earlier reports pointing to the logic of basing city-regional authorities on metropolitan transport institutions[39] and the DfT appeared convinced by the arguments in favour of reform.

Another White Paper

The key publication of the final Blair term was the local government White Paper of October 2006.[40] This document followed many earlier ones and provided arguments for mild experimentation or change to local government. The key proposals were: first, to extend the use of Local Strategic Partnerships, allowing councils to lead an array of local institutions (e.g. health providers, the police and social landlords) and pool some budgets. Second, to introduce a 'community call for action', allowing neighbourhoods to demand that the council or other service providers deliver services in a particular way within a local area. Third, there should be a greater use of neighbourhoods and parish-level government. Fourth, new models of leadership should be introduced, including additional elected mayors or fixed-term executive leaders. Finally, the government suggested that in shire areas, where there continued to be two tiers of local government, authorities should consider moving to a single tier of 'unitary' councils.

None of these ideas was new. All had, in one form or another been around for some years. The difficulty for the new Secretary of State, Ruth Kelly, was that she was operating at the start of a prolonged interregnum

[37] New Local Government Network, *Evolution and Devolution in England How Regions Strengthen our Towns and Cities*, by Ed Balls, John Healey and Chris Leslie (London: NLGN, 2006).

[38] Department for Transport, *Strengthening Local Delivery: The Draft Local Transport Bill*, vol. I: *A Consultation*, Cm. 7043-I (London: TSO, 2007).

[39] Tony Travers and Stephen Glaister, *Local Transport: How Small Reforms Could Make a Big Difference* (London: LGA, 2006).

[40] Department for Communities and Local Government, *Strong And Prosperous Communities The Local Government White Paper*, Cm. 6939-I (London: TSO, 2006).

between Tony Blair and Gordon Brown. The White Paper was cautious and offered a number of possible reforms which, as described, could either lead to a relatively radical reform or, alternatively, virtually none. By the time Blair left office, the process of reform was left unresolved.

The Lyons Inquiry

The Blair government's decade-long, tentative efforts to suggest reforms to local government finance had, from 2004, centred on the Lyons Inquiry. Lyons finally reported in March 2007. Having worked within well-understood political constraints, the report was a modest set of proposals[41] that its author believed to be 'developmental', rather than the 'big bang' advocated by commentators such as Simon Jenkins.[42]

Lyons accepted that council tax, introduced by the Conservatives in 1993, should be retained, though there might be modest reforms to make the tax paid by households relate more closely to different property prices. There should be a revaluation of the tax base. Moreover, ministers should no longer use capping to limit council tax rises from year to year. The business rate, nationalised by the Tories in 1990, should remain a centrally determined tax, but there might be a local supplement. Local income tax should be further explored, with a view to assigning part of it to local authorities in the longer term. Smaller taxes, e.g. on tourism, and charges, e.g. on waste, should be considered. There should be greater incentives for councils to build up their council tax and business rate yield; authorities should be allowed to keep part of any growth in the tax base.

The government rejected Lyons' proposals on capping, a revaluation and new taxes. A supplement to business rate was accepted, as was the possibility of charging households for waste and other environmental problems. Overall, there was no suggestion that the funding of local government could be radically changed. Tony Blair handed over the system to his successor where John Major had left it a decade before.

London

Blair's radicalism in relation to devolution continued in a modest way in the capital after 2005. The government introduced legislation[43] to

---

[41] Sir Michael Lyons, *Lyons Inquiry into Local Government* (London: TSO, 2007).
[42] Simon Jenkins, *Big Bang Localism – A Rescue Plan for British Democracy* (London: Policy Exchange, 2004).   [43] *Greater London Authority Bill* (London: TSO, 2006).

strengthen the powers of the Mayor of London and, to a lesser extent, of the London Assembly. The most important new powers affect planning and housing. In future, the Mayor would be able to override the largest borough planning decisions, to give permission for a project the borough had rejected. Hitherto, the Mayor had only been able to veto such projects, not to give them planning permission in the face of borough opposition. The new housing powers would allow the Mayor to allocate resources for affordable and social housing within the capital, a function previously overseen by central government. The Mayor's powers to appoint some board members and to give directions to the fire authority were also amended.

The London boroughs opposed the Mayor's additional powers on the grounds that they strengthened the metropolitan level of government at the expense of the local. The capital's government model remained less devolved than in Wales or Scotland, but was well in advance of the powers available at the city-wide or regional level elsewhere in England. Blair's attempt at devolution had failed in England, though London suggested that at some future date another government might try again.

Conclusions

The third Blair government faced a local government system that was, year on year, slipping away from Labour control. As had happened during the Conservatives' long period in power up to 1997, the cumulative effect of 'mid-term losses' left the Labour Party with around 5,500 councillors in 2007. When they had taken office, they had had just under 11,000 councillors: under Tony Blair, half the party's elected members had disappeared. In the south of England, only a few pockets remained, in London and other urban centres such as Brighton, Reading and Stevenage.

After a decade of New Labour, much of local government performed well according to the Audit Commission's independent analyses. Compared to Whitehall's relentless bad news stories, e.g. the need to break up the Home Office, local government in 2007 was a place of sunlit performance uplands.

Some good decentralising reform was achieved by New Labour. The 'prudential rules' system of capital control was a significant improvement on the belt-and-braces system inherited from the Tories. Devolution to Scotland, Wales and London represented a genuine diffusion of power. The removal of compulsion from competitive tendering was sensible and pro-local. Ministerial rhetoric towards local government has generally been co-operative and benign.

But underlying the Labour decade has been the reality that well-intentioned ministers from Hilary Armstrong to Phil Woolas via Nick Raynsford found themselves unable to convince the Treasury or service-sponsoring departments to abandon their vice-like grip on local government. Whitehall had been able to block many attempts to shift power away from the centre into the hands of even the best councils. The lack of funding reform following the Lyons Inquiry, the nationalisation of school funding and the aggressive use of targets all attest to the Blair decade's continuation of the centralisation that had flourished for years previously. In the UK 95% of all taxation is paid to the Exchequer.

As a result, a decade of consultation documents, White Papers and think-tank output has left local government with the drift to central control largely unchecked and with no reform to funding arrangements. The failure to bring about radical change during two parliaments when Blair had very large majorities represented a significant failure to focus on a key constitutional issue.

Looking ahead to the next ten years, it is virtually impossible to imagine governments being elected with the kind of majorities enjoyed by Labour since 1997 – and with such a weak opposition. Tony Blair missed a major opportunity to decentralise Britain.

5

Central government

PAUL FAWCETT AND R. A. W. RHODES

Introduction

Since the Fulton Committee's report in 1968 there has been a constant stream of initiatives from Labour and Conservative governments aimed at strengthening central government and reforming the civil service. Many now belong to the dustbin of history, their labels redolent of times past. Who now remembers or cares about CPRS, MINIS, FMI, the '3Es', Next Steps agencies, and citizens' charters? A sceptic might remark that nothing persists except the persistent drive for reform.[1]

Even against this backcloth of frenetic activity, one word captures the Blair government's handling of the central machinery of government – hyperactive. However understood, whatever the results, nobody can deny there has been much activity. This chapter tells three stories of central change: the centralisation story, which claims the changes sought to increase the power of the Prime Minister at the expense of cabinet and the departments; the management story, which claims the attempt to reform the civil service foundered on Blair's lack of policymaking and management skills; and the governance story, which argues the Prime Minister is locked into webs of dependence that undermined his initiatives. Finally, we essay an overall assessment.

The centralisation story

The trend to executive centralisation is seen by many commentators as widespread in parliamentary government. For example, Poguntke and Webb argue that executive presidentialism occurs when there is a shift of

---

[1] On these several labels and a history of reform, see Peter Hennessy, *Whitehall*, rev. edn (London: Secker and Warburg, 2001); and Andrew Massey and Robert Pyper, *Public Management and Modernisation in Britain* (Houndmills: Palgrave Macmillan, 2005).

'political power resources and autonomy to the benefit of individual leaders' and 'a concomitant loss of power and autonomy of collective actors like cabinets'.[2] Such centralisation was on New Labour's agenda before they came to power. For example, Peter Mandelson and Roger Liddle argued there was a need 'for a more formalised strengthening of the centre of government' that 'provides the means of formulating and driving forward strategy for the government as a whole'.[3] Journalists, academics and insiders also agreed that Blair sought to centralise power in No. 10.[4] For example, Jonathan Powell, Chief of Staff at the Prime Minister's Office, famously warned senior civil servants to expect: 'a change from a feudal system of barons to a more Napoleonic system'.[5] Blair's No. 10 aides asserted that 'Cabinet died years ago', claiming they wanted 'to replace the Department barons with a Bonapartist system'.[6] So, this section recounts the story of Blair's search for a stronger, centralised executive.

Structural changes to both the Prime Minister's Office and the Cabinet Office are the main ways in which Blair has sought to centralise policymaking. These included an increase in special advisers, a strengthening of the Prime Minister's Office's role in managing the media and policymaking, and the emergence of a 'Prime Minister's department that-will-not-speak-its-name',[7] otherwise known as the Cabinet Office.

Special advisers

There were six special advisers working in the Prime Minister's Office shortly before Labour came to power. After a sharp increase in the number of appointments following Labour's general election victory, there was a more gradual rise which finally levelled off in mid-December 1999 when twenty-five special advisers worked in No. 10. Most appointments were in

[2] Thomas Poguntke and Paul Webb (eds.), *The Presidentialization of Politics: A Comparative Study of Modern Democracies* (Oxford: Oxford University Press, 2005).

[3] Peter Mandelson and Roger Liddle, *The Blair Revolution: Can New Labour Deliver?* (London: Faber and Faber, 1996), p. 240.

[4] For a review of the relevant literature and citations see Mark Bevir and R. A. W. Rhodes, 'Prime Ministers, Presidentialism and Westminster Smokescreens', *Political Studies*, 54, 2006: 671–90.

[5] *Daily Telegraph*, 8 December 2001, cited in Anthony Seldon, *Blair* (London: The Free Press, 2004), p. 437.

[6] Dennis Kavanagh and Anthony Seldon, *The Powers Behind the Prime Minister. The Hidden Influence of Number Ten* (London: HarperCollins, 2000), p. 291.

[7] Peter Hennessy, 'The Blair Style and the Requirements of Twenty-First Century Premiership', *Political Quarterly*, 71, 2000: 386–95.

the Policy Directorate, which meant that it was staffed by non-civil servants, each shadowing a particular department or policy area.

Two special advisers had prominent roles; Jonathan Powell, and Alistair
Campbell, the Director of Communications and Strategy. Both were given
line management powers over civil servants and, while the post of Chief of
Staff was not new, the role that Jonathan Powell played as head of the
Prime Minister's Office was unprecedented in scope. The Prime Minister
also appointed unpaid advisers who reported directly to him. The most
notable example was John Birt. He was the Prime Minister's part-time
Strategy Adviser, located in No. 10. His work was shrouded in some
secrecy until freedom of information requests led to the publication of
some sections of his reports.

Special advisers were also appointed across government, although
concern over their growing numbers and cost led to a cap of two special
advisers for each minister. The only exception to that rule was the
Treasury where ministers were able to draw on the advice not only from
their own appointments but also from the special advisers appointed to
the Council of Economic Advisers. Although there were always several
members of the Council, it was not the collective body its name implied.
Members of the Council worked alongside the Treasury officials who
were responsible for developing policy in their own area of expertise. The
general growth in special advisers, especially in the Prime Minister's
Office, led to charges of centralisation and politicisation of the civil
service 'through the back door'.[8]

Politicians and civil servants consistently deny there is any politicisation, associating that phrase with overt party political beliefs, but there
are other interpretations. Advisers inject party politics into the advice
process of departments. So the role of civil servants changed from providing advice to putting together packages of advice from several sources.
As Gus O'Donnell recently commented, civil servants could no longer
claim a 'monopoly on wisdom' but must instead earn their place 'as principal policy advisers'.[9]

Individual advisers also played a prominent role in departmental policy
deliberations. For example, Andrew Adonis of the Prime Minister's Policy

---

[8] See Larry Elliott, Patrick Wintour and Kevin Macguire, 'Tensions at the Top', *The Guardian*, 16 April 2002, pp. 10–11; and Tony Blair, 'Special Advisers', *House of Commons Written Ministerial Statement by the Prime Minister*, 24 July 2006, cc. 86–92.

[9] Gus O'Donnell, 'Our 21st Century Civil Service – Creating a Culture of Excellence', Public Service Reform Conference, QE II Conference Centre, London, 6 June 2006, at: www.civilservice.gov.uk/publications/doc/psr_speech060606.doc.

Directorate often intervened to influence education policymaking, although some insiders opined acidly that 'if anyone knew Andrew was behind a policy, it immediately made people suspicious'.[10] The post has also become a springboard to high government office. Prominent examples include: Andrew Adonis (who became Parliamentary Under-Secretary of State for Schools in the Department for Education and Skills in May 2005); Ed Balls (who became Economic Secretary to the Treasury in May 2006); and David Miliband (who became Secretary of State for Environment, Food and Rural Affairs in May 2006, having previously held various ministerial positions).

Strengthening media management and policymaking

Spin, or less pejoratively news management and presenting government policy, is a long-standing part of the responsibilities of the Prime Minister's Office, but this role was strengthened after May 1997. A change to the Ministerial Code required ministers to clear all major interviews, press releases and policy statements with No. 10 before they were released to the media. The Office was also strengthened by creating a Strategic Communications Unit, which coordinated the release of departmental statements to avoid clashes. It was staffed by a mixture of special advisers and civil servants.

A few months after Labour's second electoral victory, the Prime Minister made more institutional changes to No. 10. The Prime Minister's Private Office was merged with the Policy Unit to form a new Policy Directorate. Its key functions were day-to-day liaison with Whitehall departments and writing briefs and speeches for the Prime Minister. It was also involved in developing short-term policy in the Prime Minister's priority areas, such as the Respect agenda, announced after the 2005 general election. A new position of Director of Communications and Strategy was also created to oversee the work of the Strategic Communications Unit, the Press Office and the Research and Information Unit. Its stature and influence weakened following the resignation of Alistair Campbell and the recommendations of the interim report of the Phillis Review of Government Communications.[11] Campbell's replacement was not given line management powers over civil servants and overall responsibility for government

---

[10] Cited in Seldon, *Blair*, p. 642.
[11] Government Communications Review Group, *Interim Report* at: http://archive. cabinetoffice.gov.uk/gcreview/News/interimreport.pdf.

media strategy and personnel was handed over to a new Permanent Secretary of Government Communications based in the Cabinet Office.

Supporting the Prime Minister

The Cabinet Office was always a ragbag of functions bequeathed to it by former prime ministers. Blair added to the ragbag, although he broke with tradition in the number of units created and the speed of change. Early efforts focused on tackling cross-cutting issues. Blair appointed an assortment of taskforces, working parties, commissions, 'policy Czars', policy forums and policy action teams.[12] Various cross-cutting units were also established or moved to the Cabinet Office, including the Social Exclusion Unit; the Women's Unit; the Anti-Drugs Coordination Unit; the Freedom of Information Unit; and, more recently, the Office of the Third Sector. Most of these units changed their names to reflect changed priorities or responsibilities and many were transferred out of the Cabinet Office to other departments. For example, the Social Exclusion Unit started life in the Cabinet Office at the beginning of December 1997, transferred to the Office of the Deputy Prime Minister at the end of May 2002, only to return to the Cabinet Office in June 2006, with a revised name and remit. These changes show how Blair sought to control government functions without bothering himself with too many of the operational details. As Peter Hennessy noted, 'Number 10 is omnipresent'.[13]

The second wave of initiatives sought to develop strategic policy for the Prime Minister. Initially, Blair set up the Performance and Innovation Unit (PIU) (launched on 28 July 1998) and the Prime Minister's Forward Strategy Unit (PMFSU) (launched on 22 June 2001). After the second general election victory of June 2001, an Office of the Deputy Prime Minister was established in the Cabinet Office with several new units in the department, including the Prime Minister's Strategy Unit (PMSU); the Prime Minister's Delivery Unit (PMDU); and the Office of Public Sector Reform (OPSR).

The PMSU was formed from a merger of existing strategy units, including the PIU and the PMFSU. It had three roles: strategic reviews and policy advice on the Prime Minister's domestic policy priorities; helping departments develop effective strategies and policies, and identifying and

---

[12] Andrew Taylor, 'Hollowing out or Filling in? Taskforces and the Management of Cross-cutting Issues in British Government', *British Journal of Politics and International Relations*, 2, 2000: 46–71.

[13] Peter Hennessy, 'The Blair Style of Government', *Government and Opposition*, 33, 1998: 15.

disseminating thinking on emerging issues and challenges. It worked in project teams organised around five clusters: public service reform, home affairs, economy and infrastructure, welfare reform, and social justice and communities. It increasingly took on work formerly carried out by one of the policy-specific, cross-cutting units, yet it always remained relatively small. At its peak, there were no more than ninety people working in the Unit and by mid-May 2005 it contained some fifty-five people. The work-force was drawn from the civil service, the private or voluntary sectors, and the wider public sector.

It is difficult to assess the impact of the PMSU. It published some ninety reports between May 1999 and March 2007 but it also conducted many confidential projects. Despite the claim that its reports were not official statements of government policy, they often framed the public policy debate. Its work had direct effects on government policy and the delivery of services: for example, the conclusions of the Energy Review.[14] By the end, it had a central and growing role. It was responsible for developing reform of the public services. It was also heavily involved in the six policy reviews the Prime Minister launched in October 2006. Its role was to develop big policy for the 'whole' of government, not just on a particular issue.[15] It also enjoyed broad support. It received a positive report from the House of Commons Public Administration Committee and the Conservative Party's Democracy Task Force.[16] By the prevailing standards for such units, its position was, and remains, secure. However, it is hard to judge its effectiveness because it was not the only strategic unit in the core executive undertaking such work. The Treasury always played an important role (see below).

Supporting the cabinet

The Cabinet Office under Blair had the usual secretariats: economic and domestic, European, defence and overseas, and intelligence. There has been a tendency to focus on the glamorous strategy units and ignore the long-standing, even dull, work of the Cabinet Office. That is a mistake. Contrary to assertions about the 'death of cabinet', the Cabinet Office

[14] Prime Minister's Strategy Unit, *The Energy Review* (London: Cabinet Office, 2002).
[15] For information on the Prime Minister's Policy Reviews see: www.cabinetoffice.gov.uk/policy_review/index.asp.
[16] Public Administration Select Committee, *Governing the Future*, 2006–07, HC 123-I (London: TSO, 2007); and Conservative Party Democracy Task Force, *An End to Sofa Government* (London: Conservative Party, 2007).

Secretariat continued to perform its traditional coordinating role. Of course, it was subject to the same pressures for change. Some of these changes were to meet the policy commitments of the Blair government. For example, a Constitution Secretariat was created immediately after the general election in May 1997 to coordinate the government's wide-ranging programme of constitutional reform, notably the work on devolution, freedom of information, House of Lords reform and human rights. Other changes were less significant, examples of administrative evolution, such as the change in name of the Ceremonial Branch to the Ceremonial Secretariat in 2001.

The most notable reforms were in security, intelligence and emergency-related matters. Two developments are noteworthy. First, a new post of Intelligence and Security Coordinator was created in June 2002. The Coordinator became the Prime Minister's principal adviser on security, intelligence and emergency-related matters, assuming responsibility for functions previously discharged by the Cabinet Secretary. He was responsible for day-to-day oversight of the Intelligence and Security Secretariat, providing the Prime Minister and other senior ministers with timely, accurate and objectively assessed intelligence from across government and the intelligence agencies. In November 2005, the newly appointed Permanent Secretary, Richard Mottram, also became Chair of the Joint Intelligence Committee and the title of the post was changed to Permanent Secretary, Intelligence, Security and Resilience.

Second, the new permanent secretary was also responsible for overseeing the work of the Civil Contingencies Secretariat which was created in July 2001 when the Cabinet Office merged its existing emergency planning units with those from the Home Office. Its main role was to prepare for and respond to crises and major emergencies. It worked on incidents such as avian influenza as well as the London bombings of July 2005. In short, there was a major expansion of the Cabinet Office's work in both intelligence and security, and emergency planning. The new post of Permanent Secretary, Intelligence, Security and Resilience, was created as a link between these two areas of work.[17]

---

[17] At the end of March 2007, the Prime Minister announced the creation of a new Ministry of Justice and a strengthening of the Home Office's role in security and counter-terrorism. Most of the security and intelligence functions of the Permanent Secretary for Intelligence, Security and Resilience will remain intact and the 'Cabinet Office will retain its role [in] supporting the Prime Minister on national security and counter-terrorism'. But in the ever-changing world of strengthening central capability, it is wisest to conclude that observers should 'watch this space'. See www.cabinetoffice.gov.uk/publications/reports/government_changes/doc/machinery_govt.doc.

It is hard to escape the conclusion that here was a government intent on centralising policymaking. The aim of the Cabinet Office, as a Prime Minister's department in all but name, was to allow Blair to remain on top, if not in detailed touch. However, it was still abundantly clear that the Prime Minister 'never [really] succeeded in finding a structure that suited him'.[18]

The management story

As Richard Wilson observed: 'The reality is that the Civil Service has long been under pressure from politicians to reform, beginning with Harold Wilson, who set up the Fulton Committee 40 years ago'.[19] Improving public sector management was always central to these reforms. Under Blair, as under previous governments, the spate of initiatives continued unabated. As Antony Part, former Permanent Secretary at the Department of Industry testily asserted: 'Then, as now, the administrative class spent most of their time initiating or implementing changes. It was – and is – their characteristic function, a point that has been overlooked by a number of prominent people who ought to know better.'[20] Managing change was to remain a characteristic function of the administrative class just as the search for management change was to remain a preoccupation of the political class. We now tell the story of Blair's search for a civil service with better management skills.[21]

The reform process began with the Modernising Government White Paper, with joined-up government as its flagship innovation. This agenda mutated into the 'delivery agenda' by the general election victory of June 2001. The government presented these shifts as a naturally evolving process. In contrast, others protest that: 'It's a succession of knee jerks . . . They are not standing back and defining what they mean. Phrases like

---

[18] Seldon, *Blair*, p. 694.

[19] Richard Wilson at: www.telegraph.co.uk/opinion/main.jhtml?xml=/opinion/2007/01/16/do1601.xm.

[20] Antony Part, *The Making of a Mandarin* (London: Deutsch, 1990), p. 20.

[21] On the reforms of the Blair government, see Tony Bovaird and Ken Russell, 'Civil Service Reform in the UK, 1999–2005: Revolutionary Failure or Evolutionary Success?', *Public Administration*, 85, 2007: 301–28; Paul Fawcett, *Power in UK Central Government – Centralization and Coordination under the Blair Government* (Houndmills: Palgrave Macmillan, 2008 forthcoming); and David Richards, *New Labour and the Civil Service: Reconstituting the Westminster Model* (Houndmills: Palgrave Macmillan, 2007).

"joined-up government", and the "Third Way" don't mean anything.'[22] The result was a frustrated civil service, seeking a clear sense of direction amid the plethora of detailed changes.

The Modernising Government agenda was diffuse, although the theme given the greatest prominence was joined-up government.[23] The White Paper sought to develop a framework that government could use to co-ordinate its activity. Institutional fragmentation and the attendant problems of coordination had already been noted by Robin Butler, Blair's first Head of the Home Civil Service, on his retirement:

> I do worry that the management reforms of the last decade may have focused our energies very much on particular objectives, particular targets, performance indicators in return for resources and delegations. And that we have in some measure taken our eye off what we used to be good at – and still can do – which is working more corporately across the boundaries. And it may be, and I'd regret it, that the personnel reforms that we have introduced have also given people a sense that they work more for Departments rather than for the wider Civil Service.[24]

So, a new language gained currency and we talked about joined-up government, holistic governance and partnerships.[25] It was but a phase. As the Public Administration Committee of the House of Commons commented:

> The 'Modernising Government' programme as a whole is complex and has multiple elements. It is not always clear where the really key priorities are, with the resulting danger that civil servants will endeavour to work methodically on all of them at once. This is a great virtue; but it is also a considerable disability in terms of putting first things first. In our view the immense checklists contained within the 'Modernising Government'

---

[22] See Office of Public Services Reform, *Putting People at the Heart Of Public Services* (London: Cabinet Office, 2005), p. 6; and Cabinet Office official cited in Hennessy, *The Blair Revolution in Government* (University of Leeds: Institute for Politics and International Studies, 2000), p. 9.

[23] See Cabinet Office, *Modernising Government*, Cm. 4310 (London: TSO, 1999); and Cabinet Office and Performance and Innovation Unit, *Wiring It Up* (London: Cabinet Office, 2000).

[24] Robin Butler at: www.open.gov.uk/co/scsg/conference/rw_xscript.htm.

[25] For a critical review of joined-up governance see Vernon Bogdanor (ed.), *Joined-Up Government* (Oxford: Oxford University Press, 2005); Christopher Pollitt, 'Joined-up Government: A Survey', *Political Studies Review*, 1, 2003: 34–49; and David Richards and Martin J. Smith, 'The "Hybrid State": New Labour's Response to the Challenge of Governance', in S. Ludlam and M. J. Smith (eds.), *Governing as New Labour* (London: Palgrave, 2003).

programme need to be converted into a much stronger definition of what the key priorities for action are, with clear responsibilities assigned for delivering them.[26]

Following Blair's second election victory, there was a clear shift in direction. The new focus was on 'delivery'. It was a policy shift that led to further institutional reform. Two new units were created in the Cabinet Office – the Office for Public Service Reform (OPSR) and the Prime Minister's Delivery Unit (PMDU), which we discuss below. The OPSR developed and promulgated the 'philosophy' of the delivery agenda. It also advised the Prime Minister on the ways of implementing reform in the public services and the civil service. It covered all public services including local government. It was at the heart of the delivery agenda. Nevertheless, the lack of a White Paper underpinning the delivery agenda means that its development has to be tracked through a series of policy papers, speeches and statements.[27] So the principles of the delivery agenda were not always clear, mainly because they evolved over time. Even at the start, the Cabinet Office website was less than specific in announcing the end of the Modernising Government programme and the arrival of the delivery agenda:

> Thus delivery of better, modern public service is the Government's key priority for its second term. This is not easy; one commentator has said, 'There is no drama in delivery . . . only a long, grinding haul punctuated by public frustration with the pace of change.' Failure will not be tolerated, nor will mediocrity.[28]

The clearest statements of the principles underpinning the early phase of the delivery agenda can be found in two separate documents. The first document, *Reforming our Public Services: Principles into Practice*, was published by the OPSR in March 2002. It outlined the 'Prime Minister's four principles of public sector reform': national standards to ensure that people have the right to high-quality services wherever they live; devolution to give local leaders the means to deliver these standards to local people; more flexibility in service provision to meet people's rising expectations; and greater customer choice.[29] The second document, *Putting*

---

[26] House of Commons Public Administration Select Committee, *Making Government Work: The Emerging Issues*, 2000–01, HC 94 (London: TSO, 2001), para. 42.

[27] See, for example, Office of Public Services Reform, *Reforming our Public Services – Principles into Practice* (London: Cabinet Office, 2002).

[28] Cabinet Office, 'The Second Phase of Public Sector Reform: The Move to Delivery', at: http://archive.cabinetoffice.gov.uk/eeg/secondphase.htm.

[29] Office of Public Services Reform, *Reforming our Public Services*, p. 3.

People at the Heart of Public Services, contained much of the same rhetoric.[30] In July 2004, each of the main delivery departments also published their own five-year strategies, which sought to identify how the Prime Minister's principles of public sector reform could be incorporated into the front-line delivery of services. Alas, the reform was beset with the usual problems. As Jill Rutter, head of the Strategy and Sustainability Directorate at the Department for Environment, Food and Rural Affairs commented, one of the main shortcomings of the five-year strategies was the persistent problem of a 'lack of integration'.[31]

The general principles informing the delivery agenda were also outlined by Michael Barber, the Prime Minister's former Chief Adviser on Delivery in his comments about education:

> Between 2001 and 2005 what Blair increasingly hankered after was a way of improving the education system that didn't need to be constantly driven by government. He wanted to develop self-sustaining, self-improving systems, and that led him to look into how to change not just the standards and the quality of teaching, but the structures and incentives. Essentially it's about creating different forms of a quasi-market in public services, exploiting the power of choice, competition, transparency and incentives, and that's really where the education debate is going now . . . At the political level Blair really understands this challenge, but it is highly controversial – within the Labour Party and nationally.[32]

And in February 2004, the Prime Minister outlined what delivery meant for him:

> The principal challenge is to shift focus from policy advice to delivery. Delivery means outcomes. It means project management. It means adapting to new situations and altering rules and practice accordingly. It means working not in traditional departmental silos. It means working naturally with partners outside of Government. It's not that many individual civil servants aren't capable of this. It is that doing it requires a change of operation and of culture that goes to the core of the Civil Service.[33]

[30] Office of Public Services Reform, *Putting People at the Heart of Public Services.*
[31] Public Administration Select Committee, *Governing the Future*, Q444.
[32] 'Education Reform Lessons from England'. An interview with Michael Barber at: www.educationsector.org/analysis/analysis_show.htm?doc_id=344385. See also Michael Barber, *Instruction to Deliver. Tony Blair, Public Services and the Challenge of Targets* (London: Politico's, 2007).
[33] Speech by Tony Blair to the 'Civil Service Reform, Delivery and Values' event, 24 February 2004, at: www.number-10.gov.uk/output/Page5399.asp.

Blair also emphasised the principle of earned autonomy, which involved 'giving greater freedoms to high performing providers and focusing regulation, inspection and associated interventions on poor performers'.[34]

Similar principles have informed Blair's third term of public sector reform. The closure of the OPSR in January 2006 led to its functions being transferred to the PMSU. While the PMSU no longer described the government's overall approach to public sector reform as the 'delivery agenda', its 'self-improving' model of reform clearly encompassed many of the same principles.[35] The model sought to develop a more coherent narrative of public sector reform. It brought together several reform initiatives already being implemented and it returned to old favourites like joined-up government.

The PMSU model identified four components of public sector reform: top-down performance management pressure from government; greater competition and contestability in providing public services; greater pressure from citizens through choice and voice; measures to strengthen the capability and capacity of civil and public servants and of central and local government to deliver improved public services. However, there was also a new emphasis on choice and voice or 'bottom-up pressures of choice, personalisation, voice and user engagement' to ensure that 'public service users' needs, preferences and aspirations are transmitted directly to and acted upon'.[36] These principles were reaffirmed in the Prime Minister's policy review of public services. It restated the 'governing idea of the next phase of reform' that 'services need to be personalized according to the needs and preferences of users'. It also had a renewed emphasis on the role of the state as a commissioner of services. The aim was to create:

> self-improving institutions of public service, independent of centralised state control, drawing on the best of public, private and third sector provision. These institutions must be free to develop in the way they need to, responsive to the needs and preferences of citizens, and with a flexible workforce that is able to innovate and change. Out of this vision will come a new concept of modern public services: one built around the user of the service.[37]

[34] Prime Minister's Strategy Unit, *The UK Government's Approach to Public Service Reform – A Discussion Paper* (London: Cabinet Office, 2006), p. 41.   [35] *Ibid.*, p. 23.
[36] See *ibid.*, chs. 4 and 7; and Public Administration Select Committee, *Choice, Voice and Public Services*, 2004–05, HC 49-I (London: TSO, 2005).
[37] Prime Minister's Strategy Unit, *Building on Progress: Public Services* (London: Cabinet Office, 2007), pp. 30 and 7.

It is too early to comment on the significance of these ideas. Because so much changes, so often, with no evaluation, it is impossible to say whether any changes will, or could be, effective.[38] Much will now depend on Gordon Brown. It is clear the frenetic activity originating in No. 10 has not stopped him from advancing his own agenda for public sector reform, masquerading as spending reviews, the efficiency agenda and strategic reviews (see below).

The delivery agenda not only developed policy principles but also targets. For service deliverers and middle-level managers, the focus was on delivering against performance targets. As the Prime Minister's policy review stated: 'to drive up standards, and to tackle inequalities, the immediate focus was on stronger top-down performance management'.[39] The Prime Minister's primary institutional mechanism for doing this was the PMDU. It began life tracking how well departments were performing against their Public Service Agreement (PSA) targets in 'key delivery areas'. These included health (waiting times for in-patient treatment and accident and emergency), education (levels of secondary school performance, including GCSE results), transport (cutting train delays) and criminal justice (including street crime and the inflow of illegal asylum-seekers). It provided progress reports to the Prime Minister on each of these areas and intervened if it was felt that departments might fail to deliver.[40] Over time, the Unit's remit extended to cover all PSAs, although it continued to focus on the Prime Minister's top priorities. The Cabinet Secretary also gave it oversight of the Capability Review Programme, which assessed the capacity of departments to deliver their objectives (see below). The problem in assessing the PMDU is that it was only one of several mechanisms used by the core executive to track progress against PSAs.

Running across both the modernising and delivery agendas was an ever-present desire to improve public sector management. All four of Blair's Cabinet Secretaries entered office with new ideas on the best way to reform the civil service. The Prime Minister delivered several speeches on the subject.[41] So civil service reform has always been high on the agenda

[38] For a review of the available evidence, see Lesley Hodgson, Catherine M. Farrell and Michael Connolly, 'Improving UK Public Services: A Review of the Evidence', *Public Administration*, 85, 2007: 355–82.

[39] Prime Minister's Strategy Unit, *Building on Progress*, p. 23.

[40] Michael Barber, 'How Blair Avoided a Mugging as Street Crime Left Big Cities Unsafe', *The Times*, 15 May 2007, at: www.timesonline.co.uk/tol/news/politics/the_blair_years/article1790129.ece?print=yes.

[41] See Blair, speech at 'Civil Service Reform, Delivery and Values' event; Gus O'Donnell, 'Gus' Vision', at: www.civilservice.gov.uk/reform/index.asp; Andrew Turnbull, 'Valedictory

and there was a general concern to improve leadership and professional skills. For example, Gus O'Donnell talks about his: 'vision . . . for a civil service that exudes pride, pace, passion and professionalism – the Four Ps as I call them – that together can keep the civil service relevant and effective'.[42]

Throughout, the problem was that the Prime Minister had no clear idea of how to bring about that improvement. He made it clear that leadership was central to public service delivery and, where successful leadership could not be found in the public sector, then government would look to the private or voluntary sectors irrespective of the policy area in question. There was also a general belief that the private sector performed better than the public sector, but there was no clear direction that successive Cabinet Secretaries could follow. The result was a constant stream of individual reform initiatives clustered around five themes: leadership; skills training and employee secondments; individual performance management and reward; diversity; and better recruitment practices and career development. Few of the initiatives stood the test of time. As the Cabinet Office's Capability Review concluded:

> Cumulatively, these findings reflect the need for a clear operating framework running across the complex and varied business of the Department. This has seriously weakened – particularly in the area of Civil Service reform – its impact in delivering change through other departments, as departments are faced with a series of unprioritised, or sometimes competing, central Civil Service initiatives.[43]

The last schemes were the Capability Review Programme (CRP) and the drive to improve professional skills. The CRP was launched in October 2005. It assessed seventeen departments against a 'model of capability' which focussed on three areas – leadership, strategy and delivery. The PMDU provided oversight but the reviews were carried out by teams of external reviewers drawn from the boards of other government departments, the private sector and the wider public sector. The first reviews identified key areas for improvement in departments and set out actions to improve the department's performance in those areas. As the CRP website states: 'The overarching aim is to achieve a Civil Service

Footnote 41 (*cont.*)
   Lecture', 27 July 2005, at: www.civilservice.gov.uk/publications/rtf/sat_valedictory_lecture. rtf/; and Richard Wilson, 'Portrait of a Profession Revisited', *Public Administration*, 81, 2003: 365–78.   [42] O'Donnell, 'Gus' Vision'.
[43] Cabinet Office, *Capability Review of the Cabinet Office* (London: Cabinet Office, 2006), p. 22.

which is better at delivery – that can deliver its existing targets, understand its future challenges and rise to meet them efficiently and effectively.'[44]

The Professional Skills for Government Programme was launched in September 2005. This scheme aimed to give civil servants 'the right mix of skills and expertise to enable their Departments or agencies to deliver effective services'.[45] In place of the generalists, three new career groupings were introduced – corporate service, operational delivery and policy delivery. There was also a new assessment framework, which required civil servants to demonstrate skills and experience in such areas as people management, financial management, programme and project management, analysis and the use of evidence.

The plethora of reform initiatives was not always seen as significant in the departments. As one official commented: 'the relatively subtle changes which have taken place in the reform agenda between 1999 and now don't seem worthy of close analysis from our end of the telescope'.[46] However, the restless search for reform provided continued evidence of a floundering and directionless political and administrative class. As Richard Wilson, the former Head of the Home Civil Service, lamented:

> I would not want to claim that the manner in which we implemented all these reforms over the years was a model to emulate. There was not enough overall vision or strategic planning. Too often it was uncoordinated, with different parts of the centre of government launching similar initiatives simultaneously or at a pace which long-suffering managers in departments found difficult to handle.[47]

Blair was dissatisfied with the performance of the civil service but he never knew what he wanted. This lack of direction was just as evident in his constant renaming and refashioning of central departments.[48] He was a Prime Minister in search of a toolkit for steering the heart of government, but he never found one he could use effectively.

---

[44] 'Civil Service Capability Reviews – Background', at: www.civilservice.gov.uk/reform/capability_reviews/background.asp.
[45] 'Professional Skills for Government', at: http://psg.civilservice.gov.uk/content.asp.
[46] Cited in Bovaird and Russell, 'Civil Service Reform in the UK', p. 319.
[47] Richard Wilson, 'The Civil Service in the New Millennium', valedictory speech, May 1999. See also Richard Wilson, Tomorrow's Government Lecture (London: Constitution Unit, 2006).
[48] On the extent of these changes see www.civilservice.gov.uk/management/statistics/changes/index.asp; and the individual reports at: www.civilservice.gov.uk/management/statistics/news/index.asp.

The governance story

The governance story provides an alternative to the Westminster model. It highlights the place of networks in British politics, the informal authority of which supplements and supplants the formal authority of government. It stresses the horizontal and vertical networks of interdependence in which the core executive is embedded.[49] In this section, we focus on the horizontal networks of Westminster and Whitehall and the story of the rival courts of Brown and Blair. We argue that the core executive cannot be seen as a single decision centre focused on Blair. Rather, it is a set of overlapping networks and central institutions that are all too often confounded by central fragmentation. The Blair reforms of the centre sought to impose the desired degree of coordination, but he was just one actor among many interdependent ones in the networks that criss-cross Whitehall, Westminster and beyond. So now we tell the governance story of the Blair government.

If the Cabinet Office is all about using soft levers, such as influence, support and partnerships, then the Treasury is its opposite, controlling as it does the hard levers, most notably the power of the purse. It was, and will remain, a prominent actor in the core executive. While the court politics, personality clashes and rivalry between Blair and Brown have been the subject of relentless commentary, important institutional changes, which did not provoke the same media interest, also took place. The intertwining of court politics and institutional change meant there was not only a second centre of coordination but also a second wellspring of civil service reform.

As soon as he took up office, the Chancellor made it clear that he wanted the Treasury to extend its reach far beyond its traditional Ministry of Finance role. He outlined what he expected his department to do in a speech to the Institute of Fiscal Studies: 'A Labour Treasury would need to be not just a Ministry of Finance, but also a Ministry working with other departments to deliver long-term economic and social renewal.'[50] The Department fleshed out these comments in a memorandum that it submitted to the Treasury Select Committee:

[49] See: R. A. W. Rhodes, *Understanding Governance* (Buckingham: Open University Press, 1997); and for a review of the debate see R. A. W. Rhodes, '*Understanding Governance Revisited*', *Organization Studies*, 28, 2007: 1–22.

[50] Gordon Brown, 'Modernising the British Economy: The New Mission for the Treasury', speech, Institute of Fiscal Studies, London, 27 May 1999, at: www.hm-treasury.gov.uk/ newsroom_and_speeches/speeches/chancellorexchequer/speech_chex_270599.cfm.

With the macroeconomic framework now firmly established, more resources can be directed towards examining microeconomic issues. Evidence-based microeconomic and distributional analysis is essential to underpin the Treasury's output – from Budget tax measures through developments in competition policy and analysis of poverty issues to work on reform of the legal aid system and deciding transport priorities.[51]

This theme became constant. The Treasury was: 'not simply concerned with controlling spending, but also with achieving value for money and with using spending programmes to make the economy work better'.[52] More colloquially, the former Treasury Permanent Secretary, Terry Burns, explained the change of emphasis by saying that: 'macro-economic policy is very boring . . . so . . . we are getting very interested in social policy'.[53]

This change of direction was given institutional expression.[54] Macroeconomic policy, which used to be important enough to have its own directorate, was moved to the International and Finance Directorate where it sits with several other sections. The role of the Public Services and Growth (PSG) Directorate grew. It still comprised the spending teams shadowing departments, but it now combined that role with tracking performance against PSAs and efficiency targets. It also housed the Enterprise and Growth Unit, which worked on competition and economic regulation, corporate and private finance, enterprise and science and industry. At various times, other teams worked on microeconomic policy, including productivity; competition, regulation and the energy market; regulatory reform; financial services reform; and public sector pay and efficiency. Special-purpose teams were also created to support the work of the independent reviews discussed below. The remit of all these units led the Treasury to take an interest in a much wider scope of issues and the Treasury has relished this diversification.

The Brown Chancellorship was also notable for its reform of public expenditure control. He introduced spending reviews and a new performance management framework. PSAs were set for individual departments and for cross-cutting issues. Performance against them was

---

[51] Treasury Select Committee, Minutes of Evidence, Annex 1, Treasury Aims and Objectives, 2000–2001, 11 May 2000, at: www.publications.parliament.uk/pa/cm199900/cmselect/cmtreasy/492/0051103.htm.

[52] See 'Guide to the Centre of Government', at: http://archive.cabinetoffice.gov.uk/roleofcentre/treasury.htm.

[53] Treasury Select Committee, HM Treasury, 2000–01, HC 73-I (London: TSO, 2001), para. 39.

[54] For more detail, see Paul Fawcett, 'New Labour's Treasury – Ten Years On', Public Administration (submitted).

monitored by several parts of the core executive: the PMDU in the Cabinet Office; the spending teams based in the PSG Directorate; the PSX Cabinet Committee; and separate bilateral stocktakes between ministers and the Prime Minister on specific areas, and the Chief Secretary to the Treasury on more general topics. As Paul Boateng, a former Chief Secretary to the Treasury, claimed, the Treasury has: 'some responsibility, in some sense, for *all* PSA targets'.[55]

Despite this admission, there remains a lack of clarity over how the Treasury and departments devise PSAs, as well as the incentive effects, especially when targets are either minima or not met.[56] PSAs are best viewed as a tool providing the Treasury with a 'legitimate' reason for continued or extended intervention in departmental affairs. It also provided the Treasury with a reason to demand an unprecedented amount of data from departments.[57] As a Senior Treasury official explained, the effect is that the Treasury: 'plays a much more proactive and strategic role in the development of policy in Whitehall'. Of course, the Treasury would not be the Treasury without acerbic asides, so he added: 'This, of course, has had a positive impact on this enthusiasm for joined-up government.'[58] Given the increased spending on health and education, the Treasury saw this role as a natural extension of its powers and a necessary control on departments.

The Treasury was also heavily involved in public service reform through its efficiency programme. It was a different agenda to that of the PMSU but just as important. The efficiency programme can be traced to several reports commissioned by the Treasury. They included the Gershon Review, the Lyons Review, the Hampton Review, and the Varney Review.[59] The overall aim was to achieve the headline target contained in the

---

[55] Treasury Select Committee, *Performance Targets and Monitoring*, 2004–05, HC 331-i, Q83 (London: TSO, 2005), emphasis added.

[56] Oliver James, 'The UK Core Executive's Use of Public Service Agreements as a Tool of Governance', *Public Administration*, 82, 2004: 397–419.

[57] HM Treasury and Cabinet Office, *Devolving Decision Making: Delivering Better Public Services: Refining Targets and Performance Management* (London: TSO, 2004).

[58] Private information.

[59] Peter Gershon, *Releasing Resources for the Front-line: Independent Review of Public Sector Efficiency* (London: TSO, 2004); Michael Lyons, *Well Placed to Deliver? Shaping the Pattern of Government Service: Independent Review of Public Sector Relocation* (London: TSO, 2004); Philip Hampton, *Reducing Administrative Burdens: Effective Inspection and Enforcement* (London: TSO, 2005); Cabinet Office, *Transformational Government – Enabled by Technology*, Cm. 6970 (London: TSO, 2005); Cabinet Office, *Transformational Government – Implementation Plan* (London: Cabinet Office, 2006); David Varney, *Service Transformation: A Better Service for Citizens and Businesses, A Better Deal for the Taxpayer* (London: TSO, 2006).

Gershon Review of £21.5 billion of efficiency savings by 2007–8. Each of the subsequent reports looked at particular ways of achieving that aim. More recent reports, starting with the Cabinet Office's Transformational Government Strategy,[60] have combined the efficiency drive with a renewed emphasis on joining up front-line services.[61] In the lexicon of management speak there is little that is new. Both the Varney Review and the earlier Modernising Government White Paper identify the same obstacles to joined-up government while calling for better coordination.[62]

Clearly the efficiency programme was a Treasury-driven agenda. It wrote the reports. It chaired the two main cabinet committees (on Efficiency and Relocation and Electronic Service Delivery). It was responsible for overseeing the efficiency agenda in the Office of Government Commerce before it was moved in-house.[63] The scope of the efficiency programme was broad, so it had important consequences for all the public sector. In short, the PMSU and the Treasury public sector reforms ran concurrently. They co-existed. They were not coordinated, nor could they be, because one agenda was driven by Blair and the other by Brown.

Finally, the Brown Chancellorship also played a strategic policy role using two types of policy reviews. First, there were internal reviews focusing on cross-cutting issues of government policy, reporting to the Chief Secretary to the Treasury, but sometimes published in partnership with another department. There were typically six or seven reviews for each spending review. Eight policy areas were the subject of multiple reviews. They accounted for thirty-seven of the forty-two policy reviews, including seven reviews on young children and older people; six reviews each on crime (including drugs), the voluntary sector and local government finance and rural and regional policy; four reviews on science; three reviews on employment and benefits policy and foreign affairs; and two reviews on housing supply.

Second, there were independent reviews, usually headed by someone from outside government and typically published with one or more departments, but with a secretariat drawn from, and based in, the Treasury. The reviews included the Stern Review on the Economics of

[60] Cabinet Office, *Transformational Government*.
[61] Varney, *Service Transformation*, pp. 8 and 31–2.
[62] Compare, for example, Varney, *Service Transformation*, p. 17, with Cabinet Office and Performance and Innovation Unit, *Wiring It Up*; or the specific example of Varney, *Service Transformation*, pp. 89–90 with Cabinet Office, *Modernising Government*, pp. 22–33.
[63] HM Treasury, *Transforming Government Procurement* (London: TSO, 2007), p. 20.

Climate Change (joint with the Cabinet Office); the Eddington Transport Study (joint with the Department of Transport); the Leitch Review of Skills (joint with the Department for Education and Skills); the Barker Review of Land Use (joint with the Department of Communities and Local Government); and the Wanless Review of Health Trends.[64]

In sum, the Treasury sponsored much strategic work that would normally have been produced by a central strategic unit in the Cabinet Office. The Chancellor or the Chief Secretary to the Treasury, rather than the Prime Minister or cabinet, were directly associated with these reviews. The Treasury and not the Cabinet Office provided the secretariat support for them. As the former Cabinet Secretary Andrew Turnbull explained, the consequence was that the Treasury became a policy department:

> The reviews have varied a lot in quality. Some are actually quite good. But a lot of them are HMV – His Master's Voice – and are really written to order. The Wanless report on health spending was a good example of that. And that has changed the relationship between the Treasury and colleagues, and changed the way the Treasury works, making it a policy department.[65]

These changes were as much about the court politics of Blair and Brown as they were about public sector reform. In an unguarded moment, Andrew Turnbull commented on 'Brown's ruthlessness' and 'the more or less complete contempt' with which the Treasury treated ministerial colleagues. Treasury control had come 'at the expense of any government cohesion and any assessment of strategy'.[66] No matter how commentators interpret either the court politics of the two rivals or Brown's Treasury reforms, it is clear the Treasury's redefinition of its role altered the way central government worked. It also illustrated the limits of focusing on the Prime Minister and his machinery for coordination. If we do so, we miss the problem that central coordination was undermined by competing centres of policymaking. It caused 'dilemmas and sometimes

---

[64] HM Treasury and Cabinet Office, *The Economics of Climate Change – The Stern Review* (Cambridge: Cambridge University Press, 2006); HM Treasury and Department for Transport, *The Eddington Transport Study* (London: TSO, 2006); HM Treasury and Department for Education and Skills, *Prosperity for All in the Global Economy – World Class Skills* (London: TSO, 2006); HM Treasury and Department for Communities and Local Government, *Barker Review of Land Use Planning* (London: TSO, 2006); and HM Treasury, *Securing our Future Health: Taking a Long-Term View* (London: HM Treasury, 2002).

[65] Nick Timmins, 'Highlights of Turnbull Interview', *Financial Times*, 20 March 2007, at: www.ft.com/cms/s/7a58bfa0-d6d7-11db-98da-000b5df10621.html.

[66] Nicholas Timmins, 'Stalinist Brown', *Financial Times*, 20 March 2007, p. 1.

downright confusion' in the departments because ministers and officials had 'to pick their way across a minefield'.[67]

Conclusion – the net Blair effect

New Labour built on the reforms of previous governments and the scale of its activity is as daunting as it is frenetic. What do our stories tell us about the net Blair effect on central government of all this activity?

The centralisation story tells us there is often a gulf between intervention and control. Blair intervened often, but rarely to great effect. For all the talk of a presidential Prime Minister, the most striking facts about the heart of the machine under Blair are the continued relevance of the constitutional verities of cabinet government and the elusiveness of coordination.

The claim that bilateral, or sofa decision-making, was pre-eminent and that cabinet government was in decline was premature. Cabinet, and especially its infrastructure of committees, thrived. As Rentoul noted, 'a lot of the business of government continued to be done in cabinet committees'.[68] The number of cabinet committees grew. It was deliberate policy to give 'a more central role to Cabinet Committees in Government', particularly in dealing with 'cross-cutting, cross-departmental issues'.[69] In January 1998 there were twenty-seven committees but they gradually increased in number until November 2004 when there were fifty-nine. In 2006, there were between forty-four and forty-nine ministerial committees, excluding the five Policy Review Working Groups. Blair also chaired more committees the longer he was in office. He chaired five in January 1998, ten in November 2004, peaking at sixteen in December 2005, but only dropping by one to fifteen in December 2006. He also chaired the five Policy Review Groups. In short: 'there has been much more use of cabinet as a sounding board' and cabinet now 'regularly receives presentations on major new policy development'.[70] Blair's critics single out the decline of

---

[67] Michael Barber cited in Philip Webster and Peter Riddell, 'Brown "Must Use his Honeymoon Period to Strengthen Power of PM"', *The Times*, 15 May 2007, at: www.timesonline.co.uk/tol/news/politics/the_blair_years/article1790129.ece?print=yes.

[68] See John Rentoul, *Tony Blair: Prime Minister* (London: Little, Brown, 2001), p. 544; and Turnbull, 'Valedictory Lecture'.

[69] No. 10 Downing Street, 'Cabinet Committees, Press Briefing', at: www.number-10.gov.uk/output/Page7542.asp.

[70] Geoff Mulgan interviewed on 'Looking Back at Power', BBC Radio 4, 5 September 2005, at: www.bbc.co.uk/radio4/news/look_back_at_power.shtml; and Turnbull, 'Valedictory Lecture'.

the cabinet's policymaking and coordination functions for special criticism, yet it has been clear for over a half of a century that these functions have been carried out by several central agencies of the core executive including, but not limited to, the cabinet. The cabinet persists in four forms: as the constitutional theory of ministerial and collective responsibility; as a set of rules and routines; as a political bargaining arena between central actors; and as a component of the core executive.[71]

We also know that, despite strong pressures for more proactive coordination throughout Western Europe, the coordination activities of central governments remain modest. Such coordination has four characteristics. First, it is 'negative, based on persistent compartmentalisation, mutual avoidance and friction reduction between powerful bureaux or ministries'. Second, it occurs 'at the lower levels of the state machine and [is] organised by specific established networks'. Third, it is 'rarely strategic' and 'almost all attempts to create proactive strategic capacity for long-term planning . . . have failed'. Finally, it is 'intermittent and selective . . . improvised late in the policy process, politicised, issue-oriented and reactive'.[72] In sum, coordination is the 'philosopher's stone' of modern government, ever sought, but always just beyond reach, all too often because it assumes both agreement on goals and an effective central coordinator.[73]

The management story adds the 'central flaws' of prime-ministerial 'inexperience', 'lack of clarity about both means and ends' and 'confusion about the role of central government' to our understanding.[74] As Richard Wilson observed to Blair back in 1997, 'Your problem is that neither you nor anyone in Number 10 has ever managed anything.'[75] The same point was made ten years later by Michael Barber:

> All Prime Ministers face their constraints, from their Cabinets, departments and the 'official view', but in Tony Blair's case there has been the major personal one that, prior to entering Downing Street, he had

[71] Patrick Weller, 'Cabinet Government: An Elusive Ideal?', *Public Administration*, 81, 2003: 74–8.

[72] Vincent Wright and Jack E. S. Hayward, 'Governing from the Centre: Policy Co-Ordination in Six European Core Executives', in R. A. W. Rhodes (ed.), *Transforming British Government*, vol. II: *Changing Roles and Relationships* (London: Macmillan, 2000), p. 33.

[73] Harold Seidman, *Politics, Position and Power*, 2nd edn (Oxford: Oxford University Press, 1975), p. 190.

[74] Peter Riddell, 'Blair as Prime Minister', in A. Seldon (ed.), *The Blair Effect* (London: Little, Brown, 2001), pp. 38–9; Peter Riddell, *The Unfulfilled Prime Minister* (London: Politico's, 2005), p. 41.   [75] Cited in Seldon, *Blair*, p. 629.

never run a government department, or even been a junior minister. As a consequence, he had a huge amount to learn about how organisations, especially large bureaucracies, work.[76]

Blair's weaknesses included a lack of follow-through: 'He intervenes, persuades, and then forgets'. He lacks 'policy making and management skills'.[77] So although he wants results 'he finds it hard to understand why things can't happen immediately' and he is frustrated when 'waiting for the pay-off and he doesn't have time'.[78]

The Cabinet Office is not exempt from this sweeping criticism. The Capability Review commented that its 'overall performance, particularly as seen by its major partners in other government departments, is variable. Successes also tend to be attributed to particular units, not to the Cabinet Office as a department.'[79] It added that this critical assessment:

> reflects the gap between the current capability of the Cabinet Office and the task it faces in the future. For much of the Cabinet Office's work, there is either ambiguity over the scope of its role and powers, or overlap between the work of various units. Clearer remits and business models are essential if the Cabinet Office is to exert effective leverage over service delivery from its position in the centre.[80]

In a similar vein, the Public Administration Select Committee commented on the 'difficulty in determining priorities' in the 'highly complex organisation of the Cabinet Office itself, with a profusion of small units and divisions all exercising surveillance and issuing instructions from the centre of government'.[81]

The governance story points to a net Brown effect. A key characteristic of the period 1997–2007 is the vulnerability of the Prime Minister, like all prime ministers, to both national and international events; the contingency of 'events, dear boy, events'. To compare Blair pre-Iraq and post-Iraq is to see that prime-ministerial pre-eminence comes and goes. Add the court politics of the Brown–Blair rivalry and we have a picture

---

[76] Michel Barber, 'Why Giving the Prime Minister More Power, Not Less, Must Be New Leader's First Step', *The Times*, 14 May 2007, at: www.timesonline.co.uk/tol/news/politics/article1784690.ece?print=yes.   [77] Seldon, *Blair*, p. 692.

[78] Official cited in Hennessy, 'The Blair Revolution', p. 10.

[79] Cabinet Office, *Capability Review*, p. 14.

[80] Cabinet Office, *Capability Reviews Tranche 2: Common Themes and Summaries* (London: Cabinet Office, 2006), p. 17.

[81] Public Administration Select Committee, *Making Government Work*, para. 42.

of a government in which barons vie for favour in the court of a would-be president as dependent on them for support as they are on him for favours.[82] In addition, the greatest baron was Gordon Brown who constructed 'a command Chancellorship – not seen in Whitehall since Neville Chamberlain occupied Number 11 Downing Street, when Stanley Baldwin was at Number 10 in the 1920s and 1930s'.[83]

So the centre of government was characterised, not by prime-ministerial centralisation, but by two men each presiding over their territory, which was ever more jealously guarded. Brown was 'immovable', 'dominating his own territory' with 'jagged defences designed to repel any invader, including the Prime Minister'. So 'they were not interested in submerging their differences in outlook, but in making an exhibition of them'.[84] At times, Brown was 'the official opposition to Blair within the very heart of the Cabinet'.[85] One result was a bifurcated centre. The Treasury set the strategic agenda across government, engaged in specific policy development and monitored progress against targets to a previously unprecedented extent. There was significant overlap and competition with the Cabinet Office and the PMSU. But there was one major difference. The Treasury had the hard levers, the Cabinet Office did not. 'He who pays the piper calls the tune', and Brown's reforms commanded the undivided attention of departments. Having witnessed visitations by both the Delivery Unit and the Treasury to the departments, it was clear whose views carried the greatest weight. The Treasury was greeted with a caution and care bordering on white-knuckle nerves. In all too sharp contrast, the Delivery Unit was accorded a polite, urbane reception.[86] The Brown–Blair rivalry is not just about personalities and court politics. It is about who controls the heart of the machine and the Treasury won. Brown's reform agenda was fuelled by his political agenda. It will be interesting to see whether his successor can sustain the reform momentum when Brown is Prime Minister or whether No. 10 will become the undisputed wellspring of reform.[87]

[82] On the 'oestrogen-fuelled', '*Girl's Own*, comic book' view of life at the No. 10 court, see Francis Beckett and David Hencke, *The Blairs and their Court* (London: Aurum Press, 2004).

[83] Peter Hennessy, 'Rulers and Servants of the State: The Blair Style of Government 1997–2004', *Parliamentary Affairs*, 58, 2005: 9.

[84] James Naughtie, *The Rivals: The Intimate Story of a Political Marriage*, rev. edn (London: Fourth Estate, 2002), p. 352.

[85] Robert Peston, *Brown's Britain* (London: Short Books, 2005), p. 353.

[86] Private information.

[87] For a discussion see Patrick Diamond (ed.), *Public Matters – The Renewal of the Public Realm* (London: Politico's, 2007).

Tony Blair's record on central reform could be likened to a permanent revolution but few flowers grew to maturity. Of course, there was change. But as one senior figure said: 'Blair confuses the civil servants around him . . . On the civil service he doesn't know what he wants. They say, in effect, "Tell me what *you* want and *we'll* do it." But he keeps saying different things. Richard Wilson finds it very difficult the way the Prime Minister jumps around.'[88] Moreover, politics, value clashes, interests, cultures, symbolic games and accountability all limit the usefulness of private sector management techniques in the public sector. Civil servants are not venal, or even reluctant, when implementing such reforms. But the brute fact is that top civil servants are political administrators, not managers. Their job is to take care of their minister. If there is failure, it is not a failure of leadership by Permanent Secretaries but a failure of political leadership because the Prime Minister and ministers did not know what they wanted. There was no consistent vision and it was a recipe for, and a classic example of, muddling through.

[88] Hennessy, 'The Blair Revolution', p.9.

The Constitution

PHILIP NORTON

One area in which there was a clear divide between the parties in 1997 was that of constitutional reform. The Conservatives were defenders of existing arrangements. Labour advocated a major overhaul of the nation's constitutional arrangements. The party's proposals did not figure at the forefront of the party's election manifesto – they appeared on pages 32 and 33 – but they presaged a major change in the constitutional landscape of the United Kingdom. Although the implementation of the proposals was not exhaustive, by May 2007 the British Constitution was very different from that which existed when Tony Blair entered Downing Street.

Labour's proposals

By the 1990s, the basic tenets of the British Constitution had not changed substantially since the emergence of a cabinet-centred Westminster model of government in the late nineteenth century.[1] UK membership of the European Communities in 1973 was the only major change of recent decades to challenge some of the basic principles. Otherwise, the constitutional landscape for much of the past century had been largely undisturbed and, for a good part of the period, had not figured on the agenda of political debate.

Demands for change began to be heard in the 1960s and 1970s. There was evidence of a growing discontent with the system of government, especially in parts of the United Kingdom distant from London. The Labour government appointed a Royal Commission on the Constitution in 1969: its report in 1973 recommended that 'devolution could do much to reduce the discontent'.[2] During the 1970s and 1980s, there were

---

[1] Philip Norton, 'The Norton View', in David Judge (ed.), *The Politics of Parliamentary Reform* (London: Heinemann Educational Books, 1983), pp. 56–61.

[2] Royal Commission on the Constitution 1969–1973, vol. I: *Report*, Cmnd 5460 (London: HMSO, 1973), para. 1102, p. 331.

increasingly vocal calls for a Bill of Rights and for electoral reform. A Labour government in the 1974–9 parliament sought, unsuccessfully, to implement devolution in Scotland and Wales. In 1988, on the tercentenary of the Glorious Revolution, the constitutional reform movement Charter '88 was founded. It collected to its banner not only longstanding reformers of the centre but also leftist intellectuals and party activists.[3] It advocated a new constitutional settlement for the United Kingdom, with wide-ranging changes to be embodied in a written Constitution.

The Conservative response under the premierships of Margaret Thatcher and John Major was to resist demands for change. They embraced the traditional approach to constitutional change: that is, advocating the Westminster model.[4] John Major was a particularly vocal advocate of maintaining the Union.[5] Others putting their heads above the parapet to join the debate were John Patten and Douglas Hurd.[6] To assuage demands for devolution, there were some changes to parliamentary procedures to give Scotland a greater voice at Westminster, but the basic message was one of defending the extant Constitution. It may not be the ideal (though many thought it was) but it was the real and it was deemed to deliver benefits that would be destroyed by the changes demanded by Charter '88.

In contrast, Labour's stance was radical, although it varied over the years. Under Michael Foot's leadership, the party adopted a socialist approach to constitutional change.[7] In order to create 'a democratic socialist society in Britain', its commitments included withdrawal from the European Community and the abolition of the House of Lords. This approach was modified under the leadership of Neil Kinnock and John Smith. Smith, in particular, moved the party away from a socialist to a liberal approach to constitutional change,[8] more in line with the policies advocated by Charter '88. He had been a key figure in Labour's devolution legislation in the 1970s,[9] 'but Smith's plans for constitutional change went

[3] Philip Norton, 'In Defence of the Constitution: A Riposte to the Radicals', in Philip Norton (ed.), *New Directions in British Politics* (Aldershot: Edward Elgar, 1991), pp. 147–8.
[4] See Philip Norton, *The Constitution in Flux* (Oxford: Martin Robertson, 1982), pp. 279–87.
[5] See e.g. John Major, *Scotland in the United Kingdom* (London: Conservative Political Centre, 1992).
[6] Douglas Hurd, *Conservatism in the 1990s* (London: Conservative Political Centre, 1991); John Patten, *Political Culture, Conservatism and Rolling Consensus* (London: Conservative Political Centre, 1991).
[7] Norton, *The Constitution in Flux*, pp. 263–7. See also Geoff Hodgson, *Labour at the Crossroads* (Oxford: Martin Robertson, 1981).
[8] Norton, *The Constitution in Flux*, pp. 275–9.
[9] Mark Stuart, *John Smith: A Life* (London: Politico's, 2005), pp. 74–94.

far beyond Scotland, and were to be extended across the whole country'.[10]
Though sceptical of electoral reform, he embraced devolution, House
of Lords reform, the incorporation of the European Convention on
Human Rights into British law, regional government, and a Freedom of
Information Bill. Following publication of the Plant report on electoral
reform, he committed the party to a referendum on the subject.

After John Smith's death, Tony Blair sought to maintain the commitment to constitutional reform. In his 1994 Leadership Election Statement,
he committed a future Labour government to legislate in the first year
for a Scottish Parliament. He also supported the creation of a Welsh
Assembly, an elected second chamber, the entrenchment of rights for
every citizen in a Bill of Rights for Britain, and a reform of parliamentary
procedure. 'We should', he declared, 'also make the case for regional government in England.' He said he fully supported the party's commitment
to a referendum on the issue of the electoral system for the House of
Commons.[11] These views were developed by Peter Mandelson and Roger
Liddle in *The Blair Revolution: Can New Labour Deliver?* in 1996,[12] though
they argued for removing hereditary peers from the House of Lords rather
than an immediate move to any elected element – 'perhaps there could be
a directly elected element with an avowedly regional element'.[13]

Labour's election manifesto in 1997 largely embodied these views. It
attacked the Conservative record – 'the Conservatives seem opposed to
the very idea of democracy' – and the system of government: 'Our system
of government is centralised, inefficient and bureaucratic.' There was, it
declared, 'a crisis of confidence in our political system, to which Labour
will respond in a measured and sensible way'.[14] The headline commitments were:

End the hereditary principle in the House of Lords;
Reform of party funding to end sleaze;
Devolved power in Scotland and Wales;
Elected mayors for London and other cities;
More independent but accountable local government;
Freedom of information and guaranteed human rights.[15]

[10] *Ibid.*, p. 293.
[11] Tony Blair MP, *Change and National Renewal*, Leadership Election Statement 1994
      (London, 1994).
[12] Peter Mandelson and Roger Liddle, *The Blair Revolution: Can New Labour Deliver?*
      (London: Faber and Faber, 1996), pp. 189–210.   [13] *Ibid.*, p. 205.
[14] New Labour, *Because Britain Deserves Better* (London: Labour Party, 1997), p. 32.
[15] *Ibid.*, p. 33.

Though not in the headline commitments, the manifesto also committed the party to a referendum on the voting system for the House of Commons. An independent commission on voting systems would be appointed early to recommend a proportional alternative to the first-past-the-post system. On regional government, it noted that there was no uniform demand for directly elected regional government. 'In time we will introduce legislation to allow the people, region by region, to decide in a referendum whether they want directly elected regional government. Only when clear popular consent is established will arrangements be made for elected regional assemblies.' As the party did not wish to create a new layer of government, a predominantly unitary (and cost-neutral) system of local government would be created. On Northern Ireland, the cross-party approach would be maintained to try to find a political settlement that could command both sides of the community in the province.

Devolution to Scotland and Wales was to take place 'once established in referendums'. Blair had decided in favour of referendums, despite misgivings on the part of some Labour MPs, in order to demonstrate support for devolution. In a separate section, on Britain's international role, the manifesto also committed the party to holding a referendum on Britain joining a single currency. The referendum would be the third and final stage of acceptance, following approval by the cabinet and by parliament.[16] Referendums were no longer novel to the British Constitution, but only one had been held previously on a UK-wide basis.

What did the government deliver?

Blair thus entered office with a substantial set of proposals for constitutional reform. In his second term, he also generated proposals, not embodied in the party manifesto, for the creation of a supreme court and the disappearance of the substantive role of the Lord Chancellor. To what extent, then, were these several commitments met? The record of Blair's decade can be summarised as follows.

Devolution

The government moved quickly to introduce legislation to provide for referendums in Scotland and Wales. The Scottish referendum delivered decisive majorities in favour of a parliament and for it to have tax-raising

[16] *Ibid.*, p. 38.

powers. The Welsh referendum, in contrast, was less than decisive. On a 50% turnout, 50.3% voted 'Yes' and 49.7% voted 'No'. The Scotland Act 1998 devolved executive and legislative powers, other than in reserved areas, to an elected parliament in Scotland and the Government of Wales Act 1998 devolved some executive powers to a National Assembly for Wales. Devolution soon became an established part of the constitutional landscape. In a speech in February 1998, Conservative leader William Hague accepted that devolution was going to happen and that there was no point in seeking to turn the clock back. The process of devolving powers successfully was facilitated by the fact that one party was dominant in Westminster, Holyrood and Cardiff, and that many of those involved in setting up the new bodies sat or had sat in Westminster.[17] Some further powers were transferred to the National Assembly for Wales – and the National Assembly separated from the executive (having previously been united as a body corporate) – under the Government of Wales Act 2006.

Human rights

The government published a White Paper, *Rights Brought Home,* and then followed it with the introduction of the Human Rights Bill, embodying the ECHR in UK law. The measure was passed in 1998, with its principal provisions taking effect in 2000. The Act made it unlawful for any public authority to act in a way that was incompatible with Convention rights. Higher courts were empowered to issue declarations of incompatibility where there was deemed to be a breach. By the end of 2003, the courts had issued declarations of incompatibility in fifteen cases, though five of these were overturned on appeal. Parliament enacted various changes to bring the law into line with the declarations of the courts. These included the Gender Recognition Act 2004, conferring rights on those who changed gender, and – as we shall see – various anti-terrorist provisions.

House of Lords reform

The 1997 manifesto committed the party to an 'initial, self-contained reform' to remove the hereditary peers from membership of the House.

[17] See Constitution Committee, House of Lords, *Devolution: Inter-Institutional Relations in the United Kingdom,* Second Report, 2002–03, HL Paper 28.

This was to constitute the 'first stage in a process of reform to make the House of Lords more democratic and representative'. The House of Lords Act 1999 removed all bar ninety-two of the hereditary peers from membership of the House. (The ninety-two were retained as the result of a deal between the Tory leader in the Lords, Viscount Cranborne, and the Lord Chancellor, Lord Irvine of Lairg, designed to smooth the passage of the Bill through the Lords and act as a spur to later reform.) Under goading from Cranborne, the government also moved to consider what should comprise stage 2. It appointed a Royal Commission under a Conservative former cabinet minister, Lord Wakeham. The Commission recommended three options for a partially elected chamber.[18] Though the government in its 2001 manifesto said it would seek to implement the recommendations of the Wakeham report 'in the most effective way possible', it failed to gain much support for its proposal, published in a November 2001 White Paper,[19] for a House with 20% of its members elected. It then handed over responsibility to a joint committee of both Houses, which identified seven options for reform of composition. Both Houses voted on the options in February 2003. The Lords voted for an all-appointed House and against all the other options. The Commons was unable to muster a majority for any of them. The issue returned to the agenda in 2006, and in 2007 the government published a White Paper advocating a House with half of its membership elected and half appointed.[20] In March 2007, both Houses again voted on reform options. The Lords voted again (but by a bigger margin) for only the all-appointed option, while in the Commons there were majorities for an 80% elected and a wholly elected House.

Elected mayors for London and other cities

The government achieved passage of a Bill authorising a referendum in London on whether Greater London should have an elected mayor and authority. In the referendum, a large majority (72%) voted 'Yes', albeit on a small turnout (34%). The Greater London Authority Act 1999 established an elected mayor and a twenty-five-member Assembly. The two were elected separately under an unusual hybrid system of government. The mayor enjoys some executive powers, subject to scrutiny by the

[18] Royal Commission on Reform of the House of Lords, *A House for the Future*, Cm. 4534 (London: TSO, 2000).
[19] HM Government, *Completing the Reform*, Cm. 5291 (London: TSO, 2001).
[20] HM Government, *The House of Lords: Reform*, Cm. 7027 (London: TSO, 2007).

Assembly. The successful candidate for mayor, Ken Livingstone, was elected as an independent in 2000, having been suspended from the Labour Party, but was later admitted to membership and re-elected in 2004 under the party label. The policy of rolling out elected mayors to other cities proved less successful. The Local Government Act 2000 required councils covering populations of 85,000 people or more to create a new structure, selecting one out of three options. These included a directly elected mayor. In practice, the overwhelming majority opted for an indirectly elected leader and cabinet, the closest option to the status quo. Fewer than twenty opted for an elected mayor. Where elected mayors do exist, they have broadly similar powers to those of indirectly elected council leaders.[21]

Reform of party funding

The government commissioned a report on the funding of political parties from the Committee on Standards in Public Life. The Committee reported in 1998 and, following a White Paper in 1999, the government achieved enactment of the Political Parties, Elections and Referendums Act 2000. The Act inter alia established an Electoral Commission, provided for the registration of political parties, and imposed restrictions on the sources of donations: money could not be received from non-EU and anonymous donors and parties had to report donations to the Electoral Commission. A limit was also placed on parties' expenditure in election campaigns. The measure, however, failed to still controversy over party funding. The blocking by the House of Lords Appointments Commission of certain nominations for peerages in 2006 led to allegations of honours being awarded in return for donations, resulting in a police investigation. The Prime Minister was one of those interviewed. Some of the donors were investigated for making loans to the Labour Party at less than commercial rates (not permitted under the Act). As a result, provisions were included in the Electoral Administration Act 2006 to regulate loans to political parties, including a reporting regime, and an inquiry into party funding established under Sir Hayden Phillips, a former permanent secretary in the Lord Chancellor's Department.

---

[21] Colin Copus, 'Local Government', in Bill Jones *et al.*, *Politics UK*, 6th edn (Harlow: Pearson Education, 2007), p. 577.

Electoral reform

An independent commission on the electoral system was appointed under Liberal Democrat peer Lord Jenkins of Hillhead. It reported in October 1998, recommending a system known as AV +.[22] The Alternative Vote was to be employed in single-member constituencies, accounting for 80–85% of the membership, but with a number of top-up members to ensure some element of proportionality. The report attracted opposition from the Conservative Party and from Labour MPs committed to the existing first-past-the-post system. Tony Blair adopted a fairly neutral stance on the recommendations, much to the dismay of the Liberal Democrats, and no measure was brought forward to provide for a referendum. The Labour manifesto in 2001 noted that new electoral systems had been introduced for the devolved assemblies, the Greater London Assembly, and the European Parliament elections. 'We will review the experience of the new systems and the Jenkins report to assess whether changes might be made to the electoral system for the House of Commons. A referendum remains the right way to agree any change for Westminster.' These words were basically repeated in the 2005 manifesto. By May 2007, a desk study of the consequences of the new electoral systems had not been completed, although an independent commission had published such a review in 2004.[23]

Local and regional government

The government created regional development agencies (RDAs) to encourage economic regeneration in the regions. The move to establish elected assemblies came in 2002, when the Deputy Prime Minister, John Prescott, published a White Paper, proposing referendums on a regional basis, beginning in those regions where the demand appeared to be greatest. Initially, referendums in three regions were planned, but this was then reduced to one. It was held in the North-East in 2004 and resulted in a 78% 'No' vote. On local government, the government published three White Papers and enacted, as we have seen, the Greater London Authority Act 1999 and the Local Government Act 2000. The latter required all councils with populations of 85,000 or more to move from the old

---

[22] Independent Commission on the Voting System, *The Report of the Independent Commission on the Voting System*, Cm. 4090-I (London: TSO, 1998).
[23] Independent Commission on PR, *Changed Voting Changed Politics: Lessons of Britain's Experience of PR since 1997* (London: Constitution Unit, 2004).

committee-based system of decision-making to one in which there was a clear division of executive and scrutiny functions, more resembling national government in which a cabinet is scrutinised by parliamentary committees.

Freedom of information

The government published a White Paper, *Your Right to Know*, in December 1997 and invited comments. A draft Freedom of Information Bill was published in 1999 and subjected to pre-legislative scrutiny. The Bill was then introduced and enacted as the Freedom of Information Act 2000. The Act created a statutory right of access to information held by public authorities, though with certain exemptions, including particular classes of information; some other information could be exempted as a result of a prejudice test. An applicant not satisfied with a response to a request under the Act could apply to the Commissioner for Information to determine whether the authority in question had acted in accordance with the provisions of the Act.

In order to give departments and other public bodies time to prepare for its implementation, the Act did not come into force until 1 January 2005. In the first quarter of the year, departments of state received a total of 7,733 information requests. (The figures cover 'non-routine' requests, excluding information given out in the course of routine business.) The Ministry of Defence received the largest number (1,843). Of a total of 13,427 requests made to all monitored bodies, 2,413 were deemed to fall within exempted categories. The most commonly applied exemption was that relating to the formulation of government policy.[24]

Northern Ireland

The government maintained a bipartisan approach to resolving the problems of Northern Ireland. Tony Blair witnessed two major outcomes during his premiership. The first was the Good Friday Agreement. Following substantive negotiations between the different parties, agreement was reached and embodied three strands: a Northern Ireland Assembly with devolved executive and legislative powers, with all sections of the community able to participate; a North–South ministerial

---

[24] *Freedom of Information Act 2000: Statistics on Implementation in Central Government, Q1: January – March 2005* (London: Department for Constitutional Affairs, 2005).

council; and a British–Irish Council. It also included sections on rights and equality of opportunity, and envisaged paramilitary decommissioning of arms within two years. The agreement was then endorsed, by large majorities, in referendums on both sides of the border on 22 May 1998. An assembly was elected and, following some tensions within the province, a power-sharing Executive was appointed in 1999. However, there were clashes over the pace of decommissioning by the IRA and splits within the ranks of the Unionist parties. The Assembly was twice suspended. After a re-convened Assembly in 2006 failed to make progress, the British and Irish premiers set a deadline of 24 November 2006 for agreement to be reached. In October, the government brought together the various parties from the province at St Andrews in Scotland and produced proposals for power-sharing and a deadline for the restoration of devolved government. Parliament gave legislative effect to the agreement. A referendum was held to endorse the agreement in March 2007 and, after a six-week extension of the deadline, agreement was reached on 26 March between the Democratic Unionist Party, now the dominant Unionist party in the province, and Sinn Fein, with DUP leader Ian Paisley being nominated as First Minister and Martin McGuinness of Sinn Fein as Deputy First Minister. After thirty years of violence in the province, the agreement was hailed as historic, arguably the most important constitutional achievement of the Blair premiership.

A supreme court

In June 2003, Downing Street announced that the position of Lord Chancellor was to be abolished and a new supreme court to be created. Advice revealed that such changes could not be achieved immediately – the Lord Chancellor was mentioned in a large number of statutes and other documents – and a Constitutional Reform Bill was introduced. The House of Lords referred it for scrutiny by a select committee. It was eventually enacted as the Constitutional Reform Act 2005. It created a Judicial Appointments Commission, ensuring greater transparency in judicial appointments. Its other provisions were more controversial. Despite some opposition from the House of Lords, the Lord Chancellor was no longer required to be a senior lawyer and peer, and was no longer to be the presiding officer of the House of Lords. (In 2006, the Lords elected a Lord Speaker, Baroness Hayman.) It also established a supreme court, thus detaching the existing highest court of appeal from the House of Lords. The Act stipulated that the court would come into being once the Lord

Chancellor had confirmed that the new court building was ready. This was expected to be in October 2009.

Referendums

The holding of referendums, actual or promised, became a significant feature of the constitutional landscape. As we have seen, referendums were held in Scotland, Wales, Greater London and Northern Ireland. UK-wide referendums were promised on a new electoral system and in the event of the government recommending that the UK join the single currency. The Local Government Act 2000 also provided that the introduction of an elected mayor was dependent on a local referendum, triggered either by the council or by a petition of 5% (10% in Wales) of the electors. An attempt to amend the Political Parties, Elections and Referendums Bill in 2000 to provide for a referendum on any proposed legislation 'of first-class constitutional significance' failed. Nonetheless, it was apparent that future proposals for major constitutional change were likely to face demands to be subject to a referendum. As Derek Scott, a former Downing Street adviser, recorded: 'Towards the end of the Convention on the Future of Europe, several key advisors told Tony Blair that it would not be possible to hold the line against a referendum on the EU constitution.'[25]

The Blair premiership thus saw an array of significant changes to the Constitution. The list is not exhaustive. There were a range of other changes. The Electoral Administration Act, for example, lowered the age at which one could stand for election to public office. (The first eighteen-year-old candidate stood in the May 2007 local elections.) A Commissioner for Judicial Appointments was appointed in 2001. Legal aid was reformed. There were various changes to the structures and procedures of the House of Commons as well as the House of Lords. There were various attempts by the government, thwarted in the House of Lords, to reduce the number of jury trials. As we shall see, there were also attempts to change some of the measures enacted. The foregoing adumbration, though, comprises the most significant changes enacted during the Blair premiership and all, bar the provisions of the Constitutional Reform Act, relating to the promises made when Tony Blair entered office.

[25] Derek Scott, *Off Whitehall* (London: I. B. Taurus, 2004), p. 246.

Assessment

What, then, are we to make of the changes wrought during the Blair premiership? There are four generalisations that can be made. First, they changed the contours of the Constitution but fell short of delivering everything that was promised. Second, some of them had significant unintended consequences. Third, they lacked coherence. Fourth, and most significantly in terms of Blair himself, they were marked by a sense of detachment from the Prime Minister. They are changes that will be associated with Tony Blair but changes in which he invested little intellectual commitment.

Falling short

The effects of the changes on the Constitution were notable and, in combination, dramatic. Combined with British membership of the European Communities in 1973, they constitute a constitutional upheaval unparalleled in modern British history. The period from 1970 to 2000, according to Robert Stevens, 'provided a practical and psychological transformation comparable with the earlier constitutional revolution' of 1640 to 1720.[26] As he noted, there had been other major changes to the Constitution in between, but they had been free-standing measures and not part of a period of constitutional restructuring. The two terms of a Blair premiership had resulted in such a restructuring. Scotland had a parliament for the first time in 300 years. The Human Rights Act added a major judicial dimension to the Constitution, bringing judges more to the fore in the determination of public policy. The devolution legislation had a similar effect, since the higher courts became, in effect, constitutional courts for the different parts of the United Kingdom. The second chamber was transformed into a chamber of predominantly life peers, undoing several centuries of history.

There were, though, problems in delivering the full raft of measures promised in 1997. Some did not enjoy the wholehearted support of the Prime Minister, the cabinet or Labour MPs. Tony Blair, like John Smith, was not persuaded of the case for electoral reform. Paddy Ashdown has recorded the extent to which he was willing to set up the Jenkins Commission but not then to endorse its findings.[27] The Freedom of

[26] Robert Stevens, *The English Judges* (Oxford: Hart Publishing, 2002), p. xiii.
[27] Paddy Ashdown, *The Ashdown Diaries*, vol. II: *1997–1999* (Harmondsworth: Penguin, 2002), pp. 120–4, 306–19.

Information Bill was a contentious issue in cabinet. The first minister given responsibility for it, Chancellor of the Duchy of Lancaster David Clark, wanted to go further than many of his ministerial colleagues and was out-manoeuvred in cabinet. ('David Clark was sat on by Derry, by Ivor, by Jack, by all and his white paper will be delayed until the summer is over'.[28]) Responsibility passed to the Lord Chancellor, Lord Irvine, who achieved passage of a far less stringent Act than he, and proponents of freedom of information, had wished. The cabinet was divided over Lords reform, Irvine favouring an all-appointed House[29] and Blair, having previously endorsed an elected chamber, coming down against election in 2003 but then endorsing Jack Straw's efforts to find agreement on a partly elected House in 2007. Proponents of election, such as Peter Hain, were pitted against advocates of an all-appointed House, such as John Prescott, John Reid and David Blunkett.[30] Few in government, other than John Prescott, appeared to be enthusiastic about regional government. Prescott's White Paper in 2002 was a cautious document and it was not clear to what extent powers were going to be devolved from central government as opposed to sucked-up from local government.

The result was a constitutional settlement that was only partial and that delivered on no particular approach to constitutional change. John Smith had come closest to embracing the liberal approach to constitu-tional change, as advocated by Charter '88. Blair inherited the Smith mantle, guarded over by Lord Irvine, and delivered on part of the agenda but not all of it. Many aspects were seen as unfinished business, such as Lords reform and a new electoral system, and others were seen as botched or incomplete reforms, such as the Freedom of Information Act.

Unintended consequences

Many of the changes had effects that were not intended. Unintended is not the same as unforeseen, as some critics did claim that some reforms would invite trouble.[31] The most significant problems arose in relation to devolution and the Human Rights Act. The Labour Party had been per-suaded to support devolution in the 1970s – though many in the party continued to oppose it – and the motivation was to see off the challenge from the Scottish National Party (SNP), which was emerging as the

---

[28] Janet Jones, *Labour of Love* (London: Politico's, 1999), p. 102.   [29] *Ibid.*, p. 139.
[30] See e.g. David Blunkett, *The Blunkett Tapes* (London: Bloomsbury, 2006), pp. 445, 783–4.
[31] See e.g. the CPC National Policy Group on the Constitution, *Strengthening the United Kingdom* (London: Conservative Political Centre, 1996).

biggest threat to Labour north of the border. Devolution was ostensibly justified on the grounds that, by allowing decisions to be made more closely to the people, those in Scotland and Wales would not feel alienated as they had been by decisions taken in London. This was the basis of the recommendations of the Kilbrandon Commission. As already noted, the early years saw devolution bedding in without too many problems. However, by the time Tony Blair announced his departure, the political situation in Scotland and Wales was unravelling.

The SNP saw a surge in electoral support in 2007 and emerged as the largest party in the May elections to the Scottish Parliament: the party, under Alex Salmond, formed a minority administration. Labour also lost its majority in the National Assembly for Wales. The problem of relations between Whitehall and the devolved bodies was exacerbated by the fact that the government had not sought to keep in good working order the mechanisms that had initially been created, such as the Joint Ministerial Council (JMC), to deal with possible conflict between the different administrations in the UK.[32] The government was thus ill-prepared for a period of potentially strained relations. The changing political situation occurred against a background of survey data showing that people in England were not overly wedded to keeping Scotland in the Union. An ICM poll in November 2006 found that 59% of English respondents favoured Scottish independence; 48% also wanted to see Wales and Northern Ireland separated from England.[33]

The Human Rights Act was to be the cause of tension between the executive and the courts. The most significant clashes occurred over anti-terrorism legislation. In December 2004, in the Bellmarsh case, the House of Lords held that powers in Part 4 of the Anti-Terrorism, Crime and Security Act 2001 breached Convention rights. The government achieved passage, after some difficulty, of the Prevention of Terrorism Act 2005, which was designed to meet the court's objections. During passage of the Bill, the Joint Committee on Human Rights queried whether its provisions for control orders, empowering the Home Secretary to restrict the movement of particular individuals, also fell foul of the ECHR.[34] In two cases in 2006, Mr Justice Sullivan held that control orders breached

[32] See Constitution Committee, House of Lords, *Devolution: Inter-Institutional Relations in the United Kingdom*, Second Report, 2002–03, HL Paper 28.
[33] P. Hennessy and M. Kite, 'Britain Wants UK Break Up, Poll Shows', *Sunday Telegraph*, 26 November 2006.
[34] Joint Committee on Human Rights, *Prevention of Terrorism Bill*, Tenth Report, 2004–05, HL 68/HC 334.

Convention rights. He said that he had taken into account protecting the public from acts of terrorism, but 'human rights or international law must not be infringed or compromised'.[35] (The same judge later held that nine Afghans who had hijacked a plane in 2000 could remain in the UK.) In August 2006 the Appeal Court upheld the ruling in respect of the second case involving six control orders.

Each of the decisions was attacked by ministers. Following the Bellmarsh case, Foreign Secretary Jack Straw claimed the law lords were 'simply wrong' to imply that detainees were being held arbitrarily and said that it was for government to decide how Britain could best be defended from terrorism. In August 2005 Tony Blair announced new powers to combat terrorism and declared that 'the rules of the game are changing': should legal obstacles arise, 'we will legislate further including, if necessary, amending the Human Rights Act . . . and apply it directly in our own law'.[36] Home Secretary John Reid and his predecessors, Charles Clarke and David Blunkett, were also among those criticising the decision of the judges. The Lord Chief Justice, Lord Phillips of Worth Matravers, felt the need to defend the judges – he emphasised that the judges were doing their job of applying the law and enforcing the rule of law: 'It is the law that has changed.'[37] The Lord Chancellor, Lord Falconer of Thoroton, also felt the need to defend the judges and, following a review of the Human Rights Act by his department,[38] the Prime Minister conceded that it would not be possible to amend it.

The relationship was further complicated in May 2007 with the creation of a Ministry of Justice. Senior judges were concerned about the effect on the independence of the judiciary, not least in terms of protecting the budget of the courts and ensuring that their views were heard in government. The Lord Chancellor, Lord Falconer, engaged in discussions to reach agreement with the judiciary on protecting its position, but when Tony Blair left office he did so at a time when relations between executive and the courts were notably strained, and with his Home Secretary, John Reid – speaking at a G5 summit in the USA on 11 May

[35] A. Travis and A. Gillan, 'New Blow for Home Office as Judge Quashes Six Terror Orders', *The Guardian*, 29 June 2006.

[36] Prime Minister's Press Conference, 5 August 2005, www.number-10.gov.uk/output/Page8041.asp.

[37] Constitution Committee, House of Lords, *Meeting with the Lord Chief Justice*, Fourteenth Report, 2005–06, HL Paper 213, Q59.

[38] Department for Constitutional Affairs, *Review of the Implementation of the Human Rights Act* (London: Department for Constitutional Affairs, 2006), www.dca.gov.uk/peoples-rights/human-rights/pdf/full_review.pdf.

2007 – calling for a change in human rights legislation to protect people against terrorism. The law, he declared, needed modernising. 'We need leadership to do this. It can't be left solely to the lawyers.'[39]

There were also problems with the Freedom of Information Act. Not all ministers and MPs appreciated its effects. In 2007, senior Conservative MP David Maclean achieved passage in the Commons of a Private Member's Bill to exempt parliament from its provisions. The ostensible reason was to protect the privacy of MPs' correspondence with constituents; critics claimed it was in order to prevent continuing publication of MPs' expenses. In May 2007, Trade and Industry Secretary Alistair Darling wrote to the Lord Chancellor asking for the legislation to be reviewed: in his view, it did not sufficiently protect policy advice to ministers.[40] As Philip Cowley records elsewhere in this volume, reform of the House of Lords produced behavioural changes that were unexpected. The Political Parties, Elections and Referendums Act 2000 failed to put an end to concerns over party funding. Very few mayors were elected: where they were, electors frequently elected someone outside the political mainstream. Not only were the generation and passage of some of the measures of constitutional reform far from smooth, but neither were the consequences.

Lacking in coherence

The reforms listed in the 1997 manifesto were individually significant and, in combination, had a notable effect on the contours of the British Constitution. Those measures, however, were not grounded in any clear view of what type of Constitution Labour wanted to create for the United Kingdom. There was no coherent approach to constitutional change embodied in the manifesto and hence no reference point for the particular measures that were introduced. They were essentially disparate and discrete measures, with little thought given to the relationship between them and how they fitted into a view of constitutional change.

Ministers avoided attempts to get them to identify a coherent approach. Responding to a debate in the House of Lords in 2002, Lord Chancellor Lord Irvine of Lairg conceded that the government did not have an all-embracing definition of a Constitution and argued that it

---

[39] 'Reid Urges Human Rights Shake-up', BBC News Online, 12 May 2007, http://news.bbc.co.uk/1/hi/uk_politics/6648849.stm.

[40] 'Minister Wants "Secrecy for MPs"', BBC News Online, 24 May 2007, http://news.bbc.co.uk/1/hi/uk_politics6689031.stm.

proceeded 'by way of pragmatism based on principle, without the need for an over-arching theory'.[41] He enunciated three principles:

> The first is that we should remain a parliamentary democracy with the Westminster Parliament supreme and within that the other place the dominant partner. Secondly . . . we should increase public engagement in democracy, developing a maturer democracy with different centres of power where individuals enjoy greater rights and where government is carried out closer to the people . . . Our third principle is that the correct road to reform was to devise a solution to each problem on its own terms.[42]

The first two of these principles were not necessarily compatible in determining clearly where political power should reside and the third was not so much a principle as a get-out clause. The confused approach was reflected in practice: on devolution, power was to be given to Holyrood, but 'Blair told Irvine that he did not want a plan that seemed in any way to impinge on Westminster's ultimate sovereignty'.[43] It was not the basis for identifying precisely where the government were going.

Irvine, however, was arguably the only member of the cabinet with a clear interest in constitutional affairs. When he left government in acrimonious circumstances in 2003, there was no one to continue his work. Responsibility for constitutional affairs was never drawn together within the remit of a single cabinet committee. Irvine's successor was appointed to head a new Department of Constitutional Affairs (DCA), but that remained essentially a Lord Chancellor's Department, a fact implicitly conceded when it was transformed in 2007 into a Ministry of Justice. When it existed as the DCA, not all constitutional issues fell within its remit: though junior ministers in the Scotland and Wales Office were in the DCA for pay and rations, they answered to the relevant Secretaries of State. In 2006, responsibility for Lords reform moved from Lord Falconer to the Leader of the House of Commons, Jack Straw. There was thus no clear institutional framework for addressing the Constitution qua Constitution and, after 2003, no one within government with a clear interest in doing so. What constitutional measures that were introduced after Irvine's departure were very much free-standing measures, reinforcing the apparent fragmentation of the nation's constitutional arrangements. When it came to having a coherent view of constitutional change, there was no leadership from the top.

---

[41] *House of Lords Debates*, vol. 642, c. 691 (18 December 2002).   [42] *Ibid.*, c. 692.
[43] James Naughtie, *The Rivals* (London: Fourth Estate, 2001), p. 176.

Detachment

The 1997 reforms were promised by Blair but not originated by him. They owe more to John Smith and Lord Irvine than they do to Tony Blair. Smith, as we have seen, embraced a wide-ranging agenda of constitutional change. As Anthony Seldon noted in his biography of Blair, Irvine was 'committed to fulfilling Smith's legacy'.[44] He was assiduous in seeing measures through,[45] though not always to the extent he would wish, and suffered, according to Ivor Richard, from not being a very good committee chairman.[46] When he left government, there was no one to take the lead. Blair for his part was not intellectually engaged. He was prone to prevarication. 'Waiting for Blair is like waiting for Godot', wrote Paddy Ashdown.[47] According to one senior politician, whenever he saw Blair and raised the issue of the Constitution 'his eyes just glazed over'.[48] Though Blair could engage where action was needed to achieve a particular outcome, as in Northern Ireland, that was to achieve a very particular goal, and usually involved the oratorical and negotiating skills at which Blair excelled: there was no conception of seeking to achieve a broader, coherent constitutional goal. Blair had no clearly defined view of a desired constitutional landscape and never articulated one.

Blair's lack of interest was graphically illustrated in a Commons debate in July 2000 on a motion on parliamentary reform moved by William Hague. Blair derided Hague for devoting valuable parliamentary time to the issue. 'He could have discussed jobs, the economy, schools, hospitals or even crime. I do not know whether people in his pubs and clubs are discussing pre-legislative scrutiny, but they are not in mine.'[49] It was a populist approach that failed to engage with the issue or even to appreciate its relevance to the health of the political system.

Blair entered office having no previous experience of government and never showed any intellectual curiosity as to why the relationships at the heart of government worked in the way that they did. He eschewed established forms of decision-making in favour of what came to be termed 'sofa government': decisions being made by a small group in an informal setting – 'a loose, fluid group which takes momentous decisions over

[44] Anthony Seldon, *Blair* (London: The Free Press, 2004), p. 205.
[45] See Constitution Committee, House of Lords, *Changing the Constitution: The Process of Constitutional Change,* Fourth Report, Session 2001–02, HL Paper 69, pp. 10–11.
[46] Jones, *Labour of Love,* p. 78.   [47] Ashdown, *The Ashdown Diaries,* vol. II, p. 255.
[48] Senior MP and Privy Counsellor to author.
[49] *House of Commons Debates,* vol. 353, c. 1097 (13 July 2000).

coffee in the "den" and does not trouble with such bureaucratic, Old Labour formalities as taking minutes'[50] – and largely by-passing cabinet[51] and other organs of government. This created problems in the running of government, but also reflected a wider lack of engagement with the rationale for the existence of the Westminster model of government. It also created problems for the future. By severing existing links at the heart of government, it also generated vulnerability. 'He has severed the element of trust and interdependence that previously characterised British government. Coupled with the absence of any clearly honed ideology, this means that if things start going wrong he is in danger of not being able to mobilise support, either in terms of ideological commitment or of institutional loyalty.'[52]

Conclusion

Tony Blair presided over major changes in the nation's constitutional arrangements. They did not go as far as initially envisaged in 1997 and they had a number of unintended consequences, generating tensions with the political system, not least but not exclusively between ministers and the courts.[53] They changed the contours of the British Constitution, but without any clear view of the type of Constitution that was being created for the United Kingdom. At no point could the government identify a constitutional end point or a coherent intellectual approach to constitutional change. Major constitutional change took place during Blair's watch – it is likely to be one of the principal things for which the Blair premiership is remembered – but it is not something for which Blair himself was principally responsible. It was left to others to deliver.

[50] Francis Beckett and David Henke, *The Blairs and their Court* (London: Aurum, 2004), p. 195. See also Naughtie, *The Rivals*, p. 104.
[51] See e.g. Clare Short, *An Honourable Deception* (London: The Free Press, 2004), pp. 70–1.
[52] Philip Norton, 'Governing Alone', *Parliamentary Affairs*, 56(4), 2003: 558.
[53] See *ibid.*, pp. 551–6.

7

Media management

RAYMOND KUHN

First as Leader of the Opposition (1994–7) and then as Prime Minister (1997–2007), Blair was careful to pay considerable attention to the task of managing the media. This involved Blair and his advisers – most notably Alastair Campbell, his press secretary between 1994 and 2003 – in the pursuit of different but complementary communication objectives: first, setting the news agenda by promoting some stories and downplaying others; second, ensuring that issues were framed in as positive a fashion as possible; and, finally, projecting an upbeat image of New Labour in general and Blair's leadership in particular. This obsession with media management was understandable. The UK political communications environment of the Blair era was characterised by the twenty-four-hour news cycle, an explosion of media outlets, notably rolling news channels and internet websites, a phalanx of journalists hungry for insider information and a broad range of political actors, including parties and pressure groups, functioning in competition with the core executive as sources for the media. In the promotional culture of a 'public relations democracy', managing the media was a necessity – not an option – for Blair and New Labour.[1]

For several years, Blair's media management activities met with considerable success. However, towards the middle of his first term as Prime Minister, journalists' stories critical of the government's attempts to control the news agenda began to replace comments which in the main had previously been full of praise for the professionalism of New Labour's media machine. 'Spin' increasingly provided the narrative frame for much of the media's coverage of government initiatives, as journalists revealed the behind-the-scenes process of news management to their audiences. As a result, long before the fall-out from the Iraq War completely tarnished

[1] Aeron Davis, *Public Relations Democracy: Public Relations, Politics and the Mass Media in Britain* (Manchester: Manchester University Press, 2002).

the government's reputation for truth-telling, one of the defining characteristics of Blair's leadership of New Labour in the eyes of many voters was the close and negative association with sound-bites and 'spin'.

Aiming to keep the media on message

It was during Blair's leadership of the party in opposition that New Labour acquired a reputation for its skilful handling of the media. Blair built on reforms introduced by his immediate predecessors to strengthen the power of an inner core elite based around the dominant position of the leader both to make policy and take charge of the party's strategic communications with the press and broadcasting.[2] In the eyes of this inner core, the formulation of policy and its communication to the electorate were not distinct, separate activities but rather had to be managed in an integrated, holistic fashion. Changes in party organisation were accompanied by a cultural shift whereby communication was regarded as central to the way in which New Labour functioned: the Millbank model of 'command and control'. Moreover, day-to-day media management was part of a broader exercise in political marketing whereby the New Labour brand was promoted in the electoral marketplace.[3]

After its 1997 election victory New Labour transferred into government the techniques of news management it had honed in opposition. As a result, ministers and their special advisers were constantly engaged in seeking to harness the media in the task of promoting the government's achievements to the electorate through positive imagery generation and symbolic construction.[4] During Campbell's tenure in charge of the Prime Minister's communication operations, the New Labour government's strategic approach to media management was characterised by three key features: centralisation, professionalisation and politicisation.[5]

[2] Colin Hughes and Patrick Wintour, *Labour Rebuilt* (London: Fourth Estate, 1990); Richard Heffernan and Mike Marqusee, *Defeat from the Jaws of Victory* (London: Verso, 1992); Eric Shaw, *The Labour Party Since 1979: Crisis and Transformation* (London: Routledge, 1994).

[3] Philip Gould, *The Unfinished Revolution: How the Modernisers Saved the Labour Party* (London: Little, Brown, 1998); Jennifer Lees-Marchment, *Political Marketing and British Political Parties: The Party's Just Begun* (Manchester: Manchester University Press, 2001); Dominic Wring, *The Politics of Marketing the Labour Party* (Basingstoke: Palgrave Macmillan, 2005).

[4] Nicholas Jackson O'Shaughnessy, *Politics and Propaganda* (Manchester: Manchester University Press, 2004), pp. 172–89.

[5] Bob Franklin, 'The Hand of History: New Labour, News Management and Governance', in S. Ludlam and M. J. Smith (eds.), *New Labour in Government* (Basingstoke: Macmillan, 2001), pp. 130–44.

First, Campbell put in place in No. 10 a highly centralised organisation which sought to coordinate governmental communications and impose a single message from the top down. For example, government ministers who did not adhere to the rules whereby major interviews and media appearances had to be agreed in advance with the No. 10 Press Office quickly found themselves reprimanded by Campbell. In addition, any minister or adviser he regarded as being 'off message' was treated with suspicion. During the first Blair administration, for instance, Gordon Brown's press officer at the Treasury, Charlie Wheelan, frequently came into conflict with Campbell because of his tendency to brief the media on his own initiative to promote the Chancellor's interests. The feuding between these two New Labour 'spin doctors' continued until Wheelan was forced to resign at the start of 1999 over his alleged role in leaking information about Peter Mandelson's home loan from Geoffrey Robinson.[6]

Second, a highly professional engagement with news management was evident in the various innovations introduced by Campbell in Downing Street. These included the establishment of a Strategic Communications Unit to coordinate government news announcements across departments so that a clear, focused policy message was distributed to the media on any particular day. Former journalists, such as David Bradshaw (*Daily Mirror*) and Philip Bassett (*The Times*), were employed to ensure that a media rather than bureaucratic mindset informed the process. In terms of trailing policy announcements, the rebuttal of critical statements, the 'pre-buttal' of opposition criticisms not yet disseminated in the public sphere, the proactive planting of stories via favoured journalists and speedy reaction to possible negative stories, the New Labour government's media management operations pushed back the frontiers, going further than any of its predecessors in Britain and even acquiring a glowing reputation abroad.[7]

Campbell was in many respects the personification of this professionalisation of governmental news management. As a former journalist and political editor at the two *Mirror* titles and *Today*, Campbell knew the world of the news media, and particularly tabloid journalism, from the inside. He did not have to second-guess what journalists might do with a lead; he knew from his own experience how a story would play in different media outlets. Campbell's attention to detail became legendary,

[6] Nicholas Jones, *Sultans of Spin* (London: Gollancz, 1999), pp. 259–80; Andrew Rawnsley, *Servants of the People* (London: Hamish Hamilton, 2000), pp. 210–34.
[7] Steven Barnett and Ivor Gaber, *Westminster Tales: The Twenty-first-century Crisis in Political Journalism* (London: Continuum, 2001), pp. 106–13.

as did his facility for the appropriate sound-bite, such as the 'people's princess' used by Blair on the occasion of Princess Diana's death in 1997. Moreover, Campbell was highly valued by journalists as a source because of his well-known proximity to Blair in the inner circle of key ministers and top advisers.[8] He was the first No. 10 press secretary to attend cabinet meetings on a regular basis and he acquired the reputation of having more influence in decision-making than some policy advisers.[9]

Campbell was not averse to browbeating and bullying those journalists who he thought were not giving Blair and New Labour fair treatment. He also exploited the rivalry in the lobby system of briefings by favouring some journalists at the expense of others.[10] Certain correspondents, for example, were given advance notice of material that the government wished to bring into the public sphere in the expectation that in return the government would receive positive coverage.[11] The Murdoch newspapers were a good example of this exchange relationship. On a day-to-day basis Trevor Kavanagh, the political editor of *The Sun*, was the recipient of insider nuggets of information – such as the date of the 2001 general election – ahead of their being made available to other parliamentary lobby journalists. In return, the Murdoch press provided a good platform for New Labour, while Blair had numerous articles published under his personal byline. Another tactic employed by No. 10 was to bypass lobby correspondents by targeting regional newspapers, women's magazines and ethnic minority publications so as to get its message across as unfiltered as possible to different sections of the electorate.

During Campbell's stewardship the procedures of the lobby system also underwent important structural reform. While the televising of its proceedings continued to be rejected on the grounds that this would give too much publicity to the Prime Minister's official spokesperson, briefings were now carried out on an on-the-record basis and from March 2000 a selective summary of the briefing was made available on the internet. In 2002 a further reform was introduced, whereby the morning sessions were opened up to a wider cross-section of journalists, including specialist and foreign correspondents. The Prime Minister also started to

[8] Peter Hennessy, *The Prime Minister* (Harmondsworth: Penguin, 2001), pp. 476–538.
[9] Peter Oborne, *Alastair Campbell: New Labour and the Rise of the Media Class* (London: Aurum, 1999), p. 161; Andrew Roth, 'The Lobby's "Dying Gasps"?', *British Journalism Review*, 10(3), 1999: 22.
[10] Bill Hagerty, 'Cap'n Spin *Does* Lose his Rag', *British Journalism Review*, 11(2), 2000: 13–14.
[11] Ivor Gaber, 'Lies, Damn Lies . . . and Political Spin', *British Journalism Review*, 11(1), 2000: 69.

hold monthly press conferences, which were 'on the record, televised, accessible to a much wider range of journalists than the lobby (including overseas journalists) and unrestricted in subject matter'.[12] Campbell argued that these American-style reforms were a genuine attempt to be more open with the media and less 'buttoned up' about the next day's headlines. However, according to some leading lobby journalists, the government's aim was to minimise the disruptive potential of the traditional lobby correspondents who were accustomed to 'grilling' a government spokesperson on a particular issue in comparative secrecy. Some lobby correspondents feared that the new media briefings would become more orchestrated by government, for example through the choice of journalists invited to ask questions and in the lack of opportunity to engage in sustained interrogation, and so give ministers more power to shape the news agenda.

Finally, politicisation of news management was evidenced by three important developments. First, Campbell was allowed to give orders to civil servants. This meant that he could adopt a more overtly partisan approach in his relationship with the media than had formally been the case with his predecessors. Second, Campbell's belief that the non-partisan civil servants acting as ministerial press officers in the Government Information Service (renamed the Government Information and Communication Service) would be insufficiently proactive in pushing the government's case with the news media led to many of them being weeded out and replaced in the early months of Blair's first term. Third, and most controversially, the New Labour government significantly increased the number of politically appointed special advisers in government departments, several of whom fulfilled a proactive partisan media relations role which sometimes brought them into conflict with government information officers steeped in a civil service culture of political neutrality.[13]

End of the long honeymoon

The New Labour government enjoyed an extended honeymoon period with much of the news media, which extended well into Blair's first term. As the novelty of a New Labour administration wore off, however, the government's approach to news management ran up against a 'media

[12] Colin Seymour-Ure, *Prime Ministers and the Media* (Oxford: Blackwell, 2003), p. 170.
[13] Barnett and Gaber, *Westminster Tales*, pp. 116–24; Margaret Scammell, 'The Media and Media Management', in A. Seldon (ed.) *The Blair Effect: The Blair Government 1997–2001* (London: Little, Brown, 2001), pp. 520–6.

logic' whereby in a highly competitive media system, driven by the relentless pursuit of audiences and advertisers, decision-making in newsrooms
focuses attention on those stories which satisfy criteria of newsworthi-
ness. News stories increasingly tended to emphasise conflict and disunity,
negative events and Labour personalities in trouble. For instance, the
persistent in-fighting at the heart of the executive between Blair and
Brown and their respective supporters provided good copy for political
journalists, several of whom were happy to side with either the Prime
Minister or the Chancellor of the Exchequer in their newspaper columns.

Some of the toughest news management tests for the New Labour government were in the area of scandal and impropriety, hardly surprising in
the light of New Labour's attacks on Conservative sleaze during the final
years of the Major premiership. Sometimes the government's exercise in
damage limitation was successful. For instance, potentially explosive
stories, such as Robin Cook's affair with his secretary or the resignation of
Ron Davies following his nocturnal wandering on Clapham Common,
were skilfully dealt with by New Labour's media handlers to minimise any
adverse publicity for the government.[14] Other stories proved more
difficult to manage. The Ecclestone affair, which concerned large secret
donations to the Labour Party,[15] and allegations of abuse of position
made against a succession of ministers, including Geoffrey Robinson,
Peter Mandelson and Keith Vaz, revealed the capacity and willingness of
the news media, particularly broadsheet newspaper journalists, to initiate
and pursue stories highly critical of leading New Labour figures.
Coverage of both Mandelson resignations from the cabinet had all the
hallmarks of a media feeding frenzy.

From around the beginning of 2000 New Labour's capacity to shape
the news agenda and influence the framing of coverage started to run into
difficulties as a series of highly problematic issues come on to the political
and policy agendas. The Millennium Dome fiasco, the successful campaign for the mayorship of London by the rebel Ken Livingstone standing
as an Independent against the official Labour candidate, the protest
against the rise in fuel taxation by lorry drivers and the foot-and-mouth
crisis in the countryside were all issues which New Labour found difficult
to manage in news terms in the run-up to the 2001 general election.

In 2000 Campbell passed on the onerous responsibility of the twice
daily lobby briefings to two career civil servants and assumed a more
strategic role as Director of Communications and Strategy at No. 10. This

[14] Jones, *Sultans of Spin*, pp. 244–52.   [15] Rawnsley, *Servants of the People*, pp. 89–105.

move was designed to take Campbell away from routine front-line contact with journalists and to remove him from an environment where his increasing frustration with the coverage afforded New Labour frequently spilled out into abrasive comments to journalists. Campbell argued that the real spinners in the interrelationship between government and news media were the journalists and that as a result the government's message was being distorted in various media outlets.

Blair and newspaper partisanship

A key objective of Blair as party leader and Prime Minister was to try to win over and then retain the support of as much of the national press as possible for New Labour. The size of this task should not be underestimated. At every post-war general election prior to the 1997 contest a higher percentage of national newspapers (as measured by circulation figures) than voters had supported the Conservative Party. Moreover, the intensity of anti-Labour sentiment, especially in the pro-Conservative 'redtops' (popular tabloids) and 'blacktops' (middle market papers), had been particularly noticeable during the Thatcher premiership, much to the discomfiture of the Labour leadership. In pursuing his objective, Blair benefited from the disintegration of the relationship between the Major government and much of the traditional Conservative press in the wake of the events of 'Black Wednesday' in 1992 when the pound had been forced out of the European Exchange Rate Mechanism by intense financial speculation. This disenchantment of many newspapers with the Conservatives opened up the possibility of a realignment of newspaper support in favour of the Labour Party. Neutralising traditional press opponents or, even better, bringing them round to supporting the New Labour project were more realistic options for Blair than hoping for the entry of new pro-Labour papers into the market.[16]

In the run-up to the 1997 general election New Labour was extremely successful in disarming the guns of the Tory press and even winning some national newspapers over to its cause. In addition to disillusionment with the perceived failures of the Major premiership, four factors help to explain the apparently remarkable change in newspaper partisanship during Blair's term as Leader of the Opposition.[17] First, Labour's ideological

[16] Sean Tunney, *Labour and the Press: From New Left to New Labour* (Brighton: Sussex Academic Press, 2007).
[17] Brian McNair, *Journalism and Democracy* (London: Routledge, 2000), pp. 146–55.

repositioning to appeal to the electoral centre ground made it a more acceptable alternative party of government for some newspaper propri-etors and editors. As a result, little remained of the 'loony left' type of story which had been such a feature of tabloid coverage in the 1980s.[18] Moreover, Blair personally was regarded as a strong and effective leader who was playing a key part in strengthening the party's appeal to the electorate of 'Middle England'. This combination of forceful leadership in the service of ideological moderation was a winning combination in the eyes of many newspaper proprietors and editors.

Second, under Blair's leadership New Labour in opposition actively set out to curry favour with sections of the national press, especially the Murdoch papers.[19] This was in marked contrast to the late 1980s when Labour had boycotted News International titles following the company's prolonged dispute with its workforce over the introduction of new tech-nology. As part of the charm offensive, Blair flew halfway around the world to give a speech to News International executives. In addition, New Labour seemed prepared not to attack the commercial power of leading media companies. For instance, speculation was rife that in return for support from Murdoch's newspapers, an incoming Labour government would not introduce tough cross-media ownership legislation. While there may not have been an explicit deal between Murdoch and Blair that *The Sun* would support Labour 'in return for promises that a Labour gov-ernment would leave Rupert's British media empire alone',[20] at the very least a tacit understanding emerged between Blair and Murdoch on this issue.

Third, a more sophisticated approach to news management ensured that New Labour's attacks on Conservative government policy were skil-fully prepared for journalists across a whole range of issues. These included the running of the National Health Service, rail privatisation, the huge salary increases and perks of the heads of private utilities, and the Conservative government's record on tax and sleaze.

Finally, as New Labour's electoral fortunes improved and opinion polls showed them pulling well ahead of the Conservatives, newspapers had good commercial reasons for modifying their attitudes towards the party so as to stay in tune with the views of their readers. In a competitive market, refusing to support a popular party in newspaper columns would

[18] James Curran, Ivor Gaber and Julian Petley, *Culture Wars: The Media and the British Left* (Edinburgh: Edinburgh University Press, 2005).
[19] Andrew Neil, *Full Disclosure* (London: Pan, 1997); Joy Johnson, 'Rupert's Grip?', *British Journalism Review*, 9(1),1998: 13–19.   [20] Neil, *Full Disclosure*, p. xxv.

have done little to boost circulation figures among voters, many of whom were eager for a change of government.

The 1997 election campaign witnessed an apparent sea-change in the partisan allegiances of several leading newspapers.[21] Overall six out of ten national dailies supported Labour in 1997, compared with only three out of eleven in 1992. So too did five of the nine national Sunday titles, as against a mere three five years earlier. Indeed, 'the support in 1997 placed Labour for the first time in a position of disproportionately high circulation compared to its share of the vote: 62% of circulation and 44% of the vote, compared with the Conservatives' 33% of circulation and 31% of the vote'.[22] The single most important contributory factor to this change was the decision by *The Sun* to overturn more than twenty years of pro-Conservative sympathies and move straight across into the pro-Labour camp. Because of its huge circulation and its unbridled hostility to Labour since the mid-1970s, the support for New Labour expressed by *The Sun* in 1997 had immense symbolic significance, even if its impact on voting behaviour is open to question. Yet the qualitative nature of the shift in newspaper partisanship in the 1997 campaign should not be over-stated. *The Sun* was the only national daily which moved straight across from openly supporting the Conservatives in 1992 to calling for a Labour victory five years later.

In the 2001 campaign even more national titles supported Labour than in 1997, giving the impression that press support leant heavily towards Labour to the detriment of the Conservatives.[23] However, despite the massive quantitative advantage Labour enjoyed in terms of both number of titles and circulation figures, in qualitative terms newspaper support for Labour during the 2001 campaign 'was generally subdued, often qualified and sometimes critical'.[24] By the time of the 2005 general election, Labour's support in the press had declined, with the two *Express* titles and the *Sunday Times* returning to back the Conservatives. The complexity of newspaper partisanship remained evident, with traditional newspaper party loyalties being subjected to strain in the wake of Blair's handling of the Iraq War issue. There was strong evidence of negative partisanship,

[21] Margaret Scammell and Martin Harrop, 'The Press', in D. Butler and D. Kavanagh, *The British General Election of 1997* (Basingstoke: Macmillan, 1997).

[22] Colin Seymour-Ure, 'Newspapers: Editorial Opinion in the National Press', in P. Norris and N. Gavin (eds.), *Britain Votes 1997* (Oxford: Oxford University Press, 1997), pp. 80–1.

[23] David Deacon, Peter Golding and Michael Billig, 'Press and Broadcasting: "Real Issues" and Real Coverage', *Parliamentary Affairs*, 54, 2001: 666–78.

[24] Margaret Scammell and Martin Harrop, 'The Press Disarmed', in D. Butler and D. Kavanagh, *The British General Election of 2001* (Basingstoke: Palgrave, 2002), p. 156.

often expressed in highly personalised terms of anti-Blair (for instance the *Daily Mail*), although criticism of the Prime Minister by several newspapers (including the *Daily Mirror*) did not necessarily persuade them to support the Conservative alternative in 2005.[25]

Under Blair's leadership, therefore, it is clear that New Labour was successful in decoupling longstanding ties of support between certain newspaper titles and the Conservatives. At the same time, press support for Blair and New Labour was less committed and wholehearted than that enjoyed by Thatcher and the Conservatives during the 1980s. Some newspapers, such as the *Telegraph* and *Mail* titles, were never won over to the New Labour cause. *The Sun* provided conditional support, but on the issue of Europe could be – and frequently was – extremely critical of any initiative that smacked of supranational integration. In 1998 it even portrayed Blair as 'the most dangerous man in Britain'[26] because of his stance on the single currency, and five years later led on its front page with the headline 'Blair surrenders Britain to Europe' in commenting on his stance on the EU constitution.[27] Moreover, *The Sun* was generally more supportive of Blair personally than of New Labour as a whole.

As some newspapers drifted away from New Labour in tandem with Blair's diminishing electoral popularity, it was clear that the Blair era had not seen a structural realignment of national newspaper partisanship but rather a more muted partisan de-alignment. Faced with declining circulations in highly competitive market sectors, newspapers have become more fickle in unconditionally backing a particular party. Party leaders increasingly have to negotiate for newspaper support on an issue-by-issue basis with owners and editors who keep as close an eye on public opinion and consumer trends as do politicians.

The mediatisation of Blair's leadership

In the highly developed political communication networks of advanced democracies, key political actors such as heads of government and leaders of the major parties have to devote a considerable amount of time and energy to news media activities. One aspect of this attentiveness concerns the projection and maintenance of a well-defined leadership image in the mediated public sphere. This is because the media have exerted an

---

[25] John Bartle, 'The Labour Government and the Media', in J. Bartle and A. King (eds.), *Britain at the Polls 2005* (Washington, DC: CQ Press, 2006), pp. 124–50.
[26] *The Sun*, 24 June 1998.   [27] *The Sun*, 15 May 2003.

important influence on the emergence of a clear 'leadership dimension in contemporary British politics' which 'has established the meaning and value of leadership as a political issue in its own right'.[28] As voters have become less aligned with political parties, the role of the leader in influencing electoral perceptions, attitudes and behaviour has grown. A popular leader, like Blair in 1997, attracts voters, while an unpopular one, like Blair in 2005, repels them.

Much of the British news media, notably the tabloid press and television, tend to personalise political issues and to focus overwhelmingly on the role of leadership figures in their coverage of politics. Prime Minister's Question Time in the House of Commons, for example, is an occasion for the two main party leaders to go head-to-head in a competitive contest in front of the television cameras, with an edited version of their exchange being served up in the main evening news programmes and in press coverage. Journalists frequently evaluate the performance of the two leaders as they would boxers in a championship fight, assessing whether either managed to land a knockout punch, while opinion polls constantly measure the public's evaluation of leadership performance. More importantly, many policy issues are now presented and interpreted by the media through the prism of their impact on a leader's authority and electoral popularity. While there is no single template for success in the mediatisation of leadership, an image that is weak, blurred or incoherent is potentially highly damaging.

Blair not only understood this media dimension of contemporary political leadership, but sought to use it to his advantage in a way that his predecessor as Prime Minister, John Major, had rarely been able to do. For instance, Blair's capacity to come over well on television was recognised as a distinctive electoral asset by many party members who supported him in the 1994 contest for the Labour leadership.[29] More important than his telegenic and rhetorical skills, however, was Blair's ability to convey through the media an image of leadership which was consonant with public expectations. Blair tried with considerable success to portray himself as a combination of decisive political leader and everyday family man, and through media management 'to define the private so as to fit a public image'.[30] This constructed image thus combined both 'formal authority and the ordinary "blokeishness" that is so central to his

---

[28] Michael Foley, *John Major, Tony Blair and a Conflict of Leadership* (Manchester: Manchester University Press, 2002), p. 5.

[29] Nicholas Jones, *Soundbites and Spin Doctors* (London: Cassell, 1995), p. 157.

[30] Seymour-Ure, *Prime Ministers and the Media*, p. 45.

style'.[31] During his first term as Prime Minister one commentator argued that a crucial part of the success of Blair's style was 'his capacity to, as it were, "anchor" the public politician in the "normal person" – the necessary posturing and evasions of politics are it seems at least partially redeemed by Blair's capacity to reassert constantly his normal, decent, likeable personality'.[32]

Blair actively and consciously sought to focus media attention on his self-ascribed role as a strong leader by deliberately associating himself with high-profile policy proposals across the range of government activities. In a memo leaked to the media in the spring of 2000, during a period when the government was going through a bad news trough, 'he asked his aides to provide him with "headline grabbing initiatives" on touchstone issues that would change public perceptions of the government'.[33] Blair's highly proactive stance during the war in Kosovo in 1999 and his unflinching 'shoulder to shoulder' support for President Bush in the 'war on terror' in the aftermath of the events of 11 September 2001 were eloquent media manifestations of Blair playing the role of international statesman. Television news footage of the Prime Minister talking to British troops on active duty in the Balkans, or visiting 'ground zero' in New York, can be seen as created media events where good pictures were the principal object of the exercise. In addition, Blair was not averse to displaying a tough side to his mediated persona in statements on domestic policy issues such as crime and anti-social behaviour. Yet Blair also cultivated a concerned, emotional side to his image, evident when he talked about the 'caring' issues of education and health as well as his feelings as a father.

As a modern political leader, Blair did not just use traditional news media genres to get his message across. In a communications environment characterised by the fragmentation of audiences into niche sectors and the decline in popularity of traditional means of political communication such as television news programmes, Blair was open to the use of new media outlets and genres. For instance, he was the first British Prime Minister to use the internet to reach out to the electorate and to seek to get his message across to the public without having to go through the potentially distorting intermediary filter of the journalistic process of selection and construction. The internet may not yet have established

[31] Alan Finlayson, 'Elements of the Blairite Image of Leadership', *Parliamentary Affairs*, 55, 2002: 593.
[32] Norman Fairclough, *New Labour, New Language?* (London: Routledge, 2000), p. 7.
[33] Butler and Kavanagh, *The British General Election of 2001*, p. 27.

itself as a routinised medium of political information for much of the electorate – in the 2005 general election, for example, 'only 8 per cent of the public claimed to have paid "a lot" or "some" attention to politics online'.[34] Yet notwithstanding this, the internet provides a platform for a politician to express views which may then be taken up by journalists working in the mainstream media. Certainly the impact of the internet on the mediatisation of political leadership in the contemporary era cannot simply be evaluated by the number of visits by members of the public to a website. It is likely, for instance, that more voters have heard of the 'WebCameron' initiative through traditional media coverage in newspapers, radio and television, than have accessed the Conservative leader's site directly themselves.

In addition to using the internet, Blair also exploited non-traditional genres in mainstream media to get his message across and to maintain his image – for instance, in appearances on television chat shows such as *Richard and Judy* and *Parkinson*. In early 2003 he went on MTV as part of his campaign to make the case for the war against Iraq. Politicians argue that these sorts of media appearances are necessary to reach out to those sections of the electorate, such as young voters, who do not regularly access more traditional media formats for the coverage of politics. This may well be true. At the same time, in the eyes of critics such media appearances are exploited by politicians in the hope that they will escape tough questions from professional political journalists and bypass hostile interviewers.

Blair's mediated image involved a complex mix of values, including competence, firmness and fairness. He made much of his personal integrity, emphasising the notion that he was a leader who could be trusted. The aftermath to the 2003 Iraq War did much to tarnish this constructed image, as Downing Street's role in preparing the case for war was called into question by some media outlets, including most controversially the BBC, and the question of whether Blair had knowingly misled the British public became a topic of public debate. These events were a reminder that the media may help undermine a leader's carefully crafted image just as effectively as they can reinforce it.

Almost a year before the 2001 general election, for example, Blair was given a slow handclap by sections of the audience as he was making a speech at the annual conference of the Women's Institute. Television

---

[34] Dennis Kavanagh and David Butler, *The British General Election of 2005* (Basingstoke: Palgrave, 2005), p. 173.

news coverage that evening showed an obviously embarrassed Prime Minister failing miserably to get his message across to the representatives in the conference centre. The story in the next day's newspapers concentrated not on the government's proposed policy initiatives – the formal substance of the speech – but rather on this very public failure of prime-ministerial communication, the resonance of which was hugely amplified by being shown on television. Two years later, stories in the *Spectator* magazine, the *Evening Standard* and the *Mail on Sunday* that No. 10 had intervened to try to enhance the Prime Minister's role at the funeral ceremony for the Queen Mother conveyed the impression of an arrogant Blair trying to hijack the occasion for his own purposes. The fallout from the episode was again damaging to the Prime Minister's reputation.[35] In similar vein, when Blair appeared on various audience-participation programmes in early 2003 to make the case for British involvement in military intervention in Iraq, he was subjected to some very hostile questioning from members of the public, and at times the Prime Minister looked visibly shaken by the experience. The strength of his own convictions and of the audience's views were clearly in evidence.

The Iraq War

The war in Iraq was the single most controversial issue of Blair's premiership and as such was a key test for the government in its relations with the media. Prior to the launch of the coalition offensive, the government sought to use the news media to prepare public opinion for the impending war and mobilise support for an armed invasion. Several newspapers were willing to act as more or less uncritical transmission belts for the official line regarding Iraq's possession of weapons of mass destruction. In particular, the government's claim in its September 2002 dossier that these weapons could be used by Saddam Hussein's regime within forty-five minutes of an order being given to deploy them was given significant prominence in news coverage. Misleading newspaper headlines about Britain's vulnerability to an attack by Iraq were allowed to go uncorrected by ministers and officials, who instead could allow themselves to be self-congratulatory regarding the success of the dominant news framing.

In contrast to much of the press on the Iraq issue, the BBC was regarded by Campbell as being significantly 'off message' in this crucial period in the run-up to the outbreak of armed conflict. Animosity

[35] Peter Oborne and Simon Walters, *Alastair Campbell* (London: Aurum, 2004), pp. 303–12.

between No. 10 and the Corporation built up over a period of weeks and came to a head over allegations made on 29 May 2003 by the defence and diplomatic correspondent Andrew Gilligan in a two-way exchange with John Humphrys on the Radio 4 *Today* programme that the government had knowingly misinformed the public in presenting its case for war. In particular, in a phrase that was to reverberate for months afterwards, Gilligan claimed that, according to his unnamed source, the government had ordered the contents of the September dossier 'to be sexed up'. This broadcast, which indirectly led a few weeks later to the suicide of the government scientist and former weapons inspector, Dr David Kelly, was seized on by Campbell as an instance of inaccurate reporting, which he argued typified much of the BBC's coverage prior to, during and immediately after the war. While the government may have chosen to hit out at the BBC in an attempt to divert attention away from other war-related issues, such as the controversy surrounding the failure to find weapons of mass destruction in Iraq, there is little doubt that the government's anger with the Corporation was real and that in showing its ire in public one of its aims was to send a warning shot across the BBC's bows.

Gilligan's comments were at the heart of the inquiry led by Lord Hutton into the circumstances surrounding Kelly's death. The Hutton Report, published at the start of 2004, controversially exculpated the government from responsibility for Kelly's suicide and instead directed its fire at the BBC.[36] With regard to the issue of the preparation of the September dossier, Hutton exonerated Campbell from the 'sexing up' charge. With regard to the conduct of the BBC, Hutton was damning. Gilligan's allegations on the *Today* programme were deemed to be 'unfounded'; the BBC's editorial system was 'defective'; BBC management was at fault 'in failing to investigate properly the Government's complaints' regarding the Gilligan broadcast; and the governors were criticised 'for themselves failing to make more detailed investigations into whether this allegation reported by Mr Gilligan was properly supported by his notes and for failing to give proper and adequate consideration to whether the BBC should publicly acknowledge that this very grave allegation should not have been broadcast'.[37] The publication of the Hutton Report was swiftly followed by the resignation of the chairman of the BBC Board of Governors, Gavyn Davies, the Director-General,

---

[36] Lord Hutton, *Report of the Inquiry into the Circumstances Surrounding the Death of Dr David Kelly C.M.G. by Lord Hutton*, HC 247 (London: TSO, 2004) and www.the-hutton-inquiry.org.uk/content/report/index.htm.   [37] *Ibid.*, pp. 212–14.

Greg Dyke, and Gilligan himself. The Hutton Report, however, was widely reported as a whitewash, especially in the quality press, and despite its official verdict it singularly failed to clear the air on the issue of whether the government had played fair with the media and the public in making the case for war.

The discrediting of the 'spin' culture

During Blair's second term one incident in particular appeared to many to exemplify the unacceptable face of the New Labour government's approach to news management: the Jo Moore affair. The exploitation of the events of 9/11 as a 'very good day to get out anything we want to bury' seemed to exemplify a cynical downside to the concern with favourable media coverage.[38] For some critics Moore personified everything that was wrong with New Labour's approach to public communication: too much emphasis on presentation and spin; the short-circuiting of official channels of communication by non-accountable special advisers, always seeking to secure maximum partisan advantage from every ministerial announcement; and the amorality of the belief that all is fair in news management, with the only criterion of success being the quality of the subsequent media coverage.

The Jo Moore affair acted as a catalyst for a structural overhaul of the government's approach to media relations. In early 2004 the report of a review group chaired by Bob Phillis, chief executive of Guardian Media, argued that there had been a three-way breakdown in trust between government and politicians, the media and the general public, which had led to popular disillusionment and voter disengagement from the democratic process. In particular, the aggressive approach of Labour and 'their increased use of selective briefing of media outlets, in which government information was seen to be being used to political advantage, led to a reaction from the media that has produced a far more adversarial relationship with government'.[39] On the particular issue of the use of special advisers by New Labour, the report commented that many of them 'concentrate their limited time on the political reporters in the "lobby" and on a handful of specialists . . . this has created an "inner circle" of reporters who have good access, but a disenfranchised majority who do not'.[40]

---

[38] Raymond Kuhn, 'Media Management', in A. Seldon and D. Kavanagh (eds.), *The Blair Effect 2001–5* (Cambridge: Cambridge University Press, 2005), pp. 94–111.

[39] Bob Phillis, *An Independent Review of Government Communications* (London: TSO, 2004), p. 7, and www.gcreview.gov.uk.   [40] *Ibid.*, p. 10.

Among the twelve specific recommendations of the Phillis report was one for a stronger communications structure at the centre, headed by a new permanent secretary, and a clearer definition of the roles of the Prime Minister's official spokesperson – a Civil Service appointment – and that of his politically appointed Communication Director. Phillis thus supported two separate but complementary communications teams at the centre of government: one a strong civil service-led communications unit, based in the Cabinet Office, and the second a well-resourced communications team supporting the Prime Minister, based at No. 10 and including both civil servants and political appointees. Phillis also recommended that the Prime Minister's Director of Communication should not have Order in Council powers that enable special advisers to manage civil servants.

With regard to the system of lobby briefings, Phillis argued that the system was no longer working for either the government or the media, with ministers and officials complaining about media distortion and deliberate misrepresentation, while journalists complained about information 'being used as the currency in a system of favouritism, selective release and partisan spinning'.[41] Phillis recommended that the lobby briefings should be televised, with full transcripts made available promptly online and with proceedings webcast. The review also recommended that government ministers should play a bigger part in the daily briefings rather than official spokespersons, thus bringing the daily meetings closer to the model of the Prime Minister's monthly press briefings.

Blair had already accepted the break-up of Campbell's role into its constituent parts when Phillis had published its interim report in September 2003, just a few weeks after Campbell's resignation. Because of the special nature of the relationship Campbell had enjoyed with Blair, nobody could in any case have convincingly stepped into the former's shoes once he had left. In that sense the style of New Labour media management after Campbell was always going to be different. In addition, however, the circumstances surrounding Campbell's departure and the widespread feeling that he had become too public and controversial a figure meant that the debate about his succession was not just confined to a question of individuals but also covered appropriate structures, norms and procedures. Campbell's replacement in the new slimmed-down post of Director of Communication at No. 10 was David Hill, who had previously been head of communications at Labour Party headquarters. Hill

[41] *Ibid.*, p. 25.

was regarded as a dedicated and intelligent professional, trusted by journalists, and a less keen advocate of pre-emptive 'spin' than his predecessor. However, he was also seen as not nearly so close to Blair.

The bigger question was whether the structural changes proposed by Phillis would work. While the recommendations in reaction to the perceived excesses of the Campbell era were understandable, some argued that the distinction between partisan and non-partisan information is fundamentally flawed. Sir Bernard Ingham, for example, contends that it is possible to have only one spokesperson at No. 10, either a civil servant or a party political appointee. Gaber not only agrees with this criticism, but also argues that the Phillis recommendations simply strengthen the communication power of Downing Street: 'Phillis has based many of its recommendations on the unsustainable assumption that this Government's communication effort is weak and uncoordinated and that the remedy lies in the path of greater centralisation.'[42]

Conclusion

Blair's legacy in the field of media management is a mixed one. With regard to his leadership role, he certainly recognised the significance of the media in an age in which public performance, presentational skills and 'looking the part' are aspects of politics no longer simply confined to the few weeks of official election campaigns. During his short period as Leader of the Opposition and then the first couple of years of his premiership Blair came across particularly well on television as the embodiment of a new type of political leader: a young, family man, at ease with the cameras, unbridled by the old politics of left–right ideological conflict, firm in his values and pragmatic in policy choices. In this context it is hardly surprising that some see in David Cameron a Conservative version of the mediatised style of Blair's early years of leadership.

Blair was also successful in winning the support of key media owners and newspaper editors for New Labour. While the support of a newspaper's editorial column may not shift many readers' votes during the short period of an election campaign, the steady drip effect of negative headlines and critical commentary has over time an undoubted

---

[42] Ivor Gaber, 'Going from Bad to Worse: Why Phillis (and the Government) Have Got it Wrong', paper presented at the conference 'Can't Vote, Won't Vote: Are the Media to Blame for Political Disengagement?', Goldsmiths College London, 6 November 2003.

impact on voter perception of governmental competence and on the morale of party supporters. Benefiting from a relationship with the press based on accommodation and exchange, Blair rarely if ever had to deal with the concentrated, negative attack journalism which was so much a feature of Kinnock's period as leader of the Labour Party between 1983 and 1992.

In contrast, the critical focus on media management in the political reporting of the press and broadcasting brought the Blair premiership into disrepute. Moreover, this critique was by no means just confined to the published output of political commentators[43] or former media advisers[44] from the 'Westminster village'. More worryingly for Blair, fictionalised accounts of New Labour's obsession with 'spin' and 'control freakery' became part of popular culture through television comedy programmes and Rory Bremner's satirical impersonations. In addition, the media management activities of Blair's New Labour contributed to a sense of public unease and even cynicism about the political process in contemporary Britain. While the media themselves are sometimes held responsible for this sense of voter mistrust in politics,[45] a healthy public sphere cannot be delivered by the news media acting alone. Blair and Campbell must assume some of the responsibility for the critical state of public communication in Britain, particularly evident during Blair's second term in office.

The departure of Campbell and the much less high-profile role adopted by Hill took some of the heat out of the government's relations with the media, especially after the 2005 election. Policy successes such as the conclusion of the Northern Ireland peace agreement in 2007 even allowed the Prime Minister moments of favourable media coverage in his abbreviated third term. Yet while Blair's relations with the media after New Labour's third successive election victory were never as acrimonious as they had been during his second term, this was in part because much of the media had already consigned him to the history books. The dominant media story on Blair after the 2005 election focused on speculation about the precise date of his departure from office. Ironically for a politician so concerned with media management, Blair totally mishandled the mediatisation of his exit from No. 10 by giving journalists premature notice of his decision to quit. As a result, Blair's final months in office were marked

---

[43] Nicholas Jones, *The Control Freaks* (London: Politico's, 2001).

[44] Lance Price, *The Spin Doctor's Diary* (London: Hodder and Stoughton, 2005).

[45] John Lloyd, *What the Media Are Doing to our Politics* (London: Constable, 2004).

by considerable media sniping regarding his obsession with his legacy, as well as by speculation about the nature of a future Brown premiership. In the fast-moving world of contemporary journalism, the concern to cover the next breaking story meant that in media terms the Blair era was effectively over well before he vacated No. 10.

8

Tony Blair as Labour Party Leader

RICHARD HEFFERNAN

Tony Blair's leadership style was early on encapsulated by his boast, when leader of the opposition, that he 'led' his party while John Major 'followed' his. That observation, intended as an attack on Major's premiership, was a clear portent of the way Blair would operate, within the party and in government. Labour backbenchers cheered Blair's attack to the echo, but many came later to rue his leading Labour from the front, centring the party on his personal appeal and challenging its traditions whenever he considered it necessary to do so. This approach, for good or ill, has become the template for the modern and successful party leader. If Blair modelled himself on the popular perception of Margaret Thatcher, then David Cameron, Conservative leader since 2005, has clearly modelled his leadership style on Tony Blair. Cameron has endlessly emphasised his tough, uncompromising leadership, criticising Conservatism for being out of touch ('old' Conservatism) and his claim, 'I lead. I don't follow my party; I lead them',[1] was taken straight from the Blair playbook.

A 2007 report by the Labour Commission, an unofficial group of 'broadly representative' party members, criticised Labour for being a 'command party' where 'the leadership appoints ministers, controls parliament, manages the party and consults members'.[2] New Labour, largely the creation of Blair and likeminded colleagues, foremost among them Gordon Brown, Peter Mandelson and Alastair Campbell, sought always to keep the Labour Party on a tight rein. Being 'tiny in number . . . more a junta who had executed a coup',[3] the Blairites (and their Brownite allies)

---

[1] BBC News, 'Cameron Steps Up Grammar's Attack', 22 May 2007, http://news.bbc.co.uk/2/hi/uk_news/politics/6679005.stm.

[2] LabOUR, 'Renewal: A Two Way Process for the Twenty First Century', http://savethelabourparty.org/07_Interim_Report.pdf.

[3] Andrew Rawnsley, *Servants of the People: The Inside Story of New Labour* (London: Penguin, 2000), p. xiv.

ran the party after 1994, in the words of Blair's strategist, Philip Gould, by replacing 'competing existing structures with a single chain of command leading directly to the leader of the party . . . [and by having] one ultimate source of campaigning authority . . . the leader'.[4] Blair built on Neil Kinnock's reforms to further reinvent Labour's programmatic appeal. He did so in acknowledgement of the far-reaching changes brought about by the Thatcher and Major governments. Blair thus obliged a chastened, weakened party to recognise that winning was the only objective, and that electoral salvation lay in Labour moderating its appeal and embracing neo-liberal economics. Labour's 1997 and 2005 parliamentary majorities, the largest won by any party since 1935, owed much to Blair's ability to modernise his party and fashion a broad coalition attracting support well beyond Labour's core vote.

Blair, at his peak, was both a dominant party leader and a predominant Prime Minister. While lacking, say, the wider political impact of a Margaret Thatcher, he enormously impacted the electoral standing, programmatic objectives and, most significantly, the political direction of the Labour Party. He also changed many of the ways in which government is conducted, not least how the modern prime minister operates within Whitehall, Westminster and the wider political world. Excepting Margaret Thatcher, Blair was the longest consecutively serving prime minister since Lord Liverpool and the longest-serving Labour prime minister. Harold Wilson might also have led Labour to four election victories, but he won three only narrowly and lost another he was widely expected to win. Before Blair's 1997 and 2001 landslides Labour had only ever won two sizeable parliamentary majorities, in 1945 and 1966. Under Blair, Labour, in peril of becoming defunct in 1983, and thought by some to have become a permanent second party in 1992, was transformed from a four-times loser into a three-times winner. Facing five Conservative leaders – John Major, William Hague, Iain Duncan Smith, Michael Howard and David Cameron – Blair easily electorally outpaced the first four. Thanks in large part to him, three leaders – Hague, Duncan-Smith and Howard – became the first Conservative leaders since Austin Chamberlain never to reach Downing Street. Labour's electoral success, whatever the party's future electoral standing, is the greatest contribution Blair made to his party as its leader.

---

[4] Philip Gould, *The Unfinished Revolution: How the Modernisers Saved the Labour Party* (London: Little, Brown, 1998), pp. 240–1.

Blair-led Labour and the party system

The 1945–70 Westminster party system, the era of two-party majoritarianism when Labour and the Conservatives won some 90% of the vote between them, is long dead. The post-1974 period saw the emergence of a 'two-party-plus others' system, as other parties emerged (and re-emerged), most obviously the Liberal Democrats (and their predecessor parties, the Liberals and the SDP). This system fragmented further after 1992. Different distinct party systems emerged in Scotland and Wales through elections to the Scottish Parliament and the Welsh Assembly conducted under the Additional Member System (AMS). Labour, in addition to AMS in Scotland and Wales, introduced party list PR in elections to the European Parliament and the supplementary vote in the London Assembly (while Labour in Scotland introduced the single transferable vote in Scottish local elections), but Tony Blair's brief flirtation with electoral reform for the House of Commons ended in 1998–9, when the findings of the Jenkins Commission were kicked into touch. Electors might cast their votes more widely than Labour, the Conservatives and the Liberal Democrats in second-order elections to the Scottish Parliament, Welsh Assembly and European Parliament, but at Westminster it is still Labour or the Conservatives under single-member plurality who remain more likely to form a single-party government. This may in time be reformed by a future hung parliament and a coalition government in which the Liberal Democrats are able to leverage electoral reform from either Labour or the Conservatives.

Blair – largely the agent of Labour's electoral good fortune in 1997, 2001 and, less so, 2005 – has been a spectator of electoral (as opposed to political) realignments as much as he has participated in them. The scale of Labour's victory in 1997 put paid to any intention he might have had to form a coalition government with the Ashdown-led Liberal Democrats, something reinforced by the Liberal Democrats' subsequent drift leftwards under Ashdown's successor, Charles Kennedy. After 1997 Labour's post-socialist and pro-market policy record reflected the fact that ideological differences between the parties have narrowed significantly. Amid Labour's rise and the Conservatives' collapse, the Liberal Democrats consolidated their position as the third party in the House of Commons. After 1994, as it colonised the centre, Labour was flanked by the Conservatives (and the BNP) to its right, but found the Liberal Democrats, the SNP and Plaid Cymru on its programmatic left, together with the much less numerous Greens and, eventually, the minuscule far-left grouping, Respect. Of course, with the reviving Cameron-led Conservatives now heading leftwards (and elements in post-Blair Labour likely to urge Gordon Brown to tilt left too), it remains to be seen if these party positions persist. Blair-led Labour, by moving to the political right, undoubtedly helped further reform the British party system. It has provided the circumstances in which, in Westminster terms, the system may subsequently change further. Such change may well be likely, particularly when the 'coexistence of plurality rule and PR elections is progressively accentuating and accelerating the transformation of both voters' alignments and parties' strategies'.[5] It is, however, presently too strong a claim to suggest, as Patrick Dunleavy does, that voters for the House of Commons 'support a multiplicity of parties' for governmental office even if they may be 'disillusioned with the grip of an artificially maintained "two-party" politics'.[6]

Blair's premiership witnessed a precipitous decline in British electoral turnout, which, against a post-war average of 75%, dropped to 59% in 2001 and 61% in 2005. Electors who continue to vote are more conditional in their support for political parties than previously. Such conditionality explains (and is explained by) ongoing falls in levels of partisan identification. It reflects (and further encourages) the contemporary electoral challenges that parties face. As a result, British political parties find themselves adrift from previously established electoral moorings. As ties of attachment binding electors to parties become looser, electoral behaviour becomes more volatile and parties scramble for votes in new and innovate ways. Tony Blair's leadership style and his programmatic appeal owed much to his perception of the electoral phenomena that followed from this: first, changes in established electorates of belonging from which parties draw support; and second, the rise of judgemental voting which obliges parties to pay ever closer attention to leaders, images and issues. Blair grasped that parties now have to compete with one another by convincing an ever more sceptical electorate that they have a more attractive set of leading politicians and policies than their opponents. Blair and his boosters therefore offered the Blair leadership as the solution, given a free hand, to Labour's interrelated electoral and political crises.

---

[5] Patrick Dunleavy, 'Facing up to Multi-party Politics', *Parliamentary Affairs*, 58, 2005: 503–32, at p. 502.   [6] *Ibid.*, p. 503.

The Blair style of party leadership

Party leaders, especially when in government, have never been beholden to their extra-parliamentary party. As McKenzie long ago asserted, decision-making authority resides 'with the leadership groups thrown up by the parliamentary parties (of whom much the most important individual is the party leader), and they will exercise this authority so long as they retain the confidence of their parliamentary parties'.[7] Labour's extra-parliamentary party has only occasionally been able to tip the balance of power in its favour. This was, as in 1951–5, 1970–4 and 1979–82, usually when the party found itself in opposition following a period of government, the leadership was damaged by electoral failure, and when a critical mass of party dissidents damned the party for failing to seek policies in line with Labour's doctrine and ethos. On such occasions, however, a parliamentary leadership was able to reassert its control.

Parties, only nominally internally democratic, have always been run by their parliamentary elite. Today, however, thanks largely to changes instigated by both Blair and Neil Kinnock, Labour is more than ever run by a parliamentary leader (and his allies) nominated from among the parliamentary party and first elected by an electoral college comprising MPs, party members and members of affiliated organisations. Blair was a powerful leader because the direction of the major political parties is decided more and more by the parliamentary leadership, and less and less influenced by the wider membership.[8] Party leaders have to take note of party opinion, but are not bound by it; Blair, the beneficiary of this phenomenon, has further advanced it. Party officials now work with and to the parliamentary party leadership. Again, this is not down to Blair alone, but an ongoing trend has been exacerbated by Blair's (and Gordon Brown's) centralised control. This has established a leadership template that others, not least David Cameron, now eagerly follow.

The concept of the presidentialisation of party leaders, while it ultimately misleads,[9] owes much to the far-reaching changes enacted in the form of British political leadership. There are three interrelated features of

---

[7] Robert McKenzie, *British Political Parties* (London: Heinemann, 1964), p. 635.

[8] *Ibid.*; Richard Katz and Peter Mair, 'The Ascendancy of the Party in Public Office: Party Organisational Change in Twentieth Century Democracies', in Richard Gunther, José Ramón Montero and Juan Linz (eds.), *Political Parties: Old Concepts and New Challenges* (Oxford: Oxford University Press, 2002).

[9] Richard Heffernan, 'Why the Prime Minister Cannot Be a President: Comparing Institutional Imperatives in Britain and America', *Parliamentary Affairs*, 58, 2005: 53–70.

contemporary politics which, in Michael Foley's useful concept, help to 'stretch' the Prime Minister away from both party and government.[10] First, the personal leadership style of Blair – and of Margaret Thatcher – further centred Blair at the heart of government. Second, the media-led phenomenon of political personalisation increasingly spotlighted Blair while 'marginalizing other political actors to the periphery of public attention',[11] with the exception of Gordon Brown. Third, the 'hollowing out' of political parties, their declining membership, the professionalisation and centralisation of their mode of campaigning, granted Blair and other party leaders a firmer grip over Labour's policy agenda and political direction. Parties, Blair insisted, have now to be led by their leaders because leadership is now considered the key 'medium of political discourse and information'.[12] Labour, being so 'permanently enthralled with the projected utility and leverage of [its] actual or potential leaders',[13] invested Tony Blair with considerable authority, something which extended the autonomy of the party leader, particularly the party leader as prime minister. It may be, as Anthony King suggests, that 'the personalities of leaders and candidates matter a lot less, and a lot less often, in elections than is usually supposed',[14] but parties believe electors place a great emphasis on party leaders and this is why they place a considerable emphasis on having a dynamic leadership. As Blair himself said on more than one occasion, 'there's only one thing the public dislike more than a leader in control of his party and that is a leader not in control of his party'.[15]

Blair benefited from (but he helped further advance) the transformation of British political parties, in common with European counterparts, from mass-membership, bureaucratic parties into their present-day electoral professional 'catch-all' form. An electoral professional party, as defined by Panebianco, has the following characteristics: a central role of professionals with expertise in electoral mobilisation; weak vertical ties to social groups and broader appeals to the 'opinion electorate'; the pre-eminence of public representatives and personalised leadership; financing through interest groups and public funds; and an emphasis on issues and leadership.[16] Electoral professionalism reflects the fact that parties,

[10] Michael Foley, *The British Presidency* (Manchester: Manchester University Press, 2000).
[11] *Ibid.*, p. 293.   [12] *Ibid.*, p. 230.   [13] *Ibid.*, p. 356.
[14] Anthony King, 'Conclusions and Implications', in Anthony King (ed.), *Leaders' Personalities and the Outcomes of Democratic Elections* (Oxford: Oxford University Press), p. 220.   [15] Rawnsley, *Servants of the People*, p. 363.
[16] Angelo Panebianco, *Political Parties: Organisation and Power* (Cambridge: Cambridge University Press, 1988), p. 264.

having transformed themselves into less ideologically pure organisations, see competence and image, not ideology or policy, as the key to electoral success. They increasingly prize office-seeking over policy-seeking, particularly if they have recently been repeatedly electorally unsuccessful. Again, as a result, the party leadership, the party in 'public office', will be considered the party's principal electoral asset. In turn, leaders, none more so than Blair, assert their prerogatives and limit the institutional ties preventing them from leading the party in the way they wish. Obviously such reality is not simply the product of Tony Blair's leadership. Blair, like Margaret Thatcher before him, has been the beneficiary of an ongoing, developmental process of party transformation. More importantly, however, Blair's leadership style both reinforced and reflected these existing trends. His domination of the Labour Party, in both opposition and government, helped root further the leader-centric imperative found in British political life.

Blair's political centrality owed something to his style and electoral popularity, but owed much to what is described as the personalisation of politics. An age-old phenomenon, personalisation has reached unimagined heights in recent years, as parties are built around the party leader as prime minister or prime minister designate. The leader's centrality is clearly reinforced (but is sometimes undermined) by the impacts of modern political communications, not least by the propensity of the news media to over-report him or her. Obviously, media coverage spotlights the party leader, but need not necessarily showcase him or her. Tony Blair and David Cameron may at times have enjoyed favourable, supportive coverage when Leader of the Opposition, but William Hague or Iain Duncan-Smith did not. News media coverage reflects a reality at the same time as it amplifies that reality. Blair was empowered by being reported as a successful and a popular party leader, an asset to the Labour Party and the government. He was disempowered once the news media began to report him as unpopular and failing. In response, both as party leader and Prime Minister, Blair used the news media to advantage Labour, but he also used it to advantage himself, to set the policy agenda within the government, to demonstrate his utility to the party and/or government, and to gather troops within the party and among the public at large. Of course, in doing this, aided and abetted by Alistair Campbell and Peter Mandelson, Blair laid himself open to claims that he was a 'control freak', ensuring that 'spin' would become for Labour what 'sleaze' had been for the Major-led Conservatives.

Labour's parliamentary party as Blair's prime-ministerial base

British political parties, long subdivided into leaders, sub-leaders and non-leaders, the parliamentary and the extra-parliamentary party, are now also distinguished by distinctions within the parliamentary party, most notably between the front bench and the back bench, parliamentary leaders and followers. The 'party in public office', the party leadership, not the parliamentary party as a whole, runs the show. As Prime Minister, Blair enjoyed the institutional powers conferred by that office, but he had additional power conferred by being leader of his party. Being a strong party leader between 1997 and 2005 helped make Blair a strong Prime Minister; being a strong Prime Minister strengthened him as party leader. The two roles were inextricably linked. British parties, influenced by the majoritarian and unitary traditions of the British political tradition, are increasingly and fiercely hierarchical in form. It is the party leader – the prime minister or the prime-ministerial 'candidate' and their staffs – who, in consultation with other key party figures, draws up the manifesto presented to the electorate. Labour candidates have no positive say in policy deliberation, although those MPs who come to occupy the front bench have some say in policy implementation. At British general elections electors largely vote for a party candidate in support of the party's national political image and programmatic stance. Increasingly, some say, they do so in support of the party's candidate for prime minister. Throughout his leadership Blair used this to his advantage. As leader, Blair (and those trusted to act on his behalf) largely controlled access to the front bench, although this control was fettered by a number of factors, not least his need to appease Gordon Brown, reward friends, advantage talent and, less so than previously, balance mainstream party factions. Of course, he did not have the ability to choose his chancellor, or his deputy leader and he had, unusually, to ensure a gender and geographical balance among his ministers.

Nevertheless, Blair was advantaged, in common with all prime ministers, by the fact that his parliamentary party preferred to supply and support the government of the day rather than effectively check or balance it. While having to negotiate the various obstacles thrown up in his path by the news media, the opposition, electoral opinion and the pressure of events, Blair had carefully to manage Labour MPs, particularly his most senior parliamentary colleagues. Obviously, Blair's leadership, never subject to a formal or informal inner-party challenge, was enhanced in the eyes of MPs by being thrice endorsed by the electorate (and by the anticipation that such endorsement was forthcoming). He had to deal with the would-be challenge to his leadership from the long-standing pretender to his crown, Gordon Brown,[17] but, in spite of the growing fractiousness of the parliamentary Labour Party, something born of an ever increasing unease over government policy and evidenced in strong, significant parliamentary revolts,[18] the parliamentary party remained the mainstay of the Blair government. For the most part, the majority of backbench MPs, as likely to be spectators of Blair's government as to participate in it, toed the party line for a number of reasons, usually partisan disposition and/or policy agreement, but also careerist self-interest.

No claim can be made, however, that Tony Blair always and everywhere got his own way. He was stymied in his efforts to prevent Ken Livingstone from ultimately becoming Labour's London Mayor or Rhodri Morgan from becoming Welsh First Minister. Blair may have been able to face down his party, not least in regard to economic policy, Iraq, Afghanistan and the war on terror, labour laws, criminal justice policy, education and university funding, but limits to his authority were imposed by elements within his party. He might not, in his own words, have had a 'reverse gear', but Labour sometimes imposed speed restrictions on him. Occasionally, as in the case of British entry to the euro, ministers could route him in a different direction. All political leaders have their freedom of manoeuvre restricted by what their party and the public permit and what events allow. Blair eagerly kicked against such constraints and was remarkably successful in governing against the ingrained instincts of the Labour Party, but he still had to work with and through party colleagues who could assert their preferences and sometimes protect their interests. Of course, as Blair recognised, Labour's DNA meant that the party still drew electoral strength from leftist, progressive voters supportive of the party's perceived opposition to the Conservative Party. MPs and members instinctively sought to push Labour leftwards not rightwards. As a result, while freer than ever to direct the party in his chosen direction, Blair had still to manage his party, pay heed to its established shibboleths, and manage his base of support among the electorate at large. Clearly, parliamentary rebellions – or the threat of rebellion – limited Blair's freedom of manoeuvre. He had to

---

[17] Anthony Seldon, *Blair* (London: The Free Press, 2004); Robert Peston, *Brown's Britain* (London: Short Books, 2005).   [18] Philip Cowley, *The Rebels* (London: Politico's, 2005).

keep a substantial majority of his MPs sweet. Usually, enough of them were publicly sweet even when they were privately unhappy. Blair, despite rebellions by a minority of his MPs, often obliged loyalists to back measures they would probably have preferred not to support. This cannot, however, always be assumed. All leaders know that even the most abject worm may one day turn.

As leader Blair also benefited from the unintended consequences of the extension of the franchise to elect the Labour leader beyond the parliamentary party. This reform, while instigated by the Labour left to make it easier for the leader to be fired, strengthened, not weakened, the party leader. Formal Labour leadership challenges are extremely rare, with only three since 1945, and only one challenge, the doomed effort of Tony Benn to unseat Neil Kinnock in 1988, since the extension of the franchise. This wider franchise made it impossible for a formal vote of no-confidence in Tony Blair to have been organised, had the parliamentary party been so minded to hold one, which it was not. It makes elections time-consuming and expensive, imposes high nomination barriers and eviction costs which deter would-be challengers, and so make leaders considerably more secure in office.[19] This meant Gordon Brown, long the leader-in-waiting, would have had to mount a direct frontal assault on Blair, something that would have necessitated his resignation from the government. It would also have increased the likelihood of failure, when it was already said 'whoever wields the dagger never wears the crown'.

Blair stayed in office until 2007 relatively comfortably, the would-be 'coup' of September 2006 notwithstanding. It is not that hard to remove a failing party leader. Iain Duncan Smith was unseated by a formal vote of no-confidence by MPs in November 2003 and a decision by twenty-odd Liberal Democrat frontbench spokespersons to no longer serve under him obliged Charles Kennedy to stand down in January 2006. Of course, both Duncan Smith and Kennedy were widely seen by their MPs to have become electoral liabilities; Blair was never seen as such, not even at the very end. Short of death, scandal, demonstrable electoral fallibility or dramatic political failure, it is virtually impossible to unseat a popular and successful party leader who has no wish to go. The best that can be hoped is that the underperforming leader, long in office, can be indirectly persuaded to do so.

[19] Thomas Quinn, 'Electing the Leader: The British Labour Party's Electoral College', *British Journal of Politics and International Relations*, 6, 2005: 333–52.

Labour's changing party structures

Tony Blair radically reordered Labour policy, but did less to remake Labour's organisation. In government after 1997, other than speak at it, use it to run campaigns and occasionally seek support from it, he often ignored it. Blair made few attempts to advance the careers of his supporters and made no effort to develop an extra-parliamentary cohort. Many of the changes which empowered Blair predated him as leader. Neil Kinnock had asserted the policy-making prerogatives of the leader and his shadow cabinet, while John Smith had forced Labour to embrace 'one member, one vote' in the selection of parliamentary candidates and the election of the leader and deputy leader. Blair implemented party reforms that were imposed from the top of the party down and, in the case of women's representation and the balance of constituency and trade union voting at conference, promoted from the bottom up.[20] As an example of bottom-up reform, the introduction of quotas which 'transformed women's representation at every level of the party'[21] (not least in the House of Commons), which had been argued for since the 1980s, owed little to Blair. While being personally uneasy about all-women shortlists for parliamentary selections, he might have backed the idea, but the impetus was due to others. Similarly, when Scottish and Welsh devolution placed key policies in these nations beyond the reach of Whitehall, one additional and unintended consequence was to partially re-federalise the Labour Party, bringing new life to the Scottish and Welsh components of the national party.[22]

When changes in a party's organisational form are sponsored by the parliamentary leader they are usually 'motivated by the desire to enhance the policy making autonomy of the leadership'[23] Other than choosing between leadership nominees occasionally presented by the parliamentary party (with only four such contests being held between 1981 and 2006), Labour Party members have fewer, increasingly nominal, consultative rather than decisional rights over policy formation. Labour election campaigns are now expensively fought out at the centre, local

---

[20] Meg Russell, *Building New Labour: The Politics of Party Organization* (London: Palgrave, 2005).   [21] *Ibid.*, p. 237.

[22] Martın Laffan and Eric Shaw, 'British Devolution and the Labour Party: How a National Party Adapts to Devolution', *British Journal of Politics and International Relations*, 9, 2007: 55–72.

[23] Paul Webb, 'Party Responses to the Changing Electoral Market in Britain', in Peter Mair, Wolfgang Müller and Fritz Plasser (eds.), *Political Parties and Electoral Change* (London: Sage, 2004), p. 29.

campaigns tend to be adjuncts of the national campaign, and candidate selection is strongly influenced by the party machine.

Leaders, should they be both electorally popular and politically successful, are strengthened when they control policy, campaign strategy and the management of finance and party administration. Such leadership prerogatives, never under the sole control of the leader, are delegated to a party apparatus which is dominated by (or in synch with) the party leadership. Under Blair, Labour's general secretary essentially worked for him and his circle, not for the wider party. In 1994, having persuaded Larry Whitty to step aside, Blair explicitly told the National Executive Committee (NEC) that the appointment of Tom Sawyer as his replacement was now the responsibility of the leader, not the NEC. Sawyer, Margaret McDonagh, David Treisman and Matt Carter, all selected by Blair and his advisers, worked for Blairite officials, not the NEC. Blair's last general secretary, Peter Watt, worked with and to the Prime Minister's staff even if he had not been Downing Street's preferred candidate for the post. Previous Labour leaders, notably Harold Wilson and Jim Callaghan, had the party general secretary and other senior staff appointed by an NEC over which they sometimes had little influence. Blair's creation of the Labour Party chair in 2001, a cabinet post and a prime-ministerial appointment, angered Labour traditionalists. This attempt to coordinate the government and the party, like most Blairite institutional innovations, did not amount to much. Critics charged Blair, by appointing successive party chairs Charles Clarke, John Reid, Ian McCartney and Hazel Blears, with 'controlling' the party, but in truth the party was already under the thumb of the party headquarters. Blair's appointment of Blairite loyalist Alan Milburn as Labour's election coordinator in 2004 foundered, but only because he was perceived to be an enemy of an empowered Gordon Brown who froze him out of the campaign when the Blair–Brown 'dream ticket' became the face of Labour's election pitch.

Labour Party structures have been significantly altered under successive leaders. Under Blair the NEC, while retaining some agenda-setting functions at the annual conference, no longer has an extensive political role. It does not make policy or scrutinise government decisions and it cannot challenge ministers. It was supposedly tasked with administrating the party, but actual control over party personnel, finance and election strategy was exercised by party officials appointed by Blair or his trusted aides and reporting upwards to the Prime Minister and his staff (and often keeping the Chancellor, Gordon Brown in the decision-making loop).The Labour Party conference, under recent rule changes, can only support or reject policy proposals emerging from the NEC or the National Policy Forum. Such proposals are unamendable and take precedence over other conference decisions. Conference may debate a matter of topical importance, but the right to do so is pre-screened by party officials who successfully pressurised delegates to avoid contentious subjects, particularly Iraq after 2003. Under Blair the conference weighting of votes was reformed in favour of a 50:50 split between constituencies and trade unions, something that marked a considerable shift away from the 90:10 split that previously favoured the trade unions. This made conference more legitimate, but gave constituency delegates 'more power, but over less'.[24] Conference, for so long the party arena where left and right, the parliamentary party, constituency activists and trade union barons fought it out for control of the party, is now, like the Conservative conference, an advisory body, at best a sounding board for the leadership.

Of course, it remains to be seen if such changes persist beyond Blair. However, Labour, whose members 'retain important sanctions, whilst leaders remain in control',[25] now operates an 'individual' not a 'representational' form of inner-party consultative democracy. Organised activists have been supplanted by an atomised membership. Having always lacked the practical power to instruct the parliamentary leadership, conference effectively now lacks the theoretical right to do so, having become a 'main showcase for the Prime Minister, other members of the government and for a review of progress and achievements'.[26] Should, as happened on few occasions, the party conference vote against the leadership (such as when the 2002 party conference called for a review of PFI by 67% to 33%), ministers made it clear they would ignore the vote. Such was Blair's command of the conference – and so reliable was his base of support among a broad swathe of party members – that Robin Cook observed there had been a 'complete inversion of the traditional dynamics of conference votes. Previously the platform relied upon the trade unions to keep some grip on sanity, and to put down the more implausible constituency resolutions. Today, it is the constituency delegates who are the loyalists and who stick by the platform even when the unions are rebelling.'[27] In 2004 rail re-nationalisation was supported by some 99.5% of trade unions, but

---

[24] Russell, *Building New Labour*, p. 210.   [25] *Ibid.*, p. 283.

[26] Labour Party, *Labour into Power: A Framework for Partnership* (London: Labour Party, 1997), p. 13.

[27] Robin Cook, *The Point of Departure: Diaries from the Front Bench* (London: Pocket Books, 2003), p. 222.

only by 28% of constituency delegates. In 2006, conference opposed the government's use of private contractors in the NHS by 63% to 37%, but with constituency delegates supporting the government by 62% to 38% and trade unionists opposing by 87% to 13%. Such party conference voting patterns would have astonished Hugh Gaitskell had they happened when he was Labour leader.

Some Labour Party policy deliberation might have been entrusted to Labour's National Policy Forum, a body representing MPs, ministers, party members and trade unionists, but policy formation remained firmly under the direction of ministers and their staffs. Some suggest that the Policy Forum has 'created new sites of dialogue between leaders and members'[28] but still the leadership has 'the power of the drafter and the agenda setter, it fixes the basic parameters of political acceptability. Wants and demands that are deemed unacceptable will be suppressed or deflected via the numerous gateways operated by official gatekeepers.'[29] Labour's extra-parliamentary party makes little contribution to sifting policy options other than to endorse – and thereby legitimate – the agenda presented to it by the party leadership. Such plebiscitory democracy empowers parliamentary leaders, particularly as older-style forms of party democracy have been downgraded. Obviously, 'the often disorganised and atomised mass membership of the party . . . is likely to prove more deferential to the party leadership and more willing to endorse its proposals. It is in this sense that the empowerment of the party on the ground remains compatible with, and may actually serve as a strategy for, the privileging of the party in public office.'[30]

Party membership

While still instinctively collectivist, well to the left of Tony Blair, [31] few Labour Party members conform to the stereotypical leftist, inner-city, bedsit-dwelling, polytechnic-lecturing Trotskyists of folk memory. Under Blair Labour's membership first rose significantly, but then fell precipitously. From 265,000 in 1994 membership increased to 405,000 in

[28] Russell, *Building New Labour*, p. 7.
[29] Eric Shaw, 'The Control Freaks? New Labour and the Party', in Steve Ludlam and Martin J. Smith (eds.), *Governing as New Labour: Policy and Politics under Blair* (London: Palgrave, 2004), p. 61. See also Eric Shaw, 'New Labour in Britain: New Democratic Centralism?', *West European Politics*, 25, 2002: 147–70.
[30] Katz and Mair, 'The Ascendancy of the Party in Public Office', p. 129 .
[31] See a YouGov poll published by the LabOUR Commission, in LabOUR, 'Renewal'.

1997, but more than halved after 1997. At the end of 2002 Labour claimed a membership of 248,294; in 2003, 214,592; in 2004, 201,374; in 2005, 198,026. According to one MP, Jon Cruddas, should this rate of decline continue, Labour, having lost the equivalent of 27,000 members a year since 2000, will have no members by 2013. Eight out of ten new members apparently leave after a year. It was probably inevitable that those who signed up to Blair-led Labour before 1997 (the majority of them credit-card supporters, not active members) would fall away, but the number of members participating in party processes and events is now woefully low. In 2006 some 178,889 ballot papers were distributed in the postal ballot for the constituency section of Labour's NEC but only 36,316 were returned, a turnout of some 20%. Only 13,850 votes claimed the last available of the six places when the winning candidate won fewer votes than the person who came last in the first such election held in 1998. In 2002 only 12,000 London Labour Party members (a city with an official population of over seven million) cast a vote in the ballot to select Labour's 2004 candidate for Mayor. In two recent all-member ballots to choose the sitting MP to contest a new constituency replacing two safe Labour seats, the successful candidate was selected in Gateshead by 138 votes to 117, and in Salford and Eccles by 133 votes to 118. This second membership ballot, in a constituency which has a nominal Labour majority of 12,000, claimed a 90% turnout. Such levels of participation are the rule, not the exception.

Labour might have formed a Labour Supporters' Network, a list composed of supporters who cannot vote in internal elections or stand as Labour candidates, but a declining membership means a sharp decline in its activist base. This is at its starkest in local government. In 1997 Labour had over 10,000 local councillors, but in 2007 had less than 7,000. This councillor base, the core from which party activists are drawn, has withered as Labour has performed badly at consecutive local elections and is now at a thirty-year low. Of course, party membership across all types of party is everywhere in steep decline. Such decline is considered by many, not least by the Blair leadership, to be an unavoidable feature of modern politics. While Labour's membership decline owes something to disillusionment with Tony Blair, it also owes much to apathy and the transformation of parties into post-mass-membership organisations. There is, however, evidence which

> points to a 'push' of members away from Labour during its decade in government. For some people, their reasons for leaving were political and

directly related to a dislike of specific policy positions decided by government (the most common cited being the war in Iraq). For many others,
there is clear evidence that members felt frozen out of the policy and decision making machinery of the party.[32]

Tellingly Hazel Blears, Blair's loyalist Labour Party chair, admitted that
party members 'feel left out. They don't have a relationship with their
Labour government, other than what they read in newspapers.'[33]

Tony Blair's ideal type of party, probably one financially sustained by
the state, would be backed by supporters, not members, and run by professionals reporting to the party leadership. It would be mobilised at election time and showcase the leadership at other times. Some say that
under Blair Labour, short of state funding, came close to such a model.
Party members are both resources and obstacles for any party leadership:
resources because they provide the personnel from which party elites are
drawn, legitimise the party in the eyes of the public, comprise a campaign
resource and, most importantly, form a necessary source of revenue;
obstacles because they have to be both serviced and managed, tend to the
radical and idealistic, and expect some say in determining the party's
policy position. Blair, in common with all modern party leaders, would
have liked a mass membership and would have benefited from one, but
had no desire to delegate any form of responsibility or power to it.

Party finance

The income profile of all political parties has changed considerably over
the past thirty years. As Labour's membership has halved, its spending has
almost trebled. By 2004 some 8% of Labour's income came from
members' subscriptions and 27% from trade union affiliation fees. In
the 1970s membership subscriptions had accounted for some 49% of
Labour's income and in the 1980s trade unions provided some 75%. To
compensate for falling membership monies, while helping wean Labour
off politically damaging union largesse, Blair-led Labour sought funding
from corporations and wealthy individuals. Indeed, trade union opposition to much of Labour's policy, particularly its commitment to
Thatcherite privatisation and a flexible labour market, meant some
unions reduced the monies they provided. There is perhaps no better
proof of the Blairite transformation of the Labour Party than its reordered
financial base. Almost £66 million was donated to Labour between 2001

[32] *Ibid.*   [33] *The Guardian*, 21 February 2007.

and 2005, 64% of this still from trade unions, but with some 25% being drawn from thirty-seven individuals.[34] Large donations, solicited by Lord Levy, who was Blair's – not Labour's – personal fundraiser, came from Paul Hamlyn, Christopher Ondaatje, Lord Sainsbury (Blair's Science Minister who donated some £16 million between 1995 and 2005[35]), Bernie Ecclestone, Lakshmi Mittal and Richard Desmond, among others.

In 2006 Labour's finances prompted a political crisis with the 'cash-for-peerages' (or loans-for-honours) scandal, when it emerged that nearly £14 million had been secretly loaned by wealthy individuals, most of it funding the £18 million spent on Labour's 2005 general election campaign. Several individuals Blair had nominated for life peerages were among these donors. Tony Blair, Lord Levy and the then party general secretary, Matt Carter, knew of these loans, but Jack Dromey, Labour's elected treasurer, did not. While, under the Political Parties, Elections and Referendums Act (PPERA) passed by Labour in 2000, anyone donating £5,000 or more must be named, loans of any amount made on commercial terms do not have to be declared. Labour had breached the spirit, if not the letter, of its own legislation. It was, however, the fact that there might be some link between making a loan and being given a peerage, which was illegal under the Honours (Prevention of Abuses) Act 1925, that led to a police investigation. Lord Levy and Ruth Turner, Blair's political secretary, were arrested and interviewed under caution. Blair was also thrice interviewed (the first prime minister to be so), but as a witness not as a suspect, and he was not placed under caution. By the summer of 2007, the police had concluded their investigation, interviewing some 136 people, so it remains to be seen if charges will be brought by the CPS.

Thanks largely to PPERA and the fact that the cash-for-peerages furore makes it politically difficult to tap wealthy and corporate supporters, Labour, even under Blair, retained a financial link with the trade unions, even if its political link with the unions was not valued at the highest levels of the party. Labour's finances remain parlous. The party drew an income of £26.9 million in 2003, £29.3 in 2004 and £35.3 in 2005, set against expenditure of £24.3 million in 2003, £32.1 in 2004 and £49.8 in the election year of 2005. Although some 80% of expenditure is spent on day-to-day running costs,[36] elections impose considerable financial pressures. By 2006, following the 2005 election, Labour confirmed it was

---

[34] House of Commons Constitutional Affairs Committee, *Party Funding* (London: TSO, 2006), www.publications.parliament.uk/pa/cm200607/cmselect/cmconst/163/163i.pdf.
[35] *Sunday Times*, 23 January 2005.   [36] *Ibid.*

facing 'acute cash flow problems' with debts of some £23 million. It seems, then, that the present means of funding political parties is in dire need of reform. The inquiry chaired by Hayden Phillips, established by Blair in the wake of the cash-for-peerages affair, will play a key role in future forms of party funding, but the introduction of some form of state funding, paid for by the taxpayer, remains a very real possibility.

Blair's legacy and the limits to his party authority

Denis Healey, still nursing bruises inflicted by party infighting in days gone by, envied Blair and Brown 'their good luck in living in a Britain where the trade unions are not a serious problem and there is no important challenge either in policy or personality from the left wing. There is no Tony Benn or Nye Bevan as we used to have . . . The nearest thing to a left winger these days is Peter Hain.'[37] Blair clearly benefited from the weakness (and, to be frank, irrelevance) of the Labour left. This weakness was best typified by John McDonnell's failure to attract support for his kamikaze tilt at the Labour leadership from other than a handful of unreconstructed left MPs (Gordon Brown was nominated by 313 MPs, McDonnell by only 29). It meant that Labour's culturally relativist, thirdworldist and anti-American hard left, bereft of any economic idea, clinging to the belief in the state as planner and provider, did little but heckle the Blairite steamroller after 1994. Serious misgivings over policy aside, particularly Iraq, Blair retained the support of the Labour mainstream. As Robin Cook observed, he did so largely 'because he has delivered phenomenal popularity for the party'.[38] This did much to compensate for Blair being perceived to be 'for', but not 'of', the Labour Party. His well-crafted speeches at the party conference, a forum in which he had a 'complete mastery',[39] were always warmly and enthusiastically received. By being electorally successful, Blair was a more popular leader among Labour loyalists (less so, obviously, Labour leftists and trade unionists) than he was usually given credit for.

In the end, while Tony Blair has not been a president, he was, unlike most prime ministers, 'term-limited'. Blair's September 2004 declaration that he would seek a third term, but not a fourth was a short-term (and bitterly regretted) measure to unify the party in the run-up to the 2005

---

[37] Denis Healey, 'Why the Treasury is so Difficult', in Howard Davies (ed.), *The Chancellors' Tales: Managing the British Economy* (Cambridge: Polity, 2006), pp. 61–2.
[38] Cook, *Point of Departure*, p.79.   [39] *Ibid.*, p. 222.

election and placate his wannabe successor, the Chancellor Gordon
Brown. Blair's intention to serve out the entirety of the 2005 parliament
was soon thwarted. This owed something to ongoing news media speculation about the Prime Minister's future, but owed more to a large element
of Labour's parliamentary party deciding Blair should leave office
sooner rather than later. Some Labour MPs, leftist critics, disaffected
ex-ministers and never-promoted backbenchers, long-standing critics of
Blair, had long wanted him gone. Others, principally supporters of
Gordon Brown, wanted Blair to go so that Brown could claim his inheritance. Still others, the vast majority of them Labour loyalists, reluctantly
concluded that Blair's successor needed time to prepare for the election to
be held some time before June 2010. These different schools of thought,
all separately agitating for Blair's departure (or for a date to be set when he
would depart), came together in the would-be 'coup' of September 2006.
Then, following the resignation of a junior minister and several ministerial aides, speculation in parliament and the usual news media frenzy, Blair
declared he would leave office 'within the year' and before the 2007
Labour Party conference. Once again, as is always the case in Britain's parliamentary democracy (excluding when electors turf the government out
of office at a general election), the ultimate agents of Blair's undoing were
elements within his parliamentary party. Blair, unlike Thatcher, might
have chosen the moment of his departure, but he went earlier than he
wanted, following the urging of some Labour MPs, and when faced with a
party challenge from a ministerial colleague, Gordon Brown.

The Blair–Brown relationship, the key New Labour fault-line, was both
fractious and fruitful. Political and policy disagreements between the two,
exacerbated by their camp-followers and fuelled by media reportage, at
times disfigured and divided the government. In his having to handle
Gordon Brown we can see that party management, as ever, lay at the heart
of the most significant problem of Blair's leadership. The seeds of discord
between Prime Minister and Chancellor were set in stone from the first.
Blair, rewarding Brown for not running against him in 1994 by the
'Granita pact', granted his Chancellor a prominence which gave him too
great an independence. In hindsight Blair, who would surely have soundly
beaten Brown by a significant margin, should have allowed Brown to run
against him. Then he would not have been beholden to a beaten opponent. In government Blair shrank from clipping Brown's wings, sometimes placating him, but usually preferring to work with him or around
him on domestic policy in which the Treasury could claim an interest. On
foreign policy Blair had a much freer hand. Had, for example, Blair

moved Brown from the Treasury to the Home Office in 2005 (a move, being a would-be prime minister, he could not have refused) then Brown, not Charles Clarke, would most likely have been forced out of the government in the wake of the foreign prisoner release scandal in May 2006. With his rival beyond the race, Blair might well have managed to have stayed in Downing Street for the remainder of Labour's third term.

Of course, having been Blair's heir apparent for thirteen years is testimony to Brown's considerable political weight. Having been in the cabinet or shadow cabinet for twenty years, he led for Labour on economic policy for some fifteen years. It is remarkable that no serious alternative emerged to challenge his longstanding claim to the leadership. More remarkable still is that 313 out of 352 Labour MPs supported (for a variety of reasons, some less honourable than others) his claim to succeed Blair. How strange it should be, however, that someone denied the Labour leadership in 1994 could claim it unopposed in 2007. In contrast to Brown's virtual coronation, three heavyweights had contested the Conservative leadership following Thatcher's fall, six following Wilson's resignation and at least four serious candidates were considered by the 'magic circle' to 'emerge' in succession to Macmillan. Clearly, Blair's ascendancy did little to encourage would-be successors to emerge; it did nothing to limit the established challenge of Brown. Mentioned alternatives, among them David Blunkett, Alan Milburn and John Reid, came and went. Two possibles, Alan Johnson and the inexperienced David Miliband, declined suggestions that they challenge the heir presumptive. Indeed, despite his grasp on his party, Blair strangely seemed often to march alone. He attracted supporters, but did little to advance the careers of loyalist followers, rarely placing favourites in high offices of state – so much so that loyalists like Alan Milburn, Stephen Byers and, most strikingly, even the ultra-loyal and at one time indispensable Peter Mandelson might perhaps look back on the Blair years as a time of missed personal opportunity.

Conclusion

By 2005 Labour's electoral ascendancy, whilst delighting the party, did not instil a sense of triumphalism, nor, beyond the parliamentary party, much of a sense of purpose. Such feelings, perhaps explained by mid-term blues, sometimes seemed to reflect unease, perhaps even disenchantment with the government's record since 1997. It remains to be seen how the concept of New Labour will last beyond Blair. It might be that the phrase is retired, but not the idea it identified. In terms of legacy, Blair will be remembered both for his electoral ascendancy and for his success in modernising the Labour Party. By modernisation Blair made Labour work within the economic policy framework bequeathed by Thatcherism, reconciling antagonistic concepts such as public and private, individualism and collectivism.[40] His insistence that his government promote business and empower and liberalise, not restrict or limit market mechanisms, meant Labour championed capitalism and did not criticise it. It might well be, however, that where the Conservatives re-educated Labour on economic questions (marketisation, the importance of flexible labour markets, and the need to abandon excessive forms of tax-and-spend) before 1997, Blair-led Labour painfully re-educated the Conservative Party on social questions (support for public services, respect for personal identity and preferences, and the need to recognise such a 'thing as society') after 1997.

The greatest historical claim of 'Blairism beyond Blair' might well be Blair's style of bold, authoritative party leadership. He, perhaps more than anyone, popularised the idea that a party has to be dominated by an audacious party leader to be electorally successful. Such a leader, while still paying heed to party traditions, has to prioritise office-seeking over policy-seeking. Blair's management of the Labour Party might not have produced far-reaching formal changes in its structures and procedures, but Blair did much to further encourage the model of vertical communication from leaders to members while discouraging horizontal communication between activists and members. Blair always had three related objectives in his sights: first, to increase his autonomy from both Labour's parliamentary and extra-parliamentary party; second, to programmatically modernise the party in order to prioritise New Labour office-seeking over Old Labour policy-seeking; and, third, to professionalise and personalise Labour's mode of campaigning. The ultimate goal had to be to win elections. This approach was not Blair's invention, but having done much to further root the electoral professional party form in British politics, he dramatically entrenched it. In so doing he not only politically reoriented the Labour Party but he significantly reworked the template of modern political party leadership.

[40] See Sean Driver and Luke Martell, *New Labour* (Cambridge: Polity, 2006); Ludlam and Smith, *Governing as New Labour*; Steven Fielding, *The Labour Party: Continuity and Change in the Making of New Labour* (London: Palgrave, 2002); Richard Heffernan, *New Labour and Thatcherism: Political Change in Britain* (London: Palgrave, 2001); Colin Hay, *The Political Economy of New Labour: Labouring under False Pretences* (Manchester: Manchester University Press, 1999).

9

Social democracy

VERNON BOGDANOR

'Chirac pronounced: "Tony is a modern socialist. That means he is five miles to the right of me" – "And I'm of proud of it", said Tony (10 October 1999)[1]

I

Politicians like to see themselves as shaping the future. Historians sometimes collude with them. Yet, often, the skill of political leaders lies in accommodating themselves to their environment, rather than transforming it. There are, to be sure, occasions on which political leaders wrench history from what seemed to be its preordained course: an obvious example is Churchill in 1940. More often, however, the art of political leadership consists in giving a gloss to the inevitable. That is why biographies of prime ministers so often mislead.

In considering the 'Blair effect' upon social democracy, it is tempting to assume that Tony Blair almost single-handedly transformed the ideology of the Labour Party. Perhaps his art, however, has consisted less in transformation than in adapting Labour to changes that had already occurred in British society and in the global economy. Perhaps his skill lay in enabling Labour to administer a Thatcherite dispensation more efficiently but also more humanely than the Conservatives themselves were able to do; just as Harold Macmillan in the 1950s had been to administer the Attlee dispensation more effectively than the Labour Party. But, while Macmillan had sought to achieve his aims through indirection, Blair had launched a direct assault on Labour's shibboleths, and in particular that part of Clause 4 of the party's constitution, committing it to the nationalisation of the means of production, distribution and exchange, which he succeeded in removing in 1995. Tony Blair's 'Third

---

[1] Alastair Campbell, *The Blair Years: Extracts from the Campbell Diaries* (London: Hutchinson, 2007), p. 250.

Way' was Labour's gloss on the reforms undertaken during the long years of Tory rule under Margaret Thatcher and John Major.

When Blair became Labour leader in 1994, the party was around 20% ahead in the polls. In hindsight, its electoral victory in 1997 might appear inevitable. But, in 1994, Blair dared not take victory for granted. For Labour had held large leads in the opinion polls during the Kinnock years, only to find them dissipated when a general election approached. This was primarily because the public feared a return to the failed policies of the 1970s. Despite the fact that both Neil Kinnock and John Smith had regularly insisted, with varying degrees of plausibility, that Labour had changed, there was, so Blair believed, a residual suspicion amongst voters that the transformation of the party was but skin-deep. A symbolic act was therefore needed to show that Labour had broken with its past. That symbolic act involved the removal of the commitment to nationalisation. By the 1990s, this was little more than a recognition, however belated, of reality – the reality that history was moving in a different direction from that which had been anticipated by social democrats. For social democracy, which for the first half of the post-war period had seemed in tune with the trends of social evolution, now appeared as fustian and old-fashioned, a doctrine whose greatest days lay behind it.

At the beginning of the twentieth century, by contrast, socialism and social democracy had appeared to be the wave of the future. By the end of the century, however, the very term 'socialism' had gone out of fashion; it had been replaced by 'social democracy'. The removal of the commitment to nationalisation could be held to mark explicit recognition, belated no doubt, that Labour had become a social democratic party. But, what did social democracy consist of at the end of the twentieth century – what did it actually mean? Did it mean the same as it had meant to the revisionists of the 1950s, Hugh Gaitskell and Anthony Crosland? Was social democracy equivalent to the 'Third Way' or any of the other slogans used to describe the policies of the Blair government? Or, had the Blair government repudiated, as the former deputy leader of the party Roy Hattersley believed, social democracy as well as socialism?

In his book, *The Future of Socialism*, published in 1956, Anthony Crosland claimed that social democracy was not a fixed doctrine, nor a fixed set of policies, but a set of values, the most important of which was equality. Crosland argued that the left in Britain was congenitally prone to confusing means, such as nationalisation, with ends. Nationalisation might perhaps, so Crosland thought, prove of value in helping to achieve an egalitarian society, but it was not to be regarded as an end in itself. The aim was to achieve not a society based on public ownership but an equal society, and the policies of the Labour Party ought to be evaluated in terms of whether or not they helped to achieve this aim.

Crosland was, however, unclear, and the Labour Party has remained unclear, about what equality meant and what it entailed. It was fairly clear what Crosland did not mean by equality. He certainly did not mean equality of outcomes, for even if this form of equality were achievable, it would probably threaten liberty. Crosland believed, moreover, that inequality of reward was necessary to mobilise talent. Inequalities were a form of economic rent to be paid to people of ability. To seek to do without such a rent of ability would involve direction of labour and that would be unacceptable in a free society. Equality of outcomes, therefore, would be incompatible with the values of pluralism and liberty.

Yet, if equality meant less than equality of outcomes, it meant more than equality of opportunity. For in a society based on equal opportunity the greatest rewards would go to those with the most fortunate genetic endowment and family background. Yet, as Crosland said in *The Future of Socialism*, 'No one deserves either so generous a reward or so severe a penalty for a quality implanted from the outside and for which he can claim only a limited responsibility.'[2] A society based on equal opportunity would be a society in which there was an equal opportunity to become unequal. Moreover, those who ended with the smallest rewards would be unable to console themselves, as they could in a class-divided society, with the reflection that they had been unlucky in their social circumstances; for they would be held to have deserved their fate, a fate chillingly portrayed in Michael Young's satire, *The Rise of the Meritocracy*, published just two years after *The Future of Socialism*.[3]

There is a further objection to the idea of equality of opportunity as a basis for social democracy. For equality of opportunity rewarded only marketable skills. That, however, as Raymond Plant has argued, 'neglected a wide range of other human qualities which were vitally important for sustaining a civilized democratic society'. Social democrats 'need to positively value a wider range of skills and human virtues than those which were realized in the economy and the labour market'.[4] For social democrats, the market was a good servant but a bad master.

[2] C. A. R. Crosland, The Future of Socialism (London: Jonathan Cape, 1956), p. 236.
[3] Michael Young, *The Rise of the Meritocracy, 1870–2023: An Essay in Education and Equality* (London: Thames and Hudson, 1958). In *The Future of Socialism*, Crosland acknowledges a debt to discussions with Michael Young, on p. 235 fn.
[4] Raymond Plant, 'Crosland, Equality and New Labour', in Dick Leonard, *Crosland and New Labour* (Basingstoke: Macmillan, 1999), pp. 25–6. This paragraph is based on Plant's essay.

But if equality meant neither equality of outcome nor equality of opportunity, what did it mean? What form of equality should social democrats aim for? In *The Future of Socialism*, Crosland seemed unsure. His beliefs, it has been said, were rather similar to those of the American philosopher John Rawls, who had put forward the notion of 'democratic equality'.[5] According to this notion, inequalities could be justified only on two conditions. The first was that the positions which attracted high rewards must be genuinely open to all through processes of fair competition. The second was that they should benefit the worst-off in society, improving their position in *relative* as well as *absolute* terms. It was this idea of benefiting the worst-off in relative as well as absolute terms that distinguished the social democrat from the liberal or the conservative. For most politicians, whatever their position on the political spectrum, could agree that one important test of policy should be its effects on the *absolute* standard of living of the poorest. Most governments, whether of the left or the right argue, with more or less conviction, that their policies will help the poor. The test proposed by Crosland was more stringent than that – it was that the poorest must be made *relatively* better off vis-à-vis the rich; and that, Crosland believed, could only be achieved through redistributive taxation.

Democratic equality, then, was the end. Redistributive taxation would be one important means in helping to achieve it. About means, however, Crosland was entirely empirical; for the means towards the end of social democracy would no doubt legitimately vary in different countries and different periods.

Thus, for Crosland, and for social democrats more generally, social democracy was a doctrine subject to permanent revision. Social democratic policies needed to be looked at anew by each generation so that they could be accommodated to changes of circumstance. This was an important development in the thinking of the British left. For, in the past, socialism had seemed a closed doctrine impervious to evidence and overly reliant upon supposed laws of historical development. What these laws were depended, admittedly, upon where one placed oneself on the political spectrum of the left. For Communists, and for a few on Labour's left, the laws of history had been laid down by Karl Marx; for Ramsay MacDonald, they had been laid down in a rather cloudy way by the evolutionists, whose doctrines socialists should seek to apply to society; for Sidney Webb, most of the Fabians, and most of the leaders of Labour's

5 *Ibid.*, p. 28.

heroic age in the 1940s, the laws had been laid down by economists and sociologists who had noticed the inherent tendency of modern societies towards collectivism. It was this conception which, though rarely articulated, subconsciously influenced many social democrats until the end of the twentieth century.

If the trends of history were known, it appeared to follow that the test of a good policy was that it was in accordance with these trends; policies should, as it were, assist the flow of history, rather than seeking to arrest its development. This seemed to obviate the need to work out empirically based policies from a rigorous and realistic interpretation of what was actually happening in society. Popper, however, had taught social democrats that all truths about society were conjectural. Crosland had absorbed this lesson, although many of his colleagues did not. But the conclusion which Crosland drew was that no Labour Party policies should be set in tablets of stone. All were to remain open to questioning, provided only that the central aim of equality was retained. That alone was not open to question – or, rather, anyone who questioned it had ceased to be a social democrat.

II

By 1998, however, when Tony Blair became Labour leader after four successive election defeats, it seemed that Crosland's revisionism itself needed revising. The problem that Blair faced was that, as Eric Hobsbawm had feared when Margaret Thatcher had come to power in 1979, the forward march of Labour seemed to have been halted.[6] For most of the twentieth century, as we have seen, Labour had been sustained by the belief that its advance was in some sense guaranteed by history, by what Sidney Webb had called 'the inevitability of gradualness'. Society, so it was believed, was moving inexorably in a collectivist direction. No doubt Conservative governments would continue to be elected from time to time. Their role, however, would be confined to that of administering a dispensation shaped by Labour. Their role would be that of administering a collectivised state, as the Churchill and Macmillan governments in the 1950s had done. If Conservatives tried to go further, if they tried to roll back the state, to follow the siren calls of neo-liberals such as Hayek, they would be repudiated by the electorate. For the gains

[6] Eric Hobsbawm, in Martin Jacques and Francis Mulhern (eds.), *The Forward March of Labour Halted?* (London: Verso 1981).

secured by the Attlee government could be maintained only through state action, and the voters would surely punish any government that sought to undermine them. It was for this reason that Crosland believed that these gains – full employment, the welfare state, sharply progressive taxation and recognition of the claims of organised labour – were permanent and immune to challenge from the right.

The advent of Margaret Thatcher to power in 1979 had changed all that. For she conceived of her task not merely as one of containing the advances made by Labour, but of reversing them. Dismissed at first by many on the left as an aberration, it soon became apparent that she was engaged in instituting, in the words of John Gray, 'a modernizing project with profound and irreversible consequences for political life in Britain'.[7]

Labour, therefore, was forced to adapt its doctrines to conditions that it had never before envisaged. It now seemed that social democracy, far from being guaranteed by history, was being repudiated by it. The question is whether the Blair project has been a further stage in social democratic revisionism, or whether it has finally jettisoned the social democratic ideal of equality.

The Future of Socialism had been based on a group of interrelated pre-suppositions which had been taken for granted by most of those on the left. The first was that the state could, through intelligent macro-economic policy, secure both full employment and price stability using Keynesian methods. 'Acting mainly through the budget', Crosland had argued, 'although with the aid of other instruments, government can exert any influence it likes on income distribution, and can also determine, within broad limits, the division of total output between consumption, investment, exports and social expenditure.'[8] The state should, in Crosland's view, use its ability to control the economy to redistribute income.

This belief, though taken for granted at the time across much of the political spectrum had, nevertheless, hardly been subject to empirical testing. Indeed, even at the height of the Keynesian era, in 1968, R. C. O. Matthews, Drummond Professor of Political Economy at Oxford, had convincingly argued in an article in the *Economic Journal* that post-war full employment in Britain owed hardly anything to Keynesian techniques of pump-priming.[9] The belief that social democratic aims could be achieved by fiscal means was, therefore, quite untested.

[7] John Gray, *After Social Democracy: Politics, Capitalism and the Common Life* (London: Demos, 1996), p. 10.   [8] Crosland, *The Future of Socialism*, p. 27.
[9] R. C. O. Matthews, 'Why Has Britain Had Full Employment Since the War?', *Economic Journal*, 78, 1968: 556–69.

By the time of the IMF crisis in 1976, Labour's leaders hardly dared test it. They were already convinced that it would not work. At the 1976 Labour Party conference, Prime Minister James Callaghan spoke of:

> The cosy world we were told would go on for ever, where full employment would be guaranteed by a stroke of the Chancellor's pen – We used to think that you could just spend your way out of a recession – I tell you in all candour that that option no longer exists, and that in so far as it ever did exist, it only worked – by injecting a bigger dose of inflation into the economy, followed by a higher level of unemployment – That is the history of the last twenty years.[10]

Thus the first of Crosland's presuppositions – that the economy could be brought under control by the state – had been subverted.

Crosland's second presupposition was that the British state was beneficent, efficient and generally fit for purpose. For the social democratic programme, and in particular the redistribution of income and wealth, could be achieved only by using the state as its instrument. The power of the state would no doubt expand, but this, so Crosland believed, need not cause any worries to believers in a free society. Indeed, the expansion of the state might actually strengthen rather than weaken democracy. For, as Tom Clark has pointed out, 'increasing the share of national income consumed by state services redistributed power. The private sector was controlled through market purchases, where each *pound* had equal weight, leaving influence dependent on spending power. In contrast, the state was theoretically controlled by elections, where each *vote* was equal.'[11] The extension of state power required to secure social democracy would thus not pose a serious threat to liberty; on the contrary, it would help to increase the liberty of those with little market power.

By the 1970s, however, some on the right of the Labour Party were coming to the view that the limits of taxable capacity were being reached and that if public expenditure were to rise further, the values of a pluralist society would come under threat. Moreover, it seemed that some of Labour's supporters – better-off members of the working class, whose votes might be crucial in marginal constituencies – were also coming to be hostile to high taxation, preferring, in place of what Harold Wilson

---

[10] Cited in Kenneth O. Morgan, *Callaghan: A Life* (Oxford: Oxford University Press, 1997), p. 535.

[11] Tom Clark, *The Limits of Social Democracy? Tax and Spend under Labour, 1974–1979*, Working Paper No. 64/01 (London: LSE, Department of Economic History, 2001), p. 2, emphasis in original.

artfully referred to as the 'social wage', to retain more of their real wage in their pockets. At the time of the 1976 IMF crisis, therefore, the argument that the economic crisis should be met by a rise in taxation rather than by cuts in public services was rapidly dismissed by Callaghan and Healey, and pressed, even on the left, in a somewhat lukewarm manner.[12]

The undermining of Crosland's first two presuppositions – that the state could control the economy, and that a beneficent state could be trusted to redistribute income and wealth – meant that during the long period of Conservative rule, from 1979 to 1997, the prospects for social democracy receded into the distance. Many of the things that Crosland insisted could not happen – a return to high unemployment, regressive use of the taxation system, drastic cuts in the public services and the marginalisation of the trade union movement – did in fact happen, and proved no barrier to Conservative electoral success. By the 1990s, if not earlier, it had become clear that social democrats faced a completely changed landscape, one dominated by new techniques of economic management, accompanied by considerable scepticism as to the value of government intervention and even of expenditure on the public services. After its unexpected defeat in the 1992 general election, the Labour Party drew the lesson, whether rightly or wrongly, that electors, whatever they told the opinion pollsters, would not, in the privacy of the voting booth, support a party which proposed higher taxes to finance the public services. Improvements in the public services, therefore, would have to be found in other ways.

But there was a third presupposition that lay at the heart of Crosland's analysis. It was that social democracy could be achieved in one country. There is indeed a paradox at the heart of social democracy. For social democracy, like its ancestor, socialism, is, in essence, an internationalist doctrine. Yet, in practice, the most favourable conditions for social democracy lie in highly cohesive nation-states such as Norway or Sweden. For it depends upon a sense of social solidarity, more likely to be present in small and cohesive nations than in large multicultural societies or in any international community. That is because social democracy requires citizens to feel a sense of social obligation towards their fellows such that they are prepared to pay in taxation to secure benefits for them. The stronger the sense of community, the more likely it is that such a sense of social obligation will be felt.

---

[12] See *ibid.* for a most valuable account of the effects of the 1976 crisis on the ethos of social democracy.

William Beveridge, though far from being a social democrat, had appealed to such sentiments in his famous report of 1942. He had declared that the welfare state would give: 'concrete expression – to the unity and solidarity of the nation which in war have been its bulwark against aggression and in peace will be its guarantees of success in the fight against individual want and mischance'.[13]

Of course, even in a single state, the sense of solidarity is not always easy to achieve, and there are many who feel resentful at contributing in taxation to provide for the welfare of 'spongers'. During the 1920s, Labour MPs told Ramsay MacDonald that their own supporters, men and women in low-paid jobs, were the most stringent in demanding that 'scroungers' be denied benefits.[14] In late 1975, arguing that public expenditure cuts would not necessarily be unpopular, Denis Healey, Labour's Chancellor, told the cabinet, 'At the Labour clubs you'll find there's an awful lot of support for this policy of cutting public expenditure. They will all tell you about Paddy Murphy up the street who's got eighteen children, has not worked for years, lives on unemployment benefit, has a colour television and goes to Majorca for his holidays.'[15] The reference to 'Paddy Murphy' implies, what may well have been true, that for some Labour voters Irish immigrants were not seen as part of the national community. More recently, it has been argued that many voters do not regard non-white immigrants or asylum-seekers as part of that community, and resent being asked to contribute towards their welfare. Social democracy, therefore, would be more difficult to achieve in one country when that country was multicultural than when it was ethnically homogeneous, as seemed to be the case when Crosland wrote *The Future of Socialism*. But it would be even more difficult to achieve at the end of the century, by which time Britain had become subject to forces which lay completely outside the country – the market forces of globalisation and the rules of the European Union.

Crosland had believed that social democrats could pursue policies of their choice largely untrammelled by foreign opinion. In the 1950s, this seemed to make good sense. Britain remained a sheltered economy, protected by tariffs and exchange controls. Admittedly, the Conservatives were gradually liberalising the economy, and in 1958 they made the pound

---

[13] *Social Insurance and Allied Services*, Cmd 6404 (London: HMSO, 1942), para. 8.
[14] See Alan Deacon, *In Search of the Scrounger: The Administration of Unemployment Insurance in Britain, 1920–1931* (London: Bell, 1976).
[15] Tony Benn, *Against the Tide: Diaries 1973–76* (London: Hutchinson, 1989), p. 461, 13 November 1975.

convertible. Labour criticised the Conservatives for liberalising the economy too quickly, for some social democrats looked longingly backwards to the days of the Attlee government when, so it seemed, intelligent use of controls had helped promote economic recovery, and Britain had appeared to be an island beacon of social democratic hope in an otherwise unsympathetic world.

By the 1990s, however, it had become clear that social democracy in one country was no longer a feasible option. François Mitterrand had tried it in France in 1981, seeking to expand the economy without regard for the international markets, but its failure had pushed him back to the policy of the *franc fort* and tighter European integration. Gerhard Schroeder, when he came to power in Germany in 1998, was determined not to make the same mistake, and accepted, rapidly and with some gratitude, the resignation of his neo-Keynesian Finance Minister, Oskar Lafontaine. He too came to see in European integration a substitute for the ideal of social democracy in one country.

The progress of national economies was becoming inextricably bound up with the international economy and the pressures of the global market. Governments could no longer adopt national macro-economic policies aimed at boosting demand, without risking punishment by the markets in the form of higher interest rates and falling currencies. Tony Blair showed that he understood this when, in his Mais lecture in 1995, he said:

> We must recognize that the UK is situated in the middle of a global market for capital a market which is less subject to regulation today than for several decades.
>
>   An expansionary fiscal or monetary policy that is at odds with other economies in Europe will not be sustained for very long. To that extent the room for manoeuvre of any government in Britain is already heavily circumscribed.[16]

In addition to the constraints of the global economy, Britain, as a member of the European Union, was subject to its trading rules and to the provisions of the internal market. The European Economic Community, forerunner of the European Union, had not yet come into existence in 1956 when Crosland wrote *The Future of Socialism*; and Hugh Gaitskell, Labour's then leader, was, together with some of his leading colleagues, such as Douglas Jay and Patrick Gordon Walker, positively hostile to it, partly on the grounds that membership would inhibit the

---

[16] Cited in Edmund Dell, *A Strange Eventful History: Democratic Socialism in Britain* (London: HarperCollins, 2000), p. 568.

policies of economic planning to which a social democratic government ought to be committed. By the time that Tony Blair became Labour leader, however, Labour had become more pro-European than the Conservatives. Indeed, Blair made it clear that he wanted Britain to join the euro, an aim which he failed to achieve. Even outside the euro, however, Britain was becoming subject to rules which would make it more difficult to implement social democrat policies. The Lisbon Strategy, for example, agreed to by the then fifteen member states of the European Union in 2000, sought to achieve greater liberalisation of European economies and a reduction in state regulation. That meant further restrictions on the policy instruments available to a social democratic government. Indeed, it was fear of the extent to which the European Union was adhering to a neo-liberal agenda that persuaded many on the French left to oppose the European constitution and led to its defeat in the 2005 referendum.

These developments made it difficult to see how the social democratic value of equality could possibly be attained. For numerous studies had shown that globalisation had the consequence of increasing inequalities even within a single state, let alone between states. Globalisation allowed a few to acquire massive financial rewards, while making life more difficult for those without marketable skills. Many on the right, indeed, argued that globalisation provided a new rationale for inequality. For if the economy was to be successful, risk-taking and enterprise must be given their just reward. Inequalities, therefore, could now be justified as an inevitable consequence of the rise of global markets, the benefits of which would eventually seep down to the poor. It seemed, therefore, as if the trends of history were leading away from social democracy, not towards it.

Moreover, while globalisation had increased inequality, it had, at the same time, removed from national states those policy instruments which they would need to use to redress those inequalities. These instruments would now be forbidden by the rules of the European Union, the World Trade Organisation or similar international bodies. In *The Future of Socialism*, Crosland had deliberately confined himself to social democracy in a single state, ignoring problems of international trade and finance. That had seemed a perfectly plausible assumption in the 1950s; it had become totally implausible in the very different world of the 1990s.

The dilemma which these changes involve for social democracy have been well summarised by Dominique Strauss-Kahn, a leading figure on the French left, and a former minister in the Mitterrand and Jospin governments. The success of post-war social democracy', Strauss-Kahn has claimed,

> rests on the equilibrium between production and redistribution, regulated by the state. With globalisation, this equilibrium is broken. Capital has become mobile: production has moved beyond national borders, and thus outside the remit of state redistribution – Growth would oppose redistribution; the virtuous circle would become a vicious circle.
>
> The providential state has therefore been shaken. In these conditions, the risk is strong that it will no longer be able to control the growth of inequalities. Even worse, its disengagement at the precise moment when the mutations of capitalism are causing the growth of inequality, could lead the machinery of inequality to spin out of control.

Nevertheless, for Strauss-Kahn, the stance of the left must remain the same. For 'The Left is the agent of the permanent struggle against inequalities. To guarantee a just society, it must renew its ideology and its instruments in order to adapt them to contemporary realities. It must found a modern form of social democracy.'[17] Did Tony Blair succeed in founding this modern form of social democracy?

III

A key social democratic response to the trends of globalisation has been to argue that its central aims can somehow be achieved by a coordinated social democracy operating at the transnational level. In 2001, Tony Blair told the Labour Party conference:

> If we follow the principles that served us so well at home – that power, wealth and opportunity must be in the hands of the many not the few – if we make that our guiding light for the global economy, then it [social democracy] will be a force for good and an international movement we should take pride in leading.

It is becoming natural for social democrats to argue that, although social democracy may not be attainable at national level, it can be achieved at European level through the European Union. The policy instruments which are no longer available for redistribution at national level might become available at European level. The implication clearly is that the European Union could become an embryonic European

---

[17] Dominique Strauss-Kahn: `What is a Just Society? For a Radical Reformism', in *Where Now for European Social Democracy?* (London: Policy Network, 2004), pp. 14, 16.

government, a government which might implement social democratic policies at European level. That might perhaps have been possible in the Europe of the six from 1958 to 1973, a Europe whose governments were mostly Social Democrat or Christian Democrat, with a shared belief in the virtues of state regulation and social welfare. It is, however, utterly implausible in a Europe of twenty-seven member states which are at very different levels of economic development, and contain a wide diversity of ruling parties.

The fundamental problem is that the solidarity which is, as we have seen, a necessary precondition for the success of social democratic policies of welfare and redistribution, is hardly present at European level. Many supporters of European union, including European social democrats, hope that European institutions might create a synergy so as to create a new sense of solidarity and new habits of working together, at European level, so that a European government could somehow replicate the governments of the member states. For that to happen, however, individual states would have to accept that they could be outvoted by other states and have policies imposed upon them which they did not support. The parliamentarians of, say, France, with a government of the right, would have to accept that social democrats were in a majority in the Europe of twenty-seven member states, and could impose social democratic policies upon the French, which their national government and their national voters have rejected. Such a condition only has to be stated for its utopian nature to be recognised. Indeed, even within member states, it is not easy to secure the support of members of subordinate nationalities for policies decided by national parliaments. One important motivation behind Scottish devolution was that the Scots resented being in a permanent minority during the long period of Conservative government at Westminster between 1979 and 1997. The Scots were beginning to see themselves not as a minority in the United Kingdom but as a majority in Scotland. They would perhaps be even more upset were they to be regarded as a permanent minority in Europe. It would, however, be a consequence of social democracy at European level that Britain, like the other member states, could have policies imposed upon her that her government and electors had rejected. Such an outcome is hardly likely to prove acceptable. Social democracy at European level, therefore, is likely to remain a pipe-dream.

If the aims of social democracy have been made vastly more difficult of attainment because of the transfer of power *upwards* from national institutions, these difficulties have been compounded by the transfer of powers *downwards* to devolved bodies by the Blair government. As a result of devolution, the non-English parts of the United Kingdom – Scotland, Wales and Northern Ireland – now enjoy devolved government and a high degree of autonomy in their domestic affairs. Devolution was also offered to the English regions, but rejected by a four-to-one majority in the first region to be offered it, the North-East, thought to be most sympathetic to it, in 2004.

Devolution was a policy which Blair had inherited from John Smith, and there are those who believe that he had little enthusiasm for it. Indeed, he seems to have taken some time to grasp its full implications. In 1999, Blair berated Paddy Ashdown, the Liberal leader, for the policies the Liberal Democrats were pursuing on student support in Scotland, which were contrary to those being pursued by the government at Westminster.

> 'You can't have Scotland doing something different from the rest of the country', Blair complained.
>
> 'Then you shouldn't have given the Scots devolution', Ashdown retorted, 'specifically, the power to be different on this issue. You put yourself in a ridiculous position if, having produced the legislation to give power to the Scottish Parliament, you then say it is a matter of principle they can't use it.'
>
> Tony Blair (laughing): 'Yes, that is a problem. I am beginning to see the defects in all this devolution stuff.'[18]

Yet, if the Scottish Parliament were to follow exactly the same policies as those pursued at Westminster, it might be wondered why it should be set up in the first place.

Social democracy presupposed a strong state and a centralised state. That was why it had been opposed by leading figures on Labour's left, such as Aneurin Bevan, who, when establishing the National Health Service, rigorously set his face against any separate Welsh, Scottish or Northern Irish Health Service. It was to be a *National* Health Service, and its benefits would be provided on the basis of need and not of geography. That was also the reason why devolution had been opposed in the 1970s by Neil Kinnock, who then regarded himself as Bevan's disciple, and declared in 1976 that devolution 'could be an obituary notice for this movement'.[19] 'We shall', Kinnock argued in 1978, 'be introducing into all

---

[18] Paddy Ashdown: *The Ashdown Diaries*, vol. II: *1997–1999* (Harmondsworth: Allen Lane/Penguin, 2001), p. 446, 7 May 1999.

[19] Labour Party Conference, 1976, cited in Miles Taylor, 'Labour and the Constitution', in Duncan Tanner, Pat Thane and Nick Tiratsoo (eds.), *Labour's First Century* (Cambridge: Cambridge University Press, 2000), p. 180.

political considerations an argument that has barely figured at all in British political dialogues and discussions – We have had divisions on a class basis, but not on a geographic or nationalistic basis.'[20]

For social democrats, only a strong centralised state could evaluate the needs of different social groups and ensure that redistribution was effective. But devolution would fragment the power of the centralised state and cut it into pieces. There could not, in the ideology of social democracy, be a separate Scottish or Welsh political will; for the problems of securing equality in Scotland or in Wales were no different in nature from the problems of securing it in England. These problems should be resolved not by establishing toy-town parliaments in Edinburgh and Cardiff, but only by a strong social democratic government at Westminster.

The consequences, less than a decade after the Scottish Parliament and the National Assembly of Wales have been established, would have confirmed Aneurin Bevan's worst fears. In a number of areas of public policy – residential care for the elderly, the cost of prescriptions, student support, city academies, foundation hospitals – the dispensation in Scotland and Wales is quite different from that in England. The Scottish and Welsh devolved bodies have chosen to be more generous than Westminster; they have decided not to adopt city academies, foundation hospitals or top-up fees; they have been, it might be said, Old Labour rather than New Labour.

Yet, far from seeking to counteract these trends, the Blair government, in its final days, sought to emphasise the theme of devolution, arguing that it should now be applied to England, though in a different form from the ill-fated regional assemblies proposed for the North-East in 2004, and rejected in a referendum. The Blair government proposed 'double devolution' in England, devolution not merely to local authorities, but also to local electors who would be encouraged to use new instruments of direct participation in order to overcome what many Blairites saw as a crisis of disengagement in British democracy.[21] Whatever the merits of such a programme, it would be likely, if carried out, to increase geographical inequalities in England, not to mitigate them. It therefore runs counter to social democracy as traditionally understood, and even to the New Liberalism of the early twentieth century, which also sought to equalise welfare opportunities between those living in different parts of the

---

[20] *House of Commons Debates*, 5th series, vol. 941, c. 1540, 10 January 1978.
[21] See Geoff Mulgan and Fran Bury, *Double Devolution: The Renewal of Local Government* (London: Smith Institute, 2006).

country. It has much more in common with the Old Liberalism of
W. E. Gladstone, a devolutionist but a strong opponent of all forms of
social democracy, redistribution and state action in the economy, which
he slightingly termed 'construction', than with contemporary political
doctrines.

In his Fabian pamphlet, *The Third Way*, Tony Blair claimed that the
main aim of social democracy was the promotion of 'social justice with
the state as its main agent'.[22] It is difficult, however, to see how the state
can promote social justice if it has been fragmented and cut into pieces by
devolution.

IV

What, then, remains of social democracy after ten years of Tony Blair?
What has been the Blair effect? What is there that has been 'New' about
New Labour? Tony Blair applied the epithet primarily to Labour's new
approach to reform of the public services. For the party seemed impris-
oned in an old-fashioned mindset according to which the public sector
was inherently good and the private sector inherently bad. New Labour
sought to escape this crude dichotomy. The essence of New Labour was
that public services needed to use the techniques of private business and
the market to increase efficiency. Injections of new money into the public
services, therefore, were to be dependent upon reform. Moreover, the
state should no longer be expected to be the sole provider of public services. Thus, while schooling and treatment under the National Health
Service were to remain free at source, the business sector would be
encouraged to finance new schools – city academies – for the state sector,
particularly in the run-down inner cities; while foundation hospitals
would be allowed, and indeed encouraged, to use contracts with private
bodies to improve their services.

It is, however, somewhat odd to call all this 'new'. It is new only for
those on the left. For the Thatcher and Major governments had already
shown that public services might be best run by a mixture of private and
private money, and that the state should no longer be a monopoly
provider. These doctrines were new, therefore, only for the Labour Party.

There is, however, just one area where Blair can claim to have rejuvenated social democracy. It lies in the massive increase in public expenditure, especially on the NHS, after 2001. This led to the first increase in the

---

[22] Tony Blair, *The Third Way* (London: Fabian Society, 1998), p. 1.

public sector share of gross domestic product since the 1970s, the last period of Labour government. It had been made possible by Gordon Brown's prudential economic policies from 1997 to 2001, policies which had gained the confidence of the financial markets, and therefore allowed expansion of the public services to occur safely. The increase in public expenditure constituted a radical break with the policies of the Thatcher and Major governments, and it has transformed even the attitude of the Conservative Party to the public services. For, at the time of writing, David Cameron, the Conservative leader, is insisting that the Conservatives would follow a 'prudent' policy in government. By this he means that they would ensure that the public services were fully protected before embarking upon any programme of tax cuts. Maintaining standards in the public services would be the most important priority. Such a stance offers a striking contrast to the position taken by Margaret Thatcher as opposition leader in the 1970s, although of course tax rates were much higher then than they are today. It is possible, nevertheless, that the increases in public expenditure since 2001 will permanently shift the terms of political debate, so that the mark of prudence in a government will no longer be that it seeks to hold taxes down, but that it maintains expenditure on the public services.

Apart from this, perhaps important change, however, it is difficult to point to any other ways in which Blair has been able to breathe life into the dry bones of social democracy. This does not mean that he has not achieved good things in government; and it would be wrong to suggest that Blair's vision of social democracy, the 'Third Way', or any of the other sobriquets which it has been given, is merely a clever soundbite, designed to hide the fact that his policies have been essentially a continuation of those of the Thatcher and Major governments. Blair has tried hard to humanise the neo-liberal economy which he inherited. When John Major became Prime Minister in 1990, he indicated that he wanted to make Britain a country at ease with itself after the radicalism of the Thatcher years. Blair has sought to do the same, and has perhaps done more to help achieve this aim. For he has emphasised, to a far greater extent than the Conservatives did, the problem of social exclusion, and has sought new and more sophisticated policy instruments to combat it. There is some difficulty in evaluating the success of these instruments, however, since many of them – and, in particular, the measures taken to improve education and training – will yield their results only in the long term, and not over a period of one, or even three, parliaments. Moreover, under the Blair government, the trend towards greater inequality of incomes, apparent under the Conservatives, appears to have been halted. Nevertheless, the central concern of the Blair government has been not with securing relative equality between different social groups, but with combating social exclusion, a very different thing.

Thus it is only when seen from the standpoint of a demoralised left that Blair can be said to have rejuvenated social democracy. Seen from any other standpoint, New Labour may be regarded as a form of accommodation, designed to hide from those on the left the extent to which the party was accepting the new settlement built by Margaret Thatcher and John Major. Perhaps this is not Tony Blair's fault. For it may be the case that there is no longer, and has not been for some time, a real social democratic alternative to the Thatcher/Major settlement.

Political scientists are accustomed to distinguish between 'position' politics and 'valence' politics.[23] The 'position' politics of conflict between alternatives is a much rarer phenomenon in British politics than is sometimes thought. It was present, no doubt, in 1945 and 1979, and in 1983, the year of Labour's most catastrophic post-war defeat. Since then it has come to be replaced by 'valence' politics, a politics based upon agreement about ends, but disagreement about means. 'In our view', argue the leading students of elections in Britain, 'the most important factor underlying electoral choice is valence – people's judgments of the overall competence of the rival political parties'.[24] There has been, since 1992, broad agreement that the fundamental framework established by Margaret Thatcher, based on privatisation, a liberal economy and a weakened trade union movement, should be maintained. The point at issue at general elections since 1992 has been which party would administer that dispensation most effectively.

Tony Blair's essential skill has been to transform position politics into valence politics. For, where Labour had taken up a position in clear opposition to that of the Conservatives, that position had often been electorally unpopular. Blair insisted, therefore, that a Labour government would not run the economy in a radically different way from the Conservatives, but would run it more competently; he insisted that a Labour government would not restore the powers of the trade unions by reversing the legislation of the Thatcher years putting them under statutory control; he insisted that a Labour government would nationalise

[23] See Donald Stokes, 'Valence Politics', in Dennis Kavanagh (ed.), *Electoral Politics* (Oxford: Clarendon Press, 1992), pp. 141–64.
[24] Harold Clarke, David Sanders, Marianne C. Stewart and Paul Whiteley, *Political Choice in Britain* (Oxford: Oxford University Press, 2004), p. 9.

nothing. Indeed, the general election of 1997 was the first since the Labour Party had been formed in which nationalisation was not an election issue. The issue, rather, was what Labour would privatise, not what it would nationalise. It was not unfair for Douglas Hurd to say, that 'the Conservatives lost the 1997 election, having won the fundamental arguments'.[25] Tony Blair won elections not through a radical upsurge from below, but because he was perceived as a more competent leader than his opponents, and a leader, moreover, who would not disturb the gains that had been achieved during the period of Conservative government. Tony Blair, like Harold Macmillan, proved himself a master of the politics of a post-ideological age. Both succeeded in accommodating their parties to uncomfortable realities, even if the methods they chose were very different. But Tony Blair was also a master of the politics of a post-social democratic age.

The emasculation of social democracy followed inevitably from Blair's acceptance of the constraint of globalisation, a 'golden straitjacket' as the American commentator Thomas Friedman has called it.[26] For social democracy has always been a doctrine whose fundamental premise was that the processes of economic and social change could be controlled by government. Globalisation has, for the time being at least, undermined that premise, narrowing if not eliminating entirely scope for the politics of redistribution. The social democratic doctrine of the primacy of politics has been replaced by the neo-liberal doctrine of the primacy of economics.

There is of course no inherent reason why this new dispensation should prove permanent any more than the post-war Attlee settlement was to prove permanent. Perhaps the future will show that the post-Thatcherite settlement is just as impermanent, or perhaps an original and creative social democrat thinker will arise to formulate a new social democratic doctrine, to show a path forward for social democrats in a globalised world. But the Blair effect, while thoroughly beneficent in so many areas of public policy, has done little to controvert the proposition that social democracy no longer constitutes an effective doctrine for a modern government.

[25] Douglas Hurd, 'His Major Achievements', *Daily Telegraph*, 30 June 1997, p. 18.
[26] Cited in Sheri Berman, *The Primacy of Politics: Social Democracy and the Making of Europe's Twentieth Century* (Cambridge: Cambridge University Press, 2006), p. 209.

PART II

Economics and finance

10

The Treasury and economic policy

PETER SINCLAIR

Preliminaries

What was Tony Blair's economic legacy? Inferring the economic effects of government policy is never an easy task. We need to ask how things would have differed had policies been different. Posing that counterfactual faces challenges. There are many other influences on events, apart from what government does. Economic entities depend on choices made by countless households and firms, and these in turn reflect their resources, technologies, unobservable expectations and beliefs about future policy (and other aspects of their environment). None of these are set in stone. Then there is the speed of impact. Sometimes economic policy has quick effects. And some variables can overreact. Often, though, repercussions take many years to work out in full. This is especially true of government decisions that influence the supply side of the economy. Add to this the fact that figures we have for many of the key economic variables are measured with error and subject to regular revision. So the economic record for a recent period that we have to hand now may be seriously inaccurate, distorted by a host of other factors, and barely affected by what governments did or did not do within that interval.

Politicians claim credit when things go well. They seek scapegoats to exculpate themselves when they do not. So their own statements, and the briefings and announcements of their news managers, may give no sound basis for judgement. (Nor can we trust opposition parties, given their role to paint a picture in the bleakest hues.) There is a further problem, too. Government has many heads. The formal constitutional position may be clear (although often it is not). But how are we to assign responsibility for an outcome between the relevant minister(s), the prime minister, their various political advisers, the civil service, and other bodies to which decisions may have been delegated? And most pertinently of all, how much of the applause – or brickbats – we may feel confident enough, at this early stage, to apportion among the politicians in charge, can we pass to Tony Blair, as opposed to Gordon Brown?

The macro-economic record

We should begin with the evidence. The decade from May 1997 has seen ten years of continuous and reasonably steady economic growth. Unemployment has mostly edged downwards, to levels far below those seen in the previous twenty years. Inflation has been modest and steady, far lower and less turbulent than in the 1970s or 1980s. Interest rates have generally fallen, whether real or nominal, long or short. The stock market has trended up (although with some sharp swings). Sterling has climbed relative to most of the world's currencies, above all the US dollar and the continental currencies that metamorphosed into the euro. Most of Britain's income groups have witnessed large rises in living standards. Except at the edges of the distribution, most of these ten years saw declines in inequality and poverty by most definitions. Private consumption spending has been particularly robust.

This summary of the evidence is distinctly positive. But it needs to be seen in perspective. For most variables of interest, the contrast with Britain's experience in the quarter-century to 1997 is especially impressive. But the comparison with the 1950s and 1960s, which the Blair years so resemble in many respects, is less so. Those earlier decades displayed somewhat faster than average inflation but markedly lower average unemployment than the Blair decade. And the 'bad' years 1972–97 present a very uneven picture, with a much stronger performance in most respects towards the end than earlier on. The five years 1992–7 are very much more like the Blair years than what preceded them; and as we shall see later, this may well be no accident.

Furthermore, one important economic variable, perhaps the most important of all, registered barely any change at all after 1997. This is the trend rate of economic growth. The trend in real gross domestic product per head has remained almost constant since the late 1940s in the UK. It has remained rock solid at about 2.4% per year.[1] And to complicate matters further, there are several other leading countries that displayed the same combination of steadier growth and flat (or gently decelerating) inflation and unemployment, as Britain.

---

[1] See W. Allen, R. Batley, E. Baroudy, B. Paulson and P. Sinclair, *Growth in Britain* (University of Birmingham, mimeo, 2007).

Table 10.1. Growth and inflation in the big six OECD economies

	Annual average growth rate, 1997–2007	Annual average growth rate, 1992–7	Annual average inflation, 1997–2007	Annual average inflation, 1992–7
UK	2.7	3.1	1.7	2.2
Unweighted average of next five	1.85	1.74	1.46	2.4
France	2.2	1.1	1.7	1.8
Germany	1.5	1.3	1.5	2.3
Italy	1.4	1.3	2.3	4.4
Japan	1.2	1.5	−0.8	0.8
United States	2.9	3.5	2.6	2.7

Source: IMF, World Economic Outlook and author's calculations and forecasts.

Britain has done very well when compared with the world's five other *largest* economies. While quite similar in other respects, the United States displays a slightly lower trend in real income per head, though faster in aggregate; marked rises in inequality on most definitions; and a somewhat more disturbed series for aggregate output. Japan has hardly grown since 1991. Its general absence of inflation – and spells of price declines – are not seen, by the Japanese or by outsiders, as an achievement. Rather, they are taken to be a major weakness that their authorities have sought hard to combat. And what of Germany, France and Italy? Each of these three has seen substantially slower average growth and much higher unemployment in the Blair years.

Table 10.1 illustrates. Of the big six OECD economies, the United States grew fastest from 1997 to 2007, as it had from 1992 to 1997. (Here UK economic performance on Blair's watch, which lasted for two and a half parliaments, is contrasted with the previous parliament, 1992–7, and with those of other major countries; and inflation is defined as the percentage annual average change in the country's consumer price index.) Britain came second in both periods. Actual growth was a little slower under Blair than in the previous quinquennium. But part of this small gap results from rounding, and the strong figure for 1992–7 includes a cyclical bounce. Britain's relative growth performance also appears to have slipped across the two periods. The UK grew nearly 1.4% per year

Table 10.2. Unemployment in the big six OECD economies

	Average unemployment rate, 1997–2006	Change from 1997 to 2006	Average unemployment rate, 1992–7	Change from 1992 to 1997
UK	5.5	−1.7	9.0	−2.7
Unweighted average of next 5	7.3	−1.4	7.6	+0.9
France	9.7	−2.5	11.2	+1.6
Germany	8.1	−0.5	7.3	+2.8
Italy	9.2	−4.5	10.5	+2.5
Japan	4.6	+0.7	2.9	+1.2
United States	4.9	−0.3	6.1	−2.6

Source: as Table 10.1.

faster than a simple average of the other five from 1992 to 1997. In Blair's decade, that gap dropped to 0.9%. Average annual consumer price inflation also slowed across the two periods, in absolute terms (1.7% against 2.2%). Japan's much bigger swing, from inflation to deflation, places UK inflation above the average of the rest in Blair's years, while it had been slightly below earlier.

Table 10.2 presents unemployment figures for these six economies. Britain's moved from a relatively high (but falling) figure in 1992–7 to relatively low, and still falling, under Blair. These excellent performances result from the interplay of several factors. One was Brown's welfare-to-work policies.[2] Earlier, sterling's eviction from the European Exchange Rate Mechanism (ERM) in September 1992, and the accompanying depreciation and monetary policy loosening this permitted, were important in the mid-1990s. Perhaps the greatest influence, though, was the lagged impact of the labour market and trade union law reforms enacted by Thatcher. It was to Blair's credit, and Brown's, that political pressures to repeal them were resisted. Had they succumbed, UK unemployment in 2007 might well have been closer to rates prevailing in France, Germany

[2] Britain's tax credit schemes expanded greatly in 2003–4, from foundations first laid in 1972 with the Family Income Supplement. The idea is to top up incomes for working families with low earnings, and not to reward inactivity. Six million families now receive tax credits in Britain, so the scale is very large. But so too is the level of error and fraud: nearly £2 billion has been officially described as irrecoverable overpayments.

and Italy, all of which had generally fought shy of applying Thatcherite reforms.

Many of Europe's smaller economies, on the other hand, reveal a considerably stronger record. Growth has been much faster in the Baltic Republics, Finland, Ireland, Luxembourg, Norway and Spain than in Britain, for example. And many witnessed sharper falls in unemployment, with much the same time profile of inflation as in the UK. Other advanced countries outside Europe – Australia, Canada, Mexico, New Zealand and South Korea, for example – have also grown at not dissimilar rates to Britain's in this period, and with broadly similar (or better) records of inflation and/or unemployment. And Britain's share of world GDP, measured at current exchange rates, fell in the Blair years (as it seems to have done in every decade since the mid-Victorian era). This was mainly because of the exceptionally rapid growth of most Asian economies, especially China and India. Partly because of these countries' growing weight in the world aggregate, the long-term slide in the UK share of world output might actually have gathered pace on Blair's watch. Some slide is really inevitable: over the long haul, all else being equal, richer countries tend to grow significantly more slowly than poorer ones.[3]

So much for longer-run averages. What of the *short-run* chronometry of the Blair decade? These ten years display no periods of GDP decline, in marked contrast to the previous quarter-century of UK data. There had been serious recessions in 1973–5, 1979–82 and 1990–2, but not even mild ones in 1997–2007. No 'boom and bust', agreed; but there was unmistakably some undulation in growth. So Britain's business cycle had been squashed. But not abolished. It was in fact really quite like what it had been in the 1950s and 1960s, if more muted. Annual growth peaked at about 4% in 2000 and 2004, slipping to 2% or less in early 2002 and mid-2005. Mild business cycle peaks (points where growth returns to trend from above) can be identified in 1997–8, 2001 and 2005. At around four years, the interval between the peaks is close to the fifty-four-month periodicity detectable for 1951–73. The downswing from 2000 to 2002–3 is the sharpest cyclical phenomenon in the Blair decade. But it coincides with, and doubtless betrays influence from, very much more pronounced downswings in the GDP series in the United States, in world trade, and,

[3] This 'catch-up' phenomenon is strongly attested in most cases. See G. Doppelhofer, R. Miller and X. Sala-i-Martin, 'Determinants of Long-Term Growth: A Bayesian Averaging of Classical Estimates (Bace) Approach', *American Economic Review*, 94, 2004: 813–35, for a recent study that shows this (and much else).

above all, in each of the world's principal stock markets; and it must have been aggravated by the shock of the World Trade Center atrocity.

The verdict on this broadly satisfactory record is certainly positive. Some credit for this must certainly go to Brown, and some, less directly, also to Blair. The main achievement of the Blair–Brown partnership was perhaps to have retained key features of Thatcher's reforms (particularly lower marginal income tax rates and restrictions on the rights of trades unions) that allowed the macro-economic record to blossom. And the fact that inequalities and poverty have tended to decline somewhat on many definitions (although not all, nor consistently across the decade), and not to worsen as they quite often tended to under Thatcher, will partly reflect the impact of Brown's measures to provide more support for low-income families in work.

The euro

There are few issues of economic policy where we know Blair's views differed sharply from his Chancellor's. On many they appear largely or fully agreed: the need to avoid any increase in the top rate of income tax or the standard rate of value added tax; the virtues of the private finance initiative; the early acceptance of tight limits on public spending, and its spectacular later relaxation on health expenditure; the sedulous courting of business; the distancing from Labour's traditional allies and founders, the trades unions. But on one they differed sharply. This was the issue of whether the UK should adopt the euro.

It will have been Blair's hope, early on in his premiership, that Britain would be able, at least at some point, to join Germany, France and her other main European Union partners in the world's first great currency merger. But for Brown – who in the 1980s had been if anything less Eurosceptic than Blair – that decision was a Treasury-reserved domain. The issue was kicked into touch during the first Blair parliament. 'We conclude that the determining factor as to whether Britain joins a single currency is the national economic interest, and whether the economic case for doing so is clear and unambiguous', Brown told the House of Commons on 27 October 1997.[4] The Chancellor devised, and announced, five tests,[5] all related to aspects of potential benefit or harm

---

[4] *House of Commons Debates*, cc. 583–4.
[5] These concerned whether the UK had achieved *convergence* with Europe; whether it was *flexible* enough to adapt to the change; how UK *investment* would be affected; the impact on the UK's *financial services* sector; and the prospects for *employment and growth* in Britain.

to Britain that euro adoption might entail. On the basis of the answers to these, to be illuminated by detailed research conducted within and by the Treasury, and which the Treasury would publish, Gordon Brown would make a recommendation during a second Blair government to the cabinet and parliament. A positive recommendation by Brown would trigger votes in cabinet, then in parliament, and finally a national referendum. At any point in the chain, a negative one would bury the issue, at least for a while.

Arguments in favour of euro adoption by Britain would include several points. There would be some saving of her real resources devoted to exchanging sterling and other euro-legacy or euro currencies. There could well be a stimulus to trade[6] with euro partners. And there would be an elimination of exchange rate uncertainties associated with that trade. (Given transactions costs, maintaining separate currencies is rather like imposing a tax on trade with other countries, but an especially silly tax, which, unlike tariffs on imports, does not even have the merit of raising any appreciable revenue for government.)

Potential net welfare gains might come from heightened competition in UK markets, as price comparisons between home and EU partner firms' products became less opaque. Gaps between interest rates facing lenders and borrowers might narrow, as Britain's financial markets became more liquid. Each of the above might raise the UK's long-term growth rate, possibly even indefinitely.[7] There could also be savings in foreign exchange reserves and some consequent gain in net foreign investment income; and opportunities to reap economies of scale in central banking, and possibly to improve monetary policy processes and decisions.

There are also counter-arguments. Unifying currencies across some, but not all countries, will divert trade, very probably wastefully, from excluded countries. Exchange rate uncertainties can often be hedged against at very modest marginal cost. Your country's optimum inflation

---

[6] Some influential indirect evidence supporting this claim includes J. McCallum, 'National Borders Matter: Canada–US Regional Trade Patterns', *American Economic Review*, 85, 1995: 615–23 and A. Rose, 'One Money, One Market: Estimating the Effect of Common Currencies on Trade, *Economic Policy*, 30, 2000: 7–45.

[7] This would indeed happen in any number of endogenous growth models. See R. E. Lucas, 'Supply Side Economics: An Analytical Review', *Oxford Economic Papers*, 42, 1990: 293–316; P. Romer, 'Endogenous Technological Change', *Journal of Political Economy*, 98, 1990: S71–102; and P. Aghion and P. Howitt, *Endogenous Growth Theory* (Cambridge, MA: MIT Press, 1998).

trend may differ from your monetary union partners'. Asymmetric shocks (which have quite different impacts on you and your union partners) must mean that both you, and they, are constrained to follow a second-best, common reaction. 'One size fits all' probably implies a perfect fit for no one. Currency union requires you to surrender the option to set interest rates independently, and the option to enact or permit changes in your exchange rate. Those two options may have far from negligible domestic value.[8]

Furthermore, in Britain's case, there were the luckless dummy runs. Sterling joined the 'snake-in-the-tunnel' in 1972. Later, in October 1990, it entered the ERM. But both of these commitments – however unfortunately timed – were to prove unsustainable. Further possible complications include: wrangles about how to fix entry exchange rates for legacy currencies (the partners will have conflicting interests here, and there is no easy or agreed way of quantifying a 'fundamental equilibrium' exchange rate[9]); how to make a supranational central bank democratically accountable; how to ensure that national fiscal policies do not undermine the common currency, in the way that, for example, spending and deficits of Argentina's provincial authorities helped to destroy the country's currency board in 2001–2;[10] and seignorage allocation disputes.

From 1997 to 2003, the government's official position was 'prepare and decide'. Despite its hint of activity and resolve, only a skilled semiologist could discern much real difference between this phrase and the Major government's policy of 'wait and see'. Public opinion on the issue bobbed up and down, but showed a consistently negative majority (and no overall trend). May 1998 saw it at its smallest in the MORI opinion poll – 34% in favour, and 48% against. There was a record majority against in November 2000 (18% in favour, 71% against). Typically there were about

---

[8] With its independent currency, France could devalue its way out of the wage hikes, agreed between (then) premier Pompidou and trade union leaders, that ended its national strike in 1968. But if events ever repeated themselves under the euro, France would be doomed to suffer a haemorrhage of its external competitiveness and jobs.

[9] As explored recently, for example, by R. Driver and P. Westaway, 'Concepts of Equilibrium Exchange Rates', in R. Driver, P. Sinclair and C. Thoenissen (eds.), *Exchange Rates, Capital Flows and Policy* (London: Routledge, 2005).

[10] See A. Powell, 'The Argentine Crisis: Bad Luck, Bad Management, Bad Policies, Bad Advice', *Brookings Trade Forum* (Washington DC: Brookings Institution Press, 2003); and F. S. Mishkin, *The Next Great Globalization: How Disadvantaged Countries Can Harness their Financial Systems to Get Rich* (Princeton, NJ: Princeton University Press, 2006) for more on this.

twice as many against as in favour throughout the period from 1992 to 2003. Opposition was on the whole rather stronger among women, over thirty-fives, lower-income groups and those inclined to vote Conservative. The Conservative Party made its hostility to abandoning sterling a central plank in its 2001 general election campaign, and subsequently attributed its drubbing to undue emphasis on the issue. Nonetheless, the fact that winning a referendum on euro entry looked a hopeless prospect was clearly critical in reconciling Blair to staying out, at least for a while. It may also have helped to strengthen Brown's doubts about the wisdom of entry.

In June 2003, Brown announced his verdict to the House of Commons: 'A clear and unambiguous case for UK membership of the EMU has not at the present time been made and a decision to join now would not be in the national economic interest.' The accompanying Treasury document[11] stated that 'we cannot . . . conclude that there is sustainable and durable convergence or sufficient flexibility to cope with any potential difficulties within the euro area'. On a more positive note, Brown did announce that the country's inflation target (2.5% per year increase in the Retail Price Index, definition RPIX) would switch to one based on the Consumer Price Index (which was easier to compare with the 'harmonized index of consumer prices' watched by European Central Bank). He also declared that steps would be taken to modify Britain's housing and mortgage markets, in line with the recommendations of the Barker[12] and Miles[13] reports that he had commissioned.

Was Brown right to say no (or not yet) to the euro? It is interesting to speculate on what would have happened had (a) sterling joined at the inception (1999, with notes and coins debuting in 2002), or (b) Brown announced that his tests had been met, and (improbably) that ratification

---

[11] It was buttressed by an eighteen-volume research document, HM Treasury, 'UK Membership of the Single Currency: EMU Studies', 2003, www.hm-treasury.gov.uk/documents/international_issues/the_euro/assessment/studies.

[12] K. Barker, *Delivering Stability: Securing Our Future Housing Needs*, Final Report (London: HMSO, 2004). House prices were increasing strongly in the UK – and also in some euro area economies with faster growth, such as Ireland and Spain – to much larger multiples of income than in France, Germany and Italy, raising concerns about overall monetary stability in the short run and financial stability in the longer run.

[13] D. Miles, *The UK Mortgage Market: Taking a Longer-Term View*, Final Report and Recommendations (London: HMSO, 2004). Unlike much of the rest of the EU, Britain's mortgages were typically at variable interest rates, not rates fixed for several years. This raised worries that the transmission mechanism of monetary policy could be more violent in Britain, a special concern if interest rates were to be set with reference to euro-area-wide, rather than UK, economic conditions.

by parliament and people been followed swiftly in 2004. In either case, adding UK data to the aggregate euro area statistics would probably have led the ECB into a slightly more hawkish stance for the time profile of its policy rate. This is because UK unemployment, unlike Germany's, France's and Italy's, has been low by historical standards. But, for the same reason, the policy rate would surely have been set at lower rates than the UK's.

There is a curious (and in the author's view, needlessly restrictive) convention that policy rate changes are normally limited to twenty-five basis points (one quarter of one per cent) or multiples thereof. Partly because of this, but principally because the UK would have formed barely one-sixth of the hypothetically enlarged euro area (EA+, call it), our counterfactual thought experiment would have EA+ rates set very much closer to the ECB's than the Bank of England's actual rates. This suggests that euro participation could actually have served to overcook the UK's already relatively overheated economy. EA+ rates would also, to some degree, have deepened the doldrums for the three large euro area economies: any rise in interest rates would have intensified their prob- lems of sluggishness in production, investment and employment growth. Lower policy rates would probably also have inflamed the UK housing market, either, as in Ireland, by pushing up prices strongly in 2000–2 when they were still rather quiet (had the UK joined early on), or (with entry in 2004) by intensifying the 2003–6 giddy house price boom. And an enlarged euro would probably have seen its external value fall less than it did in 2000, and recover more slowly in 2004–6. Although the UK's mild 2000–3 downswing could have been softened somewhat by the consequences of early euro entry, the major effects would, on balance, probably have been to destabilise GDP (and inflation) in the UK and also in the euro area core. The first technical, scholarly attempt to gauge the effects of euro entry-at-inception on the UK and Sweden reaches not dissimilar conclusions.[14] Future research may of course point to a different conclusion. Or we might see some evidence of sharp increases in intra-euro area trade and in growth rates that advocates of the euro project once prophesied.[15] But there is precious little evidence of this to date.

[14] H. Pesaran, V. Smith and R. Smith, 'What if the UK or Sweden Had Joined the Euro in 1999? An Empirical Evaluation Using a Global VAR', *International Journal of Finance and Economics*, 12, 2007: 55–87.
[15] See, for example, M. Emerson, D. Gros and A. Italiener, *One Market, One Money* (Oxford: Oxford University Press, 1992).

Furthermore, there have been asymmetric shocks that have affected EU countries in different ways. Instances include the big 2004–6 jump in oil prices (relatively bullish for sterling), major differences in immigration patterns, and sharp increases in Chinese exports (neutral to favourable for some EU countries, but especially damaging for Italy, given its greater similarity in export patterns). And perhaps the biggest argument for keeping sterling out of the euro area for a while was another asymmetry. Postponing entry would allow experts to quantify actual effects and see how things worked out ('the value of waiting'). Importantly it would also preserve options. Entry, an all but irreversible commitment, could only close them.

Other financial and monetary issues

If the Blair–Brown economic policy record is crowned by its essentially negative – and judicious – decision to stand aside from the euro area, there are some positive radical changes that it introduced as well. Foremost here were granting operational independence to the Bank of England, and the creation of the Financial Services Authority to combine the supervising roles of numerous bodies, the Bank included. Both changes were announced in early May 1997, in the first days of Blair's government.

They had been prefigured in some earlier Labour policy pronouncements. But the Bank independence decision astonished observers with the speed and manner of its execution. The key idea is that politicians are inherently short-sighted – fixated by impending elections – and therefore tempted to do things that bring short-term gain at long-term cost. Among these, Barro and Gordon argued,[16] were policy decisions that affected inflation. An unexpected rise in inflation would bring extra output, profits and jobs for a while; so politicians that declared a promise to keep inflation low, the right policy for the long run, would soon misbehave and lose credibility. The output gains would be fleeting, but the extra inflation would do harm. Better, therefore, to pass monetary policy decisions to a 'conservative' central banker who made low inflation his sole priority[17] – or set the central bank a widely published, transparent, low inflation commitment (a 'target') and let it get on with it, with no political interference. Perhaps it was no accident that the astonishingly

[16] R. Barro and D. Gordon, 'Rules, Discretion and Reputation in a Model of Monetary Policy', *Journal of Monetary Economics*, 12, 1983: 101–21.
[17] K. Rogoff, 'The Optimal Degree of Commitment to an Intermediate Monetary Target', *Quarterly Journal of Economics*, 100, 1985: 1169–89.

rapid inflation rates in all the world's democracies during the second half of the twentieth century – so much higher than the approximately zero rates seen in the eighteenth and nineteenth centuries – owed much to lagged effects of franchise extensions, and the Keynesian revolution that encouraged politicians to seize the levers of monetary policy and use them to try to defend and create jobs.

Brown's move was indeed a radical departure. It accorded with the grain of the times, and followed most of the best recent academic thinking on the issue. It was welcomed by the financial markets, which promptly lowered nominal interest rates on longer-term (sterling-denominated) UK government debt sharply, demonstrating a belief that British inflation would be substantially lower as a result. But just how novel was it? In some ways, the new arrangements represented a step back to the years before 1939, or 1914, when policy interest rate decisions were taken by the Governor of the Bank of England, not the Chancellor. In others, it was a logical extension of Norman Lamont's decision in 1992 to replace the broken anchor of British monetary policy – the link to the German Mark – with a new monetary framework, inflation-targeting, which New Zealand had initiated barely three years before. And before that Nigel Lawson had wanted to grant the Bank operational independence. The fact that Lawson could not tells us how subordinate most Chancellors are, in some key issues, to 10 Downing Street. But where Thatcher forbade, Blair was to delegate, at least to the Chancellor if not to other ministerial colleagues. Perhaps Blair just preferred to involve himself in foreign affairs, in education, in health, in Ulster, and saw that his time was limited and his talents and interests better confined to those spheres. Perhaps he and Brown agreed from the start that Brown should have an untrammelled say in all matters economic. And perhaps Blair recalled how Thatcher never really recovered from Lawson's angry resignation, and determined not to repeat that error. There is probably some truth in all three of these statements.

In the new system, a Monetary Policy Committee (MPC) would meet at the Bank each month to set the UK's short-term policy rate,[18] by majority vote. The MPC consisted of the Governor and two Deputy Governors of the Bank (all crown appointees on renewable five-year terms), two other Bank officials, and four external members, chosen by the Chancellor, serving three-year renewable terms. A tenth non-voting member would be a Treasury official. So the sense in which the Bank

---

[18] Known as Bank Rate from 2006.

of England gained independence in 1997 was strongly nuanced. Furthermore, it lacked goal independence. The MPC would be charged by the Chancellor with aiming at a specific number for the rate of inflation (2.5% RPIX, later changed to 2% CPI).[19] Other objectives, such as sustaining employment and growth, were to be secondary to that. If inflation over a year strayed by more than 1% from the target, the Governor would write an open letter to the Chancellor explaining why the target had been missed, and what action might be taken to attain it later. In the ten years of Blair's premiership, coterminous with the first ten years of the MPC, just one letter had to be written, right at the end. Until March 2007, annual inflation was never more than 1% off target. The upper limit was touched in January 2007, then breached two months later, largely as a result of oil price movements.

You must have *a* nominal anchor. To see that, look at the huge jump in Britain's annual inflation rate, to 26% in 1975, which followed her pilotless exit from the snake-in-the-tunnel in 1972. But which? Monetary targets – but for which monetary aggregate, and why an indirect one when what you try to stabilise is inflation? Exchange rates – but why tie yourself to the problems of your anchor currency, and at a rate that may do you serious or persistent damage? To succeed, inflation targeting depends on trust. Workers and firms bargaining over wages need to base their calculations on a shared belief that the rate of inflation over the contract period would be close to target. And in their product price-setting role, firms need to share that belief as well. If everyone's inflation expectations are anchored at or near the target, actual inflation will average out at or near the target, too.

Inflation-targeting is something of a self-justifying hypothesis. To work, the public's trust must be earned. Any tendency for inflation to stray, on the upside (or down), has to be countered by a rise (or a fall) in the policy rate. This will tend to squeeze (strengthen) aggregate demand, and thereby limit (or strengthen) rises in pay – which should translate into lower (higher) inflation. But the medicine takes time to work: its maximum impact is felt between eighteen and twenty-four months later. And when everyone learns to expect that shocks to inflation will be countered this way, the medicine's dosage can come down. The details of the inflation-targeting framework vary from country to country. And there are many that now employ it, from Brazil, Canada, Chile, Colombia,

---

[19] The goal would be changed at most once a year. In practice it was altered just once, at the end of 2003.

Mexico and Peru in the Americas, to South Africa. In Asia it has spread from New Zealand to Australia, the Philippines, South Korea, Thailand and Turkey; Japan may join them. Iceland, Norway, Poland and Sweden are Europe's main inflation-targeters, along with Britain, and it forms an increasingly important element in the European Central Bank's monetary policy framework. It has thus far been accompanied, wherever it has been applied, by steadier and lower inflation. But this begs several questions. Among them, might inflation have fallen and steadied anyway? And what is the optimum rate of inflation?

Until 2004–5, at least, when oil prices jumped sharply, inflation has tended to fall and steady almost everywhere, and not just in inflation-targeting countries. Furthermore countries that adopted inflation targeting did so, typically, because some previous regime broke down, sometimes quite chaotically. And though we have fifteen years of experience for Britain, and three more than that for New Zealand, most inflation-targeting regimes are much younger. Scrutiny of long data spans, and of a wide spectrum of countries' experiences, is needed before we can hope to get a full picture.

So it is still too early to hope to ascertain exactly what the *added* value from inflation-targeting actually is. Furthermore, if a country operates an unsustainable fiscal policy regime, with rising ratios of debt to national income, say, no monetary framework can defend it against the grave turbulence that must eventually ensue. Another worrying point is the 'Iron Law of Contempt' in macro-economics: every generation is united, if in nothing else, in despising some aspect of the conventional wisdom of thirty or so years before. This makes one ask what it is about our current macro-economic and central banking convictions that posterity will deride us for. And experts are still debating how much of the more benign economic environment of the past fifteen years or so, not just in Britain but in so much of the world, is due to improved policy frameworks, or improved policy decisions, or better luck in the form of fewer and less sinister shocks.[20] Almost certainly, it was due to a combination of all three.

Where should the inflation target be set? The Chicago tradition, pioneered by Milton Friedman (1969), had it that inflation was best not at zero, nor at a positive value, but *negative* – minus the real rate of interest. That way 'real' money (currency in purchasing power terms) could

[20] The Treasury Select Committee held a 'Ten Years On' inquiry; its submissions are available on www.publications.parliament.uk/pa/cm200607/cmselect/cmtreasy/299/299we01.htm.

become a free good, priced at its marginal cost, assumed to be zero. In other words, nominal interest should ideally be abolished. Friedman's original argument has recently been reinforced.[21] Arguments for aiming above this, possibly for zero or even positive inflation, are essentially second-best. They are numerous. Perhaps the strongest[22] stems from two facts – first, that nominal interest rates cannot be negative, and second, that altering policy rates is the standard (and arguably indispensable) mechanism for cooling or reviving economic activity at times of macro-economic stress. Aiming way above Friedman's optimum preserves the option to reflate if needed; aiming at his optimum closes it. A low positive inflation target, just a little above zero, may be best on balance. If so, Brown's choice of numbers is commendable.

Partly to guard against any possible conflict of interest that might con-front the newly independent Bank of England, it lost two functions it had long enjoyed: managing the government's debt and supervising commercial banks. The first passed to a newly created Debt Management Office. The second transferred to another new body, the FSA (Financial Services Authority). The FSA swept up the oversight responsibilities of a dozen previously separate institutions. Brown, or his adviser Ed Balls, will have feared that the Bank might be *thought to be* torn, at some point, between the macro-economic benefits of changing policy interest rates in one direction, when keeping a big retail bank afloat might push them in the other. And the boundaries between different kinds of financial institution were becoming progressively more blurred. Separate regulators were now an inappropriate, even dangerous anachronism.[23]

One final monetary decision of Brown's was much more contentious – and ultimately (when details became public eight years later) quite embarrassing. This was his sale of a large slice of the country's gold reserves in 1999. There were actually some quite good arguments for selling some gold then. Russia and South Africa, the two main producers,

---

[21] By R. Lagos and R. Wright, 'A Unified Framework for Monetary Theory and Policy Analysis', *Journal of Political Economy*, 113, 2005: 463–84; and G. Rocheteau and R. Wright (2005), 'Money in Competitive Equilibrium, in Search Equilibrium, and in Competitive Search Equilibrium', *Econometrica*, 73, 2005: 175–202.

[22] See P. Sinclair, 'The Optimum Rate of Inflation: An Academic Perspective', *Bank of England Quarterly Bulletin*, 43, 2003: 343–51, for more on this – and for four other second-best counter-arguments to Friedman.

[23] Goodhart's contribution in R. Brealey, C. Goodhart, J. Healey, G. Hoggarth, C. Shu and P. Sinclair, *Financial Stability and Central Banks* (London: Routledge, 2001) speaks eloquently to this, but argues against applying a central bank–supervision split in developing countries.

were facing serious challenges, and might respond by selling more gold. Looking back, gold had usually proved a poorly performing asset. Falls in inflation rates around the world, and some trend to freer floating, would reduce official and private demand for gold. And industrial and dental use did not seem buoyant. Furthermore, if agents were rational and neutral to risk, expected risk-adjusted yields on gold holdings could not systematically exceed those on other, arguably more useful assets. In retrospect, however, we can now see that gold actually did very well in the ensuing eight years. It was pushed up mainly by the indirect effect of falling real interest rates (reflecting greater longevity and lighter capital taxation, inter alia), and rapid Indian growth. Yet this was not easily foreseen. The key flaw in Brown's decision was not so much the principle of selling some gold, but rather the way the gold was to be sold – not secretly, but in large pre-announced auctions. Dealers would then bid down prices in anticipation, *ensuring* that the nation would get bad prices. For a government that wore transparency on its sleeve but often concealed, as with peerage loans, what it was really doing, this was an amazing lapse. Advice was ignored. In matters like that, only a fool plays poker with all his cards face up.

The gold sale was an embarrassment, at least in the way it was handled – too deaf to advice, yet also too transparent. And in retrospect it is clear that luck was against the policy of sale in 1999. But if ill luck and refusal to listen to good advice lost the British taxpayers £2 billion or so in that case, they were amply rewarded by another astonishing success: this was the auction of the third generation of telephony licences, in 1999. This raised £22.5 billion, and drew unbridled praise from the National Audit Office, which has always been (both under Blair and earlier) much more often a source of castigation of government error than of congratulation.[24] The good fortune here was to achieve the sales just before the dot.com bubble crashed in 2000–1. But the skill was the decision to listen, and follow, advice from some of Britain's leading economic experts on the relevant technical aspects of auction theory and games in her universities. The success helped to restore Whitehall's respect for academic economists, which had been impaired by the 365 signatories to the 1981 'letter' to *The Times*, to something more like what it had been in the 1960s.

---

[24] National Audit Office, 'The Auction of Radio Spectrum for the Third Generation of Mobile Telephones', report for the House of Commons, 15 October 2001.

Taxation and public finance

Economic policy goes far beyond growth, inflation, and currency, exchange rate, banking and auction issues. One of the central functions of the Treasury is to manage the government's finances, and in particular the structure and levels of taxation, and public expenditure. In the Blair–Brown diarchy, these were domains firmly reserved to Brown. But the Prime Minister's official title is 'First Lord of the Treasury'; all Brown's key decisions were agreed in discussions with Blair, even if briefly and often at short notice; and prime responsibility for all government policy, wherever formulated and applied, rests with 10 Downing Street. Nonetheless, Blair's role in the management of the British economy from 1997 to 2007 is more pomp and theatre than reality: in Bagehot's term, the Prime Minister had become a 'dignified' rather than 'efficient' part of the Constitution in this sphere. Maybe that was wise. Blair must have ruminated on how economic disputes, many of them centred on European exchange rate matters, had worsened Thatcher's relationships with two Chancellors, Lawson and Major, and, in turn, Major's with Lamont. There were earlier examples of friction between 10 and 11 Downing Street too, such as Macmillan's difficulties with Thorneycroft and Selwyn Lloyd. Heath had worked well with – and dominated – Barber, as, to a lesser extent, Wilson had with Callaghan. But Blair would hardly play Heath when confronted with Gordon Brown.

Tax policy in the Blair years was not just remarkably conservative; it was strictly Conservative in key respects. There were 'stealth' increases in taxation – higher National Insurance contributions, increases in real taxation on motor fuel until stopped in the wake of protests in 2000, sharp real increases in council tax bills as central government tightened its funding support for many local authorities, for example – but the main feature was the absence of changes in the cynosure tax rates. The standard rate of value-added tax had been changed twice under the Thatcher–Major governments – up to 15% in 1979, and up again, to compensate for the revenue lost when council tax replaced poll tax in 1991, to 17.5%. Throughout Blair's decade, 17.5% is where it stayed. The standard rate of income tax was lowered slightly (23% to 22%, with a pre-announced cut to 20% to take effect in 2008), something that, in the twentieth century, only Conservative or Conservative-dominated administrations had achieved. The top rate of income tax, which had been cut from 83% on earned and 98% on unearned to 60% and later 40% under Thatcher, raising spirited Labour opposition at the time, was firmly held at 40%.

The main argument against a steeply increasing structure of marginal income taxes is twofold.[25] First, if everyone's utility is to count in social welfare, the top marginal rate should be zero right at the top. And second, you can think of a high marginal rate on higher incomes, with lower rates below, as providing a hefty implicit lump sum transfer to people with large earnings. Such transfers are utterly unjustified on the grounds of justice (it is the poor that need them far more) or efficiency (recipients of transfers normally react by working less). In 1999, Brown experimented with a low starting rate of income tax, 10%, but announced its forthcoming abolition in his March 2007 Budget. This was a very rare case of a Brown *bouleversement*.

Previous Conservative governments had modified the main tax on company profits, Corporation Tax (CT): allowances had been reduced to accompany a reduction in rates; and the relatively generous tax treatment of dividends, as opposed to retained earnings, became somewhat less generous. Brown's 1997 Budget continued these trends, reducing the standard rate of CT, while trimming allowances and abolishing the dividend income tax credit for pension funds (which Norman Lamont, six years earlier, had already reduced from 25% to 20%; Brown likewise completed his predecessors' task of doing away with the last chunk of mortgage interest relief against income tax). Like the gold sales, this was something that could in principle be defended *ex ante*, but, as matters turned out, proved unfortunate *ex post*. But unlike the gold sales, the politics of the issue was handled with too little explanation, not too much.

The case for lowering the tax rate and broadening the base was that the tax system would be less distorted. Put another way, an 'average' person could be presumed to benefit, sooner or later, at no loss to the Exchequer. Any move to greater neutrality in taxation would generally tend to achieve this, at least under suitable conditions. Lower rates and broader bases were a Treasury aim discernible in Brown's five Conservative predecessors as Chancellor, in the way they revised VAT, CT or income tax. Add to this the old (Labour) view that discouraging dividend distribution may spur companies into more investment, and one can see that Brown's 'pension credit raid' appeared to make some sense from several standpoints.

---

[25] The pioneering and immensely influential paper by J. A. Mirrlees, 'An Exploration in the Theory of Optimum Income Taxation', *Review of Economic Studies*, 38, 1971: 175–208, provides the key ideas here. See also A. B. Atkinson, *Public Economics in Action: The Basic Income/Flat Tax Proposal* (Oxford: Oxford University Press, 1995), who argues in favour of a flat income tax structure for similar reasons.

There is also an argument against taxing the return on capital at all. Atkinson and Stiglitz[26] demonstrate this, under particular conditions, when people work when young, and consume when young and when retired. Under rather different assumptions, with numerical simulations calibrated on the US economy, Lucas[27] shows that the permanent removal of a tax on capital income would not just lead to higher capital and output and consumption in the long run, but that the gains from this would actually outweigh the early cost (in utility terms) when consumption has to drop to pay for the extra capital. And Kaldor[28] had recommended an expenditure tax (a shift to taxing personal income net of net saving) which turns out to have possibly even more appeal than Lucas's thought experiment. Arguments of this kind may have dissuaded Brown from reducing or terminating the tax-exempt (voluntary) savings schemes for individuals he inherited from Conservative predecessors. But they can also be extended, at a pinch, to offer some justification for tax leniency towards the (involuntary) saving through defined-benefit, fully funded private pensions, with which Britain, as it happened, was far better endowed in 1997 than all but two of her EU partners.

In 2007, the Treasury was forced to reveal some internal correspondence that had warned Brown not to scrap pension dividend tax credits, for fear of lowering UK share prices, raising the cost of capital to companies, and imperilling the sustainability of such pension schemes. After share prices did start tumbling (worldwide) in 2001, many defined-benefit company pension schemes did indeed close to new employees. Britain's much envied private pension funds sickened; and some died. The £5 billion-a-year credit removal was certainly a contributory factor here. But really only a rather minor one. Much more serious, in this author's view at least, was the remorseless increase in life expectation (much of which government actuaries, and many private sector actuaries, had for mysterious reasons been too cautious to predict), the fall in long-run interest rates to which it was linked, the stock market swings, and the new accounting rules concerning return and shortfall projection (which pushed the funds into lower-yielding, 'safer' assets).

Of more enduring significance was the government's commissioning of a review of state pensions by Adair Turner.[29] This report had numerous proposals, among them to raise pension age in stages, and re-establish an

[26] A. Atkinson and J. Stiglitz, *Lectures in Public Economics* (New York: McGraw Hill, 1980).
[27] R. E. Lucas, 'Supply Side Economics: An Analytical Review', *Oxford Economic Papers*, 42, 1990: 293–316.   [28] N. Kaldor, *An Expenditure Tax* (London: Allen and Unwin, 1956).
[29] A. Turner, *A New Pension Settlement for the Twenty-first Century* (London: HMSO, 2005).

earnings link. Blair and Brown are known to have differed on the timing of the restoration of the link to earnings (which have tended on average to rise some 1.5% to 2.5% per year faster than prices). Blair is thought to have favoured a rapid change; Brown saw the advantages for the public finances in delaying it as long as possible. The eventual compromise seems to have split the difference.

Nonetheless, it is sad that Brown did not revisit his 1997 decision on tax credits when the pension funds ran into serious trouble four years later. Perhaps he thought of doing so; but at this stage the public finances were deteriorating, and an annual revenue loss of £5 billion would have been even more unwelcome than before. It is also much to the Blair government's discredit (but certainly not Brown's) that its minister, Alan Johnson, capitulated to trade union pressure in postponing, for decades, well-conceived proposals to start raising the retirement age for public servants. Given rising life expectation, this surrender in 2005 leaves a large hidden cost for future taxpayers. It also flies in the face of concepts of equity. And the fact that public servants retire typically at sixty, if not earlier, aggravates the problem further. Johnson's giveaway has far greater long-run consequences than a two-year advance in the earnings link for state pensions.

Johnson took the soft, myopic option to yield to union pressure on public servants' future retirement dates. This avoided the risk of an embarrassing strike. The grave extra burden on posterity (not just extra taxes – in all likelihood, lower capital too) would of course trouble the Treasury. But it would escape much wider notice. Furthermore, Johnson was following precedent. A year earlier, John Reid had capitulated to the BMA (British Medical Association) on hospital doctors' pay and working conditions. After Thatcher's reforms, British trade unions are best thought of as bargaining partners for government in the determination of government employees' salaries. The BMA represents such bargaining at its canniest.

From late 1999, Blair and Brown prepared for a major increase in state spending on the National Health Service. The aim was partly to reduce waiting lists, partly to plan for an ageing society with increasing medical needs, and partly to make up for what was widely perceived as many years of under-expenditure, at least by comparison with France, Germany and Scandinavian countries, and with the US, which (in 2006) spent more than twice as much on its residents' health as a share of income as Britain did. Indeed one recent paper[30] argues that America's health spending-to-

[30] R. Hall and C. Jones, 'The Value of Life and the Rise in Health Spending', *Quarterly Journal of Economics*, 122, 2007: 39–72.

income ratio is likely to double by 2050, reflecting rising life expectation and the increased relative demand for health products as income per head goes up. In the US – unlike the UK and other countries in Western Europe – much of the health spending is private. One of the biggest tragedies of Blair's government is that so much extra public spending on health turned out to have so little real effect.

One reason for this was the £12 billion (and rising) bill devoted to a big computer project for the NHS. Blair had conceived this idea himself after a brief encounter with Bill Gates. It was hurriedly agreed upon. Scrutiny was minimal. If Blair's successors do not kill it, the project might actually come to fruition one day, and, if implemented, might even succeed in increasing efficiency and cutting future costs. But the present outlook is not encouraging. The project looks likely to join the Greenwich dome and the Holyrood Parliament[31] as a spectacular symbol of one of the worst aspects of Blair's government – its gullibility, mismanagement and waste. (Ironically, however, it was probably the Holyrood scandal that may have convinced Brown and Blair that private sector construction management had to be more efficient than public sector.) Another was the consequence of the terms of the private financing initiative (PFI) applied to the funding of new hospitals, schools and London Underground maintenance. A third was the failure to develop effective mechanisms that could prevent the rapid proliferation in the number of highly paid hospital management posts. And the fourth – a particularly costly error, since it led to a sharp fall of perhaps 22% in the medical services acquired for each pound spent on hospital doctors – was Reid's outwitting by the BMA. Brown was Chancellor throughout Blair's decade at No. 10. But Reid was more typical, rarely staying at any of his posts for more than eighteen months. When up against the BMA, he was newly installed as Health Secretary. Like his master Blair, Reid was sceptical of civil servants' advice, impatient to 'settle' a complex problem, keen to be seen to 'deliver' reform and not especially skilled or interested in financial detail. The BMA read Reid like a book. Brown's reaction to their tricking him will have been devastating. Blair himself may well have failed to grasp its sorry consequences.

The private finance initiative

The PFI, on the other hand, commanded support from both Blair and Brown. For Brown, it had the merit of employing private sector skills in

---

[31] Completed after long delays and almost four times its initial budget.

ensuring that construction projects were completed on time and within budget, something that British public officials have often found challenging as far as historical records go back. Conveniently, it placed capital spending off balance sheet. On top of this, it seemed to offer a relatively dependable way of making good a generation of underinvestment in so much of Britain's public infrastructure. And to clinch matters, PFI might morph New Labour's 'third way' from fog and spin to concrete.

But there were snags. UK firms borrow at higher rates than UK governments, and this must be reflected in the rental charges the firm receives on a PFI project. The differential is non-trivial, and rarely less than 150 basis points per year. For a long-term project – and most PFI schemes, some 80 agreed in hospitals and 100 in education in the Blair years, have involved twenty-five- or thirty-year leases – this unfortunate wedge could compound into a really large gap. (A PFI partner company that charged break-even rent might have to cut construction costs by around 30% or more under the public ownership alternative for the taxpayer to secure any gain.) And for the hospitals and schools that were cajoled into doing a PFI project, the impact this would have on their cost streams might be very serious. Great strains were already manifest by the end of Blair's prime ministership. One particularly absurd consequence was that some older hospitals, not encumbered with PFI obligations and in a stronger financial position, have been threatened with closure to stem the losses in the PFI hospitals. Even if PFI hospital rent fees are so high that the authorities would otherwise be tempted to walk away from them, the PFI contracts have committed them to the rent payments. So the health and school authorities are prisoners of bad contract drafting and extraordinary naïvete on the part of Blair's ministers, civil servants and/or advisers. The public sector's inability to manage public sector investment projects was, it turned out, complemented by its inability to match the wickedly clever bargaining skills[32] of the private 'partners'' lawyers.

Worse still, ensuring that PFI projects were superior to traditional public ownership projects would turn critically on astute government contracting. The PFI company might well bully subcontracting builders into working to budget, because of its self-interest. But it would also have an interest in maximising its monopoly power later on. It could insert legal clauses in the contract to ensure reversion if use were changed, and

---

[32] D. Abreu and D. Pearce, 'Bargaining, Reputation and Equilibrium Selection in Repeated Games with Contracts', *Econometrica*, 75, 2007: 653–710, have a brilliant new primer on how repeated bargaining *ought* to work when parties are rational. Perhaps Whitehall's architects of PFI schemes might benefit from consulting it.

the status of sole supplier of maintenance services, or sole beneficiary on resale, for example. Many schools and hospitals have fallen victim to sharp practices of this kind, and subsequently rued the day they entered the PFI project. And at least one prominent PFI partner company has fled offshore to deny the Exchequer a share in its booty.

Hints of gullibility and waste were intertwined with a Thatcherite suspicion about civil servants' advice in another feature of Blair's government. This was its growing reliance on private companies for expensive consulting services. Poor Sir Humphrey had begun to perspire under Thatcher. But it was Blair who really gave him his comeuppance. The civil service was famous for its lucid, crisp judicious summaries of pros and cons, completed with an elegant and usually unanswerable argument for a particular course of action (which might well be to do nothing). Like Thatcher, Blair was apt to regard these messages, and the formal meetings for which they were prepared, as unhelpful, time-wasting, pompous obstructions. Instead, his own aides would analyse issues, feed ideas up, square them with the all-important communications supremos, and, if the need arose, call in companies to do any research legwork or complex thinking. For the companies, the task would be to produce some answers, decorated with flashy Powerpoint slides, engineered – cynics might think – as much with an eye to repeat business from the key individuals whose preconceptions they might be fortifying, as to providing dispassionate top-quality advice in the public interest. Best of all, Blair hoped, the glossy little materials from private consultants seemed to offer an escape from some of the volumes of civil service documents that filled his and other ministers' nightly red boxes.

Private computer software companies also fed royally from Blair's table. Instead of waiting to buy a proven off-the-peg system that involved minimal tweaking, ministers and officials, prompted eagerly by the companies themselves, would often insist on something bespoke and untried. The companies would aim first for acceptance in principle on a fairly modest figure and optimistic timescale, and rely on modifications to specifications, and small print inserted into contracts by cunning lawyers, to keep ramping up their fees later on. At its worst, the result, from which no one could avoid blame, least of all the relevant ministers, might involve many billions of wasted pounds. Blair's NHS computer programme scandal was one example of many. Other notable IT infelicities included serious problems with passports and with social security computerisation glitches, and the inability of DEFRA, after adopting an expensive new computer system, to pay many of the UK's farmers their dues after the EU's 2004–5 reforms to the Common Agricultural Policy. Blair could reply with some justice that many foreign governments have proved just as reprehensible, if not more so,[33] and that the private sector also suffers from contracting errors, especially in relation to computer software, which we hear less about. The National Audit Office (NAO) explores and publishes details of administrative errors in Britain, but only by government. Yes; but the NAO's reports are 'coordinated' with the offending department, and might well have been even more embarrassing had it enjoyed true independence.

Distribution at home and abroad, and over time

While the Blair years saw some extra income dribble through to a few lucky PFI and computer software bosses, most definitions reveal that economic inequality and poverty actually fell during the decade. This is interesting, because the opposite trend has been displayed in the US, with which Britain's economic experiences are so often compared. And inequality tended to rise under Thatcher, especially when measured after tax. Two important measures by the government will have played some part in Britain's record under Blair. These are the Working Tax Credit (WTC), designed to raise the incomes of working families, with and without children, and the Minimum Wage (MW). WTC represents a major refinement of, and a substantial increase in generosity in comparison with, a sequence of previous schemes, which may be traced right back to Family Income Supplement (introduced under Heath in 1972). Its aim is to raise the consumption of the *working* poor, especially those with children, rather than provide unconditional benefits, or unemployment assistance, which would tend to reduce employment. WTC is therefore 'supply-side friendly', and it owes some of its design features to Clinton's welfare-to-work policies introduced in the United States. The second was introduced *de novo*, as far as Britain was concerned, in 1999. At the time of writing, it was last raised in October 2006 to £5.35 per hour for adults.

Both measures raise controversy. With WTC, some complain that nothing is done for the working-age unemployed, who constitute a large share of the very poorest, except to raise the reward for labour force participation. Others note that there is a difficult trade-off: the more generous WTC is at low wages, the greater the financial cost, and so the greater the

---

[33] The European Court of Auditors, for example, has refused to sign off the European Commission's accounts for over ten years, because of suspicion of fraud and poor administration (usually on the part of national governments).

need to pay for it by clawing it back as earnings rise. A steep rate of claw-back is tantamount to a high effective marginal tax rate, which will discourage effort and training and longer hours of work for workers with pay a little further up the scale. A lower rate of claw-back involves reducing the disincentive effect in this region, agreed, but at the cost of spreading it further up the scale – and raising the total cost of the scheme into the bargain, which can only imply considerably higher marginal tax rates elsewhere. Brown opted for a relatively generous scheme with a relatively steep claw-back rate lower down. The balance of informed observer opinion is generally with him in this. Whether MW raises or reduces total employment depends critically on where it is set. A modest MW will tend to raise rates of pay – and, critically, *the number of jobs* available – for very low-paid workers in narrow labour markets where employers do not discriminate in the wages they pay for such workers, and find – or at least believe – that they have to raise the common rate of pay to attract extra staff. This is known as 'labour monopsony'. In markets where labour varies widely according to perceived productivity, and firms can hire any amount of labour of a particular quality at a given price, imposing a MW anywhere will either be irrelevant (for those whose productivity exceeds the MW) or unambiguously job-destroying (for those below it). Evidence on the issue is contested, but most good studies[34] tend to find that MW increases are good for raising the earnings of the low paid without endangering employment.

Brown's labour market reforms appear to have had Blair's blessing. And if they squabbled on many matters, particularly Europe, and gave their civil servants what became known as 'teebeegeebees' at times when the two men were due to meet, there were other issues, too, on which they clearly saw eye to eye. One was Africa; another, climate change. Both became increasingly important in the later years. In 2005, Brown drove through an historic set of international agreements on debt relief for the world's poorest countries, most of them in Africa, with keen support both from Blair and from the exceptionally talented Secretary of State, Hilary Benn. Blair's intervention here was important, since he will have helped to neutralise official opposition from Washington on this issue. And 2006 saw the publication of Sir Nicholas Stern's *Review on the Economics of Climate Change*, which was prepared inside the Treasury, with Brown's blessing, but as a submission in the first instance to Blair. Climate change is also a matter of distribution, of justice, but this time of

---

[34] D. Card and A. Krueger, *Myth and Measurement: The New Economics of the Minimum Wage* (Princeton, NJ: Princeton University Press, 1997) is probably the most influential US study of this.

distribution across generations, not within them. Much of Blair's final year in office was devoted to informing (and raising the profile of) the debate that threats that global warming posed for the world, and trying hard to counter the reluctance of several governments, most notably the American and the Chinese, to consider what most experts now consider appropriate, indeed urgently necessary, policy responses to them. Perhaps the two men sometimes competed for the limelight on these two issues, almost as much as they cooperated. Perhaps the view they took on both issues reflected an emotional, moral commitment to do good today that took precedence over some of the analytical longer-run complexities.[35] Perhaps, in the evening twilight of his premiership, Blair was becoming desperate to salvage a reputation so grievously tarnished by Iraq. Yet it may be that, in time, these achievements of the Blair–Brown partnership come to be regarded as no less important than the Blair years' record of macro-economic stability.

Conclusions

How new was New Labour economic policy under Blair? And how Labour? Labour participated in Churchill's coalition from 1940 to 1945, and had formed two short-lived minority governments between the wars. But it was in and after 1945 that Labour came into its own. It was in power for three spells of five to six years, usually (but not always) with a working majority: 1945–51, 1964–70 and 1974–9.

Labour devalued sterling in 1949 and 1967, and saw it depreciate sharply in 1974–6. Labour extended public ownership marginally in 1964–70 and 1974–9, and massively in 1945–51. Labour increased income tax rates in all three periods, reducing the post-tax income of top earners most. It was here that the contrast with Blair's administrations was starkest. Sterling *appreciated* by some 14 % in his decade. Labour nationalised nothing in these years, and actually continued privatisations that had begun under Thatcher. The main structure and rates of income tax were changed very little under Blair. In his decade,[36] the few changes that were enacted were mostly downwards.

---

[35] Writing off a deeply indebted debtor's debt may, for all its merits, have the unfortunate side-effect of discouraging future lending. And responding to climate change by a big jump in taxes on oil may do nothing to alleviate the problem, or curb emissions, if all it does, as argued in Sinclair, 'The Optimum Rate of Inflation', is to squeeze the price the oil seller gets.

[36] This observation is only slightly qualified by the facts that a 1% contribution, seemingly indefinitely postponable, to National Insurance has been levied since 2003 on top earnings, and the point at which the 40% rate first applies has slid, relative to incomes.

In some other respects, there is more continuity with previous Labour governments. The principle that Labour governments could not, and must not try to, spend their way to full employment was first expounded forcefully by Callaghan in 1976. It was Callaghan's premiership that saw the introduction of cash limits on departmental spending, and also of monetary targets, the rather clumsy and indirect forerunner of inflation-targeting. Brown's decision to say 'No, not yet at least' to the euro in 2003 mirrors the Callaghan government's decision to keep Britain out of the European Communities' fledging Exchange Rate Mechanism in March 1979. And Blair's successful campaign to delete Clause 4 from Labour's traditional constitution (the commitment to extend public ownership) counterpointed his predecessor Gaitskell's spirited but failed attempt to achieve this back in 1962.

Where previous post-war Labour governments had failed, Blair and Brown reasoned, was in the way they had allowed supporters' expectations about what could be achieved early on to run out of control – and then drive the government into a shaming retreat in the face of hostile financial markets. Under Blair, therefore, Labour courted big business and big finance sedulously in opposition and in power. The trades unions, Labour's traditional paymasters, were sidelined and ignored. None of the Conservative government's main anti-union legislation was repealed. Any resulting shortage in Labour's election war funds was to be filled by gifts, or later loans, with no binding commitment to repay, from very rich businessmen. And after the election victory in 1997, supporters' early hopes were restrained (and financiers' nerves soothed) by the simple device of adhering rigidly to the previous government's rather restrictive spending limits.[37] In the dark arts of public relations, it is a sacred principle to 'Get the bad news out first'. Blair and Brown obeyed this tenet to the letter.

When the lid came off, in 1999, it was not long before health spending came to be raised sharply. But a hasty John Reid, the then Health Secretary, was cleverly outmanoeuvred and succumbed to the wiles of the British Medical Association. So much of the extra money, it turned out, was lavished on extra pay in return for reduced work. Some was frittered on extra staff and extra pay for hospital administrators. And some was spent on an ambitious computerisation project, which revealed all too clearly how the Prime Minister's imagination, and distaste for slow traditional administrative procedures, could run ahead of good reason and careful decision-taking. Furthermore the Blair–Brown partnership's devotion to PFI

[37] Limits that, it is thought, the outgoing government might well have relaxed had they won the election.

projects, in health and education, at least led, unlike Scotland's new Parliament, to timely completions. But government's inability to understand the private companies' small print and fee structure was to bequeath a legacy of financial poison for the health trusts that had been induced to enter them. In these details, Blair's administration was blind and incompetent.

Yet in many, even bigger things, Brown did well. And Blair did well too, whatever his motives, by just letting Brown get on with it. In granting operational independence for the Bank, in retaining the Lawson–Thatcher tax structure and anti-union laws, and in not joining the euro, the Blair–Brown duumvirate showed considerable wisdom. They inherited a strong macro-economy from Major, and a policy framework set mainly by Thatcher. But their greatest achievement was to consolidate the revolution of their Conservative predecessors.

References

Abreu, D. and D. Pearce (2007), 'Bargaining, Reputation and Equilibrium Selection in Repeated Games with Contracts', *Econometrica*, v. 75, 653–710

Aghion, P. and P. Howitt (1998), *Endogenous Growth Theory*, MIT Press.

Allen, W., R. Batley, E. Baroudy, B. Paulson and P. Sinclair (2007), Growth in Britain, University of Birmingham, mimeo

Atkinson, A. and J. Stiglitz (1980), *Lectures in Public Economics*, McGraw Hill

Barker, K. (2004), Delivering Stability: Securing Our Future Housing Needs, Final Report, HMSO

Barro, R. and D. Gordon (1983), 'Rules, Discretion and Reputation in a Model of Monetary Policy', *Journal of Monetary Economics*, v. 12, 101–21

Brealey, R., C. Goodhart, J. Healey, G. Hoggarth, C. Shu, and P. Sinclair (2001), *Financial Stability and Central Banks*, Routledge

Card, D. and A. Krueger, *Myth and Measurement: The New Economics of the Minimum Wage*, Princeton University Press

Doppelhofer, G., R. Miller and X. Sala-i-Martin (2004), 'Determinants of Long-Term Growth: a Bayesian Averaging of Classical Estimates (Bace) Approach', *American Economic Review*, v. 94. 813–35

Driver, R. and P. Westaway (2005), Concepts of Equilibrium Exchange Rates, in *Exchange Rates, Capital Flows and Policy*, eds. R. Driver, P. Sinclair and C. Thoenissen, Routledge.

Emerson, M., D. Gros and A. Italiener (1992), *One Market, One Money*, Oxford University Press

Hall, R. and C. Jones (2007), 'The Value of Life and the Rise in Health Spending', *Quarterly Journal of Economics*, 122, 39–72

H.M. Treasury (2003a), 'UK Membership of the Single Currency: an Assessment of the Five Economic Tests', cm 5776, 9 June

H.M.Treasury (2003b), 'UK Membership of the Single Currency: EMU Studies', (http://www.hm-treasury.gov.uk/documents/international_issues/the_euro/assessment/studies)

Kaldor, N. (1956, *An Expenditure Tax*, Allen and Unwin

Lagos, R. and R. Wright (2005), 'A Unified Framework for Monetary Theory and Policy Analysis', *Journal of Political Economy*, v.113, 463–84

Lucas, R. E. (1988), 'On the Mechanics of Development', *Journal of Monetary Economics*, v. 22, 3–42

Lucas, R.E. (1990), 'Supply Side Economics: an Analytical Review', *Oxford Economic Papers*, v. 42, 293–316

McCallum, J. (1995), 'National Borders Matter: Canada – US Regional Trade Patterns', *American Economic Review*, v. 85. 615–23

Miles, D. (2004), 'The UK Mortgage Market: Taking a Longer-Term View', Final Report and Recommendations, HMSO

Mirrlees, J. A. (1971), 'An Exploration in the Theory of Optimum Income Taxation', *Review of Economic Studies*, v. 38, 175–208

National Audit Office (2001), the Auction of Radio Spectrum for the Third Generation of Mobile Telephones, Report by the Comptroller and Auditor General, House of Commons 233, 19 October

Pesaran, H., V. Smith and R. Smith (2007), 'What if the UK or Sweden had Joined the Euro in 1999? An Empirical Evaluation Using a Global VAR', *International Journal of Finance and Economics*, v. 12, 55–87.

Powell, A. (2003), 'The Argentine Crisis: Bad Luck, Bad Management, Bad Policies, Bad Advice', *Brookings Trade Forum*, Brookings Institution Press.

Rocheteau, G. and R. Wright (2005), 'Money in Competitive Equilibrium, in Search Equilibrium, and in Competitive Search Equilibrium', *Econometrica*, v. 73, 175–202

Rogoff, K. (1985), 'The Optimal Degree of Commitment to an Intermediate Monetary Target', *Quarterly Journal of Economics*, v. 100, 1169–89.

Romer, P. (1990), 'Endogenous Technological Change', *Journal of Political Economy*, v.98, S71–102

Rose, A. (2000), 'One Money, One Market: Estimating the Effect of Common Currencies on Trade', *Economic Policy*, v. 30, 7–45

Sinclair, P. (1994), 'On the Optimum Trend of Fossil Fuel Taxation', *Oxford Economic Papers*, v. 46, 869–77

Sinclair, P. (2003), 'The Optimum Rate of Inflation: an Academic Perspective', *Bank of England Quarterly Bulletin*, v 43, 343–51

Stern, N.H. et al (2006), *The Stern Review on the Economics of Climate Change*, http://www.hm-treasury.gov.uk/reviews/stern_review_economics_climate_change.

Turner, A. (2005), *A New Pension Settlement for the Twenty-first Century*, HMSO10

11

New Labour, new capitalism

ROBERT TAYLOR

'Labour as a party not only believes that economic dynamism and social justice must go hand in hand but that creating and maintaining the right environment for enterprise and wealth creation is a policy priority.'

Tony Blair launching the 2005 general election manifesto

'The challenge of globalisation needs a strong and vibrant trade union movement standing up for its members in a coherent and intelligent way.'

Tony Blair to the TUC annual conference in 2002

'The partnership between us is essential and I intend to ensure that it remains positive and firm.'

Tony Blair speaking at the Confederation of British Industry annual conference on 17 November 2003

Tony Blair spoke in Manchester on 30 April 2007 as part of his legacy tour. His subject that day was the world of paid work and the New Labour government's contribution to its evolution during his ten years as Prime Minister. In a comprehensive presentation Blair set out what he believed had always been a coherent and credible programme, designed to modernise Britain's labour markets and its employment relations in a strategic political response to the pressures imposed on the country's economy by the dynamics of globalisation and relentless technological innovation.

'Work, the fact of work and the changed nature of work were central to the government's economic and social policy from the beginning', he claimed.[1] Unlike previous Labour governments, his administration had sought to develop a new role for the state in its engagement with the wider political economy as it tried to encourage economic efficiency with social justice in the workplace. The state's primary purpose was no longer either to control or regulate, not even to protect employees from the adverse

[1] For the full text of Blair's Manchester lecture see the Downing Street website: www.gov.uk.

consequences of structural change or 'intervene to make employers more flexible' in their management of labour. Instead, modern government was needed to assist in meeting the insatiable demands of capital, to ensure private companies could compete effectively in open markets and to provide more investment in education and training to assist in ensuring that the UK could boast a high-quality, high-productivity economy. A positive approach by the state that encouraged risk-taking and wealth creation was the way forward. The New Labour project was to embrace global capitalism with enthusiasm in a radical break with Labour's troubled socialist past.

Blair's most important achievement was to identify his government with the forces of international finance capital. Under his government the City of London grew into one of the successful centres of globalisation. By 2007 nearly half the country's two million people employed in financial services were concentrated in the booming world of banks, insurance houses, venture capital companies and management consultants that populated the Square Mile and Canary Wharf in London's former dockland. Under a lightly regulatory regime, less onerous for capitalists than in the United States, Britain's capital took on an iconic status as the world's super-rich flocked to do business within its boundaries and pursue ostentatious lifestyles with a speculative explosion in property prices and conspicuous consumption. The relentless tidal wave of corporate mergers and acquisitions, the growth of private equity companies, hedge funds and venture capital firms were startling features of the Blair years. So was the upsurge in boardroom remuneration with mega pay rises and benefits, generous severance packages and lucrative share options, as London came to resemble the world of greed and power portrayed so vividly by Tom Wolfe in his *Bonfire of the Vanities* about New York in the 1990s. The inflow of Russian oligarchs who did so well out of the collapse of communism, Arab potentates and the assorted winners of international capitalism created what amounted to a new plutocratic class in Blair's Britain. The annual *Sunday Times* survey of the wealthy, argued that the 1997–2007 period was a golden age for the rich, rarely seen in modern British history. It estimated that when Blair came to power the wealth of the country's richest thousand people stood at £98.99 billion, while ten years later their wealth had climbed by an extraordinary 263% to £359,943 billion.

The Prime Minister never criticised those new 'masters of the universe' for their excesses, and the widening gap of wealth and income between themselves and the rest of the workforce that resulted. On the contrary, he himself sought their adulation and some were well rewarded with honours, perks and status. A hundred years earlier the Labour Party that Blair led had been created as an idealistic alliance of socialist societies and trade unions to challenge and seek to replace the global capitalism of that time with a socialist commonwealth based on the principles of solidarity and equality and the common ownership of the means of production, distribution and exchange.

Between 1997 and 2007 New Labour embraced the neo-liberal capitalist order, not in a defensively apologetic way but with a real sense of pride and swagger. Blair's concept of the state was for it to act as a handmaiden in the establishment of a new economic and social order, reminiscent of the one that flourished towards the end of the nineteenth century.

'The character of this new age is one of individual empowerment', Blair insisted in his 2007 Manchester lecture. It meant people at work now wanted both the state and society to 'support' and not 'control' them: 'They want to be in control.' In the Prime Minister's words, 'New Labour meant a release from the old fashioned view of the labour market.' 'Job protection through regulation was becoming out-dated', he added. The challenge facing government was now 'to make employees powerful, not in conflict with their employer but in terms of their marketability in the modern workforce'. The state's primary function was 'to equip the employee to survive, prosper and develop in markets'. The Blair approach to this new world of paid work could be summed up in two words – 'employee empowerment'.

In his Manchester lecture the Prime Minister insisted that his New Labour government – from its first day in office in May 1997 – had always sought not merely to accommodate but to embrace the underlying forces of change, fuelled by increasingly dynamic global markets. Its aim was to adapt and assist in the development of a knowledge economy in Britain through encouraging the wide use of information technology by employees and businesses. New Labour recognised the old age of manufacturing for the UK was drawing to a close, as a dramatic transformation was taking place in the world economy through the global integration of goods and services in increasingly open markets. During his ten years in 10 Downing Street Blair proclaimed that his intention was to help to govern by moving with the current of such turbulent trends so that Britain could become one of the world's leading countries in the new international economic order, open to foreign investment, deregulated and flexible, and committed to private wealth creation. By 2007 the UK had grown comparable in its attractions for foreign capital, according to the International Monetary Fund, to tax havens such as the Seychelles and the Cayman Islands.

Blair argued in his Manchester lecture that what he regarded as New Labour's radically distinctive approach to labour markets and employment relations had been clearly defined from his first days as party leader in 1994, and it reflected his hard-nosed recognition of contemporary realities. There was much truth in his assertion. Nobody could deny that the Blair attitude to capital and labour represented a definitive break with his party's ideology, ethos and traditions. In a special general election manifesto produced in April 1997 and directed at the business community, Blair set out how he intended to work closely with capital once in government. In that crucial document he made a strenuous effort both to convince as well as reassure the business community that his New Labour project, which had been jointly designed by himself and his Chancellor-to-be Gordon Brown, would not involve any return to an Old Labour-style policy agenda like that of the 1970s. It was not to concern itself with the restoration of lost trade union powers and influence. Nor was it even prepared to re-establish a strong and exclusively bilateral relationship between the state and the trade unions in the management of the political economy. Instead Blair/Brown wanted to stimulate the creation of a friendly, informal and strategic alliance with business that would aim to help boost corporate competitiveness, stimulate company investment strategies and focus on research, innovation and creativity. Blair and Brown told the business community in 1997 that a New Labour government would not make any attempt to second-guess the way they ran their affairs. This did not mean the state would remove itself entirely from the management of the political economy, but now its functions were to liberate private companies from excessive regulation and help to create the kind of competitive framework that would help them to flourish in the global economy. 'It is business not government that creates lasting prosperity', Brown's preface to the 1997 business manifesto declared. 'The job of government is not to tell people how to run their businesses but to do what it can to create the conditions in which business can thrive and opportunities for all can flourish.'[2] This was a New Labour language of 'positive engagement' with employers which had not been heard quite so bluntly before in a Labour Party document. It reflected a distinctively

[2] Draft article by John Edmonds, 'Positioning Labour Closer to the Employers', for *Historical Studies in Industrial Relations*, November 2006.

different approach by the Labour Party to the state's future relations with capital and labour that was upheld consistently during Blair's years in Downing Street.

But if New Labour's business mission for the political economy was already apparent from the project's very inception around Blair's kitchen table in his Islington home to those who chose to look, this was not widely appreciated or even recognised by many at the time, especially inside the trade unions. When elected Labour leader in July 1994, Blair was not entirely free to draw up the kind of uninhibited pro-business labour market and employment relations strategy from scratch that he would have liked to do. He felt himself constrained then by the existence of what seemed to be formidable political barriers that stood in his path. He was compelled to accept much of the public policy agenda that had been bequeathed to him by his Labour predecessors Neil Kinnock and John Smith, even if he was often to do so with some reluctance. Later, as Prime Minister, he came to regret his earlier caution, although his successful abolition of Labour's Clause 4 from its 1918 constitution early in his leadership in 1995 had removed whatever lingering ideological commitment his party retained to the public ownership of private companies.

Most of the substantial labour market and employment relations commitments that Blair inherited had been drawn up by Labour in close collective liaison with the party's trade union allies. The promise to introduce a statutory national minimum wage to eradicate poverty pay was already contained in Labour's 1992 general election manifesto, even if the precise administrative details of how this was to be achieved had not yet been worked out. Labour had also been committed since 1992 to end the country's opt-out from the Social Chapter of the European Union's Maastricht Treaty, secured by Conservative Prime Minister John Major. This move might suggest that Britain under Blair was willing to embrace a range of new legally enforceable workplace rights that were commonplace in the rest of continental Europe. It is true New Labour's 1997 business manifesto did its best to minimise what the impact of the ending of the opt-out might mean to private companies. As it explained,

> We understand business concerns that in the future costly legislation could be imposed on Britain through the social chapter. But we have made it clear that in government we will not agree to extend qualified majority voting to social security or co-determination in the boardroom. We will keep matters concerning pay and the right to strike outside the scope of the social chapter.

In addition, Blair promised employers privately that he would make sure that their anxieties over threats to their competitiveness and to employability would receive the highest priority before any further steps were taken to introduce more EU social legislation.

Labour's commitment in 1997 to introduce legislation to make it easier for trade unions to negotiate formal recognition agreements from companies for collective bargaining purposes had been made by Blair's predecessor John Smith, but even in 1992 the Labour Party manifesto had promised to promote the right to union membership and representation, as well as new worker rights for consultation and information from companies. Blair swallowed all of this, but he made it clear to employers that such legislation was not going to be designed to advance trade union power in the name of social justice. Instead, it would be introduced in a cautious manner so that it would neither disrupt nor harm their business activities. Blair was to argue that such reforms could only be justified in what they achieved if they helped private firms to grow. Whatever fairness for workers might result from Labour's proposals, they were to be implemented in order to meet the needs of private capital and were not designed primarily to bridge any representation gap or strengthen workers' collective voice for its own sake.

Moreover Blair made it clear before the 1997 general election that a Labour government under his leadership would not give back to the trade unions all the so-called freedoms and rights they claimed to have enjoyed before the passage of eight separate pieces of legislation since 1980 under Margaret Thatcher and John Major, which had weakened their collective powers of bargaining and marginalised their influence on government. Perhaps even more importantly, Blair rejected any suggestion that New Labour would establish a close working arrangement with the Trades Union Congress, such as the Social Contract which had so dominated government–trade union relations during the 1970s. On the contrary, he told trade union leaders on many occasions, in public as well as in private, that he was determined to eradicate what he regarded as the destructive and debilitating culture of the Old Labour movement where trade unions used their financing of the party and their block votes at the annual conference to dictate what Labour should carry out when in government. Under his leadership the 'contentious' alliance of party and trade unions was no longer even going to pretend to be a formal partnership of equals. Union leaders were to be treated with politeness: at best they would enjoy a minimum respect and some informal access to Downing Street, as well as relevant government departments. But this did not mean they would be able to negotiate any special bilateral deals to their sectionalist advantage at the expense of capital. The TUC's modernising general secretary John Monks was later famously to liken the trade union presence in New Labour circles to that of 'embarrassing elderly relatives at a family reunion'. There was to be no question of creating new tripartite institutions – as was done in the 1960s and 1970s – to further a public policy agenda that would be concerned to offer the trade unions any form of co-management of the political economy. Britain between 1997 and 2007 was to remain the only country in the European Union that deliberately rejected the use of institutional partnerships or social dialogues between the state, capital and labour at national, regional or company level. Blair regarded such tripartite arrangements as corporatist, inefficient and one of the primary reasons why continental Europe's variety of social market models had grown so sclerotic in the new age of globalisation and technological change.

Moreover, in his introduction to the 1997 Labour election manifesto Blair also emphasised that if he was elected he would not repeal the anti-trade union laws of the Thatcher era: 'We make it clear that there will be no return to flying pickets, secondary action, strikes with no ballots or the trade union laws of the 1970s'.[3] Instead a framework of basic minimum rights for the individual employee in the workplace was promised in order to establish 'partnership not conflict between employers and employees'. It is true that Blair's determination not to bow the knee to trade union demands and pressures for any return to the kind of industrial relations arrangements of the 1970s was not as drastic a rupture from the views of his immediate predecessors as he might like to have implied. In 1992 Neil Kinnock had also emphasised he would not repeal Margaret Thatcher's anti-union laws.

A broad continuity of outlook with past Labour commitments also seemed apparent in Blair's initial approach to the development of labour market strategy. New Labour came into government in May 1997 with a precise and clear programme of action to deal with unemployment under the stirring slogan 'Employment opportunities for all'. It was called the New Deal – with an unacknowledged tribute to President Franklin D. Roosevelt's efforts to end the Great Depression during the 1930s in the United States. As Lord Richard Layard of the London School of Economics, and one of its main architects, recalled, the conception of this pro-active approach to Britain's unemployment problem won early

[3] *Labour Party General Election Manifestos 1900–1997* (London: Politco's, 2000), p. 347.

enthusiasm from Blair, even if the details were worked out and implemented by Brown and his Treasury team. The concept of rights and
responsibilities, of putting an end to the dependency culture of the
unemployed and socially excluded, appealed instinctively to Blair's
moralistic conception of what was right and wrong. But the focus on
policies that would energise those who wanted to work through options
of training, job subsidies, or joining environmental task forces could be
traced in Labour policy thinking back to the 1980s and perhaps even
earlier.

What was distinctively New Labour in labour market policy, however,
was that Blair brought a harsher, more moralising edge to what needed
to be done. This signalled a genuine break with past practice which
amounted to much more than the rhetoric of tough language. Blair was
always keen to identify himself with the purposes of the New Deal, which
reflected his own instinctive conviction that nobody should be able to
claim something for nothing in the world of the socially excluded, where
the focus should be on the restoration of the paid-work ethic.

From the start of the project, employment relations and labour market
strategy was always regarded inside New Labour circles as central to
Blair's strong commitment to the creation of a modern open market
economy based on individual freedom and choice rather than on any
restoration of collective institutions, the pursuit of social justice or even
the promotion of the public interest.

It is true previous Labour governments had always accepted the existence of a mixed market economy despite their commitment to the state
ownership of specific industries and vague notions of socialist centralised
planning. Labour Prime Ministers before Blair were often high-minded
pragmatists, even if too often their apparent constructive interest in
ensuring private industry thrived had always proved cautious, timid and
defensive. Such an apologetic approach was now going to change fundamentally. 'I want a country in which people get on, make a success of their
lives. I have no time for the politics of envy', wrote Blair in his 1997
general election manifesto. He wanted to help to equip Britain so that it
could prosper 'in a global economy of technological change'. The 1997
programme spoke enthusiastically of 'healthy profits' as 'an essential
motor for a dynamic market economy'.

But Blair also appeared at that time to be concerned to use the state to
improve the quality of the labour supply. Not for the first time in modern
British politics, New Labour promised that it would tackle the country's
skills problems by transforming its inadequate industrial training system

to meet the employment needs of the new economy. 'We need to win on higher quality, skills, innovation and reliability', argued the 1997 election manifesto. It spoke of creating individual learning accounts to encourage people to improve their employability by upgrading their qualifications, and the creation of a virtual University of Industry which it was promised would bring 'new opportunities to adults seeking to develop their potential'. Neither of those proposals proved to be effective in practice and they were quietly buried. Similar promises of action on skills and training had also been included in Labour's 1992 programme. Here again, New Labour did not signal as much of a radical break with the recent past as its leading enthusiasts liked to suggest. However, the tone was now certainly different. Tackling the country's historic failure in training and skills seemed to have become an integral part in the much more ambitious grand narrative of Blair's modernisation strategy to win the hearts and minds of southern England, where his party had failed to make much electoral headway for eighteen years, by appeals to the affluent and the aspirational who had formed the political base of Thatcherism.

But of course 1997 was not really to be New Labour's Year Zero. Blair inherited the most promising labour market prospects ever enjoyed by any Labour Prime Minister in British history. The two minority Labour administrations under Ramsay MacDonald between the wars had fought with little success to conquer mass unemployment in the face of an orthodox Treasury belief in the sanctity of the gold standard, balanced budgets, free trade and deflation. The second government ended up in August 1931 divided over cutting the levels of state benefit to the unemployed. In 1945 Clement Attlee's Labour government spent six years heroically trying to build a New Jerusalem out of the ruins of the Second World War, in a Britain that was virtually bankrupt, dependent on massive American aid for its recovery, and faced with a crippling arms bill after the onset of the Cold War. In October 1964 incoming Labour Prime Minister Harold Wilson inherited a huge balance-of-payments deficit and a currency that was dangerously vulnerable to international speculation. Ten years later he returned to office to lead a minority Labour government that inherited the worst economic conditions of the post-war period, with a real fear of hyperinflation and rising mass unemployment, and a trade union movement aware of its negative power to obstruct change but unwilling to shoulder national responsibilities and exercise collective restraint both in its own and the national interest.

By contrast, in May 1997 Blair and Brown were the fortunate beneficiaries of a British economic revival that had first begun under the

Conservatives in the autumn of 1992. 'The incoming government will inherit the most benevolent set of economic statistics since before the First World War', claimed the outgoing Prime Minister John Major, as he left 10 Downing Street for the last time.[4] Registered unemployment had begun to fall from the early months of 1993, mainly due to the country's abrupt departure from the European Exchange Rate Mechanism in the previous autumn. It continued to do so successively month after month over the next eight years. The pace of the decline in unemployment was actually faster during Major's last three years as Prime Minister – from 9.3% in 1994 to 6.8% in 1997. Under Blair the unemployment figure dropped from 6.1% in 1998 to 4.7% by 2004, before rising slightly. There was also evidence in the later Major years of an improvement in the perhaps more important indicator for the health of the labour market – the employment rate. Under Blair that figure never returned to the high rate achieved by Edward Heath's government in 1973, even if he declared the country's employment rate target should be 80% by 2020, much more ambitious than the one of 75% set by the European Union Lisbon Summit in 2000.

In addition, the development of a more activist labour market strategy was already proving a success under Major well before Blair's arrival in office. The introduction of the Job Seeker's Allowance to replace unemployment benefit, with its greater emphasis on conditionality so that the unemployed were to be encouraged to find work through a mixture of incentives and sanctions, signalled a more focused approach. The technological modernisation of Job Centres, carried through in 1996, laid the foundations that were to make the implementation of Labour's New Deal programme after January 1998 more effective than it might otherwise have been. There appeared to be much more continuity than change in labour market strategy, whatever the New Labour spin machine might argue.

But by May 1997 trade union leaders and others on the left had convinced themselves that once New Labour was in government it would move in a more progressive direction. Certainly at first Blair seemed prepared publicly to lean, at least tentatively, towards the European social market model. Initially both he and his Chancellor were keen to take Britain into a much closer relationship with Brussels and return the

[4] For John Major see Robert Taylor, *John Major* (London: Haus Publishing, 2006), as well as Major's own memoirs, *John Major: The Autobiography* (London: HarperCollins, 1999), and Anthony Seldon, *Major, A Political Life* (London: HarperCollins, 1997).

country to the mainstream of European democratic politics. The trade unions through the TUC – who had changed their own official attitudes to Europe six times in twenty years – had come to recognise the benefits to them of the continental approach to employment affairs after a stirring speech by EU president Jacques Delors to the 1988 Congress in support of a workers' Europe.

In the supposed competitive war between the varieties of capitalism, Blair looked to establish a hybrid version of the social market economy through a judicious mixture of rights and responsibilities for trade unions and employees underpinned by a commitment to employment opportunities for all. The Blair record in government belied much of such wishful thinking. The trade unions deceived themselves if they had thought otherwise. Increasingly both Blair and Brown were to draw far more of their inspiration for the reform of Britain's labour markets and workplaces from the American neo-liberal model of deregulation, open trade, privatisation and incentives for corporate capitalism. But this was only part of the story. A potentially substantial range of employment regulations, designed to provide employees with opportunities to claim minimum legal rights, was passed into law during the Blair years. Moreover, because it was framed with care to alleviate the anxieties of business, the resulting regulation stood a much better chance that it would take root and help to establish a new balance between capital and labour to their mutual advantage. It is not surprising that the emerging hybrid model reflected conflicting pressures, and as a result it encouraged ambiguity, confusion and scepticism.

But by 2007, beneath the surface of an often deceptive culture of material contentment, workplace Britain had become much more stressful and polarised. While most employees in work enjoyed real increases in their earnings, the persistent long working hours culture brought with it high rates of absenteeism and ill-health that was reflected in the rise in invalidity benefits. While surveys found fewer employees were worried about being made redundant, and there was lower labour turnover and greater permanency of job tenure, more work intensification seemed widespread. Strikes may have been less frequent than at any time for more than twenty years, but this did not mean employees were more satisfied.

The Prime Minister's unsettling adoration of corporate wealth seemed at odds with any recognisable moral values and principles once associated with the Labour movement. Both Blair and Brown were unwilling to challenge the excesses of boardroom sleaze, greed and corporate corruption. Much more government concern was focused on how to deal with the most socially vulnerable in the labour market – single mothers, the disabled, older male manual workers, and those millions of people who were without any recognisable skills and who suffered from low levels of literacy and numeracy. Some observers were convinced that the New Labour project was often little more than a ruthless continuation of Thatcherism and did not herald a strategic retreat from the ideological certitudes of the 1980s, especially in its response to employment relations and labour markets. Such criticism was an exaggeration. During his years as Prime Minister Blair sought to bring about a recasting of the often uneasy relationship that existed between capital and labour. It may not have looked particularly social democratic by European standards, but neither was it simply a return to the master–servant relationships of nineteenth-century sweatshop Britain. Out of the ruins of the once familiar voluntary system of industrial relations, Blair was encouraging the formation of a new hybrid to meet the challenges posed by an increasingly globalised economy. Other European governments were both attracted and repelled by the outcome. They liked to see falling unemployment and admired the labour market strategy that Blair and Brown wrongly claimed they had introduced to bring this about. But at the same time they disliked the social disintegration and moral disorder that was also widespread with rising crime, drug addiction, alcoholism and poverty that seemed to be an integral but dark side of Britain's hybrid model.

Goodbye to collectivism – hello to individualism

One of Margaret Thatcher's lasting achievements as Prime Minister was to weaken decisively trade union power and influence. She did this through her 'step by step' strategy of restrictive legislation, firm resistance to public sector trade union militancy exemplified by the crushing of the miners in the 1984–5 national coal strike, and a willingness to tolerate levels of unemployment not seen in Britain since the inter-war years that had undermined trade union bargaining strengths. The results also owed much to her readiness to champion employee individualism, as she created a more enterprising economy based on low levels of personal taxation, deregulation and privatisation.

The authors of an authoritative study of the 1980–8 period of industrial relations explained what happened:

> The Thatcher government's aim – highly controversial at the time – was to weaken the power of the trade unions, deregulate the labour market and

dismantle many of the tripartite institutions of corporatism in which trade
unions played a major part. Subduing inflation was to be given priority
over maintaining low unemployment. Reducing the role of government
and levels of public expenditure were policy goals. The free play of market
forces was to replace the search for consensus between government and the
'two sides' of industry.[5]

By 1997 Blair had accepted most of those changes. Outwardly he
promised as Prime Minister that he would provide the trade unions with
a minimal legal framework inside which opportunities would exist for
them to try and reverse their steep decline in membership and collective
bargaining coverage. He also indicated that he wanted the trade unions to
modernise themselves and become different kinds of voluntary collective
bodies through the adoption of new agendas that emphasised partnership with employers, individual empowerment, learning and skills.
Above all, he favoured a decisive reduction in the political role that the
trade unions played inside the Labour Party. What he sought was a cultural revolution in their ethos and ideology. In his first speech as party
leader to the 1994 TUC Conference Blair told the unions: 'We will be the
government and we will govern for the whole nation not any vested interest in it.' And he meant what he said.[6]

During his few years in active Labour politics as a young man Blair
came to despise much trade union behaviour, although as a barrister specialising in employment law, he was at first broadly sympathetic. In articles in the New Statesman published in the early 1980s he even defended
the closed shop, supported secondary picketing and backed solidarity
strikes. This was perhaps the price any ambitious Labour politician like
him was forced to pay in order to further their political career at a time
when the trade unions were dominant in the party. But Blair was always
untouched by the sentimentalities associated with the Labour movement.
He even came to question whether it had been sensible for the trade
unions to create a party which was overwhelmingly rooted in the exclusive interests of organised manual workers.[7] Moreover, Blair was opposed
to the politics of class, in which he feared too many trade unions were
trapped in a historic repository of resentments and antagonisms. To him
too many of them were the relics of a bygone age of cloth caps, mills
and pits, and exponents of an unattractive male macho culture that he

---

[5] Neil Millward, Alex Bryson and John Firth, All Change at Work? 1980–1998 (London:
Routledge, 2000).   [6] TUC, 2004 Report (London: TUC, 2004), p. 54.
[7] Tony Blair, 'New Britain; My Vision of a Young Country', New Statesman pamphlet, 1996,
p. 25.

believed was irrelevant to the new world of work with its growth in the importance of women employees, white-collar and private service occupations, and small private firms. His highly personalised picture of trade unions could often seem lurid, simplistic and exaggerated. It reflected a right-wing tabloid newspaper version of complex realities. Most unions were modernising themselves in order to survive and prosper throughout his years as Prime Minister. Many came to resent his populist and ignorant attitudes. But he was always doubtful about either their willingness or capacity to reform themselves as organisations in structure and beliefs. Such sceptical feelings came to shape his general attitude to those who were still Labour's principal pay-masters during his time in Downing Street.

Moreover, by 1997 Blair recognised that the trade unions had grown far weaker than at any time since the inter-war Depression. They were now once again the under-dogs, not over-mighty subjects. As long as a New Labour government did not need to introduce a national incomes policy under which trade unions could act as enforcers of wage restraint on their unwilling members, they would not be able to exercise any effective leverage over its public policies. Every Labour Prime Minister before Blair had been eventually driven by adverse circumstances into seeking a negotiated bargain with the trade unions to deal with the country's economic troubles. This was no longer an imperative for Blair in what was, during his years in government, a booming and relatively trouble-free economy. In a deliberate move, the incoming Prime Minister refused to see the TUC during his first six months in Downing Street. This demonstrated that he did not need them in order to govern, and that they were not essential for the success of the New Labour project.

But as TUC general secretaries John Monks (to September 2003) and Brendan Barber (for the later period) admitted, this did not mean that his government held the trade unions at arm's length or sought to confront them.[8] They agreed that Blair's arrival opened doors and corridors in Whitehall that had been locked to the trade union movement for nearly eighteen years. While the Department of Employment was not re-established, and no senior minister was given the specific role of representing trade union interests around the cabinet table, an informal network of personal connections and links was established between the TUC, ministers and relevant government departments. The arrangement may not have enjoyed the same status as the myriad of institutions and

---

[8] Author's separate interviews with John Monks and Brendan Barber, April 2007.

committees that had existed in the Wilson or even Attlee years, but it was far better than nothing. 'We enjoyed a steady traffic between ourselves and government on a daily basis', Barber pointed out. 'We need to keep the suggestion of hostilities between the trade unions and New Labour in perspective. What we had was not perfect but it was far better than what we had under the Conservatives.' However, Blair was keen to avoid any suggestion that this might lead to any return to the kind of institution-building that had characterised earlier Labour governments. It is true that he did not abolish tripartite bodies like the Advisory, Conciliation and Arbitration Service, the Health and Safety Commission and the Equal Opportunities Commission that had survived the Thatcher/Major era, although he cut back their budgets and reduced their activities. He also agreed to establish an independent Low Pay Commission to advise and monitor the annual upgrading of the national minimum wage after its arrival in 1998. That body, with its members appointed from among employers, trade unionists and academics, proved to be highly successful in raising the pay of the poorest workers, but it did not become a model for use in other policy areas. Blair agreed to the creation of ad hoc committees, task groups, temporary commissions, public inquiries and the like to deal with specific employment issues such as gender at work equality, pensions and training. What he would not countenance was a multilateral bargaining approach between capital, labour and the state. Blair preferred to encourage bilateral relations, with the forces of capital and labour directed through his Downing Street policy unit and relevant government departments in an often complex decision-making process of triangulation.

In adopting an openly hostile attitude to corporatist tendencies, Blair believed he was merely reflecting the changing new world of work. Increasingly de-industrialisation, occupational shifts to private service employment and away from manufacturing, and the marked decline in private sector collective bargaining coverage were creating a more individualistic, more decentralised form of industrial relations, which emphasised flexibility, pluralism and personal choice. Non-unionism was now the norm across swathes of the private sector so that only an estimated 16% of employees were organised by trade unions by 2006. Increasingly younger workers aged between sixteen and twenty-four – known as Thatcher's children – saw little point in being trade union members. Blair was also unwilling to encourage new forms of collectivism that would protect trade unions from change or provide them with exclusive rights and privileges. He was not even prepared to say that his government would encourage workers to join trade unions, even in the government's own labour force. The Prime Minister argued that trade unions were to be provided with only limited statutory freedoms and that these would be mainly designed to help in the establishment of 'strong markets, modern companies and an enterprise economy'.[9] Blair wanted trade unions outside the public sector to become less traditional collective bargainers and more learning organisations for their members, personal service providers, and partners with companies in the creation of high-performance workplaces. Modest state funds were established to assist in the creation of partnerships at work and in promoting trade union modernisation and learning. Blair's approach was far removed from the social justice and political equity concerns of Labour's past.

But despite his genuine scepticism about the willingness of trade unions to change their structures and strategies, Blair honoured his limited policy commitments, although not without some anxieties in the TUC that he would walk away from his promises. The resulting 1999 Employment Relations Act and a mildly amending measure passed three years later (The Employment Act 2002) were evidence enough of his intentions. Admittedly Blair pointed out that when implemented the proposed legal reforms for recognition would still leave Britain with the most lightly regulated labour market of any leading economy in the world. Moreover, he made it clear to the TUC that this was all the trade unions could expect from New Labour and that what was to be implemented was not to be seen as the first instalment of any strategy for trade union advance towards a final industrial relations settlement reached on their terms. He was also keen to point out that the legislation was not designed to promote the collective, but to underpin individualism in the workplace. What he sought, he claimed, was the creation of a statutory minimalist framework that steered a cautious path between the absence of minimum standards of protection at the workplace and a return to the laws of the past. It was based on the rights of the individual employee, whether exercised on their own or with others as a matter of personal choice. It also sought to match rights with responsibilities and draw a line under the issue of industrial relations law by bringing forty years of sporadic industrial strife to a close. Of course, what Blair agreed to implement fell far short of trade union aspirations. Moreover, it was based on the questionable premise that an individual in the workplace was involved in a partnership of equals with his or her employer. In fact, the rights

---

[9] *Fairness at Work*, White Paper, Cm. 3969 (London: TSO, 1997).

gained were only really achievable if employees secured effective representation either through a trade union or the services of a solicitor. Blair
seemed to accept this. Under the 1999 Act the introduction of a legal right
for a worker to be accompanied by a person of their choice in a disciplinary issue provided a means for trade unions to gain access to companies.

But the new more militant generation of union leaders elected democratically through the ballot box in 2002 and 2003 demanded much more
than this. They wanted in particular Blair's acceptance of fundamental
labour rights for workers as enshrined in core ILO conventions that had
been signed by previous UK governments. The so-called Warwick
Accords, negotiated between the Labour Party and the trade unions in
2004, assembled a list of proposals for improving workplaces, but there
were always doubts whether these modest suggestions would lead to
much energetic action by government in their implementation. Trade
union weakness – for all the bluster at Labour Party conferences – was
painfully apparent by early 2007. Union leaders threw their backing
behind a Private Member's Bill that sought some mild amendments to
existing collective labour law under the name of trade union freedom,
but this measure even failed to secure private members' time in the House
of Commons for debate after it met with strong government disapproval.
Even a Private Member's Bill – strongly backed by the trade unions – to
more effectively regulate gang-masters who were found to be exploiting
contract foreign labour expired because insufficient Labour MPs bothered to support it.

Blair often found himself in alliance with the new former communist
states of central and eastern Europe as he opposed a number of legislative
proposals from the European Union that the British trade unions
wanted – such as full rights for agency workers and an end to the
country's opt-out from the EU working time directive's attempt to
impose a maximum forty-eight-hour working week. The TUC was also
compelled to fight a marathon campaign in support of legislation to give
consultation and information rights to workers if they wanted them.
Blair was joined by employer organisations to block the passage of that
measure through Brussels in a rearguard action. The government backed
down over it eventually, but only after finding itself in virtual isolation.
But by then the measure was so watered down it made little initial impact
on most companies. 'It was a victory for us', admitted John Cridland at
the CBI.

The public sector trade unions were to prove a constant irritation
to Blair and Brown as the government pursued its privatisation drive

through what remained outside the profit-making economy, and sought to reform working practices and pay systems across the public services. The Prime Minister was upset by the unions' stubborn attempt to defend what he saw as restrictive labour practices and inefficiencies. Blair wanted to ensure value for taxpayers' money by forcing public sector workers into an acceptance of the values of the private market through the spread of private finance initiatives, competitive tendering, and the sub-contracting-out of services to private profit-makers. Trade unions fought hard to uphold professional standards in the public sector and they tried to oppose the debilitating cult of managerialism that swept through the health service and the rest of the public sector under Blair. The state selling-off of air traffic control and the London Underground aroused predictable trade union resistance, especially as it involved pouring bil-lions of pounds of taxpayers' money into the pockets of often inefficient private companies. The fire-fighters tried to defend their ways of working through strike action but were heavily defeated in 2004–5. Blair was suc-cessful in pressing for a modernisation of public sector bargaining in central and local government. New pay systems put an end to ancient inequalities between manual and non-manual workers, while gender differences narrowed and hours of work were harmonised. But by the end of his premiership Blair regretted that he had not stood up more firmly to public sector unionism in his commodification of the public services.

Blair's admiration for private sector capitalism was coupled with a will-ingness to try and influence the behaviour of companies towards their employees. It is true little was done to legislate on corporate manslaughter to make named employers liable for prosecution over accidents at work. The government's deregulation taskforce stressed the need for cutting red tape, reducing risk assessment in workplaces and placating companies who wanted to be left alone to get on with their business activities without the over-intrusion of the law.

But this did not mean that New Labour was content to unshackle employers to enjoy an undisputed unilateral power over those who worked for them. Blair also presided over what amounted to an unac-knowledged workplace revolution through a massive growth in the pro-vision of individual employee rights. Some of the measures that were introduced were based on legally enforceable directives emanating from the European Commission, but many others were not. A few owed their existence to American good human resource management practices. Others reflected Blair's view of the individualised world of paid work. It was said that much of his family-friendly workplace agenda of maternity

Table 11.1. Rights through regulated labour markets

- Qualifying period for unfair dismissal reduced from two to one year's employment tenure.
- Unfair dismissal compensation raised and index-linked.
- Outlawing of waiver clauses for unfair dismissal rights in fixed-term employment contracts.
- Rights to be accompanied by a trade union official, or anybody else, in disciplinary and grievance hearings before the employer.
- Part-time workers to have equal rights to full-time workers.
- Individual contracts for employees who want to opt out of a collective agreement.
- Extension of maternity leave rights from fourteen to twenty-six weeks' leave from the day the woman starts work, but also entitled to a further twenty-six weeks' leave.
- A right to extend unpaid maternity leave and unpaid parental leave after one year's service with an employer.
- The right to return to one's job or a suitable alternative after maternity leave.
- The right not to be treated unfavourably on return to work after maternity leave, nor to be dismissed or selected for redundancy for any reason connected with pregnancy or maternity.
- The right for up to twenty-six weeks off work for adoption leave, with a possible further twenty-six weeks.
- The right for parents to request flexible working from an employer to consider, but no automatic right to such arrangements.
- A right to 'reasonable' unpaid time off work in such cases as domestic incidents such as deaths and accidents within the family or involving dependants and friends.
- Annual paid leave for four weeks.
- Exclusion of public holidays from the length of holiday entitlement.
- Restrictions on night working to eight hours.
- Minimum daily and weekly rest periods at work.
- Measures to strengthen protections for workers under the age of eighteen.
- Right not to be discriminated against at work on grounds of gender, age, race, disablement, sexual orientation or working part-time.

Trade union rights
- Automatic trade union recognition where over 50% of the relevant workforce is in union membership.
- Trade union recognition by ballot where a majority of the relevant employees or at least 40% of the workforce vote 'yes'.
- Protection for workers from victimisation by the employer when campaigning for union recognition.

Table 11.1. (*cont.*)

- Discrimination by omission or blacklisting on grounds of trade union membership, non-membership and other activities made unlawful.
- Employers cannot recognise a non-independent ('sweetheart') union to bypass the legislation.
- Where recognition exists, the union must be consulted on training.
- Removal of the requirement to name union members in notices of industrial action.
- Dismissal of strikers taking part in lawfully organised disputes is automatically unfair for twelve weeks, and only fair thereafter if the employer is deemed to take reasonable procedural steps to try and resolve the dispute.

A more detailed coverage can be found in the TUC's *Your Rights at Work* (London: TUC, 2004), and P. Davies and M. Freeland, *Towards a Flexible Labour Market* (Oxford: Oxford University Press, 2007).

and paternity leave owed much to pressure from his wife Cherie. Cridland admitted that the dramatic growth in worker rights was to cause his own organisation some difficulties. Employers found it was relatively easy to remain united in resistance to familiar trade union collectivist demands, and to press Blair with considerable success in ensuring employer interests were looked after through the dilution, delay or even abandonment of much of what trade unions wanted. Downing Street was always willing to listen and act over business complaints about the trade union agenda. But such an approach was far less possible when it came to resistance to the creation of individual employee rights, especially when Blair argued that all he was doing was trying to help promote the emergence of civilised workplaces that would help to improve productivity and corporate performance through a strategy of economic efficiency and social justice, but framed on business terms.

For their part, many trade unions were often either hostile or ambivalent in their reaction to the individual rights agenda. Ideally they would have preferred measures that were limited only to trade union members. Now all employees would be covered by a framework of individual rights.

The real beneficiaries of Blair's individualistic workplace agenda were women, either in employment or seeking a paid job. Many of the minimum rights sought to improve their work/life balance in the face of increasing workplace stress and the feminisation of the labour force. By continental European standards the new rights may have looked limited and inadequate. But at least they seemed to recognise at last the persistence of workplace gender inequalities made worse by the growth of the female labour force and the inadequacy of earlier equal pay and gender discrimination laws, as well as the insatiable demands of companies that were unmet by the traditional nine-to-five working time arrangements and the need for part-time employees. The new emphasis on employment flexibility ensured there would be a much greater focus on women and their needs at work.

Weaknesses of the hybrid model

Blair's determination to introduce labour market and employment relations reforms in order to help capital maximise its potential was not entirely consistent. Despite his well-meaning rhetoric as Prime Minister, he surprisingly failed to devote much of his time to resolving the country's familiar intractable long-term supply-side problems, whose tangled roots lay deep in its economic history. The most serious lack of significant progress could be seen in failing to raise the quality of the workforce at the lower end of the labour market. A succession of authoritative international reports between 2000 and 2007 revealed the extent of the UK's relatively poor skills performance during the Blair years. Among advanced industrialised nations the country suffered from a particularly chronic lack of workers equipped with recognisable and adaptable intermediate qualifications. In 2006 it was still estimated that as many as a third of all adults of working age lacked any recognised skills at all, or were at best low-skilled. This was a much higher proportion than could be found in competitor countries such as France and Germany, which were often the object of the Prime Minister's scathing criticism for their supposed labour market deficiencies. The Blair record on skills and training was depressingly similar to that of his predecessors. The apparent lack of any urgent official concern for the plight of the country's millions of poorly qualified or unqualified workers remained a puzzle, especially as Blair appeared to recognise that the country's long-term prosperity lay through the creation of a more highly skilled, highly motivated labour force. A review commissioned by the government from Lord Leitch, and published at the end of 2006, urgently emphasised that the government needed to give a much greater priority to carrying through radical reforms if it wanted the UK to compete successfully in the global economy. It seemed New Labour's creation of the Learning and Skills Councils, as well as the Regional Development Agencies, had made little significant impact on the problem. The Train to Gain programme, the newly formed Centres for Vocational Excellence and government-funded employer training schemes were further attempts to deal with skill weaknesses. But by the end of his premiership this was an area where Blair could not point to much tangible advance. Hopes were pinned on the restoration of apprenticeships as well as a national training programme for employers to be launched in 2007, under which the government offered to subsidise courses for their existing employees to be up-skilled. But this seemed too little, too late. Leitch argued that despite the substantial promise of more investment and reform the UK could only expect to run to stand still by 2020 in the skills of its labour force.

Many of Blair's own advisers admitted the skills and training issue did not receive the government attention that it deserved. Lord Layard suggested it was Blair's 'greatest failure' in his labour market strategy.[10] But as an official report pointed out in 2004, 'Unless the UK has a requisite stock of skills, including entrepreneurship, innovation, managerial effectiveness and technical capability then the goal of achieving a high value added high productivity economy will remain elusive. The extent of the skills gap far exceeds recruitment problems.'[11] The long tail of poorly motivated and under-qualified workers, as well as inefficient and poorly managed private sector companies, continued to place a serious question-mark over the country's longer-term ability to secure a competitive advantage in globalising markets. Moreover the skills failure was closely related to other familiar weaknesses. As the 2004 government skills audit pointed out, 'Skills strategies go hand in hand with policies and strategies to increase levels of capital investment within companies, develop new products and processes and capture new markets.'

International comparisons did not suggest private companies were allocating sufficient of their financial resources to research and development investment. 'In recent years the aggregate amount of spending on research and development in the UK has lagged behind that of our international competitors', complained a 2004 study from the government's own Office of National Statistics. It spoke of a 'comparative lack of entrepreneurial spirit' among Britain's employers compared with the United States, and the poor quality of much of its management.[12] In 1999 the United States invested 25% more capital per hour worked than in this

---

[10] Author's interview with Lord Richard Layard, April 2007.

[11] Department of Education and Skills, *Skills Audit* (London: TSO, 2004).

[12] Craig Lindsay, *Labour Productivity, Labour Market Trends* (London: Office of National Statistics, November 2004), p. 47.

country, while France invested 60% more and Germany 32% more. In 2005 the pre-budget statement revealed that British business invested 1.24% of gross domestic product in research and development but this compared with 1.37% in France, 1.73% in Germany and 1.87% in the United States. The Treasury was compelled to admit that Britain 'was less effective at realising the commercial potential of research and business expenditure and its current aggregate level was below the average of OECD countries'. Nor was the UK impressive in its growth in innovation. In 2000 innovation companies in the country represented 62% of turnover and 54% of total employment. 'In most other European economies the shares were significantly higher', wrote Ian Brinkley at the Work Foundation.[13]

The country was rescued from such inadequacy with the dramatic growth of inward migration by mainly young workers with adaptable skills and drive from central and eastern Europe after their countries entered the European Union as full members in January 2004. In addition, British employers in both the public and private sectors were compelled to travel through the developing world in search of people who were willing to come and work in Britain in the health service and other professions. Cherry-picking expeditions at the expense of the poorest in the world were able to cover over some of the inadequacies of the country's indigenous labour force.

But Britain's continuing supply-side problems helped to explain why it still achieved relatively low levels of comparative labour productivity during the Blair years. In an April 2005 assessment the National Institute for Economic and Social Research (NIESR) concluded that there had been 'no obvious improvement' in UK productivity performance since 1997. It is true that the country was no longer falling behind France and other competitor European nations in the way it had done for the forty years after the end of the Second World War, but the NIESR noted that it was 'not obviously closing the gap with France and we have stopped closing the gap with the United States'.[14] Official figures for 2005 showed little productivity improvement either. Measured by gross domestic product per worker, the UK figure was still 26% below that of the United States and 10% less than France. The picture was little better when productivity performance was measured by gross domestic product per hour

[13] Ian Brinkley, *Defining the Information Economy* (London: Work Foundation, July 2006).
[14] National Institute for Economic and Social Research, in *National Institute Economic Review*, no. 192, April 2005.

worked. Germany, France and the United States continued to be ahead of the UK in that measurement.[15]

While the UK appeared to develop strongly as an information economy under Blair, it did not look so impressive by international comparison. In 1994 the UK invested 3.5% of its gross domestic product in knowledge activities, but by 2002 this had risen to 3.7%, only a modest 0.2% improvement over the period. The Organisation for Economic Co-operation and Development did not even classify the country as a high-investment economy. That term was used to cover Sweden, the United States, Finland, South Korea, Denmark, Japan and Canada.

A further profound weakness that persisted in the UK labour market under Blair was the existence of intractable social inequalities. The country's workforce came to represent an hourglass, with a small number of highly skilled winners at the top and a huge proportion at the bottom. A devastating report, *The Cost of Exclusion*, published by the LSE's Centre for Economic Performance for the Prince's Trust in April 2007, estimated that as many as 20% of the young aged sixteen to twenty-four in 2005 – nearly a million – were not in education, training or employment, with a calculated loss to the economy of £10 million a day. It reported that this finding showed there had been 'little change since the mid 1990s' when Blair became Prime Minister.[16] Clearly the UK had still a long way to go before it could claim success in the reconciliation of economic efficiency with social justice in a modern economy.

Back to the future? The hybrid model in perspective

Under Blair a new ill-defined hybrid market model began to emerge in the UK which was exemplified in his policies towards capital and labour. Whether the resulting mixed achievement – admired by right-wing European politicians such as French President Nicolas Sarkozy, Italy's Silvio Berlusconi and Spain's José Maria Aznar – could be copied by other countries as an effective response to globalisation elsewhere was highly debatable. Certainly evidence of any countervailing influence in the creation of an alternative political economy model was hard to find in the UK by 2007.

A century earlier, in what came to be known as the progressive era in the years leading up to the outbreak of the First World War in August

---

[15] Office of National Statistics, press release, 21 February 2007.
[16] LSE Centre for Economic Performance, *The Cost of Exclusion* (London: LSE, April 2007).

1914, the British Labour movement – among others – had sought to create a new and better world for all, but especially the manual working class. This had involved demanding the creation of regulated labour markets through the actions of an increasingly paternalistic state to protect the poor, old and vulnerable, and to eliminate the curses of poverty and unemployment. The social policy agenda was coupled with the emergence of trade unions which aimed to improve the material needs of their members through the voluntarist system of industrial relations based on autonomous trade union bargaining with employers, and the negotiation of non-legally binding collective agreements and joint consultation. Now it seemed that the New Labour project under Blair/Brown had made Britain safe for the triumph of global capitalism through rebalancing the relations between capital and labour. This was quite an achievement. Whether the results would turn out to prove stable, permanent or morally defensible was, however, quite another matter. Blair and Brown had moved Britain dramatically with the grain of market forces as they consolidated and advanced Margaret Thatcher's inheritance. They did not seriously seek to challenge any vested corporate interests outside the trade unions. Under them Labour abandoned any pretence that its purpose was the creation of a more socially equitable society rooted in the pursuit of left-wing values such as equality, liberty and fraternity. In 2007 it was to be the forces of capital and not labour in Britain who could now proclaim with a sense of triumph, 'We are the masters now.'

But the Blair effect on labour markets and employment relations was to prove more transformational than even this might suggest. During his years as Prime Minister the Labour movement virtually ceased to exist as a recognisable entity. Its institutions ossified and its social base collapsed, partly due to the continuing decline of a skilled manual working class that had provided so much of Labour's organisational and moral strength in the workplaces and in civil society during much of the last century. Rapid occupational changes in society were mainly responsible for this profound transformation, which had gathered pace after the 1970s. It was not due to the deliberate actions of Blair or anybody else in political life. But perhaps he more than most of his contemporaries sensed intuitively what was going on and responded to it by seeking to reflect the consequences of the new realities within his political project. There was more than spin and hype to this phenomenon. Blair demonstrated why the UK was unable to transform itself into a genuinely social democratic country like those in northern Europe. The individualism of the country's industrial relations and employment system reflected what were always deep and stubborn social forces that went back to the nineteenth century and industrialisation. From Ramsay MacDonald to John Smith, the Labour Party claimed that an important part of its moral purpose was to transform Britain into a classless society and to replace, or at least modify, the workings of the market economy through the creation of an economic model that was based on social justice and equity rather than profit and competition. But even in the aftermath of the Second World War, when T. H. Marshall's concept of social citizenship was widely recognised by the political class, most people seemed more concerned for their own well-being within their own private family networks and the wider civil society. Most regarded paid work as an instrumental means needed for the pursuit of a better life and were deeply sceptical, even hostile, to the role of an intrusive centralising state, however well-meaning it might be in theory. The reports of the Mass Observation surveys suggest this popular attitude was even prevalent in the age of Attlee in the 1940s.[17] The hegemony of collectivist values that underpinned successful social democracy in Nordic Europe was never to be achieved in Britain. Blair and his New Labour project recognised that to win and retain political power the Labour Party needed to capture southern England, the world of the comfortable and respectable suburbs, the new industries and the aspirational consumers of an increasingly affluent post-industrial society. New Labour's purpose was to ensure its association with those realities where capital had to be accommodated and collective labour made subordinate to the project's grand narrative. In his 2007 Manchester lecture Blair spelt out with clarity and conviction what his labour market and employment relations strategy had always been concerned to do – make the country's workers and its employers fit for purpose in an increasingly fragile and unpredictable world of globalisation, full of opportunities but also dangers. Blair turned out to be Britain's first postmodernist Prime Minister, as his attitude to capital and labour was to illustrate. It should have come as no surprise that the results were less than clear-cut, ambivalent and often disappointing. The onward march of the Labour movement had long gone into disorderly retreat and even rout. The institutions that its Labour socialist ideology had inspired all but disappeared after the 1970s. Britain was returning to the values that in part reflected an acquisitive worker individualism, which had

[17] For a brilliant exposition of this theme see David Kynaston, *Austerity Britain* (London: Bloomsbury, 2007).

emerged and been shaped in a much earlier period of its history. Blair liked to pride himself on being young and modern. In truth, he came to reflect in politics a British past that had once existed before the onset of twentieth-century collectivism and whose underlying individualistic attitudes of mind had not really gone away.

Acknowledgements

I would like to thank Geoff Norris from the Number 10 Policy Unit; John Cridland from the Confederation of British Industry; John Monks, general secretary of the European Trade Union Confederation; Brendan Barber, general secretary of the Trades Union Congress; David Coats from the Work Foundation; and Alastair Hatchett of Incomes Data Services for their help in writing this chapter. The outcome is entirely my own responsibility.

12

Transport

STEPHEN GLAISTER

Transport was not one of Tony Blair's successes. This is illustrated by the *Brief* he issued in May 2007 to the Parliamentary Labour Party, plainly intended to trumpet achievements in over his ten years. There are twenty-two pages in standard format and 'Transport' is shorter than all the others save 'Arts' and 'Africa'.

The biggest single failure of transport policy was nicely summed up by Blair himself on 1 March 2007. He had invited Richard Hammond of TV's *Top Gear* fame into No. 10 to give an interview about road pricing which was published verbatim and as a podcast on the official website[1] with the populist heading '"Hamster" tackles PM on road pricing'. During the course of this he said:

> I can see a huge problem looming up ahead . . . the amazing thing is that
> there are 6 million more cars on the road since we came to office, almost 7
> million actually from 26 million to 33 million I think it was, someone was
> telling me, and over the next 20 years there are going to be I don't know
> how many millions more.

Although this problem was obvious to many commentators ten years earlier, Blair did not see it then. He showed little interest in transport and delegated the topic to John Prescott, Deputy Prime Minister and then Secretary of State for the Department for Environment and Transport. On 6 June 1997 *The Guardian* reported that Prescott had said in a public speech, 'I will have failed if in five years' time there are not . . . far fewer journeys by car. It's a tall order but I urge you to hold me to it.'[2] A 'tall order' indeed, and one to which Blair and his government proved unwilling, or unable, to devote sufficient analysis or resources.

---

[1] www.number10.gov.uk/output/page11123.asp.
[2] Although there were subsequent claims that Prescott had not said this, he confirmed the essence of the remark in a House of Commons debate, 20 October 1998.

After the radical reforms by privatisation and deregulation of most of the transport industry under the Tory regimes the ideology had seemed straightforward to many supporters: to 'integrate', to replace new road building with rejuvenated public transport and to re-establish the role of the public sector.

But Blair initially underestimated the complexities. He delegated transport to people who did not deliver. As a result, until 2000 transport policy as implemented amounted to a continuation of Tory policies. Throughout his premiership, in so far as there was any positive control, it remained with the Chancellor and the Treasury who continued to determine crucial tax rates, rigidly constrained funds for transport operating and capital purposes, fixed the rules for local authority borrowing, promoted private provision and private finance, laid down criteria for value for money and fought for what they saw as essential national transport policy.

Blair was drawn into transport when things went badly wrong: the fuel price protests in 2000, the unresolved dispute over London Underground PPP during the 2001 general election, the collapse of Railtrack in 2001, the resignation of Stephen Byers in 2002, when one of his own 'e-petitions' on road pricing embarrassed the government, and when his wife was caught in a traffic jam. As he came to the end of his final term it was unclear who was in control of transport policy.

The importance of transport to the electorate

It took the whole of the first Blair parliament for Labour to respond to the fact that the transport interests of the electorate had been transformed over the previous three decades. Car ownership is now common. This has been the result of increasing real incomes, demographic changes and the generally falling real costs of motoring, and these trends will continue. Meanwhile public transport has become much less relevant, with the exception of some special markets such as the commute into London. Nationally, the car now accounts for 85% of all passenger kilometres (excluding walking).[3] Half the population uses a train less than once a year,[4] bus and rail each account for 6% (much less outside the London area). Rail now carries 8% of freight tonne-kilometres.

[3] Department for Transport, *Transport Statistics Great Britain*, 2006 edn (London: TSO, 2007).
[4] Strategic Rail Authority, *Everyone's Railway: The Wider Case for Rail* (London: Strategic Rail Authority, 2003).

In spite of the attention the national press gives to public transport, opinion surveys consistently show it to be surprisingly unimportant to voters. A MORI/*Evening Standard* poll ahead of the 2005 general election[5] found that healthcare (67%) and education (61%) were the leading issues in helping respondents decide which party to vote for, while public transport (26% nationally and 40% in London) was tenth. But a YouGov poll in 2007 reported that 43% thought that traffic congestion was serious on the roads near where they lived.[6] In material appearing under his own name Blair was aware of the importance of catering for motorists. But in 1997 there was little evidence to suggest that he suspected how awkward transport could become.

The 1998 Transport White Paper

In 1997 Blair delegated the day-to-day business of transport, environment, land use planning and local government to his deputy, John Prescott, and created an 'integrated', sprawling and ultimately unmanageable department for him: the Department of the Environment, Transport and the Regions (DETR). Prescott proceeded to issue a consultation paper in the summer of 1997 and, a year later, a major Transport White Paper.[7] Prescott's sentiment, illustrated in his foreword, caused concern in No. 10 in case it could be perceived as being 'anti-car':

> we needed to improve public transport and reduce dependence on the car . . . Better public transport will encourage more people to use it . . . The priority will be maintaining existing roads rather than building new ones and better management of the road network to improve reliability . . . persuading people to use their cars a little less – and public transport a little more.

The 1998 Transport White Paper was a large and glossy document but it was generally considered to have failed to resolve many issues – it was memorably dubbed 'Carry on Consulting'. It was hopelessly unrealistic in its aspirations to substitute bus and rail for the car. It presaged a major review of the national roads programme, as a result of which many schemes were withdrawn. The unintended but inevitable consequence was that road congestion would get steadily worse. The White Paper did

[5] Joe Murphy, 'Voters Care Most about Health', *Evening Standard*, 14 April 2005.
[6] *Daily Telegraph*, 26 February 2007.
[7] Department of the Environment, Transport and the Regions, *A New Deal for Transport: Better for Everyone*, Cm. 3950 (London: TSO, 1998).

have the virtue of having a consistent approach on environmental policy, the core of which was the commitment to continue a 6% per annum increase in the duty on road fuels above inflation (a policy inherited, at 5% per annum, from the Conservative government). This was enough to slow traffic growth – though not enough to reverse it. However, the 'fuel duty escalator' contained the seeds of the first transport policy catastrophe for the Blair government. This only became apparent after the July 2000 publication of Prescott's Ten-Year Transport Plan.

The 2000 Ten-Year Transport Plan

The Ten-Year Transport Plan[8] was an important attempt to recognise the long horizons involved, and Prescott was able to make the remarkable claim that he had a ten-year agreement with the Treasury on the funding for the plan. Its main features were an increase in resources for local authority transport purposes and a major shift of emphasis towards both public and hoped-for private investment in railways. There was a modest increase in budgets for investment in strategic roads which returned the levels to what they had been in the mid-1990s, before the Conservatives had cut spending, thus already marking a policy reversal on roads.

More rigorous analysis was attempted in support of the Ten-Year Plan[9] than predecessor documents with the result that the reality of the need to cater for inevitable traffic growth was recognised explicitly. This may have been due to the influence of Lord (Gus) Macdonald who had been appointed by Blair as Transport Minister with responsibility for delivering the plan.

The plan was a good concept and a good document, with proper supporting analysis. It had flaws, such as an imbalance of investment in favour of railways and against buses and roads, an unrealistic view of the capacity of the railway to carry enormously increased traffic – especially whilst it was being rebuilt – and its provision for new road capacity was still inadequate. However, these things could have been adjusted if, as had been intended, the plan had been revised every year or so as it was rolled forward.

[8] Department of the Environment, Transport and the Regions, *Transport 2010* (London: TSO, July 2000).
[9] Department of the Environment, Transport and the Regions, *Transport 2010. The Background Analysis* (London: TSO, 2000). Not surprisingly, given the novelty of the exercise, the results were mixed.

The fuel price crisis

But almost immediately things went seriously wrong. Civil protest broke out in the autumn of 2000: a rise in the world oil price, a lead given by lorry drivers in France, and the fuel duty escalator combined to cause the public to rebel. Lorry drivers obstructed access to fuel supply depots. The country suddenly came to a frightening halt. There was talk of food stocks running out within days. Fuel for buses, trains and lorries (essential to food supply) had already become scarce. There could not have been a clearer demonstration that outside London the country now depends on roads, not railways. This was a major national crisis demanding the immediate attention of the Prime Minister.

As Seldon observes, 'Taking control of events at home, such as during the fuel crisis in 2000 and the foot and mouth crisis in 2001, confirmed Blair's belief that he alone, assisted by his close team in Number 10, could solve any problem.'[10] One part of the solution was that the Chancellor was persuaded to abandon the fuel duty escalator. Amazingly, the Chancellor claimed on national radio that this change in policy would have no effect on long-term traffic growth – contrary to all the objective evidence. At a stroke this change destroyed such coherence as transport and environment policy had had.

The fuel price crisis further alerted the Prime Minister to the electoral consequences of neglecting the vast majority of transport users. Blair's 'Foreword' in the 2001 election manifesto makes no mention of environment or transport. But in the main document transport comes before health and education, under *The Productivity Challenge*:

> Labour's priority is to improve and expand railway and road travel. Our ten-year Transport Plan – offers real hope to motorists and passengers alike . . . Supertrams will transform transport in our big cities, with 25 new light rail or tram schemes . . . Motorways will be upgraded: a hundred new bypasses will reduce accidents and pollution. But environmentally damaging road schemes have been scrapped.

So there was a new balance, including prospects for further new road capacity. 'Integrated transport', an eternal cliché which was pervasive in the 1998 policy was demoted in this manifesto to the insipid 'Good transport systems offer choices across transport modes. Transport Direct – a phone and Internet system designed to plan journeys and sell tickets – will put transport services at people's finger tips.'

[10] Anthony Seldon, *Blair*, 2nd edn (London: The Free Press, 2005), p. 694.

Blair's experience with the fuel price protests was to have important ramifications for his handling of road pricing in his last few months.

The withdrawal of Prescott from transport policy and the death of the Ten-Year Plan

Seldon noted that 'Number 10 became concerned about Prescott's agenda, and was especially worried about the perception that it was anti-car, with damaging electoral consequences . . . Blair . . . worried Prescott was becoming an "unguided missile" in his huge department.'[11] The change in tone between the 1998 Transport White Paper – Prescott's document – and the Ten-Year Plan signalled a more active interest from No. 10 and the end of Prescott's reign in transport policy.

Transport officials had recognised that the plan would need to be revised and set up a continuing programme of work. Apart from faults in the plan itself, 'events' quickly made revision urgent. These included the fall-out from the fuel price crisis, from the collapse of Railtrack (see below) and a steep increase in the cost of the railways.

Much work was done by officials, and the publication of revisions to the plan was eagerly anticipated. But no revision was ever published. The plan withered after 2001 with the appointment of Stephen Byers as Secretary of State for Transport, one of several 'favoured (and non-Brownite) ministers – perhaps the most conspicuously unsatisfactory of all [Blair's] favoured ministers: his antipathy to his civil servants and his obsession with style over substance epitomised New Labour at its worst'.[12] This was well illustrated by Byers' attitude to the Ten-Year Plan. It is said that when, on his arrival, the civil service offered him a briefing on the plan he declined, dismissing it as a creation of a previous government.

So a major attempt to create a long-term transport policy and to secure 'buy-in' from the Treasury was undermined by the disinterest of the new 'Blairite' Secretary of State.

Indecision: the railways

Railways policy under Blair has proved to be indecisive, ineffective and very expensive. The costly debacle on the London Underground (see below) came about because of a vague policy delegated to Prescott and

[11] *Ibid.*, p. 416.   [12] *Ibid.*, pp. 416, 633.

hijacked by the Treasury. The failure on the national railways came about because of a disputed decision by Blair to do nothing. In opposition the party had a clear policy: 'a Labour government will make good its commitment to a publicly owned and publicly accountable railway'.[13] But Blair decided not to change the ownership or governance of the railway. This was consistent with the 1997 manifesto to keep it 'as we find it, not as we wish it to be'. So nothing much happened, although there was a propensity to draw attention to failings and for John Prescott to promise 'action', including (unrealistically) 'renegotiation' of the train operating contracts. The rapid growth in patronage which had started in 1994 continued.

Perceived failings in the structure of the railways did lead the government to announce an intention to create a new Strategic Rail Authority (SRA) in the 1998 White Paper.[14] Reform of the railways may have been close to John Prescott's heart, but it manifestly did not catch the Prime Minister's attention: the legislation proved to have great difficulty in finding parliamentary time. It took two and a half years to reach the statute book in the Transport Act 2000.

Of all the traumas experienced by the UK rail privatisation, the failure of Railtrack in autumn 2001 attracted by far the greatest public attention, although the privatised railway would have run into difficulty in any case because of the severe financial problems experienced by the train-operating companies (TOCs), unrealistic aspirations and inadequate funding to meet them.[15]

There were two major rail accidents, one in 1997 at Southall in which seven people were killed, and one in 1999 at Ladbroke Grove in which thirty-one people were killed. The extent to which privatisation may have been a factor remains controversial, but the general public laid the blame at the door of 'Tory privatisation'. In this they were encouraged by John Prescott who started the criticisms on a visit to the Southall accident site and initiated public inquiries rather than the normal ones by the Railway Inspectorate. Members of the government promised that they would discipline Railtrack, to force it to become absolutely safe whatever the cost (even though the relevant powers were vested in the independent

---

[13] Clare Short for the Opposition in SBC Warburg, *Railtrack Share Offer, Prospectus*, 1996.

[14] Christopher Foster, *British Government in Crisis* (Oxford: Hart Publishing, 2005), gives an important account of the deficiencies in policy and legislation concerning the Railways Act 1993 and privatisation in 1996.

[15] See Stephen Glaister, *British Rail Privatisation – Competition Destroyed by Politics*, Occasional Paper 23 (Bath: Centre for Regulated Industries, 2005).

Rail Regulator and the independent safety regulators). Railtrack was particularly heavily criticised in the press after the Ladbroke Grove accident.

That was a crucial turning point: with sufficient leadership government could wisely have taken the line that this was now a private industry and it was a matter for the independent safety and economic regulators to sort out. This kind of approach was illustrated by Transport Secretary Douglas Alexander in his simple factual reporting to the House of Commons on the fatal Grayrigg (Cumbria) derailment in February 2007.[16] There was no commentary and the matter was quickly forgotten. The very public intervention by ministers after Ladbroke Grove greatly heightened the general public's perception – contradicted by the evidence – that privatisation had made the railways less safe.[17]

These factors became critical after another accident, at Hatfield in October 2000, caused by the failure of a decaying rail. Four people were killed. The rail in question had exhibited symptomatic cracks before failure. Because of their Ladbroke Grove experience Railtrack feared the response from the press and from government. Consequently, after Hatfield, Railtrack all but closed the system. This destroyed the train service and with it their own business and the businesses of the train operators.

At about the same time it emerged that Railtrack had mismanaged the major procurement for the refurbishment and upgrading of the West Coast Main Line – a failure by a private company that has not often been remarked on by New Labour, so keen to allege that the private sector is more efficient than the public sector. Railtrack appealed direct to the Treasury for several billion pounds to rescue it. The Treasury started to make new grants – thus protecting Railtrack shareholders and lenders from the consequences of their board's errors.

Then, in October 2001, Stephen Byers invoked the provisions of the Railways Act 1993 to put Railtrack into Railway Administration. He appeared determined to take an opportunity to destroy the privatised shareholder-ownership structure. Although there are allegations that this move had been planned for some months, neither Byers, Brown nor Blair had thought through what new arrangements for ownership and control might look like. It was an option to encourage a conventional corporate

---

[16] House of Commons, 26 February 2007.
[17] See Andrew A. Evans, 'Rail Safety and Rail Privatisation', *Significance*, 4(1), March 2007: 15–18.

takeover of Railtrack and there were companies that showed an interest. That would have kept the structure intact and avoided the damaging hiatus that occurred.

If the Labour Party had seen this as a move to renationalise the railways, it was to be quickly disappointed. The Treasury was unwilling to find the funds necessary to buy out surviving private interests. In addition Railtrack had considerable and rapidly increasing debt – approaching £20 billion at the time of Blair's resignation – which had been classified by the Office of National Statistics as private debt, in spite of a formal financial indemnity provided by government, on the grounds that the company was under private, not public, control. The Chancellor was absolutely unwilling to countenance any move that would bring that debt onto the public balance sheet.

Railtrack lingered in administration for about a year, at considerable cost. Then government replaced it by Network Rail, a company limited by guarantee. This is run by an executive accountable to about 120 'members', many chosen to represent public or private interests including train operators, railway employees and passengers. It was described as 'not for profit', thus appearing to deal with the objection to the earning of profit in a public utility – although 'not for dividend' would have been less misleading. The company would be entirely financed by debt, supposed to be serviced out of profits.

There is considerable confusion about the governance of Network Rail: 'who is it accountable to and for what?' Indeed, in order to satisfy the crucial test that allows the debt to continue to be classified as private, off the public balance sheet, it is necessary that the public sector *not* be in control of the company – and yet government is guaranteeing the debt. Arguably, the restructuring of Railtrack into Network Rail changed little beyond obfuscating lines of accountability. The Parliamentary Transport Select Committee described it as a 'fudge'.[18]

The government was evidently dissatisfied with the new structure it had created – not least because the Treasury was surprised by the size of the liability they were faced with after the independent Rail Regulator's Extraordinary Review published in December 2003. Alistair Darling, appointed Sectary of State in May 2002 on the resignation of Byers, instigated another policy review. He explicitly and publicly recognised that, so long as anything like the current structure of the railway survives, his

---

[18] House of Commons Transport Select Committee, *The Future of the Railway*, HC145 (London: TSO, 2004), para. 13.

predecessor's attempts to weaken the position of the independent Rail Regulator had been unwise.

In July 2004 the outcome was published as a White Paper, *The Future of Rail*. The one major change proposed was that the Strategic Rail Authority would be abolished and its functions transferred to the Department for Transport. It is deeply ironic that this reversed the only change that Labour made during the whole of its seven years in power. The Railways Act 2005 divides the functions of the SRA between Network Rail and the Department for Transport. Crucially, the Conservatives had deliberately put the rail industry beyond the direct control of government, on the grounds that experience had shown that government interference had been damaging to the successful running of rail businesses. Now, for the first time in history, high-level policy is the direct responsibility of a Whitehall spending department. By 2007 civil servants were specifying and procuring new trains.

As Blair left office new procedures were being implemented under the 2005 Act, beginning the attempt to address the new problems presented by this slide from a system driven by commercial incentives to one that amounts to a mammoth task of government administration. By July 2007 the Secretary of State for Transport and Scottish ministers were required to publish a High-Level Output Statement (HLOS) and a Statement of Funds Available (SoFA). In principle this should remedy a problem that has bedevilled railways policy since the 1920s – that governments have been unwilling to discuss explicitly what they want and how much they are prepared to spend. Although it is not the place of the Office of Rail Regulation (ORR) to comment on the HLOS and SoFA, it will adjudicate on whether the money on offer is adequate to fulfil the expectations and, if necessary, negotiate a reconciliation.

This process had to mesh in some Byzantine way with two other related exercises. The ORR had started the normal process of consultation for the October 2008 Periodic Review of Network Rail's charges for the Control Period from 2009. And government as a whole was deeply emerged in the overall Spending Review 2007.

At the highest level of national policy Blair left the railways in a strangely ambiguous position. There was almost no money in current budgets for capacity enhancements – as distinct from maintenance and renewals. The government was in the throes of a particularly 'difficult' spending review, with pressures on overall spending opposing politically powerful demands from the health, education and defence sectors, so it seemed unlikely that the HLOS and SoFA process would produce new state funds for the railway.

In an interesting new development in governance, on 10 May 2006 the Prime Minister wrote a public letter to the incoming Secretary of State for Transport[19] setting out what was required of him. Once the platitudes have been discarded the letter is quite short and pithy. It contains a good diagnosis of the reasons for the anticipated growth in demand for roads and railways. But crucially this short letter has *two* separate mentions of the current constraints on public expenditure. There was an important steer here that the Secretary of State should not expect to be able to solve his problems with large quantities of new Treasury resources.

In any case, the railway was already costing the taxpayer over £4.5 billion per annum, relatively few people outside London use the railways, and it is hard to point to objective, quantitative evidence in justification. It is hard to relate railway subsidy to delivery against stated or implicit government policy objectives – such as assistance to the disadvantaged or reduction of greenhouse gas emissions where rail loadings are low.

Blair v. Brown; devolution v. centralisation.
The PPP for the London Underground

The story of the Underground Public Private Partnership (PPP) illustrates several aspects of Blair's administrations: the consequences of delegating without a coherent overall policy; the consequence of blind reliance on advice from management consultants, lawyers and business people if they are imperfectly briefed on the subtleties of public policy; the consequences of allowing policy to develop which is not supported by the evidence; the dominance of Blair, and particularly Brown, over Prescott; and a philosophical disagreement between Blair and Brown over the wisdom and feasibility of the devolution of powers to local authorities.

The PPP for the London Underground deserves attention in its own right because of its size. It is far bigger than any other PFI or PPP deal. At the time it was conceived it was bigger than all those others put together. Announced in 1998 and completed five years later, the Blair administrations forced it through in the face of several sceptical assessments by the House of Commons Transport Select Committee, one from the Treasury Select Committee, one from the National Audit Office (plus

---

[19] www.pm.gov.uk/output/Page9455.asp.

two post-completion), scepticism at the Standing Committee on the Bill and a steady stream of critical assessments from the serious press and independent commentators.

Back in 1997 there was a wide measure of agreement about the problem to be solved.[20] The London Underground was crowded and unreliable. Between £1,000 million and £2,000 million was needed to make good past failures and to adequately maintain and renew the physical assets. New rail capacity was needed.

It was taken for granted that sorting out the Underground would be delegated to John Prescott. But when he proposed an immediate straight-forward capital grant the Treasury flatly refused. Apart from the limitations due to the policy of sticking to the previous administration's spending plans for two years, the Treasury was determined to secure the same kind of managerial efficiency improvements they perceived as having been achieved under the Conservative administrations by the privatisation of the railways and the other utilities. This left Prescott in an impossible position and, arguably, he never retrieved control of policy on the Underground from the Treasury.

At this point Whitehall as a whole was at a loss to know what to do. The Treasury has steadfastly denied in public that the Chancellor and his ministers ever did anything other than give advice and support to the responsible department. But Geoffrey Robinson, who had been the Treasury's Paymaster General, helpfully revealed in a Commons debate the Treasury's lead in what happened next:

> We could skin a cat in so many ways, and when it came to public–private partnerships – which were quite innovative – there were many different options available. No. 10 had its view; the advisers to No. 10 had their view; the then Department of Transport, Local Government and the Regions had its view; I had a view; the Treasury had a view; and the Deputy Prime Minister had very strong views. We had to find a way that we could all see would carry this forward . . . I convened a group of four business men with experience of both the public and private sectors to make a recommenda-tion to us. Essentially, that recommendation is what we have today.[21]

The *Evening Standard* revealed that Robinson had said later that the busi-nessmen were chosen because they had experience of major privatisa-tions: 'they were, therefore, the very best people to advise the Government

[20] See Stephen Glaister and Tony Travers, *Governing the Underground: Funding, Management and Democracy for London's Tube* (Bath: Centre for Regulated Industries, 1997).
[21] House of Commons debate, 27 June 2002.

on what would work'.[22] They were chaired by Sir Malcolm Bates who had been the author of two reports to the Treasury about how best to develop the Private Finance Initiative. He was appointed chairman of London Regional Transport (LRT) in April 1998 in place of Peter Ford who had articulated LRT's view that the PPP proposal was close to the bottom of a list of fifteen alternative options.

Thus a major policy was developed not by the Prime Minister, not by the Secretary of State for Transport, not by the civil service, not by management consultants but by an ad hoc group of businessmen selected by a Treasury minister and against the considered policy of the board responsible for running the Underground.

Prescott announced the PPP for the Underground to the Commons in March 1998, after refinement by management consultants PricewaterhouseCoopers and the law firm Freshfields. Thirty-year contracts based on three roughly equal-sized groups of lines were to be awarded to the private sector, after a competition, for the repair, maintenance and enhancement of the fixed infrastructure, signalling and trains. Two-thirds of the employees would remain in direct public sector employment to drive the trains and staff the stations.

One embellishment authored by Prescott was an assurance that staff transferring to the private sector would have their terms and conditions protected. This was an important departure from previous privatisations and private finance deals and, arguably, it compromised one of the main sources of cost reduction that the Treasury was so keen to replicate for the Underground.

Gordon Brown and the Treasury have systematically held the line that the PPP was the sole responsibility of Prescott and his successors. But few in Whitehall or in the press saw it that way. Chair of the Transport Select Committee, Gwyneth Dunwoody, gave the following account in the Commons:

> As a Committee, we were worried that most of the arrangements for the bids had been Treasury led, to the point where Treasury officials appeared to be taking precedence over the DETR in the negotiating, and providing individuals who were themselves directly dealing with the applicants for the bids, and yet we were not able to persuade Treasury Ministers to appear before us to discuss the implications. We said very clearly that we thought that that decision undermined the work of Select Committees, simply because the House of Commons does have a responsibility not just to ask awkward questions but to obtain answers.[23]

[22] *Evening Standard*, 28 June 2003.   [23] House of Commons debate, 27 June 2002.

The Treasury refused to be scrutinised, but employees of the consultants did appear before the Select Committee to assist transport officials and ministers in explaining the policy, and on occasion they were put up to explain and justify it at briefings for the press. For instance:

> The Treasury's argument is two-fold. First . . . it does not trust London Underground's public sector management to deliver. But second, it maintains the PFI offers the advantage of transferring to the private sector the risk of maintaining the track, signalling and tunnels. 'Under PPP,' says Tony Poulter of PricewaterhouseCoopers, who is advising the government on the Underground deal, 'it was down to the private sector to sort it out, and they did . . . Bonds may have worked for the New York subway but the British public sector does not have experience of being able to write contracts that successfully deliver what is wanted. Through a PPP, with its long-term transfer of operating and financial risk, it does.'[24]

This illustrates not only that the government was using private consultants to expound and defend government policy, but also that in 1999 it was accepted on all sides that this was in fact a Treasury policy. In 2005 the press and the public remained clear that PFI and PPP policies were Treasury policies. One of many illustrations is Will Hutton's comment: 'Over the past eight years, I have had my differences with Brown . . . The Private Finance Initiative and the London Underground Public Private Partnership, in particular, are too poorly designed to advance the public interest.'[25]

The extent to which the Treasury had become seduced by what the consultants promised the PPP would deliver is apparent in the Chancellor's 1998 Comprehensive Spending Review which mentions 'the new Public–Private Partnership for London Underground (which is expected to remove the need for public subsidy from 2000/01)'.[26] Thus it was anticipated that, magically, the Underground's underinvestment problem would be solved and all need for subsidy for the Underground would be removed! The government has never revealed the analysis underlying this, even in the face of repeated demands from members of the Standing Committee of the Commons dealing with the legislation. On analysis of a six-page sketch issued by PricewaterhouseCoopers it immediately looked too good to be true.[27]

---

[24] *Financial Times*, 27 November 1999.   [25] *The Observer*, 13 March 2005.
[26] HM Treasury, *Modern Public Services for Britain, Investing in Reform* (Comprehensive Spending Review), Cm. 4011 (London: TSO, 1998), para. 8.4.
[27] See Stephen Glaister, Rosemary Scanlon and Tony Travers, *A Fourth Way for the Underground?* (London: Greater London Group, June 1998); and Stephen Glaister, Rosemary

Yet ministers and the Prime Minister took the view that PFI and PPP arrangements enabled delivery of projects which could be delivered in no other way – often seeming to imply that the private sector investor would somehow 'step in' to replace the basic funding that the taxpayer could not, or would not, provide. Thus, Geoffrey Robinson declared: '[PFI] is enabling Government to support a significant number of additional projects beyond what can be provided through the public purse.'[28] And the Prime Minister explicitly put the view that the policy was somehow providing public services that the taxpayer could not afford: 'The reason that we are engaged in this public–private investment partnership is so that the infrastructure work, which is urgently needed in the tube, can be done.'[29] and 'there is no way Government through the general taxpayer can do it all'.[30] This view, that PFI and PPP somehow entice the private sector to provide resources that the taxpayer will not provide, is plainly nonsense. But it has been put forward so often by Labour ministers that one can only assume they believe it, perhaps because they do not understand the fundamental economics behind what are, by any standards, technically complex procurements.

As the details of the implementation of the PPP were worked up a philosophical difference between Blair and Brown began to emerge. The legislation to devolve powers to a directly elected London Mayor and London Assembly were being developed in parallel. Blair's 1997 manifesto had indicated that this was to be genuine and substantive devolution. Yet the Treasury was concerned at the prospect that the new London Mayor and Authority would become profligate. Initially this was independent of the personality of the Mayor. The government's plan was to have the Underground PPP completed before April 2000, at which point the new Mayor would assume his or her powers.

In the event the negotiations for the Underground dragged on until the end of 2002, at which point, in accordance with the Greater London Act 2000, they and their liabilities were summarily imposed upon the Greater London Authority. Whether by design or by accident, the effect of the PPP was to fetter the Mayor's powers over the Underground. Thus the Blair-inspired move towards the devolution of London government conflicted with the Brown-inspired PPP solution for the London Underground. The

Footnote 27 (cont.)
    Scanlon and Tony Travers, *Getting Partnerships Going: Public Private Partnerships in Transport* (London: Institute for Public Policy Research, April 2000).
[28] Speech to a PFI conference, 27 April 1998.
[29] House of Commons debate, 6 February 2002.   [30] Labour Party Conference, 2002.

conflict between this and the fact that the successful candidate for Mayor had been elected on a ticket of explicit opposition to the PPP and with an alternative solution, formed the substance of an unsuccessful judicial review brought by the Mayor in the summer of 2002.

One thing that Blair and Brown did have in common was a difficult relationship with Ken Livingstone who won the first mayoral election in 2000. Having failed to give assurances considered adequate, Livingstone was denied the official Labour candidature and excluded from the party. He promptly stood as an independent and won easily. Blair and Livingstone repaired their relationship, but it remains to be seen how that between Brown and Livingstone develops.

Blair did make a public intervention on the Underground PPP in 1999, in the context of Ken Livingstone's alternative proposals. However, both Blair and Prescott must have been ill-advised on the facts concerning how capital had been successfully raised for some time in US cities:

> Rosemary Scanlon, a visiting research fellow at the London School of Economics and former deputy state comptroller for New York City . . . has written to Mr Blair to express concerns about his comments . . . His statement, in an interview with *The Observer* newspaper, was 'an absolute and utter untruth,' she said. In the letter to the prime minister, she explains that New York City did have a fiscal crisis in 1975. But the Metropolitan Transportation Authority, a State of New York agency, was set up as a public benefit corporation in 1981, and has since then issued more than $14bn (£8.6bn) of bonds. 'The MTA reinvestment programme, and its bond issuance, is without question a major success story in New York.' A Downing Street spokesman later . . . added: 'To saddle the city with an enormous amount of debt is a recipe for disaster.'[31]

The policy was hugely unpopular both within the Commons and outside it. Negotiations were ugly and were obviously going to continue for much longer than had been expected. Ken Livingstone was a popular figure and he had appointed Bob Kiley from New York, one of the world's best, as Transport Commissioner (chief executive of TfL). They had an alternative, tried and tested, proposal for raising capital through the issuance of bonds secured against future revenues and other sources of income; and for procuring service from the private sector through a larger number of much shorter-term contracts, which would be easier to manage and to enforce. Several alternatives were available. The Labour government had rescued the floundering (supposedly privately funded)

[31] *Financial Times*, 23 November 1999.

project to build a fast rail link between London and the Channel Tunnel by guaranteeing over £5 billion of borrowing on the markets – subsequently the rights under this guarantee were in effect exercised and the bond issue method of raising local authority capital became Treasury policy in 2004.

With the 2001 general election approaching, Blair intervened. On 2 February 2001 John Prescott and Bob Kiley reached an agreement under which Kiley would take a lead in achieving the modifications necessary to give TfL and London Underground Limited 'unified management of the Underground' – thus meeting one of Kiley's and Livingstone's core objections to the government's original proposal. Negotiations proceeded throughout February and most of March. The DETR were helpful, and with substantive input from 'Adrian Montague, head of the government's private finance initiative department',[32] and 'Lord Macdonald, a Scots media mogul bizarrely put in charge of London's surface and underground railways',[33] the government made concessions which looked as though they would make a resolution possible.

But Kiley found that the understanding he had reached with Prescott was not respected in subsequent negotiations with government representatives. Agreement was not reached by the end of February 2001 deadline, but the government made a new proposal with a deadline for agreement at the end of March. Again negotiations foundered, essentially because in Kiley's view the government was still not prepared to allow the public sector to retain direct control over maintenance activities or to hold private contractors accountable for the identifiable capital improvements.

After this breakdown London Underground resumed its negotiations on the original PPP proposal, and TfL began to prepare its case for the judicial review, due to be held on 12 June 2001 (but later delayed until 23 July). With a general election due on 7 June 2001, the Prime Minister must have been keen to find a resolution to this unpleasant dispute involving several of his senior ministers. It came on 4 May 2001 with handshakes outside No. 10 and the announcement of a new agreement whereby Kiley would be appointed to the additional position of chair of London Regional Transport, with the purpose of enabling him to 'finalise the PPP contracts for the Underground, making whatever changes within the framework of the PPP are necessary to address concerns previously raised by TfL.'[34] In a DETR press notice John Prescott said 'I am delighted that we have found a way towards unified management control within the

---

[32] *Sunday Times*, 25 March 2001.   [33] Simon Jenkins, *Evening Standard*, 28 March 2003.
[34] Transport for London, press release, 4 May 2001.

framework of the PPP.' The Prime Minister also commented, 'I warmly welcome and endorse this agreement. I've met with Bob Kiley, heard his concerns and have confidence in his ability to deliver a PPP which meets those concerns and ours and will be good for London. He will have the full support of the Government in his efforts.' Thus, apparently, both Blair and Prescott had publicly conceded the crucial 'unified management control' point.

This move was certainly successful in removing the acrimony from the issue for the duration of the general election campaign. But by early July Kiley had informed Blair and the new 'Blairite' Transport Secretary, Stephen Byers, that he had been unable to conclude an agreement with the preferred bidders and recommended that the procurement be abandoned and restarted on a new basis. With the election out of the way, Byers immediately rejected this suggestion and directed that the government's original plans proceed. By 15 July Blair was again defending the original PPP plan 'as the only way to get a "massive investment" into the ailing network'.[35] On the 17th the government summarily replaced Kiley as chairman of the LRT Board, reinstating his predecessor, Sir Malcolm Bates. The Prime Minister's official spokesman made clear that the dismissal of Kiley was a government decision, approved by Tony Blair and not a personal initiative of Stephen Byers'.

Press and parliamentary reaction was hostile, sensing that the Chancellor had never had any real intention of giving way and that Kiley's appointment had been a cynical device. An *Evening Standard* leader said that realities should not prevent 'Londoners from venting their fury on the prime minister and Mr Gordon Brown, the silent killer in the background of this debacle.'[36]

Polly Toynbee laid the blame firmly at Gordon Brown's door:

> Those who are friends of this government are appalled at this feckless squandering of good will. Most London Labour MPs and ministers privately roll their eyes in despair at what is going on in their name – the chancellor's runaway train no one else can stop . . . As I write, calls rain in from Brown's people claiming incredibly that the PPP has nothing to do with the chancellor, nothing at all. It was all John Prescott's baby – as if. Last week they told me it was all Stephen Byers's responsibility, forsooth. The chancellor's fistprint on this one is indelible: his people have done the negotiating, he is the one key player who still refuses to meet Kiley.[37]

[35] *Evening Standard*, 16 July 2001.   [36] *Evening Standard*, 18 July 2001.
[37] *The Guardian*, 20 July 2001.

Kiley and Livingstone repeatedly attempted to persuade the government that in negotiation the deal was becoming even worse value for public money. There were constructive meetings with Blair but none with the Chancellor. Kiley had requested a meeting with Gordon Brown as far back as April 2001, and felt that in a ten-minute meeting they could quickly come to grips with some of the issues. It never happened.

On 5 February 2002 the Transport Select Committee published a strongly argued report that recommended that the government not proceed with the PPP.[38] The arguments were reiterated in a Commons debate led by the formidable chair of the Committee, Gwyneth Dunwoody on 27 June 2002.

Blair did make a personal attempt to understand the issues in detail, to the extent of attempting to read and understand the many thousands of pages of draft commercial contracts. There was a rumour that at a meeting between Blair and Mayor Livingstone, in the spring of 2002, Blair showed surprise and concern about the developing long-term financial liabilities for the government and he asked his aides in No. 10 to listen to both sides of the argument and to report back.

In parliament Transport Secretary Byers seemed to say that he had an open mind pending final reports from consultants (rather than from officials) about the value for money of the deals. Unsurprisingly, when these arrived they were not definitive, but in any event the government eventually closed the deals in spring 2003. Final negotiations were painfully slow, and the terms of the contracts changed significantly with the effect of reducing the exposure to risk for the private sector, as noted by the critical report from the Public Accounts Committee (PAC) in March 2005.[39] The government's absolute commitment to completing the policy greatly weakened its bargaining position against the preferred (and, by then, effectively the only) bidders.

The *ex post* appraisals are beginning to appear. On publication of a further Transport Select Committee Report in March 2005,[40] the chair, Gwyneth Dunwoody, made the crucial point: 'I welcome the fact that the government is at last putting real money into the Tube. But I cannot see why it needed a PPP to do it.' The PAC found that the PPP had caused

---

[38] House of Commons Committee on Transport, Local Government and the Regions, *London Underground*, HC387 (London: TSO, 2002).

[39] House of Commons Committee of Public Accounts, *London Underground Public Private Partnerships*, HC466 (London: TSO, March 2005).

[40] House of Commons Transport Committee, *The Performance of the London Underground*, HC94 (London: TSO, March 2005).

years of avoidable delay, and the procurement alone had cost the taxpayer getting on for £900 million, about half in fees to advisers and consultants, and half in higher borrowing costs than an alternative promoted by Livingstone, amongst others. Transport for London has published progress reports[41] showing a mixed experience, including an emerging concern that the contractors may fail to deliver the investment programme as rapidly as they had promised and that the predictions of the consequences of lack of management control are beginning to be realised.

An editorial in *The Guardian* (1 April 2005) on the occasion of the publication of the critical PAC report summed up the sorry episode:

> One of the few dents in Gordon Brown's reputation for sound economics is his dogged pursuit of public–private partnerships for the underground in London, despite widespread criticism that it would have been much cheaper if the project had been financed by government-backed bonds. Yesterday's report by the all-party public accounts committee will do nothing to restore his reputation . . . Looking back, the whole episode looks like a triumph of dogma and personal prejudice over common sense.

As Blair approached the end of his final term the public were beginning to learn of the parlous state of the finances of Metronet (responsible for two-thirds of the Underground PPP). Successive annual reports from Transport for London had documented the progressive falling behind on the investment programme in track replacement and, especially, station refurbishments. The independent PPP Arbiter gave a 'mixed' first annual review in November 2006[42] and when asked for a preliminary view about a disputed £750 million overspend, he replied that there was evidence that Metronet had not been entirely 'economic and efficient', with the implication that the consortium would be held liable for at least some of the over-run.[43] As the *Evening Standard* and many other commentators reported, 'Metronet has been forced to admit that its handling of work has been a shambles and is under intense pressure to improve its performance.'[44] Within two days of Blair leaving office, Metronet filed with the PPP Arbiter for an Extraordinary Review of its fees, revealing that its overspend had spiralled to £2 billion in respect of the two-thirds of the

[41] London Underground, *London Underground and the PPP – The Third Year 2005/06* (London: London Underground Limited, 2006). There were similar reports for the two previous years.
[42] PPP Arbiter, *Annual Metronet Report 2006* (London: Office of PPP Arbiter, 2006).
[43] PPP Arbiter, *Treatment of Investment at an Extraordinary Review* (London: Office of PPP Arbiter, 2007).
[44] Dick Murray and Hugo Duncan, *Evening Standard*, 18 April 2007.

Underground infrastructure under its management.[45] The ratings agency downgraded some of Metronet's bonds. So Gordon Brown as Prime Minister was faced with the prospect of sorting out the problems of his own creation as Chancellor. This set of contracts is so important and so expensive that no Prime Minister could escape an involvement in a decision about whether and how to rescue it.

Further indecision over London devolution: Livingstone and congestion charging

Road user charging – or congestion charging as the London realisation was to be branded – was another transport subject where Blair showed inconsistency. Charging road users by time and location as a means of controlling traffic congestion whilst producing revenues was a long-established idea, but it had always been thought to be too politically difficult to implement (except, of course, crudely by increasing fuel duty). But the powers for local authorities to implement it were contained in the GLA Act 2000 in the case of London, and the Transport Act 2000 in the cases of other local authorities. Crucially, the legislation insists that the net revenues be applied locally for transport purposes for at least ten years.

This policy is a sensible component of devolution and it represents one of the only sources of locally generated income at the discretion of an English local authority. No doubt the 'economic-efficiency' half of the Treasury brain welcomed this move. But the 'control-of-public-spending' half certainly did not: it represented a move towards hypothecation of a 'tax' income over which the Treasury would have no control. But the battle had to be won if the policy was to have any chance of political acceptability. And it was won through the persistence of the Deputy Prime Minister.

One might have expected that Blair, apparently committed to real devolution, would have supported any local politician who sought to make use of the new powers. But once candidates for London Mayor were announced and Independent Ken Livingstone committed himself to introducing congestion charging, the policy of the official Labour Party candidate became not to introduce it. Blair and his colleagues were careful to emphasise the political and technological risks of using the powers they had themselves created. When on many occasions backbenchers asked ministers to intervene on their behalf, the answer was

[45] Dan Milmo, The Guardian, 29 June 2007.

always that this was the responsibility of the Mayor of London and the government had no powers to intervene.[46] The clear expectation was that the policy would fail spectacularly and it would all be Ken Livingstone's fault.

In the event the London congestion charging scheme went 'live' in February 2003, worked well and demonstrated to considerable interest round the world. In October 2003 Blair gave a fulsome acknowledgement:

> I was very, very sceptical but I think that it has made a difference, and I think that provided the money is ploughed back into transport, then I think it is an interesting example of how we can manage transport policy for the future. I think it is too early to evaluate all the results of it, but you have got to give credit where it is due.[47] This history seems to have been forgotten in Blair's *Brief* to the PLP of May 2007 in which he claims for himself as a 'key moment' 'congestion charge operating successfully in London'.[48]

Now it is apparent that Livingstone has become an important political ally of the Prime Minister's, as revealed in a MORI survey for the GLA.[49] Livingstone has been allowed to rejoin the Labour Party and seems to enjoy a good relationship with Blair. The growth in London bus patronage – a clear consequence of Livingstone's policies – has been sufficient to allow Blair to claim in his PLP *Brief* that 'Bus use [is] increasing year on year for the first time in decades',[50] even though the annual statistics show it to be falling outside London.[51]

It is Livingstone and the GLA that are leading the way in implementing the devolutionist Prudential Borrowing regime that allows local authorities a new freedom to borrow within limits of 'prudence'. In December 2004, with a delightful irony, Ken Livingstone successfully launched the first £200 million onto the financial markets: the government had flatly refused Livingstone's proposition that he be allowed to do precisely this as an alternative to the Underground PPP, on the grounds noted above that 'To saddle the city with an enormous amount of debt is a recipe for disaster.'[52] This was the beginning of a £3,000 million, five-year programme of long-term borrowing, and subsequent issues have proved to be in heavy demand in the markets, attracting rates of interest close to government securities and preserving excellent ratings with the ratings

---

[46] For example, see the exchange in the Commons with Richard Ottaway, 9 January 2002.
[47] *London Today*, ITV.   [48] PLP *Brief*, May 2007, p. 17.
[49] *The Guardian*, 17 January 2005.   [50] PLP *Brief*, May 2007, p. 17.
[51] Department for Transport, *Bus and Light Rail Statistics GB: October – December 2006* (London, TSO, 2007).   [52] *Financial Times*, 23 November 1999.

agencies. All this with the explicit approval of the Treasury as part of a good five-year funding agreement for London.

National road pricing

The success of London congestion charging encouraged Alistair Darling – who had been appointed by Blair as Secretary of State for Transport, to sort out the transport policy muddle left behind by Prescott and Byers – to take the idea seriously at a national level. To have been seen to be considering this would have been unthinkable a couple of years earlier, yet this kind of traffic management forms the core of the Transport White Paper of July 2004. And Blair himself wrote a foreword to it. Whilst hardly a strong endorsement for the eventual possibility of national road user charging, it is the most one could expect and it is remarkable considering the sensitivity Blair had previously shown to the power of the motoring electorate. In fact, after some hesitation, he had already given his endorsement to road pricing in 2002 in his foreword to the RAC Foundation's *Motoring Towards 2050*.[53]

Importantly, in endorsing this aspect of the White Paper Blair was endorsing the positive conclusions of the Road Pricing Feasibility Study.[54] This was a major piece of research by Department for Transport officials overseen by a steering group mainly of non-civil servants and chaired by a senior official who would, in spring 2007, rise to become Permanent Secretary at the Department for Transport and therefore to assume overall responsibility for delivering the policy on road pricing.

Blair, having given approval 'in principle' to developing national road pricing, delegated development of the policy to his Secretary of State, Alistair Darling. Further staff work was carried out and substantial sums of money were put on offer through the new 'Transport Innovation Fund' to local authorities that could be encouraged to bid for grants to assist them in implementing pilot schemes (Birmingham and Manchester being two of the most prominent candidates). When Douglas Alexander succeeded Alistair Darling, Blair's remarkable introductory letter of instruction reaffirmed that:

> Managing demand for road transport and ensuring we get the best out of
> our existing network are vital. We therefore need to advance the debate on

---

[53] RAC Foundation, *Motoring Towards 2050* (London: RAC Foundation, May 2002).
[54] Department for Transport, *Feasibility Study of Road Pricing in the UK* (London, TSO, 2004).

the introduction of a national road-user charging scheme. The successful
roll-out of local schemes funded from the Transport Innovation Fund will
be critical. I would like you to identify the other key steps for the successful
introduction of road-user charging within the next decade.[55]

Everything was consistent with Blair leading on this matter at the
highest level, securing consistency across Whitehall and delegating policy
development to the relevant departments. Then in early 2007, in the same
way as during the fuel price protests of 2000, that dozing monster 'the
motorist' reawoke. The stimulus was an 'e-petition'.[56] This system was set
up in November 2006 on the official No. 10 website. It allows the general
public to initiate a petition on more or less anything and the public can
'sign' online. Initially, many of the petitions were on trivia and poorly
supported. But 'We the undersigned petition the Prime Minister to scrap
the planned vehicle tracking and road pricing policy' received some
press coverage: it closed on 20 February 2007 with over 1.8 million sig-
natures. This caught Blair's attention. Within a day he sent a personal
email response to every signatory,[57] and, as already noted, on 1 March he
created a podcast interview with motoring journalist Richard Hammond
on the No. 10 website.[58]

These responses are significant for several reasons. First, here was a
Prime Minister announcing important policy changes though the
medium of email and podcast. Second, his replies seem to make little connection with the 2004 Transport White Paper for which he had written
the foreword and he makes little reference to the Road Pricing Feasibility
Study or the other research and policy development work that had been
carried out over several years by the Department for Transport[59] to which
he had delegated the task: 'I see this email as the beginning, not the end of
the debate ... we have not made any decision about national road
pricing'. The podcast seems to deny the existence of the thorough investigation in the 2004 Feasibility Study:

> You could decide you were going to get rid of all the other taxes and just
> have that and you could decide that it is going to be revenue neutral. Now
> all these are policy decisions that you take in the future. The only issue at
> the moment is do you want to investigate this technology as a way of
> dealing with the problem both of congestion and of how you raise money
> for transport, do you want to do it or not? And you may decide at the end of

[55] www.pm.gov.uk/output/Page9455.asp.   [56] http://petitions.pm.gov.uk.
[57] www.pm.gov.uk/output/Page11050.asp.   [58] www.pm.gov.uk/output/Page11116.as.
[59] The email does give a link which leads to comprehensive material on the DfT's website.

it you don't want to do it, but all I am saying at the moment is because you have got this additional dimension of congestion, as well as all the complexities of how you tax people in relation to transport, is it not sensible at least to investigate it?

Third, some of the Prime Minister's comments in the podcast suggest that he is not entirely clear in his own mind about the point of road pricing: 'you could charge very low amounts when you are travelling in the non-peak times and higher amounts when you are travelling at the peak times and you can do that if you want, or you might decide not to do it, but that is one way of doing it'.

Most importantly the episode laid bare the extent to which the government as a whole had failed to address some of the fundamental issues raised by road pricing, notably what would happen to the revenues raised.[60] On 19 February the junior minister Stephen Ladyman said on a radio broadcast,[61] 'The second thing people are concerned about is that it's going to be an additional charge . . . and what we are saying [is] it's going to be a charge instead of the additional road taxes . . . people . . . in most parts of Wales will actually be better off'. In other words the government had already decided that road pricing would be tax revenue neutral. This had been the line taken by senior Labour politicians on previous occasions. Yet in his email Blair says 'funds raised from these local schemes [potential pilot schemes being worked up in places such as Birmingham and Manchester] will be used to improve transport in those areas.' And in the podcast he says:

> You could decide you were going to get rid of all the other taxes and just have that and you could decide that it is going to be revenue neutral. Now all these are policy decisions that you take in the future. The only issue at the moment is do you want to investigate this technology as a way of dealing with the problem both of congestion and of how you raise money for transport, do you want to do it or not? . . . part of what you need to do is to raise money to invest in a better public transport system, because the best way of reducing congestion is if you have a better transport system . . . I could name you about five different city schemes for metro links and so on, and light rail systems, and transit systems and so on, but you have got to raise money for all of these.

---

[60] The issues are discussed in Stephen Glaister and Dan Graham, *National Road Pricing: Is it Fair and Practical?* (London: Social Market Foundation, 2006). A particularly important issue is the difference in incidence on different parts of the population implied by different policies on the use of road pricing revenue.   [61] BBC *Eye on Wales*.

It was plain that through the mechanism of the e-petition the government had managed to procure a strong public reaction against a policy that the public could not possibly have understood, not least because the government itself had not begun to resolve fundamental questions: and it certainly had not explained what is a very complex proposition.

The magnitude of the government's failure to explain its position was revealed in a YouGov survey for the *Daily Telegraph* between 19 and 21 February which estimated that '84 percent reckon either that the present Government's sole motive in advocating road pricing is the desire to raise revenue (48 per cent) or that it is one of the Government's motives, along with the desire to reduce congestion and pollution (36 per cent).' Commenting on the whole episode Anthony King remarked that 'If road pricing turns out not to be the present Government's poll tax, it will only be because neither this administration nor any other administration is likely to go anywhere near it.'[62]

This poor management by No. 10 of what could have been a truly radical development of transport policy has undoubtedly weakened the chances of its implementation in the foreseeable future. As Blair himself observes in his podcast: 'Well as I say this is years in advance, but having gone through the fuel protest, I think it is highly unlikely that you will find politicians in the future putting something forward if people just are completely rebelling against it.'

Blair's personal interventions

If Blair showed a general disinterest in high-level transport policy he showed himself to be perfectly willing to intervene when he was personally affected. In the autumn of 2002 Transport for London was engaged in a quantity of road works in preparation for the introduction of congestion charging. One Friday afternoon some contractors at Vauxhall left work, leaving behind unattended but defective temporary traffic lights. The Prime Minister's wife was seriously delayed in the ensuing traffic jam. Action was immediate. Blair required junior Transport Minister John Spellar to investigate, to make weekly reports and to make recommendations. After some debate about whether it would be better to remove traffic management powers and give them to a 'traffic Tsar' (which would have been a bizarre contradiction to the creation of the devolved GLA) it was sensibly decided that highway authorities such as

---

[62] *Daily Telegraph*, 26 February 2007.

the TfL required stronger powers. A Bill was announced in the November 2003 Queen's Speech and the Traffic Management Act had royal assent by July 2004. Blair could certainly make things happen in the transport policy world when he put his mind to it.

Another less benign example emerged during evidence given at the Old Bailey concerning corporate manslaughter and health and safety charges arising from the Hatfield railway accident. *The Times* reported evidence given in court that the Prime Minister had applied 'naked' pressure to Railtrack executives to lift the speed restrictions plaguing the network.[63] He had offered to 'syndicate' or share the risks. This is an extraordinary suggestion. It is that the Prime Minister was seeking to influence the professional judgement both of those accountable to their shareholders for running a private company (hence the court case) and of the independent rail safety regulators. It is also unclear what 'syndicating' the risks might mean in practice: had the Prime Minister's requests contributed to a subsequent fatal accident it is hard to see that there is a mechanism in law whereby the Prime Minister could have somehow taken over culpability from those accountable for running a safe railway. If the government or parliament were discontented with the way Hatfield had been handled, then the appropriate response would have been to legislate with due process.

Crossrail is another becalmed major project that Blair took a personal interest in. This is a proposal for a large new underground railway joining Heathrow and points west of London with Stratford and Canary Wharf in the east via Paddington and Liverpool Street. First approved by the Thatcher administration in 1989 as a solution to crowding in central London, and latterly forming a centrepiece of Ken Livingstone's solution for dealing with growing demand, *Transport 2025*,[64] this project has had several hundred million pounds spent on planning and design work but no government has been willing to find the funds to build it. Quite early in Blair's first term his advisors in the No. 10 Policy Unit showed an interest in the scheme. Blair appeared to be convinced of the case. His personal letter to his new Secretary of State for Transport in May 2006 includes 'we need to ensure that we have identified a clear way forward on Crossrail, consistent with sensible handling of the Bill currently before Parliament.'[65] But he could not secure from the Treasury the firm commitment necessary towards the £16 billion estimated cost of the scheme:[66]

[63] *The Times*, 12 March 2005.
[64] Transport for London, *Transport 2025* (London: TfL, November 2005).
[65] www.pm.gov.uk/output/Page9455.asp.
[66] Christopher Adams, *Financial Times*, 8 March 2007.

In a private meeting with a delegation of business and trade union leaders led by Ken Livingstone, London's Mayor, Mr Blair sought to dispel fears that the government had gone cool on the £10 bn [in 2002 prices, more recently estimated at about £16 billion] railway, saying that it was 'absolutely committed . . . The prime minister . . . believes a decision in principle can be made on Crossrail ahead of this year's comprehensive spending review.

Blair's growing interest in transport

In transport policy documents prior to 2001, if there was a foreword it would be by the Secretary of State for Transport and Deputy Prime Minister, John Prescott. After 2001 it seems that Blair had realised a need to take a closer personal interest. That Blair wrote a warm foreword to *Motoring Towards 2050*, an independent report by the RAC Foundation was remarkable. The 2004 Transport White Paper also has a foreword by the Prime Minister which is only 25% shorter than the Secretary of State for Transport's own preface. It shows the extent to which Blair had sought to impose his own view. The first substantive paragraph includes: 'Over 100 road schemes have been completed. The M25 is being widened . . . we want to see Crossrail in London, road widening and bypasses to tackle the worst areas of congestion.' It would have been unthinkable to start a major transport policy statement in this way during Blair's first term.

So by the beginning of his second term Blair had realised that transport was a problem and that he had lost faith in the ability of his Secretaries of State or the Chancellor to solve them. He decided to become more directly involved, and to do that he strengthened the resources available to him directly. Lord Birt had silently attended a Cabinet Office seminar in November 2001 where academics and other experts had been invited to express their views about the long-term issues in transport, without having been told that this was essentially an initial briefing for Birt. The No. 10 website records a press briefing by the Prime Minister's official spokesman (PMOS):

> Asked to clarify exactly what it was about Lord Birt which had so impressed the Prime Minister that he believed he could solve the country's transport problems, the PMOS said it was important to make a distinction between what the Forward Strategy Unit (FSU) – of which Lord Birt was a member – was and was not doing . . . we had set up a small unit within Government composed of people drawn from different backgrounds who could look at some of the longer term issues facing our public services ten or twenty years down the line.

Asked the difference between the FSU and the Policy Unit, the PMOS said that the FSU's role was to look at issues ten or twenty years hence. The new Policy Directorate's role was to look at the short and medium terms.[67]

The Leader of the Opposition was quick to articulate a general concern, particularly within the civil service, that transport policy development was becoming confused and unaccountable.[68] The Commons Select Committee on Transport complained about the way the normal systems of scrutiny were being evaded by Birt's position.[69] Lord Birt had not accepted an invitation to provide oral evidence to their inquiry into the Ten-Year Plan. Noting that a couple of members of Lord Birt's team were being paid for by the transport department they expressed the view that it is important that those engaged in policy should be accountable to parliament through the select committee system.

Neither papers written for Birt, nor reports written by Birt for the Prime Minister, have been made public. But it became known that one proposal emanating from Downing Street was for a new network of tolled motorways. This idea was scotched by Alistair Darling on taking office as Transport Secretary.[70]

Press appraisals of Birt's role[71] reported a lack of clarity over how, or if, Birt's access translated into real power. They also reported irritation in the civil service that Blair had quietly created what was effectively a Prime Minister's department in which Birt, unelected and unaccountable through civil service codes, was a key part. They noted that the number of consultants hired by the government had exploded, just as it did at the BBC in the Birtian days. It is reported that senior civil servants moaned about the increase in management consultancy 'Birtspeak' in communications from what is referred to disparagingly as 'the Centre'.

As if in confirmation of the suggestion that the Chancellor felt threatened on transport policy by the 'blue skies thinking' seeping from No. 10, in his March 2005 Budget Gordon Brown announced yet another transport policy initiative.[72] Sir Rod Eddington was to advise ministers on the impact of transport decisions on Britain's productivity, stability and growth beyond 2015. Although technically a joint exercise between Treasury and Transport, the terms of reference read like 'Treasury-speak'.

[67] 8 January 2002.   [68] House of Commons, 23 January 2002.
[69] House of Commons Transport Committee, press notice, 31 January 2002.
[70] *Daily Telegraph*, 2 June 2002.
[71] David Hencke, *The Guardian*, 27 January 2005, and Rachel Sylvester, *Daily Telegraph*, 10 January 2005.   [72] *The Guardian*, 17 March 2005.

It is likely that the exercise was partly motivated by the Treasury in an attempt to influence the Department for Transport to change the way it spends its budgets in favour of what the Treasury would see as better value for public money.

Sir Rod Eddington's review[73] reasonably said that the way to obtain the best value from a limited public budget is to select the schemes with the greatest benefits in relation to their costs. He reviewed a portfolio of schemes, but careful reading of his report does not reveal strong support for increasing expenditure on railways. And as one press report noticed, 'three-quarters of the 186 projects . . . Sir Rod Eddington considered which showed the benefits outweighed the costs involved were road schemes. Just 14 were rail improvements, the rest involved trams, buses, walking and cycling proposals.[74]

Conclusion

In his introduction to *The Code of Practice on Consultation*,[75] Tony Blair wrote 'effective consultation is a key part of the policy-making process'. The episodes related in this chapter illustrate that if there is not effective consultation then the process is unlikely to make successful policy. They support Seldon's view[76] that 'Tony Blair has never been a man who has liked or felt a need to consult widely'. Each of the episodes exhibits some or all of the following: lack of a clear overall policy direction; parallel development of closely related policies in several parts of Whitehall, including a nebulous constellation of bodies in and around No. 10 Downing Street; a willingness to ignore or deny evidence; a reliance on commercial management consultancy and individual advisers rather than accountable ministers and their civil servants; a failure carefully to develop policy and then legislation over a reasonable period of time; an unwillingness to publish or consult on a substantive written account of draft legislation giving the reasoning in support of it; and a reluctance to be exposed to scrutiny.

Had scrutiny and critique been heeded, then some of the mistakes might have been avoided. The 1998 Transport White Paper proposed more consultation rather than specific legislation (except for the creation of the SRA, which took two and a half years to enact), but the generic

[73] Sir Rod Eddington, *The Eddington Transport Study* (London, TSO, 2006).
[74] Juliet Jowit, *The Observer*, 17 December 2006. The evidence has subsequently been published at www.dft.gov.uk/about/strategy/eddingtonstudy/pubeddingbase.
[75] Cabinet Office, 2003.   [76] Seldon, *Blair*, conclusion to 2nd edn, pp. 695–7.

policies it proposed did not square with the facts of the situation or the reality of electoral sentiment. There soon had to be U-turns on road building, fuel duties and later on road pricing which destroyed such coherence as there was.

The Ten-Year Plan was a good concept and it did have high-quality public documentation. However, the necessary revisions in the light of unexpected events never happened, and a good idea died for lack of attention when Byers, the Treasury and the Prime Minister all lost interest.

The development of the PPP for the London Underground, the destruction of Railtrack, its replacement by a new form of company, and the process adopted for the next review of the railways policy were all matters of national significance, involving considerable commitments of public money over many years. Parliament was inadequately involved in both cases. Public money was spent on management consultants, yet much of their work was – and remains – confidential. Proposals were published without prior consultation. Rather like the rail privatisation Bill of the early 1990s,[77] the Railways Act 2005 was not well defined in advance and had to be put together 'on the hoof' in parliament.

There was much turbulence in transport policy during Blair's terms of office but little progress. The Prime Minister's initial attempt to delegate failed. John Prescott at the DETR generated several genuinely new policy initiatives but they were undermined by No. 10 or blocked by the Treasury because they were unrealistic, unpopular or not consistent with Treasury policies on the use of the private sector, on control of public expenditure, on public borrowing and on the needs of the economy. Blair was drawn into attempting to make transport policy in Downing Street, with little help from the Chancellor.

On Blair's resignation it was unclear where, if anywhere, the real initiative lay. Symptomatic is the growing number of internal and official advisory bodies attempting to develop transport policy outside the official Department for Transport, including internal units in the Treasury and in Communities and Local Government (formerly the Office of the Deputy Prime Minister), the Prime Minister's Strategy Unit in No. 10, and the Commission for Integrated Transport advising the Department for Transport. As Blair left power his government had stimulated and received reports relevant to transport from four major independent studies. In addition to Sir Rod Eddington's review on transport there was Sir Nicholas Stern's review on the economics of climate change, Kate

[77] See Foster, *British Government in Crisis.*

Barker's review of land use planning and Sir Michael Lyons' inquiry into the future of local government.[78] It was not clear how either the outgoing or the incoming Prime Minister intended to make a coherent response to these important and substantive documents. Political scientists may be able to offer comment on what it says about the state of government to have so many overlapping and concurrent policy reviews by independent outsiders. Overall, the effect has been substantial additional centralisation of powers over transport policy in the hands of the Prime Minister and, separately, the Chancellor but with little clarity about how they ought to be used.

Alistair Darling's 2004 Transport White Paper did take a sensible long view. Whilst it took great care not to give any hostages to fortune by quoting numbers, it did, with the endorsement of Blair in his foreword, realistically set out major conflicts that future governments would have to deal with. It presaged a process for forcing government to reveal a coherent position on funding the railways (which was timed to come to a head just after Blair left office). In particular, it showed the beginnings of the unavoidable debate about how best to address the insatiable wish of the electorate to move around in their own private vehicles. Unfortunately this was thrown into disarray by No. 10's stimulation and then mismanagement of a public debate about national road pricing. Meanwhile the biggest ever Public Private Partnership for the London Underground, which Blair and Brown had spent so much money and effort forcing through over five years, was looking distinctly precarious. A satisfactory resolution of the conflicts – if there can ever be such a thing – will require a return to an analysis of the facts, clear policy subject to scrutiny, building unheard-of public consensus and considerable leadership.

[78] Sir Rod Eddington, *The Eddington Transport Study* (London, TSO, 2006); Sir Nicholas Stern, *The Economics of Climate Change* (Cambridge: Cambridge, 2006); Kate Barker, *Review of Land Use Planning* (London: TSO, 2006); Sir Michael Lyons, *Lyons Inquiry into Local Government* (London: TSO, 2007).

13

Industrial policy

NICHOLAS CRAFTS

Introduction

The starting point for this chapter is to consider what is meant by 'industrial policy' and what might be its rationale. The traditional notion was that government should intervene to promote manufacturing as a whole or key industrial sectors to widen the country's industrial base and to increase the rate of growth of manufacturing output and productivity. These objectives could be pursued through subsidies or tax breaks to investment, encouragement of mergers that created 'national champion' firms, state ownership and protectionist policies. In this guise, 'industrial policy' reached its apogee in the 1970s.

Economists might see a rationale for such interventionist policies in terms of seeking to correct market failures. For example, while free trade and specialisation along lines of comparative advantage represent an efficient allocation of today's economic resources, it may imply neglecting infant industries with high productivity growth potential and positive externalities in the future. Advocates of traditional industrial policies would frequently argue that they were needed to counter the 'short-termism' of British capital markets. And a more radical approach might have entailed the creation of new financial institutions or more direct state control of investment decisions.

By the mid-1990s, government policy was focused on 'competitiveness'. This was defined in terms of 'the degree to which it can, under free and fair market conditions, produce goods which meet the test of international markets, while simultaneously maintaining and expanding the real incomes of its people over the long term'. In effect, this places productivity performance at the heart of the matter. This was made more explicit under the Blair government through its emphasis on 'the Productivity Agenda'. These more recent incarnations of supply-side policy retain the stress on raising the long-run growth of productive potential in the economy through encouraging investment and innovation but with increasingly less emphasis on the special role of manufacturing and without the overt protectionism and dirigisme that many traditional Labour thinkers would have wanted.

A very interesting aspect of the design of supply-side policies intended to raise the long-run rate of economic growth is the role of competition policy. In the 1970s, this was seen as unimportant, and Schumpeterian arguments that large firms with market power did more R & D, achieved economies of scale, and thus were good for productivity, often held sway. During the 1990s, empirical research by academic economists undermined these claims and pointed to the importance of competition as an antidote to principal–agent problems (managerial slack) in firms with weak shareholders and thus as a stimulus to the rapid adoption of improved products and processes. So, whereas in the earlier post-war period competition policy was seen as an irrelevance or possibly an obstacle to faster growth, in the recent past its role in improving productive efficiency, as well as addressing the consumer losses from firms' market power, has been increasingly recognised.

The Labour Party and industrial policy in the early 1990s

By the early 1990s, the context of industrial policy had changed considerably compared with 1979 when Labour was last in government. On the external front globalisation had advanced significantly, with increased competition from Asian manufacturers and much greater international mobility of capital. On the domestic front, the Thatcher government had moved away from the interventionist policies of the 1970s, allowed market forces to downsize manufacturing, implemented privatisation on a large scale, introduced industrial reforms and reduced marginal rates of direct taxation. 1970s-style industrial policy had received a seriously bad press in terms of incurring substantial costs but few benefits while propping up losers rather than picking winners.[1]

Labour could respond either by reinventing interventionist policies or, in effect, accepting the thrust of Thatcherite policies and seeking to refine them. Until Gordon Brown became Shadow DTI Minister late in 1989 the former seemed to be the preferred option. A vision of a new industrial

---

[1] See the assessments by Derek Morris and David Stout, 'Industrial Policy', in Derek J. Morris (ed.), *The Economic System in the UK* (Oxford: Oxford University Press, 1985), pp. 851–94, and Aubrey Silberston, 'Industrial Policies in Britain, 1960–1980', in Charles F. Carter (ed.), *Industrial Policy and Innovation* (London: Heinemann, 1981), pp. 39–51.

policy was proposed by the Policy Review Group under Bryan Gould, Brown's predecessor. This stressed the need for a pro-active industrial policy under the auspices of a 'developmental state' and envisaged the creation of a much more powerful DTI responsible for industrial strategy along the lines of the Japanese MITI and a long-term commitment of substantial funds to key manufacturing sectors through a new National Investment Bank.[2]

By the time of the 1992 election, there had been a significant shift towards a greater reliance on tax incentives rather than the creation of new institutions, but the party's rhetoric still stressed the need for industrial policy to modernise the manufacturing base. When Brown became Shadow Chancellor in 1992 this move was accentuated, and between then and the 1997 election the shadow Treasury came to dominate the shadow DTI.[3] Tony Blair aided and abetted this outcome by moving Robin Cook from the DTI brief to Shadow Foreign Secretary. At the 1997 election, Labour's manifesto had effectively abandoned traditional industrial policy; proposals for a super-DTI and a National Investment Bank were no longer on offer.[4] Thus, Blair's leadership consolidated the move that was already under way to something much closer to American-style rather than Japanese-style policy.

In 1992 Labour was still promising to return essential services to public ownership as and when funds permitted. By 1997, this promise had been dropped and replaced by making essential services accountable. In the meantime, in an important symbolic move, the old Clause 4 which committed the Labour Party to large-scale public ownership had been revised in 1995 to refer to belief in a dynamic economy in which the enterprise of the market would be joined with the forces of partnership and cooperation.

With regard to globalisation, Blair set a tone in a 1996 speech that marked a big departure from the protectionist tendencies of the 1980s in stating that the driving force of economic change today is globalisation and that New Labour's economic philosophy was to accept globalisation and work with it.[5] Similar sentiments were repeated in the 1997 manifesto.

[2] These proposals are set out in Keith Cowling, 'The Strategic Approach', in Industrial Strategy Group, *Beyond the Review: Perspectives on Labour's Economic and Industrial Strategy* (London: The Labour Party, 1989), pp. 9–19.
[3] See the account in Colin Hay, *The Political Economy of New Labour* (Manchester: Manchester University Press, 1999), ch. 4.
[4] The evolution of policy between 1992 and 1997 is well reviewed in Richard Hill, *The Labour Party and Economic Strategy, 1979–97* (Basingstoke: Palgrave, 2001), pp. 111–23.
[5] Reported *ibid.*, p. 44.

Policy since 1997

When Labour won a landslide victory in the 1997 election, it was possible
to wonder whether in government it would revert to 'Old Labour' policies.
The answer to this question soon became apparent and is a resounding
'No'. 1970s-style policy was conspicuous by its absence in that there was
no nationalisation programme, no move to subsidise manufacturing
investment, no counterpart of the National Enterprise Board, no return to
high marginal rates of direct tax, no attempt to resist de-industrialisation
by supporting declining industries and no major reversal of industrial
relations reform. Overall, there was certainly no desire to reinstate the de
facto policy veto held by the trade unions that had characterised that
period. Implicitly, the Thatcher supply-side reforms had been accepted.

One episode underlines both the distance that Labour had travelled
since the 1970s and the failure of earlier interventionist policies, namely,
the collapse of MG Rover with the loss of about 6,000 jobs just before the
2005 election. It is generally agreed that this company, the rump of
British Leyland which was nationalised in 1975, and received £3.5 billion
of public money in subsidy between then and 1988 when it was sold to the
private sector, failed through a history of low productivity and inadequate product development.[6] Now the approach of the DTI was to try to
broker a takeover by the Shanghai Automotive Industry Corporation
and, in this context, to provide a loan of £6 million to keep the
Longbridge plant open for just one more week. This was probably ill-
judged, but taxpayers escaped very lightly by earlier standards.[7]

Following the 1997 election, Blair continued to allow Brown to run
supply-side policy. In this area the Treasury rather than the DTI has
dominated, and the Treasury has become increasingly involved in microeconomic rather than macro-economic policy. The focal point has been
the productivity agenda, with no particular bias towards manufacturing
as somehow special. In opposition, as Shadow Chancellor, Brown made a
much-derided reference to 'post-neoclassical endogenous growth theory'
in a 1994 speech written by Ed Balls. In office, insights from modern
growth economics have been central to the way that productivity policy
has been framed.

---

[6] A good summary of the state's involvement with this company over thirty years is in Nigel
Berkeley, Tom Donnelly, David Morris and Martin Donnelly, 'Industrial Restructuring
and the State: The Case of MG Rover', *Local Economy*, 20, 2005: 360–71.
[7] A report by the National Audit Office, *The Closure of Rover* (London: TSO, 2006), concluded this was the case.

The main thrust of this approach is that growth of output and productivity depends on investment in physical and human capital and on innovation. Decisions to invest and to innovate respond to economic incentives such that well-designed policy can raise the growth rate a bit. This implies that government needs to pay attention to direct tax rates, to undertake investment that complements private sector capital accumulation, to support activities like R & D where social returns exceed private returns, and to facilitate competitive pressure on management to adopt cost-effective innovations. These ideas are clearly reflected in the 'five drivers' of productivity growth which were articulated initially by the Treasury in 2000.[8] These are investment, skills, innovation, competition and enterprise.

HM Treasury publications on productivity are based on this framework and like to announce progress in each of these areas. The current summary points to the stability delivered by the post-1997 macroeconomic policy framework and an increase in public capital spending as positives for investment, additional public expenditure on schooling and expansion of higher education as good for skills, the introduction of the R & D tax credit in 2001 as promoting innovation, the reform of competition policy in two Acts in 1998 and 2003 as stimulating competition and enterprise being encouraged by reforms to corporate taxation and by reductions in the burden of regulation.[9]

Evaluating productivity policy

There is no doubt that the new approach of inflation targeting by the Monetary Policy Committee has been associated with very stable macroeconomic conditions compared with other periods; the volatility of GDP growth since the introduction of inflation targeting has been about two-thirds that of the previously most stable period during the Bretton Woods years.[10] It is less clear that this will have a positive impact on growth since the empirical literature has struggled to identify robust effects.[11] As

---

[8] HM Treasury, *Productivity in the UK: The Evidence and the Government's Approach* (London: TSO, 2000). This is placed explicitly in the context of endogenous growth economics in Nicholas Crafts and Mary O'Mahony, 'A Perspective on UK Productivity Performance', *Fiscal Studies*, 22, 2001: 271–306.

[9] HM Treasury, *Productivity in the UK 6: Progress and New Evidence* (London: TSO, 2006).

[10] Luca Benati, 'UK Monetary Regimes and Macroeconomic Stylised Facts', Bank of England Working Paper no. 290 (2006).

[11] See the review of the evidence in Stefan Norrbin and Pinar Yigit, 'The Robustness of the Link between Volatility and Growth of Output', *Review of World Economics*, 144, 2005: 343–56.

Table 13.1. Investment/GDP (%)

	1976/8	1994/6	2003/5
France	22.3	17.8	19.3
Germany	20.3	21.2	17.5
UK	18.8	15.3	16.5
USA	18.3	16.9	18.5

Source: OECD, *Historical Statistics, 1960–1986* (Paris: OECD, 1988), and *National Accounts* (Paris: OECD, 2006).

table 13.1 reports, investment as a share of GDP has increased by about one percentage point compared with the mid-1990s but is still lower than in other major economies.

Similarly, the academic literature suggests that the R & D tax credit should increase R & D and total factor productivity (TFP) growth. A careful study of its possible impact suggested there was a strong case for its introduction in that it would be cost-effective and might raise TFP growth in the long run by 0.3% per year.[12] However, there is no study available so far that has quantified the actual impact for the UK, and UK R & D in 2004 was actually slightly lower as a percentage of GDP than it had been in 1995 (1.9% compared with 1.7%).

The expansion of educational provision has had favourable implications for productivity. The skill level of the UK labour force has been increasing quite rapidly; in 2004 15% of workers in the market economy were high-skilled and 14% low-skilled compared with 8% and 30%, respectively, in Germany.[13] This reflects in particular the much greater proportion of graduates in the UK labour force and has its origins in the Conservative period. The graduate wage premium continued to increase until 2000, since when it has been constant.[14]

The new view of competition policy as central to improving productivity performance is the most radical change. This represents a move to a rules-based system with ministerial discretion removed, pro-active powers for the competition authorities and serious penalties for anti-competitive behaviour. The adoption of a substantial lessening of competition tests for

[12] Rachel Griffith, Stephen Redding and John van Reenen, 'Measuring the Cost-effectiveness of an R & D Tax Credit for the UK', *Fiscal Studies*, 22, 2001: 375–99.

[13] Estimates from www.euklems.net.

[14] Stephen Machin and Anna Vignoles, 'Education Policy in the UK', Centre for the Economics of Education Discussion Paper no. 0057 (2006).

mergers removes the public-interest gateways allowed in earlier legislation. It is too soon to assess the impact of these reforms on productivity growth, but the evidence that competition is good for productivity growth is strong and the experience of the 1956 Restrictive Practices Act suggests that there could be a significant positive effect.[15] The OECD has constructed indicators of product market regulation which are designed to reflect the extent to which the regulatory environment is conducive to competition, and empirical work shows that this indicator is associated with better productivity performance.[16] Here the UK has continued to have the best overall score in the OECD.

Business may well feel that policy towards enterprise has been less convincing. Reducing administrative burdens of regulation is at most an aspiration, and the British Chambers of Commerce claim that the additional costs of regulation since 1998 now amount to over £55 billion. The statutory rate of corporate tax was reduced from 33 to 30% in 1997 and to 28% in 2007. Here the UK has been following a general trend reflecting greater capital mobility as globalisation progresses, but has been outpaced by other EU countries. This is perhaps unfortunate since, as evidence of the effects of reductions in corporate tax has accumulated, it now seems likely that the revenue-maximising rate is below 30%.[17]

Table 13.2 captures some of the flavour of New Labour supply-side policy. There is continuity from the Thatcher reforms in terms of relatively little subsidy for industry and light regulation of product market entry. Taxation has edged up but remains well below levels in the high-tax European countries. In the absence of a return to protectionism, New Labour has seemed content to see further de-industrialisation, and employment in industry fell from 26.7% of the labour force in 1997 to 22.1% in 2005 (table 13.3). It is reasonable to see the overall picture as one of building upon the approach of the Conservatives, but important improvements have been made, notably in terms of competition policy and the R & D tax credit.

[15] The classic reference is Stephen Nickell, 'Competition and Corporate Performance', *Journal of Political Economy*, 104, 1996: 724–46; on the impact of the 1956 Act, see George Symeonidis, 'The Effect of Competition on Wages and Productivity: Evidence from the UK', *Review of Economics and Statistics*, forthcoming.

[16] See the review of the evidence in Nicholas Crafts, 'Regulation and Productivity Performance', *Oxford Review of Economic Policy*, 22, 2006: 186–202.

[17] For data on corporate tax rates and an assessment of the elasticity of revenues, see Michael Devereux, 'Developments in the Taxation of Corporate Profit in the OECD since 1965: Rates Bases and Revenues', paper presented to the Alliance for Competitive Taxation (2006).

Table 13.2. Some aspects of supply-side policy

(a) State aid/manufacturing GDP (%)

	1981/6	1994/6	2005
France	4.9	1.8	1.5
Germany	3.0	3.8	1.7
UK	3.8	0.9	0.9

(b) Product market regulation (1–10)

	1978	1998 (1)	1998 (2)	2003
France	10.00	7.17	4.17	2.83
Germany	8.67	4.67	3.17	2.33
UK	8.00	2.33	1.83	1.50
USA	6.17	2.67	2.17	1.67

(c) Distortionary taxes/GDP (%)

	1975	1995	2004
France	23.2	31.2	32.3
Germany	25.8	26.8	24.6
UK	26.5	22.7	24.5
USA	20.0	22.9	20.8

Sources:
State aid: European Commission, *2nd Survey of State Aids* (Luxembourg: European Commission, 1990), *6th Survey of State Aids* (Luxembourg: European Commission, 1998) and *State Aid Scoreboard* (Luxembourg: European Commission, 2006).
Product market regulation: 1978 and 1998 (1) from Paul Conway and Giuseppe Nicoletti, 'Product Market Regulation in the Non-manufacturing Sectors of OECD Countries: Measurement and Highlights', OECD Economics Department Working Paper no. 530 (2006); 1998 (2) and 2003 from Paul Conway, Veronique Janod and Giuseppe Nicoletti, 'Product Market Regulation in OECD Countries, 1998 to 2003', OECD Economics Department Working Paper no. 419. Higher scores denote more regulation.
Distortionary taxes: OECD, *Revenue Statistics, 1965–2005* (Paris: OECD, 2006), based on definition in Richard Kneller, Michael Bleaney and Norman Gemmell, 'Fiscal Policy and Growth: Evidence from OECD Countries', *Journal of Public Economics*, 74, 1999: 171–90.

Table 13.3. Structure of employment (%)

	Agriculture	Industry	Services
1979			
France	8.9	36.1	55.0
Germany	5.4	44.2	50.4
UK	2.7	38.6	58.7
USA	3.6	31.2	65.2
1997			
France	4.4	25.3	70.3
Germany	2.9	34.8	62.3
UK	1.9	26.7	71.4
USA	2.7	23.9	73.4
2005			
France	3.5	22.6	73.9
Germany	2.4	30.0	67.6
UK	1.4	22.1	76.5
USA	1.6	19.8	78.6

Source: OECD, *Labour Force Statistics* (Paris: OECD, 2006).

The productivity record since 1997

It is instructive to distinguish between real GDP per person and real GDP per hour worked. The latter is a measure of labour productivity whereas the former reflects differences in demography, labour force participation and unemployment, as well as output per unit of labour input.

With regard to real GDP per person, as table 13.4 reports, there was an increase of about 0.5 percentage points per year compared with the Conservative years from 1979 to 1997 and growth in the period 1997 to 2006 was appreciably faster than in either France or Germany. The result is that by 2006 the level of real GDP per person was higher than in those countries and the change in relative positions since 1979 has been quite striking. The UK was already on course to overtake France before 1997 but had to improve its performance to do so after 1997.

Trends in real GDP per hour worked have been somewhat different. Since 1997 there has been a small decrease in its growth rate, as table 13.4 shows, which has been quite similar to that in France though well ahead of the German rate. There has been an acceleration in American labour productivity growth which none of these European countries was able to

Table 13.4. Real GDP per person and per hour worked

(a) Levels (UK = 100)

(i) Real GDP per person

	1979	1997	2006
France	113.7	103.8	98.6
West Germany	115.9	106.7	
Germany		95.3	87.1
USA	142.7	140.7	136.2

(ii) Real GDP per hour worked

	1979	1997	2006
France	119.0	119.4	118.6
West Germany	121.9	128.1	
Germany		102.5	97.7
USA	139.1	115.1	118.5

(b) Rates of growth (% per year)

(i) Real GDP per person

	1979–97	1997–2006
France	1.40	1.83
West Germany	1.45	
Germany		1.39
UK	1.92	2.41
USA	1.84	2.04

(ii) Real GDP per hour worked

	1979–97	1997–2006
France	2.40	2.00
West Germany	2.67	
Germany		1.53
UK	2.39	2.08
USA	1.32	2.40

Source: Groningen Growth and Development Centre and the Conference Board, *Total Economy Database, January 2007* (2007), www.ggdc.net.

match. The gap in the level of real GDP per hour worked between the UK and France (and probably West Germany) is still much the same as in 1979 at around 20%. Seemingly, then, UK performance in terms of productivity has been less impressive than in terms of GDP per person.

The difference lies in employment patterns. Increasingly over time, the workings of French and German labour markets have tended to exclude low-productivity workers who are too expensive to be employed (especially young people) or for whom early retirement is a very attractive option. Making a correction for these labour market distortions would reduce the current gap in real GDP per hour worked by about 8 percentage points, whereas no such correction would have been warranted in 1979.[18] Thus the underlying productivity gap with France and West Germany has fallen since 1979. Similarly, the apparent decrease in UK labour productivity growth since 1997 is probably accounted for by lower unemployment.

HM Treasury's approach to productivity has clearly focused on increasing hours worked as well as output per hour worked on the basis that at the margin an hour worked is worthwhile provided that the extra output is worth as much to the employer as the cost to the worker of the hour worked, even if this reduces average labour productivity. It might then be reasonable to give more weight to the increase in the growth of real GDP per person rather than the decrease in growth of real GDP per hour worked since 1997.

A closer look at productivity growth in the market economy

Although most discussions of economic growth relate to the whole economy, including both private and public sectors, it is informative, especially in the present context, to examine performance in the market economy. This is partly because there are well-known difficulties in measuring public sector output but also because the marketed sector is the locus of industrial policy.

Table 13.5 reports the results of a growth-accounting exercise for the market economy. Growth accounting is a technique to decompose the growth of output into contributions from increases in factor inputs (capital, labour, etc.) and from TFP. This latter is the residual after the

---

[18] This comment and the following discussion is based on the estimates in Renaud Bourles and Gilbert Cette, 'Les évolutions de la productivité "structurelle" du travail dans les principaux pays industrialisés', *Bulletin de la Banque de France*, 150, 2006: 23–30.

Table 13.5. Sources of market economy real GDP growth (% per year)

	Hours worked	ICT capital inputs	Other capital inputs	Labour quality	TFP	Real GDP	Real GDP/ hours worked
France							
1980–95	−0.4	0.3	0.6	0.5	0.8	1.8	3.0
1995–2004	0.4	0.5	0.5	0.4	0.7	2.5	2.0
Germany							
1980–95	−0.4	0.2	0.7	0.2	1.2	1.9	2.4
1995–2004	−0.5	0.5	0.5	0.1	0.5	1.1	1.7
UK							
1980–95	−0.6	0.5	0.7	0.3	1.6	2.5	2.9
1995–2004	0.4	1.0	0.5	0.5	0.9	3.3	2.7
USA							
1980–95	1.0	0.5	0.6	0.2	0.7	3.0	1.9
1995–2004	0.3	0.8	0.6	0.3	1.7	3.7	3.1

Source: Mary O'Mahony and Catherine Robinson, 'UK Growth and Productivity in International Perspective: Evidence from EU KLEMS', *National Institute Economic Review*, 200, 2007: 79–86.

input contributions have been accounted for and results from improvements in technology and/or efficiency. In this case, the contribution from growth in labour inputs is further divided into that from hours worked and that from improvements in the quality (skills) of the labour force.

Table 13.5 also displays the rate of growth of output per hour worked in the market economy and this is a good starting point for this closer look at productivity growth. Here it is noticeable that in the post-1995 period the UK has clearly outperformed France and Germany as productivity growth in those countries has dipped markedly, but there has also been an acceleration in the United States which has outperformed the UK.

Turning to the sources of UK output growth in the 1995 to 2004 period, several features are noteworthy. First, a strong contribution from improvements in labour quality is confirmed. Second, there was also relatively rapid growth in ICT capital inputs (computers, software, telecoms). Third, TFP growth decreased compared with the previous period and was well below the rate achieved by the United States, although exceeding French and German rates.

The context for productivity growth since the mid-1990s has been the advent of ICT as a new general-purpose technology with the potential for substantial productivity advance in services. This was the mainspring of the revival of productivity growth in the United States, and service sectors which use ICT intensively, such as retail distribution and financial services, account for faster productivity growth in the United States than in the large European economies post-1995.[19]

Compared with many European countries, the UK has been well placed to take advantage of the opportunities of the ICT era. This was a legacy of the Conservative years rather than a creation of New Labour. The rapid expansion in the number of college graduates matches the requirements of the new technology, while it is also apparent that ICT-using services have contributed most to productivity growth in countries with low product-market regulation.[20] Moreover, empirical investigation has found that ICT investment is discouraged by strong employment protection because this makes the reorganisation of work, which is central to realising the productivity potential of ICT, very expensive.[21] Indeed, Jean-Philippe Cotis, OECD Chief Economist, sees a UK productivity paradox: 'Why on earth isn't UK productivity catching up faster, given economic theory, good UK policies and comparatively low productivity levels to start with?'[22]

The solution to this paradox may be as follows. First, UK productivity performance has been stronger than Cotis allows once it is recognised that scope for catch-up is less than would be suggested by the raw data on the productivity gap (once labour-market distortions are taken into account) and that productivity growth in the market economy has been considerably faster than in the economy overall. Second, the relatively large difference between rates of labour productivity growth in the

[19] Robert Inklaar, Mary O'Mahony and Marcel Timmer, 'ICT and Europe's Productivity Performance: Industry-level Growth Account Comparisons with the United States', *Review of Income and Wealth*, 51, 2005: 505–36.

[20] On the value of human capital in exploiting ICT, see Timothy Bresnahan, Erik Brynjolfsson and Lorin Hitt, 'Information Technology, Workplace Organization and the Demand for Skilled Labor: Firm-level Evidence', *Quarterly Journal of Economics*, 117, 2002: 339–76; on the relationship between regulation and productivity growth from ICT-using services, see Giuseppe Nicoletti and Stefano Scarpetta, 'Regulation and Economic Performance: Product Market Reforms and Productivity in the OECD', OECD Economics Department Working Paper no. 460 (2005).

[21] C. Gust and J. Marquez, 'International Comparisons of Productivity Growth: The Role of Information Technology and Regulatory Practices', *Labour Economics*, 11, 2004: 33–58.

[22] Jean-Philippe Cotis, 'Economic Growth and Productivity', paper delivered to Annual Conference of the Government Economic Service (2006).

marketed sector and the whole economy reflects the rapid expansion of public sector employment under New Labour. Third, OECD measures of product market regulation may underestimate barriers to entry in the UK because they do not reflect the strictness of the planning laws. A sector in which this has had a big effect is retailing, where it has been estimated that a ban on out-of-town developments imposed in 1996 reduced TFP growth in the sector by 0.4% per year or about an eighth of the whole post-1995 slowdown in TFP growth reported in table 13.5.[23]

All this indicates that the government's pursuit of productivity improvement has been less single-minded than a reader of Treasury publications on the topic might suppose. This seems to be the perception of the business community as reflected in competitiveness surveys. Between 1997 and 2007 the UK fell from eleventh to twentieth in the rankings of the *World Competitiveness Yearbook* while the UK score for 'the ease of doing business fell from 79% of the best in the world to 45% of the best in the world over the same period.[24] Relaxing planning laws was a key recommendation of the high-profile 1998 McKinsey report on how to improve productivity performance, which was quietly buried. Similarly, the expansion of public sector employment has been controlled much less rigorously than it might have been. So perhaps the final explanation of the Cotis Paradox is that while productivity policy has been good it has not been that good.

Conclusions

Industrial policy and its metamorphosis into productivity policy is an area that has been controlled by Gordon Brown since the early 1990s. By the time Tony Blair became leader it was already clear that 1970s-style industrial policy or a British MITI were off the menu. Brown's reaction to Thatcherite reforms was quietly to accept them and seek to build from there.

The subsequent evolution of policy has been informed by mainstream academic economics. The most significant new development in the approach to productivity policy has been the recognition of the importance of competition. This has been reflected in major legislation in the form of the 1998 Competition Act and the 2003 Enterprise Act. It is, however, too soon to say what will be the impact of these reforms.

[23] Jonathan Haskel and Raffaella Sadun, 'Entry Regulation and Productivity: Evidence from the UK Retail Sector', Ceriba Working Paper (2007) at www.ceriba.org.uk.
[24] IMD, *World Competitiveness Yearbook, 2007* (Lausanne: IMD, 2007).

UK productivity performance since 1997 has been good but not really outstanding by international standards. Growth of real GDP per person has been a bit higher and growth of real GDP per hour worked a bit lower than under the Conservatives. Labour productivity growth has been underpinned by the adoption of the new technology of the ICT age, and this has been facilitated by the expansion in numbers of graduates and a largely conducive regulatory environment. These conditions were part of Labour's inheritance from the previous government and it is unlikely that productivity performance would have been very much different under the Conservatives. Market services rather than manufacturing have been central to productivity outcomes and this has meant that, in contrast to conventional wisdom in the late 1980s, the United States has seemed a more relevant model than Japan.

PART III

Policy studies

14

Law and the judiciary

MICHAEL BELOFF

Blair and the law

Tony Blair was by profession a barrister, but his early entry to parliament prevented him, as it prevented Margaret Thatcher, from leaving more than modest footprints in the law, or emulating Asquith, the only other twentieth-century Prime Minister with a background in the Inns of Court. He specialised in employment litigation, and between 1977 and 1983, his years of practice, ten of the cases in which he appeared were of sufficient importance to be published in a series of law reports.[1] His brief life in Chambers left him with two significant legacies, one professional, one personal. He found in the Temple both his first Lord Chancellor Derry Irvine and his wife Cherie (Booth). Blair, with his average second-class degree from Oxford obtained a tenancy at the expense of Cherie with her brilliant first from LSE.[2] This episode, reflective of the male public school ethos of the Bar at the time, did not impede her (she was elevated to Silk in the last year of the Major government) from enjoying a highly successful career at the Bar, but instilled in him no long-term ambition to achieve the same.

His labour law experience was responsible for his first major front-bench appointment under Neil Kinnock, shadowing Michael Howard, the

---

[1] *Thomas Marshall (Exports) Ltd* v. *Guinle* [Chancery Division] [1979] Ch. 227; *The Royal Naval School* v. *Hughes* [Employment Appeal Tribunal] [1979] IRLR 383; *Methven* v. *Cow Industrial Polymers Ltd* [Court of Appeal] [1980] ICR 463; *International Sports Co. Ltd* v. *Thomson* [Employment Appeal Tribunal] [1980] IRLR 340; *Brooker* v. *Charrington Fuel Oils Ltd* [County Court] [1981] IRLR 147; *Marley Homecare Ltd* v. *Dutton* [Employment Appeal Tribunal] [1981] IRLR 380; *Abbotts and Standley (appellants)* v. *Wesson-Glynwed Steels Ltd* [Employment Appeal Tribunal] [1982] IRLR 51; *United City Merchants (Investments) Ltd* v. *Royal Bank of Canada* [Court of Appeal] [1982] QB 208; *Nethermere (St Neots) Ltd* v. *Gardiner* [Employment Appeal Tribunal] [1983] ICR 319; *BL Cars Ltd* v. *Lewis* [Employment Appeal Tribunal] [1983] IRLR 58.
[2] Initially at Crown Office Row, then in 1981 at Harcourt Buildings when Irvine set up his own set. Anthony Seldon, *Blair* (London: The Free Press 2004), pp. 48–9, 63–5.

Secretary of State: but later he displayed no particular appetite for engaging with legal issues, apart from voicing populist philosophy – 'the rules of the game have changed' – in the area of crime and punishment (in which he had no professional background) which appeared from time to time at odds with the public statements of his wife.[3] When Sullivan J. quashed a refusal of leave to remain in the United Kingdom of an Afghan acquitted of charges of hijacking aircraft,[4] the Prime Minister commented 'It's not an abuse of justice for us to order their deportation, it's an abuse of commonsense frankly to be in a position where we can't do this.' (The Court of Appeal subsequently commended the judge for 'an impeccable judgment'.[5])

In his valedictory PLP *Brief* dated May 2007, compiled to celebrate ten years of a Labour government, law is only mentioned in conjunction with order. The summary under the rubric of the Constitution lists the enactment of the Human Rights Act 1988 (HRA) but otherwise makes no reference at all to the significant changes to the judiciary and civil legal system of the same decade.

Blair and the lawyers

If Blair had no particular affection for the law, he had no inbuilt animosity towards lawyers; and the legal culture of the Blair era was dominated by a web of relationships reminiscent of those charted in the late Anthony Sampson's *Anatomy of Britain* in which everyone who counted seemed to be connected to everyone else.

Lord Irvine had been his and Cherie's pupil master. Philip Sales, who served from 1997 as Junior Counsel to the Crown (Common Law) (or Treasury Devil), came from Irvine's old set at 11 King's Bench Walk (KBW), as did three High Court Judges, Patrick Elias, Richard Field and Brian Keith. Irvine appointed (without advertisement) as his special adviser Gary Hart, a former partner of the prestigious city firm Herbert Smith, and godfather to the Blairs' daughter, prompting an unsuccessful tribunal claim of sex discrimination from Jane Cohen, a legal aid lawyer.[6]

Lord Irvine's successor was, if anything, an even closer ally, as he was a former flatmate of the Prime Minister. Lord Falconer, who started in

---

[3] Michael Beloff QC, 'The Concept of Deference in Public Law', *Judicial Review*, 2006: 213, paras. 1 and 2.

[4] *R (on the application of S)* v. *Secretary of State for the Home Department* (2006) EWHC 111 (Admin.).

[5] 2006 EWCA Civ 1157 para. 50. Cf. Tony Blair, 'Shackled in the War on Terror', *Sunday Times*, 27 May 2007.   [6] *Lord Chancellor* v. *Coker*, *The Times*, 3 December 2001 (CA).

government service as Solicitor-General (and survived responsibility for the Millennium Dome), emerged as the country's senior legal figure, when in 2003 Lord Irvine was dismissed in a manner as peremptory as that with which Harold Macmillan disposed of Lord Kilmuir forty years before during the Night of the Long Knives. He came from the blue-chip chambers at Fountain Court, as did the Attorney-General Lord (Peter) Goldsmith QC. Lord Irvine appointed another Fountain Court alumnus Lord (Tom) Bingham, as Senior Law Lord, and Lord Falconer appointed his own former pupil master Lord Justice (Mark) Potter, a commercial lawyer, as president of the Family Division. Shortly after Cherie Booth became a founding member of Matrix Chambers in 2000, another member, Ken Macdonald QC, became Director of Public Prosecutions.

There were further filaments of friendship in the legal web. Henry Hodge, a former solicitor, husband of Minister of State Margaret Hodge, was made chairman of the Immigration Appeals Tribunal and a High Court Judge. The Blairs holidayed at the French chateau belonging to David Keene, who was promoted to the Court of Appeal. New Labour life peers included a trio of QCs: Baroness (Helena) Kennedy,[7] Lord (Tony) Grabiner (chairman of the Board of Governors of LSE) and Lord (Dan) Brennan (a member of Matrix).

In no instance could even the most acerbic critic complain that the appointees lacked qualifications for their office, and in several instances the post-holder was outstandingly eligible, but there was substance to the impression that New Labour's legal establishment was an extended family.

The fulcrum of change: the Constitutional Reform Act 2005 (CRA)

Pivotal to the Blair administration's reform of the legal system was the replacement of Lord Irvine by Lord Falconer on the Woolsack. The precise reasons for this wholly unanticipated reshuffle have not yet been revealed. Lord Irvine was, for all the faux pas over Wolsey and wallpaper, still in his formidable Lord Chancellarial prime, and could reasonably have expected to remain in office until the end of Blair's second term, if not beyond. The best guess is that David Blunkett, then an influential Home Secretary and an unrestrained critic of judges over their over-liberal (as he saw them) attitudes to crime and immigration – perennially sensitive issues for the

[7] However, she became a fierce critic of the Blairite approach to civil liberties and the justice system: see Helena Kennedy, *Just Law* (London: Chatto and Windus, 2004).

Home Department[8] – resented the Lord Chancellor's constitutionally proper defence of judicial independence, and confronted the Prime Minister with an unenviable choice of which to retain in his cabinet. The changes later embedded in the CRA were a camouflage for, or at any rate a consequence of, not a cause, of Lord Irvine's demise and there is little evidence that there had been any advance thought about them.

The fact that the office of the Lord Chancellor was purportedly abolished by press release (unavailingly, given its various roots in statute) speaks volumes for the administration's assessment that (as Stalin said of the Pope) the judges' moral authority was not supported by any divisions. In looking-glass mode, consultation took place after, not before, the event.

The CRA itself commenced (unusually) with a Statement of Values. Section 1 provided that the CRA does not adversely affect 'the existing constitutional principle of the rule of law' or 'the Lord Chancellor's existing constitutional role in relation to that principle'. The dimensions of that duty were not defined; nor was the content of the values to be protected[9] – although during the debate between the judiciary and the executive over the establishment of a Ministry of Justice in the last weeks of the Blair regime, it was suggested that allegations of its breach might be deployed as 'a nuclear option'.

The major changes engineered by the CRA were:

- the abolition of the triple role of Lord Chancellor;[10]
- the replacement of the Lord Chancellor by the Lord Chief Justice as head of the judiciary;
- the projected detachment of the Appellate Committee of the House of Lords from parliament and its reconstitution as a Supreme Court in name (as it had been for some while, in fact) so reflecting a continental concept of separation of powers;[11]
- the creation of a Judicial Appointments Commission (JAC) (coupled, inevitably with a Judicial Appointment and Conduct Ombudsman).

---

[8] See, for precedents in the Major years, Joshua Rozenberg, *Trial of Strength* (London: Richard Cohen Books, 1997).

[9] Although Section 3 contains a list of provisions designed to immunise the judiciary from practical interference while ensuring in terms of resources political support. See Lord Bingham of Cornhill KG, 'The Rule of Law', the Sixth Sir David Williams Lecture, Cambridge, November 2006, in *Cambridge Law Journal*, 66, March 2007: 67.

[10] Influenced indirectly by the Strasbourg decision *Mc Connell* v. *UK* 28488/95 impugning the triple role of the Bailiff of Guernsey.

[11] Lord Mance, 'Constitutional Reforms, the Supreme Court and the Law Lords', *Civil Justice Quarterly*, 66, 2006: 127.

In anticipation, a revivified Judges Council[12] approved the terms of a concordat reached between the Lord Chief Justice and the Lord Chancellor as to who had responsibility for what, the negotiation of which survived Lord Woolf's public description of Lord Falconer as 'a cheerful chappy' – an observation not designed to cause offence but one which clearly did so.

The functions of the Lord Chancellor, developed over a millennium, spanned, at the commencement of the first Blair administration, the legislative executive and judicial spheres of government. He was a member of the Upper House, its Speaker and a senior cabinet minister, and he presided over the Appellate Committee of the House of Lords. He had responsibilities for overseeing court administration, making appointments to the bench at all levels (including the lay magistracy) and of Queen's Counsel, and overseeing the funding of legal services. To this, during Lord Irvine's tenure, was added implementation of the HRA and in 2001 responsibility for constitutional affairs (previously within the Home Office fiefdom).

The single most significant feature of Lord Falconer's time as Lord Chancellor was his (staged) abdication of the very powers to which Lord Irvine had so tenaciously clung. The title of Lord Chancellor lingered on, symbolic not substantial, the consequences of a minor revolt in the House of Lords; but the smile on the face of the Cheshire cat had more connection with the animal itself than the titular Lord Chancellor has with the traditional holder of the office.

The judiciary

Lord Irvine sat only rarely as presiding judge in the House of Lords or Privy Council.[13] Lord Falconer never did and since April 2006 he (and his

---

[12] Lord Justice Thomas, 'The Judges' Council', *Public Law*, 2005: 608.
[13] House of Lords
    Modahl v. *British Athletic Federation Ltd* [2002] 1 WLR 1192
    Boddington v. *British Transport Police* [1999] 2 AC 143
    Director of Public Prosecutions v. *Jones (Margaret)* [1999] 2 AC 240
    Carmichael v. *National Power Plc* [1999] 1 WLR 2042
    Murray v. *Foyle Meats Ltd* [2000] AC 51
    Uratemp Ventures Ltd v. *Collins* [2002] 1 AC 301
    AIB Group (UK) Ltd v. *Martin* [2002] 1 WLR 94
    B. (A Minor) v. *Director of Public Prosecutions* [2000] 2 AC 428.
  Privy Council
    David Alexander Schiller (Appellant) v. *(1) HM Attorney-General for Gibraltar (2) The Captain of the Port of Gibraltar (Respondents)* (1998) LTL 11 September 1998 (unreported elsewhere).

successor) has been debarred from doing so. Power to appoint judges was surrendered to a Judicial Appointments Commission (JAC); and to an equivalent body to appoint Queen's Counsel. The new and more significant title of Secretary of State for Constitutional Affairs (replaced on 9 May 2007 by Secretary of State for Justice) indicated that for the future the role was political. And while mandated by the CRA to defend judicial independence and by the Courts Act 2003 to maintain an efficient court system,[14] the incumbent may do so without any experience of the legal system as a practitioner, or any knowledge of it as an academic, since the future qualification for the office will merely be the possession of such experience as the Prime Minister considers appropriate.[15]

The Lord Chief Justice assumed the title of 'President of the Court of England and Wales' with the statutory duty of representing the judiciary's views to parliament and government, overseeing the deployment of individual judges, allocating work within the courts, and ensuring that appropriate structures are in place for the training and support of judges.[16]

The removal of the Lord Chancellor from the summit apart, there were no major changes in the hierarchy – Lords of Appeal in Ordinary, Lords and Lady Justices in the Court of Appeal, High Court Judges, Circuit Judges (and Recorders[17]), District Judges and Deputy District Judges. The surrender by the Lord Chancellor of his judicial functions led to the Vice-Chancellor in the Chancery Division becoming the Chancellor.[18] The Courts Act 2003 introduced new post-holders, the Head and Deputy Head of Civil Justice. The CRA did the same for Criminal Justice and Family Justice. The Official Referee's Court was rebranded the Technology and Construction Court, and the Crown Office list the Administrative Court.

The Supreme Court will consist of twelve judges. The current Lords of Appeal will become the first members of the new court and will thereupon cease to be entitled to sit in parliament. They will be called 'Justices

---

[14] A uniform system of court administration was established in 2005 as Her Majesty's Court Service (HMCS).

[15] He has also left the Woolsack, as the House of Lords now selects its own Lord Speaker.

[16] The CRA also contained new provisions for disciplining of judges.

[17] In the wake of *Starrs* v. *Ruxton* (2000) SLT 2000 the Scottish system of temporary sheriffs was held incompatible with the right to an 'independent and impartial Tribunal' under Article 6 of the European Convention on Human Rights (ECHR), because of the vulnerability of their posts to executive influence. In Gilbertian fashion all assistant recorders were collectively upgraded to recorders.

[18] The AJA 1999 (see below) established the post of Vice-President of the Queen's Bench Division.

of the Supreme Court' and the senior members will be president and deputy president. They will inherit the jurisdiction of the House of Lords and of the Privy Council in devolution matters. Reflecting yet again the impact that architecture has on the legal system, the court will not come into being until it can be properly housed – the preferred (by the government) venue for the new court is Middlesex Guildhall. Not all Law Lords supported their detachment from parliament[19] or even their physical relocation;[20] some did,[21] others hedged their bets. 'There can be no doubt', wrote the Senior Law Lord, 'that since June 2003 the mountains have laboured mightily: it remains to be seen whether they have brought forth a mouse, or a valuable measure of overdue reform or a monster.'[22]

Lord Bingham of Cornhill was the first judge since Lord Alverstone to bring off the career coup of becoming both Master of the Rolls and Lord Chief Justice (in charge first of civil, then of criminal justice). Both his successors, Lord Woolf of Barnes and Lord Phillips of Worth Matravers, did the same. This double, once as rare as the cup and league double in football, rapidly achieved the status of a norm – and in the same era. Lord Bingham, however, went further and procured a treble, becoming Senior Law Lord in 2000. This position was thus given new status. Previously, it was allotted on the principle of Buggin's turn.

Other personal (as distinct from institutional) innovations during the Blair era included the first woman Law Lord or Lady (Baroness Hale of Richmond in 2004). In 1997 there was only one female Lord Justice (Butler-Sloss), but she was followed by (Mary) Arden, (Brenda) Hale, (Janet) Smith and (Heather) Hallett (The Crown Court Act 2003 Section 63 belatedly introduced the title 'Lady Justice'). (However, there were neither at the start nor the finish of the Blair years any ethnic minority representatives in posts above the circuit bench save for Mrs Justice (Linda) Dobbs[23].) Lawrence Collins became the first solicitor to be appointed directly to the High Court in 2006 and then to the Court of

---

[19] Lord Cooke of Thorndon, 'The Law Lords: An Endangered Heritage?' *Law Quarterly Review*, 119, 2003: 49.

[20] Lord Hope of Craighead, 'A Phoenix from the Ashes? Accommodating New Supreme Court', *Law Quarterly Review*, 121, 2005: 253.

[21] Lord Steyn, 'The Case for a Supreme Court', *Law Quarterly Review*, 118, 2002: 382.

[22] Lord Bingham of Cornhill KG, 'The Old Order Changing', *Law Quarterly Review*, 122, 2006: 211.

[23] In 2005 there were 10 women High Court Judges out of 107; 67 women Circuit Judges out of 626; 197 women benchers out of 1,414; 85 District Judges out of 433. The information on ethnic minorities is less robust, but at circuit level representation is 10%; at district level 30%.

Appeal in 2006. Sir Jack Beatson was the second High Court Judge (after Lady Hale) to have been appointed whose primary previous occupation was as an academic (latterly as Rouse Ball Professor of English Law at Cambridge).

In 1998 High Court appointments were for the first time advertised. In 1999, in the wake of Sir Leonard Peach's report, an Advisory Commission for Judicial Appointments was established. An audit carried out by that body chaired by Sir Colin Campbell in 2003 found the present system 'seriously lacking in transparency or accountability'. As a result of this critique, as well as for reasons of constitutional propriety, the JAC was set up with effect from April 2006 to select candidates for judicial office in England and Wales across all areas of the judiciary, from High Court Judges to non-legal tribunals, and to recommend one candidate for each vacancy. The new rules gave the Lord Chancellor a right of single rejection for which he has to provide reasons: he cannot select an alternative candidate. The JAC consists of fifteen persons: a judge, a solicitor, a barrister, a tribunal member and a JP with a lay majority. The lay chair, Baroness Prashar, was the former Civil Service Commissioner.

The JAC set itself three objectives – to define merit; to identify fair and effective assessment methods; and to encourage a wider range of applicants.[24] The definition of merit comprises five core qualities and abilities with seventeen supportive behaviours. Intelligence, integrity, scholarship, analytical skills and judgement, authority and articulateness are naturally paramount; but mandatory criteria such as patience, courtesy and sensitivity to other cultures and gender might well have excluded many celebrated judicial figures in even the recent past.

The system represents a sea-change from that which prevailed in May 1997 when the Lord Chancellor, after what in another context were famously called 'the customary processes of consultation' among the senior judiciary, picked, chose and invited himself. A wholly closed system has been replaced by a more open one. However, there is no doubt that the unduly modest (and indeed the unduly arrogant) will be deterred by the very need to apply for fear that any rejection may somehow become public, and others, suffering from neither of these qualities, by the sheer complexity of the system (supported, as it is, by a huge bureaucracy). It remains to be seen how much the constituency of these (especially at the High Court level and above) will differ from the beneficiaries

---

[24] Baroness Usha Prashar, 'Judicial Appointment – A Quiet Revolution', *The Barrister*, Easter Term issue, 2007.

of the abandoned methodology and, in particular, whether that constituency more accurately reflects the national demographic,[25] and, to the extent that it does so, does not concurrently compromise what its chairman has described as 'the outstanding reputation of our existing office holders'.[26]

Judges' pay

The new arrangements for appointment do not in any way qualify either judicial security of tenure or the principle that judges' pay cannot be diminished during their term of office, legacies of the Act of Settlement 1701.[27] For the future, under the new constitutional arrangements the amount of salary 'is to be determined by the Lord Chancellor with the agreement of the Treasury', the one with responsibility for the rule of law, the other for the wealth of the nation.

As a matter of practice the Senior Salaries Review Body (SSRB) with its Judicial Sub-Committee makes recommendations to the Lord Chancellor,[28] which are usually if not always accepted.[29] In the other two groups within the SSRB's remit (senior civil servants and senior officers of the armed forces) there was a move towards performance-related pay but it was rejected for the judiciary for fear of compromising judicial independence.

Those who had taken the Queen's shilling did not during the Irvine/Falconer years in fact express major worries about their pay packet. Only in 2005 was there a minor (at any rate compared with *les événements* of 1931[30]) crisis when the judges sought exemption from legislation in force from April 2006 which imposed a lifetime limit on tax relief allowed

---

[25] Lord Falconer has consulted on a proposal to permit judges below the level of the High Court to return to practice as a means of encouraging women in particular to seek judicial appointment (although he made it clear that he would not himself be the beneficiary of any such rule). [26] Baroness Prashar, 'Judicial Appointment'.

[27] Michael Beloff QC, 'Paying Judges: Who, Whom, Why, How Much?', Neill Lecture 2006, in *Denning Law Journal*, 30, 2006: 1.

[28] Lord Williams of Mostyn QC (then Chairman of the Bar Council, later a poacher-turned-gamekeeper as Attorney-General, and finally, before his premature death, Leader of the House of Lords) called it 'dangerous to have an allegedly independent body which is then overruled by politicians'. Speech at Bar Conference, September 1992.

[29] After my own retirement to its chairmanship in 2003 there was a temporary purge of lawyers, a small, but not uninteresting indication of the waning influence of the judiciary, which had traditionally insisted that only lawyers could understand their special needs.

[30] Robert Stevens, *The Independence of the Judiciary* (Oxford: Clarendon Press, 1993), pp. 52–3.

on pension benefits – said to breach their legitimate expectations on appointment – but were mollified by Lord Falconer's stealthy and well-spun announcement, in an act of political legerdemain, that he would spend an extra £9 million a year on judges' pay and pensions.[31]

However, as the gap between the earnings of top practitioners (the pool of recruits) and judges widened, there was a perceptible trend, already apparent at the start of the 1990s, of those invited to take up High Court appointments declining to do so – something almost unthinkable even thirty years ago. In 2001–2 nineteen High Court judges were appointed, but six refused. As the Sub-Committee reported in 2002:'This significant figure – almost a third of the number of those appointed – calls into question whether there was an increasing pattern of refusals which indicates future difficulties in attracting appropriate appointees.'[32]

Law officers

The decline in numbers of practising barristers who were concurrently MPs (a phenomenon whose explanation lies beyond the scope of this chapter but whose heyday was in the Edwardian era almost a century ago) meant that the tradition that the Law Officers were in the Commons was for the first time broken. John Morris MP QC, a Secretary of State for Wales in the last Labour administration, was succeeded as Attorney-General by Lord (Gareth) Williams of Mostyn QC and, when the latter became Leader of the House of Lords, by Lord Goldsmith QC. Lord Falconer QC was the first Solicitor-General and he was succeeded by Harriet Harman, a solicitor (so, paradoxically, aligning title with title-holder). She was then made a QC and so was Mike O'Brien after her.

Before 1997 the Solicitor-General used to act as the Attorney-General's deputy and carried out functions delegated by the latter. Since the Law Officers Act 1997, which made the roles interchangeable, the two ministers could divide the duties between themselves as they saw fit, but custom, if nothing else, preserved a vertical rather than a horizontal relationship. They have achieved functional but not political parity.

The Attorney-General continued to appoint the Director of Public Prosecutions (DPP), oversee the work of the Serious Fraud Office (SFO) and the Treasury Solicitor's Office (TSO), and represent the Crown Court

---

[31] Beloff, 'Paying Judges', p. 17.
[32] Cm. 5389-11, para. 4.26, discussed in Frances Gibb, 'Low Point for High Court Appointments', *The Times*, 5 March 2002.

in major international litigation and trials of the constitutional dimension. Lord Goldsmith, an accomplished advocate, was particularly engaged by this aspect of his role. But it was during his tenure that the position of Attorney-General as a member of the government, yet simultaneously its independent legal adviser, came increasingly under scrutiny. His advice, allegedly in contradiction to his first impression, that the invasion of Iraq in 2003 would be lawful;[33] his role in halting the inquiry into corruption linked to the sale of BAE systems to Saudi Arabia;[34] and his assertion in 2007 that he retained a necessary part in any decision as to whether or not Blair allies could be charged in relation to the receipt by the Labour Party of undisclosed loans by putative peers, prompted suggestions that his office should be decoupled from government altogether. The seed planted in the dying months of the Blair administration may flower in the post-Blair era.

The criminal justice system

During the period under consideration both criminal and civil court structures and systems were subject to intense scrutiny. A review of the Criminal Courts of England and Wales (2001) was carried out by Lord Justice Auld, and many of its recommendations were implemented in the Courts Act 2003. A key proposal that Crown Courts and Magistrates Courts should be amalgamated into a single court was, however, rejected; moving together was preferred to merger. The Criminal Justice Act 2003 made practical provisions for ensuring that fewer cases went to the Crown Court.

A single Commission of Peace for England and Wales was created to give JPs a national jurisdiction, though in practice they will continue to sit in local justice areas. But concurrently ninety-eight local courts closed,[35] increasing numbers of legally qualified District Judges (previously stipendiary magistrates) sat together with or in place of lay justices, and authority in many areas with implications for delivery of justice was transferred from the justices to their clerks. There was in consequence a growing sense that, notwithstanding repeated statements by Lord Chancellors to the contrary, there was a hidden agenda emanating from the Home Office to abolish the very system of lay justice.

---

[33] A decision whose legal merit was questioned by many eminent lawyers: see e.g. Lord Alexander of Weedon QC, Tom Sargant Memorial Lecture, 10 October 2003 at the Law Society, and Professor Philippe Sands, Lord Mischon Memorial Lecture 2005, at UCL.

[34] Which prompted a judicial review by two public interest bodies – unresolved at the point of writing.   [35] *The Magistrate*, May 2007.

Juries, however, remained talismanic. The Home Office consultation paper in July 1998 considered unavailingly the abolition of right to jury trial in respect of a range of offences, including grievous bodily harm and theft. Provisions of the Criminal Justice Act 2003 which allow a trial by judge alone where there is a 'real and present danger' of jury-tampering, or in complex fraud cases where the interests of justice are thought to require it, are yet to be brought into effect. Concern continued to be expressed as to whether juries – another amateur institution in a professional world – were the best instrument of justice, barely mitigated by the abolition of various immunities for jury service including counter-intuitively those of barristers and judges (in the Criminal Justice Act 2003).

One major fraud trial ('the Jubilee trial') collapsed under its own weight in 2006 at a cost to the public purse of £60 million, and the prospect of a system straining under the burden of an ever increasing number of lengthy terrorist trials (for which a special panel of twenty-one judges was created) prompted further anxiety.[36] But the civil liberties lobby in parliament retained the upper hand (especially in the Upper House) to defeat or compel withdrawal of tentative government efforts at diminishing the role of juries.

The subject of 'Crime and Penal Policy', the fruit of the criminal justice system, is dealt with elsewhere in this volume.[37] From the perspective of the judiciary, 'the torrent of criminal legislation'[38] posed problems in practice as well as of principle, as successive Home Office ministers struggled to give useful meaning to the Blair first mantra 'tough on crime'. Lord Justice Rose spoke for many when in the course of one of his judgments he described the provisions of the Criminal Justice Act as 'labyrinthine' and 'astonishingly complex',[39] adding for good measure in another case that they were 'deeply confusing,'[40] and concluding 'we find little comfort or assistance in the customary canons of construction for determining the will of Parliament which were fashioned in a more leisurely age and at a time when elegance and clarity of thought and language were to be found in legislation as a matter of course rather than exception'.

Judges remained concerned at the end as at the outset of the Blair administration that their purpose to make the punishment fit the crime

---

[36] See the account of the experience of one juror in the bomb plot trial, *The Times*, 3 May 2007, p. 6.   [37] See chapter 15, p. 318.   [38] Lord Bingham, 'The Rule of Law', p. 9.

[39] *R* v. *Lang* (2005) EWCA Crim 2864 2006 1 WLR 2509, para. 16.

[40] *R (Crown Prosecution Service)* v. *South East Surrey Youth Court* (2005) EWHC 2929 (Admin) 2006 1 WLR para. 14.

was being impaired by legislative incoherence, political pressure and lack of prison space.

Civil justice system

Auld followed Woolf. The Civil Procedure Act 1997 (providing a statutory foundation for the Report of Lord Woolf into 'Access to Justice') received the Royal Assent in February 1997, just before the demise of the Major administration. It was enacted against a background of continuous change in civil justice: judicial case management, alternative dispute resolution (ADR), conditional fees for personal injury and insolvency cases were already part of the legal landscape.

But if the Conservative government was the midwife, the Blair government was the nurse of the new civil procedure rules (CPR) which came into effect on 26 April 1999 and were described as 'a new product code with the overriding objective of enabling the Courts to deal with cases justly'. They were infused with the concepts of proportionality – the devotion of time and money not in excess of that required by the issues at stake[41] and equality of arms – that, so far as practicable, parties should be on an equal footing – and designed to eliminate delay, expense and complexity. There were provisions to promote settlement[42] and to mitigate the traditional adversarial culture. Judges were to manage cases both pretrial and at the trial; and were no longer to allow parties (and their lawyers) to dictate the pace of legislation. Under the rules there were developments of group litigation orders (GLO) and the representative action, stopping short, however, of full-blown class actions, US-style.[43] Archaic phrases were removed from the vocabulary of the rules, although not all changes clarified, and traditionalists regretted the replacement of pithy Latinisms with more ponderous Anglo-Saxon prose.

Before 1997 appeals in civil cases from the County Court and the High Court were generally heard by the Court of Appeal. Sir Jeffrey Bowman identified the work load of that court as excessive.[44] Part IV of the Access to Justice 1999 Act (AJA 99) reformed the system. In civil and family cases

---

[41] Small claims were allocated to a fast track and there was a multi-track for more complex litigation.

[42] Simon Roberts 'Settlement as Civil Justice', *Modern Law Review*, 63, 2000: 739, a step not far enough according to some. Rachel Smithson, 'Some Difficulties with Group Litigation Orders – and Why the Class Action is Superior', *Civil Justice Quarterly*, 2005: 40 (see also 212).   [43] Smithson, 'Some Difficulties'.

[44] Report to the Lord Chancellor by the Review of the Court of Appeal (Civil Division) 1997.

permission is normally required to appeal any first-instance decision and more appeals are dealt with at a lower level than before.

The consistent themes in the reorganisation of court business in the civil and in the criminal field during the Blair years were flexibility in deployment of judicial resources, the allocation of cases to the lowest appropriate level, and the increasing involvement of judges in adminis- tration at the expense of judging. Beneath the surface of formal adjudica- tion by judges there developed an emphasis on ADR,[45] encouraged by the Lord Chancellor's Department (LCD) (subsequently renamed the Department of Constitutional Affairs and latterly the Department of Justice) and indeed blessed by the courts themselves,[46] not only arbitra- tion but mediation, conciliation and negotiation.[47]

Only Coroner's Courts survived the tide of the reform and a Bill is pro- posed for the next session of parliament to modernise the last relic of a medieval legal system whose peculiarities were exposed in contentious litigation over the format of the inquest into the death of Diana Princess of Wales.[48]

Legal aid

The AJA 1999 provided for two new schemes to replace the existing legal aid scheme whose origins lay, like the National Health Service, in the post-war Atlee administration, and which was similarly subject to increasing strains as demand outweighed capacity. A Legal Services Commission (LSC) was established to create, maintain and develop a Community Legal Service for civil and family cases. It has a duty to use its resources reflecting the priorities set by the Lord Chancellor to secure the best possible value for money and to liaise with other funders of legal ser- vices. The Commission was also to be responsible for a Criminal Defence Service (for the first time in England) providing a Public Defender Service (PDS).[49]

---

[45] Alternative Dispute Resolution (ADR 1999).
[46] *Cowl* v. *Plymouth CC* [2002] 1 WLR 803, *Dunnett* v. *Railtrack Plc* [2002] 1 WLR 2434.
[47] See Henry Brown and Arthur Marriott, *ADR Principles and Practice*, 2nd edn (London: Sweet and Maxwell, 1999).
[48] *R (on the application of Paul and others)* v. *Deputy Coroner of the Queen's Household and Assistant Deputy Coroner for Surrey; R (on the application of Al Fayed)* v. *Deputy Coroner of the Queen's Household and Assistant Deputy Coroner for Surrey* [2007] 2 All ER 509.
[49] Derek O'Brien and John Arnold, 'Salaried Defenders and the Administration of Justice Act 1999', *Modern Law Review*, 63, 2000: 394.

Publicly funded legal services could only be provided by those who held Legal Service Commission contracts (building on a franchising system in place since 1994) to those who survived both a merits and means test. Previously lawyers were paid after the event, calculated by reference to time expended on the case; thenceforth they were to be paid by block contracts with prices fixed in advance. But the contract system necessarily limited suppliers and inevitably imposed regulatory and administrative burdens on solicitors.

From 1 April 2005 there was a mandatory system of fixed fees covering all types of controlled civil work, except immigration. When graduated fixed fees were introduced for family and criminal work, barristers took the view that they were being denied 'proper remuneration' and voted to abandon the cab-rank rule for cases subject to the system. There was even a brief strike.[50]

A letter to *The Times* on 30 November 2006 from a Law Society Council member suggested that the rise in legal aid spending was not the result of professional inefficiency but 'bureaucracy imposed upon solicitors by the Legal Services Commission; more and more legislation, policies and initiatives; sloth and incompetence in the manner that cases are investigated and considered for charge; poor listing practices in the Magistrates Courts and the Crown Courts; incompetent management of the Courts along with too many managers and not enough people processing the work'. Fixed fees, it was suggested, led to fixed amounts of time and effort devoted to the work.

But whatever its cause, the fact of the rise was undisputed and in July 2006 Lord Carter presented a Review of the Legal Aid Programme at the invitation of the Lord Chancellor, which made sixty-two recommendations for a move to a market-based approach (a characteristic Blairite concept). Among the key ones were: best value tendering for legal aid contracts based on quality, capacity and price from 2009; new responsibilities for the Law Society and the Bar Council to enhance the quality of the legal aid supplier market; fixed fees for solicitors carrying out legal aid work in police stations to encourage more efficient practices, including cutting costs related to waiting and travelling times; revised graduated fees for Crown Court advocates and a new graduated fee scheme for Crown Court litigators to reward earlier preparation and resolution of cases; tighter control of very high cost criminal legal aid cases; standard fees for civil and family legal help, and new graduated fees for solicitors in private law family and childcare proceedings.

---

[50] See further restrictions contemplated by the Criminal Defence and Services Act 2006.

The Law Society criticised the complexity of the LSC's draft contract terms. The Bar applauded the revised advocacy graduated fee scheme (RAGFS) in place in April 2007, which ended a decade of diminution (in real terms) of the value of fees for defence work, and a redistribution from long cases (which enabled a few barristers to earn enviable sums from the public purse) to 1–10 day cases, but objected to proposed rates for long complex cases, and price competitive tendering (PCT). Both branches of the profession were united in their concerns about the future of publicly funded legal provision. 'We are facing', the president of the Law Society recently wrote, 'the long term under-funding of an impoverished legal aid system and the additional threats posed by the government's foolhardy timetable for changes in the legal system'.[51] Both the professions anchored their criticism in the needs for the vulnerable (those accused of crimes,[52] in family disputes, or seeking welfare benefits) to be properly represented.

The government, while careful not to suggest that the criticism was fuelled by professional self-interest, contended that the ever growing demands for legal services were putting intense pressure on the national economy, but like Harpagon in Molière's *L'Avare*, who aspired to a better table at a lower cost, claimed less convincingly that better justice could be provided at less expense. A variety of judicial review challenges, claiming in particular that the reforms will put small firms servicing minority communications out of business, are in the pipeline.[53]

The AJA 99 also affected reforms in relation to the private funding of litigation.[54] Conditional fee agreements were extended in 1999 to all civil (except family) cases. Both the uplift payable for successful cases and litigation insurance premiums could be recovered in costs from the other side. Third parties became entitled to establish funds to support litigation, also on a conditional basis. While supporters of the measures argued that they increased access to justice for those too rich to qualify for public funds, but not rich enough to pay for lawyers, critics warned against the spur to 'ambulance chasers' and the potential for conflicts of interest between client and lawyer.[55]

[51] Fiona Woolf, 'What Price Justice?', *The Barrister*, Easter issue, 2007.
[52] The Criminal Defence and Services Act 2006 enables regulations to be made to give the Legal Services Commission powers to grant and withhold rights to representation in criminal proceedings. Section 2 provides the right for representation to be granted only where the individual satisfies the criteria of financial eligibility.
[53] Frances Gibb, 'Is This an Unseemly Rush to Change?', *The Times Law*, 1 May 2007, p. 26.
[54] See the consultation paper 'Access to Justice and Conditional Fees' (LCD, 1998).
[55] Desmond Ryan, 'Conditional Fee Agreements: Strutting their Stuff Around – A Circle that Cannot be Squared', *Civil Justice Quarterly*, 2001: 29.

Tribunals

The report of Sir Andrew Leggatt, former Lord Justice of Appeal[56] – the first serious review since the Franks Report 1957[57] – identified a system of adjudication, outside the boundaries of the ordinary court system, which had 'grow'd like Topsy', and was in consequence topsy-turvy. Leggatt recommended a common administrative service: the grouping of existing tribunals into nine divisions, with each related to a single subject area, each with its appellate tier (providing appeals on points of law and thereafter to the Court of Appeal). As was usual with reports of this period, not *all* his recommendations were accepted,[58] but a new tribunal service accountable to the Department of Constitutional Affairs (DCA) was launched in April 2006 without the need for legislation,[59] and a Tribunals Courts and Enforcement Bill has been introduced into parliament.

The Bill reflects many of the principles applied elsewhere to reforms of the court system, importantly involvement of the JAC in the appointments process; interchangeability of roles (for example, Circuit Judges will be automatically tribunal members); a duty on the Lord Chancellor to provide administrative support; carefully limited two-tier appeal rights; and, less importantly, the re-designation of legally qualified members as tribunal judges.

Some tribunals will share a common administration, and the leadership of the Senior President of Tribunals, but their jurisdictions will remain autonomous, the employment tribunals (and the Employment Appeal Tribunal) because of the nature of the cases that come before them, involving one party against another (unlike most other tribunals which hear appeals from citizens against decisions of the state), the Asylum Immigration Tribunal (AIT 2005) because (unlike the other tribunals) it has a single-tier appeal only.

The government had originally intended to immunise the AIT's decisions from judicial review, but retreated in the face of massive opposition from all parts of the political spectrum.[60]

---

[56] *Tribunals for Users. One System, One Service* (London: TSO, 2001).   [57] Cm. 218.

[58] See Department of Constitutional Affairs, *Transforming Public Services: Complaint, Redress and Tribunals* (London: DCA, 2004).

[59] Guevara Richards and Hazel Genn, 'Tribunals in Transition: Resolution or Adjudication', *Public Law*, 2007: 116.

[60] Andrea Le Sueur, 'Three Strikes and It's Out', *Public Law*, Summer 2004: 225.

Inquiries

The Blair years saw a series of controversial inquiries of different origins. Lord Hutton's into the death of Dr David Kelly was non-statutory; the Bloody Sunday Inquiry chaired by Lord Saville was set up under the Tribunals of Inquiry (Evidence) Act 1952. But the lack of coherence prompted the Inquiries Act 2005, so as to provide a new framework by which a minister can establish an inquiry into events that have caused public concern, endowed with appropriate coercive powers to commandeer documents and to summon witnesses. Inquiries will generally sit in public, but (controversially) there is a discretion to hold them in private. The issue of diverting judges from their judicial function was not addressed in the Act directly; the provision requiring a minister to consult the Lord Chief Justice about such appointments may put a brake on the practice but will not bring it to a stop. Lawyers as a class may (like politicians) be unpopular: judges retain substantial respect, but it is doubtful if it is enhanced by their deployment in such extra-curricular exercises.[61]

The professions

The AJA 99 accelerated the thrust of the Courts and Legal Services Act (1990) and enshrined the principle that lawyers with appropriate qualifications and subject to appropriate rules of conduct should be able to exercise full rights of audience in all proceedings. It provided for the Lord Chancellor to authorise bodies other than the Law Society to grant rights of audience and to authorise their members to conduct litigation (including the Chartered Institute of Patent Agents, the Institute of Trademark Attorneys and the Institute of Legal Executives). This did not, however, affect overmuch the Bar's dominance in advocacy, and it countered the challenge by changing its rules so that barristers could in certain circumstances accept instructions directly from clients rather than through solicitors.[62]

In 2003 Lord Irvine dramatically suspended the system by which he had annually selected (on the Queen's behalf) successful applicants for the rank of Queen's Counsel in the wake of a critical report by Sir Colin Campbell. However, despite fears (in the profession) that the status would be forever abolished, in 2006 it was reinstated by Lord Falconer, but with the Lord Chancellor excluded from the selection process, which

---

[61] Iain Steele 'Judging Judicial Inquiries', *Public Law*, Winter 2004: 738.
[62] The AJA 1999 established a system of practising certificates for barristers.

was now handed over to an independent panel. A fee of £2,500 is now required for an application, but this did not appear to deter ambitious applicants, and in 2006 out of 175 successful ones there were thirty-three women and ten from ethnic minorities. Honorary Silk was bestowed more frequently than before on senior solicitors and academics.

The professions were not immune to the modernising spirit of the age. Already by 1997 the traditional position at the Bar whereby pupils (apprentice barristers) paid their pupil masters had been reversed. Now scholarships of ever increasing size were offered by sets of chambers to counter the attractions of the substantial salaries paid by blue-chip city firms to newly qualified solicitors. The Bar indeed adopted a rule which prohibited unfunded pupillages (although, as an example of the law of unintended consequences in action, it may have worked against those from non-traditional backgrounds). School placement programmes to promote the Bar as a career to new constituencies and a Bar Vocational Course (BVC) loan scheme negotiated with major banks are part of the current Bar Council agenda.[63] A committee chaired by Lord Neuberger is examining the virtue of further reforms.[64] Whether outreach programmes, any more than those of the ancient universities, will dispel the perception of a closed professional shop, engendered by anachronistic media representation and the concerns of law lecturers in the newer universities, has yet to be seen.

To negotiate the shoals of anti-discrimination law, Chambers adopted far more rigorous systems of assessment for aspirant pupils and tenants, and for the most part recognised the guidance of the Pupils Applications Clearing House (PACH) and its descendant (OLPAS), designed to introduce some order and equity into what had previously been an anarchic system in which Chambers competed unscrupulously against each other for the best and brightest recruits, like football club managers seeking out teenage players.

For barristers and solicitors alike, continuing professional education became mandatory – swelling the ranks of conference organisers, complementing an increasing emphasis on practical training before and at the stage of pupillage at the Bar or articles as solicitors. Pro bono work became fashionable.

Transfers between the two branches of the profession increased – Herbert Smith and Co. became the first City firm to employ two QCs – while

---

[63] Geoffrey Vos QC, 'A Programme for the Future Success of the Profession', *The Barrister*, Easter Term issue, 2007: 1.
[64] The Neuberger Interim Report was published on 5 April 2007.

traffic in the reverse direction was still more common. Relations between the professions improved, even if the Bar insisted that its code of conduct, including the cab-rank rule, ought to be applied to all advocates, while in major firms Chinese walls had to be constructed so as to avoid conflicts of interest. Responding to globalisation, there were mergers between City firms, and between them and their many US (or continental) equivalents. Clifford Chance's merger with the US firm Rogers and Wells created the world's first billion-dollar practice.[65]

Despite all these internal modernising initiatives, in July 2003 the DCA concluded that the regulatory framework in England and Wales was 'outdated, inflexible, over-complex and insufficiently accountable or transparent', and commissioned Sir David Clementi to investigate.

He duly proposed an independent officer for legal complaints and a legal standards board to oversee the profession; permission for barristers to enter into partnerships with solicitors; and permission for non-lawyers to manage and own legal practices. A Heineken approach designed to allow the legal services to reach hitherto unreached parts seemed destined to result in a Tesco law. While he recommended that in any such new-style law company (alternative business structures (ABS)) qualified lawyers should be in the majority, the government have opted for unlimited external ownership and investment, taking, in the view of some critics, the lawyers out of the law. Bridget Prentice, the Minister for Constitutional Affairs, notoriously equated the purchase of legal services with the purchase of baked beans.

The Legal Services Bill currently before parliament sets out proposals for a new regulatory framework – the Legal Services Board (LSB), which will authorise front-line regulators, the Bar Council and the Law Society to carry out day-to-day regulation, provided they meet LSB standards. In tandem there will be a new Office for Legal Complaints (OLC) to handle complaints for the whole legal profession. Given the fact that the professions had already sought to separate their representatives from the regulatory rules, this excited the concern that the Falconer legacy to the legal profession would be regulation, regulation, regulation.

None of this impeded an inexorable upward trend in qualified lawyers. In July 2004 there were 121,165 qualified solicitors – a growth of 50% in

[65] Some described and decried the metamorphosis of the legal professions into legal businesses with both sets of Chambers and solicitors seeking to provide a corporate in-house service which might be other than in the best interests of clients. Sir Gavin Lightman, 'A Legal Profession for the Twenty First Century', *Civil Justice Quarterly*, 22, 2001: 235.

the decade. Women constituted 39,199 – an increase of 120%; ethnic minorities 8,031 – an increase of 2.2% up to 9%. At the same time there were 11,564 barristers in independent practice, of whom 8,153 were men and 3,411 were women (these included 1,078 QCs, of whom 991 were men and 87 were women).

Lawyers' law

While changes in the legal system and its institutions are matters for the political arms of government, changes in the law itself are shared with the judicial arm. In this context the conventional view relegates the judiciary to a minor role. The legislature can affect changes in areas previously controlled by the common law. The judiciary, by contrast, cannot affect changes in legislation. The sovereignty of parliament is said to be a constitutional fundamental.

This picture requires continued modification for three main reasons. Firstly, the impact of the United Kingdom's accession to the Treaty of Rome involved the traversing of a legal Rubicon: thenceforth the laws of the United Kingdom were subordinate to a higher norm. This development preceded the Blair administration by a quarter of a century, but despite the rhetorical rejections of a European superstate from many of its prominent figures, the Prime Minister included, leaving the European Union was never an option on the table and Luxembourg (the European Court of Justice) as well as Brussels (the European Commission) impinged ever further on the national substantive law in a host of areas ever more loosely connected with a common market.

Secondly, the domestication of the ECHR by the Human Rights Act 1998 (HRA) with effect from 2 October 2000 gave judges the novel power to declare that duly enacted legislation itself was incompatible with Convention rights, or else face defeat at the hands of the European Court of Human Rights in Strasbourg. The power was rarely used, partly because the HRA simultaneously imposed on the judges the duty to interpret legislation so as to make it compatible with Convention rights 'so far as possible' reading words into or out of a statutory scheme. On some occasions they effectively undermined the very thrust of the legislation itself, for example by reinstating the right of persons accused of rape to cross-examine the alleged victim on her previous sexual experience.[66]

---

[66] *R* v. *A* [2000] 1 AC 45.

The HRA, by annexing most Convention rights, involved the national court in deciding such open-textured and politically freighted questions as to what interference with them was 'necessary in a democratic society', stimulating a debate as to whether (and when) the judiciary should show deference to executive or legislative choice.[67]

The HRA has thus substantially added to the weapons at the disposal of an already activist judiciary, extending the control of executive action by means of the machinery of judicial review,[68] corralling and sometimes frustrating the wishes of the government. Because the courts are also identified by the HRA as public authorities, it also invigorated the development of the common law.

In many areas judges' use of the HRA has been relatively uncontroversial. Sidling in where parliament has feared to tread, the courts have effectively created a right of privacy in cases involving persons from model Naomi Campbell[69] to the Prince of Wales,[70] while simultaneously extending the boundaries of freedom of expression, especially where political speech[71] is involved.

More controversially, spurred on by decisions from Strasbourg the courts have abrogated the Home Secretary's role in determining how long prisoners sentenced to life imprisonment should serve.[72] They have modified the interpretation of various statutes to protect the rights to a fair trial and the presumption of innocence.[73] They have launched a series of torpedoes at the government's desire for stricter control of immigration and restrictions on asylum-seekers.[74] David Blunkett counterattacked: ' I am personally fed up with having to deal with a situation where Parliament debates the issues and the Judges then overturn them.'

In *A v. Secretary of State for the Home Department*[75] the House of Lords determined that detention without trial of suspected foreign terrorists was incompatible with the HRA, being both disproportionate and

---

[67] See Beloff, 'The Concept of Deference'.
[68] Michael Beloff QC, 'Judicial Review – The State of the Art', *Jersey Law Review*, February 2003: 29.   [69] *Campbell* v. *Mirror Group Newspapers Ltd* [2004] 2 AC 457.
[70] *Prince of Wales* v. *Associated Newspapers Ltd* (2006) EWCA Civ 1770.
[71] *Jameel (Mohammed)* v. *Wall Street Journal Europe Sprl.* 2006 UKHL 44, [2006] 3 WLR 642. *Reynolds* v. *Times Newspapers Ltd* [2001] 2 AC 127.
[72] *R* v. *Secretary of State for Home Department ex p. Anderson* 2002 UKHL46.
[73] Though not to the point of absurdity: *Brown* v. *Stott* [2003] 1 AC 681 (no violation of the privilege against self-incrimination in compelling a defendant suspected of drink-driving to identify herself as the driver of the car).
[74] *R (European Roma Rights Centre)* v. *Immigration Officer at Prague Airport* [2005] 2 AC 1.
[75] [2005] 2 AC 68.

discriminatory. Lord Bingham of Cornhill explained how the balance of constitutional power was struck:

> It is also of course true, that Parliament, the executive and the courts have different functions. But the function of independent judges charged to interpret and apply the law is universally recognised as a cardinal feature of the modern democratic state, a cornerstone of the rule of law itself. The Attorney General is fully entitled to insist on the proper limits of judicial authority, but he is wrong to stigmatise judicial decision-making as in some way undemocratic.

On 25 July 2006 the Prime Minister commissioned a review of the Human Rights Act – although, as with not a few Blairite initiatives, words do not appear to have been followed by prompt action. It left untouched the substance of the Act and merely counselled against its overenthusiastic use.

Thirdly, in the course of rejecting a challenge based on the nuances of the Parliament Acts of 1911 and 1949 to legislation banning hunting with hounds, two of the Law Lords hinted that in extreme circumstances they would refuse to give effect to legislation which offended (in their view) basic constitutional values, reflecting a philosophy of judicial authority last articulated by Sir Edward Coke in the seventeenth century.[76] Lord Steyn said:

> The supremacy of Parliament is still the general principle of our constitution. It is a construct of the common law. The judges created this principle. If that is so, it is not unthinkable that circumstances could arise where the courts may have to qualify a principle established on a different hypothesis of constitutionalism. In exceptional circumstances involving an attempt to abolish judicial review or the ordinary role of the courts, the Appellate Committee of the House of Lords or a new Supreme Court may have to consider whether this is a constitutional fundamental which even a sovereign Parliament acting at the behest of a complaisant House of Commons cannot abolish.

These dicta represented a high-water mark in the development of judicial review prompted by a variety of factors, but, most relevantly for present purposes, by a reaction against an ever more intrusive state and an imbalance of political forces where (as during the Thatcher era) one party enjoyed such numerical supremacy in the House of Commons as to render MPs effectively unable to provide redress for citizens' grievances.[77] The judiciary at the same time revivified the

---

[76] R (Jackson) v. Attorney General (HL(E)) [2006] 1 AC 262 at 302–3.
[77] Lord Woolf 'Judicial Review – The Tensions Between the Execution and the Judiciary, Law Quarterly Review, 118, 1998: 579.

ancient tort of misfeasance in public office;[78] developed the concept of exemplary damages for abuse of public power;[79] formulated a principle of legality holding that not only ambiguous but general words were incompetent to infringe an existing constitutional principle;[80] while beating a measured retreat from the rule in *Pepper* v. *Hart*[81] which had allowed them to use, in strictly limited circumstances, ministerial statements as an aid to the construction of statutory provisions, but had involved indirectly an albeit modest qualification of their independent role as interpreters. Lord Irvine had indeed anticipated the possibility that the judges might seek to subvert the Blair agenda. In a lecture given in 1996 he inveighed against judicial supremacism,[82] but without noticeable impact.[83]

The law developed too in a subterranean way, uninfluenced by the political agenda. The judges continued, indeed completed, the journey away from a literal and towards a purposive and contextual construction of contracts[84] and statutes;[85] they conceived the technique of prospective overruling of earlier decisions;[86] and they eroded the boundaries between domestic law and international law.[87] They expanded the boundaries of negligence to embrace the performance by public authorities of statutory functions[88] and revoked the immunity of advocates from suits for negligence.[89] They also promoted equality of the sexes in the distribution of assets on divorce.[90]

---

[78] *Three Rivers DC* v. *Governor and Company of the Bank of England* (No. 3) [2003] 2 AC 1.
[79] *Kuddus* v. *Chief Constable of Leicester Constabulary* [2002] 2 AC 122.
[80] *R* v. *Secretary of State for the Home Department ex p Pierson* [1998] AC 539, 575 per Lord Browne-Wilkinson; *R* v. *Secretary of State for the Home Department ex p. Simms* [2002] 2 AC 115, 131 per Lord Hoffmann.   [81] [1993] AC 573.
[82] Lord Irvine of Lairg, 'Judges and Decision-Makers. The Theory and Practice of Judicial Review', ch. 9 in *Human Rights, Constitutional Law and the Development of the English Legal System* (London: Hart, 2004), at p. 158.
[83] I have already mentioned examples in the context of a discussion of the Prime Minister's own thinking and of the demise of Lord Irvine; for other examples see Lord Lloyd of Berwick, 'The Judges and the Executive – Have the Goalposts Been Moved?', Denning Lecture 2005, in *Denning Law Journal*, 2006: 79.
[84] *ICS* v. *West Bromwich Building Society* [1998] 1 WLR 896.
[85] *Inland Revenue Commissions* v. *McGuckian* [1997] BTC 346.
[86] *Re Spectrum Plus Ltd* 2005 UKHL 41, [2005] 3 WLR 58.
[87] See e.g. *R (on the application of Al Skreini* v. *Secretary of State for Europe and Commonwealth Affairs)* [2006] EWHC Cir. 1279.
[88] *Barret* v. *Enfield London Borough Council* [2001] 2 AC 550. *Phelps* v. *Hillingdon London Borough Council* [2001] 2 AC 619.   [89] *Arthur J. S. Hall* v. *Simons* [2002] 1 AC 615.
[90] *McFarlane* v. *McFarlane* [2006] 2 AC 618: and the much reported *Charman* case in May 2007.

In one sphere they could indeed claim to have prompted legislative reform. In denying redress to a young man who in defiance of a council warning notice dived into a shallow lake and broke his neck, Lord Hobhouse of Woodborough uttered some trenchant words which[91] found echoes in the government's subsequent Compensation Act 2006, mandating courts to take account of the possible deterrent effect of imposing liability for negligence, and which itself spawned in 2007 rules for the compulsory registration of claims-handling companies.

The Ministry of Justice

In a final effort to embed his legacy the Prime Minister announced that a Ministry of Justice was to be established on 9 May 2007 to bring together Her Majesty's Courts Service, the Tribunals Service and the current responsibilities of the DCA with the National Offender Management Service – including criminal law and sentencing policy. The Office of Criminal Justice Reform (OCJR) and the Ministry of Justice will have complete departmental oversight of civil and family justice as well as key elements of constitutional and rights-based policy such as data protection and the HRA. A simultaneous circular letter from the Lord Chancellor stated that the Ministry of Justice would strengthen further the already strong judicial–executive relationship set out in the concordat.

But despite the New Labour newspeak with which this initiative was proclaimed, senior judges, who once more were not consulted in advance, were concerned that stronger safeguards to ensure their independence were required under the proposed regime. They feared that unless the budget for the courts was ring-fenced, it would be consumed by the demands of the prisons and the probation service; that they would be forced to tailor sentences according to available prison space; and that the Minister of Justice (the Lord Chancellor) would face judicial review

---

[91] In *Tomlinson* v. *Congleton Borough Council* [2004] 1 AC 46 at p. 97:

> In truth, the arguments for the claimant have involved an attack upon the liberties of the citizen which should not be countenanced. They attack the liberty of the individual to engage in dangerous, but otherwise harmless, pastimes at his own risk and the liberty of citizens as a whole fully to enjoy the variety and quality of the landscape of this country. The pursuit of an unrestrained culture of blame and compensation has many evil consequences and one is certainly the interference with the liberty of the citizen.

proceedings before the very judges whose budget he controls,[92] creating an unseemly picture of conflict of interest.

The themes

Ad hoc as many of changes in the architecture of the law during the period appeared to be, there was an underlying rationale, reflected in Lord Hewart's oft-misquoted dictum, 'justice must not only be done but must manifestly and undoubtedly be seen to be done', betokening an increased sensitivity to the appearance, as well as the actuality, of justice. This underlay the demise of the Lord Chancellor as judge, the projected demise of the Law Lords, and the threat to the traditional role of the Attorney-General, as well as the insistence that the professions (if not, in Adam Smith's phrase, conspiracies against the laity, not their natural servants) could not independently police their own.

The editors of the ninth edition of Walker and Walker's *English Legal System*[93] wrote, 'The last 7 years since the 8th Edition of this book have seen wholesale changes and reform in virtually every aspect of the Legal System.' The tenth edition will be able to identify yet further change. Whether the changes are improvements time alone, and as always, will tell. For at the end of the three Blair administrations the same issues dominated the legal agenda as at the start, with the same inherent tensions of continuity against modernisation, merit against diversity, justice against economy.[94] Triangulation has provided no final answers.

The future

The changes made to the system during the Blair era are not likely to be reversed. Powers separated will not be conjoined. While the litigation culture still remains essentially adversarial, with outcomes dependent upon the dedication of resources and the forensic performance of counsel, there will continue to be a move away from a court-based system of dispute resolution and the traditional emphasis on oral

[92] Lord Woolf, 'Judicial Independence not Judicial Isolation', Clifford Chance Lecture at the University of Essex, April 2007. Gibb, 'Is This an Unseemly Rush to Change?'; David Pannick: 'Preventing the Ministry of Justice Causing Injustice', *The Times Law*, 8 May 2002.   [93] Published by Oxford University Press, April 2005.
[94] Lord Phillips of Worth Matravers LCJ, in his Lecture to the Judicial Studies Board, 2007, was the senior, but not the solitary voice, who saw a legal system, if not starved of resources at any rate undernourished.

advocacy.[95] New forms of dispute resolution will increasingly supplant it, whether it be via new administrative tribunals, proliferating ombudsmen (in both the public and private sectors) or mediation and its cousins. The civil service will continue to encroach upon judicial territory. It may be that a lighter touch of regulation will find favour with a Conservative administration; but the laicisation of the administration of the law will prove to be an irreversible trend.

As Mr Blair departed the scene with a controversial Ministry of Justice in its first weeks of operation, a Legal Services Bill still to reach the statute book, and, from their respective perspectives, judges, barristers and solicitors up in arms about both, he may console himself that no one could accuse him of undue favouritism to the profession of which he remains a member.

[95] For an elegiac expression of regret Michael Beloff QC, 'Advocacy. A Craft under Threat', the Espeland Lecture 2003, Oslo.

15

Crime and penal policy

TIM NEWBURN AND ROBERT REINER

Introduction: Tougher than the rest?

Crime and crime control have been pivotal to the New Labour project from the outset. The 'Blair effect' on crime policy began not in 1997 when Tony Blair became Prime Minister, nor with his 1994 election to the Labour Party leadership, but in 1992 when John Smith appointed him Shadow Home Secretary.

The significance of Blair's impact can only be appreciated in the long-term context of the post-Second World War politics of law and order. Crime had not been a partisan political issue until the early 1970s,[1] although specific aspects, notably capital punishment, were always controversial.[2] The politicisation of law and order became marked during the late 1970s, in the run-up to Margaret Thatcher's 1979 general election victory. Her sharp attacks on Labour's alleged 'softness' in relation to crime and disorder gained a huge electoral dividend: opinion polls show that no other policy put Labour so far behind the Conservatives.[3]

In the late 1980s hints emerged of a cooling of partisan conflict about crime, as both parties sought to develop more pragmatic policies. Labour realised that some of their traditional approaches (such as commitment to a strong civil libertarian stance, and to addressing the deep causes of crime) were electoral liabilities despite their intrinsic merits. For their part the Conservatives – embarrassed by unprecedented increases in crime and disorder – explored more effective crime prevention policies, rather than just ratcheting up police resources and

---

[1] David Downes and Rod Morgan, 'No Turning Back: The Politics of Law and Order into the Millennium', in M. Maguire, R. Morgan and R. Reiner (eds.), *The Oxford Handbook of Criminology* 4th edn (Oxford: Oxford University Press, 2007), pp. 201–40.

[2] T. Morris, *Crime and Criminal Justice Since 1945* (Oxford: Blackwell, 1989); M. Ryan, *Penal Policy and Political Culture in England and Wales* (Winchester: Waterside Press, 2003).

[3] Downes and Morgan, 'No Turning Back', p. 204.

punishment.[4] This pragmatic consensus was short-lived. It ended in 1992, as Tony Blair, newly appointed Shadow Home Secretary, began to capture the law-and-order issue from the Conservatives, and Michael Howard (who became Home Secretary in 1993) vigorously defended this Tory fiefdom.[5]

The key turning point came in 1992/3 with Blair's pledge to be 'tough on crime, tough on the causes of crime'.[6] Ironically, this legendary soundbite may have been 'borrowed' from its original author Gordon Brown.[7] But whatever its provenance, it resonated with the national soul-searching about crime and moral decline following the tragic murder of the Liverpool toddler James Bulger in February 1993. The beauty of the slogan was to hit all bases at once, balancing the populist desire for puni-tiveness with effective security against victimisation. Its ambiguities allowed people to see what they wanted. Did 'tough on crime' mean evi-dence-led crime prevention that worked, or harsh punishment of crimi-nals? Was 'tough on the causes of crime' a nod to the traditional social democratic idea that crime had deep social root causes? Not according to recent exchanges between Blair and David Cameron over gun crime. The Tory leader blamed a 'badly broken' society (forgetting how much of the damage was due to his predecessor, Margaret Thatcher, who had denied that there was such a thing as society). Tony Blair saw the problem as having very specific, limited causes, requiring policing solutions. But the ultimate political value of Blair's soundbite lay in its sub-text: a double whammy of toughness locked into one short, sharp sentence, cutting at a stroke the accusation that Labour was 'soft and flabby on crime' (in the words of the 1992 Conservative election manifesto).

Blair's tough talk put the Conservatives on the defensive, inaugurating a new phase in the politics of law and order: deep consensus about tough crime control but fierce conflict about which party is tougher. We will explore the 'Blair effect' on crime and criminal justice policy, analysing crime trends and patterns, the politics of law and order, the development and effectiveness of criminal justice policy, and the extent to which changes can be attributed to the Blair government.

[4] Robert Reiner, *Law and Order: An Honest Citizen's Guide to Crime and Control* (Cambridge: Polity, 2007) pp. 122–3, 130–1.
[5] Tim Newburn, ' "Tough on Crime": Penal Policy in England and Wales', in M. Tonry and A. Doob (eds.), *Crime and Justice 36* (Chicago: University of Chicago Press, 2007).
[6] Tony Blair, 'Why Crime is a Socialist Issue', *New Statesman*, 25 January 1993.
[7] Neal Lawson, ' "Reid"ing the Riot Act: New Labour, Crime and Punishment', *Renewal*, 14(3), 2006: 1; Catherine Bennett, 'Blair and Brown Keep Talking About Being "Tough on Crime". And By Tough They Mean, You Know, Tough-ish', *The Guardian*, 29 March 2007.

Boom or bust? crime trends under New Labour

During the 2005 election campaign Labour's literature postulated a triumph in the war against crime. 'When Labour came to power in 1997 we inherited a grim legacy. Crime had doubled [since the 1970s] . . . Overall crime is down by 30 per cent on 1997 . . . violent crime by 26 per cent.'[8] Michael Howard (as Conservative leader) attacked with directly contradictory figures: 'When I was Home Secretary crime fell by 18 per cent . . . Under Mr Blair . . . Overall crime is up by 16 per cent. Violent crime is up by over 80 per cent.'[9]

Neither the Labour nor the contradictory Conservative claims were lies: just different damned statistics. Labour's success story was based on the British Crime Survey (BCS); the Conservative rebuttal used the police-recorded statistics. Not surprisingly, the validity of these different data sets has become politicised. The public do not buy either good news story – the BCS regularly finds that some two-thirds of the population believe crime is rising nationally.[10]

So what *has* happened to crime under New Labour? The limitations of the police-derived figures have long been known. There is a vast 'dark figure' of unrecorded offences, because victims may not report crimes to the police, the police may not record them, and many crimes occur with no individual victims who *could* report them. So apparent trends in the statistics may reflect changes in the reporting and recording of crime rather than actual levels of offending. Nothing more could safely be said until the advent of victim surveys, in particular the BCS, launched in 1981.

The headline story of crime trends over the last half-century is the massive rise in the police-recorded rate. It rose from less than half a million offences per annum in 1955 to a peak of 5.5 million by 1992, falling back to 4.5 million in 1997 when Labour took office. But by 2003/4 the rate reached just under 6 million – the highest ever, declining to just over 5.6 million in 2005/6.[11] This supports the Conservative charge that overall crime increased under New Labour. But contrasting the police-recorded statistics with victim surveys suggests a more complex picture, putting the Conservative years in a much worse light.

---

[8] *Tackling Crime* (London: Labour Party, 2005), p. 2.
[9] 'Action on Crime' in *Conservative Manifesto*, February 2005, pp. 1–3.
[10] Alison Walker, Chris Kershaw and Sian Nicholas, *Crime in England and Wales 2005/6* (London: Home Office, 2006), p. 35.   [11] *Ibid.*, p. 14.

Three distinct phases can be distinguished on the basis of the victim survey evidence, within what otherwise appears to be a relentless rise in the recorded crime rate since the mid-1950s:[12]

1955–83: recorded crime rise

Until the 1970s there was no other measurement of trends apart from the police statistics. But during the 1970s the General Household Survey (GHS) began to ask about burglary victimisation. Its data showed that most of the increase in recorded burglary was due to greater reporting by victims. Between 1972 and 1983 recorded burglaries doubled, but victimisation increased by only 20%.[13] Victims reported more burglaries, mainly because of the spread of household contents insurance. This cannot be extrapolated necessarily to other crimes, or even to burglary in previous decades, but the GHS indicates that the increased rate for this highly significant crime was mainly a recording phenomenon, up to the early 1980s. It is plausible that this applied to volume property crimes more generally.

1983–1992: crime explosion

The BCS in its first decade showed the reverse: although recorded crime increased more rapidly between 1981 and 1993 than BCS crime (111% compared to 77%), the trends were similar. By both measures crime rose at an explosive rate during the 1980s and early 90s, the Thatcher and early Major years (see figure 15.1).

1993– : ambiguously falling crime

From the early 1990s the trends indicated by the police statistics and the BCS began to diverge. The BCS continued to chart a rise until 1995, but the police data fell from 1992 to 1997. Insurance companies made claiming more onerous, thus discouraging reporting by victims, and more 'businesslike' managerial accountability for policing implicitly introduced incentives to keep crime-recording down. So Michael Howard's success in reducing crime was mainly a recording phenomenon (see fig. 15.1).

---

[12] Reiner, *Law and Order*, ch. 3.
[13] Mike Hough and Pat Mayhew, *Taking Account of Crime: Key Findings from the Second British Crime Survey* (London: Home Office, 1985).

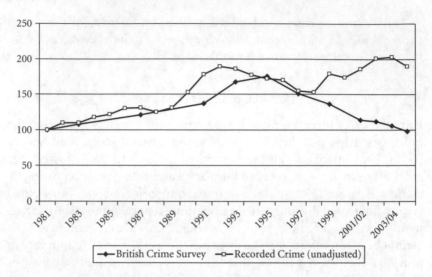

Figure 15.1. Indexed trends in crime, 1981–2004/5.

After New Labour came to power in 1997 the two measures continued to diverge – but in the opposite direction. The BCS fell from 1995 to 2005, since when it has remained roughly at the level of the first BCS conducted in 1981. The police-recorded statistics, however, began to rise again from 1998 up to 2004, since when they have declined a little.[14]

The rise in the recorded rate was due overwhelmingly to two major changes in police procedures for counting crimes: new Home Office Counting Rules in 1998, and the 2002 National Crime Recording Standard (NCRS). These reforms boosted the recorded rate substantially compared to what would have been measured previously.[15] This was a predicted consequence of the changes, because the 1998 rules made 'notifiable' a number of offences (such as common assault) that hitherto had not been included in the recorded rate, and the NCRS mandated the 'prima facie' rather than 'evidential' principle, requiring police to record 'any notifiable offence which comes to the attention of the police' even in the absence of evidence supporting the victim's report.[16]

[14] Walker *et al.*, *Crime in England and Wales 2005/6*, p. 19; Jorgen Lovbakke, Paul Taylor and Sarah Budd, *Crime in England and Wales: Quarterly Update to December 2006* (London: Home Office, 2007).

[15] This is shown by the alternative calculations using both methods in Walker *et al.*, *Crime in England and Wales 2005/6*, p. 19.

[16] John Burrows, Roger Tarling, Alan Mackie, Rachel Lewis and Geoff Taylor, *Review of Police Forces' Crime Recording Practices* (London: Home Office, 2000), p. 31.

The counting rule reforms are explicable only by concern in the early optimistic days of New Labour to develop evidence-based crime policy, even at the price of a politically sensitive rise in recorded crime. A further recent revision in 2006 restores some discretion to the police not to record offences reported to them in the absence of supporting evidence.[17] This would reduce the recorded rate, other things being equal.

The BCS is free from the particular problems that make the police figures unreliable as a measure of trends. However, it is not (and has never claimed to be), a definitive index. It necessarily omits many offences: homicide, the supreme example of personal victimisation; crimes with individual victims who are unaware of what happened (such as successful frauds); crimes against organisations or the public at large; consensual offences such as drug-taking, and other serious examples. Its sampling frame excludes certain highly victimised groups such as children under sixteen and the homeless. So the government's tendency to treat the BCS as definitive is as problematic as the earlier exclusive reliance on the police statistics.

Within the falling overall crime level, murder and other serious crimes of violence have increased. During the early 1990s there were around 650 homicides recorded per annum in England and Wales. Since 1997 this has increased to over 700, and, in most years since the millennium, well over 800 (although the figures were inflated by specific cases such as the Harold Shipman victims recorded in 2003/4), declining to 765 in 2005/6 (including those who died in the July 2005 bombings). In 1997 8% of all recorded offences were categorised as 'violent' (roughly similar proportions had characterised the crime statistics for decades), but by 2005/6 this had increased to 22%. Recorded robberies have continued to rise, as have drug offences according to the latest statistics.[18] So the trends are certainly not as rosy as the BCS suggests.

Cross-dressing: the turbo-politicisation of law and order

During the 1970s and 80s the parties were deeply polarised on matters of fundamental principle concerning crime and criminal justice. Labour embraced a species of Clintonian criminology – 'it's the economy,

---

[17] Home Office, *Counting Rules for Recording Crime*, at: www.homeoffice.gov.uk/rds/countrules.html, General Rule A.
[18] Lovbakke *et al.*, *Crime in England and Wales: Quarterly Update to December 2006*, p. 3.

stupid': crime was attributed primarily to economic deprivation and injustice. Tory policy was to toughen deterrence. New Labour sought to triangulate these poles. The 1997 Labour manifesto made this plain: 'On crime, we believe in personal responsibility and in punishing crime, but also tackling its underlying causes – so, tough on crime, tough on the causes of crime, different from the Labour approach of the past and the Tory policy of today.'

By the time Labour came to power in 1997 they had developed a raft of crime control policies, combining toughness with smart, evidence-led, joined-up, workable measures, and even some significant gestures towards Old Labour attachment to civil liberties (above all the 1998 Human Rights Act). This was epitomised by the 1998 Crime and Disorder Act, a quintessential 'third way' synthesis. The Act's Janus-faced tough/smart policy combination was encapsulated in its restructuring of youth justice: systematic, evidence-based attempts to address and prevent offending by early prediction of risks and appropriate remedies, coordinated by inter-agency local Youth Offending Teams, and centrally by the Youth Justice Board.[19] Alongside this, however, were a variety of new powers for the police and the courts to control youth crime and disorder, such as ASBOs, child curfew schemes, abolition of *doli incapax*, detention and training orders. The net result was an increase in the use of custodial penalties for young offenders.

From 1992 onwards New Labour transformed the political landscape, reflecting broader shifts in world politics. During the 1970s and 1980s neo-liberal and neo-conservative political parties, ideas and policies had become dominant in the Western world, but they were fiercely if unsuccessfully contested. On a world scale the New Right's ascendancy was completed by the 1991 fall of the Soviet Union. But what really embedded the global hegemony of neo-liberalism was the acceptance of its economic and social policy framework by the erstwhile social democratic or New Deal parties of the West. The embrace of the 'third way' by the Clinton Democrats and New Labour marked a new consensus, sounding the death-knell of the post-war mixed-economy Keynesian settlement that conservative parties had accepted in the early 1950s. Blatcherism was Butskellism in reverse. This was epitomised by the new deep consensus about law and order, a fundamental acceptance of what can be called the crime-control complex, with these core elements:

---

[19] Rod Morgan and Tim Newburn, 'Youth Justice', in Maguire *et al.*, *The Oxford Handbook of Criminology*.

Crime is public enemy no. 1

Crime, disorder – and since 2001, terrorism – are seen as *the* major threats to society and to individual citizens, by the public and politicians. MORI has conducted polls on what people see as 'the three most important issues facing Britain today' for more than thirty years. In the early 1970s, when law and order was emerging as a political issue, less than 10% rated it amongst the top three. By 1977 this had increased to 23%, and as high as 41% during the pre-election months in 1979. In the 1980s and early 1990s it generally fluctuated between 10% and 20%. But after 1993 – despite falling crime levels – the proportion putting crime in the top three issues was often above 30%. Since 2001 crime has consistently been rated a leading concern, rivalled only by 'terrorism' and 'race relations/immigration' – cognate issues in the tabloid world of law-and-order discourse, and merging into a new all-encompassing obsession with 'security'.[20]

Individual not social responsibility for crime

In the crime control consensus, crime is seen unequivocally as the fault of offenders, stemming from their free choice, individual or cultural pathology, or intrinsic evil. It is certainly *not* caused by social structural factors. This was expressed most bluntly in 1993 by the then Prime Minister John Major: 'Society needs to condemn a little more and understand a little less.' Tony Blair has frequently echoed these sentiments, as when he regretted that 'the left, by the 1980s – had come to be associated with the belief that the causes of crime are entirely structural . . . we had eliminated individual responsibility from the account'.[21]

Foregrounding victims over offenders

The victim has become the iconic centre of discourse about crime, ideal-typically portrayed as totally innocent. Crime discourse and policy are a zero-sum game: concern for victims precludes understanding – let alone sympathy for – offenders. This has become a central theme of Blair's speeches on criminal justice.

[20] Ian Loader and Neil Walker, *Civilizing Security* (Cambridge: Cambridge University Press, 2007).
[21] Tony Blair, 'Our Citizens Should Not Live in Fear', *The Observer*, 11 December 2005, p. 30.

The purpose of the criminal justice reforms is to re-balance the system radically in favour of the victim, protecting the innocent but ensuring the guilty know the odds have changed . . . our first duty is to the law-abiding citizen. They are our boss. It's time to put them at the centre of the criminal justice system. That is the new consensus on law and order for our times.[22]

Crime control works

Since the early 1990s can-do optimism has reinvigorated law enforcement agencies around the world. Policing and punishment *work*. Criminal justice professionals and conservative politicians celebrate this as a triumph of common sense over the 'nothing works' pessimism and over-sensitivity to civil liberties that are said to have hampered crime control in the late twentieth century.[23] Blair's speeches have encapsulated this:

> Looking back, of all the public services in 1997, the one that was most unfit for purpose was the criminal justice system . . . there was a resigned tolerance of failure, a culture of fragmentation and an absence of any sense of forward purpose . . . We halved the time to bring persistent juvenile offenders to justice. We introduced the first testing and treatment orders for drug offenders. We introduced and implemented a radical strategy on burglary and car crime which cut both dramatically. We toughened the law. As a result, on the statistics we are the first Government since the war to have crime lower than when we took office . . . Building on these foundations, we started to become a lot more radical in our thinking. We introduced the first legislation specifically geared to Anti-Social Behaviour. We asked the police what powers they wanted and gave them to them . . . We have introduced mandatory drug testing . . . We have established the first DNA database . . . a new framework for sentencing. Probation and prisons are to be run under one service. Community penalties are being radically re-structured. And we have 12,500 more police than in 1997.[24]

High-crime society normalised

Popular culture and routine activities have become increasingly focused on crime risks and the perception that we live in a 'high-crime society'.[25]

---

[22] Speech launching the Home Office *Five-Year Strategy for Criminal Justice*, 19 July 2004, at: www.number-10.gov.uk/output/page6129.asp.

[23] Franklin Zimring, *The Great American Crime Decline* (New York: Oxford University Press, 2007), ch. 2.

[24] Speech launching the Home Office *Five-Year Strategy for Criminal Justice*.

[25] David Garland, *The Culture of Control* (New York: Oxford University Press, 2001), pp. 161–3.

Crime concerns have penetrated everyday life,[26] paradoxically enhancing fear rather than security.

> The home owner who sets her alarm each time she leaves the house is constantly reminded of the possibility of burglary during her absence. Likewise the ubiquitous signs warning that . . . CCTV cameras are in operation, or guards patrolling are akin to anxiety makers advertising the risks of crime at every turn . . . The more provision for security is made, the more people regard as normal or necessary, and the greater their anxiety when it is not available.[27]

Backing the bobbies

Despite the many scandals that have beset them, and survey evidence about declining public trust, the police remain a bedrock mantra of security,[28] and all parties have to support and strengthen them to demonstrate their tough-on-crime credentials. There has been a remorseless growth of police powers, without corresponding safeguards, the Human Rights Act of 1998 constituting the only – increasingly beleaguered – balance. New powers to intercept communications, conduct covert operations, stop and search and arrest, and new public order offences were created in the early years of New Labour by the Police Act 1997, the Crime and Disorder Act 1998, the Regulation of Investigatory Powers Act 2000, the Terrorism Act 2000, and the Criminal Justice and Public Order Act 2001. In 2002 the Home Office conducted a review of PACE, to provide a 'useful tool supporting the police and providing them with the powers they need to combat crime'. Accordingly safeguards for suspects have been eroded. The Criminal Justice Act 2003 authorised detention for thirty-six hours for all (not just 'serious') arrestable offences, and added criminal damage to the possible grounds for stop and search. The Serious Organised Crime and Police Act 2005 created a power of arrest for all offences, enhanced powers of search and fingerprinting, and allowed for civilian custody officers, overturning the PACE requirement that they should normally be police sergeants. In Blair's last month as Prime Minister new proposals have been floated to create a power for police to stop and question

---

[26] Jonathan Simon, *Governing Through Crime* (New York: Oxford University Press, 2007).
[27] Lucia Zedner, 'Too Much Security?', *International Journal of the Sociology of Law*, 31(1), 2003: 165.
[28] Robert Reiner, *The Politics of the Police*, 3rd edn (Oxford: Oxford University Press, 2000), chs. 2 and 7; Ian Loader and Aoghan Mulcahy, *Policing and the Condition of England* (Oxford: Oxford University Press, 2003).

anyone, without any requirement of 'reasonable suspicion'.[29] The pressures on the police to achieve results have intensified in the new crime control climate, and they are armed with new powers unfettered by safeguards. This reduces the legal accountability of the police, despite the enhancement of the complaints process represented by the Independent Police Complaints Commission that became operational in 2004.

Serious and organised crime control

In common with other governments around the world, New Labour has been concerned about a perceived growing threat of serious and organised crime, seen increasingly as linked with terrorism, although the definition, measurement and character of organised crime remains elusive and controversial.[30] This has been a major stimulus to police reorganisation, accentuating a long-standing trend towards the centralisation of core detective functions. The main measure has been the creation of the Serious and Organised Crime Agency (SOCA) by the Serious Organised Crime and Policing Act 2005. The Agency, established initially with 4,200 staff, amalgamated the functions of the earlier National Criminal Intelligence Service (NCIS) and National Crime Squad (NCS), together with the investigative branches of the Immigration Service and HM Customs and Excise (now the Revenue and Customs Service), arguably representing 'a paradigm shift in British policing'.[31] SOCA has a number of other important characteristics that set it apart from the main UK constabularies. SOCA's first director-general was drawn from the police service, having previously led the NCS, but the first chair of the SOCA board, Sir Stephen Lander, was ex-Director-General of MI5, indicating the emergence of a hybrid agency, working as a policing body but specialising in covert and intelligence-gathering activity. SOCA will have officers permanently stationed abroad working with and within intelligence agencies in other jurisdictions, and will include investigators from other UK agencies. SOCA is a non-departmental public body, not a police force, and its staff are civilians not police officers, although they have considerable designated powers. As an NDPB (non-departmental public body) it

[29] 'Minister's Plan for New Stop-And-Question Powers Takes Senior Officers by Surprise', *The Guardian*, 28 May 2007, p. 4.
[30] Michael Levi, 'Organised Crime and Terrorism', in Maguire *et al.*, *The Oxford Handbook of Criminology*.
[31] Clive Harfield, 'SOCA: A Paradigm Shift in British Policing', *British Journal of Criminology*, 46(4), 2006: 743–61.

is governed by a board with a majority of non-executive members and, unlike the majority of police forces, is answerable directly to the Home Secretary rather than to a police authority. It thus consolidates the trend towards increasing central control of policing at the expense of the local authority element of the traditional tripartite accountability structure, as well as the growing populism of policy-making – 'public concern' about issues will be ascertained by analysing 'the amount of column inches in the press'.[32] These centralising and pluralising trends are evident in relation to policing generally, encapsulated above all in the 2002 Police Reform Act, and the (as yet abortive) amalgamation programme.[33]

New times, new crimes

New Labour has been repeatedly jolted into new 'tough' laws and initiatives by media-driven moral panics, and since 2001 – and *a fortiori* 2005 – the threat of terrorism. Michael Tonry has documented no less than thirty-three such get-tough-on-crime initiatives announced between June 2001 and May 2003 alone, with thirteen 'crime summits' between 1999 and 2003.[34]

So far has New Labour gone in prioritising 'tough on crime' over 'tough on the causes of crime' – let alone civil liberties – that in recent years the Conservatives have (perhaps opportunistically) resurrected some Old Labour nostrums. During the 2005 general election, for example, they pledged to reinvigorate local police accountability with elected police commissioners – reversing the party's 1980s positions. In the 2005 parliamentary debate on government proposals to allow ninety days' detention for terror suspects, the Conservatives joined with Labour rebels to defeat the measures on civil liberties grounds, arguing they undermined 'Britain's freedoms'.[35] They also criticised Labour for politicising the police by encouraging the Metropolitan Commissioner, Ian Blair, and other chief officers to lobby in support of the government proposals – a remarkable switchover of positions from the 1980s. Since David Cameron became Conservative leader this political cross-dressing has become even more marked, with Cameron repeatedly emphasising the social roots of crime – above all in his keynote 'hug a hoodie' speech,[36]

---

[32] Sir Stephen Lander, Chair of SOCA, interview in *The Independent*, 10 January 2005, p. 29.
[33] Tim Newburn and Robert Reiner, 'Policing and the Police', in Maguire *et al.*, *The Oxford Handbook of Criminology*.
[34] Michael Tonry, *Punishment and Politics* (Cullompton: Willan, 2004), pp. 41–7.
[35] 'Blair Defeated on Terror Bill', *The Guardian*, 9 November 2005.
[36] 'Show More Understanding of Hoodies, Urges Cameron', *The Guardian*, 10 July 2006.

though he has more recently sought to distance himself from that sentiment.[37]

'Tough, with immediate bite': criminal justice policy-making

Criminal justice policy-making under Blair has had a number of hallmarks. First, and very much in contrast with 'Old' Labour policy, the overriding tendency has been to define deviance up. Second, there has been a profound shift in which the centre of government – No. 10, the Cabinet Office and special advisers – has become increasingly important in the framing of policy. Finally, crime has been used – almost more than any other public policy issue – as a means of constructing and managing the image of government generally, and the Prime Minister more particularly.

Defining deviancy up?

In 1993, New York Senator Daniel Moynihan published an influential report in which he talked of 'defining deviancy down':[38] rising crime and deviance led to such behaviour being generally viewed as 'normal', so that the public (and police) had become overly tolerant of previously unacceptable forms of conduct. Despite Margaret Thatcher's hard-line rhetoric, the criminal justice policies pursued by her Home Secretaries had been something of a phoney war, certainly compared to New Labour's crime policy, which has defined deviancy up since 1997 (a trend already under way with the Major government's reaction to Blair's post-1993 seizure of the toughness agenda).[39]

This can be seen in the sheer weight of criminal justice legislation since 1997. Ignoring laws containing crime-related provisions but primarily aimed at other matters, there were well over forty major Acts of Parliament on criminal justice and penal policy between 1997 and 2006. It has been estimated that more than 3,000 new criminal offences have been created since 1997, one for every day the Blair government has been in power.[40]

---

[37] 'Don't Hug a Hoodie, Says Cameron', BBC News 17 May 2007, http://news.bbc.co.uk/1/hi/uk_politics/6665017.stm (accessed 20 May 2007).

[38] Daniel Patrick Moynihan, 'Defining Deviancy Down: How We've Become Accustomed to Alarming Levels of Crime and Destructive Behaviour', *American Scholar*, 62(Winter), 1993: 17–30.   [39] Reiner, *Law and Order*, pp. 129–39.

[40] Nigel Morris, 'Blair's "Frenzied Law-Making"', *The Independent*, 16 August 2006.

Defining deviancy up is also visible in the criminalisation of social policy. Matters previously defined as 'social problems' are defined as 'crime problems', and crime prevention or reduction becomes a central, sometimes overriding, goal of social policy.[41] This is perhaps most visible in the areas of asylum and immigration, where government policy is now inextricably tied to crime and security. Similar observations, however, might be made about housing, education and welfare policy, each of which is increasingly permeated by crime control concerns. Thus, a central goal of local government and housing policy is now the creation of 'safe and sustainable communities'[42] and a core aim of education policy has become the reduction of failure in adult life as indicated by such risk factors as repeat offending and drug use.[43]

New Labour's most substantial policy developments in this regard are what have become known as its anti-social behaviour and Respect agendas. From his earliest days as Shadow Home Secretary Blair appeared convinced that tackling 'incivilities' as well as crime should be a core government responsibility, much influenced by James Q. Wilson and George Kelling's 'Broken Windows' arguments.[44] In 1997, in response to a question about his view of zero tolerance by the editor of the *Big Issue,* Blair said, 'It is important that you say we don't tolerate the small crimes. It says you don't tolerate the graffiti on the wall . . . Obviously, some people will interpret this in a way which is harsh and unpleasant, but I think the basic principle is here to say: yes it is right to be intolerant of people homeless on the streets.'[45]

It was New Labour's initial flagship law-and-order legislation – the 1998 Crime and Disorder Act – which introduced ASBOs. Their reach has subsequently been extended by the Criminal Justice and Police Act 2001, the Police Reform Act 2002 and, crucially, by the Anti-Social Behaviour Act 2003, adding substantially to the powers available to the courts, the police and local authorities. The establishment of an Anti-Social Behaviour Unit and a 'Respect Task Force' under the direction of the outspoken Louise Casey – previously the government's 'homelessness

---

[41] Adam Crawford, *Crime Prevention and Community Safety* (Harlow: Longman, 1998).

[42] HM Government, *Five Year Plan. Sustainable Communities: People, Places and Prosperity* (London: ODPM, 2005).

[43] Department for Education and Skills, *Five Year Strategy for Children and Learners* (London: DfES, 2004).

[44] James Q. Wilson and George Kelling, 'Broken Windows: The Police and Neighbourhood Safety', *Atlantic Monthly*, March 1982, pp. 29–38.

[45] 'Clear Beggars from Streets, Says Blair', *The Times*, 7 January 1997.

czar' – ensured that the issue became, and remained, a high-profile one. In a short period, 'ASBO' became part of everyday vocabulary. Government priority has clearly been to increase the use of such measures. In a speech to Anti-Social Behaviour Co-ordinators in 2004, Blair said, 'The challenge I gave you last year was to make sure you used [your legal powers]. You have risen to the challenge in a hugely impressive way. And I want to thank you all.'[46]

Labour has not neglected its pledge to be tough on the causes of crime. Initiatives such as Sure Start and child-poverty-related policies, the various community regeneration programmes, and the attempts to improve support for working parents and for early years education, attack some of the social conditions conducive to offending, and should not be underestimated. Yet the overwhelming message from government on law and order has remained that tough crime-fighting policies are key. In its concern to jettison Old Labour's tendency to 'define deviance down', New Labour has swung inexorably in the other direction: redefining social ills as problems of crime and social order, and extending the reach of the criminal justice system into ever greater parts of community and family life.

'Yes, Prime Minister'

The nature of criminal justice policy-making has also changed markedly in the last decade. There have been substantial changes within the Home Office, culminating in the splitting of the department into two parts. Crucially, the centre of gravity in criminal justice policy-making has shifted, with the Prime Minister and the Cabinet Office occupying an increasingly important role. Significant changes in the Home Office had already begun under Michael Howard's tenure as Home Secretary between 1993 and 1997. Senior civil servants of long standing have been replaced by individuals drawn from other areas of public life, often with little experience of policy-making. The policy-making process in this field has become more politicised[47] with the emphasis on 'delivery' driving performance. Political, policy and special advisers have become more prominent, as has No. 10 and the Cabinet Office.

---

[46] Quoted in Rod Morgan, 'With Respect to Order, the Rules of the Game Have Changed: New Labour's Dominance of the 'Law And Order' Agenda', in Tim Newburn and Paul Rock (eds.), *The Politics of Crime Control: Essays in Honour of David Downes* (Oxford: Clarendon Press, 2006), p. 101.

[47] Ian Loader, 'Fall of the "Platonic Guardians" ', *British Journal of Criminology*, 46(4), 2006: 561–86.

Blair's role has been central. Seemingly ill at ease leaving home affairs to his Home Secretaries, Blair surrounded himself with policy teams and advisers, producing a stream of ideas and initiatives, by no means all well thought through. Controversially, in 2000 the ex-Director-General of the BBC, John Birt, became an unpaid special adviser to the Prime Minister, where his responsibilities included drawing up a '10-year crime plan'.[48] Although there is no evidence that Burt's eventual report[49] had much impact,[50] it is the fact of his appointment – with no experience in the field, and working directly to the PM rather than the Home Secretary – that is significant. As noted earlier, there have been regular 'summits' in Downing Street to debate the latest crime problems, and several reviews of crime policy conducted outside the Home Office, all suggesting that Blair perceived crime policy as central to his government's and his own success.

Smart and tough? PR and penal policy

Central to the shift from 'Old' to 'New' Labour was the utilisation of public relations techniques in the presentation of the party and policy initiatives. From the famous 'tough on crime, tough on the causes of crime' soundbite onwards, image management has played a significant role. This had three main aspects: creating and announcing policy in ways that are expected to play well in the tabloid press; using crime announcements to divert attention from other 'bad news' stories; and, crucially, using crime initiatives as a regular vehicle for placing stories that aim, at least in part, to convey positive (tough) messages about the Prime Minister.

Gaining attention

New Labour took much from the Clinton Democrats. Writing in 1993, Patricia Hewitt and Phillip Gould suggested that 'the lessons which the British left can learn [from the US] are not so much about *content* – although there is valuable intellectual exchange already under way – as

---

[48] 'Birt Becomes Number 10 Adviser', http://news.bbc.co.uk/1/hi/uk_politics/1483994.stm (accessed 21 May 2007).

[49] The report is available at: www.cabinetoffice.gov.uk/foi/pdf/crime.pdf.

[50] It has been said that it was Birt who alerted Blair to the significance of drugs in relation to crime, and he certainly produced a later report on the topic, not all of which has been published. It does not seem to have had any impact on policy. Cf. Alan Travis, 'Prescribe Free Heroin: Birt's Secret Advice to Ministers', *The Guardian*, 9 February 2006.

about *process*.[51] Ensuring that headlines aimed at 'Middle England' (what the Clintonites called the 'working middle class' in the US) displayed sufficient 'tough-on-crime' credentials was a central concern. Consequently, tough-sounding terminology such as 'zero tolerance' and 'three strikes and you're out' were regularly deployed in speeches and newspaper articles by Blair and successive Home Secretaries.[52] Punitive rhetoric has been an ever-present feature of New Labour's method.[53] Writing for, and to, the tabloid press was also a core tactic, to announce policy initiatives or, occasionally, to respond personally to criticism.[54]

Diverting attention

Particularly when under pressure Blair's administrations have sought to hide bad news by making 'new' policy announcements or quickly suggesting new initiatives. From the start crime has been central to such tactics. In early 1999 the controversial 'three strikes and you're out' provision for burglary, introduced as part of Michael Howard's 1997 Crime (Sentences) Act but put on hold by Jack Straw, was suddenly activated in the midst of the row over Peter Mandelson's home loan.[55] More recently, as the story of the Home Office's mishandling of foreign national prisoners was beginning to unfold, the Prime Minister and new Home Secretary immediately announced a series of initiatives, including the possible introduction of a paedophile notification scheme along the lines of the US Megan's Law (an idea floated and rejected several years previously), as well as another proposed 'radical overhaul' of the criminal justice system to 'safeguard the human rights of victims at the expense of offenders'.[56]

Framing Blair

In the years leading up to the 1997 election victory, crime worked well for Blair. His speech after the murder of James Bulger, and the 'tough on crime' sound-bite, powerfully illustrated how effective crime stories could be in the positive presentation of self to the electorate. Once in

[51] Patricia Hewitt and Phillip Gould, 'Lessons from America: Learning from Success – Labour and Clinton's New Democrats', *Renewal*, 1(1), 1993: 45–51.
[52] Tim Newburn and Trevor Jones, 'Symbolising Crime Control: Reflections on Zero Tolerance', *Theoretical Criminology*, 11(2), 2007: 221–43.
[53] Norman Fairclough, *New Labour, New Language* (London: Routledge, 2000).
[54] 'Rattled: Blair Pens 975 Words to *The Sun* in his Defence', *The Sun*, 2 May 2000.
[55] www.guardian.co.uk/guardianpolitics/story/0,,321637,00.html (accessed 21 May 2007).
[56] 'Blair to Launch Overhaul of Criminal Justice', *The Guardian*, 16 June 2006.

power, Blair continued to use the media in this way, with increasingly mixed results. Ill-thought-through initiatives, such as marching offenders to cashpoint machines, were spotted for what they were, and sat uneasily with longer-term Home Office policies. Perhaps the best illustration emerged from another attempt to hide a bad news story by a policy announcement. In a handwritten memo written in April 2000 – but leaked some time later – Blair made clear his preferred strategy:

> On crime, we need to highlight the *tough* measures: compulsory tests for drugs before bail . . . the extra number of burglars jailed under 'three strikes and you're out'. Above all, we must deal *now* with street crime . . . When the figures are published . . . they will show a small – 4 per cent – rise in crime. But this will almost entirely be due to the rise in levels of street crime – mobile phones, bags being snatched. This will be worst in London. The Met Police are putting in place measures to deal with it; but as ever, we lack a tough *public* message along with the strategy. We should think now of an initiative, e.g. locking up street muggers. Something tough, with immediate bite that sends a message through the system . . . But this should be done soon and I, personally, should be associated with it.[57]

Blair's long-standing interest in crime policy, and his early successes in using it to party and personal advantage, have coloured New Labour criminal justice policy. Much of the government's 'initiativitis' in this area, and its tendency to undermine medium and long-term policy programmes with short-term, apparently knee-jerk initiatives – or, indeed, merely 'kite-flying' for a quick headline – can be laid at Blair's door. Ironically, for an administration so wedded to image-management as a core component of governing, the consequence has been a confused and at times incoherent public presentation of criminal justice policy-making.

What worked? New Labour's criminal justice balance sheet

As outlined earlier, according to the BCS there have been substantial drops in overall crime levels in the past decade: over a third between 1997 and 2006. During this time the Blair governments were hyperactive in the law-and-order sphere, talking tough, passing legislation, creating new offences, and making enforcement against low-level incivilities a central plank of their strategy. One consequence has been an extraordinarily

---

[57] *The Sun*, 17 July 2000; the full text of the memo is available at: http://news.bbc.co.uk/ 1/hi/uk_politics/836822.stm (accessed 21 May 2007).

rapid expansion in the numbers in custody (from around 62,000 in 1997 to 80,000 by 2006[58]), as well as greater numbers receiving community sentences. How do the trends in crime and punishment relate to each other, and what other factors do we need to take into account in understanding these trends?

Growing penal severity has not resulted from increasing crime, but because the sanctions imposed by the courts have become harder. A first-time domestic burglar had a 27% chance of being sent to prison in 1995. By 2000 this had risen to 48%. In addition, average sentence lengths for such offenders rose from sixteen to eighteen months. Over half of the increase in custodial sentencing was for people with no previous convictions. Similar trends can be seen in relation to community penalties: two-thirds of the increase between 1991 and 2001 involved offenders with no previous convictions.[59] There is no evidence of any substantial increase in the number of offences being brought to court, or that those offences being prosecuted are more serious than before.[60] Rather, it appears that the post-1993 second-order consensus on punitive crime policy is the major factor behind the punishment binge.[61]

There is growing evidence that sentencers are affected not only by the legislative context in which they work but also by the general mood, the penal zeitgeist.[62] Although sentencers in Britain are significantly more protected from public opinion than their peers in, say, the United States, they are by no means entirely insulated. Given the general political mood in the last decade or more – one of largely unrelieved populist punitiveness – there can be little surprise that decision-making in the courts has resulted in ever harsher treatment of offenders.

Have the substantial increases in punishment brought about the crime drop? Here, research evidence is reasonably consistent: the substantial increases in incarceration do have a bearing on the crime drops measured in the UK and elsewhere, but only a relatively small one. Although there are several ways in which imprisonment might plausibly have an effect on crime rates – via the rehabilitation of offenders sentenced to custody, or through a deterrent effect on the population generally or more specifically on those punished – it is the incapacitation effect that seems most

---

[58] Rod Morgan and Alison Liebling, 'Imprisonment: An Expanding Scene', in Maguire *et al.*, *The Oxford Handbook of Criminology*, pp. 1100–1.

[59] Sir Patrick Carter, *Managing Offenders, Reducing Crime* (London: TSO, 2003).

[60] Michael Hough, Jessica Jacobson and Andrew Millie, *The Decision to Imprison: Sentencing and the Prison Population* (London: Prison Reform Trust, 2003).

[61] Reiner, *Law and Order*, ch. 5.   [62] Newburn, 'Tough on Crime'.

likely to have the greatest impact. However, the research results are not overly impressive. Evaluating such effects some years ago, a previous head of the Home Office's research unit concluded that a 'change in the use of custody of the order of 25 per cent would be needed to produce a 1 per cent change in the level of crime'.[63] More recently, the Home Office concluded that the prison population would need to increase by 15% for a crime reduction of 1%,[64] but this probably overestimates the incapacitation effect.[65]

If massive increases in levels of punishment, particularly incarceration, were the primary cause of the crime drop then this should be most visible in the United States, where substantial drops in overall crime since the mid-1970s (though violent crime only dropped since the early 1990s) have been accompanied by more than a sixfold increase in the incarceration rate. A number of very careful research studies have produced estimates ranging from around 10%[66] to 25%[67] of the crime drop being attributable to the dramatic increase in incarceration.

Comparative research casts further doubt on increased punishment as the prime suspect in the crime drop. Crime rates in the majority of English-speaking and European countries show a similar trend to England and Wales: rising since the 1950/1960s until the early to mid-1990s, and then levelling off or falling.[68] However, this was not accompanied everywhere by a punishment surge. Notably, Canada[69] and Scotland,[70] neighbours of the US and England, achieved similar crime declines without substantial increases in imprisonment. Similarly, although there have been drops in crime, imprisonment rates have remained relatively stable in

[63] Roger Tarling, *Analysing Offending* (London: HMSO, 1993), p. 154.
[64] John Halliday, *Making Punishments Work* (London: Home Office, 2001).
[65] Anthony Bottoms, 'Empirical Research Relevant to Sentencing Frameworks', in A. Bottoms, S. Rex and G. Robinson (eds.), *Alternatives to Prison* (Cullompton: Willan, 2004), pp. 66–72.
[66] John Donohue and Peter Siegelman, 'Allocating Resources among Prisons and Social Programs in the Battle against Crime', *Journal of Legal Studies*, 27(1), 1998: 1–43.
[67] William Spelman, 'The Limited Importance of Prison Expansion', in Alfred Blumstein and Joel Wallman (eds.), *The Crime Drop in America* (New York: Cambridge University Press, 2000).
[68] Michael Tonry and David P. Farrington, 'Crime and Punishment in Western Countries, 1980–1999', in Michael Tonry (ed.), *Crime and Justice: A Review of Research* (Chicago: University of Chicago Press, 2005).
[69] Anthony Doob and Cheryl Webster, 'Countering Punitiveness: Understanding Stability in Canada's Imprisonment Rate', *Law and Society Review*, 40(2), 2006: 325–68.
[70] David J. Smith, 'Crime and Punishment in Scotland', in Michael Tonry and David P. Farrington, *Crime and Punishment in Western Countries, 1980–1999* (Chicago: Chicago University Press, 2005).

Germany, Japan and Belgium. One is forced to conclude that any assumption 'that there is a simple, common, or invariant relationship between the crime patterns that befall a country and the number of people it confines is wrong. Faced with similar crime trends, different countries react in different ways.'[71]

If increased imprisonment provides only a very partial explanation of the crime drop, what of policing and crime prevention? Here the evidence is more positive. Analysing the very substantial 1990s drop in crime in New York City, Zimring recently concluded that the 'best estimate of the level of crime reduction achieved [by the policing changes in the city] is between a quarter and a half the recorded decline'.[72] Even if this is accurate – and others have questioned the policing impact[73] – there are many American cities that experienced substantial declines in crime without similar policing changes. More importantly for our purposes, the policing reforms in England have been quite unlike those undertaken in New York. Nevertheless, it remains plausible that the substantial increases in police numbers in England, together with improved working practices, have had a crime reduction impact. Add to this the reforms of the youth justice system (though there is some dispute over the extent of reduction in reoffending resulting from these[74]), and one has at least a partial explanation of the crime decline under New Labour.

But this is far from the whole story. The very fact that crime rates have been falling in most developed economies, although their criminal justice and penal polices vary markedly, suggests that single, grand-narrative explanations are implausible.[75] Under New Labour there has been a series of important socio-economic changes aimed at reducing 'social exclusion' which have had an important bearing on trends in crime. Falling unemployment, reductions in child poverty, and a slight drop in income inequality (but only back to approximately 1997 levels),[76] are undoubtedly important factors in any explanation of crime trends under New Labour. Indeed, a recent review by the Prime Minister's Strategy Unit concluded that 80% of the crime reduction was attributable to economic

---

[71] Michael Tonry, 'Determinants of Penal Policies', in Tonry, Crime and Justice.

[72] Zimring, The Great American Crime Decline, p. 151.

[73] See, for example, Andrew Karmen, New York Murder Mystery (New York: New York University Press, 2000).   [74] Morgan and Newburn, 'Youth Justice'.

[75] Michael Tonry, Thinking about Crime (New York: Oxford University Press, 2005); Reiner, Law and Order, chs. 4 and 5.

[76] Mike Brewer, Alissa Goodman, Alistair Muriel and Luke Sibieta, Poverty and Inequality in the UK: 2007 (London: Institute for Fiscal Studies, 2007).

factors, although this estimate is somehow omitted from the version of the report currently on the cabinet website, which concentrates almost entirely on criminal justice solutions.[77]

Conclusion: New Labour crime control: a success that dare not speak its name?

The evidence reviewed above suggests that a raft of socio-economic changes, together with some criminal justice reforms, account for much of the crime decline under New Labour. Is this success in crime reduction vindication of the pledge to be tough on crime *and* tough on the causes of crime? Up to a point, but given the staggering explosion of crime under the Conservatives, things really could only get better. Moreover, the aspects of criminal justice policy that worked have been smarter policing and prevention, rather than the hardening of punishment. And the sotto voce, limited reduction of social exclusion, poverty and inequality by stealth is better described as slightly stern, rather than tough, on the causes of crime.

The paradox of New Labour is that it only appears comfortable with the first half of its epochal mantra. Blair as Shadow Home Secretary in 1992/3 spearheaded a remarkable achievement for New Labour, capturing the law-and-order issue from the Tories. The lasting impact of this is shown by David Cameron's efforts to win it back with mellower rhetoric than his predecessors as Conservative leader. Ironically, it has been New Labour that shifted the balance increasingly to tough policy and practice, away from the more complex approach it started with.

One consequence of the obsession with 'tough-on-crime' rhetoric and, to a lesser degree, practice, is that the public appears largely ignorant of the extent of the crime decline. Blair in particular has consistently emphasised the bad news, the 'need' to repeatedly modernise the criminal justice system to make it 'fit for purpose' in the twenty-first century. This breast-beating is counter-productive, suggesting – against all the evidence of greater power, resources and targeting – that the system is badly broken, thus stoking public anxieties.

Majoritarian electoral systems do require centre-left parties to capture a substantial section of the middle-class vote. Arguably they must allay middle-earners' fears about redistribution at their expense by tough

[77] Enver Solomon *et al.*, *Ten Years of Criminal Justice under Labour: An Independent Audit* (London: Centre for Crime and Justice Studies, 2007), p. 14.

leadership espousing middle-class values against the left of the party.[78] *Sun*-worshipping law-and-order policies and tight central control follow from this logic. Nonetheless it is arguable that the huge Labour majority in 1997 indicated support for more liberal and just policies (still implicit in some survey evidence) that could have been tapped by Labour to modify law-and-order ideology rather than embed it.[79] That this was the path not taken owes more to Blair's evident personal belief in the narrowest interpretation of his mantra, rather than a logical necessity imposed by globalisation and neo-liberalism. The commitment to toughness paradoxically made New Labour's record in overall crime reduction a success that dare not speak its name, for fear of tabloid attacks on it as soft and out of touch. Increasingly ruthless and shrill assaults on civil liberties have fed the fears that purportedly justify them, and undermined the policies that succeeded in containing crime to some extent. In a kind of Gresham's Law, tough but only marginally effective policing and punishment tactics have elbowed out attacks on the causes of crime that could provide more deep-rooted security.

[78] David Soskice, 'Follow the Leader', *Prospect*, May 2007, pp. 48–51.
[79] Peter Wilby, 'Thatcherism's Final Triumph', *Prospect*, October 2006, pp. 28–31; Reiner, *Law and Order*, pp. 171–2.

16

Immigration

SARAH SPENCER

Immigration, in the run-up to the 1997 election, was not an issue Labour was keen to discuss. Critical of the impact of Conservative measures, it was nevertheless convinced that immigration was an issue on which it could only lose votes. Labour did, moreover, agree with the Conservatives that tough immigration controls were essential for good race relations. Its intention was simply to mitigate some of their harshest effects. Labour's manifesto commitment was thus modest, affirming the importance of 'firm control' while promising to remove certain 'arbitrary and unfair' results: just six lines addressed the issue which would later preoccupy the Prime Minister, asylum, promising 'swift and fair' decisions to tackle the backlog and crack down on fraud. There was no mention of labour migration where Labour was fundamentally to change the parameters of policy and debate. In contrast to other major policy areas, Labour thus came to power with no vision, no policy goals, no anticipated 'third way'.

The Conservatives' legacy was a backlog of 52,000 asylum cases and a tabloid press convinced that the vast majority were 'bogus', drawn to Britain, in the language of Michael Howard, because it was a 'soft touch'. For the public, immigration was not a salient issue in the 1997 election, just 3% rating it among the top three concerns facing Britain.[1] The opportunity to give the backlog cases the right to stay, when the mistakes of the previous administration could have been blamed, was nevertheless rejected. A major computerisation failure and pre-election staff cuts in the Immigration and Nationality Directorate (IND), coupled with rapidly rising asylum applications ensured that the backlog grew rapidly to 125,000 by 1999. Asylum numbers would dominate the Home Office agenda and preoccupy the Prime Minister until, by 2005, he was finally satisfied that they were under control.

[1] Ipsos Mori *Political Monitor: Long Term Trends* www.ipsos-mori.com/polls/trends/issues.shtml#2007.

Meanwhile, with little public acknowledgement, the Conservatives had quietly overseen a steady increase in the number of work permits to meet skill shortages in the health service, teaching and parts of the private sector, including a growing number of multinational inter-company transfers. Big business, however, was critical of a bureaucratic, slow and unpredictable work-permit system, later to prove ripe for reform by an incoming administration with a business-friendly deregulation agenda.

The limited ambition in the 1997 manifesto was reflected in a White Paper, *Fairer, Faster, Firmer,* the following year.[2] The subsequent Immigration and Asylum Act 1999 continued the path the Conservatives had set, extending measures to prevent and deter asylum-seekers from reaching the UK. Only at the margins, in the removal of the much criticised 'primary purpose' rule,[3] and later in cutting waiting times for families wanting to come to the UK, did Labour alleviate some of the negative impact of entry controls, responding to pressure from ethnic minorities, not least in the Home Secretary Jack Straw's own constituency. While the number of migrants arriving for family reunion and marriage continued to rise, this early focus of reform was quickly eclipsed by the two groups of migrants which dominated Blair's period in office, asylum-seekers and migrant workers.

Asylum

The nightly TV pictures of asylum-seekers from Calais's Sangatte refugee camp scaling fences to board trains bound for Dover in 2001 was a visible symbol of government's inability to control migration. But the pressure began much earlier, with disturbances in seaside towns and complaints from local authorities in the south-east that they were shouldering an unfair burden in welfare provision and electoral risk. Applications rose from 32,500 in 1997 to a high of 84,000 in 2002 (ranking sixth, per capita, across the EU).

Media pressure to act was relentless, egged on from 2002 by the 'think-tank' Migration Watch, and often misinformed; the debate polarised between those convinced all applicants were abusing the system and those convinced they should all be allowed to stay. The Opposition rammed home its advantage, proposing extreme, unworkable 'solutions'.

[2] Home Office, *Fairer, Faster, Firmer, A Modern Approach to Immigration and Asylum*, Cm. 4018 (London: TSO, 1998).
[3] The primary purpose rule put the onus on those seeking entry on grounds of marriage to show that the primary purpose of the marriage was not to gain entry to the UK.

Ministers and special advisers speak of this period as 'extraordinarily tense' and 'consistently problematic', with the 'media onslaught unrelenting'. Only in such a climate could asylum have remained on the agenda of the cabinet meeting held two days after 9/11 in 2001.

David Blunkett, Home Secretary from 2001 to 2004, saw the threat not as asylum-seekers per se but as their impact on a public already unsettled by the pace of change, fearful of crime and resentful of newcomers accessing resources which they themselves needed. Mindful of the surge in right-wing parties elsewhere in Europe, he saw tough measures as essential to prevent such a drift in the UK. He felt 'grossly misinterpreted by the liberal left', who failed to support him in that approach.[4]

The evolving strategy was threefold: to raise the barriers to asylum-seekers reaching the UK; to restrict access to work, benefits and health-care as a deterrent; and to increase the through-put of cases at IND while limiting access to appeals. A senior adviser to the Prime Minister during this period says, 'The Government realised that if you want to get numbers down you have to prevent people arriving in the first place. You can do what you like to try to make life more unpleasant for people once they got here but that was never going to reduce the overall numbers.'[5]

The 1999 Act had extended penalties on transport providers which delivered passengers with no right of entry to the UK, and visas were introduced for countries from which numbers of applicants were rising.[6] The measure which had the most immediate impact, however, was the closure of the Sangatte refugee camp. Talks with the French government achieved minimal cooperation until Nicolas Sarkozy, with whom David Blunkett had an immediate rapport, took charge. Agreement to close the camp was reached in December 2002.

Convinced that asylum-seekers were attracted to the UK in part by access to welfare benefits, the 1999 Act had replaced benefits with a controversial voucher system. TGWU leader Bill Morris led a successful coalition of protest, damning a 'cruel' system that had 'deepened the misery of

---

[4] Rt Hon. David Blunkett MP, Home Secretary 2001–4, interviewed by the author on 17 April 2007, from which other quotes in this chapter are also taken.

[5] Interviewed by the author on 23 March 2007, from which other quotes in this chapter are also taken.

[6] The number of countries from which visas were required was extended from 19 in 1991 to 108 in February 2005. *Joint Refugee Council and Oxfam Response to the Home Affairs Select Committee Inquiry into Immigration Control* (London: Refugee Council and Oxfam, 2005), p. 4.

those in need while lining the pockets of supermarkets and black market-eers'.[7] Cash benefits at 70% of regular income support were restored for those who would otherwise be destitute but legislation in 2002[8] withdrew support from asylum-seekers who did not apply on arrival ('S55', later overturned by the courts) and the 'concession' that asylum-seekers were allowed to work after six months was withdrawn in July that year.[9] Although numbers were falling by 2004, another Act[10] further limited access to an appeal, while regulations excluded failed asylum-seekers from accessing secondary healthcare.

Reducing the backlog of cases could only be tackled by faster pro-cessing at the IND. Critics argued that 'front-loading' the system to enable case-workers to make fast but also fair decisions would prove the best deterrent to those without a strong claim to refugee status. The IND was, however, singularly ill-equipped to provide it. When Barbara Roche took over as Immigration Minister in July 1999 she was told that there were only fifty case-workers trained to handle asylum cases, in a year when there were 71,000 applications.[11] Public expenditure controls had been deemed to prevent rapid investment in this area, though Maeve Sherlock, former Treasury adviser and later head of the Refugee Council, is convinced that a well-argued case to the Treasury to 'invest to save' would have proved convincing. The cost of maintaining asylum-seeker families, and of funding appeals, was hugely counter-productive in terms of cost, loss of political capital and the effect on the lives of the families concerned. 'If you had front-loaded a lot of those costs you would have ended up with a much fairer, faster, and more efficient system. The busi-ness case was overwhelming.'[12]

In practice, reform was slow. As the number of applications rose, so did the backlog, and it was brought down only by fast-tracking cases at the expense of quality of decisions, the number of successful appeals rising to more than one in five by 2002. A fundamental overhaul of the case-handling system was finally initiated in 2005. Meanwhile, a series of 'backlog clear-ance' exercises had quietly processed long-standing applications through to

[7] Bill Morris, 'Are Civil Liberties at Risk? Yes, Says Bill Morris', *The Observer*, 30 September 2001, http://observer.guardian.co.uk/libertywatch/story/0,,561488,00.html.
[8] The Nationality, Immigration and Asylum Act 2002.
[9] Later restored for those still waiting for a decision after twelve months, in line with EU Directive 2003/9/EC.
[10] The Asylum and Immigration (Treatment of Claimants, etc.) Act 2004.
[11] Barbara Roche, interviewed by the author on 5 April 2007, from which other quotes in this chapter, except where stated, are also taken.
[12] Maeve Sherlock, interviewed by the author on 4 April 2007.

a discretionary right to stay. Fiona Mactaggart, Race Relations Minister from 2003 to 2005, is convinced nevertheless that this humane solution to the backlog was not an option until the government had restored a level of public confidence in its capacity to deal with unfounded claims. 'The salience of immigration and race issues was so high it had the capacity to take off. It didn't because we didn't do things like amnesties.'[13]

Blair's preoccupation

Blair was mindful of asylum as a growing issue during the first term but by 2002 it absorbed an increasing amount of his time. 'By the end of 2002 the situation was unsustainable', a senior adviser to Blair says: 'We were just getting slaughtered on asylum. It wasn't unusual for there to be an asylum story on the front page of a tabloid every day of the week.' Asylum became one of the top ten delivery priorities for the PM's Delivery Unit and a constant focus of his stock-takes and briefings. Looking back, Blunkett says: 'I think one of the things that over the ten years affected Tony most of all was the idea that the government should be seen to be powerless; that issues such as this were out of our hands, that there was nothing we could do, and would therefore be dubbed inadequate or incompetent.'

Wholly unconvinced by arguments from lawyers and officials that more radical measures – including large-scale detention – were not feasible, Blair consistently challenged the Home Office to do more. Blunkett's adviser Nick Pearce, who was present at many such meetings, compares Blair's style to throwing a ball into the distance, leaving officials and advisers to scurry over and bring it back to a sensible place, only to have him throw it again: 'he would continually push as far as you could go on an issue, get 20% of what he wanted, then push again and get another 20% and just keep doing it'.[14]

Blair stunned the Home Office by announcing on *Newsnight* in February 2003 that asylum applications would be halved within a year. While numbers were beginning to fall, this was wildly ambitious. Blunkett was not confident it could be achieved and recalls 'gentle words' with Blair; his biographer intimates that the conversation was more heated.[15] Blunkett nevertheless characteristically used the Prime Minister's commitment to

[13] Fiona Mactaggart MP, interviewed by the author on 22 March 2007, from which other quotes in this chapter are also taken.
[14] Nick Pearce, Special Adviser to the Home Secretary 2001–4, interviewed by the author on 16 March 2007, from which other quotes in this chapter are also taken.
[15] Stephen Pollard, *David Blunkett* (London: Hodder and Stoughton, 2005), p. 278.

lever cooperation from other departments. Blair, having used this tactic successfully to galvanise action, did so again in 2004, promising to reach the 'tipping-point' – a greater number of removals of failed asylum-seekers than new applicants each month – and then insisted on tougher measures in the Asylum Bill of that year to achieve it. 'The tipping-point was a good rhetorical device', Mactaggart argues. 'Nobody was getting around to deporting them – it made the system get around to it and that did help change people's views.'

Blair's role was also pivotal in silencing opposition from other departments – from Lord Chancellor Derry Irvine on curtailing asylum appeals, the Foreign Office on extending visa controls and sceptical cabinet colleagues on ID cards. A senior adviser confirms: 'The advantage of having the PM involved was that you could bring around the table departments which had not been that cooperative on some of the things the Home Office wanted to do. That made a big difference.'

Dispersal

The 1999 Act had also provided for the dispersal of asylum-seekers away from the south-east and the National Asylum Support System (NASS) was set up in 2000 to manage it – an ambitious scheme to create a welfare and accommodation system for a transient, diverse population with significant needs. Highly centralised, with little buy-in from local authorities and hence reliant on private landlords, and dispersing asylum-seekers to areas where local residents themselves experienced multiple disadvantage, the system was beset with difficulties from the start. The Home Office had no previous relationship with local authorities, no experience of housing provision, and no infrastructure to organise the transport of people at short notice. Pearce says: 'The whole thing was mad – a Thomas Cook model: give them a voucher and put them on a bus.' The consequence was asylum-seekers arriving in local communities with scant preparation for the services they would need nor the reaction of their neighbours.

Blunkett sought to replace dispersal with a system of accommodation centres, removing asylum-seekers from local housing, education and health provision, an idea earlier rejected by Straw following violent attacks on such centres in Germany. Strong opposition from Brown on cost grounds, a rare example of Treasury opposition on migration matters, and public resistance in areas designated for the new centres, relegated the idea to a pilot scheme.

Success?

A cursory look at asylum figures would suggest that the government achieved its overriding objective: the number of applications fell sharply after 2002 to 49,000 the following year, the beginning of a steady decline to 23,500 in 2006. The backlog was, by 2006, no longer significant. (Removal figures remained more stubborn, never coming close to the number told they had no right to stay.)

It is an open question, however, to what extent the control or deterrent measures led to the fall in applications, relative to the impact of events beyond the government's control in the conflict zones from which the majority of asylum-seekers came. Insiders and critics are in a level of agreement that the imposition of visa controls contributed to falling numbers from countries such as Zimbabwe where there was no improvement in the conditions causing people to flee; but the end of the war in former Yugoslavia and the peace process in Sri Lanka, for instance, also contributed.

Advisers themselves question whether welfare benefits were ever an incentive for asylum-seekers to choose Britain (the academic evidence suggested not)[16] and hence whether their withdrawal had any impact other than to leave many destitute. Blunkett himself thinks there are measures, such as the power to remove the British-born children of failed asylum-seekers, on which he expended considerable political capital, but 'hasn't made any difference at all'. Nor is it known how many would-be asylum-seekers, deterred by a slow system that provided neither work nor adequate welfare support, chose not to apply but to work illegally instead in a labour market with employers ready to overlook the immigration status of those willing to do the job.

Measures to prevent asylum-seekers reaching the UK did, however, breach the spirit if not the letter of the UK's obligations under international law, including the fledgling Human Rights Act.[17] How many of those prevented from reaching the UK had a genuine need for protection will never be known. Restrictions on benefits and the right to work were severely criticised on humanitarian grounds and as counter-productive, public resentment focusing on asylum-seekers' dependence on the taxpayer and visibility on street corners with nothing to do. The Joint

[16] Vaughan Robinson and J. Segrott, *Understanding the Decision Making of Asylum Seekers* (London: Home Office Research Study 243, 2002).
[17] Shami Chakrabati, 'Rights and Rhetoric: The Politics of Asylum and Human Rights Culture in the United Kingdom', *Journal of Law and Society*, 32(1), 2005: 131–47.

Committee on Human Rights concluded in 2006 that: 'by refusing permission for asylum-seekers to work and operating a system of support which results in widespread destitution, the treatment of asylum-seekers in a number of cases reaches the Article 3 ECHR threshold of inhuman and degrading treatment'. . .[it] falls below the requirements of the common law of humanity and international human rights law'. [18] Blunkett insists criticism of this kind considers only one side of the argument – the rights of individuals not the wider public good: 'We were dealing with individual rights of course but we were dealing with public policy as well. You had to see the two in balance if you weren't in the end to destroy any kind of confidence in what a democratic government was trying to do.'

Public hostility

In contrast to the expansion of labour migration, Labour's asylum reforms required primary legislation, ensuring a consistently high profile for a contentious and divisive political debate. Blair and successive Home Secretaries were convinced that maintaining a high profile for the tough measures they were taking was the way to reassure the public that they were bringing migration under control. Polling evidence shows this was not successful. A window of opportunity in the first three years, when no more than 10% rated immigration and race in the top three issues facing Britain, was lost as it rose to 27% in 2001, and reached 39% as asylum numbers and the media fever pitch reached their peak in 2002. By April 2007, as Blair prepared to announce his resignation, 36% of the public rated immigration and race issues second only to crime. Eurobarometer data confirmed that where immigration is separated from broader race issues, concern remains as high: 40% of the UK public in 2006 rated immigration *the* most important area of concern. Across the EU as a whole, immigration came fourth.[19]

The reasons for this are not difficult to see. The public did not hear messages direct from ministers but via the press, and the tabloids continued to headline anti-asylum-seeker stories on a regular basis, despite

---

[18] Joint Committee on Human Rights, *The Treatment of Asylum Seekers,* Tenth Report of Session 2006–2007, vol. I, *Report and Formal Minutes,* HL Paper 81-1, HC 60-1 (London: TSO, 2007), p. 41.

[19] Ipsos Mori, *Political Monitor: Long Term Trends;* Eurobarometer 66, *Public Opinion in the EU,* Autumn 2006, http://ec.europa.eu/public_opinion/archives/eb/eb66/eb66_uk_exec.pdf.

falling numbers. Second, the rhetoric of new measures to tackle asylum, emphasising abuse of the system, reinforced the perception of asylum-seekers as a threat, not people in need of protection. Finally, the public did not, as the government had anticipated, readily tell the difference between an asylum-seeker, a migrant worker or an international student in their neighbourhood. Pearce says,

> With hindsight, we weren't communicating in the way the public were thinking. Locality has more impact than we realised – people talking to their friends and neighbours – and there was a naivety in thinking they would understand the different categories of migrant as we did. Even if they heard the message, the effect of the tough rhetoric was to wind up their concerns, not reassure them. We should have taken down the temperature and worked with local authorities and the local press to change attitudes. But the pressures at the time were immense.

Mactaggart agrees that the rhetoric was damaging: 'It created a belief that claiming asylum was an abusive act, against the community. The rhetoric told them that they had something to worry about. It didn't reassure people. And the way we treated asylum-seekers was also damaging.' Don Flynn, director of the Migrants' Rights Network, suggests that the government's style of politics provided a context in which latent anxieties about migrants could be mobilised: 'It assumed in 1997 that the electorate would always respond to immigration negatively, at a time when public opinion was as sanguine on the issue as it had ever been. If Blair had brought migration within his modernising rhetoric he could have led a progressive current within public opinion which undoubtedly existed.'[20] Roche argues, however, that even by the time she became Immigration Minister in 1999, it was already very difficult to change the terms of the debate. There was no interest in positive messages, such as the refugee integration strategy. 'It was positive, progressive stuff – on refugee doctors for instance – but there was little interest in that.'

Immigration 'control' to 'managed migration'

In contrast to asylum, Blair initially had little concern about labour migration. Employers critical of the work-permit system were soon satisfied by relaxation of work-permit controls and streamlined procedures, enabling skilled migrants to fill vacancies in the public and private sectors. Eager to

---

[20] Don Flynn, director of Migrants' Rights Network, interviewed on 21 May 2007, from which other quotes are also taken.

shift the focus of political and media debates, it was on these migrants that Roche focused in a path-breaking speech to the Institute for Public Policy Research (ippr) in September 2000. Emphasising the economic and social benefits of migration to the UK, she said: 'we are in competition for the brightest and the best talents, the entrepreneurs, the scientists, the high technology specialists who make the global economy tick . . . the evidence shows that economically driven migration can bring substantial overall benefits both for growth and the economy'.[21]

'I wanted', she says now, 'to be the first Immigration Minister to say "immigration is a good thing", that we are a nation of migrants. But it has to be legal, and it has to be well managed.' It was only with the arrival of Blunkett at the Home Office after the 2001 election, however, that Roche's theme was reflected in a marked shift in language and policy from that of immigration 'control' to 'managed migration'. A report commissioned by the Prime Minister from his Performance and Innovation Unit had set out the evidence and rationale for a shift in approach, a report received with some enthusiasm at the Treasury, if less so within IND itself.[22]

Blunkett came into office having overseen the growth in labour migration at the Department for Education and Employment. With the break-up of that department he took this responsibility with him to the Home Office, bringing recognition of the economic benefits of migration into a department that had traditionally focused only on keeping migrants out. It created the opportunity to join up policy on family migration, asylum and migrant workers for the first time.

Blunkett saw that policy on labour migration and asylum could not be addressed in isolation. High job vacancy rates and the lack of legal channels for migrants to take those jobs were both encouraging illegal immigration and lengthening the asylum queues. Conversely, clamping down on illegal migration and asylum would mean closing off some sources of much needed labour. He recalls discussing it with Brown because the Treasury was 'very jumpy': 'We knew that if you didn't have very substantial legal routes for working in this country our economy would be closed down.'

The growth in work permits had, moreover, been a tangible demonstration that labour migration flows could be managed and had, at that stage, aroused little opposition. Within days of taking office Blunkett had

[21] Barbara Roche MP, 'UK Migration in a Global Economy', presentation to ippr event, 11 September 2000.
[22] S. Glover, C. Gott, A. Loizillon, J. Portes, R. Price, S. Spencer, V. Srinivasan and C. Willis, *Migration: An Economic and Social Analysis*, RDS Occasional Paper 67 (London: Home Office, 2001).

announced his intention to open up new skilled and low-skilled routes for legal migration in order to 'undercut the people smugglers'. The willingness to open up low-skilled routes, and the overt intention to use this to avoid migrants resorting to alternatives, was a significant departure from past Labour and Conservative policy. 'My view was that legality breeds confidence in the system, illegality undermined all that we were trying to do and encouraged the theory that everything was falling apart which the right wing press reinforced over and over again.'

A 2002 White Paper, *Secure Borders, Safe Havens: Integration with Diversity in Modern Britain,* thus sought for the first time to set out an integrated approach. Largely written by Blunkett and Pearce, in the face of some incomprehension in the IND, it anticipated opening up labour migration channels; further restrictions on asylum-seekers; and developing a new approach to citizenship as a tool of integration for those remaining in the long term. Published within months of the events of 11 September 2001, and in the midst of constant media pressure on asylum, it was already clear that control measures would dominate debate. Reform of labour migration did not, however, require primary legislation, enabling controls to be relaxed under the radar of media interest. Growing recognition in the Treasury of the contribution migrants were making to economic growth and productivity ensured pressure on IND officials to cut red tape. 'The Treasury was always pro migration', Pearce says. 'You could always count on their support.' New schemes were introduced for the highly skilled to enter without a job offer and the number of work permits rose from 29,000 in 1997–8 to 68,000 in 2001–2, holding steady above 59,000 each year since.[23]

Labour shortages in hospitality and food processing led to an entry scheme for low-wage jobs and to more seasonal agricultural workers. Working holiday-makers, once restricted to part-time non-professional work, were allowed greater mobility in the labour market, as were overseas students. Employers eager to access low-skilled migrants welcomed the initiatives but, significantly, had applied little pressure for them, suggesting that they were experiencing little difficulty finding irregular migrants, including asylum-seekers, who were willing to do the work.[24]

[23] Report of the United Kingdom SOPEMI correspondent to the OECD, 2006, www.geog. ucl.ac.uk/mru/docs/Sop06_final_200207.pdf.

[24] See research findings in Bridget Anderson, Martin Ruhs, Ben Rogaly and Sarah Spencer, *Fair Enough? Central and Eastern European Migrants in Low Wage Employment in the UK* (York: Joseph Rowntree Foundation, 2006), on employers willing to 'bend the rules' to employ irregular migrants.

Independent research showed that the growth in migrant labour was bringing benefits to the UK labour market and the Treasury, albeit modest (except for the firms and public services otherwise unable to get staff) and that fears about the impact on wages and unemployment were proving unfounded.[25]

EU enlargement

It was in that context that the decision was taken to open up Britain's labour market to nationals of the new EU member states on 1 May 2004. Anticipating that the net total who would take advantage of this opportunity could be in the region of 20,000 a year, the decision initially aroused little political or public interest. Only in the weeks leading up to 1 May did media anticipation that a significant number of Roma might come, and that migrants might choose to live on benefits rather than work, lead Blair to focus on the issue. Blunkett stood firm, insisting that the migrants were needed for low-skilled jobs which would otherwise be taken by illegal migrants. A compromise was reached: a Worker Registration Scheme, recording the migrants' employment and monitoring their highly restricted access to benefits – a scheme which had the downside of recording those arriving but not those returning home, thus inflating the figures.[26] Nevertheless, the net figure was undoubtedly greater that the government had anticipated, as was the impact on local communities and local authorities in areas lacking experience of migration.[27] Once again, research confirmed benefits for the UK economy (with some evidence that these are recognised by a minority of the public);[28] if not always acceptable working conditions for the workers

[25] Jeremy Kempton, *Migrants in the UK: Their Characteristics, and Labour Market Outcomes and Impacts*, RDS Occasional Paper 82 (London: Home Office, 2002). The evidence on the impact on source countries, meanwhile, is mixed: remittances from migrants can contribute to development goals but recruitment of professionals in some cases exacerbates an unwelcome brain drain. Select Committee on Development, *Migration and Development: How to Make Migration Work for Poverty Reduction,* Report of the Sixth Session, HC 79-1 (London: House of Commons, 2004).

[26] 630,000 registered between May 2004 and March 2007. *Accession Monitoring Report A8 Countries, May 2004–March 2007* (London: Border and Immigration Agency/DWP, 22 May 2007).

[27] See Audit Commission, *Crossing Borders, Responding to the Local Challenges of Migrant Workers* (London: Audit Commission, 2007).

[28] *Sunday Times* poll, August 2006, found 14% strongly agree that immigration is generally good for Britain and a further 29% tend to agree.

themselves.[29] 'The objective was always to meet the needs of the economy', Don Flynn, says. 'It did not take into account the needs of the migrants themselves.'

Free movement for EU nationals nevertheless had one effect on migrants which passed almost unnoticed. For those who had been working in the UK illegally before 1 May 2004, the decision to allow free movement was in effect an amnesty, transforming them overnight into EU citizens with a right to live and work in the UK.

Media reaction to the number of Eastern Europeans, coupled with the pressures on local services, ensured that citizens of the two newest EU member states, Bulgaria and Romania, were not allowed free access to the UK labour market in 2007. The economics said yes, but the politics no. With a Home Secretary, John Reid, now keen to impose restrictions, Blair played little part in the decision.

The spotlight had earlier focused on Bulgaria and Romania when a junior IND official alleged that staff had been told to fast-track visas from those countries. Home Office Minister Beverley Hughes unwittingly misled the House of Commons that she had been unaware of claims that fraudulent applications were slipping through the net. Costing the minister her job in April 2004, the incident also exposed the complexity of the labour migration system: a plethora of different categories of entry and a weak enforcement regime, leaving the system vulnerable to abuse.

At the Labour Party conference that year Blair announced a 'top-to-bottom' analysis of the immigration system. Charles Clarke, now Home Secretary, went on to launch a five-year developmental plan, *Controlling our Borders, Making Migration Work for Britain*, three months before the 2005 general election. With a dual focus on strengthening border controls and a points system to streamline the more than eighty different channels for entry to work, it launched migration policy into a third-term managerial phase, subsequent policy statements[30] optimistic that biometric technology and efficient administration could finally bring inherently unpredictable migration flows under control.

[29] N. Gilpin, M. Henty, S. Lemos, J. Portes and C. Bullen, *The Impact of Free Movement of Workers from Central and Eastern Europe on the UK Labour Market* (London: Department of Work and Pensions, 2006); Anderson et al., *Fair Enough?*
[30] Immigration and Nationality Directorate, *A Points-Based System: Making Migration Work for Britain* (London: TSO, 2006); Immigration and Nationality Directorate, *Fair, Effective, Transparent and Trusted: Rebuilding Confidence in Our Immigration System* (London: Immigration and Nationality Directorate, 2006).

International students

Labour migration had not been the first immigration channel overhauled to meet the needs of the economy. Fees paid by international students were of growing significance in higher education and in 1999 Blair launched an ambitious scheme for the UK to attract 25% of the English-speaking student market, a 100% increase in students. Visa restrictions were relaxed and students allowed access to the labour market while studying. By 2004, the UK had achieved 24% of the global market, the income from fees to higher education institutions growing from £622 million (1997–8) to £1,275 million (2003–4). The absurdity of forcing graduates trained at British universities to return home before applying to work in the UK was gradually ended, allowing them to switch into skilled labour migration schemes, not least in Scotland where the Scottish Executive's 'Fresh Talent' initiative sought migrants to reverse Scotland's declining population. In 2006 Blair launched a successor scheme, concerned at growing competition for students from abroad.[31]

Benefit or threat?

Ministers and advisers insist that the events of 9/11, while having a profound affect on the Home Office and the political climate, had not radically shifted immigration or asylum policy because, Pearce says, 'politicians and officials know, despite the press agenda, that terrorism and migration are only very remotely connected'. It is indeed striking that security considerations post-9/11 did not affect the opening up of new labour market channels nor the expansion in student numbers.

Within months of 9/11, nevertheless, the Anti-terrorism, Crime and Security Act had provided for the indefinite detention of foreigners suspected of involvement in terrorism, replaced, following a legal challenge, by control orders in 2005. Blair's personal response to the London bombings in July 2005 included the promise that any asylum-seeker involved in terrorism would be denied refugee status, a measure enacted in 2006 along with substantial provisions for information-sharing among transport, immigration and police authorities. Further legislation in 2007 will increase the policing powers of immigration officers, allow access to tax

---

[31] See overview of UK policy and data on international students in Alan Findlay and Alexandra Stam, 'International Student Migration to the UK', Georgetown University, March 2006, www.12.georgetown.edu/sfs/isim/Event%20Documents/Sloan%20Global%20Competition%20Meeting/Findlay-UK.pdf.

data to identify illegal immigrants and require foreign nationals to have biometric identification cards, while enabling the automatic deportation of some offenders.[32] Finger-printing of all visa applicants will be introduced by 2008 and electronic checks on those leaving and entering by 2014. In his last speech as leader to the party conference, Blair said the question is 'how we reconcile openness to the rich possibilities of globalisation with security in the face of its threats', arguing that biometric ID cards 'are not a breach of our basic rights, they are an essential part of responding to the reality of modern migration'.

In Blair's final years it was evident that the positive language on the benefits of migration, albeit rarely projected to the public at large, was being overtaken by the language of harm. This was perhaps most evident in Reid's enforcement strategy in 2007 which proposed 'Immigration Crime Partnerships' at the local level to target rogue employers, now subject to criminal penalties, and migrants working illegally.[33] With asylum numbers under control, the focus had now shifted to illegal immigrants, the number of whom the government had, under pressure, estimated to be between 310,000 and 570,000.[34] The Conservatives had introduced civil penalties on firms which employed people without permission to work but, failing to resource a system of inspection, ensured that the enforcement would be little more than symbolic. In Labour's first term there were only thirty-four successful prosecutions.

The introduction of ID cards was intended, inter alia, to enable employers and service providers to establish each individual's immigration status, extending immigration control from Heathrow to the hospital gate. Initially sceptical, Blair endorsed the proposal at the Labour Party conference in 2003. Given Treasury opposition, it may now not proceed. Meanwhile the 2006 Act extended the civil penalties on employers and enforcement units made periodic well-publicised raids. The growing use of detention triggered a series of critical reports, including from HM Inspector of Prisons, on poor conditions and failure to meet welfare needs. In a rare move to protect migrant workers, following the

---

[32] Immigration, Asylum and Nationality Act 2006; UK Borders Bill 2007.

[33] *Enforcing the Rules: A Strategy to Ensure and Enforce Compliance with our Immigration Laws* (London: Home Office, March 2007), www.ind.homeoffice.gov.uk/6353/aboutus/enforcementstrategy.pdf.

[34] Described by Home Office Minister, Tony McNulty, as the government's 'best guess'. BBC News Online, 'Illegal Immigrant Figure Revealed', 30 June 2005, http://news.bbc.co.uk/1/hi/uk_politics/4637273.stm.

Morecombe Bay tragedy and a concerted campaign by trade unions, the Gangmasters (Licensing) Act 2004 regulated migrant employment agencies in the agriculture and fisheries industries. A growing campaign for an amnesty for those who had been working in the UK for four years later won the support of trade union and church leaders.

EU cooperation

Blair's government was acutely aware that many EU member states faced similar challenges and that the measures those states took – or failed to take – impacted on the UK. Significant energy was invested in securing cooperation in strengthening external border controls and data-sharing. Nevertheless, the government negotiated an opt-out from EU immigration and asylum measures, allowing it to cherry-pick those that suited its objectives. While providing a forum for negotiation, the EU was thus less a driver of UK policy than an occasional means to achieve it.

Integration and citizenship

Innovative race equality legislation to address systemic discrimination in the public sector followed a public inquiry Straw instigated into the failure of the police to apprehend the killers of Stephen Lawrence, the victim of a racially motivated murder in South London. The focus of Straw's new equality strategy and of the social cohesion initiatives that followed riots in northern towns in 2001, were, however, on second- and third-generation ethnic minorities, not newcomers to the UK. While nominally part of the same department, officials responsible for the 'integration' of migrants – to the limited extent that responsibility existed – were not part of the cohesion team. Nor did ministers, until the establishment of the temporary Commission on Integration and Cohesion in 2006, hint that it might be time to bring migrants within cohesion strategies at the local level.

Back in 2000, the government had consulted on a limited integration strategy for refugees, *Full and Equal Citizens*, subsequently further developed in 2005. Providing somewhat limited support to refugees in finding accommodation and employment, the new strategy had its critics. Yet the recognition it accorded that refugees may need assistance in the integration process was not extended to other migrants: family members, labour migrants or students. 'The difference', an official told the author in 2006, 'is that we have obligations to refugees under international law and that they could not plan their lives here. For other migrants, if it does not work out, they know where to catch the bus home.'

The evidence suggests, nevertheless, that failure to consider the needs of new arrivals and their impact on local services, or to provide a sceptical public with an explanation for the demographic change they see around them, has proved short-sighted.[35] 'My regret', Blunkett says, 'is that we didn't move fast enough in 2002 towards emphasising and supporting much greater social integration programmes. We didn't put enough time and resources into positive measures at a local level.'

Only for those seeking citizenship did the government take a new approach, introducing citizenship classes, tests and ceremonies for those applying for naturalisation and latterly tests for those given indefinite leave to stay, the intention being that this will 'contribute to mutual understanding and common values of tolerance and respect'.[36] Significant new resources were provided for English-language tuition, but competing demands on the skills budget later led to cuts in free provision. Long waiting lists remain for access to classes in many parts of the country.

Blair's interest in the integration agenda grew after the 2005 London bombings, focusing on Muslims and ethnic minorities rather than on migrants per se. In a valedictory speech on 'multiculturalism and integration', however, he explicitly included migrants, whose 'extraordinary contribution' he acknowledged, arguing that respect for diversity must be tempered by acceptance of 'common, unifying, British values'.[37]

Immigration and Nationality Directorate

The inability of the IND to follow through from legislation to delivery was an enduring theme throughout the decade, to the deep frustration of the Prime Minister. That it did prove possible to overhaul the administration of the work-permit system at an outpost in Sheffield only deepened frustration at the IND's inability to transform the handling of asylum casework in Croydon. Successive governments' preoccupation with cutting immigration numbers, a culture of reaction to events, and the

---

[35] See Audit Commission, *Crossing Borders*; and Sarah Spencer, Martin Ruhs, Bridget Anderson and Ben Rogaly, *Migrants' Lives Beyond the Workplace: Central and East Europeans in the UK* (York: Joseph Rowntree Foundation, 2007).

[36] Advisory Board on Naturalisation and Integration, www.abni.org.uk/about/background/index.html.

[37] Tony Blair, 'Our Nation's Future, Multiculturalism and Integration', speech to the Runnymede Trust, 8 December 2006, www.number-10.gov.uk/output/Page10563.asp.

perception of the IND as a career backwater had, it seems, led to a department unable to think strategically or to join up related policy areas, even
within the Home Office itself. The foreign prisoners' fiasco that ended
Charles Clarke's period at the Home Office in 2005, and arose from the
failure of the IND and the Prison Service to communicate on the deportation of foreign-born prisoners, was only one visible example. Clarke
had overseen changes in the IND, including importing senior people with
operational experience from outside government, but did not last to see
the fruits of those reforms.

The frustration at the lack of both efficiency and transparency in case
management was felt as deeply by immigration lawyers, who pressed
repeatedly for migrants and their representatives to receive a better
service. One suspects it was not this concern that Reid had in mind when
he told the Home Affairs Select Committee in 2006 that his department
was 'not fit for purpose', instigating a review of the IND which finally led
to its separation in April 2007 into the Border and Immigration Agency.

The Blair effect

Blair must shoulder some responsibility for the party's failure to anticipate Britain's emerging position within the global movement of people –
the inevitability that migration would have a growing economic and
social impact in Britain – and consequently for the government's lack of
vision and strategic objectives on taking power in 1997. Nevertheless,
faced with significant skill and labour shortages, Blair showed a courage
in opening up the UK's labour market that was lacking in most of his
European counterparts. He leaves Britain on the map as a country which
is firmly open to labour migration in a way that seemed inconceivable
only a decade ago. When an ippr report in 1994 argued for the economic
benefits of migration to be recognised, and suggested lessons could be
learnt from countries of immigration such as Canada, it was a voice in the
wilderness.[38] That view is now mainstream, and in a global economy it is
unlikely that openness to labour migration – at different levels and in
different forms – will be reversed. The job of government is no longer
simply to control and exclude. 'Even the Tories will not row back on this',
Pearce says: 'there has been a shift in the political landscape which is here
to stay'.

[38] Sarah Spencer, *Strangers and Citizens: A Positive Approach to Migrants and Refugees*
(London: Rivers Oram, 1994).

Blair made little attempt, however, to convince the public of the rationale for this new approach. Positive messages from Home Office ministers on the economic benefits of labour migration were drowned by the negative messages on asylum. Convinced that the public would only be reassured by tough messages and action on asylum, Blair gave it an extraordinary amount of his personal attention. In the period 2001–2004, a senior adviser says he attended more than fifty meetings Blair held on asylum, some lasting three to four hours, and doubts there was any single issue other than Iraq on which he had as many meetings:

> It was the sheer drive, having set that Newsnight target that he put into delivery. If left to their own devices the Home Office would not have driven on asylum as much as they did. The Home Office is so driven by day to day events that, without pressure to keep going on an issue for months and months on end, it just doesn't happen. There was a consistent pressure from the PM which they couldn't ignore.

To the extent that the external controls and exclusion from work and benefits did contribute to the fall in asylum numbers, Blair must therefore take some credit. To the extent that those measures eroded the refugee protection regime, preventing individuals in need of protection from reaching Britain and leaving some of those who did destitute, he must share responsibility.

The issue on which Labour focused in its 1997 manifesto, the treatment of family members, should not be overlooked in assessing Blair's legacy. The 'primary purpose' rule had cast suspicion on anyone entering the UK for marriage, and the impact of correcting that injustice, Mactaggart, insists, was 'iconic', as was the decision in 2002 to restore citizenship to British Overseas Citizens whose right of entry had been withdrawn: 'They had been deprived of their citizenship. We gave it back to them. It was the morally right thing to do. We could change a rule and have a positive impact on people's lives.' With the focus by then on asylum, the government got little credit for righting this 'historic wrong'.

Giving substance to the acquisition of citizenship may also prove to have more than symbolic significance if those who acquire it feel a stronger sense of acceptance in British society. The failure to develop a strategy to address the needs of the 1,500 migrants who arrive in the UK each day and their impact on local communities was a surprising omission that left local authorities in a policy vacuum from which they have yet to emerge.

Blair inherited an Immigration and Nationality Directorate incapable of strategic planning, efficient casework management or effective enforcement. Coping with six major Acts of Parliament in less than ten years arguably exacerbated its difficulties.[39] Frustrated that successive attempts at administrative reform did not deliver, Blair's insistence on results finally led to the IND's rebirth as the Border and Immigration Agency in 2007. It remains to be seen whether that will deliver the efficiency and joined-up administration that eluded it while in the Home Office. Leaving overall responsibility in a rump Home Office, now focused almost exclusively on security and policing issues, does not bode well for a policy that needs to have broader economic, social, human rights and international development objectives.

A clear lesson from the Blair decade is that migration cannot be managed solely through tighter controls and tougher enforcement when the powerful draw of jobs, education, family or a place of safety make migration an aspiration some will risk all to achieve. In this, the literature shows, Britain's experience mirrors that of other industrialised countries: policies which do not take account of the long-term dynamic of migration processes in source and receiving countries, of the actual motivations of migrants or the strength of demand for their labour, and which overestimate the impact of regulation, tend to fail.[40] Migration cannot be turned on and off like a tap.

Blair's overriding objective was to convince the public that migration was under control and to neutralise immigration as a political issue. In that he undoubtedly failed, polls showing public concern rising throughout his period in office, reinforced by the measures and rhetoric that were meant to reassure. That outcome, and the lessons that could be learnt from it, are his most enduring legacy to his successor. An immigration debate that revolves on numbers, that concedes that rising numbers are a threat per se, cannot be won. For the public and sections of the media any number is too many; and numbers are not within the government's control. Labour failed to shift the debate into more constructive territory in the early years when it had the greatest chance to succeed. When Blair left office there was still no sign that it seriously intended to try.

---

[39] Immigration and Asylum Act 1999; Anti-terrorism, Crime and Security Act 2001; Nationality, Immigration and Asylum Act 2002; Asylum and Immigration (Treatment of Claimants) Act 2004; Immigration, Asylum and Nationality Act 2006; UK Borders Bill 2007.

[40] Stephen Castles, 'Why Migration Policies Fail', *Ethnic Studies*, 27(2), 2004: 205–27.

17

Schools

ALAN SMITHERS

Blair came to power in 1997 with improving education as his declared passion, and believing he knew how to do it. He had tacitly accepted the major planks of Conservative reform – the national curriculum, national tests, regular inspections and financial delegation to schools – although his party had opposed all of them at the outset. But even so he believed there was a vital missing ingredient: the engine to drive up standards. And he thought he knew what it was. Governments had traditionally contented themselves with policy and legislation. He wanted his government to accept responsibility for 'delivery' as well, and he had been persuaded that targets and monitoring were the way to do it.

Within a week of the 1997 election, a Standards and Effectiveness (SEU) unit had been set up in the Department for Education and Employment (DfEE, as it was then). It had specific tasks including 'improving and sustaining standards of attainment' and 'monitoring performance in education and intervening where necessary',[1] but it was intended also as a catalyst to change the culture of a civil service which 'had little truck with the idea of delivery'.[2] Within two weeks, ambitious national targets for the literacy and numeracy of eleven-year-olds had been declared and David Blunkett, the Secretary of State, was tempted into admitting 'his head would be on the block'[3] if they were not met (which famously became reported as he would resign). This was the first public indication that Blair's education ministers would be judged not only on political nous but also on how well pupils did.[4]

Blair's education policy was not all plain sailing, but his struggles were more with his own backbenchers than the main opposition party. His first act as leader in July 1994 was to kick into touch the recommendations

---
[1] Department for Education and Skills, Standards Site, Standards and Effectiveness Unit, www.standards.dfes.gov.uk/seu/.
[2] Stephen Pollard, *David Blunkett* (London: Hodder and Stoughton, 2005), p. 228.
[3] *Ibid.*, p. 256.   [4] *Ibid.*, p. 263.

of the education commission set up in the wake of the 1992 election defeat under the then shadow Secretary of State, Anne Taylor. Her document, *Opening Doors to a Learning Society*, proposed, among other things, scrapping league tables, bringing grant-maintained schools back under local authority control and replacing A-levels by a general diploma. A particularly thorny issue was – and is – the organisation of secondary education. Old Labour is implacably opposed to academic selection and has long wanted to see the abolition of the remaining grammar schools, in spite of their popularity and achievements. Blair thought he had found a convenient way of sidestepping the issue by adopting the mantra 'standards not structures'. He could also see the political potential in this respect of the Conservative's diversity agenda. Far from an untidy mix of schools being a problem, it could be argued that the different types were necessary to give parents choice. With money following pupils, schools would compete for parental preferences and this would reinforce targets in levering up standards.

For his plans to succeed Blair needed to find extra funding and here he had to contend with Gordon Brown, his Chancellor of the Exchequer, who wanted to devote the available money to his own pet, but costly, scheme of tax credits. There was also a dire shortage of teachers and it was feared that school staffing was near to collapse. Moreover, the Thatcher and Major governments had left unfinished business, in particular with regard to the role of the local education authorities and qualifications reform. Blair nevertheless felt very confident that education could be transformed. He had a strong team, carefully laid plans, and the government was riding high in popular support. He had every hope that his tenure would come to be celebrated as the time when England's education really did become world-class.

Ten years on we can see how it has all worked out. The numerical targets enable us to make a quantitative assessment. We can also track what happened to diversity and choice in secondary education, the social agenda, the teaching profession, the curriculum and qualifications, autonomy and accountability, and how much extra money was made available. This chapter complements the reviews of Blair's education policies made immediately after the first and second terms of office.[5] The themes and conclusions remain much the same, but we are now able to

---

[5] Alan Smithers, 'Education Policy', in Anthony Seldon (ed.). *The Blair Effect* (London: Little, Brown, 2001), pp. 405–26; and Alan Smithers, 'Education', in Anthony Seldon and Dennis Kavanagh (eds.), *The Blair Effect 2001–5* (Cambridge: Cambridge University Press, 2005), pp. 256–82.

take in the broad sweep of Blair's thirteen years as Labour leader. We begin by considering the people who helped to shape his thinking.

People

Blair was particularly fortunate in his first Education Secretary, David Blunkett, who served for three years in the shadow cabinet and the whole of the first term. Blunkett was of the left and acted as a bridge between Blair and Labour activists, but importantly he was also open to new ideas. It was Blunkett's powerful speech that helped to ward off an impending defeat from the floor at the 1995 Labour Party Conference over grant-maintained schools. Blunkett and his aide Conor Ryan were in on the meetings of the small group that helped Blair to clarify his thinking and shape it into policies. Together they wrote, in consultation with Blair's advisers, much of the major policy documents, *Diversity and Excellence* and *Excellence for Everyone*, which provided the platform for the first years in office. David Blunkett, in turn, was fortunate in his permanent secretary Michael Bichard, who unusually had been appointed from outside the civil service and was very receptive to Blair's ideas on delivery.

Beside Blunkett, the key players were David Miliband, Michael Barber, Andrew Adonis and, less directly, Cyril Taylor. Miliband and Barber were there from the very beginning. Miliband was brought in from the Institute of Public Policy Research and Labour's Social Justice Commission to help put together Blair's manifesto for the 1994 leadership contest, and he soon became Blair's head of policy. In 1994, he had edited a book, *Re-inventing the Left*, which became the 'set text for New Labour intellectuals'.[6] He played a major role in drafting both the 1997 and 2001 manifestos, and in 2001 he was himself elected an MP. In no time he emerged as the Minister for School Standards, where he stayed till December 2004.

Barber, chair of education in Hackney, former Labour candidate for Henley, and professor at the London Institute for Education, drafted some of Blair's early important speeches on schooling. It was Barber who laid the foundations for two of the main prongs of Blair's education policy. He was a keen advocate of targets. In *The Learning Game* (1996), personally endorsed by Blair, he held out a vision of 'the power of ambitious targets . . . to provide a real opportunity to generate excitement and enthusiasm across society'.[7] Both Blair and he had been very impressed

---

[6] Andrew Rawnsley, 'Heir to Blair?' *The Observer*, 20 October 2002.
[7] Michael Barber, *The Learning Game* (London: Victor Gollancz, 1996), p. 261.

by the way David Simon and John Browne (both soon to be ennobled) were using targets to turn British Petroleum from an also-ran into a world leader. Barber also came up with the phrase that was so often to be repeated in the early days, 'standards matter more than structures',[8] at a select gathering including Miliband, Blunkett and Ryan, in Blair's office in the Commons in January 1995.

Barber was appointed special adviser to the DfEE immediately after the 1997 election victory and soon afterwards he became the first head of the SEU. Its focus on delivery and outcomes, particularly through the literacy and numeracy targets and strategies, was counted a great success and Blair sought to extend the approach across departments. In 2001 Barber moved to No. 10 (later relocated to the Treasury in the spirit of bridge building) as head of the Prime Minister's Delivery Unit. Originally it was intended to monitor progress on seventeen priorities, but these were whittled down to eight key objectives, including secondary school performance.[9] Each objective became the focus of a high-level meeting in the cabinet room every six weeks or so, chaired by Blair and attended by the secretary of state whose responsibility it was, with Barber – 'Mr Targets'[10] – making the initial presentation. Although remaining close to Blair, Barber left government service in 2005, rewarded with a knighthood.

Adonis, a don, journalist and social democrat, came to Blair's notice, it is said, when in the run-up to the 1997 election he wrote an article in *The Observer*[11] urging Blair to become his own Secretary of State for Education. He was recruited to become education adviser and rapidly became so important that articles began to appear suggesting that he, not Blunkett, was de facto Education Secretary.[12] They clashed notably over Chris Woodhead, the edgy Chief Inspector of Schools, whom Blunkett did not want to re-appoint, although instructed to do so by Blair via Adonis. Adonis replaced Miliband as Blair's policy chief for the second term, and at the beginning of the third term he was elevated to the House

[8] Anthony Seldon, *Blair* (London: The Free Press, 2005), p. 243.
[9] Peter Hyman, *1 out of 10: From Downing Street Vision to Classroom Reality* (London: Vintage, 2005), pp. 175–6. The other seven main objectives were NHS waiting times; cancer/coronary heart disease; the patient experience; railway reliability; the tube; crime, especially street robbery; and asylum.
[10] Andrew Grice, ' "Mr Targets" on a Mission to Reform Whitehall', *The Independent*, 6 January 2003; and Michael Barber, *Instruction to Deliver: Tony Blair, the Public Services and the Challenge of Delivery* (London: Politico's, 2007).
[11] Andrew Adonis, 'Let Blair Be His Own Education Chief', *The Observer*, 15 December 1996.
[12] Francis Beckett, 'Which of These Two Men is the Real Education Secretary? (Not the One You Think)', *New Statesman*, 16 October 2000.

of Lords so that he could become an education minister. There, as in his other roles, he shaped and drove forward Blair's plans, but with even more clout, and it could be argued that his influence has been more profound than that of anyone in education since 1945. Adonis was succeeded as Blair's education adviser at No. 10 by Conor Ryan, who had been David Blunkett's right-hand man.

Perhaps the most surprising of the major influences on Blair's education policies was Cyril Taylor, who in the memorable words of Peter Wilby, 'has surfed, without apparently pausing for breath, from the high tide of Thatcherism to the uplands of New Labour'.[13] Not a member of Blair's inner team, Taylor has done perhaps more than anyone to flesh out Blair's vision of diversity in secondary education. A former Conservative parliamentary candidate for Keighley and member of the Greater London Council, he was asked by Margaret Thatcher to organise a conference for industrialists at the Festival Hall on youth unemployment. They persuaded her that the solution to the twin problems of low educational performance in the inner cities and the shortage of scientists and engineers was to set up city technology colleges (CTCs) in partnership with business. When business did not play its part – only fifteen CTCs eventually got off the ground mainly at the taxpayers' expense – Taylor hit on the idea of enabling existing schools to achieve specialist technology status through additional funding.

Taylor met Blunkett in 1995 in relation to the controversy over grant-maintained schools, which at first were the only ones eligible to bid for this extra money, and converted him to the cause. A little later he travelled with Blair up to Darlington to open a specialist school and evidently sold him the idea also. When Blair came to power, instead of winding up the scheme as he might well have done, specialist status became the cornerstone of his secondary education policy. Taylor became a close ally of Adonis and together they pushed through the diversity agenda. By the end of Blair's premiership, a trust set up by Taylor and partly funded by the government had over four-fifths of English secondary schools affiliated to it. Taylor, knighted in 1989 for education services by Margaret Thatcher, received a second knighthood in 2004 from Labour. In all he had served ten secretaries of state.

Blunkett held the education brief for seven years, but following his short-lived promotion to the Home Office, secretaries of state came and went, with four at the helm from 2001 to 2007 – Estelle Morris, Charles

[13] Peter Wilby, 'A Different Sort of Missionary', *The Guardian*, 18 July 2006.

Clarke, Ruth Kelly and Alan Johnson. They had to play themselves in and brought their own personalities and priorities to the role (Charles Clarke, for example, disbanded the SEU). During the second term, not surprisingly, education policy began to drift and, impatient to see his education project embedded before he left office, Blair made Adonis a minister in an attempt to secure its future.

The rivalry between Tony Blair and Gordon Brown was a recurring theme of New Labour, but as far as education policy was concerned their spheres of interest were different. Brown directed his attention to skills and employment, and his main impact on schools was as their paymaster. Brown shared Blair's enthusiasm for targets and began making public service agreements with the spending departments in which they would agree certain outputs for the money received. In the case of the Department for Education and Skills (DfES, as it became in 2001) this was for a 2% a year improvement in the proportion of young people achieving five good GCSEs.

Targets and delivery

The thing about Labour's targets is that they provide clear benchmarks. At first, ministers and officials thought they had every reason to be confident. The percentage of pupils reaching the expected levels for eleven-year-olds rose by 12 percentage points in English and 10 percentage points in maths from 1997 to 2000, and they seemed well on course to meet the targets of 80% in English and 75% in maths by 2002. Figure 17.1 shows that the numeracy and literacy scores of eleven-year-olds went up year by year. Barber was encouraged to the point that he boasted to an American audience that 'large scale reform is not only possible but can be achieved quickly'.[14]

A closer look at the data, however, raises doubts about whether it was the targets that were making the difference. Scores in fact rose more rapidly in the final years of the Conservative government when no targets were set, and science without a national target followed the same trajectory as English and maths. Even the meaning of the rising scores has been questioned. An analysis by Peter Tymms, a professor of education at the University of Durham,[15] suggested that the increases were specific to the

[14] Michael Barber, 'Large-scale Reform is Possible', *Education Week*, 15 November 2000.
[15] Peter Tymms, 'Are Standards Rising in English Primary Schools?' *British Educational Research Journal*, 30, 2004: 477–94.

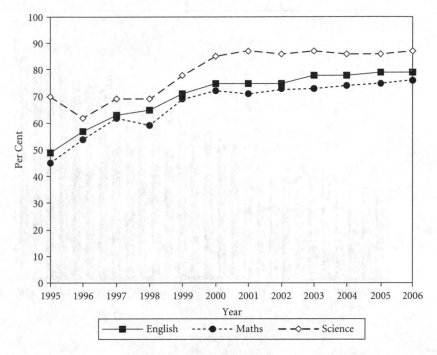

Figure 17.1. Percentage of eleven-year-olds achieving level 4 or higher
Source: DfES, *National Curriculum Assessments at Key Stage 2 in England (Provisional, 2006)*, National Statistics First Release SFR 31/2006 (London: DfES, August 2006), table 1.

tests used and did not show up to the same extent in more general measures. He was supported by the Statistics Commission which concluded that 'the improvement in KS2 test scores between 1995 and 2000 substantially overstates the improvement in standards in English primary schools over that period'.[16] This was hotly disputed by the DfES which demanded the Commission 'revisit your conclusions on the Peter Tymms article and set the record straight'.[17] The DfES argued that the school test results were borne out by international studies, but that too is open to doubt.[18]

---

[16] Statistics Commission, *Measuring Standards in English Primary Schools: Report by the Statistics Commission on an Article by Peter Tymms* (London: Statistics Commission, 2005).

[17] David Normington, *Measuring Standards in English Primary Schools: Report by the Statistics Commission on an Article by Peter Tymms, 21/02/05* (London: DfES, 3 March 2005).

[18] Alan Smithers, *Blair's Education: An International Perspective* (London: The Sutton Trust, 2007).

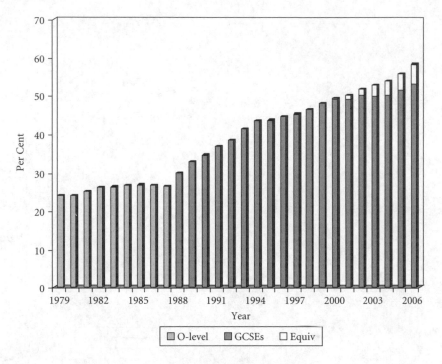

Figure 17.2. Percentage of five good GCSEs or equivalent
Sources: Alan Smithers 'Do Better Results Mean Worse Exams?' *Managing Schools Today*, 22–27 September/October 2005, and BBC News 'Five Good GCSEs Obtained by 59%', 19 October 2006, http://news.bbc.co.uk/1/hi/education/6065436.stm.

The examinations at the end of secondary schooling were also subject to targets. On the face of it, they could be claimed to be driving up performance. Figure 17.2 shows that, in 2006, 59.0% of pupils obtained five good GCSEs or equivalent against 45.1% when Labour came to power. It is not quite the rate of increase specified in the Treasury's public service agreement with the DfES, but nevertheless encouraging. But what part have targets played? Taking a longer view, figure 17.2 also shows that the percentage achieving five good grades has increased every year since 1988 when the GCSE came on stream. In so far as it is possible to detect an effect of Blair's policies, it is that schools have been increasingly turning to GCSE equivalents to boost their results. When belatedly the government included English and maths in the GCSE performance measure, it came as quite a shock to discover that the percentage achieving five good passes dropped sharply, falling to only 45.8% in 2006.

The complexities in interpreting the results of the key stage tests and examinations suggest that it was unwise for the government to stake its reputation on them. Not only can it become embarrassing, as when Estelle Morris, Blunkett's successor, felt she had to resign, but it also tends to distort education as schools strive to make the numbers come right irrespective of whether what they are doing is educationally sound.[19] It also became hard for the government to look at the results dispassionately. As was once perceptively remarked, 'those who have so committed themselves in advance to the efficacy of the reform . . . cannot afford honest evaluation'.[20] When I come to summing up Blair's tenure I shall be arguing that attempting to improve education through target-setting was misguided.

School organisation

I shall also be arguing that there is a fundamental flaw in the other main arm of Blair's schools policy: diversity. When Blair came to power, among all the other school types, there were fifteen city technology colleges and 245 specialist schools (mainly in technology, but also in foreign languages, sports and performing arts), the fruits of two not very successful Conservative policies. Blair had a choice: to abandon them or to adopt them. Urged on by figures apparently showing that they boosted results, which Sir Cyril Taylor[21] kept producing, he decided to stay with them, tentatively at first, with, in 1997, the aim of 450 more specialist schools by the end of the parliament. But by the second term they had become central to Blair's secondary education policy. The target was raised first to 1,500, then 2,000, and eventually it was envisaged that all secondary schools would have a distinctive ethos. The range of possible specialisms was progressively extended and in 2003 Taylor's Technology Schools Trust became the Specialist Schools Trust.

But it is not altogether clear in what sense they are specialist. The science schools, for example, were not even able to select 10% of their pupils, generally did not have better-qualified staff or facilities in science, and their science results were often less good than those of schools with

[19] Warwick Mansell, *Education by Numbers: The Tyranny of Testing* (London: Politico's Publishing, 2007).

[20] Donald Campbell, 'Reforms as Experiments', *American Psychologist*, 24, 1969: 409–29.

[21] Cyril Taylor and Conor Ryan, *Excellence in Education: The Making of Great Schools* (London: David Fulton Publishers, 2005), pp. 77–9.

other specialisms.[22] Schools were keen to become specialist because it meant extra money – a 1,000-pupil school could expect to receive £616,000 over four years. To be accepted as such they had to raise £50,000 of private sector sponsorship and then submit a bid to the Secretary of State detailing how they would raise their performance overall, increase achievement in their specialism, and work with at least six partner schools. The DfES tended to see this as a very good process for schools to go through and thought of it more as a general school improvement programme than setting up schools with distinctive curricula. But it left parents faced with a confusing, incomplete, and in practice meaningless array of specialisms, apparently requiring them to think what subjects (including business and enterprise) would be best for their child from the age of eleven.

Some schools were failing so badly that it was thought that there was nothing for it but to start again. The city technology college concept became adapted to this purpose, re-branded by Adonis first as 'city academy' and then just 'academy'. Academies were set up as independent schools funded directly by the government. In return for about 10% of the capital funding (which could be reduced on negotiation) a sponsor is given control of the board of governors and ownership of the land and buildings (which revert to the local authority if the academy closes), and the school employs its own staff and sets its own admission arrangements. Academies emerged in 2000 from the Fresh Start initiative in which schools with less than 15% of the pupils achieving five A*–C grades at GCSE three years in succession would be considered for closure or replacement. But it is evident that they became increasingly prominent in Blair's thinking. By the time he left office he had set a target of 400, when there was nowhere near that number of schools so bad they had to be closed. Blair had come to see academies as desirable in their own right, influenced in part by the success and popularity of state-funded independent schools in other countries, notably the Netherlands.[23] Academy status was opened up to encompass some private schools, and local authorities were encouraged to become sponsors. Manchester found it cost-effective to open eight. In 2005, Taylor's Trust was handed the academies and once more it changed its name, this time to the Specialist Schools and Academies Trust.

[22] Alan Smithers and Pamela Robinson, *Physics in Schools and Colleges: Teacher Deployment and Student Outcomes* (Buckingham: Carmichael Press, 2005), p. 16.
[23] Organisation for Economic Cooperation and Development, *Learning for Tomorrow's World: First Results from PISA 2003* (Paris: OECD, 2004), table 5.19, pp. 436–7.

New Labour, to the dismay of the old guard and its backbenchers, was also more than accepting of the fee-paying sector. On taking office, the first Blair government contented itself with meeting its manifesto commitment to phase out the assisted places scheme. By 2000 it was prepared to go on record as saying that it liked independent schools, and in major speeches Blair expressed his wish to modernise the comprehensive principle so that maintained neighbourhood schools would come to rival the independent schools in their 'first-rate teaching and facilities'.[24] At first, Blair appeared to do little to bridge the independent/state divide other than making available a small amount of funding for partnerships. But as his term drew to a close it became clear that he was coming at it from both directions: seeking to open up independent schools through a new Charities Act which required them to demonstrate their public benefit; and creating more free-standing schools in the maintained sector. An independent school head in London admitted that if the academies were allowed to select pupils it would be the end of schools like his.[25] The Education and Inspections Act in 2006 paved the way for yet another type of school, the 'trust school': schools remaining within the maintained sector but supported by an independent foundation. The Act enabled schools, either individually or collectively, to form trusts with organisations ranging from universities to businesses. Like the sponsors of academies, the trusts would, through the governing bodies, manage the land and assets, employ staff and set admissions criteria. The Bill was not uncontroversial with Labour backbenchers, but Adonis was able to get it through with Conservative support. As Blair left office the first schools to acquire trust status were being revealed.

The drive towards school independence left the local education authorities in an even more ambiguous position. Their powers had been progressively stripped away by the Thatcher and Major governments, but they were expecting to be given a leading role once more by the incoming Labour government. Their hopes were raised when the funding of the grant-maintained schools was channelled back through them. But Blair, convinced by Adonis who had discussed it at length with Woodhead, pushed for wholesale reform against a reluctant Blunkett and the DfEE.[26] With Blair out of office the LEAs are still there, but even more constrained. The Education and Inspections Act left them with the role of

[24] Smithers, 'Education Policy', p. 424.
[25] Alan Smithers and Pamela Robinson, *School Headship: Present and Future* (London: National Union of Teachers, 2007), p. 70. [26] Pollard, *David Blunkett*, pp. 233–4.

commissioning rather than providing education. As their functions were reduced, local authorities increasingly merged their education and social services departments, often under the latter. But the ambivalence remained, with local authorities being among the organisations able to set up academies and form trusts.

Social justice

Having taken upon itself the responsibility of running the education system, the Blair governments brimmed over with ideas for increasing 'delivery' through reform, modernisation and innovation. Not all were directed towards educational excellence. Blair, heavily influenced by the report of Labour's Social Justice Commission, written by Miliband together with the deputy chair Patricia Hewitt, herself to become a cabinet minister, saw education as the way to a more inclusive society. In November 1998 the DfEE issued a mission statement declaring that its twin goals were 'an inclusive and fair society' and 'a competitive economy'.[27] Inclusion became the watchword and the number of special schools for those with disabilities declined as more of their pupils entered mainstream schooling.[28] A cross-departmental Social Exclusion Unit reporting directly to the Prime Minister was launched and it embarked on a 'ConneXions' (sic) initiative to keep more young people in education and training to the age of eighteen. In the face of widespread truanting, the first Blair government introduced a raft of measures involving learning mentors, learning support units, pupil referral units and the short-lived 'Truancy Buster' awards.

The individual initiatives of the first term took on a coherent shape in the second. Prompted in part by the horrific death in 2003 of Victoria Climbié, the government embarked on what it saw as an integrated approach to the well-being of young people from birth to the age of nineteen. In *Every Child Matters* (ECM), it set out five goals: every child was to be provided with support to be healthy; stay safe; enjoy and achieve; make a positive contribution; and achieve economic well-being. A Children's Act in 2004 required all organisations involved in children's services, including schools, hospitals, the police and voluntary groups, to work

[27] Department for Education and Employment, *Learning and Working Together for the Future: A Strategic Framework to 2002* (London: DfEE, 1998).

[28] Department for Education and Skills, *Schools and Pupils in England, January 2006 (Final)*, National Statistics First Release SFR38/2006 (London: DfES, 2006), table 1, shows that the number of LEA-maintained special schools declined from 1,153 in 1997 to 1,033 in 2006.

together to achieve these aims. The Act also gave children more say in their futures, and in 2005 the first Children's Commissioner for England was appointed.

As part of its programme to deliver ECM the government promoted the development of extended schools, providing from 8.00 a.m. to 6.00 p.m. all the year round what it termed 'wrap-around childcare'. This included parenting and family support, study support and clubs, swift and easy referral to specialist services such as speech therapy, and community use of facilities. Schools were also encouraged to open children's centres, bringing together early education, childcare, and health and family support, with a target of 3,500 by 2010. The government's concern for pupil welfare also extended to setting up the School Food Trust, which saw into law recommendations on healthy eating made in the wake of Jamie Oliver's television programmes. The more extensive use of, and the extensions to, school facilities led the government to question who should be running them. It commissioned a report[29] which suggested that the nature of schooling had changed so much that chief executives with a broad range of leadership and management skills rather than traditional headteachers were required. But this aroused concerns that learning and teaching would be in the hands of people who did not know enough about education, and whose priorities were elsewhere.

Teachers and staffing

When Blair came to power headteachers were not the school staffing issue at the forefront of his mind. There was a severe shortage of classroom teachers as a result of both under-supply and excessive wastage. Not only was there the manifesto commitment to reduce class sizes, but all the schools policies were at risk. Blunkett, who had been a teacher himself, recognised that the salary scale was not good enough, but he was neither allowed, nor did he want, to give a hefty pay rise all round. In *Teachers: Meeting the Challenge for Change*, launched in 1998 with a foreword by Blair, Blunkett proposed performance-related pay to reward and motivate good teaching. A bonus, later incorporated as an upper pay scale, was introduced for teachers who on appraisal could cross a performance threshold. But in the event nearly all the 197,000 teachers who applied received the bonus, and the main effect was to create a longer and more

---

[29] Department for Education and Skills, *Independent Study into School Leadership by PriceWaterhouseCoopers* (London: DfES, 2007).

generous pay scale. In addition, Blunkett introduced incentive payments for graduates to train as teachers, with extra payments to those in maths, science and information technology. But these had not had time to take effect by the 2001 election and headteachers were complaining loudly that they did not have enough teachers. Some were threatening to close their schools for part of the week. Worried that the issue could lose them votes, the Labour Party put a commitment to recruit an extra 10,000 teachers into the 2001 manifesto.

In parallel with a push to improve teacher recruitment through the Teacher Training Agency (from 2005, the Training and Development Agency for Schools) by, among other things, developing ways of training on the job, the re-elected government also sought to stem the flow out of the profession. It accepted the recommendations of a review[30] that it had commissioned for reducing teachers' workload. These centred on transferring a number of tasks from teachers to assistants. It also guaranteed teachers a minimum of 10% of the school week free of classroom duties, but unfortunately it did not fund schools to appoint the necessary extra teachers, so raising the prospect of assistants doing the actual teaching. This was fiercely opposed by the National Union of Teachers who would not sign up to the 'Workload Agreement', and also the National Association of Headteachers, when they subsequently withdrew. Nevertheless, the reforms rolled on and in the manifesto for the 2005 election the Labour Party claimed that there were 28,000 more teachers than in 1997. This involved some careful presentation since there were only 8,700 extra qualified teachers, but there were 13,000 additional unqualified and trainee teachers in schools.[31] Much to the relief of the government the electorate accepted the spin and teacher supply did not loom large in the 2005 election. When Blair left office, in spite of continuing teacher shortages in inner-city schools and subjects like maths and physics, he was able to claim recruitment had been improved, and staffing schools was far less of a problem than the one he had inherited.

As well as tackling recruitment and retention directly, the first Blair government also attempted to underpin teaching as a profession by establishing a General Teaching Council (GTC) along the lines of the doctors' professional governing body. It was pressed for by Barber and

[30] PriceWaterhouseCoopers, *Teacher Workload Study*, www.teachernet.gov.uk/management/remodelling.

[31] Department for Education and Skills, *School Workforce in England, January 2005 (Provisional)*, National Statistics First Release SFR17/2005 (London: DfES, April 2005), table 1.

accepted by Blunkett, but resisted by the DfES civil servants who did not want to give away any power. The upshot was that it emerged as a pale shadow of what it could have been, weakened by poorly drafted legislation and with reserved places for the unions when it ought to have been independent of them.

At about the same time, a staff college for headteachers, the National College for School Leadership (NCSL), was established. It too got off to an uncertain start and a government review in 2004 found that it needed to achieve 'greater role clarity, outcome focus, goal clarity and efficiency'.[32] Both the chairman and the chief executive left, and those who replaced them were galvanised into seeking to satisfy those expectations. It was helped by being given teeth when its main qualification, the National Professional Qualification for Headship (NPQH), was made compulsory for new headteachers of state schools from 2009. NCSL also energetically promoted itself by raising concerns about the supply of headteachers and introducing a whole raft of courses for emergent, established, advanced and consultant school leaders, as well as entry to headship. It argued that the impending shortfall was so severe that school leaders would have to be drawn in from other fields. It was supported by the GTC and in November 2006 the newly appointed Chief Inspector of Schools, Christine Gilbert, added her voice.[33] These warnings, along with the claim that the change in the nature of schooling made it necessary, put the future of headship in the spotlight, but it remained unfinished business on Blair's departure.

Curriculum and qualifications

The outgoing Conservative administration in 1997 left on the table the Dearing review of 16–19 education. The first Blair government put it out to formal consultation and plumped for one of the options. Under the grandiose title of *Curriculum 2000* it retained A-levels but modularised them and introduced a half-way house, the Advanced Subsidiary (AS). Passes and top grades leapt, but schools complained that sixth-form studies had become a continual exam. There were teething problems in introducing the new arrangements, which led to a succession of inquiries chaired by Mike Tomlinson who had taken over briefly from Woodhead

---

[32] Department for Education and Skills, *End to End Review of School Leadership Policy*, prepared by the Review Team (Nottingham: National College for School Leadership, 2004).

[33] Alex Frean and Alex Blair, 'Business Executives Could Save Badly Run Schools, Says Ofsted', *The Times*, 23 November 2006.

as Chief Inspector of Schools. He successfully defused the row over A-levels and was given the wider remit of 14–19 reform by Charles Clarke, the then Secretary of State.

The Tomlinson Working Group took a long time, but in doing so won over most of the educational establishment to its ultimate proposal of scrapping A-levels and GCSEs in favour of a diploma embracing all qualifications. Miliband had been one of the authors of the original proposal for a 'British Bac' and both he and Clarke encouraged Tomlinson. But Tony Blair, as he made clear in his first speech as leader, wanted to retain A-levels. It is difficult, therefore, to see why he allowed Tomlinson so much time for his ideas to take root, other than being massively distracted by Iraq and such issues as university tuition fees. He had been reassured by Miliband and Tomlinson that A-levels were safe, but perhaps speciously because while the content would be retained the qualification itself would not.

Clarke and Miliband were there to officially receive the Tomlinson report, but both were soon moved to other posts and it fell to the new Secretary of State, Ruth Kelly, to break the news on Blair's behalf that the government was rejecting the main thrust of the Tomlinson proposals. It was, however, going to put in place a 14–19 strategy providing personalised learning (another of Miliband's hobby-horses) and involving schools, further education and employers working together to provide a range of opportunities alongside A-levels, including new vocational diplomas and apprenticeships. But the schools struggled to cooperate because they had been put into fierce competition by the diversity agenda. Education 14–19 on Blair's departure was still work-in-progress. In a speech to the 2006 Labour Party Conference Brown said he wanted the school-leaving age to be raised to eighteen, and in January 2007 the DfES confirmed that by 2015 all young people will have to be engaged in education or training to that age.[34] It was not clear what sanctions would be employed against those who were not.

The government under Blair was not only keen to restructure education 14–19, but also made changes to nursery education, and the primary and secondary curriculum. On taking office it honoured its promise to scrap the Conservative's nursery voucher scheme, and by 2000 it had made available a free nursery place for every four-year-old. By 2004 there was on offer a place for every three-year-old whose parents wanted it.

---

[34] BBC News, 'School Leaving Age Set to be 18', 12 January 2007, http://news.bbc.co.uk/1/hi/education/6254833.stm.

Tests for five-year-olds were introduced, and the government seemed to be looking increasingly to the early years as a means of tackling the persistent rump of children, particularly boys, leaving primary schools unable to read, write and add to the expected standards. In primary education, after the big push on literacy and numeracy, the DfES issued *Excellence and Enjoyment* in which it sought, not entirely successfully, to broaden out primary education by re-emphasising music, the arts, creativity, PE and sport, and introducing a modern foreign language. Schools were also asked to identify 'gifted and talented pupils' for master classes, but without being provided with a reliable means of doing so.

In contrast to the battles over the content of the national curriculum when it was introduced in 1988, it was modified with little fuss under Blair. At the secondary level, citizenship, personal, social and health education (PSHE), careers education and work-related learning were added to the Conservative's original ten-subject curriculum plus religious education. The requirements for the individual subjects were slimmed down and some subjects, such as a modern foreign language, were made optional after fourteen. It is one of Blair's achievements that in his ten years in office the national curriculum came to be accepted as a normal part of the school landscape.

Autonomy and accountability

A key issue in the relationship between central government and schools is how to strike an appropriate balance between autonomy and accountability. Michael Barber, drawing inspiration from a paper published by the Centre for Educational Outreach and Innovation at Columbia University,[35] persuaded both Blunkett and Blair that the answer was 'strategic management', in which top managers (the government) and 'local educators' (headteachers) both have 'a unique and important contribution to make'. The 'former holds the big picture' and 'the authority to intervene when things go wrong', while schools 'having the close up picture' are 'free to determine means and proximate ends'. Fine in theory, but it led to a deluge of directives from the centre (322 in 1998 alone), described with feeling by one headteacher as 'independence with a big thick collar and chain'.[36]

[35] Center for Educational Outreach and Innovation, *Re-Centralization or Strategic Management?* (New York: Teachers College, Columbia University), cited in Pollard, *David Blunkett*, p. 251. [36] Smithers and Robinson, *School Headship*, p. 71.

The government under Blair held schools to account in two main ways: the test and examination scores in relation to the targets, as we have already discussed; and external inspections. The inspection service was beefed up by the Conservatives as the Office for Standards in Education (Ofsted) in 1992. The process initially involved a four-year cycle, but under Blair it was first replaced by a six-year cycle and then radically changed as part of a *New Relationship with Schools*.[37] The inspection now turned on a detailed self-evaluation form (SEF) that the school is responsible for updating and having ready as a basis for a two-day Ofsted inspection at short notice. It became mainly a check on what the form contained rather than classroom observations, making reported results even more important. Headteachers have felt increasingly prey to poor pupil results and inspection reports, making many senior teachers unwilling to take on the role. It was compared to being a football manager, but without the huge salaries and pay-offs.[38]

Funding

Unlike many areas of policy, Blair was given a relatively free run on schools by Brown. But the Chancellor relished the power his role as paymaster gave him. Funding for education was tightly constrained in the first two years, but generous later. In order to establish a reputation for prudence Brown kept to Conservative spending plans for the years 1997–9, even though, as Kenneth Clarke his predecessor admitted, the Tories themselves would probably not have done so. This presented difficulties for Blunkett and his Schools Minister Stephen Byers, who could not move as fast as they or No. 10 would have wished. In an attempt to be seen to be doing good they continually announced and re-announced new initiatives, a habit which New Labour found hard to break. Brown did find an extra £19 billion for education for the period 1999–2002, but rather over-egged the amount by reaching this figure through triple counting. In the 2000 Comprehensive Spending Review the Chancellor also introduced pockets of money to be paid directly to schools for them to use as they wished. But at the end of the first Blair government the percentage of GDP devoted to education was still less than it had been under John Major in 1995.

[37] Department for Education and Skills, *A New Relationship with Schools*, www.teachernet. gov.uk/management/newrelationship/.
[38] Smithers and Robinson, *School Headship*, p. 80.

In contrast, in the second term the government boosted education (and also health) spending.[39] From £21.43 billion, in 1997–8, schools current expenditure in real terms had risen to £23.48 billion in 1999–2000 and to £34.36 billion in 2005–6, an increase of 60%. The extra funding did not always find its way into schools, since a not inconsiderable sum was held back to fund initiatives and pay consultants. The Blair governments also wanted to fund on a 'something for something' basis, with schools bidding for money from various pots. This led to some schools drawing on their staffing budgets to employ full-time bid writers. The government's move to three-year budgets was popular, since with annual settlements, perhaps made partway through the financial year, they could find themselves lurching from relative comfort to crisis, such as when there was a panic over teacher redundancies in 2003–4. The Chancellor seems to have shared Blair's enthusiasm for delivery through targets and used them in signing Public Service Agreements (PSA) with government spending departments, including education. But in practice these were largely meaningless, other than allowing the Chancellor some control and to claim the expenditure was investment, since there was no clawing back when the targets were not met.

Government funding for school buildings more than doubled from £1.26 billion in 1997–8 to £3.02 billion in 2005–6, with the rolling out of the *Building Schools for the Future* programme – again subject to bidding. New school buildings were also provided through the private finance initiative (PFI), whereby the public sector rents on long leases premises built by the private sector. Whether PFIs have intrinsic benefits as the government has claimed is contestable, but they did enable schools to be built immediately on a live-now-pay-later basis. While Blair's first term in office was disappointing in terms of school funding, the second more than made up for it. The share of the GDP spent on education[40] rose from 4.8% in 1996–7 to 5.7% in 2006–7.

Summing up

As his time in office came to an end Tony Blair was distinctly bullish.[41] He claimed to have overseen, among other things, higher academic

[39] Department for Education and Skills, 'Replies to Questions Sent by the Committee on 5 June 2006', House of Commons Education and Skills Committee, *Public Expenditure. Fifth Report of the Session 2005–06*, HC1201, Ev 43–46, table A.

[40] Treasury figures from http://csr07.treasury.gov.uk/spending/areas/education.

[41] See, for example, the transcript of Tony Blair's speech to the Specialist Schools and Academies Trust, 30 November 2006, www.number-10.gov.uk/output/Page10513.asp.

achievement in primary and secondary schools, the embedding of
diversity leading to high-quality choice of school, the recruitment of a
motivated and highly qualified teaching profession with increased
prestige, and the funding of state-of-the-art buildings and equipment.
Table 17.1 bears him out to some extent. Scores in tests and examinations have indeed risen, there is now a greater variety of schools, there
are more teachers, and extra money has been found. But table 17.1 also
contains hints that the situation is not so rosy. There were more day
pupils in independent schools in 2007 than in 1997 in spite of the
rising costs and a decreasing school age population, and one wonders
why parents were prepared to fork out so much if the state sector
had improved as dramatically as Blair claimed. More children were
truanting and one wonders why they should not want to be in school
when it is there for their sake. And while there are more recruits to
the teaching profession, more are leaving. The claim to have established a genuinely post-comprehensive schools system is also open to
question.

Blair's policy of creating different types of schools for parents to
choose from has been welcomed in many quarters, not least by the
Conservatives from whom it was taken over. But it suffers from a central
weakness, which neither party has been able to resolve. That is: what
happens when more parents want their child to go to a school than can be
accommodated? Independent schools hold competitive entrance examinations, an option not open to most state schools. Blair first attempted to
provide a fair basis for admissions through a code for which schools were
'to have regard', but it was clear from the differences in school intakes
that various kinds of social selection were going on. The Education and
Inspections Act 2006 strengthened the code by specifying that schools
must 'act in accordance with' it, requiring the government to spell out
what was possible, including that places could be decided by ballot.
However, this proved mightily unpopular with parents, particularly those
who felt they could manipulate the old system. Brighton announced that
it would take advantage of the provision,[42] but the council was booted out
in the May 2007 elections.

The diversity which Blair prides himself on as having embedded presents parents with a confusing and incomplete mix of specialist schools,
faith schools, academies, trust schools and other school types without a

[42] BBC News, 'Schools to Give Places by Lottery', 28 February 2007, http://news.bbc.co.uk/1/
hi/education/6403017.stm.

Table 17.1. Ten years on

	1997	2006/7
Test and exam scores[a]		
KS 2 English level 4	63.0%	79.0%
KS 2 maths level 4	62.0%	76.0%
KS 2 science level 4	69.0%	87.0%
5 A*–C GCSEs	45.1%	59.0%
A-level passes	87.8%	96.6%
A-level A grades	15.7%	24.1%
Schools[b]		
Specialist	245	2,695
CTCs/academies	15	46
School staffing[c]		
Qualified regular teachers	396,200	417,600
Teacher turnover	35,700	46,000
Pupil:teacher ratio primary	23.4	21.8
Pupil:teacher ratio secondary	16.7	16.5
Teaching assistants	60,600	162,900
Other support staff	79,200	142,000
Pupil:adult ratio primary	17.9	12.4
Pupil:adult ratio secondary	14.5	11.4
Pupils[d]		
Unauthorised days absence from secondary schools	5,354,000	6,956,000
Not in education, employment or training age 17	47,690	62,650
Day pupils in independent schools	395,940	441,758
School funding[e]		
Capital	£1.26 billion	£3.02 billion
Current	£21.43 billion	£34.36 billion
Per pupil	£2,970	£4,590

Sources:
[a] Department for Education and Skills, *National Curriculum Assessments at Key Stage 2 in England, 2006* (Provisional) National Statistics First Release SFR31/2006; Department for Education and Skills, 'Jim Knight Puts English and Maths at the Heart of Driving up GCSE Results', press notice, 11 January 2007;

Table 17.1 (*cont.*)
table 1; annual publications of InterBoard Statistics, compiled by the Centre for
Education and Employment Research at the University of Buckingham.
[b] Specialist Schools and Academies Trust, press release, 3 April 2007,
www.specialistschools.org.uk.
[c] DfES, *School Workforce in England*, January 2007 (Revised), tables 2, 15 and 16;
Local Government Analysis and Research, *Survey of Teacher Resignations and
Recruitment 1985/6–2005*, Report 39, December 2006.
[d] Department for Education and Skills, *Pupil Absence in Maintained Secondary
Schools in England in 2005/06*, National Statistics First Release SFR35/2006, 21
September 2006; Department for Education and Skills, *Participation in
Education, Training and Employment by 16–18 Year Olds in England, 2005 and
2006*, National Statistics First Release SFR22/2007; table 5, 26 June 2007.
[e] House of Commons Education and Skills Committee, *Public Expenditure*,
Fifth Report of the Session 2005–2006, HC1201, Ev 43–6, tables A and
extended 8.4.

fair way of deciding who gets into where. While undoubtedly some
schools have improved considerably during Blair's watch, insufficient
attention has been given to the overall shape of the system, so it is hard to
claim that state education provides equivalent opportunities for all children. An imperfect market has been created that is hard to reconcile with
equity, which at the outset Blair declared to be one of his twin goals.
Everyone wears clothes but of different quality; compulsory education
has gone the same way.

There are also reasons for challenging Blair's celebration of the rising
test and examination scores. He was clearly right to tackle literacy and
numeracy in the primary school and to be concerned about educational
standards. One would not want to deny that the rising scores reflect some
real improvements and a number of failing schools have been turned
round or replaced. But the chosen method of relentless pressure from the
centre through targets and league tables with a real prospect of being relegated out of existence is flawed. Blair may have been persuaded by his
advisers and friends in business that targets were the key to raising performance. But test and exam scores are not a product in the sense that
barrels of oil or tins of baked bins are; they are surrogates for the education we hope is taking place. Treating the scores as products has turned
schools into something like exam factories. Thus while results may have
gone up, the narrow focus has inflicted collateral damage. Truancy
increased (see Table 17.1). Behaviour became a major concern, with

scheme after scheme being tried.[43] Employers continually complained that school leavers lacked 'soft skills'.[44] The UK came bottom of twenty-one developed nations in UNICEF's 2007 Report Card on child well-being.[45] It also became more difficult to attract headteachers to state schools because they felt vulnerable to the targets and league tables, and burdened by the numerous initiatives thrown at them.

I sense that Blair himself, in spite of his upbeat pronouncements, is somewhat disappointed with his legacy in education. From 'education, education, education' at the outset, schools came relatively low down among the achievements claimed. During his time in office other priorities have emerged – notably, Iraq, Afghanistan, Northern Ireland, global warming, world poverty, Africa and the environment. But he has also been in the grip of numerous societal changes which will have had a bearing on the way schools operate, among them the fluidity and variety of family life; the loss of deference; the changing script for women; alternative forms of employment; immigration leading to multiculturalism and multi-faith communities; and a revolution in information technology. It has also not been fully understood that over half the variance in pupil performance is associated with pupil characteristics such as ability and background and only about a tenth can actually be linked to schools.[46] This must have been very frustrating for a person impatient for change.

Blair's ten years as Prime Minister have certainly had a considerable impact on schools, but whether for good or ill history will decide. On the plus side, I would put embedding the national curriculum, tests, Ofsted and financial delegation inherited from the Conservatives; the literacy and numeracy strategies in primary schools; the improvement of individual schools, particularly some poorly performing ones; the extra funding for schools, both for buildings and recurrent expenditure; and keeping A-levels. On school staffing I am ambivalent, since the overall figures mask acute shortages in challenging schools and some subjects. Moreover, the workload reforms were botched to some extent by not

[43] BBC News, 'Behaviour Lessons for Teenagers', 30 April 2007, http://news.bbc.co.uk/1/hi/education/6607333.stm.
[44] Chartered Institute of Personnel Development, 'Employers Are Prioritising School Leavers' "Soft Skills" Says Survey', 25 August 2006, www.trainingreference.co.uk/news/gn060825.htm.
[45] United Nations Children's Fund Innocenti Research Centre, Report Card 7, *An Overview of Child Well-Being in Rich Countries* (Florence: UNICEF, 2007).
[46] Jeff Searle and Peter Tymms, 'The Impact of Headteachers on the Performance and Attributes of Pupils', in James O'Shaughnessy (ed.), *The Leadership Effect: Can Headteachers Make a Difference?* (London: Policy Exchange, 2007), pp. 18–19.

funding the extra teachers needed to implement them. And the jury is still out on much else. I would particularly question the pursuit of diversity of schools as an end in itself. A system of compulsory education surely needs a coherent shape serving all children, rather than a free-for-all among different school types. At the end of the first Blair government, I thought that Blair had wanted to make too many changes at once; at the end of the second I doubted the substance was there. Looking back over the whole thirteen years we can see that flaws in two of the cardinal ideas – pressure from the centre through target-setting and diversity of schools – stand out as major reasons for the achievements being less than might have been hoped.

18

The health and welfare legacy

NICK BOSANQUET

The state of UK health services in 1997 was characterised as one of crisis. Famously its future leader and the nation lived through 'twenty-four hours to save the NHS'. In 1997 the crisis was seen mainly in terms of long waiting times. Later came assessment in terms of under-funding, low levels of spending in relation to the European average, and poor outcomes in terms of key disease areas such as cancer and heart disease. Later still came a different assessment in terms of poor value for money and lack of incentive. Thus within the Blair premiership there were three different policy phases which we will note as Blair (1997) Blair (2000) and Blair (2003).

These policy changes were heading into a health environment which was showing much more rapid change across all developed countries than in the previous four decades. A new wave of high-benefit programmes was bringing benefits to patients but stretching funding in all systems. There were moves worldwide towards a greater focus on prevention and away from hospital treatment. Survival was improving but bringing a new challenge of reducing disability and improving quality of life.

Blair (1997) was mainly set by the priority for containment of public spending. The decision was taken to stick with the previous government's plans for public expenditure, both for the total and for detailed allocations. However, within this constraint some initiatives were taken. There were the National Service Frameworks starting with that for coronary heart disease.[1] Promising but short-lived were the Health Action Zones (HAZ) with special stress on lifestyle change in deprived areas. In addition there were targets for reducing waiting times for elective treatment and a stronger emphasis on public health with the appointment of a Minister for Public Health and a particular emphasis on reducing

---

[1] Department of Health, *National Service Framework for Coronary Heart Disease* (London: DoH, 2000).

smoking. These policies were mainly developed from within the Department of Health led by Health Secretary Frank Dobson, who was not a member of the Blair inner circle. There appears to have been little direct involvement in them by the Prime Minister.

Paradoxically these policies were beginning to show quite positive results. Much of the gain from the *National Service Framework for Coronary Heart Disease* came before the large increase in funding which marked out the Blair (2000) approach: and the HAZ were beginning to secure strong involvement from local communities. The public health focus was showing success in changing public attitudes to smoking in public places even though levels of smoking fell rather slowly. More questionable, however, was the decision to omit the target for reducing obesity which had appeared in the previous government's *Health of the Nation* report.[2] This period also saw the foundation of the National Institute for Health and Clinical Excellence (NICE) and the start of an independent regulator to review standards through the health service. Both NICE and the principle of independent regulation were to endure.

The key steps to the Blair (2000) approach included a winter crisis in 1999 over admissions, a personal letter from Frank Dobson spelling out the absolute requirement for more funding for the NHS, and a series of meetings with clinicians and health professionals which raised the issues of under-funding and poor outcomes. Among them was a meeting with key clinicians in cancer services reporting on poor outcomes and lack of availability of drug therapies particularly in breast cancer treatment. The experience of a patient – Mavis Skeet – whose operations in Leeds were cancelled several times, was also influential in terms of raising the political temperature. The trigger for action was a personal intervention by Lord Winston, a leading expert on reproductive medicine and a Labour peer. His interview in the *New Statesman* in January 2000 seemed to have been motivated partly by concerns about the care for his elderly mother. He expressed very wide concerns about the funding of the NHS:

> It is not good enough to say we're going to spend £20 billion over 35 years or whatever. Do we want a health service that is steadily going to deteriorate and be more and more rationed and will be inferior on vital areas such as heart disease and cancer, compared to our less well-off neighbours?[3]

[2] Department of Health, *Seventeenth Report: Health of the Nation, A Progress Report Together with the Proceedings of the Committee Relating to the Report and the Minutes of Evidence, and Appendices* (London: DoH, 1997).

[3] Mary Riddell, 'The New Statesman Interview – Robert Winston', *New Statesman*, 14 January 2000.

The personal influence of the Prime Minister was great in the two later policy periods concerned with funding and reform. His involvement in the period before 2000 was mainly concerned with waiting lists and their public presentation. The next two phases were very much the personal initiatives of the Prime Minister. In early 2000 there was a new commitment to reach European levels of funding. To this the Department of Health added *The NHS Plan* for using the funding which was driven by the Health Secretary Alan Milburn and which set out a ten-year programme of investment in training more doctors in new medical schools, building new hospitals and introducing IT around the theme of NHS modernisation.[4]

The key direction was that of building capacity. *The NHS Plan* did begin with some discussion of whether the NHS was capable of delivering change: but at this stage these doubts and reservations did not affect the main policy theme of adding to capacity. These changes were accompanied by a series of targets which were monitored in detail by a delivery unit based in No. 10 and headed by Professor Michael Barber. This unit produced data which gave the Prime Minister a much closer contact with service performance in a more detailed way than had been the case with any previous administration. The relentless message of these targets for the health service was that activity and improvement were taking place very slowly. By 2001 there were beginning to be unfavourable reviews of productivity change in the NHS and by the start of 2002 it became clear that the first stages of increased funding had not increased activity or reduced waiting times at all.

The targets, together with the influence of No. 10 policy advisers, led to the second key Tony Blair conversion which was to the role of competition. This began from the summer of 2001, helped by difficult contacts with patients in Birmingham during the election campaign. The patient day in Birmingham was also the scene of a major argument between Prime Minister and Chancellor over a passage in the manifesto that was permissive of independent Treatment Centres.

It was after the 2001 election that the Prime Minister began to describe the NHS as a 1948-style institution which had to change. It was also after the election that a series of incidents convinced ministers that it would be much better if local managers had more freedom to manage. One clinching incident here was when there were parliamentary questions to the

---

[4] Department of Health, *The NHS Plan: A Plan for Investment, a Plan for Reform*, Cm. 4818 (London: HMSO, 2000).

Secretary of State about the problems of the mortuary in Bedford Hospital.

Out of this changing direction came some new policies: patient choice, money following the patients (payment by results), the Foundation Trusts and Independent Sector Treatment Centres (ISTCs). Foundation Trusts were a hybrid between the German not-for-profit hospital and the Scandinavian community board. They may also have been influenced by a visit which Alan Milburn made to Spain in the summer of 2002 where a press release mentioned the rather different Spanish concept of foundation hospitals.

The reform agenda picked up speed from 2002 to 2005, helped along by a powerful team of advisers within Downing Street. It was accepted that the NHS was affected by triple nationalisation: in funding, resource allocation and in provision. Policies were developed for more pluralism and some competition on the supply side, thus beginning to modify one kind of nationalisation.[5]

The aim was set for a programme by independent Treatment Centres which would account for 15% of procedures, thus creating a longer-term market which would sustain investment and innovation. The Foundation Trust Bill was passed through parliament, even if only by two votes in the Commons, and Foundation Trusts began to show distinctly better performance in financial management and quality of care. The financial problems of the Bradford Trust were resolved by the regulator and local management without involving central government. A new paper also restyled *The NHS Plan* as an NHS improvement plan and set out a coherent programme for the redesign of the service to give more patients choice and to improve care for patients with long-term medical conditions.[6]

This promising reform programme was, however, slowed by the emergence of immediate and pressing problems with financial deficits. The NHS found itself faced with large amounts of new funding – cash increases of 8–9% a year on average and 12–15% for some deprived areas. A vast amount of funding and new staffing was poured into a system which had a very weak capacity to manage or to use new funds in an effective way. Even if there had been strong management capacity it would have faced a very serious problem in the shortage of specialised resources and staffing available for purchase in the short term. The extra

[5] Nick Bosanquet, *A Successful National Health Service* (London: Adam Smith Institute, 1999).
[6] Department of Health, *The NHS Improvement Plan: Putting People at the Heart of Public Services* (London: DoH, 2004).

funding was not synchronised with the new hospitals and the additional doctors. In the event the funding was mainly spent on new employment contracts and on increased staffing, which was criticised by the House of Commons Health Select Committee as having been excessive and haphazard.[7] This was one more sign of the lack of synchronisation between the plans at the centre and the actual decisions taken locally.

The policy changes also led to management overload for all and great resistance for some. The most bitterly contested were those for ISTCs where the Prime Minister's key policy was faced with delaying actions at all levels – from the Treasury concerned about the possible effects on PFI schemes, from the Department of Health, and from local health managers concerned about destabilisation of local hospitals.

The introduction of these new policies was further shaken by the unexpected new crisis over deficits which came to be the key policy issue for two years. There were a number of reviews of why this had come about, of which the most comprehensive was by the department's Chief Economist.[8] This showed that the main reason for the deficits was the uncontrolled expansion in staffing numbers of 120,000 beyond the targets set in *The NHS Plan*. In the background was the low priority given to financial control before the problem of deficits was realised. To many it seemed hard to explain how a service where spending in cash terms had tripled from £30 billion in 1997 to £90 billion in 2007 could be in a situation where many organisations were in financial deficit with about 10% of Trusts near administration or insolvency by any normal standards.

By 2007 the ten Blair years in the health service were widely assessed but with an extraordinary degree of variation between different groups. Opinion surveys of voters and surveys of NHS staff were generally negative. Opinions by recent patients were positive, as were those by health service researchers and opinion-formers. An editorial in the *Health Service Journal* summed up this consensus view that 'Blair had saved the NHS'.[9] Yet a reformed NHS with patient choice, immediate access and a pluralism of providers seemed a long way off. If Blair had saved the NHS it was hardly the NHS envisaged in the most creative phase of 2001–5.

The achievements of the Blair years were seen in terms of improved outcomes, lower waiting times, improved funding and better staffing.

---

[7] House of Commons Health Committee, *NHS Deficits, First Report of Session 2006–07*, vol. I, HC 73 (London: HMSO, 2006).

[8] Department of Health, *Explaining NHS Deficits, 2003/04 – 2005/06* (London: DoH, 2007).

[9] 'It Was a Difficult Journey, but under Blair the NHS was Saved', *Health Service Journal*, 3 May 2007.

Improved outcomes: The claims here were particularly strong for heart disease and cancer that the specific decisions had saved thousands of lives. Certainly there was significant progress but it was difficult to attribute specific causation. The improvements in outcomes for heart disease and cancer were part of an international trend which began in the early 1990s. The rate of change in outcomes showed little increase over the Blair period, nor was there anything very distinctive about the UK record compared to that achieved in other systems, including those with lower proportions of government funding. The conclusion of an independent review by the OECD was that 'on some outcomes, the effect of higher spending is less clear: premature cancer deaths and heart/circulatory diseases have continued to decline, but not faster than during the 1990s'.[10]

Waiting times. There was certainly success in reducing the numbers waiting from over 1 million to 700,000 but this was waiting on a highly particular basis at the point of entry into the health system. There were still long waits for those needing further treatment or those with recurrent disease. Many of these patients with very serious problems would still have to wait up to six months for a first appointment. There were also long waiting times for non-consultant appointments, such as for digital hearing aids where by 2007 there were 300,000 people on the waiting list, with some waiting two years or more. Waiting times were also long for less-popular or high-profile diseases such as mental illness and COPD which were not affected by targets. For mental health there was still little access to low-cost non-drug interventions such as cognitive behavioural therapy.

Improved funding. One of the most significant commitments was to improve NHS funding. In the 2002 and 2004 Budgets, the government pledged to increase health expenditure by 7.4% a year in real terms between 2002–3 and 2007–8. The Department of Health's estimate is that health spending will be 9.5% of GDP in 2007–8. If health spending were to continue at the same rate of growth for two further years it would be 10.5% of GDP in 2010.

The GDP deflator, however, underestimates the true scale of NHS inflation. It is the most general measure of price change in the economy rather than a measure of the real resources actually available to local

---

[10] OECD, *OECD Economic Survey 2005, United Kingdom* (Paris: OECD, 2005).

health services. A more realistic measure of such increases would deflate by a change in NHS specific costs. The planned increase in funding ran into a problem which had been predicted as early as 18 January 2000, two days after the original pledge to raise spending to European levels: 'Pouring more money into a monopoly provider such as the NHS simply puts up costs because suppliers to the NHS will charge more.'[11]

Before 1999 the two indices were showing little divergence. From 2001, however, they began to diverge and the NHS specific cost index rose 4–5% a year until 2004. Thus the increase was 4% a year in real terms rather than 7% during the first period of the spending increase. In principle it would be possible to reduce the impact of these NHS-specific changes by shifting expenditure to lower-cost inputs but in practice local managers generally lack the flexibility to do this.

From 2001 to 2006 the NHS came to show a major problem of stagflation. The Keynesian remedy of a large increase in expenditure was no longer chosen for the economy as a whole but still remained a key policy within the public sector. There was a deep inconsistency in New Labour between its perspective on the economics of the private sector and what was regarded as the key priority for the NHS. In many areas the combination of large tax-funded expenditure increases with the central planning of output was regarded as dangerous and completely outmoded. But in the NHS this was regarded as the only feasible and effective way of organising the service.

The outlook to 2010 is for an increase in commitments against this limited increase in real spending. In essence the commitments set out in *The NHS Plan* will become very important claims on funding.

The old system of funding capital spends on a pay-as-you-go basis set up a conflict between revenue and capital spending. Indeed, if the government had continued with the old system it would have been difficult to increase revenue spending at the pace that has occurred. At least a half of the real-terms increase would have had to be committed to the additional capital expenditure, even before allowing for the problems of increases in development costs which were such a notable feature of public sector hospital projects in the past.

The new PFI-based system, however, raises additional cost commitments for the future. These are particularly as a result of the repayments on the capital, which are much higher than the capital charges on the older buildings. In addition there are the costs of installing and running

[11] Nick Bosanquet, 'How to Save the NHS in 12 Months', *Daily Mail*, 18 January 2000.

new technology in these hospitals, which on all international evidence from the OECD and from the US are likely to be heavy. There may be some offset to the cost increases if the new service providers can run services more efficiently, or replace retiring staff covered by Regulations on Transfer of Undertakings and Protection of Employment with staff on different contracts.

The main immediate impact of PFI schemes is likely to be through higher capital costs which, in the initial period, are at least 15% higher. Some of the early schemes have been able to reduce costs through refinancing in a period of falling interest rates, but this is unlikely to be an option for later schemes which are likely to proceed during a period of rising interest rates.

Beginning in 2007, the NHS faced the challenge of paying the annual costs of these schemes. There will be some help from the fact that most of these are fixed-price contracts while the total NHS expenditure will still be rising. In the long term, with indexation generally only at the RPI, these payments will be less onerous. By 2010, however, the NHS will have to find £2 billion to cover the annual charges on the new PFI schemes, some of which will be additional to current spending.

Evidence from the early PFI schemes at Norwich, Dartford, Carlisle, Worcester and the West Middlesex in London shows that the coming of local PFI schemes has also had short-term effects which were threatening both to financial balance and to the Trusts' ability to compete. The Trusts are all facing serious deficits and their performance against targets for waiting times has been poor. By 2007 the position had worsened. Of the fifteen large schemes then in operation ten were rated as weak by the Healthcare Commission for financial management and use of resources, four as fair and only one as good. Most were rated as weak because of their deficits.

At best the new hospitals face a running-in period when there will be many management problems in new systems and equipment. Beyond the initial period, however, they will face intense competition from Foundation Trusts and from Treatment Centres which will have had several years' start and the chance to build customer relationships. The new hospitals are likely to have higher costs at a time when the national tariff and greater competition will be driving costs down. Large hospitals may begin to look like battleships in a submarine wolf pack. They may also face a situation of decline in referrals and admissions. Referrals by GPs have already fallen in each of the last two years and the additional workload has come from referrals between consultants within the hospital system. For the future it should be possible to reduce referrals and admissions through the new primary care contract and through more integrated care.

The choice programme will probably have led to a reduction in waiting times as has happened with cardiac surgery in the south-east where the choice programme has led to the elimination of waiting times. The new PFI hospitals will be seeking to cover higher costs in a situation where demand has reduced and market power has shifted to the buyer. The PFI principle as such was highly positive but it could be used in a more modular, flexible way. The effect of central planning of the location of hospitals was to leave the NHS with hospital costs which threatened investment in the closer-to-patient services which were the preferred model after 2002.

Between now and 2010 the NHS faces a round of new contracts – but it has also had to deal with the full cost effects of increases in manpower from earlier decisions on central planning. Among key areas of change are:

Agenda for Change. This involved the regrading of the whole NHS work-force to provide a consistent set of differentials. The estimated cost is likely to be around 0.5–1.0% of the wage bill in the first phases, with some higher gradings being offset by the lower grading of support staff.

The new consultant contact. This has a running-in period when a new incremental scale may come into effect giving higher returns to more experienced consultants. The immediate increase in the salary bill is likely to be about 10%, while the increase in career earnings is estimated by the British Medical Association to be around 16%. In addition there will be activity-based supplements for additional sessions.

Increases in staffing. More important for pressure on costs and expenditure will be the increased numbers of staff. Numbers of medical students have risen by 50% and many will seek employment. The NHS total staffing number is likely to rise by at least 40% by 2010 compared to 2000. As *The NHS Plan* proposed: 'The next few years will see a major expansion in staff numbers in the NHS. This expansion has to be sustained. The increases we are making in training numbers will provide for further staff expansion in future years.'[12]

[12] Department of Health, *The NHS Plan*, p. 55.

These changes have come about before the increases in staff numbers under *The NHS Plan*. There will be a 50% increase in the number of medical graduates annually by 2010 and a 30% increase in the number of nursing graduates. Even allowing for likely increases in staff turnover and in retirements, there is likely to be a significant increase in the number of doctors and nurses. Increases in these groups usually lead to increases in supporting and technical staff. Unless numbers of funded posts continue to rise, there would either be medical/nursing unemployment or lack of adequate support at a time of expanding activities.

From 1999 to 2005 staff numbers rose by 25% and then began to show a slight fall as the NHS came under greater financial pressure. Such increases in staffing run the risk of cramping local initiative in service development. They increase the cost base for local funders and reduce the amount available for alternative suppliers. Thus any realistic development of pluralism will be difficult against this background of rising costs of directly employed staff.

Such increases may also make it more difficult to fund the working capital and infrastructure, which would allow staff to work more productively. The new staff may be frustrated by the lack of equipment and supporting systems. While most employers are reducing staff numbers in order to ensure better support and investment in the use of staffing time, the NHS is spending more on staff, mainly on lifetime employment tenure.

The expansion will be particularly strong in groups with the highest pay levels. Over the ten years 1993–2003, numbers of consultants rose from 16,598 to 27,754 (an increase of 67%). There have also been rapid increases in the number of nurses in high grades or consultant status and in managers in the more senior groups. Over a period when it has become more possible to carry out substitution with the use of less highly paid staff, the NHS hospital service has swung towards higher costs.

The pattern of staffing development has been very different in primary care where there is less central planning and more local decision-making on staffing. Over the period 1993–2003 the number of GPs rose by 9% while the number of practice nurses rose by 30%.

Overall the increase in staff numbers will raise the relative costs of the service. It is undeniable that there will be some gains in service standards. The question is whether they could have been achieved at lower cost and whether a different mix of staff and support might in fact have led to larger gains in service standards.

Health inequalities. It had long been recognised that there are differences both in outcomes and in access and these have continued. Following a heart attack intervention rates were 30% lower in the lowest socio-economic groups than in the highest.[13]

On some measures inequality has increased. Recently the Department of Health has noted that the relative gap in life expectancy has increased by 1% for males and 11% for females between 1995–7 and 2002–4. The relative gap for infant mortality also increased. The infant mortality rate was 19% higher than in the total population in 2002–4 for the more deprived group of Primary Care Trusts (PCTs) compared with 13% higher than in the baseline period of 1997–9. Inequalities also widened in primary care. By 2005, 66% of the most deprived PCTs were more than 10% below the England average for numbers of GPs – an increase from the position in 2002 when 48% of the most deprived GPs were below the England average.[14]

There was a significant transfer of funds, with some PCTs in deprived areas getting a funding increase 50% higher than the average from 2005 to 2008: the challenge for PCTs was to target policies so as to make a real difference to these inequalities. Similarly the government reiterated the policies of adding private sector providers in deprived areas.[15] It remains to be seen whether this would be enough to make a difference.

Public health. For public health the Blair years will be remembered for a great public success and some private regression. The success was the restriction on smoking leading to a ban on smoking in public enclosed spaces. The regression was in numerous indicators of lifestyle which were well set out by the Prime Minister himself in one of his farewell speeches: 'Obesity is rising rapidly. One in four adults and children in the UK is obese and rising. The social effects of alcohol abuse are widespread and worsening. An estimated 1.7 million people in the UK have type 2 diabetes. 10% of NHS resources are used to treat diabetics. This could double by 2010. And it is avoidable.'[16]

The policy future was seen in terms of public–private partnership with Jamie Oliver's campaign on school dinners as a prototype. There was

---

[13] Julian Le Grand, 'The Blair Legacy? Choice and Competition in Public Services', Lecture to the London School of Economics, 2006.
[14] Department of Health, *Tackling Health Inequalities: Status Report on the Programme for Action – 2006 Update of Headline Indicators* (London: DoH, 2006).
[15] Department of Health, *Our Health, our Care, our Say, a New Direction for Community Services* (London: DoH, 2006).
[16] Tony Blair, speech on healthy living, Nottingham, 26 July 2006.

some success in raising the consumption of fruit and vegetables by children. The Prime Minister looked forward to 'a vast untapped potential out there for still greater partnership between public, private and voluntary sectors'. His hope for the next ten years was that the health debate would shift so that it was about 'prevention as much as cure, about personal responsibility as much as collective responsibility, about the quality of living as much as life expectancy'.[17] The last three years of the government in fact saw little sign of this shift as the day-to-day financial problems of the NHS loomed large; but the future agenda was well defined.

The agenda was also well set for reducing social exclusion in the future with an emphasis on early intervention and personal support through direct payments giving much more freedom to carers or older adults. Under the Blair administration direct payment had been piloted.[18] The success in reducing child poverty was not accompanied by any distinctive success with those groups that were hardest to reach. For example, the chances of people with long-term mental illness in getting help with housing or with returning to work showed little improvement, with 50% still reporting they had received little help and 80% still being out of the workforce. There was also little success to report in improving opportunities for children in care. As the Prime Minister said: 'We need to be frank. We are not yet succeeding. One in 10 children in care get five good GCSEs compared to six out of 10 of other children. Only 6% make it to higher education compared to 30% of all children.'[19] The government certainly deserved credit for bringing the concept of social inclusion to the fore as a key policy aim, but there remained a very difficult challenge for the future.

In general the Blair government tended to concentrate on health services. Its policies for social services built on the earlier shift to a mixed economy of care. Spending rose faster than before but only at about half the rate of spending in the NHS. An excellent independent regulator reported progress in access and quality. The mixed economy led to a greater flexibility in developing new services. For example, increased access to intensive home care was almost entirely met by private providers, as was care for people with the most severe learning disabilities. Social services showed lessons about the gains to a real mixed economy which were generally unheeded for the NHS.

[17] *Ibid.*   [18] Tony Blair, *Our Nation's Future – Social Exclusion*, 5 September 2006.
[19] *Ibid.*

Developing NHS IT. The aspiration of acquiring an electronic patient record was a noble one. Connecting for Health could point to some results including the introduction of access to broadband and digital transmission of X-rays in the London area – but the programme as a whole by 2007 was a long way behind schedule. It has also changed direction, aiming to develop previous legacy systems rather than replace them.[20] The previous achievements of GPs had been underestimated and the top-down approach had not worked well. The aspiration was highly praiseworthy but an approach which emphasised local initiative as well as system integration would have got results far more quickly at a far lower cost.

The missing dimension – reliable international comparisons

The changes were affected by the crucial problems faced by central planners that they may be implementing yesterday's system. While *The NHS Plan* pointed to a huge centralised system, international experience was moving in a totally different direction.

The first funding wave of *The NHS Plan* was based on comparisons of NHS spending as compared to GDP shares in the rest of Europe. The policy conclusion was that the UK should move with extreme speed to spend more than the European average. Such comparisons ignored some crucial 'health warnings' about international comparisons.

Health systems can be divided into those with a strong primary care base as against those with direct access to specialist care and fee-for-service. As Table 18.1 shows, the spending levels for the first type of system, at 8–9% of GDP, are well below those for the second type, at 10–12%. Yet all studies of population health, treatment outcomes and patient access show that the first type of system delivers results which are at least as good and in many dimensions better than the second.

Recent research on the US health maintenance organisation Kaiser Permanente sponsored by the Department of Health has itself confirmed that the first type of system in a regional context can indeed deliver very effective results. The original research showed that on an adjusted PPP basis the NHS spent $1,784 per head while Kaiser Permanente spent $1,984 per head.[21] These results were fully adjusted for differences in the

[20] Richard Granger, Director General of IT for the NHS, oral evidence to the House of Commons Health Committee, 26 April 2007, HC 422–i.
[21] Richard Feachem *et al.*, 'Getting More for their Dollar: A Comparison of the NHS with California's Kaiser Permanente', *British Medical Journal*, 324, 2002: 135–43.

Table 18.1. Growth of expenditure on health 1990–2001, health
spending as percentage of GDP

	1990	2001
Primary care-led systems:		
Denmark	8.5	8.6
Finland	7.8	7.0
Netherlands	8.0	8.9
New Zealand	6.9	8.1
Spain	6.7	7.5
Sweden	8.2	8.7
United Kingdom	6.0	7.6
Fee-for-service-led systems:		
Belgium	7.4	9.0
France	8.6	9.5
Germany	8.5	10.7
Switzerland	8.5	10.9
United States	11.9	13.9

Source: OECD Health Data, 2004

age composition of patients and in the differences in the range of services
provided by the two systems. Later comparisons sponsored by the
Department of Health showed that: 'For the 11 causes selected for study,
total bed use in the NHS is three-and-a-half times that of Kaiser's stan-
dardized rate.'[22]

The level of spending generated in the first system reflects the costs of
providing certain services involving primary care access, referral and pro-
tocol-driven secondary care. If this system is associated with higher levels
of spending, this implies either higher costs than could be prudently
managed or higher levels of activity. There is good international evidence
that high levels of health spending are often associated with the flat of the
curve – with waste and low quality in care. Detailed criticisms have been
made, for example, of the low standard of cancer care in Germany and the
poor quality of prescribing in France. An OECD summary concluded
that: 'While richer countries tend to spend more on health, there is still

[22] Chris Ham *et al.*, 'Hospital Bed Utilisation in the NHS, Kaiser Permanente and the US
Medicare Programme: Analysis of Routine Data', *British Medical Journal*, 29, 2003:
1257–60.

great variation in spending among countries with comparable incomes. Even more importantly the highest spending systems are not necessarily the ones that do best in meeting performance goals.'[23]

Canada supplies a particularly strong example of how funding without reform may in fact lead to increases in waiting times and greater access problems. Between 1993 and 2003, average waiting times have risen 70% over a period when real spending per head rose 21%, in constant 1995 dollars, from $1,836 to $2,223. New Zealand has had similar problems, with a 40% increase in real-terms spending from 2000 to 2006 but a fall in the number of elective procedures and a rise in waiting times. Thus higher levels of spending are often taken to conceal problems of low productivity.

A more considered international comparison would certainly have pointed to a strong case for some additional funding. UK spending was in fact below the GDP shares found in tax-funded/primary care-led systems. There were also serious deficiencies in some key areas of care where a combination of new incentives with extra funding was required. The international evidence, however, pointed to a phased increase in spending to 8–9% of GDP. The increase to 10–11% of GDP was not supported by international evidence.

The Blair diagnosis of under-funding was also hard to reconcile with UK capability in primary care, its potential for lower-cost public health programmes and the targeting of health spending on most cost-effective programmes through NICE. It also tended to concentrate management attention on the spending of extra funding rather than on making better use of the funding that was already there. The various NHS plans have ignored the real lessons of international experience which were recently summarised by the OECD:

> Ultimately increasing efficiency may be the only way of reconciling rising demands for health care with public financing constraints. Cross-country data suggest that there is scope for improvement in the cost-effectiveness of health care systems. This is because the health sector is typically characterized by market failures and heavy public intervention, both of which can generate excess or misallocated spending. The result is wasted resources and missed opportunities to improve health. In other words, changing how health funding is spent, rather than mere cost cutting, is key to achieving better value.[24]

---

[23] OECD, *Towards High Performing Health Systems* (Paris: OECD, 2004).
[24] OECD, *OECD Health Systems – Measuring and Improving Performance* (Paris: OECD, 2004).

Table 18.2. Waiting times for publicly funded patients in Spain (days)

	1992	2000
Cataract surgery	68.0	47.6
Cholecystectomy	103.4	53.8
Hernia	84.6	48.3
Prostatectomy	119.4	42.7
Vaginal hysterectomy	71.9	52.5
Knee arthroscopy	51.4	53.8
Hip replacement	271.4	59.8
Knee replacement	91.3	63.4
Varicose veins	232.8	50.6

Source: OECD, Health Care Systems – Lessons from the Reform Experience
(Paris: OECD, 2003).

The case for this modified target has been strengthened by the evidence of the possible impact of incentives within primary care-led systems. Without shifts in funding as shares of GDP such systems can deliver very clear improvements in access and service. The achievements in reducing waiting times in Spain between 1992 and 2000 are a clear example.

The OECD attributes most of the decline to the use of financial incentives in achieving waiting time targets which were introduced after 1998. A similar approach to financial incentives, allied to expansion in service, was adopted in Denmark, leading to a fall in median waiting times for cardiac procedures from thirty days in 1997 to fifteen in 2001, a period in which waiting times in the UK rose rapidly.

Within the UK, reform has shown very positive results where it has been tried. Key areas where changes adapted from Scandinavia have been introduced include the introduction of new financial penalties/incentives for reducing delayed discharge and the choice programme for cardiac and other surgery in London.

Since local councils have faced cost penalties in paying for prolonged admissions, the numbers of patients staying in hospital unnecessarily are now more than 4,000 lower than in 2001. The Secretary of State has said:

> A massive reduction in delayed discharges was the equivalent of adding eight extra hospitals to the NHS. In fact more beds were created through incentives than the total additional beds planned through extra funding (2,500) over the next decade . . . These figures suggest that the introduc-

tion of the reimbursement scheme seems to have provided the extra incentive we needed to maintain momentum.[25]

In London, between 2002 and 2004, 12,500 patients were offered a choice of where their treatment should take place and 7,480 accepted it.[26] Among the results have been that:

- South-east London Treatment Centres in Orpington and Bromley now have spare capacity and began advertising for patients from February 2004.
- Private hospitals in the area have become concerned about declining patient numbers.
- The National Heart Hospital, bought to increase NHS capacity in cardiac surgery, found that it was short of patients because waiting lists had been reduced by the choice programme and it had to convert to non-surgical uses.

Thus within a very short time the choice programme was successful in reducing waiting times even before new capacity in Treatment Centres was introduced. There was similar success with choice in surgery for cataracts in the south of England.

There has also been a tendency to attribute success to funding when it should have been attributed to reform. Thus, in coronary and heart disease, the government stresses that the fall in the death rate – 41% over the last decade – is the result of NHS modernisation. Much of the work in introducing the National Service Framework and extending the use of statins, however, has been carried out in primary care where spending has been rising more slowly. And within secondary care waiting times for cardiac surgery have been reduced, mainly as a result of the choice programme.

The National Audit Office has come to a similar conclusion in regard to accident and emergency services. Its recent report found that the Department of Health had allocated less than £30 million per year to improving A&E services compared to an annual spend on those services of over £1 billion. Rather than extra funding, A&E departments have improved waiting times by developing new working practices, in particular by treating patients with minor injuries quickly rather than making them wait until patients with more serious injuries have been treated

[25] Department of Health press release, 'Dramatic Fall in Delayed Discharges', 17 May 2004.
[26] Department of Health press release, 'NHS in London Advertises for Patients', 4 February 2004.

('see and treat'), by giving more clinical responsibility to experienced nurses and by improving access to diagnostic services.[27]

Within the service for cancer patients, there has certainly been some improvement in access and survival for patients with breast cancer. Better funding of new drug therapies is likely to have contributed, but research in the US has clearly shown that detection of cancer at an earlier stage through screening is the most important reason for better survival. The successes in improving survival owe more to long-term investment, since the 1980s, in what is now one of the world's most advanced systems for population screening, than to funding increases under *The NHS Plan.* So far, indeed, the results of funding increases have been disappointing. A survey by the Royal College of Radiologists in 2003 indicated that waiting times have not improved since 1998, and that only a minority of patients are receiving treatment within recommended waiting times.[28] A later review showed that by 2006 radiotherapy services were only delivering 61% of the recommended levels of treatment.

The future of the NHS will be one of great funding pressure. *The NHS Plan* and the following four years have seen the announcement and design of future policies and commitments. In the next phase these new policies will actually have to be funded. However, the problem is greater than that of short-term funding pressure due to the inconsistency between the various key policies. The NHS must manage the effects of five key policies:

- the introduction of competition between providers through standard tariffs where money follows the patient;
- the rising costs of the hospital system through PFI and new staff contracts;
- a range of new providers, including Treatment Centres and Foundation Trusts, operating to much more compelling budgetary incentives by which they have to increase activity in order to survive;
- a strong supply response to the new primary care practice contract resulting in many more services at a higher cost;
- commitments to integrated care for chronic illness through Evercare and other systems.

This range of policies results from the gradual shift from central planning towards local initiative. The PFI schemes are the result of central

---

[27] National Audit Office, *Improving Emergency Care in England* (London: NAO, 2004).
[28] Royal College of Radiologists, *Equipment, Workload and Staffing for Radiotherapy in the UK 1997–2002* (London: Royal College of Radiologists, 2003).

Table 18.3. The policy framework to 2010

Policy	Comment
National tariffs	Full introduction in 2007. Paid at standard rates with gainers (costs below tariff) and losers.
New consultant contract and Agenda for Change	Long-term costs (improved lifetime pay and leave allowances) will be greater than immediate costs.
PFI schemes	
New providers	First wave of contracts will be ending in 2010. Treatment Centres and Foundation Trusts with room to expand activities (such as Royal Marsden and Bradford) will be gainers under the national tariff.
The new GMS contract	Strong supply response in next two years and on to 2010.
ICT development costs over next five to seven years	
Care integration and better management of chronic illness	

planning, whereas the new GP contract will create a great deal of scope for local enterprise. Its results will depend on local negotiation rather than a central plan. The inspiration for the contract in fact came from local initiatives in improving services for coronary health disease in Kent and other areas which owed little to national policy. In return for acceptance of quality standards GPs have in fact regained some the freedoms which they had under fund-holding.

The NHS will be under great financial pressure and it will also be dealing with a much more unpredictable series of financial problems as new programmes develop. Managers will be dealing with the local impacts of strongly inconsistent policies and commitments. Hospitals with higher costs in staffing and capital will be seeking to increase activity. Treatment Centres will be seeking to expand contracts and activities. PCTs will be seeking to fund extended services in primary and more integrated care outside hospitals.

The most immediate financial problems are likely to arise with hospitals themselves. There is a high risk that spending to purchase more activity from the hospitals will crowd out investment in care integration.

Conclusions

In official doctrine *The NHS Plan* was presented as an assured long-term macro success, which will be reached through temporary friction in problems over waiting times, access and quality. Such problems are usually attributed to past under-funding. Friction was created by the timing of the NHS change itself. Reform denotes incentives aimed at increasing value from existing spending; funding is about additions to the resources available. Reform seeks to increase productivity from the existing core while funding makes marginal changes to staffing and capacity. Since 2000 funding and reform have often been presented since as being simultaneous and complementary, but in reality funding has come before reform.

By 2010, total expenditure will be 10.5–11.0% of GDP, which will be well above the European average and more than 50% higher than the GDP shares of Scandinavia and New Zealand. On a worldwide basis the public sector share of spending is likely to be the highest of any system.

The NHS will be facing serious affordability problems from commitments on PFI schemes, staffing, the GMS contract and Treatment Centres. There will be tension between these commitments and funding for innovations and new therapies. It will be difficult to fund both the unfinished agenda set by NICE and National Service Frameworks and the new therapies that will be emerging in the future.

The failure to use reform earlier means that waiting time targets will be reached much later and at much greater cost. The reform experience in the UK and other systems would indicate that the six-month waiting time target could have been reached in 2004 instead of 2005 and the three-month target in 2006 instead of 2008 – earlier results which would have benefited thousands of patients.

The 2005 waiting time target has only become even remotely attainable because of new programmes introduced when it was clearly not going to be achieved. Independent Sector Treatment Centres, introduced from 2003 onwards, were not even mentioned in *The NHS Plan* in 2000. If these new programmes had been combined far earlier with incentives for the core health service, the waiting list targets would have been much more easily and quickly achievable. As it is, it will be almost the end of the whole decade of *The NHS Plan* before the NHS begins to approach minimum international standards in waiting time and access.

Experience both internationally and in the UK shows that reform, based on changing incentives, can improve access significantly. Waiting times in Spain and Denmark have fallen sharply since new financial incentives were introduced. In the UK, reforms such as financial penalties for prolonged hospital admissions and patient choice have been successful.

There has been a tendency to attribute success to funding where it should have been attributed to reform, particularly in regard to cancer services, coronary heart disease and accident and emergency services.

The funding-first decision has perverse effects for the UK as a whole. Public funding is now rising twice as fast as private. There is a high risk that the cost increases will crowd out the spending which would be required for new and unpredictable changes in therapies and technology. The NHS may be stuck with long-term spending on yesterday's systems.

There is also the risk that the high rate of increase in spending will not be sustainable if the growth of GDP falls to 2% a year or if other priorities emerge. The increase in health spending has been funded in part by a reduction in the growth of social security spending and an actual reduction in defence spending. There is much that is positive about the aim of a patient-centred service with more focus on long-term illness. There is much to admire about the commitment and dedication of staff in the NHS. In terms of the UK's longer-term social and economic challenges, however, the level of spending projected for 2010 represents poor value for money. With reform followed by some additional funding the UK could have a major improvement in access and effectiveness for 8–9% of GDP. That would be 2% of GDP – around £20 billion in today's prices – less than under current plans.

In the period 2001–5 the Blair government set a new direction for the health service involving patient choice, more rapid access, new incentives and more pluralism in providers. In many ways this was a highly promising agenda for change which fitted to the long-term challenges of working with a different age structure and higher expectations in a different kind of society; but this programme was introduced alongside the previous commitments to massive increases in funding, staffing and the building of new hospitals. The new reform plan aimed at flexibility, but this would take investment in new services. The investment margin was taken over by the cost increases already in the system. The Blair era threatened to create a future in which the NHS was locked into long-term contracts for obsolete hospitals and unaffordable increases in staffing. Among the most pressing problems were those of the likely discrepancy between numbers graduating from medical schools and the number of funded posts. By 2012, 6,000 people a year will be graduating from medical school but only 2,000 doctors will be retiring.

The Blair era also left a legacy of serious problems in quality of care. The NHS, in common with other health systems worldwide, was affected by the challenge of providing care for patients who were often much sicker and were being treated by more complex and demanding procedures. The rise in hospital-acquired infection was only one sign of the problems. There were also large numbers of patients at risk from thrombosis, which was estimated by the Department of Health to cause 25,000 deaths a year in hospitals. There were also many complaints about medical errors and about the quality of care for elderly patients admitted with a medical emergency. It was far from clear how the NHS would develop the confident caring skills to deliver any guarantee of care for patients. Survey evidence may have created a false sense of optimism as it did not cover patients who had died and many who had experienced serious complications. The mid-period reforms set the right way forward in minimising in-patient admissions and giving people, especially elderly patients, more support in their own homes, but the drives from the cost momentum and the payment-by-results system were to treat more and more patients in hospitals. Thus incentives were increasing hospital workloads even when hospitals were having great difficulty in delivering safe care.

For the NHS The Blair era represented an attractive aspiration for a service based on patient choice. It was developed with great power and eloquence but on closer examination the concepts were being realised only partially or not at all. The Blair legacy scored well on intentions but the likely legacy of results for successors was likely to be most troublesome. There was also a missing economic sense with little concern about value for money. The extreme case of input fixation was in Blair's pronouncements on staffing where increases in staffing numbers were held to be achievements in themselves, irrespective of whether they contributed very much to productivity or whether they created balanced teams.

There were real achievements in terms of improved access for care. Waiting times for cardiac surgery fell from two years to three months, and waiting for elective treatments was a maximum of six months by 2007, and was likely to be eighteen weeks in many areas by 2008. There were also some attractive new projects for walk-in centres in primary care. Yet many of these gains were due to reform – the introduction of competition and choice – and had come well before the funding increases. The Blair premiership saw gains in service access for some groups of patients but the question is whether these could have been achieved at much lower cost and a greater strengthening of the capacity of local management to deliver change.

The Blair era scored most highly on its eloquent definition of new ways forward and placing these new policies against wider themes of social change. It scored perhaps inevitably low for interest span, as no prime minister can in the face of national and international challenges take any consistent interest in any one departmental programme. Blairism was also associated with a certain amount of wishful thinking and, for health, an unwillingness to face up to unpleasant realities. For example, a more realistic approach might have scaled back on the cost commitments in *The NHS Plan* in order to allow more investment for the reform programme. The ability to communicate was great and while in place was used to great effect, but the ability to sustain change and regulation against a background of strong opposition was only fitfully there.

The Blair era left the NHS in a state of tension between *The NHS Plan* momentum and later reform policies. Most of the extra capacity and the new incentive structures were in place with the potential to generate some considerable improvements. The money was no longer with government but had been transferred to the Primary Care Trusts. Practice-based commissioning aimed to restore local initiative to GPs. There were major problems in dealing with the cost increases in the hospital system. The task for Blair's successors was to move to a system with much stronger local capability for securing value from the vast funds now going into the NHS.

19

Equality and social justice

KITTY STEWART

Thatcher's legacy, Blair's response

The society Labour inherited when it took power in 1997 looked dramatically different from the one it had left behind in 1979. During the Thatcher years economic growth had disproportionately benefited the better-off, leading to a widening gulf between rich and poor. The scale of the change can be seen in historical context in figure 19.1. Poverty more than doubled between 1979 and 1991, with families with children most deeply affected: between one in three and one in four children lived in relative poverty in 1997. Inequality measures such as the Gini coefficient show a similar pattern.

Some of these changes could be put down to global forces, including a growing premium for skilled workers as technological progress shifted the pattern of labour demand. Demographic change was important too, with increasing numbers of children growing up in one-parent households. But policy under Margaret Thatcher was also crucial. Curbs on trade union power and an end to the minimum wages councils had removed a floor on wages, while the move to linking benefits to price levels rather than incomes had left those without work, from pensioners to the unemployed, increasingly far behind. At the same time, changes to tax policy had shifted the burden of taxation from the rich to the poor, for example through reductions in the top rate of income tax accompanied by a greater reliance on indirect taxes. By the early 1990s the UK had moved from being one of the more equal European countries to one of the most unequal, more comparable on poverty and inequality measures to the United States than to Europe. The wider consequences of this shift were reflected in a number of other indicators: teenage pregnancy and homelessness were among the highest in Europe and there were high social-class differentials in infant mortality and other health indicators.[1]

---

[1] See e.g. Commission on Social Justice/IPPR, *Social Justice: Strategies for National Renewal* (London: Vintage, 1994); John Micklewright and Kitty Stewart, *The Welfare of Europe's Children: Are EU Member States Converging?* (Bristol: Policy Press, 2000).

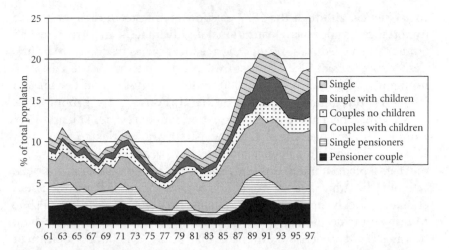

Figure 19.1. Population with below half average income by household type 1961–97
Source: John Hills, *Inequality and the State* (Oxford: Oxford University Press, 2004),
figure 3.1; updated from Alissa Goodman, and Steve Webb, *For Richer, For Poorer: The
Changing Distribution of Income in the United Kingdom 1961–1991* (London: Institute
for Fiscal Studies, 1994).
Note: Share of population living below 50% equivalised mean income, before the
deduction of housing costs. Other figures and tables in the chapter use the slightly
different poverty line of 60% equivalised median income, but this is not available for
the long-run series.

What was the response of the Labour Party under Tony Blair to these
enormous challenges in areas close to its traditional values and priorities?
Three phases can arguably be identified. In opposition in the mid-1990s,
the party had gone out of its way to avoid association with the poor and
disadvantaged and to ditch its reputation as the party of tax-and-spend.
Hard hit by successive election defeats, the shift towards the centre
ground had begun under Neil Kinnock and John Smith, but accelerated
under Blair's leadership. When Blair took over in 1994 he made it clear
straight away that he intended the party to 'build a new coalition of
support, based on a broad national appeal that transcends traditional
electoral divisions'.[2] Between 1994 and 1997 Labour worked hard to distance itself from the unions, steered clear of being drawn into pledges on
spending and abandoned any commitment to full employment. The run-
up to the 1997 election saw hardly a whisper of poverty, inequality or

[2] Tony Blair, *Socialism*, Fabian Pamphlet 565 (London: Fabian Society, 1994), p. 7.

social justice, although the 1997 election manifesto did emphasise the importance of addressing educational disadvantage – in 1996 Blair had famously listed 'education, education, education' as his top three priorities for government. The manifesto also promised to introduce a national minimum wage and to get 250,000 under-twenty-fives off benefit and into work. But to make it quite clear that this was a 'New' Labour Party, which could be trusted with the nation's finances, in January 1997 Gordon Brown guaranteed that the party would stick to very tight Conservative spending plans for the first two years of a Labour government, and pledged not to raise either the basic or top rates of income tax.

From the time Labour took office, however, social justice issues climbed quickly up the agenda. Blair's first major speech as Prime Minister outside the House of Commons was made from a Peckham housing estate, where he promised that under a Labour government there would be 'no forgotten people and no no-hope areas'.[3] In August 1997 the creation of the Social Exclusion Unit was announced, with a starting brief to examine school exclusions, rough sleeping, poor areas, teenage pregnancy and sixteen- to eighteen-year-olds not in education or training. At the Treasury, one of Gordon Brown's first priorities was a welfare-to-work programme: the windfall tax on privatised utilities – the only major new source of funds available during the first two years in office – was used to fund the New Deal for Young People and the New Deal for Lone Parents. Brown was also keen to make sure paid work made financial sense: on the day after the election he instructed civil servants to start developing plans for a tax credit scheme for the working poor, formally announced in the March 1998 Budget as the Working Families Tax Credit (WFTC). A commission to establish a starting level for the minimum wage was also established in the first few weeks in office.

Then in March 1999, at a lecture to commemorate William Beveridge, Blair made his now infamous pledge, not just to reduce but to *eradicate* poverty among children: 'Our historic aim – that ours is the first generation to end child poverty forever . . . It is a 20 year mission, but I believe it can be done.'[4] Sources inside the Treasury suggest that not even the civil servants who wrote the speech were expecting this and that it was a last-minute and unilateral decision taken by Blair. Certainly the assembled

---

[3] Tony Blair, Speech at the Aylesbury Estate, Southwark, 2 June 1997.
[4] Tony Blair, 'Beveridge Revisited: A Welfare State for the 21st Century', in Robert Walker (ed.), *Ending Child Poverty: Popular Welfare for the 21st Century* (Bristol: Policy Press, 1999), p. 7.

academics and journalists were taken by surprise; Polly Toynbee of *The Guardian* has since described the pledge as 'astounding'.[5] Where did this announcement come from? Its timing coincided with the end of the commitment to stick with Conservative spending plans, but also with the emergence of a growing body of evidence underlining the long-term scarring effects of childhood poverty. Research results such as those released by the Treasury at about the time of the Beveridge speech made it clear that real opportunities of later success in education and the labour market were vastly reduced for children growing up poor.[6] This tied in with a growing emphasis from Blair on the importance of individual opportunity. In a pamphlet on the 'Third Way' in 1998, he had declared the four values 'essential to a just society' to be 'equal worth, opportunity for all, responsibility and community',[7] and opportunity had since become a government watchword. The pledge to end child poverty indicated a genuine commitment to giving disadvantaged children a fairer start in life.

The child poverty pledge was followed up with concrete interim targets. Successive budgets reformed the tax-credit and benefit system and made it steadily more generous for families with children, for the remainder of Labour's first term and throughout the second and third terms. There were also considerable increases in investment in services for young children and in education. But while children were at the heart of the government's anti-poverty strategy, 1999 also marked the start of a broader attack on social injustice. In September, the first in an annual series of government audits of poverty and social exclusion indicators was published: *Opportunity for All*.[8] It promised an 'integrated and radical policy response' to the combined problems of childhood deprivation, worklessness, health inequalities, fear of crime, poor areas, poor housing, pensioner poverty, ill-health and isolation, and discrimination on grounds of age, ethnicity, gender or disability. A raft of policies followed, of which the most significant are summarised here:[9]

[5] Polly Toynbee, 'Time to Talk the Talk', *The Guardian*, 29 November 2002.

[6] Centre for Analysis of Social Exclusion (CASE)/HM Treasury, *Persistent Poverty and Lifetime Inequality: The Evidence*, CASE Report 5 and HM Treasury Occasional Paper 10 (London: London School of Economics and Political Science and HM Treasury, 1999).

[7] Tony Blair, *The Third Way: New Politics for the New Century*, Fabian Pamphlet 588 (London: The Fabian Society, 1998), p. 3.

[8] Department of Social Security, *Opportunity for All: Tackling Poverty and Social Exclusion* (London: DSS, 1999).

[9] For more detail, see John Hills and Kitty Stewart (eds.), *A More Equal Society? New Labour, Poverty, Inequality and Exclusion* (Bristol: Policy Press, 2005).

- welfare-to-work programmes, the national minimum wage and tax-benefit changes favouring low-income families with children, both in and out of work;
- investment in childcare and in nursery education for three- and four-year-olds; in Sure Start programmes for under-fours in deprived areas; and in longer and more generous maternity leave;
- substantial increases to education and health funding, including changes to funding formulae in favour of poorer areas;
- 'floor targets' for achievement in employment, crime, education, health and housing in the most disadvantaged areas, backed up with serious funding through the National Strategy for Neighbourhood Renewal and through a number of additional targeted programmes such as Sure Start and the Excellence in Cities programme for schools – the aim being to meet a pledge arguably even more ambitious than the pledge on child poverty: 'within 10–20 years, no-one should be seriously disadvantaged by where they live';[10]
- education maintenance allowances, paid to those who remain in education between sixteen and eighteen, aimed at increasing the low educational achievement of young people from low-income households;
- Working Tax Credits for childless couples;
- improvements in benefits for disabled children and adults;
- for pensioners, an increase in the means-tested income minimum and the extension of means-tested help higher up the income scale through the Pension Credit; additional special measures including winter fuel allowances, free eye tests, free TV licences and increased income tax allowances;
- some action to reduce inequalities in outcomes between ethnic groups, such as Ethnic Minority Achievement Grants to local authorities to improve educational attainment.

   The scope and scale of action outlined here is certainly very different from anything that could have been anticipated from the election manifesto of 1997. Yet while some of the priorities continued throughout – for instance, tax credits for families with children became more generous each year right up to and including the Budget of 2007 – the final years of Blair's leadership can be seen as representing a third and more disappointing phase. While Blair described the 2005 Queen's Speech as 'quintessentially New Labour: economic prosperity combined with social

---

[10] Social Exclusion Unit, *New Commitment to Neighbourhood Renewal: National Strategy Action Plan* (London: Cabinet Office, 2001), p. 8.

justice', the public sector reform agenda was given far greater emphasis during the third term than any policies to tackle disadvantage. In May 2005 Blair used his first press conference after the election to argue that 'our task is to deepen the change, accelerate reform and address head-on the priorities of the British people in the NHS, schools and welfare reform ... [Reform] means driving innovation and improvement through more diverse provision and putting people in the driving seat'; something of a contrast to the Peckham speech of June 1997.[11] Towards the very end of his leadership, in April 2007, it was on public sector reform, not social justice, that his close friend Lord Falconer said Blair wished he had moved more quickly.[12]

A related point is that the agenda went just so far and no further. A number of issues remained strictly off limits, even after the record second-term landslide and the third-term victory, after which Blair himself had nothing to lose. Non-disabled adults without children were expected to work, with little patience (and falling benefits) for those who found work difficult. Asylum-seekers (and their children) faced increasing exclusion, from benefits, from work, from local authority housing and from education. But perhaps most striking is the issue of overall income inequality: the focus remained clearly and explicitly on the situation and opportunities available to those at the bottom, and on the income gap between the bottom and the middle. The incomes of those at the top end of the distribution were never considered relevant. These omissions are serious, and have resulted in a mixed record for Blair: he leaves behind a country with less poverty, in which many people face more promising opportunities than before, but one in which inequality of outcome is greater than it has ever been, with consequences for the next generation, and with implications for how we see ourselves as a society. In this chapter we look at changes during the Blair years to income poverty and income inequality and at policies designed to improve life chances through investment in early years services, education and health. For discussion of Labour's broader record in addressing disadvantage in poor areas, ethnic inequalities and low political participation, and its treatment of asylum-seekers, the reader is referred elsewhere.[13]

---

[11] Cited on the BBC News website, 12 May 2005, http://news.bbc.co.uk/go/pr/fr/-/1/hi/uk-politics/4540723.stm.

[12] Nicholas Watt and Patrick Wintour, '"He Has Proved Incredibly Resilient"', interview with Lord Falconer, *The Guardian*, 30 April 2007.

[13] See relevant chapters in Hills and Stewart, *A More Equal Society?*

Poverty

Reducing both child and pensioner poverty was an important goal for Labour under Blair, with a wide range of measures introduced to raise income for each group. However, concern did not extend to the working-age population without children, and specifically those without work. This section looks at what happened to levels of poverty for each of these three groups in turn, and considers how far government policy can be said to be responsible.

Children

Table 19.1 shows the change in the share of children living in poverty between 1996/7 and 2005/6, the latest year for which figures are available. Figures are given both before and after housing costs (BHC and AHC); each measure has advantages, but the Blair government adopted the BHC indicator as its measure of choice.

It is clear that there were substantial drops in child poverty over the period as a whole, especially for households with at least one member in work. These changes are particularly significant when one considers that this is a relative poverty line, measured as a share of median income, and the median itself rose rapidly over the period. Measures of material deprivation show more striking improvements in real living standards, even among those who remained below the poverty line: the share of the income poor who said they were behind in paying bills fell from 41% to 31% between 2000 and 2004; while the share who could not keep their home warm fell from 18% to 12%.[14]

However, progress was not sufficient for the government to meet its first target of reducing relative child poverty by one quarter between 1998/9 and 2004/5. Furthermore, as table 19.1 also shows, much of the improvement had been achieved by mid-way through the second Labour term: between 2003/4 and 2005/6 the overall rate of child poverty was in fact steady or even slightly increasing. It should be noted that this disappointing result came as a surprise not just to government, but also to researchers and commentators, who were predicting right up to early 2005 that the target would narrowly be

---

[14] Maxine Willitts, *Measuring Child Poverty Using Deprivation Indicators*, DWP Working Paper 28 (London: Corporate Document Services, Department for Work and Pensions, 2006). Willitts uses a poverty measure of 70% of median income BHC.

Table 19.1. Child poverty 1996/97–2005/06 (%)

	Before housing costs				After housing costs			
	1996/7	2003/4	2005/6	% change 1996/7–2005/6	1996/7	2003/4	2005/6	% change 1996/7–2005/6
Lone parent, full-time (%)	11	7	7	−36	16	10	14	−13
Lone parent, part-time (%)	27	20	17	−37	44	30	30	−32
Lone parent, no work (%)	64	59	56	−13	86	78	75	−13
Couple, one FT, one no work (%)	22	16	17	−23	28	22	26	−7
Couple, one or both PT (%)	53	50	44	−17	62	57	53	−15
Couple, both no work (%)	71	64	64	−10	79	77	74	−6
All children (%)	**27**	**22**	**22**	**−19**	**34**	**29**	**30**	**−12**
All children (million)	**3.4**	**2.9**	**2.8**		**4.3**	**3.7**	**3.8**	

Source: DWP, *Households Below Average Income 1994/5–2005/6* (London: DWP, 2007), table E3.1; Mike Brewer, Alissa Goodman, Alistair Muriel and Luke Sibieta, *Poverty and Inequality in the UK: 2007*, IFS Briefing Note 73 (London: Institute for Fiscal Studies), tables 5 and 6.

Note: Share of children living in households with equivalised income below 60% of the median before and after the deduction of housing costs.

met.[15] The flagship anti-poverty strategy, the tax credit programme, had been made increasingly generous annually from its introduction in 1999, with a particularly sharp increase in April 2003 aimed directly at meeting the 2004/5 goal. In 2005/6 £17 billion was paid out on tax credits – around 1.5% of GDP.[16] Let us consider both the contribution of policy to the fall in child poverty witnessed in table 19.1 and the explanation for the failure to meet the first child poverty target.

Labour's child poverty strategy was based heavily on promoting employment, through active labour market programmes such as the New Deal for Lone Parents (and more recently the New Deal for Partners), through investment in childcare, and through a series of policies intended to 'make work pay', including the national minimum wage, reforms to tax and National Insurance which favoured low earners and – most significantly – the system of means-tested tax credits. In particular, the Child Tax Credit (CTC) introduced in April 2003 integrated the systems of support for children in households in and out of work, in principle removing many of the benefit disincentives and uncertainty surrounding the move into a job – although at the cost of creating high effective marginal tax rates higher up the income scale (see chapter 10). The level of worklessness among households with children – the highest rate in the industrialised world when Labour came to power – fell steadily, as indicated in table 19.2, though it remains high by international standards. A strong underlying economy – itself to at least some degree attributable to Labour's macro-economic management – was an important factor, but supply-side policies increasing the incentives for parents to work also appear to have been effective.[17]

At the same time, tax credit and benefit changes (including those mentioned above as well as increases to universal Child Benefit and to the length and generosity of maternity pay) substantially lifted the incomes

[15] Mike Brewer, *Will the Government Hit its Child Poverty Target in 2004–5?* Briefing Note 47 (London: Institute for Fiscal Studies, 2004); Holly Sutherland, *Poverty in Britain: The Impact of Government Policy since 1997. An Update to 2004–5 Using Microsimulation* (Cambridge: Microsimulation Unit, University of Cambridge, 2004).

[16] National Audit Office (NAO), *HM Revenue and Customs 2005–06 Accounts: The Comptroller and Auditor General's Standard Report* (London: TSO, 2006).

[17] For example, tax credit changes between 2000 and 2003 are estimated to have raised lone-parent employment by 3.4 percentage points, and that of fathers in couples by 0.9 percentage points, but to have had a slight disincentive effect for mothers in couples. See Richard Blundell, Mike Brewer and Andrew Shephard, 'The Impact of Tax and Benefit Changes between April 2000 and April 2003 on Parents' Labour Supply', IFS Briefing Note 52 (London: Institute for Fiscal Studies, 2004).

Table 19.2. Worklessness and children

	Children under 16 in workless households		Children in workless households by family type	
	1000s	%	Of all children in lone-parent households (%)	Of all children in two-parent households (%)
Spring 1996	2.4	19.9	58.4	10.0
Spring 1998	2.2	18.5	56.5	8.2
Spring 2000	2.0	16.6	52.5	6.8
Spring 2002	2.0	16.8	51.1	6.8
Spring 2004	1.9	16.1	49.3	6.1
Spring 2006	1.7	15.3	46.8	6.2

Source: Office for National Statistics, 'Work and Worklessness among Households: Time Series', Tables 3(i) and 3(ii). Online edition: www.statistics.gov.uk/statbase/Product.asp?vlnk=12859 (downloaded May 2007).

of families in all types of employment situations, reducing poverty for most groups – as indicated in table 19.1 – with families with a single earner benefiting most. Researchers at the Institute for Fiscal Studies (IFS) estimate that rising incomes for households in given employment situations were responsible for around 80% of the total change in poverty rates during Labour's first two terms, while movements into work explain much of the rest.[18]

Why were these policies not sufficient to meet the child poverty target, despite optimistic predictions? Forecasting economic change is notoriously difficult, and in the case of a relative child poverty measure small errors can have a big impact on results, both because many children are positioned just above and below the poverty line, and because the future poverty line itself is unknown and dependent on median income, which is even harder to control and predict than the incomes of poorer households. Any combination of the assumptions made about earnings, profits, rent, interest rates, tax and employment behaviour may lie behind the shortfall. The IFS initially suggested that part of the explanation may have been an overestimation of tax credit take-up in forecasts,

---

[18] Jonathan Shaw, 'Eradicating Child Poverty', Briefing Note (London: Institute for Fiscal Studies, 2007).

but recent administrative figures indicate that take-up of Child Tax Credit was high, at between 93% and 98% among low-income working families in 2004/5, up from 91–95% in 2003/4.[19] Another, rather different, issue raised by the IFS is that the household survey data used by the government to track child poverty (the Family Resources Survey) appear to under-record receipt of tax credits, perhaps because they are sometimes made as one-off payments and may not show up in the month in which the household is surveyed. This problem has worsened sharply since 2001/2: by 2004/5 the gap between administrative data and FRS data had reached nearly £5 billion, or almost one-third of total expenditure on tax credits.[20] As administrative data are a more robust indicator of tax credit spending than survey data, this suggests that child poverty may have fallen by more than official data suggest.

If this is the case, it poses serious questions about the government's ability to measure child poverty accurately in the future, particularly as tax credits become an increasingly important part of the anti-poverty strategy. But the challenges for the future clearly do not stop with measurement issues. A 2006 report by the Joseph Rowntree Foundation estimated that additional spending of at least £4 billion a year in tax credits would be needed to lift enough children over the poverty line to meet the 2010 target of halving child poverty.[21] Whether or not a Brown government succeeds in finding these resources, it is disappointing that a bigger dent has not yet been made in the mountain of poverty illustrated in figure 19.1, and disappointing that the government was unable to point unequivocally to a 25% reduction in child poverty by 2004/5. However, it is also undeniable that real and substantial progress was made for poor children under Blair. Perhaps not least of his government's achievements was David Cameron's announcement that a future Conservative government would also have the reduction of relative child poverty as a goal.[22] That a Conservative leader would make such a commitment – indeed, would even accept the concept of poverty as relative – would have been quite inconceivable when Labour took office.

[19] Mike Brewer, Alissa Goodman, Jonathan Shaw and Luke Sibieta, *Poverty and Inequality in Britain: 2006*, IFS Commentary 101 (London: Institute for Fiscal Studies, 2006); HM Revenue and Customs, *Child Tax Credit and Working Tax Credit Take-up Rates 2004–05* (London: HMRC, 2007).

[20] Brewer *et al.*, *Poverty and Inequality in Britain: 2006*.

[21] Donald Hirsch, *What Will it Take to End Child Poverty? Firing on all Cylinders* (York: Joseph Rowntree Foundation, 2006).

[22] Helene Mullholland and agencies, 'Cameron: Poverty is a Moral Disgrace', *The Guardian*, 24 November 2006.

Pensioners

Over a quarter of pensioners lived in relative poverty in 1997. Prior to Blair's leadership, Labour had been keen to restore the link between pensions and earnings broken by the Thatcher administration – this was a central plank in both the 1987 and 1992 manifestos. But by 1997 the policy had been dropped in favour of a broad statement that 'all pensioners should share fairly in the increasing prosperity of the nation'. The first two years of Labour government saw very few policy measures aimed explicitly at pensioners, with the exception of annual Winter Fuel Payments of £100, introduced in November 1997.

However, from April 1999 a series of reforms aimed to improve living standards for the poorest pensioners. Income Support for pensioners was rebranded the Minimum Income Guarantee (MIG) in 1999, with above-inflation increases and a commitment to increase MIG in line with earnings rather than prices, which was repeated in the 2001 manifesto. In 2003 the MIG was renamed again (and made more generous) as the guarantee element of the Pension Credit, and the 2005 manifesto and then the 2006 Pensions White Paper continued the commitment to earnings-uprating into the long term. By April 2004 the guarantee element was equivalent to around 25% of average earnings for a single person – the level the basic state pension would have been if the link with earnings had not been broken. The difference, of course, is that the Pension Credit is means-tested. At the same time, some new universal benefits in kind such as free eye tests and TV licences were introduced, and there were also small increases in the basic state pension. The 2006 White Paper pledged to re-link the latter to earnings by the end of a fourth Labour term.

If the guarantee element of Pension Credit continues to be linked to earnings it will remain just above the poverty line for a single person, though still just below for a couple. Its impact is clear: the level of pensioner poverty has fallen steadily and substantially, from 29% in 1996/7 down to 17% in 2005/6, measured after housing costs, representing a fall of more than 40%.[23] This can be seen in figure 19.2, which also shows that most of the change took place during Blair's second term, as would be expected given the timing of reforms. Measured before housing costs, the decline is less dramatic, but poverty still fell by 15%, down from 25%

---

[23] Department for Work and Pensions (DWP), *Households Below Average Income 1994/5–2005/6* (London: TSO, 2007). The poverty line is 60% of equivalised median income.

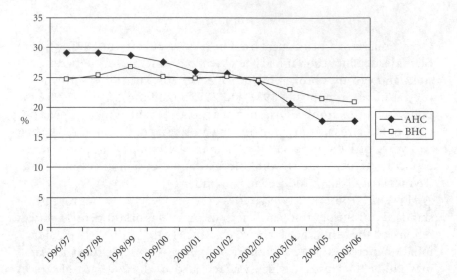

Figure 19.2. Share of pensioners living below the poverty line before and after
housing costs
Source: DWP, *Households Below Average Income 1994/5–2005/6.*
Note: Percentage of pensioners living in households with income below 60% of the
equivalised median before and after housing costs.

to 21%. It is striking that by 2003/4, on the AHC measure, a pensioner
was less likely to live in poverty than a non-pensioner for the first time
since the early 1980s recession, and the gap widened in each of the subsequent two years.[24] Not all the decline in pensioner poverty can be attributed to government policy: there is also a cohort effect, as new retirees
tend to be better off than the older pensioners they replace. But the IFS
estimate that the cohort effect accounts for only one-quarter of the
poverty reduction over the period, with rising incomes accounting for
three-quarters.[25]

If all pensioners claimed the Pension Credit, poverty would have fallen
even more quickly – after all, poverty in single-pensioner households has
in principle now been abolished. In fact, while take-up of the guarantee
element increased substantially in the year after its introduction in 2003,
in 2005/6 between 19% and 30% of eligible pensioners still failed to

[24] Mike Brewer, Alissa Goodman, Alistair Muriel and Luke Sibieta, *Poverty and Inequality in
the UK: 2007*, IFS Briefing Note 73 (London: Institute for Fiscal Studies, 2007).
[25] Brewer *et al.*, *Poverty and Inequality in Britain: 2006.*

claim.[26] This compares with between 6% and 17% of the non-pensioner population eligible for Income Support.[27] In many cases the amounts unclaimed are quite substantial, with one-third of non-claimants eligible for more than £50 a week.[28] Research commissioned by the DWP in 2004 and 2006 into the causes of low take-up found the most common obstacle to be perceived ineligibility: many pensioners did not think they would qualify, perhaps because they were home-owners, lived with adult relatives or had been turned down for assistance in the past.[29] Some were put off by a complicated application process; others were worried about going through the process only to be turned down, as they did not want to appear 'greedy'. A positive finding of the research was that very few people were unaware of the existence of the Pension Credit, in contrast to an earlier finding that 57% of entitled non-recipients of MIG were unaware of benefits payable to people on low income.[30] In 2006 the National Audit Office concluded that the Pension Service had made 'real and substantial progress' since 2002 'using new and well-thought through approaches' to ensure that more pensioners received their entitlements, although still more could be done to reach the most disadvantaged.[31] Continued low take-up highlights the key problem with reliance on means-tested benefits to tackle poverty, but it remains true that poor pensioners have vastly improved financial support available to them in 2007 compared to 1997, and that imaginative efforts are being made to make sure all of them benefit in practice.

Working-age households without children

The situation of working-age households without children was conspicuously absent from government targets and indicators under Blair. This is not to say that nothing was done to improve living standards for low-income households without children. The extensive agenda aimed at

---

[26] DWP, *Pension Credit Estimates of Take-up in 2005–06* (London: DWP, 2007).

[27] DWP, *Income Related Benefits: Estimates of Take-Up 2004/2005* (London: DWP, 2006).

[28] DWP, *Pension Credit Estimates of Take-up in 2005–06*, figure 1.2.

[29] C. Talbot, L. Adelman and R. Lilly, *Encouraging Take-up: Awareness of and Attitudes to Pension Credit*, DWP Research Report 234 (London: DWP, 2004); K. Bunt, L. Adams and C. Leo, *Understanding the Relationship between the Barriers and Triggers to Claiming Pension Credit*, DWP Research Report 336 (London: DWP, 2006).

[30] Cited in Maria Evandrou and Jane Falkingham, 'A Secure Retirement for All? Older People and New Labour', in Hills and Stewart, *A More Equal Society?*

[31] NAO, *Progress in Tackling Pensioner Poverty: Encouraging Take-up of Entitlements* (London: TSO, 2006).

helping people into work and at making work pay encompassed non-parents as well as parents. Some of the measures, such as the national minimum wage and reforms to tax and National Insurance contributions at the bottom of the income distribution, benefited all low earners. There were also a series of New Deal programmes for specific groups, covering young people, the long-term unemployed aged twenty-five plus, and disabled people (compulsory for the first two groups, voluntary for the latter); these appear to have had positive though limited impacts.[32] Smaller initiatives strengthened the employment rights of part-time and temporary workers, and helped address low pay in the public sector.[33] Perhaps most strikingly, in April 2003 the Working Tax Credit was extended to include households without children: with this move the government effectively began to subsidise low wages in general, not just where a low wage is insufficient to support children. In one of the last acts of Blair's premiership, the Welfare Reform Act of May 2007 introduced substantial reforms to Incapacity Benefit, including both much more support for work-related activity and training and the threat of benefit sanctions for the first time for those refusing to participate.

What about the level of financial support for those who remain without work? Reforms to the benefit system raised incomes for the most severely disabled, while introducing a greater degree of means-testing. These reforms were largely welcomed by disability campaigners, although there is concern that benefits are poorly advertised and difficult to access.[34] Incapacity Benefit rose only in line with the retail price index, lagging behind the change in the poverty line over most of the period, though making gains in the most recent years. Other out-of-work benefits (Job Seeker's Allowance and Income Support) were adjusted through the decade for price inflation excluding housing costs, meaning a steady deterioration in relation to average earnings. A single person on Income Support in 1997/8 received weekly benefit equivalent to about 40% of median income after housing costs – well below the poverty line. By 2005/6 this share had fallen to just 31%. This contrasts sharply to the sit-

[32] See Giacomo Georgi, 'The New Deal for Young People Five Years On', *Fiscal Studies* 26(3), 2005: 371–83; Bruce Stafford with others, *New Deal for Disabled People: Third Synthesis Report – Key Findings from the Evaluation*, DWP Research Report 430 (London: DWP, 2007).

[33] See Donald Hirsch, 'Welfare in Work: The Missing Link in Welfare Reform', in Kate Bell (ed.), *Staying On, Stepping Up: How Can Employment Retention and Advancement Policies be Made to Work for Lone Parents?* (London: One Parent Families, 2006).

[34] See Gabrielle Preston (ed.), *A Route out of Poverty? Disabled People, Work and Welfare Reform* (London: Child Poverty Action Group, 2006).

Table 19.3. Poverty among households of working age without children 1996/7 to 2005/6 (%)

	Before housing costs		After housing costs	
	1996/97	2005/06	1996/97	2005/06
All working-age adults without children	12	13	17	17
Single/couple one or more FT self-employed	13	12	15	18
Single/couple all in FT work	2	2	3	4
Couple, one FT, one PT work	1	3	2	5
Couple, one FT work, one not working	7	10	10	14
Single/couple no FT, one or more PT work	18	19	24	25
Workless, head or spouse unemployed	50	54	67	64
Workless, other inactive	29	35	43	45

Source: DWP, Households Below Average Income 1994/5–2005/6, table F4.

uation in Sweden, for example, where out-of-work benefits for all family types sit safely above the poverty line.[35]

The result was that, despite rising employment, poverty among working age households without children failed to fall during Labour's time in office, as shown in table 19.3. Tax credits and other measures intended to make work pay appear to have had an impact on encouraging employment (which is why we see a stable overall figure despite increased risk in each category), but they have not managed to prevent rates of poverty from rising even for those in work. Among those without work, nearly two-thirds of households in which the head is unemployed lived below the poverty line after housing costs in 2005/6, alongside nearly one-half of those in other inactive households (including those claiming incapacity and disability-related benefits).

How worried should we be about such high levels of poverty among non-working households without children? Should non-disabled adults

---

[35] See Christina Behrendt, At The Margins of the Welfare State: Social Assistance and the Alleviation of Poverty in Germany, Sweden and the United Kingdom (Aldershot: Ashgate, 2002).

not be expected to support themselves without reliance on state benefits? There is a pragmatic reason for concern about current levels of out-of-work benefits: it cannot be easy to look for work under financial constraints that make basic requirements such as suitable clothes and transport costs problematic. There is also an ideological concern about the nature of an inclusive society. Many of those with caring responsibilities for dependants other than children, those in poor health but not severely disabled, and those who simply find participating in working life difficult on standard terms experienced Blair's decade as one of gradually deepening poverty. Unease at the situation of people in these categories is compounded by the fact that poverty has risen even among *working* households without children, casting doubt over the idea that non-working households could move out of poverty if they only chose to do so: individuals currently on Incapacity Benefit or Income Support are likely to have fewer skills and face greater barriers to work than those already in employment.

Life chances

As already noted, evidence of the impact of poverty in childhood on an individual's future opportunities appears to have been central to the commitment to end child poverty. At the same time, the Blair government also recognised the importance for life chances of non-income factors, in particular education. Alongside income transfers and work-promotion initiatives it invested heavily in education, including policies aimed at furthering children's development from the very earliest years; and to a lesser extent in children's health. It was a long-term strategy, aimed at creating a new generation of adults more skilled than the current one, in stronger health and better placed to bring up their own children free from poverty. The long-term nature of this goal means a full assessment of the strategy's success or failure will not be possible for many years, but this section examines the policies that were introduced and looks at early evidence of the difference they are making.

The early years strategy

There were four key elements to early years policy. Taken together, they represent a sea-change in the support, services and opportunities available to pre-school children and their parents, with government taking major responsibility for this age group for the first time.

First, the increase in the level of statutory maternity pay and the expansion of paid maternity leave first to six then to nine paid months (with a view to an eventual extension to a year's paid leave) followed research evidence indicating that the best place for a baby is at home with a mother who wishes to be there. This is certain to have enabled more children of low-income working parents to spend more time with their mothers in the first few months of life (although it appears that the same rate of compensation for two weeks' paid paternity leave has been too low to encourage many fathers to take it up).

Second, the Blair government fulfilled an early commitment to provide a free part-time nursery place to all three- and four-year-olds, following evidence of the central importance of pre-school education for school-readiness and later academic and social outcomes, particularly for children from disadvantaged backgrounds. By 2002, just 7% of children from social classes IV and V were not receiving any nursery education, compared to 17% in 1997. Third, there were some moves to improve the quality of formal childcare, including much greater regulation under the Ofsted umbrella and the creation of a new graduate Early Year's Professional status with training starting in 2006 – small but positive steps towards raising the overall status, pay and conditions of childcare workers.

Finally, there were the set of Sure Start policies – first, Sure Start Local Programmes (SSLP); later, Sure Start Children's Centres. SSLP brought a raft of initiatives to children under four in the 500 most disadvantaged wards, with local Sure Start boards initially operating independently of local authority control to determine how best to provide parenting support, play, learning and childcare experiences, primary health care and advice, and support for children and parents with special needs. Preliminary evaluation of the local programmes (and the evaluation team stress that it is really too early for assessment) found modest evidence of more positive parenting in Sure Start areas, although not among the most deprived families.[36] Sure Start was also widely popular with parents: in research conducted by the Centre for Analysis of Social Exclusion with parents in deprived areas it was one of very few government initiatives spontaneously mentioned as having made a positive difference.[37] Ironically, its high profile and positive image led to what

---

[36] National Evaluation of Sure Start (NESS), *Early Impacts of Sure Start Local Programmes on Children and Families*, NESS Research Report 13 (London: TSO, 2005).

[37] See Anne Power and Helen Willmot, 'Bringing up Families in Poor Neighbourhoods under New Labour', in Hills and Stewart, *A More Equal Society?*

some have seen as a dilution of the original programme, although the government has sold it as spreading the benefits across the country: since April 2006 SSLPs have come under local authority control as Sure Start Children's Centres, with additional centres developing from other government initiatives including Neighbourhood Nurseries and Early Excellence Centres. There were 1,000 Children's Centres by September 2006, with plans for one in all 3,500 wards in England and Wales by 2010, and the idea is that they bring together childcare, early education, health, employment and family support under one roof. Substantial resources are being directed to them, with total spending of £3.2 billion between 2004 and 2008; this represents somewhat reduced funding per centre compared to the budget for the original 500 SSLPs, although whether disadvantaged areas suffer will depend on how funding is distributed. Again, it is early for assessment, but a recent National Audit Office report into existing centres found quality of services high and improving, although not all centres were doing all they could to reach the most disadvantaged groups.[38]

Education

Tackling educational disadvantage was an early priority for the Blair government. Since the low point of 1999, when the commitment to stick to Conservative spending plans came to an end, the share of GDP spent on education has risen steadily, from 4.5% to planned spending of 5.6% in 2007/8. This shifted the UK up the international spending range: 5.6% is getting close to the share spent in, for example, France in 2003 (5.8%), though it still falls well short of the spending share in Denmark (6.7%) and Sweden (6.5%). At the same time, the formula for allocating resources to Local Education Authorities was revised, increasing the share to those with most deprived populations, although only by half the level recommended in the PriceWaterhouseCoopers report commissioned by the Department for Education and Skills to guide the reform. In part the decision not to implement the full recommendation was driven by the fact that the LEAs themselves each have their own internal allocation formulae, meaning there is no way of ensuring that the extra resources reach the most needy schools.

There were also a number of targeted initiatives, including Excellence in Cities (EiC), which provides funding for learning mentors and for

---

[38] NAO, *Sure Start Children's Centres* (London: TSO, 2006).

provision for gifted and talented pupils in the most deprived third of LEAs, and the Ethnic Minority Achievement Grant (EMAG), supporting a range of programmes benefiting schools with high concentrations of minority ethnic pupils. EiC has been found in early evaluations to have had a positive effect on school attendance and mathematics attainment, with the greatest impact in the most disadvantaged schools.[39]

Classroom-based reform focused on standards, continuing with Conservative-designed policies such as literacy and numeracy hours, regular formal testing and league table publication; the latter now include measures of 'value-added', making them better reflections of a school's performance rather than simply its social and academic intake. In addition, Labour pursued its 1997 election pledge to ensure that no child aged five to seven was taught in a class with more than thirty pupils. Between 1997 and 2007 the share of all primary school children in such classes came down sharply, from 33% to 14%, although 1.4% of the five to seven age group are still taught in larger classes.[40]

What was the combined impact of these policies on inequality in educational attainment? There is some evidence of catch-up to 2001 in the performance in Key Stage tests of 'rich' and 'poor' schools (those in which respectively less than 5% and over 40% of pupils qualify for free school meals).[41] The government discontinued the publication of these data from 2001, but since 2002 we have been able to look at pupil performance directly. Figure 19.3 shows the share of pupils from different ethnic groups achieving five or more GCSEs at grades A*–C (the triangles and circles in the figure), along with the performance of pupils eligible for free school meals relative to that of other pupils (the bars); this last has been called the 'poverty penalty'. The figure shows both that the average performance of black, Pakistani and Bangladeshi pupils is catching up with that of white pupils, and that the relative performance of those receiving free school meals has improved substantially within each ethnic group. These changes are impressive for a four-year period, although the poverty penalty remains serious, particularly for the white population: in 2006

[39] Stephen Machin, Sandra McNally and Costas Meghir, 'Excellence in Cities: Evaluation of an Education Policy in Disadvantaged Areas', NFER Working Paper January 2006 (Slough: National Foundation for Educational Research, 2006).

[40] DfES Time Series Data (http://www.dfes.gov.uk/rsgateway/DB/TIM/m002007/ts-prim-cs.pdf).

[41] Abigail McKnight, Howard Glennerster and Ruth Lupton 'Education, Education, Education . . .: An Assessment of Labour's Success in Tackling Educational Inequalities', in Hills and Stewart, A More Equal Society?

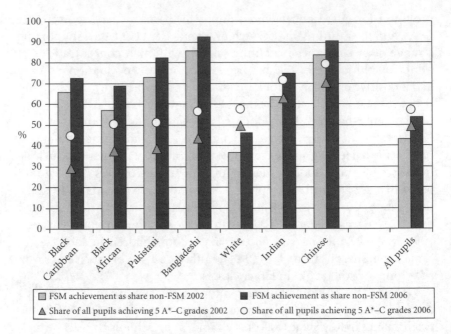

Figure 19.3. Disparities in educational achievement by ethnicity and free school meal status: share of pupils achieving at least five GCSEs at grade A*–C 2002 and 2006 and 'poverty penalty' for each ethnic group.
Source: Department for Education and Skills (DfES) Statistical First Releases: http://www.dfes.gov.uk/rsgateway/DB/SFR/s000448/table49-52.xls (for 2002) and http://www.dfes.gov.uk/rsgateway/DB/SFR/s000693/Addition1V1.xls (for 2006).

white pupils eligible for free school meals were still less than half as likely to achieve five A*–C grades as their non-eligible classmates.

Interestingly, when we look further down the education system, the story is more complicated. At earlier key stages smaller disparities are observed across both ethnic group and free school meals status, but there is less unambiguous evidence of improvement between 2002 and 2006, with the poverty penalty widening slightly overall in writing at age seven and in mathematics and science achievement at eleven. This raises doubts about whether the rate of change illustrated in figure 19.3 will be sustained.

Health

Health inequalities were subject to considerable attention during the first two Labour terms, with a series of assessments and reviews following the report of the independent Acheson inquiry.[42] Four months before the 2001 election the government announced two health inequalities targets: the first to reduce the difference in life expectancy between areas with the lowest life expectancy and the average; and the second to reduce the gap in infant mortality between manual groups and the population as a whole by at least 10% by 2010. Policies, however, were thinner on the ground – to the extent that a 2004 Treasury review concluded that 'after many years of reviews and government policy documents, with little change on the ground, the key challenge now is delivery and implementation, not further discussion'.[43]

The main policy emphasis was on overall levels of health and increased spending on health care. Health spending rose as a share of GDP from 5.7% in 1998 to 9.4% in 2006 – and, as for education, funding formulae were reformed to channel more resources to disadvantaged areas. In addition, Health Action Zones were set up, aimed at developing local programmes to tackle health inequalities in collaboration with social services, voluntary and business organisations and local communities. However, despite strong evidence of the importance of childhood health as a driver of health in adulthood, there was no overarching health strategy for children. The policy for very early childhood relied mainly on Sure Start, with Public Service Agreements to reduce low birth weight, emergency hospital admissions, smoking in pregnancy and re-registrations with the child protection register in Sure Start areas (covering just one-third of poor children). There were also small initiatives such as the National School Fruit Scheme, which provides every schoolchild aged four to six with a daily free piece of fruit; and increases in funding to improve the quality of school lunches in the aftermath of chef Jamie Oliver's high-profile campaign on the issue. At the tail end of the Blair premiership, the 2007 Budget announced the extension of child benefit to women from week twenty-nine of their pregnancy – a welcome recognition that a child's health is affected by maternal nutrition well before birth.

In practice, the share of babies born at low birth weight rose slightly across social classes between 1997 and 2004.[44] The social class differential

[42] Department of Health (DoH), *Independent Inquiry into Inequalities in Health Report* (London: TSO, 1998); DoH, *Saving Lives: Our Healthier Nation* (London: TSO, 1999); DoH, *Tackling Health Inequalities: A Programme for Action* (London: DoH, 2003). For further discussion see Franco Sassi, 'Tackling Health Inequalities', in Hills and Stewart, *A More Equal Society?*

[43] Derek Wanless, *Securing Good Health for the Whole Population* (London: HM Treasury, 2004), cited in Sassi, 'Tackling Health Inequalities'.

[44] A rising share of babies born with low birth weight can reflect technological advances which enable more premature babies to be kept alive at birth, so should not in itself be

rose between 1997 and 1999 and fell back thereafter, leaving no change overall: in 2004, as in 1997, children from social classes 5–8 were one quarter more likely to be born weighing less than 2.5 kilograms than children from classes 1–4. The class differential in infant mortality increased slightly between 1997 and 2005, though it peaked in 2003: in this case progress has been made for all groups, but gains have been a little greater for higher social classes. The most recent data on spatial differences in life expectancy are also discouraging: the gap between England as a whole and the poorest fifth of local authorities widened by 2% for males and 8% for females between 1995–7 and 2003–5.[45] For adults it is arguably much too early to judge the impact of any recent changes, given both lags in data and the speed with which policy might be expected to affect health outcomes. But the lack of progress in reducing health inequality for young children is more worrying – both because the challenge of reducing later inequality after an unequal start is far greater, and because young children's health ought to be quick to respond to effective policy.

Income inequality

Reducing the level of overall income inequality was explicitly *not* a goal for the Blair government. Blair repeatedly emphasised that his concern was with the bottom half of the income distribution rather than the top half, and with 'equality of opportunity' not 'equality of outcome'. As he put it in a Fabian Society pamphlet in 2002, 'We favour true equality: equal worth and equal opportunity, not an equality of outcome focused on incomes alone.'[46] Or, more colourfully, on *Newsnight* in 2001: 'It's not a burning ambition of mine to make sure that David Beckham earns less money.'[47]

In practice, figure 19.4 shows that incomes rose marginally faster for the poorer groups than for the richer groups during the Blair era. This

Footnote 44 (*cont.*)
  seen as a negative trend: the social class differential is more informative. Data for low birth weight and infant mortality is from the Office for National Statistics (Childhood, Infant and Perinatal Mortality Statistics for England and Wales, Series DH3).
[45] DoH, *Tackling Health Inequalities: 2003–05 Data Update for the National 2010 PSA Target* (London: DoH, 2006).
[46] Tony Blair, *The Courage of our Convictions: Why Reform of the Public Services Is the Route to Social Justice*, Fabian Ideas 603 (London: Fabian Society, 2002), p. 2.
[47] Cited in Tom Sefton and Holly Sutherland, 'Inequality and Poverty under New Labour', in Hills and Stewart, *A More Equal Society?*

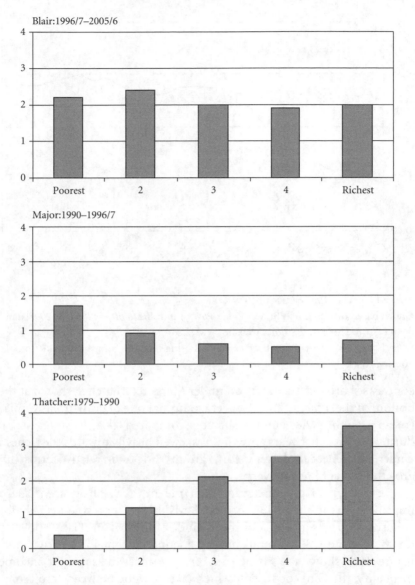

Figure 19.4. Real income growth by quintile group under Tony Blair, John Major and Margaret Thatcher (% per year).
Source: Brewer *et al., Poverty and Inequality in the UK: 2007*, table 4.
Notes: Averages in each quintile group correspond to the midpoints, i.e. the tenth, thirtieth, fiftieth, seventieth and ninetieth percentile points of the income distribution. Incomes have been measured before the deduction of housing costs.

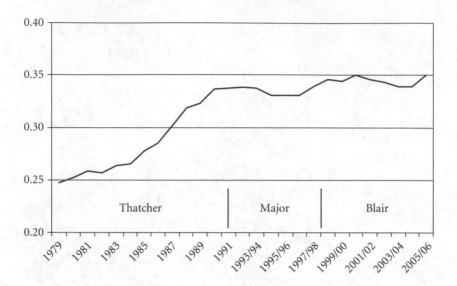

Figure 19.5. The Gini coefficient 1979–2004/5
Source: based on figure 8 in Brewer *et al.*, *Poverty and Inequality in the UK: 2007*; data from Institute for Fiscal Studies website (www.ifs.org.uk).
Note: The Gini coefficient has been calculated using incomes before the deduction of housing costs.

contrasts sharply to the situation under Margaret Thatcher, shown at the bottom of the figure. While the average annual rate of growth was similar (mean growth of 2.8% under Thatcher compared to 2.3% under Blair), during the Thatcher years growth was skewed heavily towards the richest. Under John Major the lower income groups did best in relative terms, but growth was very low for everyone.

The pattern of growth under Blair meant, as we have seen, sharp improvements in the real living standards of the poorest, especially for children and pensioners, and more modest declines in relative poverty for these groups. But overall income inequality remained fairly static. Figure 19.5 shows the change in one summary measure of income inequality, the Gini coefficient, which takes a value between zero (complete equality) and 1 (if one person receives all the income and the others nothing). The Gini rose slightly during Blair's first term to reach a record level of 0.35 in 2000/1. It fell slightly in the second term, but by 2005/6 it was back up to the 0.35 high.

Why has inequality not fallen, despite the many measures taken – successfully – to raise the incomes of the poorest? For one thing, this was largely a time of strong economic growth, and in such periods inequality tends to rise. Certainly tax-benefit changes have had difficulty keeping up with rapid increases in median incomes, which is why relative poverty indicators have fallen much more slowly than indicators using a fixed income poverty line. But more importantly for the Gini measure, income at the very top of the income distribution – in particular among the richest 1% or even 0.5% of individuals – increased far more quickly than average. The income shares of both the top 1% and the top 0.5%, which had been falling throughout the century for as far as records go back, have been on the increase since the early 1980s, with a particularly sharp rise since 1998.[48] This has not affected poverty indicators (measured against the median) but has influenced inequality indicators which reflect the full distribution, such as the Gini. The major contributor to income inequality is earnings inequality, and this continued to widen after 1997, particularly in the top half of the distribution: the ratio between the earnings of those at the ninetieth percentile and those at the median reached an all-time high of 2.0 in 2003, although it dropped very slightly thereafter.[49] Growing income inequality also contributed to rapidly widening disparities in wealth. Excluding housing assets, the share of wealth owned by the richest 10% of the population rose from 57% to 63% in the two decades to 1996, and then from 63% to 71% in the following seven years under Labour; the share belonging to the top 1% also increased sharply.[50]

Micro-simulation by Tom Sefton and Holly Sutherland indicates that the Gini coefficient in 2004/5 was significantly lower than it would have been if the 1997 tax-benefit system had been left in place and only adjusted for inflation: the reduction in the Gini compared to that scenario is about one-third of the size of the rise of the previous twenty years.[51] The Gini is also lower than it would have been under a more generous scenario, in which the 1997 system was adjusted for average income growth, though the impact in this case is reduced by about half. In sum, while tax-benefit changes under Labour were quite strongly redistributive, they worked against the tide of pre-tax and benefit growth in earnings, and were only sufficient to prevent further increases in inequality, not to reduce it.

[48] Anthony B. Atkinson, *Top Incomes in the United Kingdom over the Twentieth Century*, University of Oxford Discussion Papers in Economic and Social History 43 (Oxford: University of Oxford, 2002).
[49] Sefton and Sutherland, 'Inequality and Poverty under New Labour'.
[50] ONS statistics at www.statistics.gov.uk/cci/nugget.asp?id=2. Housing assets are more evenly distributed than other wealth, but the time trends are very similar.
[51] Sefton and Sutherland, 'Inequality and Poverty under New Labour'.

Of course, Labour could have taken measures to try to limit the growth of earnings inequality. The government could have attempted negotiation to address rising rates of city pay and bonuses, which have grown on Blair's watch to levels unacceptable to many. Or it could have moved beyond the quiet redistribution which has funded tax credits for the low-paid through hidden measures such as the non-indexation of tax rate bands (dubbed 'redistribution by stealth') and introduced a higher rate of income taxation. This was ruled out in each of Blair's three parliaments by manifesto commitments not to raise either the basic or the top rate of income taxation – a pledge first made in the nervousness before the 1997 election and repeated at each subsequent election. There would have been clear pragmatic gains to be made from a higher rate, raising resources to fund further reductions in child poverty, for example. But a real attempt to tackle incomes at the top and bring income inequality down would also have made an enormous difference in itself to the shape of British society in 2007. Blair's position that the incomes of the rich are of no relevance to the rest of the country other than as a source of envy is difficult to defend. One manifestation of their importance is the annual contribution of city bonuses to record levels of house price inflation since 1997, which have fast created a new wealth divide between those who already own homes or stand to gain from a housing inheritance and those who do not. Just in themselves, such wildly differing levels of remuneration, far beyond anything which may be justifiable on meritocratic grounds, are unfair and are seen as unfair, creating a sense of injustice which affects individual morale and national solidarity.

Blair's legacy: a more equal society?

It is undoubtedly the case that Blair's Labour government took the levels of poverty and social injustice plaguing Britain in the 1990s extremely seriously – far more seriously than many would have expected when Labour came to power on a fairly modest manifesto in 1997. The evidence sketched out in this chapter points to intervention across a very wide range of areas – addressing child and pensioner poverty, worklessness and educational disadvantage, improving the opportunities available to very young children and their parents, and tackling the multiple problems facing people living in deprived neighbourhoods. In many cases policy has seen considerable success; in other areas less so. It is always possible to argue that more could and should have been done, but a look back to figure 19.1 reminds us of the scale of the task that Labour faced. Overall Britain is a fairer and more equal society in 2007 than it was in 1997, and it is almost certainly far more equal than it would have been after another ten years of Conservative government.

What was Blair's personal contribution to these changes? Most obviously, his unexpected pledge to eradicate child poverty had an enormous impact. Without such a pledge it is unlikely that benefit changes favouring children would have developed as far or as fast, or been given such priority – although a committed Gordon Brown in the Treasury was arguably more important in ensuring delivery. More generally, the 'opportunity for all' agenda, with its emphasis on the importance of tackling disparities in life chances from birth onwards, appears to bear Blair's stamp.

At the same time, however, it is difficult not to look back at the Blair decade with a sense that the opportunity for even greater change was missed. Early on, many who wanted to see Labour tackle overall inequality as well as poverty believed that Blair was holding back for fear of upsetting the electorate, but as the decade progressed it became more than clear that this was not a Prime Minister unwilling to take on an unpopular policy and stick by it in the face of widespread opposition. It is apparent now that there were limits to Blair's commitment to social justice, and his main priorities lay elsewhere. If his mission had only been a different one – if it had led him to take on inequality as his enemy – he might have left behind an entirely different landscape.

20

Culture and attitudes

BEN PAGE

After a decade in power most politicians' popularity is in decline. Tony Blair's was no exception. However, focusing only on the popular and media mood towards the end of his term in office risks missing the wood for the trees. We should look back at the man and his standing with the British public with respect – at least in the period 1994–2002. Ratings of Blair's performance in Opposition were virtually unprecedented in polling history. Compare his performance as Leader of the Opposition with the four Conservatives, including David Cameron, who followed him in this role (Figure 20.1).

From the time he assumed leadership of the Labour Party, Blair's personal rating was one of the highest recorded. And after he became Prime Minister, he was the most popular Prime Minister recorded in the post-war period, with his ratings exceeding those of Mrs Thatcher for a considerable period of tenure (Figure 20.2).

By 1999 his historically high level of approval was in decline and apart from a boost at the time of terrorist attacks and the early days of the Iraq War, it drifted downwards. In October 1997 just 6% thought Blair was out of touch with ordinary people; by the time he announced his resignation 51% thought so. But in those first two years in office he was far more popular than Mrs Thatcher was whose reputation and indeed premiership, ironically, was saved only by a war.

What went wrong? In a word Iraq, and the Hutton Enquiry after it, together with possibly unmeetable expectations on the public services agenda. In October 2000 46% of the populace rated Blair trustworthy. In September 2006 the figure was 29%.

In one sense Britain's falling out of love with Tony Blair was inevitable. In 1997 expectations of what a Labour government would do were high – and with the benefit of hindsight almost impossible to meet. Given the need to gain credibility on the management of the economy and to avoid income tax rises, Labour stuck to Conservative spending plans that

Q How satisfied or dissatisfied are you with the way...
is doing his job as...?

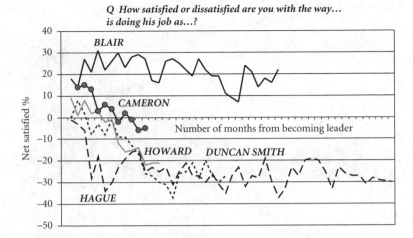

Figure 20.1. Blair in Opposition
Base: c. 1,000 British adults interviewed 3rd week of the month

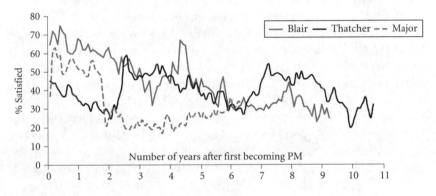

Figure 20.2. Satisfaction: Blair vs Thatcher / Major
Base: c. 1,000 GB adults each week

Kenneth Clarke has stated would have been unlikely to have actually been followed. So one of the great ironies of Blair's premiership is that despite public hopes for higher spending on public services, overall aggregate expenditure as a percentage of the economy did not return to the levels of John Major's last year in office until after Blair had been *premier for five years*. In this sense his resignation speech acknowledgement that both his and the country's expectations had been too high seems right (Figure 20.3).

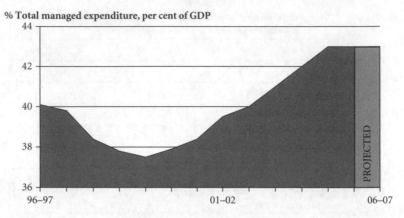

% Total managed expenditure, per cent of GDP

Figure 20.3. They spent the money. . . . .

In the heady dawn of 1997, few among the public expected Labour would follow Conservative spending plans for the first few years, with real rises in expenditure only starting well into their first term in office.

Secondly, overall judgements about public attitudes to Tony Blair have to be made in response to a world which, in his own words, fundamentally changed in his second term. When one looks at the issues the British public say concern them, he was right. Concern about immigration/race relations increased twelve fold from 3% (June 1997) to 36% (April 2007) as asylum and migrant numbers rose dramatically at the end of the twentieth century. With 9/11 and the subsequent wars in Afghanistan and Iraq, followed by Britain's own home-grown 7th July bombings, concern about defence/foreign affairs increased from only 2% to 27% of the public citing it as the key issue facing Britain over the same time period, with huge spikes in concern at the time of key events.

This combination of security issues in the broadest sense, Blair's relationship with the US 'war on terror' and his personal relationship with George Bush will colour judgements about his performance – and until there is a settled view about the outcome of Iraq, it is unlikely there will be one on Blair either (Figure 20.4).

It is also worth reflecting on those concerns that effectively vanished under Tony Blair. One of the reasons that Labour achieved a historic third term, was because the 'issue' that had dominated British politics in the previous two decades – the economy – was vanquished as a concern. During Blair's time as Prime Minister, concern about unemployment dropped from 39% (June 1997) to 8% (April 2007) (Figure 20.5).

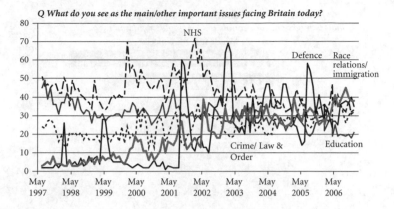

Q What do you see as the main/other important issues facing Britain today?

Figure 20.4. Rise of security
Base: c. 2,000, adults aged 18+ per month

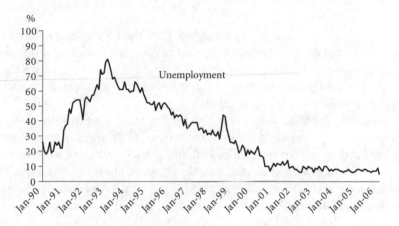

Figure 20.5. Falling concern about unemployment
Source: Ipsos MORI political aggregates. Base: c. 2,000 adults aged 18+ per month

It was the relatively successful management of the economy that allowed public service investment, and created an implicit, if not acknowledged, feel-good factor. Blair got little credit for the ongoing removal of the one issue that had kept the British public awake at night in the early 1990s. At the time of his departure from office, 60% of people thought Britain was getting worse as a place to live – the comparative figure under Thatcher in 1988 was only 40%. Nevertheless when one compared how the British felt about their own personal circumstances in

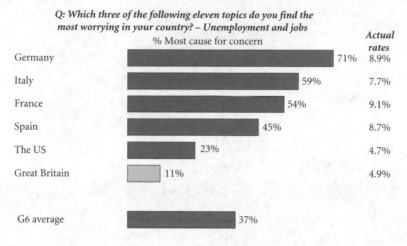

Figure 20.6. Most worrying issues nationally – Unemployment and jobs
Ipsos MORI G6 study – 1000 interviews by telephone May 2006

2006, they were markedly more positive than their European neighbours and other major economies (64% said they were confident about their own prospects in 2006, compared to only 36% in France and 54% in Germany) and personal concern about unemployment was dramatically lower than elsewhere (Figure 20.6).

However, the Blair boom was not equally shared , with some sections in society experiencing 'turbo-consumerism', and others, particularly in the most deprived communities benefiting less – although all groups in society saw a rise in incomes. For some, particularly those in the City which now accounts for 8.8% of the UK's total GDP, spending power increased dramatically. Overall there was a widening of the gap between 'the haves', 'have nots' and the 'have-yachts'. While overall incomes rose under Labour, the decade saw polarisation along wealth and cultural lines, with the wealthiest 10% claiming a larger and larger share of overall income. And with conspicuous consumption the order of the day in much of the popular media, Britain used consumer credit to meet its aspirations for instant gratification. In 2006 some 107,288 people in the UK were declared insolvent – an increase of over 40,000 from 2005. Household debts soared, with consumer credit keeping the economy afloat (Figure 20.7).

More generally, Blair's meritocratic boom did not make us any happier. The proliferation of media channels and the rise of reality programmes which gave everyone – whether they were talented or not – a

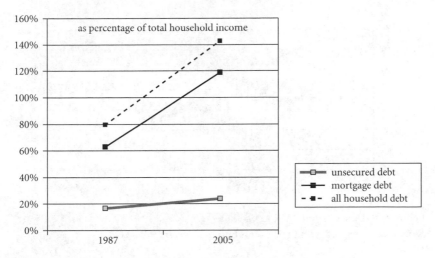

Figure 20.7. Mortgaged to the hilt. . . . .

chance to become famous meant that for many it was no longer about keeping up with the Joneses, but aspiring to keep up with the Beckhams, the footballer and singer couple who epitomised 'celebrity' culture during much of this period. This was not necessarily a new phenomenon, but it was exacerbated during the Blair years. A popular culture of upward comparison was not a prescription for feeling good about ourselves given that so many people, failing to achieve their aspirations, might regard their life as second-best.

The Blair years saw a surge in interest in the study of well-being, with Cabinet Office studies on what would increase national happiness, a spate of media coverage and a diverse range of books, with titles like 'Status Anxiety', 'Happiness: lessons for a new science', and 'Affluenza'. The leader of the Opposition, David Cameron, as part of his recasting of the Conservative party, said in May 2006: 'Well-being can't be measured by money or traded in markets. It's about the beauty of our surroundings, the quality of our culture, and above all, the strength of our relationships. Improving our society's sense of well-being is, I believe, the central political challenge of our lives.' The data suggested he might have had a point (Figure 20.8).

In his contribution to the publishing genre on happiness, *Affluenza* (2007), Oliver James comments on what he cites as a causal link between economic inequality and incidences of emotional distress and the rising numbers of the UK population turning to medication. In 1997, around

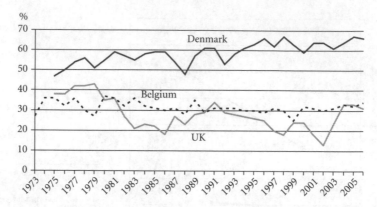

Figure 20.8. Danes happier, UK less so
Source: Very satisfied with their lives – Eurobarometer 1973–2006

6.5 million prescriptions were written for selective serotonin reuptake inhibitors; this figure had risen to 13.3 million by 2002. Furthermore, recent figures suggest that one in six adults has a neurotic disorder such as anxiety or depression.

None of these phenomena are exclusive to Blair's Britain and need to be weighed up against overall public attitudes. Firstly, supporters of Blair and Brown's management of the economy would, no doubt, point to economic growth as signs of success and argue that wealth-creation did not prevent the government making significant inroads into tackling child poverty (albeit that it still had a lot to do to meet its target of zero poverty by 2020). Certainly, income inequality and poverty did not feature as a key spontaneous concern for the public and Britons were relatively less concerned about domestic poverty compared to citizens of other major European countries. In 2007 a quarter of Britons cited poverty and social inequality among the three most worrying issues, compared to nearly half of Germans (Figure 20.9).

In fact, despite the pressures, and growing separation of the very rich from the very poor, Britons seemed quite tolerant of high levels of income inequality. They were far less likely than citizens of most other European countries to feel strongly that the government should reduce income inequality, despite the UK having the highest levels of inequality among major European countries.

As he left office, 46% of the public still thought that Blair's government had been good for them personally and only 35% thought it had been bad for them – a positive net score of +11. Thatcher's figure on this measure

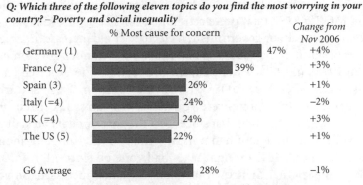

Figure 20.9. Most worrying issues nationally – poverty and social inequality
Source: Ipsos Global Consumers and Citizens Monitor. February 2007. Base: c. 1,000 interviews in each country

was negative: minus 2. But at the same time, while 46% of people thought Mr Blair's government had been good for the country as well, another 43% thought it was bad, yielding a 'net' figure of +3. Under Thatcher, the net figure when she left was +12.

One question is whether Blair truly achieved a fundamental shift in the nature of politics. If Mrs Thatcher's economic liberalism, destruction of corporatism and introduction of free market flexibility to large areas of the economy and British life is now generally seen as irreversible, Blair's investment in public services and social justice can also be seen as a new paradigm. With the Conservative Party under David Cameron in 2006 offering to match or outspend Labour on key public services in Britain, and the Liberal Democrats arguing for tax rises, it may be that in time, we will come to see Blair's years as a turning point. In early 2006 research showed an important, albeit not decisive, shift in attitudes towards egalitarianism. When Mrs Thatcher was in office during the 1980s, the majority of the British public preferred a society 'which allows people to make and keep as much money as they can' (52%) rather than one 'which emphasises similar incomes and rewards for everyone' (40%). By 2006, the public were more evenly divided (46% and 48%) between the individualistic and collective approach.

In fact, public attitudes were ready for many of Blair's more popular policies before he arrived on the scene. In 1997 the British Social Attitudes study recorded that some 75% of the public said they favoured tax rises for public service improvements. Of course, Tony Blair pledged not to increase income tax rates in 1997, but the electorate never really believed him: in MORI's 1997 final pre-election poll for *The Times*, 63% said they expected that a Labour government, if elected, would increase income tax, only 3% lower than the 66% who had expected a Kinnock government to do so in 1992 (and 17% lower than the proportion who expected Labour to raise taxes after May 2005). It was the same in 2001: as early as December 1999, the public were convinced that taxes had risen under Labour – only 28% thought that since 1997 the government had kept taxes down while 57% thought it had not. By January 2001, 'thinking about all forms of taxation', 48% thought taxes had gone up since 1997 'for most people' and 41% that their own personal taxes had increased. So voters elected Tony Blair with a landslide in 1997, expecting him to increase taxes, and re-elected him in 2001 believing that his government had done so, and did so again in 2005.

What was different was that at each of his victories Blair had the credibility to deliver a policy for which there had actually been considerable public support throughout the 1990s. One reason why Tony Blair was elected three times and Neil Kinnock never was – apart from the weakness of the Conservatives and the economic situation – was simply perceived competence. Evidence from the British Election Survey suggests that Labour's defeat in 1992 had resulted not from opposition to the idea of tax rises but from distrust of a Kinnock government's ability to spend the money raised wisely and efficiently. In contrast, Blair and Brown's most visible tax rises, e.g. National Insurance rises for the NHS, were supported and generally perceived to be necessary, with satisfaction with local health services rising for much of his time in office. It was only in 2006, towards the end of Blair's tenure, that serious doubts in the public mind erupted over whether public spending in the NHS was being wasted and the belief arose that the Conservatives would be more competent to manage public services and indeed the economy , whereas at the 2005 General Election Labour were *still* seen as better placed to manage public spending (Figure 20.10).

A culture of spin and the trust deficit

One of the many criticisms of Blair's government was that it was preoccupied with the 'packaging of politics' or, in other words, spin. The word has become indelibly associated with him, and in 2007 even Peter Mandelson confessed that presentation took precedence over policy at times.

Spin in itself is nothing new: the Labour Party set up its first press and publicity department in 1912. What is new, however, is the high profile of

Q *Do you think a Labour or a Conservative Government*
would be most effective in getting good value for the public money it spends?

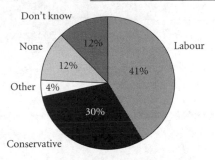

Figure 20.10. Value for money from Labour?
Base: 1,005 British adults 181, 15–18 April 2005. Source: MORI/Financial Times

the personnel involved at the heart of government in managing the message (Alastair Campbell, Charlie Whelan, Peter Mandelson and Jo Moore became 'household' names during Blair's premiership) and also the prominence that has been attached to presentation. While survey trends going back decades suggest it is wrong to talk about a new crisis of trust in government under Blair, there were significant and worrying declines in some aspects of trust in institutions and in straightforward electoral participation, with Blair's second two victories won on some of the lowest turnouts ever. Many government initiatives over this period attempted to address this, both by trying new ways of making the act of voting easier – postal voting, and experiments with online and other approaches – as well as measures to allow greater accountability and transparency, for example the Freedom of Information Act, but overall these often made no headway whatsoever in the face of a hostile media which found itself in a Mexican standoff with the government, and general disengagement from party politics.

Trust in the government and Blair specifically was a key issue in the 2005 general election. Debate tended to focus on the information that was used to make the case for the war in Iraq, but this set the context for much more general statements about how government generally could no longer be trusted to provide high quality, accurate and unbiased information. Indeed, one of the key Conservative posters of the campaign was '*If he's prepared to lie to take us to war, he's prepared to lie to win an election*'.

Of course, lack of trust in politicians was not a new phenomenon. As the chart below shows there was very little change in levels of trust in

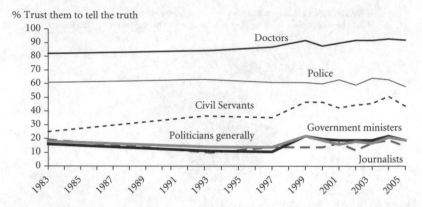

% Trust them to tell the truth

Figure 20.11. Trust in individual professions
Source: MORI/BMA

many professions from the 1980s onwards, with government ministers and politicians always bumping along the bottom of the graph. Indeed, the only notable shift in Blair's term was the general increase in trust in civil servants, something of a surprise given the negative focus of most media coverage of government 'bureaucrats'. Comparisons with other European countries also showed that the UK was not unusual, with around average levels of trust in our politicians (Figure 20.11).[1]

However, there were some significant declines in specific aspects of trust in the UK which do suggest a shift in opinions. For example, as seen in the chart below, trust in Tony Blair since 2000 saw a significant decline, although this was most rapid before 2002 (when the Iraq War began), and of course attitudes towards prime ministers generally decline through their terms in office.

Trust in the government to act in the interests of the country rather than their party seems rather more erratic, with a marked increase following the general election in 1997, followed by an even sharper decline from 1999 to 2001. It is likely that the terrorist attacks in 2001 and the general election contributed to something of a revival, but the decline following was equally sharp, and by 2003 the proportion who said they trusted the government to act in the interests of the country was half that seen in 1986 (Figure 20.12).

Sir Alistair Graham, Chairman of the Committee for Standards in Public Life, set up following scandals over 'Cash for Questions' under the

---

[1] This is seen in both the European Social Survey and Eurobarometer studies.

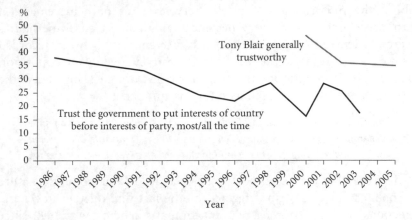

Figure 20.12. Trust in the Prime Minister and Government
Source: MORI/BSA

Conservative administration of the 1990s, claimed Blair's legacy will be 'as closely associated with the loss of public trust'[2] as John Major's was with sleaze. In one sense the data seems to support this view. By 2005, six in ten did not feel that the government used official figures honestly or that official figures were produced without political interference.[3] And whereas nearly half of people (48%) in 1998 felt the government was upholding high standards in public life, this fell to 35% at the time of Blair's resignation – not a total collapse, but certainly a significant fall.[4] There was undoubtedly much greater awareness among the general public of the *packaging of politics* – or more commonly spin – than there was in the 1990s. Quotes such as the one below from MORI's qualitative research over this period suggest how suspicious the public became, and how difficult it will be for future prime ministers to rebuild public trust in government:

> *Everything – there's spin on it. Even when you don't think it has got spin, it's got spin on it.*[5]

One observable trend during the Blair decade was that as the delivery of public services came to the front of political debate, and with the media as much as the official Opposition acting as chief inquisitor, statistics

[2] Interview with the Sunday Times, March 2007.
[3] ONS Survey 2005.
[4] Ipsos MORI survey of 961 adults,11–13 May, 2007.
[5] Participant in MORI focus group, September 2004, quoted in 'Who Do You Believe?' a MORI report of 2005.

about the performance of public services and the achievement of promised targets for delivery became highly contested. Crime figures were particular examples of this, with discrepancies between recorded crime and figures from the British Crime Survey used by the opposition and the media to score points. A leader article from the Daily Mail in the run-up to the 2005 election illustrates this approach:

> He (Blair) blithely brushes aside his own official evidence and seizes on quite separate figures to assert that violent crime is down. Confused? You're meant to be. Manipulating statistics to muddy the waters is a New Labour speciality.

Indeed the Blair years saw widespread general concerns about the nature of political life in Britain, triggered by the fact that turnout in general elections tumbled. The most relevant comparison here is with 1992, since Blair's influence was already acting in the electoral sphere in his 1997 victory before he had taken office as Prime Minister. At the 1992 general election, 78% of the electorate went to the polls; in 2001 and 2005 turnout had fallen almost by a quarter, to 59% and 61% respectively.

It is almost irresistible to compare the 35% of the electorate that Neil Kinnock lost with in 1992 and the 36% of Blair's third victory thirteen years later. Widespread disengagement with the politics as practised by both main parties was evident, despite the fact that interest in politics per se was virtually unchanged at around six in ten of the public – ever since the 1970s (Figure 20.13)!

Falling turnout was the tip of the iceberg of a wider phenomenon of falling political participation: Blair left political party membership much lower in 2007 than in 1997, but this may be misleading, since membership in 1997 was inflated by a temporary boost in Labour membership tied into popular enthusiasm for the first Blair government, and this conceals a less dramatic but much longer-term trend. Most significant was the falling number of activists available to the parties on the ground, whether fighting national or local elections, and the ageing profile of those who remained. This is not in any sense a consequence of the Blair government, although his efforts to reverse this decline had little impact, and participation in the new elections that Blair created – various referenda over devolution and for the Scottish Parliament and Welsh Assembly, and in the Mayoral elections in London – did not see a surge in political participation either. One is left feeling that personal contact between party campaigners and voters, which research shows is still one of the strongest predictors of turnout, may simply be an option that was no longer available to the campaign planners except on a much smaller

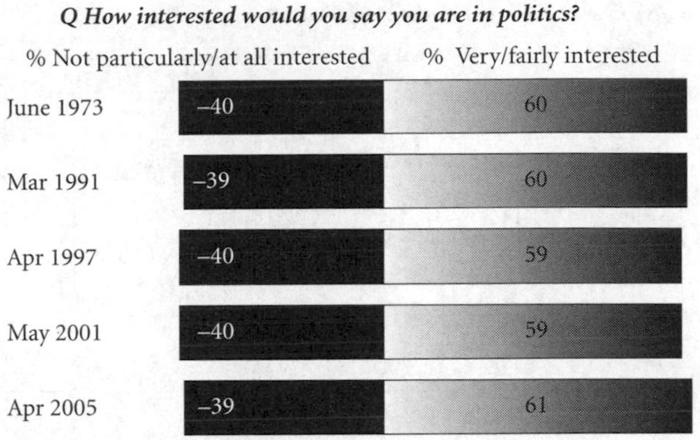

Q How interested would you say you are in politics?

% Not particularly/at all interested   % Very/fairly interested

June 1973	–40	60
Mar 1991	–39	60
Apr 1997	–40	59
May 2001	–40	59
Apr 2005	–39	61

Figure 20.13. Interest in politics over time
Base: c. 2,000 British/UK adults 18+. Source: MORI/JRRT/Electoral Commission, Times, FT

and more concentrated scale, with campaigns fought hard in marginal seats, and voters in the rest feeling neglected.

Public services

Billions spent, but what did the public notice? Blair promised to dramatically improve, modernise and above all 'reform' public services, in particular education and the NHS. He promised to be tough on crime and its causes. His track record was decidedly mixed, although how much he personally can be held responsible for this is unclear.

Taking each of these services in turn, in some ways education was Blair's biggest success story in terms of public opinion, where by putting in some universal targets and initiatives like the literacy hour, as well as investment, overall public concern about the area fell markedly. During the Blair years parental satisfaction with their children's schools generally rose in MORI's local surveys for hundreds of individual councils, although there was little comprehension of the Academy programme (Figure 20.14).

At the same time attainment rose and then plateaued – and there remained deep class divides in terms of attainment and expectation, as a survey commissioned for the Sutton Trust towards the end of Blair's term confirmed, with the social background of children's parents still impacting massively on their expectations of future attainment. In 2006, for example only 4% of upper middle-class parents (AB) believed their own

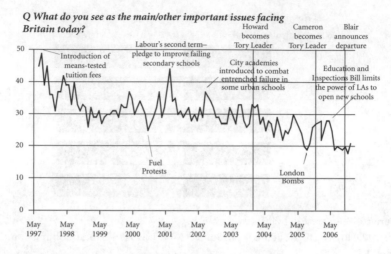

Figure 20.14. Concern about education
Base: c. 1,000 British adults each month age 18+

child would finish their academic career only with GCSEs, compared to 25% among working class (DE) parents.

In contrast, on *the* key issue of the National Health Service, at least in terms of public opinion, Blair saw initial recognition of success fall apart, following the 2005 general election. He seemed to regard this as an inevitable stage of reform, but at the time he left office, public pessimism about the future of the NHS was higher than at any point in his tenure, and for the first time in polling history the Conservatives were seen as having better policies on the NHS than Labour, despite being fairly circumspect about what these policies were (Figure 20.15).

News of ward closures, redundancies and cut backs following the measures needed to avert a repeated NHS deficit were to blame. At the time of Brown's National Insurance rises in 2002, more people expected an improvement than a decline (net score of +14%) in health services in Britain. By the time Blair left most expected the NHS to get worse (net score of −30%) – with 16% of the population expecting the NHS to get 'much worse'.[6]

Ironically, given the rise in NHS spending, the biggest public concerns about the NHS remained a lack of resources and investment, linked to a long-standing belief that there was still a shortage of doctors and nurses

---

[6] Ipsos MORI Delivery Index 2001–2007

Q Thinking about the NHS over the next few years do you expect it to get better/worse?

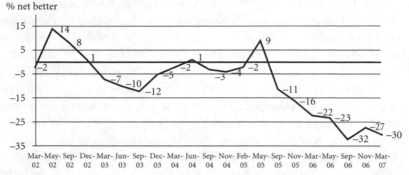

Figure 20.15. Long-term decline in expectations of the NHS
Base: c. 1,000 British adults

and that the NHS suffered from bureaucracy. Some of these views were strongly linked to political beliefs – Conservative voters were far more likely to feel the issue was bureaucracy, for example – but voters of all persuasions were worried about staffing levels.

How much was the overall public mood based on reality? The challenge facing anyone in charge of the NHS is that in terms of public and patient confidence, the national picture is nearly always much worse than the local one. If one moves from looking at anxieties about the direction of the health service nationally, patient satisfaction with actual healthcare told a more positive story. From winter 2002, overall public satisfaction with the NHS averaged around 60% and was rising gradually. The proportion satisfied with GPs was even higher, averaging around 81%. The news was also positive for hospitals: net satisfaction (percentage satisfied minus percentage dissatisfied) with out-patient, in-patient and accident and emergency services all showed positive trends.

Furthermore, the trends showed consistently that the people who actually *used* NHS services were more positive than the public in general: when Blair left office some 91% of patients experiencing in-patient services cited it as excellent or very good.[7] Nor were the public negative about Labour's health policies per se. Despite the furore in the Labour Party and the health professions about many NHS reforms, in particular

---

[7] MORI and Ipsos MORI Tracking Research for the Department of Health 2000 –2006: see www.dh.gov.uk. See also patient satisfaction data recorded by individual Trusts at www.healthcarecommission.org.uk.

Foundation Hospitals, and the involvement of private sector providers in the NHS, the public broadly backed Blair's reforms. Numerous studies by Ipsos MORI found that people were happy to be treated in the private sector provided the NHS paid, and that most believed that increasing choice would have a positive impact on the quality of healthcare. However, 'choice', while central to Blair's plans for using contestability to drive improvements, was not embraced with open arms by the public. While it was not seen as a bad thing per se, it was a long way down most of the public's list of desired improvements, and not received in the same almost totemic way that it was used by the government.

Indeed one of the problems for Blair was a lack of clarity about whether 'choice' was a moral good in its own right, something deeply valued by the public, or a means to an end – i.e. of introducing competition where the state was the monopoly supplier of a service. At the time of Blair's departure, it was still the case that the majority of patients being referred into the acute sector by GPs were NOT being offered a choice of specific hospitals, but this was not a reason for dissatisfaction.

So why the public gloom about the NHS? It was, in part, the 'perception gap' which plagued Labour as it attempted, not just to turn round public services, but also *be seen to have done so.* Tony Blair explained it to Labour's Spring Conference in March 2004:

> There is much scratching of the head in political circles over this apparent paradox. People who feel personally optimistic in Britain; but collectively pessimistic. They say their own health care in the NHS is good; but the NHS in general is bad. Their schools are good; but education is bad. They are safer; but the country is less safe. Their future is bright; but the nation's is dark.

The Prime Minister may well have been specifically referring to a MORI survey for the Department of Health conducted between November 2003 and February 2004. This found that while 67% of the public agreed that 'My local NHS is providing me with a good service', only 48% would admit that 'The NHS is providing a good service nationally'. This translated to 59% of the sample saying they were 'satisfied' with the NHS, and yet only 30% agreeing that 'The government has the right policies for the NHS'.

This gap between local experience and perception of how a key service was performing nationally was to bedevil the later years of Blair's government. It was particularly acute over issues around crime and immigration, and reflected the government's problems in persuading the media to take any assertions it made about its achievements at face value. The

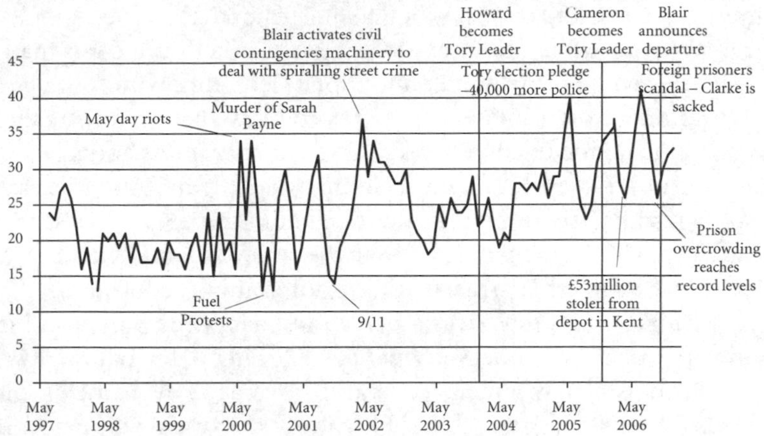

Q *What do you see as the main/other important issues facing Britain today?*

Figure 20.16. Concern about crime/law and order
Base: c. 1,000 British adults each month age 18+. Source: Ipsos MORI

public, who were basing their attitudes more on what they heard from the media and from people who worked in public services, were not just judging *actual services they received*, but their *impressions* of them every-where else as well.

On crime, there were very mixed results. It grew in prominence during Blair's decade, even as statistics suggested it was down. In 1992, following a clear focus on crime by the Labour Party and Tony Blair ('tough on crime, tough on the causes of crime'), the perceived gap between the two parties narrowed and indeed Labour took a slight lead. And yet, by 2000, the familiar pattern had been restored and once again, Labour was viewed as second-best on crime (Figure 20.16).

Indeed crime and violence remained a higher priority for the British public than in many other European countries and the US, and was con-sistently since 1997.

At the same time, the government spent an unprecedented amount on the Criminal Justice System (CJS) and by 2007 spent more per head on law and order than any other country in the OECD. And to a large extent, Blair spent this money on areas and issues that, it would seem, would meet public demand. There were, for example, more police officers than ever before, neighbourhood policing was a priority, average sentences were increased and greater powers introduced to help tackle anti-social behaviour.

The outcome was that actual crime rates have fallen since 1997, with crime overall reduced by 35% – but no one believed the government: only one in five were willing to accept that crime was falling and less than half (43%) believed there are more police.[8] Blair left office with confidence in the government on crime lower in this country than in any of the five major countries included in Ipsos MORI's regular international tracking study, including the USA, France, Germany and Spain. And this was not simply a result of an unpopular government in the UK not being trusted on all its activities – the public had a higher level of confidence than these same countries in other areas including, for example, education.

As with the NHS, there was a perception gap – the public had more confidence in how crime was managed locally than nationally. The explanation is partly media coverage: coverage on crime is biased towards the negative, a fact that is likely both to explain why perceptions are more negative than actual trends and influence national rather than local opinion. Other reasons for misconceptions between local and national opinion include a natural 'hometown favouritism', where people tend to believe that those who live in their local area share values and behaviours.

But as importantly, there are high-profile or 'signal crimes' that have a greater impact on perceptions than other crimes, and these did not decrease. For example, during Blair's watch, crimes resulting in injury from firearms went up over four-fold and homicides up 23%. Although the numbers directly affected by these were very small, media coverage was enormous.

Finally, back on the issue of contested statistics, it seems likely that the definition of crime in the public's mind incorporates far wider issues than the official definition, with for example, some being influenced by their views on terrorism and ASB (anti-social behaviour). As these rose in prominence, then crime was also seen to have increased. Indeed one of the marked trends in public opinion during this period was around anti-social behaviour. Local surveys repeatedly showed that what people most saw as a key issue was facilities for teenagers, and low-level disorder. Initiatives like ASBOs were supported by the public (82% agreed with their use), but overall had little impact on feelings of safety. Indeed Blair's Respect Campaign, while working at a local level, and campaigns around zero tolerance, while appealing to widespread concerns, also served to remind people of the issue. At the end of 2006, right across England, ASB and

---

[8] ICM and MORI research for the Cabinet Office 2004/5.

activities for teenagers remained the number one local concern in the government's BVPI surveys in every English local authority.

It was in one of the areas where there were fewer targets (an early ten-year plan was publicly abandoned) and less direct involvement by the Prime Minister that in fact public opinion became more optimistic rather than pessimistic during his term in office – public transport. Here there was an early disaster with the inherited privatised rail network, the Hatfield crash, and the renationalisation of Railtrack, but in the meantime, led by London, real investment in bus services and new rolling stock and renewal of the rail network gradually saw transport recede as a key public concern. Indeed in London the proportion of people citing it as one of the worst things about the city fell from 35% in 2001 to 15% by late 2006,[9] and the same series saw a rise, to 81% in the proportion of Londoners describing it as an easy city to get around. By the end of Blair's term in office, only three people in a hundred were citing it as a key national issue, whereas five years earlier 22% had done so. From 2003, there was a rise in public optimism about public transport. Traffic congestion remained seen as a key issue, and surging fuel prices remained a 'feel bad' factor, but it was not anywhere near the challenge that reforming the NHS posed Blair (Figure 20.17).

Finally, one of the biggest shifts in public opinion during the Blair years was rising concern, initially about asylum-seekers, legal and illegal, and then race, multi-culturalism and immigration of all sorts (Figure 20.18). By the end of Blair's premiership this was frequently seen as the biggest issue facing Britain, although how much was driven by media coverage as opposed to actual experience was unclear – while only 18% per cent saw it as a big problem in their own area, some 76% saw it as a national problem. But nevertheless, the pace of change was unsettling in some communities, such as Barking and Dagenham – the local authority which became more diverse more quickly than anywhere else in the UK and voted BNP in large numbers. The whole debate around immigration was media-led, with the average Briton estimating that 22% of the UK population was born abroad (in 2003 the actual figure was 6%), and with 78% disagreeing that the government was open and honest about migration.

The government was more criticised on this issue than virtually any other, and the British became more concerned than any other

[9] Ipsos MORI/GLA Annual London Surveys 2001–2006: see http://www.london.gov.uk/mayor/annual_survey.

Q *Thinking about public transport over the next few years do you expect it to get better/worse?*

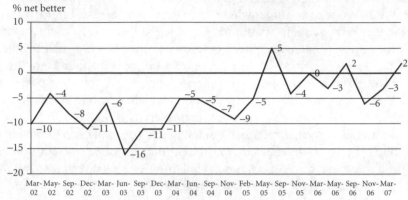

Figure 20.17. Public transport: overall trend is up since 2002
Base: c. 1,000 British adults

Q *What do you see as the main/other important issues facing Britain today?*

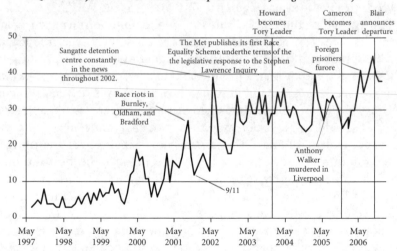

Figure 20.18. Concern about race relations/immigration
Base: c. 1,000 British adults each month age 18+. Source: Ipsos MORI

Q Which three of the following eleven topics do you find the most worrying in your country? – Immigration control

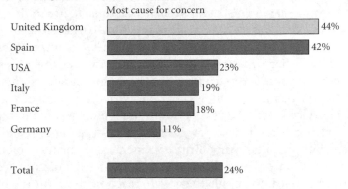

Figure 20.19. Most worrying issues nationally – Immigration control
Source: Ipsos MORI International Social Trends Monitor, Nov 2006. Base: c. 1,000 interviews in each country

major economy, and (Figure 20.19) were more likely than most European neighbours to feel that their country was absorbing more immigrants than similar-sized countries. The arrival of home-grown terrorism saw a debate over multiculturalism.

But while a tiny minority of Muslims in the UK harboured radical views, what is striking, even after the July 2005 bombings, was that although a sizeable minority of British people were uneasy about multiculturalism, the majority were not, and there was a good deal of common ground between different groups. There was strong support for many policies to encourage integration, among both Muslims and everyone else alike: the idea that would-be citizens should pledge their primary loyalty to Britain (76% support and 73% of Muslims), accept the authority of British institutions (91% to 93%), integrate fully into British society (69% to 73%) and accept the rights of women as equal citizens (95% to 94%) – these all show high levels of agreement on both sides. An overwhelming majority of all groups thought immigrants should be *made* to learn English (90% support, as opposed to 82% support amongst the population as a whole). Application of Norman Tebbit's Test showed that nine in ten Britons and Muslims agreed British sporting success made them proud.

Asked if they thought multiculturalism is a mistake that should be abandoned, the nation as a whole (68%) and British Muslims (74%) both *disagreed*. Where there were differences of view was around culture and traditions. Both groups agreed on using English, respecting British laws and institutions, and accepting that Britain is primarily Christian. They both agreed that new arrivals should 'integrate'. But forced to chose between two statements, either *'People who come to live in Britain should adopt the values and traditions of British culture'* or *'People who come to live in Britain should be free to live their lives by the values and traditions of their own culture'* sharp differences were present between British Muslims and the rest of Britain. Six in ten Britons thought immigrants should become basically British in all senses (58%, but 35% did not). Amongst British Muslims views were the other way around – most wanted to retain their own culture. What Britain saw in this period was a hybrid and evolving future, but retaining many 'British' principles of fairness, tolerance and democracy. Only a minority of zealots on both sides did not accept that, despite the tensions. While there were reactions both on the liberal left and among more radical Muslim groups over the Blair government's reactions to the terrorist attacks, in one sense what is striking is that actually society remained pretty much in vague agreement about what Britishness meant – even if opinion formers toiled over it.

Blair and public sector staff

One of the key impacts on public confidence in public services was public sector staff themselves. One of the most ironic aspects of public opinion during the Blair years is that the millions employed in the public sector experienced considerable increases in pay – for example 64% more pay for teachers alone, and GPs becoming some of the best paid in the world – yet became increasingly negative about their employer. By 2007, public sector staff were as likely to say they planned to vote Conservative as they were to vote Labour, a reversal of Labour's huge lead among this group in 1997, and this in turn impacted on public perceptions.

One of the biggest challenges for Blair, after spending hundreds of millions on extra pay and injecting new resources, was his inability to persuade public sector staff that his plans would improve services rather than simply open them up to the private sector, or save money without decreasing quality (Figure 20.20).

In particular, with over a million people in the NHS who went home every night to friends and family to tell it 'like it is', Blair's government faced a real challenge. As the NHS under Blair shows, and indeed so does all the textbook research on employee motivation, increasing pay does not build motivation. Instead, showing that you value, respect, and listen to people, and have a clear simple narrative are much more effective – but

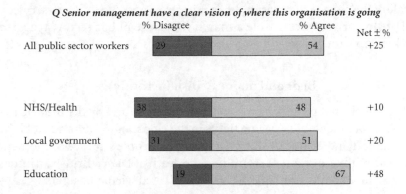

Figure 20.20. Attitudes to senior management
Base: All public sector workers (921), NHS/Health (216), Local government (149) and Education (227) workers in Britain Oct. 2005, Feb. 2005 and April 2006, excludes self-employed

on many of these aspects, Blair's government was on either a deliberate or accidental collision course. The result was that up to 70% of the most trusted public servants in Britain – GPs – were negative about the direction of NHS reform to their patients and community.

The impact of technology

Blair's years saw the internet, mobile phones and recently user-generated content revolutionise many aspects of our culture – Blair embraced much of this technology as offering improvements in public services, greater power to ordinary people and faster, easier access to public services. Under Blair internet access grew from some 40% to 60% plus, digital interactive TV took off from nowhere reaching 80% plus of households, and the web finally came of age. While this can be overstated, in terms of its impact, given that only some 8% of working-class pensioners were online by the time he left office, nevertheless, as part of its modernisation of Britain, Blair's government spent millions on projects to give all school children internet access, to improve government websites and to ensure all public services were accessible either online or by phone. In one sense one could argue that much of this investment had little impact on user experience, where expectations rose considerably. Over the six years from 1998 to 2004, the proportion of the public saying public services failed to meet their expectations increased from 40 to 51%, but this obscures the scale of the change that was under way in terms of accessibility to services, where the private sector stole a march which the public sector struggled to keep up with.

Blair and major British institutions

Blair was elected promising to modernise Britain, and by the time he left office, fewer men were wearing tights in the House of Commons. But how did underlying attitudes shift? Despite his 'people's princess' moment and the dramatic events surrounding the death of Diana, British attitudes to the monarchic principle actually remained virtually unchanged – apart from a small wobble in the aftermath of her death, only 20% of people wanted a republic in 2006 – the same as in 1986. Indeed attitudes to many key British institutions actually changed relatively little under Blair. While devolution in Scotland and Wales fundamentally changed the landscape, it is hard to talk of a shift in public attitudes that would anywhere near match up to the rhetoric of modernisation, except in terms of ongoing scepticism about national politicians.

Similarly, the BBC, despite a fairly ferocious battle with the government over the Kelly affair and the resignation of its Chairman, remained trusted, and confidence in it was little changed. By August 2003, as the Kelly affair broke, the BBC was more trusted than Blair and has remained so since (Table 20.1).

Despite modernising parliament and the end of the hereditary principle in the Lords, overall attitudes moved less than one might have expected. Overall attitudes towards the way Britain was governed did not really improve, although neither did they fall as precipitously as some commentators would have us think. For example with a popular vote for devolution in Scotland, and Wales, one might have expected public support for their local assemblies – but actually five years on in 2004, 36% of Scots thought their new parliament had achieved nothing at all, and fewer than one in ten thought it had achieved a lot.

One of the challenges Blair faced was that in some ways, the country was less willing to change than he was – on the NHS, for example, around three quarters of the population consistently believed that it should be maintained at whatever cost – with this figure hardly varying despite constant efforts at reform, introduction of more private sector provision, reconfiguration and so on.[10] The idea, popular in Downing Street, that it

---

[10] Ipsos MORI research for Department of Health 2000–2006

Table 20.1

Base: All British adults 18+ (982)	Trustworthy %	Not trustworthy %	Don't know %	Net trustworthy % ±
Tony Blair	41	49	10	−8
Alastair Campbell, the Prime Minister's Director of Communications	14	60	−26	−46
Andrew Gilligan, the BBC journalist	32	30	38	+2
Geoff Hoon, the Defence Secretary	24	45	30	−21
The BBC	59	26	15	+33

needed physically recasting, with a major reduction in state-controlled healthcare (as opposed to state-provided) only appealed to between one in four and one in five people. Indeed one of the things that stands out in an examination of the British over this period is how deep-rooted and unchanging values were.

Culture and the arts

In June 1998 Blair invited the key art world figures to a No. 10 summit on Labour's policy on the arts. As Nicolas Serota, who opened Tate Modern under Blair, put it in an interview in *The Guardian*: 'The long freeze on arts funding begun by the Conservatives was over, thanks to a three-year settlement worth an extra £290m. Museums, galleries and the performing arts all benefited. It meant Tate Modern would be able to open with free admission.'

Although Blair and his government spent their first five years having constant problems with the Dome, the arts did see major investment, and with free admission and Lottery money, there was a revival of museum and gallery attendance. Box office numbers in the seven major regional theatres rose by nearly 40% in the five years to 2007, and similarly there were nearly 30 million extra visits to England's national museums

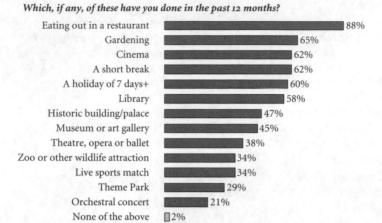

Which, if any, of these have you done in the past 12 months?

Eating out in a restaurant — 88%
Gardening — 65%
Cinema — 62%
A short break — 62%
A holiday of 7 days+ — 60%
Library — 58%
Historic building/palace — 47%
Museum or art gallery — 45%
Theatre, opera or ballet — 38%
Zoo or other wildlife attraction — 34%
Live sports match — 34%
Theme Park — 29%
Orchestral concert — 21%
None of the above — 2%

Figure 20.21. Leisure Habits of the British Public
Base: All British adults aged 15+ (1.010). May 2003

and galleries, five years after entry charges were scrapped. Consider the world's most successful modern art museum, Tate Modern. It had over 4 million visitors in 2006, compared with just over 2 million visitors to New York's much longer-established Museum of Modern Art.

More generally the consumption of arts, books and film all rose, as did consumption of all types: eating out continued to rise in prominence, and during this period London's restaurants, and indeed those across the country, improved to a point where several made it into international lists of the top fifty worldwide (Figure 20.21).

But if Blair's government boosted participation in the arts, it made less progress in widening access – there was a boost in people from working-class backgrounds visiting museums and galleries, but so too in visits by the traditional middle classes.

While the Dome was reviled by most critics and the media, overall public attitudes towards Labour's arts spending seem to have been benign. 'The past 10 years have given the arts the stability to behave creatively,' said Christopher Frayling in 2007: 'People talk about the golden age of the 1950s, but it's nothing compared to now. Then there were 26 organisations funded by the Arts Council. Now there are 1,100.'

Despite ire at the later freezing of expenditure after the initial rise in investment, Blair's three administrations were widely regarded as investing in cultural excellence, at least by their most obvious beneficiaries. The Tate's Serota argues that excellence and vibrancy goes beyond theatre: 'in architecture, the visual arts, theatre and in writing, the work that's been produced has been admired internationally to a degree that hasn't been the case for most of the second half of the century.'

So despite the arts fraternities' more general suspicion of Blair, and despite their near universal revulsion at the invasion of Iraq, there has not been the same visceral hatred of the 1980s, characterised by Elvis Costello imagining Thatcher's burial with relish in 'Tramp the Dirt Down'.

It may not have been a golden age, but as far as the public were concerned, there was more of it, and ageing facilities have been revitalised, boosted by Millennium spending, and ratings of quality of life in the centres of British cities, where the grand projets were concentrated, rose.

The rise and rise of celebrity culture

In 1996, Peter Mandelson and Roger Liddle, in The Blair Revolution, set as the central aim of Blair's government the re-creation of Britain as a 'young' country. Even before his election, Blair sought to identify with the icons of Britain's resurgent pop scene. In early 1995, Blur's singer Damon Albarn was invited to meet Blair at the Commons. Once in office, with 'Cool Britannia' parties in Downing Street at the start of his term of office to his holidays with ageing pop stars, Blair enjoyed and participated in the cult of the celebrity that saw *X Factor*, *Big Brother*, and shows like *I'm a Celebrity, Get Me Out of Here* come to dominate mainstream entertainment. Even in a 2003 interview with Saga magazine to celebrate his 50th birthday, Blair said: 'I feel I should graduate to classical music, properly. But the truth is, I'm more likely to listen to rock music. I listen to what the kids play.'

Blair was keen to communicate that he was culturally in tune with the public – describing himself as a 'regular guy', sharing his tastes in music (his *Desert Island Discs* selection, for example, managed to incorporate practically every major musical genre from Debussy through to the Darkness) and, in 2007, taking part in a TV comedy sketch, albeit for charity, asking the character Catherine Tate whether he looked 'bovvered'.

And for a time, this flirtation with popular culture worked. Oasis came out in full support of Tony Blair, a story which was picked up in the press with many papers leading with the headline 'What's the story? Don't vote Tory'. Some went even further: Paul Conway, Managing Director of Virgin Records said of Blair 'here is a person of our generation who understands us . . . it's like when Kennedy dawned on the politics of America'.

However, as the grim realities of governing got in the way, it was hard for the increasingly mistrustful general public to see Blair's fraternising as anything other than a highly polished marketing campaign. Even by March 1998, the NME had accused Labour spin-doctors of stealing British culture and repackaging it 'under a brand name'. Jarvis Cocker said: 'It would have been better had the Tories won the election.' The invasion of Iraq saw many of those celebrities who had been so lavishly entertained at Downing Street take to the stage in protest.

But Blair's flirtations with celebrity culture were only a symptom of a trend that came to dominate many aspects of British popular culture. *Big Brother* first came onto British TV in the summer of 2000 and quickly caught the public's imagination; around sixteen million votes were cast throughout the second series shown in 2001 – only ten million fewer than bothered to turn out and vote in the election that same year. Clearly, the popularity contest that was taking place inside Elstree was as important to many as the one at Westminster. Celebrity has always been with us, of course, but the 'democratisation' of celebrity was distinctive under Blair. The growth of reality television over this period presented viewers with people like themselves, who, regardless of whether they had any kind of talent, had their fifteen minutes of fame at worst, or became millionaires. And, given that over the past decade events internationally were, at times, simply extraordinary, is it any wonder the British began to relish mundane escapism?

Of course, this change in the nature of celebrity and our shift in aspirations cannot be attributable to Tony Blair. Instead, it is more a result of the proliferation of media channels, the ongoing digital revolution, and the constant and unremitting self-reference that this allows, as well as the ongoing decline of deference. But Blair can be seen as part of this preoccupation with appearance and presentation. After Blair's resignation speech Gordon Brown was quick to differentiate himself by stating that 'we're moving from this period when celebrity matters . . . people are wanting the concerns that they have discussed in a rounded way' – although shortly after making this statement he himself decided to appear on primetime TV to present an award for the 'Greatest Briton Ever', and had already been drawn into the debate over Jade Goody's remarks on *Big Brother* the previous year.

Going green?

Blair leaves office with it clear that climate change is under way and public concern starting to reflect this. His decade saw an unprecedented

Q *What do you see as the main/other important issues facing Britain today?* – *pollution/environment*

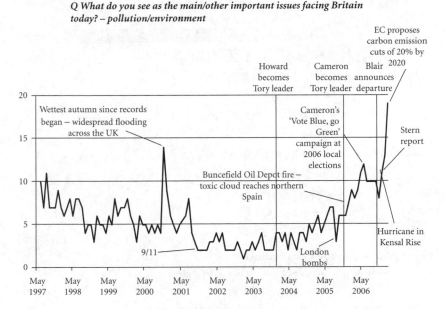

Figure 20.22. Issues Facing Britain: Environment
Base: c. 1,000 British adults each month age 18+. Source: Ipos MORI

growth in environmental debate, regulation and awareness in Britain. It was established on the agendas of Whitehall, town halls, boardrooms, newsrooms and schools throughout the country – and a number of government-supported organisations were established to promote environmental behaviour to consumers (WRAP) and business (Carbon Trust). However, the change can easily be overstated, and Blair's influence was by no means clear-cut (Figure 20.22).

The only time the British public rated 'the environment' as *the* single most important issue facing Britain was in 1989, when 35% said they were concerned about it. For most of the Blair years, fewer than one in ten people saw it as crucial and it was only towards the end of the Blair decade that it really took off, even then sitting well below concerns around crime or immigration. In March 2007, despite Al Gore's *Inconvenient Truth* being one of the biggest grossing documentaries ever, despite a blizzard of media coverage, despite rapid increases in recycling and local recycling policy being a key issue in the local elections of 2007, most people in Britain said they were doing nothing about it personally (Figure 20.23).

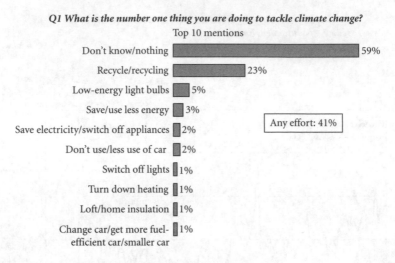

Q1 What is the number one thing you are doing to tackle climate change?
Top 10 mentions

- Don't know/nothing — 59%
- Recycle/recycling — 23%
- Low-energy light bulbs — 5%
- Save/use less energy — 3%
- Save electricity/switch off appliances — 2%
- Don't use/less use of car — 2%
- Switch off lights — 1%
- Turn down heating — 1%
- Loft/home insulation — 1%
- Change car/get more fuel-efficient car/smaller car — 1%

Any effort: 41%

Figure 20.23. Effort to tackle climate change
Base: 2,130 British adults, 9–15 and 23–29 March 2007

Admittedly when the public were asked what was happening on a global scale it was far more prominent – but terrorism still outstripped global warming by a considerable margin (40% vs 23%) in 2007.

Nevertheless, even if public opinion only shifted towards the end of his term in office there were some real shifts in public behaviour – nearly always more due to coercion than persuasion. To take one example: the volume of recycling in Britain increased dramatically. This is mainly thanks to concerted efforts by local authorities, Blair's government and the EU – and crucially did not depend on 'winning hearts and minds'.

Another key issue was Congestion Charging. While one of Blair's many volte-faces was over the competence of Ken Livingstone as Mayor of London, Livingstone was, once elected, given the space to lead the way on one of the largest road charging schemes in the world and then be returned to office with 55% of Londoners giving him their first or second preference votes in 2004, and outright hostility to the charge switched round to grudging acceptance.

There were marked shifts in consumer trends. As Blair left office fair trade, ethical, cruelty-free, organic and such products were quite the thing, with many succeeding despite their premium pricing. But it is hard to discern a distinctive Blair effect in this – much of the change is the evolution of existing trends. In the late 1980s, 'green' brands and products sprang up quickly – but many of them carried the burden of higher prices and the perception of inferior quality. Only gradually did this perception change and they became fashionable – witness celebrities driving Toyota Prius cars.

So what has been 'the Blair effect' in this area in the last decade? In one sense Blair's policies on the environment were deeply contradictory – despite overwhelming evidence of its impact, he saw no reason why his own or anyone else's flights should be strictly limited, and presided over a massive growth in air travel by Middle England. But the pursuit of self-made, self-reliant, self-determining 'Mondeo Man' voters had gone hand-in-hand with a far more collectivist approach (of which environmental legislation is one product), albeit more slowly than any of the experts in climate change might have liked.

Conclusions

Overall, Blair was as much shaped by events and public opinion as shaping them. Despite the accusations over spin, despite disappointment over the war and public services, more people gave him the benefit of the doubt, and if they knew how publics in other major countries felt, might have been more charitable. One can argue about the effectiveness of his reform and investment policy in public services, regret the missed opportunities, but from the point of view of the public at large, there was a feeling that he, more than any of his predecessors in office, benefited them personally.

21

Higher education

JOHN O'LEARY

Higher education provides one of the enduring mysteries of Tony Blair's 10 years in office. Why, when his mantra of 'education, education, education' focused so tightly on schools and nurseries, did he risk the future of his administration on a half-hearted reform of university funding? Whether through misjudgement, stubbornness or genuine radicalism, his proposals for top-up fees came closer than foundation hospitals, trust schools, or even the war in Iraq to bringing a premature end to his premiership.

In his resignation speech at Trimdon Labour Club, Blair recalled the introduction of £3,000 undergraduate tuition fees as 'deeply controversial and hellish hard to do' although he insisted that he had been 'moving with the grain of change around the world'.[1] Yet, for most of his time in office universities took a back seat to more pressing educational concerns, as successive public spending settlements demonstrated. Indeed, the shorthand of 'schools and hospitals', used in later years to underline the government's priorities, was probably a more accurate reflection of reality than the more familiar 'education, education, education'.

Fees were a recurring theme of the Blair years, however. They were high on the new Prime Minister's agenda after the 1997 general election, when the main parties had been happy to 'park' the question of how to pay for the much-expanded and increasingly expensive university system by commissioning Sir Ron (subsequently Lord) Dearing to chair a higher education inquiry.[2] The subsequent report made 93 recommendations on subjects as diverse as academic pay to the machinery of quality assurance, but is (mis)remembered almost exclusively for recommending the end of 'free' higher education.

---

[1] Resignation speech, Trimdon Labour Club, Sedgefield, 10 May 2007.
[2] *Higher Education in the Learning Society,* The National Committee of Inquiry into Higher Education, July 1997. ISBN: 1 85838 253 X.

In fact, although Dearing wanted graduates to meet part of the cost of full-time higher education when they could afford it, the recommendation was coupled with the restoration of grants for those from low-income families. David Blunkett, the Education Secretary throughout Blair's first term in office, quietly buried key parts of the package under pressure from the Treasury. Up-front fees of £1,000 a year were duly imposed, without grants but with less resistance than many had expected from Labour MPs. This may have been at least partly because means-testing ensured that a minority of students would be charged the full amount and many others would pay nothing at all. But that easy ride through the Commons may have sown the seeds of subsequent miscalculations over fees.

Labour's inheritance

Universities were never convinced that they received the full value of the new fee income following adjustments to their block grant, but the injection of cash allowed ministers to begin to reverse more than a decade of cuts in funding per student. There was plenty to reverse: annual 'efficiency gains' combined with sharp growth in student numbers had seen unit funding for full-time students drop by 36% between 1989 and 1997.[3] The student population had more than doubled in that time, as the polytechnics were first released from local authority control and then allowed to become universities in 1992. Student maintenance grants were gradually reduced and replaced by loans, albeit at a zero real rate of interest. There had been other important reforms, such as the establishment of external quality assurance, but the Tory years were remembered in universities largely for budget cuts and underfunded expansion.

There could hardly be a more authoritative picture of the higher education system inherited by the incoming Labour government than that recorded in the 2,000-page Dearing Report. The committee noted that 'almost all' public funding for capital expenditure had ceased in 1993 and a cap placed on any further growth in the number of undergraduates. Further reductions in unit costs would be required to meet Conservative spending plans. 'The concern now is that short-term pressures to reduce costs, in conditions of no growth, may damage the intrinsic quality of the learning experience which underpins the quality of UK awards.'[4]

---

[3] *The Future of Higher Education*, Cm. 5735, January 2003, p. 18.
[4] *Dearing Report*, summary report, p. 11.

Dearing concluded that UK higher education could take 'justifiable pride' in extending opportunities to 1.6 million students while maintaining its international standing in research, innovating in teaching and learning, and becoming more cost-effective. But the proportion of GDP devoted to higher education remained low and he warned of an imminent funding gap of more than £500 million with a backlog of essential capital work amounting to some £9 billion.[5] In short (which the Dearing Report was not), Labour was inheriting an overstretched higher education sector that was in urgent need of renewal. The process of transformation from an elite to a mass system was taking place in a haphazard manner, as universities adjusted to constantly changing signals from the Treasury and the Education Department.

Ministerial teams

Dearing's 93 recommendations landed on the desks of David Blunkett and his Higher Education Minister, Baroness (formerly Tessa) Blackstone, until the 1997 election Master of Birkbeck College London. As an insider, she was a popular choice in universities and, like her boss, she served the whole of Blair's first parliament. But, though Blunkett's preoccupation with primary education left his formidable understudy with a largely free rein, the low priority given to universities restricted the scope for innovation. The first term in higher education was mainly about fire-fighting, from the implementation of tuition fees to battles over Oxbridge.

The second term was altogether more turbulent for higher education policy, as for other areas of education. Although Blunkett was succeeded by another schools specialist in Estelle Morris, higher education had become more of a concern in Downing Street. With Margaret Hodge a combative force as Higher Education Minister, the new team appeared less sure-footed than its predecessor. It was to last less than two years, although this rather than the Blunkett/Blackstone marathon stint was nearer the norm for post-war education ministers of all parties.

Blair's third ministerial pairing was by far the most active in higher education. Charles Clarke arrived as Education Secretary in mid-negotiation on the introduction of top-up fees but, as a former president of the National Union of Students and briefly as a higher education consultant, he had a confidence that many previous holders of his office lacked in

---

[5] *Dearing Report*, main report, p. 269.

dealing with university issues. Alan Johnson, his Higher Education Minister, could scarcely have had a more different background, having left school at 15. In a parliamentary party packed with graduates, the lack of any contact with universities was expected to count against him, but a combination of charm and political acumen won over rebellious colleagues and vice-chancellors alike. The pairing was so successful in piloting fees legislation through the Commons against the odds that both won promotion – Clarke to the poisoned chalice of the Home Office and Johnson into the Cabinet as Work and Pensions Secretary, a rare advancement for a higher education minister.

By then, the political heavy lifting was over where higher education was concerned. Ruth Kelly came and went as Education Secretary with little involvement in university affairs, while Kim Howells enjoyed a similarly uneventful few months as Higher Education Minister before the 2005 election. Alan Johnson made a triumphal return to the department as Education Secretary for the final months of the Blair era, but left most university business to his Higher Education Minister, Bill Rammell, who had effectively swapped jobs with Dr Howells.

After sometimes stormy relationships with ministers during the Thatcher years, universities and union leaders enjoyed a reasonable rapport with most of the Blair appointees. Vice-chancellors of the most prestigious institutions and a select few others with the right political links would lobby No. 10 directly, but gripes about the Department for Education and Skills more often concerned its perceived powerlessness than any refusal to listen. Conscious of its strong focus on schools, the department belatedly strengthened its higher education directorate in 2003, appointing Sir Alan Wilson, the former Leeds University vice-chancellor, as its first Director General. But by then, the key decisions of the Blair years had been taken.

The early years

Responding to the Dearing Report took up much of Labour's initial period in office where higher education was concerned. Its tenth anniversary, like that of Tony Blair's arrival in office, prompted a spate of reassessments of the report's impact. Sir David Watson, in an inaugural lecture as Professor of Higher Education Management at the University of London's Institute of Education, claimed a number of successes for the committee of which he was a member. They included a more structured approach to partnership between universities and industry, more

attention to teaching and learning, systematic funding to widen participation in higher education and improved university governance. But
Sir David did not believe that the central idea of the report – that of a
'compact' in which institutions would gain increased security in return
for greater accountability and responsiveness to a range of stakeholders –
had been realised. Funding levels have fallen far short of the sums needed
to provide such security, let alone to implement the measures that
Dearing considered necessary to produce a world-class higher education
system (rather than a few world-class institutions).[6]

The first and most obvious example of this trimming came with the
fees package announced in the government's response to the report. The
decision to make fees payable upfront, rather than wait up to twenty years
for graduate contributions to put the scheme into credit, at the same time
as completing the transition from student grants to loans, stored up
political trouble. Means-testing had to be introduced to avoid pricing
hundreds of thousands of natural Labour supporters out of higher education and universities were given £40 million for hardship funds for students who had exhausted their loan entitlement. The system was so
unpopular in Scotland that its abolition was a central plank in the coalition between Labour and the Liberal Democrats after devolution. The
Cubie Report,[7] commissioned by the new Scottish Parliament, paved the
way for the abolition of upfront fees with a more modest £2,000 total
contribution payable by graduates in instalments. But it would not be
until 2004 that similar measures were agreed in England.

The other pressing concern of those early days was an issue that
Dearing deliberately fudged because of its political sensitivity: that of
college fees at Oxford and Cambridge. The report's proposed review of the
'substantial addition to the standard funding for institutions of higher
education' represented by college fees[8] was taken up enthusiastically by
Lady Blackstone, who was accused of anti-Oxbridge bias in a lengthy and
sometimes bitter campaign to preserve the £35 million in extra funding for
tuition. Robert Stevens, the Master of Pembroke College, Oxford, accused
her of setting out to 'eviscerate' the universities.[9] It was the first example of
the love/hate relationship that was a recurring theme of Labour's dealings
with the ancient universities. Gordon Brown, an Edinburgh University

---

[6] *Whatever happened to the Dearing Report?* Professorial lecture, 6 February 2007,
    www.ioe.ac.uk/publications.
[7] *Student Finance: Fairness for the Future,* 21 December 1999.
[8] *Dearing Report,* main report, p. 300 (19.46).
[9] John O'Leary, 'Ministers out to Ruin Oxbridge, Says College Head', *The Times,* 13 July 2001.

graduate with little time for the pretensions of the English elite, made his position clear at the 1997 Party conference: 'When at Oxford and Cambridge, half of the places still go to the private schools, it is time to modernise and extend opportunity by redistributing resources.'[10] But Oxford-educated Blair was more sympathetic and a compromise was found, under which a steadily reducing sum would be paid to the universities centrally for allocation to the colleges.

The row over college fees proved to be the shape of things to come, as the government in general – and Brown in particular – veered between steering policy to promote research at the UK's two pre-eminent universities and pressing them to broaden their admissions. Brown was prepared to find £69 million, without giving rival universities the opportunity to compete, for a research partnership between Cambridge and the Massachusetts Institute of Technology.[11] But six months later he would ignite the greatest single higher education controversy of the Blair years with ill-informed criticism of Oxford over the rejection by Magdalen College of Laura Spence, a well-qualified candidate for medicine from a Tyneside comprehensive. The teenager had been predicted (and subsequently achieved) five A grades, but was said by the college to have interviewed badly in comparison with other equally well-qualified applicants, some of whom were also from comprehensives. Nevertheless, Brown condemned the decision as 'scandalous' and blamed 'an interview system more reminiscent of the old school network and the old school tie than justice'.[12] It was an incident that scarred relations, not just with Oxford, but with universities generally, who felt themselves being bullied into complying with the government's agenda to widen participation.

Universities were already subject to 'performance indicators' that included the proportions of entrants from state schools, from the lowest socio-economic classes and from areas of low participation in higher education. Those who lagged furthest behind national averages were named and shamed by their funding councils, which offered a 5% premium (as Dearing had proposed) on those recruited from poor areas. Yet it was the government's own policy on tuition fees that was most obviously holding back working-class participation, at least among the mature students who had flocked to the polytechnics and their successor

[10] 'Oxbridge to be Stripped of Some of its Glitter?' BBC News, 15 December 1997.
[11] Tom Buerkle, 'Institute will Promote New High-tech Businesses in Britain', *International Herald Tribune*, 9 November 1999, p. 1.
[12] Alexandra Frean, John O'Leary and Philip Webster, 'Brown Goes to War over Oxford Elite', *The Times*, 26 May 2000, p. 1.

institutions in the 1990s. While fees had made little difference to sixth-
formers' enthusiasm for degrees, the Treasury felt obliged to fund a £68
million package to revive interest among older applicants.

If Brown had left his mark on the higher education debate in the Laura
Spence affair, Blair's first-term moment had already happened and
was almost equally unexpected. Although there had been discussions in
a small group of ministers, civil servants and advisers about ways of
increasing England's historically low rate of participation in post-school
education, Blair's announcement of a new target came out of the blue.
Rather than use the traditional benchmark of participation by 18-year-
olds, he set a goal of 50% of the population experiencing higher education by the age of 30, giving universities until 2010 to reach the target.
This had the merit of including mature students, who were in the majority in new universities, but it was such a novel concept that the Education
Department at first could not even give the current position. It turned
out to be 43% and efforts to bridge the gap dominated higher education
policy for years to come.

The 50% target rapidly became a rod for the government's back, particularly when combined with a requirement to recruit more students
from poor backgrounds. The figure was symbolic and had no detailed
rationale in economic or social terms, but it was sufficiently ambitious to
require concerted action. For all the evidence of similar growth in other
developed nations, public opinion was never convinced of the need for
half the population to go to university, particularly when there was a
shortage of plumbers and other skilled tradespeople. With most of the
growth coming in new universities, which were responding to student
demand with new types of vocational degrees, critics rounded on so-
called 'Mickey Mouse' courses like surf science and golf course management. Similar debates were taking place in other parts of the world – in
Australia, for example, they were known as 'cappuccino courses'. In the
UK, media studies became the object of particular scorn, despite bur-
geoning demand for places and obvious employment opportunities.

With the Tories making political capital on the perceived dumbing
down of higher education, David Blunkett took on the task of setting out
Labour's vision in a speech at Greenwich University in February 2000. In
a location chosen to echo Anthony Crosland's famous blueprint for the
polytechnics, Blunkett defended media studies and launched the two-
year foundation degrees that were seen as the engine of further expansion, while setting out higher education's role in the knowledge economy
and placing it in the context of globalisation. An important part of the

message was that Labour's expanded higher education system would not be of the ivory tower variety, but would serve the economy with modern, vocational courses, many of which would be delivered in the workplace.

Surprisingly, however, Blunkett immediately eclipsed his own speech with a scarcely coded warning at the subsequent press briefing about the dangers of top-up fees. They would not be imposed while he was Education Secretary, he volunteered after ignoring the topic in his speech, but he would not be Education Secretary for ever. There could have been no clearer indication of the struggle that was taking place at the top of government and which would dominate education policy in Blair's second term. Blunkett had accepted the inevitability of tuition fees in 1997, but fought a successful rearguard action against taking the next step towards American levels of payment. He did not believe that universities or the Treasury could fund bursaries on the scale necessary to preserve access for students from low-income families. Against the expectations of many around him, Blunkett even won a manifesto promise that Labour would not introduce top-up fees in the next Parliament. But the commitment for the longer term would barely survive his departure from the Education Department and, ironically, it was the unpopularity of the original fees regime that hastened the arrival of higher charges.

The second term

Blair returned from the 2001 election campaign shocked at the antipathy that he had encountered towards tuition fees. In another unexpected intervention, he used his party conference speech to announce joint Treasury/Education Department reviews of student support and higher education funding.[13] Hasty briefing suggested that among the options was the return of universal student grants, an indication of the confusion surrounding the announcement, rather than any realistic assessment of the likely outcome. Months of in-fighting followed, during which the overlapping nature of the reviews inevitably led to them merging and moving in the direction of top-up fees. The exercise might have started as a response to student poverty, but concerns for the state and future standing of the leading universities gradually took over. Andrew (now Lord) Adonis, Blair's main education adviser, and Roy Jenkins, Chancellor of Oxford University and one of the Prime Minister's mentors, were instrumental in

---

[13] Ben Russell, 'Review of University Tuition Fees Ordered in Drive to Attract Working-class Students', *The Independent*, 3 October 2001.

convincing him that there was no alternative to top-up fees if British universities were to compete with their much richer American rivals. And the fees should be variable so that the best universities could charge more than the rest and also distinguish between different courses if they chose. The private returns from a university degree were sufficient to justify a more substantial contribution from the student, it was argued, as long as higher education remained affordable for those of limited means.

But the early fee models suggested that Blunkett's concerns on this score had been well-founded. Students would continue to pay upfront and the threshold for fee waivers would be much lower than in the original fee regime. Estelle Morris, who had replaced Blunkett as Education Secretary, was not opposed to higher fees, but was uncomfortable with the idea of the state paying more to support some students than others and worried that the scheme, as proposed, would further limit access. She warned Blair that such proposals would be unacceptable to many Labour MPs and supporters of the party in the country, pressing instead for the original fee to be doubled and support for needy students to be maintained. When Morris resigned, in September 2002, it was over her own assessment of her stewardship of her department in the wake of controversies over A levels, individual learning accounts and primary school tests. But some of her colleagues still believe that fees would have pushed her to the brink if she had not gone then.

Charles Clarke, Morris's successor, immediately put down a marker for what were to be tough negotiations with the Treasury by letting it be known that he had been 'attracted' by the idea of a graduate tax, although he had an open mind on the subject. Since Adonis and the No. 10 team had been championing fees, while Gordon Brown was said to favour a graduate tax, the suggestion was political dynamite. Blair wanted universities to set their own fees and keep the income, while Brown naturally preferred a system that would keep the Treasury in control. At a breakfast meeting at *The Guardian*'s offices, Brown painted top-up fees as a deterrent to working-class students and expressed doubts about universities' ability to manage the cash injection that fees would bring.[14]

Clarke may have appeared to be siding with the Brown camp, but his real purpose was to ensure that any new system included a switch from upfront charges to income-contingent repayment after graduation. Having secured a delay in the promised November publication of a White

---

[14] Patrick Wintour, 'Chancellor at Odds with Blair over Top-up Fees', *The Guardian* p. 1, 20 November 2002.

Paper, Clarke eventually achieved not only the deferred payment model, but also a much more generous package of student grants and bursaries. By the time the White Paper was published in January 2003, the maximum fee had also been limited to a comparatively modest £3,000 a year. [15] This fell far short of what some of the more prestigious universities were demanding – Sir Richard Sykes, Rector of Imperial College London had told his governors that at least £10,500 a year would be needed for under-graduate courses to break even[16] – and even in the run-up to publication of the White Paper, £5,000 a year was a live option. Behind-the-scenes advice from the Higher Education Funding Council for England was that £3,000 a year was unlikely to produce the market that Blair desired, but this was considered to be the most that Labour MPs would support.

In the event, both judgements proved to be correct. Both the Conservatives and Liberal Democrats opposed the proposals at the heart of the Higher Education Bill, while more than 100 Labour back-benchers eventually signed an Early Day Motion condemning variable fees. The Lib Dems had opposed fees in all their guises and, while many Conservatives found their party's stance opportunistic and inconsistent with its free market principles, few Tory MPs were prepared to help save the government's skin. There followed months of explanation, argument and arm-twisting in the Labour ranks. Backbenchers disliked the princi-ple of top-up fees and, although the scheme would not be implemented until the following parliament, many felt that the Bill breached their manifesto commitment. A number of concessions were made, including the proposed establishment of an Office of Fair Access to protect the interests of low-income families. Although cast as a politically correct ogre on the Tory benches and in the press, Oftoff (as critics labelled the agency) proved to be a distraction, making almost no impact on the way in which fees were introduced on the ground.

Although feelings over fees ran high in the Labour Party, there is no doubt that anger over Iraq helped stoke up opposition to the Bill. The issue became a proxy for wider political concerns as prominent allies of Gordon Brown – some with little track record of involvement in education debates – emerged among the leading rebels. Brown made an eleventh-hour appeal to his supporters to back the Bill and was cred-ited with saving it when Nick Brown, the former Chief Whip and close

---

[15] The Future of Higher Education, Cm. 5735, p. 9.
[16] Rebecca Smithers, 'Leak Reveals University Plan to Levy £10,500 Fees', The Guardian, 18 October 2002.

confidant of his namesake, switched sides on the morning of the vote. Even then, the result could hardly have been closer. Clarke made one more concession (a review after three years) and Alan Johnson delivered a crucial handful of waverers with a well-judged closing speech. But Hilary Armstrong, then Chief Whip, warned Blair that the vote would be lost and, even as MPs filed through the lobbies, the Prime Minister was consulting Johnson on which of them would call for a subsequent vote of confidence. Victory by only five votes for a party with a majority of 161 was so precarious that even the committee stage and final reading could not be taken for granted, although the Bill was never in such danger again.

Top-up fees were no panacea for the hard-pressed universities, which were required to hand back up to a third of the extra income in bursaries. Those with high research costs dismissed them as a drop in the ocean, while even Clarke put the total income from fees at only £1 billion a year when Dearing had put higher education's funding shortfall at £9 billion.[17] But an important principle had been established and Brown also guaranteed that fee income would be in addition to the normal increases in government grant, set for the first year at 6% in real terms. When the fees were finally introduced, in September 2006, applications dropped – but only in comparison with the unusually high figures in the previous year, when many mature students brought forward their study plans to avoid the higher charges. By the second year of the scheme, new records were being set for applications and even some of the critics had to admit that students were taking the change in their stride.[18] The 50% target (now reduced to 'working towards' this level) was still a long way off and the policy of widening participation among under-represented socio-economic groups was no further forward, but neither had it been blown completely off course, as many had predicted. As revolutions go, top-up fees proved less than earth-shaking, but the battles of 2004 may turn out to have long-term significance.

Beyond fees

From outside the university world, it may feel as if tuition fees and the expansion of student numbers were the sum total of Blair's achievements

[17] House of Commons Education and Skills Committee, Oral Evidence, 14 January 2004.
[18] Peter Knight, 'Why We Should All Think like 17-year-olds', *Education Guardian*, 17 April 2007.

in higher education – and they certainly were the dominant themes. But a few other initiatives – some successful and others not – deserve at least passing examination. Like other areas of public policy, higher education was by no means exempt from the spin and exaggeration for which New Labour became notorious. In this field, however, the more grandiose the description, the more prone it was to failure. Three government-sponsored 'universities' were created, for example, but none survives in its original form. The University for Industry – more a creature of Brown than Blair – never focused on university-level courses and only became a mass provider of adult education when it switched to the 'learn direct' rubric. The lesson was not learned with the NHS University, which was wound up in 2005 after a brief attempt to expand and coordinate health service training. In between came the UKeU, an e-learning consortium announced in David Blunkett's Greenwich speech, which closed in 2004 after spending some £50 million and attracting a mere 900 students worldwide.

To some extent, the same could be said of foundation degrees, another feature of the Greenwich speech. Much more like Higher National Diplomas than degrees, they were a further example of the misconception that changing an educational label could transform the status of unglamorous products. By April 2007, there were more than 40,000 applications for foundation degrees, but many were for courses that were substitutes for diplomas. Although growing in popularity and consistent with the government's desire to expand workplace learning, foundation degrees would not make the contribution originally anticipated to meeting Blair's 50% participation target.

The institutional map continued to change as well, although less dramatically than under the Tories' promotion of the polytechnics. Charles Clarke created a new category of teaching universities, dropping the traditional insistence on research and allowing smaller colleges to apply for enhanced status. By 2007, almost a dozen colleges had joined the universities' ranks and more were poised to follow. They included the first universities for more than 100 years to have formal religious associations, in former Church of England teacher training colleges.

Some of the other higher education initiatives of the Blair years remain works in progress. A rash of committees followed the 2003 White Paper, on subjects such as fairer admissions, reducing bureaucracy, and boosting universities' endowments. There was some progress subsequently in reducing red tape and encouraging more systematic fundraising by universities, but the centrepiece of admissions reform –

post-A-level applications – was watered down and still had not been finalised when Blair left office. Overall regulation certainly increased over the decade, although a lighter touch was applied in some areas – notably quality assurance, where published reports on every subject area were discontinued in England and Northern Ireland when the first round was completed in 2001. Wales had already taken this step, while Scotland continued with less burdensome reports, demonstrating the increasing differences between the home countries after devolution.

In two areas of higher education policy that were particularly important to Blair, however, there was a UK-wide approach. The first was even given the title of the Prime Minister's Initiative when it was launched in 1999, challenging universities and further education colleges to increase the number of students from outside the EU to 75,000 by 2005. The target was met a year ahead of schedule and a second phase, seeking another 100,000 students, was launched in 2006. Although the sums of money committed to the initiative were relatively small, Blair's involvement sent beneficial signals to overseas governments and immigration authorities. While the policy may have tapped into a global trend, increased reliance on overseas student fees represented a significant change in the economy of UK higher education during his period in office.

The other major concern for both Blair and Brown was the ability of leading UK universities to compete internationally in research. This, both men agreed, could only be done effectively by further concentrating research funds on a small proportion of universities. Labour inherited the Research Assessment Exercise, which involved panels of senior academics sitting in judgement on their peers' work. Although expensive, it had the effect of channelling researchers towards the leading departments, which were rewarded with both the status and the funding to recruit the best before the exercise was repeated. Charles Clarke would have taken concentration still further, identifying a small institutional elite, rather than allowing departments from all universities to compete, but his White Paper instead demanded a (short-lived) extra category of sustained excellence. Throughout the Blair years, the RAE was accused of distorting universities' priorities because no similar pool of money existed to reward good teaching. But it was not until 2006 that the Treasury, which had protected research funding to a surprising degree and promised much more for science, intervened to demand a less cumbersome system.

The Opposition

However moderate the achievements, there was a certain consistency in Labour's higher education policy in the ten years following 1997. Successive models of tuition fees established the principle of co-payment by graduates for degree courses, expansion of opportunity was a constant demand and research funding was protected and concentrated. The same could not be said of the Opposition, at least where the Conservative Party was concerned. The Liberal Democrats stuck by their promise to avoid fees through taxation – initially from their planned extra penny on income tax and later from enhanced rates for high earners only – although they wavered over the desirability of further expansion of student numbers. The Conservatives, by contrast, had three different policies in four years and were heading for another as Blair retired from office.

Having (like Labour) avoided the need for a detailed policy in 1997 by subscribing to the Dearing Review, the Tories went into the 2001 election promising large sums to endow an unspecified number of universities and set them free from state control. Credited to Michael Portillo, as Shadow Chancellor, the plan was to use the income from the sale of mobile telephone licences and future privatisations to provide as many endowments as could be afforded for universities that would agree not to raise fees. Since this was the very freedom that most of the likely contenders wanted, and there was no certainty how many universities could be released from the shackles of the state, the approach did not survive long into the next parliament. By May 2003, Iain Duncan Smith was promising to scrap fees altogether, call a halt to expansion and purge 'Mickey Mouse degrees'. Michael Howard, as his successor, was expected to drop Tory opposition to fees but, perhaps because of the perceived popularity of the party's stance among middle-class voters, set about modifying it instead. The Conservatives went into the 2005 election still promising to halt expansion, scrap the Office for Fair Access and abolish fees, but admitting that interest rates on student loans would have to go up instead. Only when David Cameron arrived as leader did the party accept top-up fees and recognise that limiting access to higher education conflicted with Tory principles of freedom of the individual. Although still to be finalised, Conservative policy – as in schools – began to look remarkably similar to Labour's.

Blair or Brown?

The two dominant figures of New Labour may have fallen out over top-up fees and had different priorities for the expansion of higher education, but there was more consensus over the general direction of policy than in many areas. Although he has declared that education will be the 'passion' of his government, Brown's public pronouncements on the universities have been few and far between. There have been notable exceptions, such as his intervention in the Laura Spence affair, but in most respects he can be judged on actions rather than words. While access to higher education has been an important part of his agenda for social justice, scientific and medical research has been his priority – with a predictable accent on the contribution to economic prosperity. From the review of science and engineering skills that he commissioned from the late Sir Gareth Roberts to Richard Lambert's report on universities' links with business and industry, Brown has acted independently, but without suggesting a likely departure from the direction of travel over the past ten years. Indeed, he conceded at the launch of a pamphlet by Lambert on European universities that the 1.1% share of gross domestic product spent on higher education would have to rise. With the proportion in the US already at 2.6%, he was prepared to 'enter debate' on increasing public funding and to consider an increase in the £3,000 cap on top-up fees after 2009.[19]

Blair, by contrast, has set out his vision for universities on several occasions, notably in a speech to the Institute for Public Policy Research on the eve of voting on the Higher Education Bill. This perhaps came closest to explaining why he was prepared to risk everything for top-up fees. Higher education, he said, was 'as important to our society and economy as the big "extractive" industries of the past – and just as important to our nation's future in providing the raw material, in terms of skills and innovation, that individuals and whole industries will require to succeed'.[20] Explaining away the contrast with Labour's 2001 manifesto pledge not to introduce top-up fees, he described a 'learning process' that had taken place over the previous two years, ignoring his responsibility for the sector over the four years before that. However, he did admit that he had been wrong to reject Dearing's proposed package of grants and fees.

[19] Toby Helm, 'University Fees Likely to Rise, Says Brown', *Daily Telegraph*, 6 June 2006.
[20] Tony Blair, 'A Fair Future For All: Labour's University Reforms', 14 January 2004.

Blair's emphasis on universities' central role in the knowledge economy was characteristic of his government's largely utilitarian view of higher education. Charles Clarke became embroiled in controversy after suggesting that universities could no longer rely on the 'medieval concept' of a community of scholars to justify substantial state investment and now had to demonstrate that they were contributing to national prosperity. Once Blair had been convinced that a step change in funding was necessary to unlock the potential to make that contribution effectively – and that variable fees represented the only feasible route – what he saw as Old Labour opposition only stiffened his resolve. He might not have persevered if he had known that the risk of defeat was quite so great, but the influence of Iraq made such fine margins almost impossible to predict accurately. For all the delays, there was never a point at which he considered withdrawing the reforms.

The legacy

For many in higher education, whether students or staff, the Blair years were a disappointment. Students felt betrayed by the imposition of tuition fees, while staff felt undervalued and expected more investment, particularly in the early years of Blair's premiership. But, although there was no return to pre-Thatcher staffing levels and the pressures of expansion continued to change the student experience, universities were in a better state after ten years of Labour government than in 1997. With a new-found confidence that belied ministerial doubts about their managerial competence, universities made their own inroads into Dearing's £9 billion backlog of capital projects. Few of the growing number of universities were without their prestige building project in 2007, usually funded by their own borrowing rather than government grant. Student numbers had continued to grow and UK universities' international standing remained high: fledgling international rankings showed the leading universities second only to their richer American rivals for research excellence.

Blair's policies had imposed seemingly irreconcilable strains on the higher education system, seeking to ensure preferential treatment for those at the top of the research tree while demanding both expansion and an intake that was more socially diverse at all types of university. Yet the sector survived intact, with little evidence of the social engineering that became a media obsession and occupying a more prominent position in the life of the nation. The outlook for the post-Blair era may be no more comfortable, particularly as the number of 18-year-olds begins to decline in England: universities will continue to play second fiddle to schools in any government's spending priorities and the cap on top-up fees will almost certainly remain lower than many would like. But higher education is now recognised as a global market in which the UK is a leading player.

Inevitably, Blair's premiership will be remembered in higher education mainly for top-up fees. Judged by his original aims of creating a market that would bring significant benefits to Oxbridge and the other leading universities, they cannot yet be seen as a success. But the reform changed the character of higher education in England with minimal disruption and will no doubt pave the way to more substantial change in years to come.

PART IV

Wider relations

22

The national question

IAIN MCLEAN

Introduction

The more perceptive tributes to Tony Blair on his retirement stressed how *Gladstonian* he was. Up to a point. Like W. E. Gladstone, the towering figure of late nineteenth-century politics, Tony Blair was driven by religious conviction. Like Gladstone, he pursued a liberal interventionist foreign policy. Gladstone demanded that the Turks should be driven bag and baggage out of Bulgaria. His biggest foreign-policy disaster was the death in Khartoum in 1885 of General Gordon, who had been pursuing an (actually unauthorised) campaign against an Islamist insurgent.

Gladstone announced in 1868, when invited to take office for the first time, 'My mission is to pacify Ireland', before returning to chop down a tree at his north Wales estate. Like him, Tony Blair drew his core support from the peripheral regions of the UK – Scotland, Wales and northern England. Like Gladstone, Tony Blair carried out his mission to pacify Ireland. The last month of his premiership saw the utterly improbable sight of Ian Paisley and Martin McGuinness laughing out loud as they prepared to take power together in Northern Ireland (see chapter 23). Unlike Gladstone, Tony Blair had no particular empathy with northern Britain, except perhaps in Sedgefield, Co. Durham. As shown in other chapters of this book, New Labour had to conquer southern England to govern, and Tony Blair's true mission was to pacify Isleworth. Other New Labour figures – Gordon Brown, John Prescott – stood for Labour's northern English and Celtic bases.

As many commentators have remarked, the huge constitutional changes that occurred in Scotland and Wales during Tony Blair's time came almost casually. Blair showed some interest in process, but very little in policy. Devolution was a policy he inherited.

Scotland and Wales in 1994

That New Labour came to power in 1997 committed to devolving power
to Scotland and Wales was the work of three people – Blair's predecessor
John Smith, and his leaders in Scotland and Wales, Donald Dewar and
Ron Davies. Of these, Smith and Dewar truly believed in devolution in
and for itself. John Smith had been Devolution Minister during the
Callaghan Labour government's failed attempt to grant devolution to
Scotland and Wales between 1976 and 1979. Donald Dewar's promotion
had been blocked by the fiercely anti-devolution Willie Ross, Labour's
Scottish Secretary up to 1976. Ron Davies was a late and reluctant
convert. Dewar and Davies recognised that devolution could bring electoral advantage, but must be handled carefully. In this Dewar was much
more successful than Davies.[1]

Dangerously called the Callaghan government's 'flagship' policy, devolution was holed below the waterline in February 1977. A group of
Labour backbenchers, led from the north-east of England, killed the original Scotland and Wales Bill by combining with the opposition to defeat a
timetable (guillotine) motion. As the Geordie[2] rebels saw it, a Labour
government was proposing to reward the Scots for voting SNP (Scottish
National Party) and punish the Geordies for voting Labour. They had a
point. Labour's turn to devolution had occurred between the two elections of 1974. Labour politicians in London then suddenly realised that
expected SNP gains could damage both the Union and Labour's chances
of forming a government. It usually depended on Scotland for its majority. In October 1974, the SNP won 30% of the vote in Scotland, but only
eleven of Scotland's seventy-two seats. It would only take a few percentage points more in the popular vote, which it was getting in 1975 polls, for
the electoral system to flip from punishing the SNP to rewarding it. On as
little as 35% of the Scottish vote, evenly spread, the SNP would have won
a majority of the seats in Scotland under the Westminster first-past-the-
post system. Therefore the Scots had to be bought off.[3]

[1] For John Smith (1938–94) and Donald Dewar (1937–2000), see their respective entries in
the *Oxford Dictionary of National Biography* on-line at www.oxforddnb.com. Ron Davies
stood down from the National Assembly in 2003. He later left the Labour Party. In 2007 he
ran as an independent in his former constituency, coming third.
[2] Inhabitant of Tyneside. Perhaps from the name of George Stephenson who was born in
Wylam, near Newcastle.
[3] For full details see Iain McLean and Alistair McMillan, *State of the Union* (Oxford: Oxford
University Press, 2005), pp. 160–70.

This was ancient politics. It was what Unionist and Conservative governments had been doing in Ireland, later in Northern Ireland, since 1886, and in Scotland since 1918. In Ireland, it was called 'killing Home Rule with kindness'. It failed to kill Home Rule, and most of Ireland became independent in 1921. But it continued to work in Scotland and what was left of Ireland. As a result, in 1977 public spending per head in Scotland was higher than in the northern region of England, although Scotland was richer and (the Geordies maintained) the north of England had problems of social deprivation just as severe as Scotland's. Nothing has changed – see table 22.4 below.

The damaged Callaghan flagship ploughed on, but sank in sight of port, taking its whole company with it. The Bill was split into separate Bills for Scotland and Wales. Further Labour backbench rebellions imposed two more hurdles. First, devolution was not to be ratified unless confirmed by a referendum in the relevant territory. Second, in those referenda, devolution was not to be ratified unless 40% of the electorate voted for it. This was splendid hypocrisy, as far fewer than 40% of the electorate had voted for the then (or any other post-war) government. It worked for the rebels. Welsh devolution crashed to an 80/20 defeat. Scottish devolution was narrowly carried in the referendum, but the Yes vote fell far, far short of the 40% threshold. In March 1979, the fading SNP had to challenge the government in a confidence motion. This was when the now hackneyed phrase 'turkeys voting for Christmas' first appeared in UK political speech. The government lost the confidence motion by one vote, forcing the 1979 general election. Margaret Thatcher's victory in that election killed devolution stone dead.

Or so it seemed. The entire Scottish political class had been preparing for devolution for five years. When the incoming government abruptly dismissed it, nothing happened. This signalled that the demand for devolution had been broad but not deep. Probably, it was mostly a demand for more – more of whatever was going. It was rational for the Scots to demand that, and rational for the UK government to concede it.

However, at the ensuing Conservative general election victories in 1983 and 1987, the party's relative position in Scotland weakened. After a revolt by people in big houses facing sharp rate increases, the Conservatives had piloted the community charge ('poll tax') in Scotland ahead of England. In 1987, all the Scottish ministers involved in introducing the poll tax there lost their seats. This was probably coincidence – the poll tax disaster had barely begun to register with the electorate at the time. But by

1989, with this and other causes of resentment against Margaret Thatcher bubbling up, the fact that unpopular policies were being imposed by a government that held only ten of the seventy-two seats started to register. The SNP, with three MPs, denounced Scottish Labour MPs as the 'Feeble Fifty'. A collection of Scots worthies formed a Scottish Constitutional Convention, supported by Donald Dewar and the Labour and Liberal Democrat parties, but not the Conservatives or the SNP. The Constitutional Convention reported in 1995. It recommended a 129-seat Scottish Parliament, comprising one first-past-the-post MSP from each Westminster constituency and regional lists crafted so that the overall party balance was proportionate to the regional votes cast. This is the Additional Member System (AMS), as also practised in Germany and New Zealand, which was to flummox many commentators in 2007. The parliament was to have the power to vary the standard rate of income tax up or down by 3p in the pound. But the basic block of money for public spending on devolved services would continue to be an un-earmarked grant from the Treasury to Scotland, calculated under the existing Barnett formula (explained below). The Convention therefore proposed that the Scots should – at least mostly – spend tax revenues that other people raised.[4]

Wales was different. It always is. The 1979 referendum had shown up a cruel gulf between Welsh-speaking and English-speaking Wales. People in the first wanted to protect their language and culture, and supported devolution. People in the second – about 80% of Wales – saw the language more as a threat than as an opportunity. Quietly constructive language policies, and a lot of killing with kindness in the shape of the huge subsidies from mostly English taxpayers to S4C (Sianel Pedwar Cymru, the Welsh-language public TV station), had defused the politics of language by the mid-1990s. However, the hegemonic Labour Party in Wales included many politicians who saw devolution as a distraction. This may have been for low reasons of wanting to keep their seats, and/or for the high reasons articulated by Labour's most charismatic Welshman Aneurin (Nye) Bevan (1897–1960). In Bevan's view, socialism was about redistribution from the rich, wherever they lived, to the poor, wherever they lived. The task of a socialist movement was to seize the levers of power and ensure that the redistribution took place. In this perspective,

[4] For the Constitutional Convention, see *ibid.*, pp. 172–3. For the poll tax in Scotland, see D. Butler, A. Adonis and T. Travers, *Failure in British Government: The Politics of the Poll Tax* (Oxford: Oxford University Press, 1994), pp. 129–36.

devolution to poor regions of the UK was at best pointless and at worst counter-productive.

So when John Smith died suddenly in 1994, there existed a blueprint for devolution in Scotland, which he had publicly backed. There was nothing in Wales. Between then and Labour's victory in 1997 the plans had to be worked up. There is no evidence that Tony Blair took an active part before the 1997 election campaign. He left it to Dewar and Davies, with the English implications to be left for later. Donald Dewar's task was easy, as he had a blueprint to hand. He had himself been one of the initiators of the Constitutional Convention. The arrangements in the Scotland Act 1998 are exactly as proposed by the Constitutional Convention – both in what they enact (especially electoral reform and the division of responsibility between Edinburgh and London) and in what they overlook (finance, and representation of Scotland at Westminster). Some people, less far-sighted than Dewar, complained that the AMS electoral system would deprive Labour of a majority in the Scottish Parliament. Dewar himself described it as 'the best example of charitable giving this century in politics'.[5] However, its true purpose was to deprive the *SNP* of a majority in the Scottish Parliament. Dewar had absorbed the lesson of the near-miss of 1974 and 1975. In the Scottish Parliament, the SNP cannot win a majority of seats unless it gets almost 50% of the vote. Therefore, Scottish independence has many thresholds to cross.

Ron Davies had the heirs of Nye Bevan to fight. They included Neil Kinnock, the Welsh leader of the Labour Party before Smith, still very influential in Wales. With no constitutional convention to guide him, Davies settled for the most that the factions in the Welsh Labour Party could agree on. This was an assembly that would have the powers to make secondary but not primary legislation in devolved areas. Secondary legislation means statutory instruments issued under Acts of Parliament. If the National Assembly wanted something that required an Act of Parliament, it must ask the UK government and House of Commons for it.

In 1996–7 Tony Blair made his only direct interventions into Scottish and Welsh devolution. In 1996, he and George Robertson (the shadow Secretary of State for Scotland: Dewar had temporarily moved to social security) insisted that there would be not one but two referendum questions on the Constitutional Convention proposals. The first would ask

---

[5] *Parliamentary Debates*, vol. CCCXII, 6 May 1998, col. 803.

whether voters wanted a Scottish Parliament; the second whether they agreed with the 3p-in-the-pound tax power. In the 1997 election campaign, Blair went further. Visiting Edinburgh a month before polling day, he told the political correspondent of *The Scotsman*:

> '[S]overeignty rests with me as an English MP and that's the way it will stay'. Mr Blair also ruled out the use of a Scottish Parliament's tax-varying powers, which he likened to those of an English parish council, in the first term of a Labour government . . . [H]is five-year pledge of no rise in the basic and standard rates of tax applied to 'Scotland as well as England'.[6]

Alex Salmond, the SNP leader, accused Blair of burying the Claim of Right (the summary of the Constitutional Convention). What indeed was the point of offering a 3p-in-the-pound tax and then promising not to use it?

However self-contradictory, Blair's actions held off a Conservative threat to make the 'tartan tax' an effective slogan. In the 1997 general election, the Conservatives were wiped out in both Wales and Scotland. The first-past-the-post electoral system had its usual exaggerative effects. Table 22.1 shows the votes and seats won by the parties in Scotland and Wales at each election between 1997 and 2007.

The referenda took place in September 1997. Both the parliament and its tax powers were comfortably ratified in Scotland. In Wales it was a damn close-run thing. In fact the *No*es were ahead all night, until the final county to report – Carmarthen, a Welsh-speaking rural area – swung it for *Yes*. The data are in table 22.2.

The Scottish result proved that devolution was, as Smith had claimed, 'the settled will of the Scottish people'. The Welsh result proved that it was anything but the settled will of the Welsh people. However, devolution is path-dependent. Once it has arrived, it stays. The Conservatives, who opposed it, have adapted to it in both countries. Their PR systems give the Conservatives seats that they cannot win at Westminster (table 22.1). All the lobby groups on domestic policy now split their operations among London, Edinburgh and Cardiff. The Scottish Parliament and the National Assembly for Wales, constituted by the Scotland Act and the Government of Wales Act 1998, came into existence in 1999. They were to have fixed terms of four years. Table 22.3 gives the details of each

---

[6] J. Penman, 'Real Power Will Stay with MPs in England, Blair Tells Scotland', *The Scotsman*, 4 April 1997.

assembly. Details for 2007 are the latest available, as this chapter went to press in mid-May, two weeks after the elections.

The rapid turnover of First Ministers has many causes, but only one is relevant to this chapter.[7] Tony Blair disapproved of Rhodri Morgan, who would have succeeded Davies in 1997 or 1998 if individual Labour Party members in Wales had had their way. Instead, Blair used the party's machinery and trade union block votes to impose Alun Michael as First Minister. However, Michael resigned in 2000 ahead of a vote of confidence in the National Assembly which Labour lost, to be replaced by Morgan. Tony Blair admitted, 'I got that judgment wrong. Essentially you have got to let go of it with devolution.'[8] It took him three years to realise that.

Scotland and Wales in 2007

By May 2007, Scotland and Wales had had three national elections each (tables 22.1 and 22.3). In Scotland, Labour governed jointly with the Liberal Democrats in the first two parliaments. In 2007, the SNP gained a one-seat plurality over Labour and formed a minority administration with Green support. The two parties together hold only 49 of the 129 seats, and there is one nationalist-leaning independent. In Wales, Labour has always governed, usually in a minority or with Liberal Democrat support (for part of the first Assembly).

So the first thing to evaluate is the effect of the electoral system. Tony Blair is no friend of proportional representation (and nor is Gordon Brown, at least for the House of Commons). And yet he was content to have PR embedded in the Scotland and Wales Acts (as it is, for quite different reasons, in Northern Ireland: see chapter 23).

As already noted, PR for Scotland was a product of Donald Dewar's statecraft. It has blocked the possibility of the SNP declaring a victory for

---

[7] For narratives of the progress of devolution in Scotland and Wales, see Iain McLean, 'The National Question', in A. Seldon (ed.), *The Blair Effect: The Blair Government 1997–2001* (London: Little, Brown, 2001), pp. 429–47, and 'The National Question', in A. Seldon and D. Kavanagh (eds.), *The Blair Effect 2001–5* (Cambridge: Cambridge University Press, 2005), pp. 339–61; and A. Trench (ed.), *Has Devolution Made a Difference? The State of the Nations 2004* (Exeter: Imprint Academic, 2004). The Trench volume summarises the quarterly monitoring reports from the Constitution Unit, University College, London, since 2001. For the latest available see www.ucl.ac.uk/constitution-unit/research/devolution/devo-monitoring-programme.html.

[8] *The Observer*, 9 April 2000, as quoted by Lewis Baston, 'The Party System', in Seldon, *Blair Effect*, p. 166.

Table 22.1. Votes and seats in Scotland and Wales, 1997–2007

Scotland

	House of Commons 1997				Scottish Parliament 1999				House of Commons 2001			
	Vote Share	Seats	Seat Share	Seat/Vote	Vote Share	Seats	Seat Share	Seat/Vote	Vote Share	Seats	Seat Share	Seat/Vote
Labour	45.6	56	77.8	1.71	36.2	56	43.4	1.20	43.9	56	77.8	1.77
Lib Dem	13.0	10	13.9	1.07	13.3	17	13.2	0.99	16.4	10	13.9	0.85
SNP	22.1	6	8.3	0.38	28.0	35	27.1	0.97	20.1	5	6.9	0.35
Conservative	17.5	0	0.0	0.00	15.5	18	14.0	0.90	15.6	1	1.4	0.09
Other	1.8	0	0.0	0.00	7.0	3	2.3	0.33	4.0	0	0.0	0.00
	100.0	72	100.0		100.0	129	100.0		100.0	72	100.0	

Wales

	House of Commons 1997				National Assembly 1999				House of Commons 2001			
	Vote Share	Seats	Seat Share	Seat/Vote	Vote Share	Seats	Seat Share	Seat/Vote	Vote Share	Seats	Seat Share	Seat/Vote
Labour	54.7	34	85.0	1.55	36.6	28	46.7	1.28	48.6	34	85.0	1.75
Lib Dem	12.4	2	5.0	0.40	13.0	6	10.0	0.77	13.8	2	5.0	0.36
Plaid Cymru	9.9	4	10.0	1.01	29.5	17	28.3	0.96	14.3	4	10.0	0.70
Conservative	19.6	0	0.0	0.00	16.2	9	15.0	0.93	21.0	0	0.0	0.00
Other	3.4	0	0.0	0.00	4.8	0	0.0	0.00	2.3	0	0.0	0.00
	100.0	40	100.0		100.0	60	100.0		100.0	40	100.0	

Scotland

	Scottish Parliament 2003				House of Commons 2005				Scottish Parliament 2007			
	Vote Share	Seats	Seat Share	Seat/Vote	Vote Share	Seats	Seat Share	Seat/Vote	Vote Share	Seats	Seat Share	Seat/Vote
Labour	32.0	50	38.8	1.21	39.5	41	69.5	1.76	30.7	46	35.7	1.16
Lib Dem	13.6	17	13.2	0.97	22.6	11	18.6	0.82	13.8	16	12.4	0.90
SNP	22.4	27	20.9	0.94	17.7	6	10.2	0.57	32.0	47	36.4	1.14
Conservative	16.1	18	14.0	0.87	15.8	1	1.7	0.11	15.3	17	13.2	0.86
Other	16.1	17	13.2	0.82	4.4	0	0.0	0.00	8.3	3	2.3	0.28
	100.0	129	100.0		100.0	59	100.0		100.0	129	100.0	

Wales

	National Assembly 2003				House of Commons 2005				National Assembly 2007			
	Vote Share	Seats	Seat Share	Seat/Vote	Vote Share	Seats	Seat Share	Seat/Vote	Vote Share	Seats	Seat Share	Seat/Vote
Labour	38.3	30	50.0	1.31	42.7	29	72.5	1.70	30.9	26	43.3	1.40
Lib Dem	13.4	6	10.0	0.75	18.4	4	10.0	0.54	13.3	6	10.0	0.75
Plaid Cymru	20.5	12	20.0	0.98	12.6	3	7.5	0.60	21.7	15	25.0	1.15
Conservative	19.6	11	18.3	0.94	21.4	3	7.5	0.35	21.9	12	20.0	0.91
Other	8.3	1	1.7	0.20	4.9	1	2.5	0.51	12.3	1	1.7	0.14
	100.0	60	100.0		100.0	40	100.0		100.0	60	100.0	

Notes: Vote share in Scottish Parliament and National Assembly for Wales: unweighted average of constituency vote and list vote for each party

Sources: BBC Election websites 2001, 2005, 2007; Electoral Commission; Constitution Unit; A. Trench (ed.), 'Has Devolution Made a Difference? The State of the Nations 2004' (Exeter: Imprint Academic, 2004), Fig. 4.7

Table 22.2. Scotland and Wales: referendum results, 1997

	Yes to parliament	No to parliament	Yes to tax powers	No to tax powers	Turnout
Scotland 11.09.97	74.3	25.7	63.5	36.5	60.4
Wales 18.09.97	50.3	49.7	n/a	n/a	50.1

Table 22.3. The Scottish Parliament and National Assembly for Wales since 1999

Dates	Governing party	First Minister
Scottish Parliament 1999–2003	Labour–LD coalition	(1) Donald Dewar (Lab.) (2) Henry McLeish (Lab.) (3) Jack McConnell (Lab.)
Scottish Parliament 2003–7	Labour–LD coalition	Jack McConnell (Lab.)
Scottish Parliament 2007–11	SNP minority administration with Green support	Alex Salmond (SNP)
National Assembly for Wales 1999–2003	Lab minority administration, later Lab–LD coalition	(1) Ron Davies (Lab.) (2) Alun Michael (Lab.) (3) Rhodri Morgan (Lab.)
National Assembly for Wales 2003–7	Labour (in minority by end of parliament)	Rhodri Morgan (Lab.)
National Assembly for Wales 2007–11	Lab minority administration	Rhodri Morgan (Lab.)

Notes: For seat totals controlled by each party, see table 22.1. LD = Liberal Democrats.

independence after winning a majority of seats. The SNP is very like the Bloc and Parti Québecois, the separatist parties in Canada. Its popularity rises and falls as that of the locally dominant party falls and rises. But support for sovereign independence always runs behind support for the party.[9] In the 1992 Westminster election it campaigned for 'Scotland Free in Ninety-Three' and gained no seats. (It increased its share of the vote, but in the wrong places, and lost a by-election gain.) Alex Salmond, who first became leader in 1990, then downplayed independence (but kept out of the Constitutional Convention) and urged voters to support devolution in the 1997 referendum. The SNP's promise to hold a referendum on independence proved a sticking point in the 2007 coalition negotiations. A deal with the Liberal Democrats broke down on this point. There is nothing like a majority in the 2007 Scottish Parliament for an independence referendum, let alone for independence.

Plaid Cymru has never posed a comparable threat to the Union, being a cultural party which dominates the Welsh-speaking areas of Wales but has trouble elsewhere. Why then was PR imposed on Wales too? Principally for consistency and, as usual, as a bit of an afterthought. There was no blueprint for Welsh devolution in 1997. Everybody expected Labour to win more than half of the votes in Wales. In fact it never has done at a National Assembly election (table 22.1).

The electoral system is actually not fully proportional in either country. Figures 22.1 and 22.2 show the ratio of votes to seats for each party in each election since 1997. In a perfectly proportional system, the ratio would always approach 1.0, except for groups that were too small to win a seat at all.

Labour still wins from the AMS system. In both countries it has always won a higher share of seats than of votes, so its ratio is always above 1.0. The nationalist parties never fully benefited from AMS until 2007, when both rose above 1.0 for the first time. So the system promoted Labour (although not as much as first-past-the-post would have done) and failed to help the nationalists until 2007. Most importantly, it has fostered coalition government, either formally or informally. Minority governments (as in 2007) cannot enact the whole of their manifesto and must deal with other parties.

To a political scientist, the most important point about coalition government is that it reduces the *win set of the status quo*.[10] The win set is the set of points that can beat the status quo. At Westminster, that usually means 'whatever the governing party's whips can persuade their

[9] See McLean and McMillan, *State of the Union*, tables 8.3 and 8.11; John Curtice, 'Restoring Confidence and Legitimacy? Devolution and Public Opinion', in Trench, *Has Devolution Made a Difference?*, figure 9.8.
[10] George Tsebelis, *Veto Players: How Political Institutions Work* (Princeton, NJ: Princeton University Press, 2002), pp. 2, 8–9.

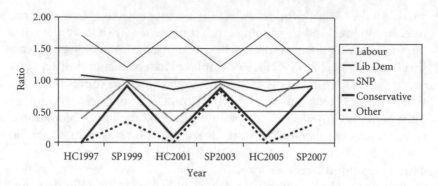

Figure 22.1. Seat/vote ratios in Scotland

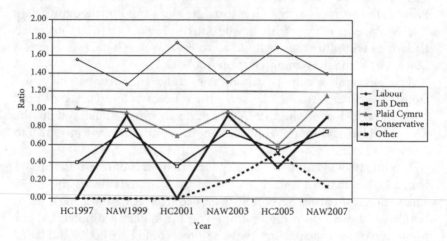

Figure 22.2. Seat/vote ratios in Wales

followers to vote for'. Therefore the win set, in a Westminster system, is large. This means that the governing party can make radical policy changes in any direction it likes, so long as it controls its own MPs and the House of Lords does not veto the change. Coalition government contracts the win set, because a majority requires support from more than one party. As a consequence, policy is more stable. Stability is neither good nor bad in itself, but merely a characteristic of the parliamentary setting. In their cross-national survey of the impact of constitutions on policy, Persson and Tabellini calculate that proportional regimes spend more on welfare policy and have higher budget deficits than majoritarian regimes such as the UK parliament. This, they argue, is because under PR there are more veto players who could veto any reduction of welfare benefits for their client groups.[11]

However, the situation in Scotland and Wales is more complicated. Both countries had new powers in 1999 to do things they could not do before. Therefore there could have been majorities that were suppressed before 1997, which could change policy radically even under a coalition government. In Scotland, there were. The Scottish Parliament has power to alter Scots law on domestic matters, and in some notable areas it has done so. It has abolished feudalism and 'poinding and warrant sales' (a form of recovery of assets from debtors). And it has established the right to roam in the countryside.[12] On the other hand, in the face of homophobic hostility, it ducked the opportunity to legislate for civil partnerships in Scotland, passing the parcel hastily to Westminster, which enacted a Scottish section in the Civil Partnerships Act 2004.

Policy initiatives in Wales have been more limited – by the National Assembly's powers among other things. The hurried design of the new institutions was radically faulty. The *primary legislation / secondary legislation* distinction completely fails to map on to the *reserved powers / devolved powers* distinction. Therefore, the Assembly lacks the legal power to do a lot of the things its majority might like to. The Assembly's Richard Commission recommended granting more powers to the National Assembly. The Government of Wales Act 2006 (2006 c.32),[13] a notable constitutional statute hardly noticed outside Wales, does some of this with effect from the National Assembly taking office in 2007. It abolishes the 'county council' model for Welsh government in the 1998 Act, and substitutes a 'government and opposition' model. It empowers the National Assembly to make quasi-Acts ('Assembly Measures') in the areas for which it is responsible. Devolution, as Ron Davies was fond of saying, is a process not an event, and the process will continue beyond the 2007 election in unpredictable ways.

---

[11] Torsten Persson and Guido Tabellini, *The Economic Effects of Constitutions* (Cambridge, MA: MIT Press, 2005), tables 6.4 and 6.7.

[12] Abolition of Feudal Tenure etc. (Scotland) Act 2000 asp 5; Abolition of Poindings and Warrant Sales Act 2001 asp 1; Land Reform (Scotland) Act 2003 asp 2.

[13] See the Assembly government's website explaining the Act at http://new.wales.gov.uk/ gowasub/gowa/?lang=en. For the Richard Commission on the Powers and Electoral Arrangements of the National Assembly for Wales (2004) and the former 'county council' model, see http://image.guardian.co.uk/sys-files/Politics/documents/2004/03/ 31/richard_commission.pdf and the Constitution Unit's Wales monitoring reports for 2004 and 2005.

However, over most of the domestic agenda, the changes made are more incremental than the abolition of feudalism and of poindings. And some important developments have been non-changes, where policy *has* changed in England.

The biggest incremental changes in Scotland have been two expensive spending commitments: the non-adoption of 'top-up' fees for university students domiciled in Scotland and the provision of free social care for the elderly. Both of these followed independent reports and were supported by coalition majorities.[14] They confirm Persson and Tabellini's claim that coalition government is associated with higher welfare spending. The Scots did both of these because they could: their formula funding, examined below, allowed up to 20% per head more spending on domestic services than in England.

Otherwise, policy change has arisen because the Scots and Welsh have not made changes that have been made in England. Neither Scotland nor Wales has league tables of school or hospital results, nor of local authority performance. Neither has introduced the quasi-market reforms of the NHS introduced in England during the second Blair administration (see chapter 18). On the whole, the results of policy divergence must be highly satisfying to Tony Blair. In England there has been much pain and many complaints from the providers of health and education. But, if the measurements can be trusted, standards have risen. Waiting times have dropped sharply, and school results have improved. In education, it is difficult to make comparisons, just because the Scots and Welsh have refused to publish league tables. But in health, they have stood still or gone backwards, even though more is spent per head on health in Wales and Scotland than in England as a whole, and (in Scotland) more than in any region of England except London. Victims of these disparities include National Assembly Health Minister Jane Hutt, although her sacking in 2005 was not directly linked to the relative failure of the NHS in Wales,[15] and three successive chief executives of the Welsh

---

[14] The (Scottish) Cubie Report on student finance, and the (UK) report of the Sutherland Royal Commission on social care, both published in 1999. The UK government rejected Sutherland's recommendation to make social care free for those whose medical condition required it, but the Scottish Executive accepted it. See Rachel Simeon, 'Free Personal Care: Policy Divergence and Social Citizenship', in Robert Hazell (ed.), *The State of the Nations 2003: The Third Year of Devolution in the United Kingdom* (Exeter: Imprint Academic, 2003), pp. 215–35. For full details of both policies, see the Scottish monitoring reports of the Constitution Unit.

[15] John Osmond (ed.), *Labour's Majority in Doubt: Monitoring the National Assembly December 2004 to April 2005* (Cardiff: IWA, and London: Constitution Unit, 2005), p. 10.

Ambulance Service, who resigned or were dismissed in quick succession in 2006.[16]

The two 'wicked issues' of devolution are finance and representation in the House of Commons. Before devolution, Scotland, Wales and Northern Ireland were each funded by a block grant from the UK Treasury. Since the early 1970s, this has been by way of the now-notorious 'Barnett formula'. It takes its name from Joel (Lord) Barnett, who was Chief Secretary to the Treasury from 1974 to 1979, although the Treasury was already using it under the previous Conservative government. Barnett served two purposes. It substituted a block grant for annual bargaining over each and every service, which the Treasury suspected the 'Celts' of using to force public spending up to an unacceptable level. In this they were backed by their territorial Secretaries of State as part of killing Home Rule by kindness. And it was designed to bring very gradual convergence towards equal public spending per head for each territory of the UK. In 1976 the Treasury also conducted a 'needs assessment' with the grudging agreement of the territorial departments. This showed that Scotland and Northern Ireland, but not Wales, were receiving public spending allocations for the services that would have been devolved under the (abortive) Scotland and Wales Bill(s) ahead of their 'needs'.

In the short run Barnett protects this relative overspending (although if the Treasury's numbers were reliable it should never have been applied to Wales). Therefore it made sense for the Constitutional Convention to say that it should continue. Its continuation was promised in the White Papers preceding the 1998 Scotland and Wales Acts, but is not in the Acts themselves, so it could be altered without legislation. In the long run, it would cause spending in Scotland and Wales to crash down below whatever their relative needs now are to a level equal per head to spending in England. This would not be fair, and would not be in the interests of either Wales or Scotland.[17]

In the long run, as Keynes said, we are all dead. However, the long run has not yet arrived. Barnett has been running for thirty years. But the

---

[16] 'Ambulance Reform "to Cost £140m"', BBC Wales, 26 September 2006, at http://news.bbc.co.uk/1/hi/wales/5378974.stm; Wales Audit Office, 'Ambulance Services in Wales', December 2006, www.wao.gov.uk/assets/englishdocuments/Ambulance_Inquiry.pdf. For a book length discussion of relative performance to 2003, see Scott Greer, *Territorial Politics and Health Policy: UK Health Policy in Comparative Perspective* (Manchester: Manchester University Press, 2004).

[17] This is a brutally concise summary. A whole book can be, and has been, written about the Barnett formula: Iain McLean, *The Fiscal Crisis of the United Kingdom* (Basingstoke: Palgrave, 2005).

Table 22.4. UK identifiable expenditure and relative GVA by country
and region, per head, 2005–6, excluding social protection

Region	£ per head	Index (UK=100)	Index GVA
Scotland	5,093	119.9	96
Wales	4,648	109.4	78
Northern Ireland	5,457	128.4	80
England:	4,099	96.5	102
North-east	4,530	106.6	79
North-west	4,415	103.9	88
Yorks and Humberside	4,109	96.7	87
E. Midlands	3,648	85.9	93
W. Midlands	3,947	92.9	89
E. England	3,475	81.8	107
London	5,288	124.5	136
South-east	3,578	84.2	115
South-west	3,747	88.2	94
UK	4,249	100.0	100

Source:
Cols. 1 and 2: Public Expenditure Statistical Analysis (London: HM Treasury
2007), calculated from table 9.11.
Col. 3: Office of National Statistics, Headline Gross Value Added (GVA) at
current prices by region.
Correlation between col. 2 and col. 3 −0.05.

latest public spending relativities, published by the Treasury in March
2007, show that Scotland still has public expenditure per head on
devolved services[18] almost 20% ahead of the UK average (table 22.4).
Wales has spending about 9% ahead of the UK average. But Wales is a relatively poor region and Scotland has roughly average income per head. If
spending were designed to counter poverty, one would expect the correlation between public spending per head (table 22.4, col. 2) and gross value
added (GVA) per head (col. 3) to be strongly negative – approaching −1.

[18] Table 22.4 excludes 'social protection', most of which comprises pensions and social security benefits. These are not devolved and are payable at uniform rates throughout the UK.
Some other identifiable expenditure, notably part of that on agriculture and fisheries, is
not controlled by the devolved administrations, but exclusion of that does not materially
affect table 22.4.

In fact it is −0.05. There is almost no correlation between the wealth of a UK region and the public spending it gets. Scotland had ample cushion, and Wales had a little, to increase welfare spending compared to England, as Persson and Tabellini predict.

The problem of representation has been acidly called 'what those with short memories call the West Lothian Question'.[19] Gladstone, who had a long memory, wrestled with it for seven years and failed to find an answer in either of his Government of Ireland Bills (1886 and 1893). The problem is: how (if at all) should a territory which has a devolved government be represented in the House of Commons? If every territory had devolution, the problem would be simple. But England does not, and the attempt to offer an elected assembly in the north-east was turned down overwhelmingly in a referendum in 2004. The House of Commons therefore doubles as the elected part of the government of the UK and of the government of England. How many MPs from Scotland and Wales should sit there, and what powers should they have?

One possibility would be to exclude them. But that would not be fair. Scotland and Wales are not independent countries. Taxation, social security, foreign affairs and defence are not devolved. For the people of Scotland and Wales to be excluded would be taxation without representation – the slogan of the rebellious American colonists in 1776.

Another possibility is what Gladstone called the 'in and out solution' – that Scottish and Welsh MPs could vote on non-devolved matters such as defence and social security, but not on devolved matters such as health and education. This is current Conservative policy. But it is unworkable. Whenever the UK party majority in the House of Commons differed from the English party majority, the government of the day would be unable to carry half its legislation. Either it would be formed by the party with a majority of seats in England, which could not tax or run foreign affairs; or it would be formed by the party with a UK majority, which could not carry its English health or education measures.

A possible solution to the West Lothian Question is to reduce the numbers but not the powers of MPs from Scotland and Wales. This has been done in a minor way for Scotland but not for Wales. Scotland has come down from seventy-two MPs to fifty-nine, which is only slightly above its population share. Wales has forty, which is far above its population share. Northern Ireland was reduced to about two-thirds of its population share of MPs between 1920 and 1979 because it had a devolved

---

[19] By the constitutional lawyer and Northern Ireland specialist Brigid Hadfield.

assembly. But when devolution there ended, its under-representation ended too. On none of the occasions since then when devolution was restored there, including the latest time in 2007, has anybody dared mention the idea of cutting its Westminster representation back again. Were this Northern Ireland solution to be again adopted, its representation in the Commons would be cut to about twelve, that of Scotland to about forty, and of Wales to about twenty-four.

Has devolution worked?

In Sir Humphrey Appleby's favourite phrase *Yes … and No*. It has worked in two main ways: containing the nationalist threat to the Union and offering a natural experiment in domestic policy. It has failed in three main ways: finance, representation and the possibility of English backlash.

Containing the nationalist threat

This may seem a surprising claim immediately after the SNP installed its first First Minister, Alex Salmond, in May 2007. However, as already noted, he will not get a referendum on independence unless a majority of the Scottish Parliament will vote for one. And if he does get it, it will only succeed if his party can buck a thirty-year trend that support for independence runs behind support for the SNP.

It is much too early to make predictions for the 2007–11 Scottish Parliament. But in the election campaign two themes were prominent. One is good for the SNP's prospects and the other is bad for them. Salmond's good move might have been copied from Leon Trotsky or Derek Hatton, the Trotskyite who led Liverpool City Council until Neil Kinnock expelled him and his friends from the Labour Party in 1985. Trotsky wanted to foment 'permanent revolution' by making popular but impossible demands of any bourgeois government. The Alex Salmond version of that was the SNP's call during the 2007 to close down the nuclear submarine base at Faslane, in a deep narrow sea loch near Glasgow. Under devolution, that is no business of the Scottish Parliament or Executive. Defence is a reserved matter, for the UK government alone. There is no realistic chance that (under a government of any party) it would agree to move its nuclear-armed submarines out of a site that is operationally ideal to one outside Scotland that would be much less suitable for hiding submarines.

But as a Trostskyite move, it was very smart. Faslane has been a site of left-wing protest for forty years.[20] Voting against Faslane was a feel-good, cheap-talk way of voting against Tony Blair and the Iraq War. As no UK government will concede the SNP demand, it can go on demanding it and inducing the good feeling.

On the other hand, the SNP's domestic manifesto was radically incoherent. It promised to spend yet more on public services with no suggestion of reforming them. Its expenditure would be funded out of oil revenues, which the SNP cheerfully assumed would continue to flow and would all flow to Scotland. Neither assumption seems plausible. The same oil revenues were double-booked to fund a capital programme for when the oil ran out. The party promised to abolish council tax in Scotland and use the 3p-in-the-pound income tax to replace it, ignoring the fact that if it abolished council tax, it would lose the council tax benefit which the UK Treasury pays to those who cannot afford the tax (or some of them). It will therefore predictably struggle to honour its manifesto promises during the 2007–11 parliament.

Devolution as a natural experiment

This is linked to the second, unforeseen, advantage of devolution to Scotland and Wales. Policy on health, education and local government has now diverged considerably across the four countries of the UK. As noted, this is more because the Scots and Welsh administrations have not changed what the English administration – i.e. the UK government acting as government of England – has changed. The second and third Blair administrations have seen a spread of control mechanisms designed to push up the performance of public services. These have included

---

[20] I grew up with this, to the tune of 'Three craws were sitting on a wa' On a cold and frosty morning':

> It's suicide to hae them on the Clyde,
> Hae them on the Clyde,hae them on the Clyde,
> Sheer suicide to hae them on the Clyde
> And we dinnae want Polaris!

> Off, off, get off the Holy Loch,
> Off the Holy Loch, off the Holy Loch,
> Off, off, get off the Holy Loch,
> For we dinnae want Polaris!

The base which in the 1960s was in the Holy Loch off the Clyde estuary is now at the more remote Faslane, on the Gare Loch.

league tables and internal markets. They have been highly controversial, and on the whole unpopular with existing providers of public services (as one would expect). There are doubts about the reliability and validity of some of the performance measures.[21] But the comparison with Scotland and Wales puts Blairite reform in England in a good light. Public services in England do more with less than in either Scotland or Wales. They cost less and deliver more. The conspicuous failures of the NHS in Wales since devolution have already claimed political scalps. Future administrations in both countries may have to make Blairite reforms – or find some other way to reform their public services.

One might expect some pressure in the opposite direction – when the devolved administrations do something good, one should expect the English to copy them. This has not happened much, for somewhat disreputable reasons. The eminent Scots historian Christopher Harvie (elected an SNP MSP in 2007) records a conversation between the leading public intellectuals of Scotland and England, John Stuart Blackie and Benjamin Jowett, in 1866: 'I hope you in Oxford don't think we hate you.' 'We don't think about you', was the reply.[22]

In the early years of devolution, some advisers to both Tony Blair and Gordon Brown became agitated about the Scottish Executive's expensive and probably unsustainable commitments to social care and cheap university fees. Others were more blasé. The policies (and demands for them) were not leaking south for two reasons. The Anglo-Scots border is thinly populated, so few elderly ladies have moved to Scotland in search of social care (and if they did it would be the Scots' problem). And the English media are more blissfully ignorant than ever before of anything happening in Scottish or Welsh politics. When the leakage was the other way (for instance, in reports during 2006 of patients from Powys being turned away by hospitals in Shropshire) the news was big in Wales but imperceptible in England.

Finance, representation, and the English backlash

The Barnett formula is unsustainable and the West Lothian Question is unanswerable. Some have argued that this does not matter as long as the

---

[21] For an introduction to this large subject, see the website of the ESRC Public Services Programme at www.publicservices.ac.uk/our_research.asp#1stSmall, on which see especially the Jacobs, O'Mahony and McLean projects.

[22] Christopher Harvie, *Scotland and Nationalism: Scottish Society and Politics, 1707–1977* (London: Allen and Unwin, 1977), p. 121.

people do not care about it. It is true that the Scots and Welsh do not care much that they are over-represented. The Scots do not care that they are over-funded for their public services. Who would? The Welsh ought to care more than they do that Barnett actually under-funds them, relative to need, but up to 2007 they have been (for such a musical nation) uncharacteristically quiet about it.

But those who say 'the people don't care, only academic fusspots do' have been looking in the wrong place. The place they should be looking is England. True, the 'English backlash' was expected to lead to a vote for an assembly in the north-east in 2004 and did not. But the area of greatest danger to the Scots is not the north-east but the south-east of England. Lobbyists in London and the south-east are increasingly saying 'We pay the taxes and don't get the services. Our tax receipts are going to those subsidy junkies in Scotland and Northern Ireland.' The numbers in table 22.4 give this claim some credence (although note that public expenditure per head in London is very high). All parties in Scotland other than the Labour Party were demanding 'more fiscal autonomy' in the approach to the 2007 elections. They meant very different things by that phrase. But they face the risk of getting what they wish for. A cool London government might say, 'All right – you asked for fiscal autonomy. Here is some. You can keep your tax proceeds – even, if you insist, the proceeds of 90% of North Sea oil taxation. In return, you can choose what public services you want out of that tax revenue. Off you go, and the best of luck.' Scotland might then become not another Quebec, but another Slovakia – surprised into independence by a larger neighbour calling its bluff.[23]

Was it anything to do with Tony Blair?

In stark contrast to Northern Ireland, Tony Blair had relatively little to do with Scottish and Welsh devolution. He inherited the commitment from John Smith. He oversaw large constitutional changes but had little input to them. As he himself said to a reporter, it took him three years to realise that having devolved power to Scotland and Wales he should not meddle in their affairs. The good bits of the constitutional change were the bits

---

[23] Iain McLean, 'Scotland: Towards Quebec or Slovakia?', *Regional Studies*, 35, 2001: 637–44; Timothy Garton Ash, 'Independence for Scotland Would Not Be Good For England', *The Guardian*, 3 May 2007. Available at www.guardian.co.uk/commentisfree/story/0,,2071089,00.html.

that the Scottish Constitutional Convention had thought through. The
bad bits were the bits they had ignored. The failings of the Government of
Wales Act 1998 were corrected by the 2006 Act. The failings of representation and finance are with us yet.

However, in retirement Tony Blair may have the last laugh. Devolution
has offered a natural experiment in public service delivery. It has tended
to show that the unpopular reforms of the second Blair term to public
services in England have worked – at least when compared to the unre-
formed public services of Scotland and Wales. The Scots and the Welsh
deserve more fiscal autonomy. When and if they get it, they will face the
real world of politics on a tight budget. Once that has happened, devolution will have come of age.

23

Ireland: the Peace Process

FRANK MILLAR

Tony Blair's Irish peace

When he entered Downing Street on 2 May 1997, Tony Blair would not have believed the extent to which two conflicts – one ancient, one modern – would shape his premiership and inform his legacy. Nor that it would be a deal with the octogenarian Reverend Ian Paisley – sealed in his last days in No. 10 – that would enable the Prime Minister to set seemingly stable peace in Northern Ireland against the violent uncertainty to which he would have to leave Iraq.

It might not have been quite what the author of the famous email had in mind months before, advising on the orchestration of Blair's farewell tour, urging him to depart the stage leaving the crowds cheering for more. Cheering crowds would have been too much to expect in Belfast, where the antagonisms and scars of bitter division and brutal conflict would not be quickly excised. Indeed some on both sides had watched in disbelief as their tribal chieftains inched toward accommodation, convinced, hoping, praying . . . that their leaders might still be engaged in an ever more elaborate version of the all-too-familiar 'blame game'.

Yet it was truly a remarkable moment at Stormont on 8 May 2007 when Blair, accompanied by Irish Taoiseach Bertie Ahern, watched Paisley and Sinn Fein's Martin McGuinness assume their joint office as First and Deputy First Ministers in Northern Ireland's new power-sharing Executive. And it would certainly be one for Blair to savour in the post-Downing Street years.

A helping hand

But Blair could hardly have failed in Northern Ireland, could he? For had nationalist Ireland not already done much of the 'heavy lifting' by the time he arrived in power? Specifically, had the IRA not ensured politics would eventually triumph after concluding that republicans could not hope to force British withdrawal and Irish unification by means of 'the long war'?

The Conservatives would insist any assessment of the Blair government's conduct of the British economy should begin with its 'inheritance'. In Northern Ireland, too, the new Prime Minister owed much to those who had gone before. It would be right in any circumstances to acknowledge the cast of characters which contributed to the promising prospect that greeted Blair on his first visit to the Province within weeks of taking office. It is also necessary to chart the evolution of the Peace Process to appreciate and contextualise the extraordinary developments that would occur on Blair's watch, and his contribution to them.

The Provisional IRA's original ceasefire of 31 August 1994 might have exploded with the bomb that killed two British civilians at Canary Wharf on 9 February 1996. However the consensus remained – not least within the Northern Ireland Office (NIO) – that the bombing as much as anything reflected republican impatience with an exhausted Major government, perceived by then to be dependent on Ulster Unionist votes in the House of Commons. Unionists inevitably saw the bomb in the City of London as proof that the IRA's 'cessation' of operations was tactical and predicated on a guaranteed – united Ireland – outcome. Those British civil servants with access to the hard intelligence instead saw a republican leadership effectively marking time pending the commencement of fresh negotiations with an incoming Labour administration. When those negotiations finally got under way, moreover, the parties would discover that the essential framework of a political settlement – including dual referendums as the means of 'self-determination' by the peoples of Ireland – had been defined by visionary SDLP leader John Hume as far back as 1990.[1]

Soon after Margaret Thatcher and then Taoiseach Garret FitzGerald signed the 1985 Anglo-Irish Agreement, Hume had engaged in a personally and politically perilous attempt to persuade Sinn Fein president Gerry Adams that IRA violence was not only immoral but counter-productive. Hume's thesis was that the Thatcher/Fitzgerald deal established for the first time British 'neutrality' on the question of the Union of Great Britain and Northern Ireland. He was mistaken. Edward Heath's government had signalled it would have no desire to impede the realisation of Irish unity, should a majority seek it.[2] And the belief that Britain

---

[1] John Hume interview, *Irish Times*, 13 January 1989.
[2] British Green Paper, 1972, IFB no. 117004987.

was 'neutral' on the constitutional issue certainly informed unionist fears through the long years of the ensuing 'Troubles'. Perhaps it did not matter in the great scheme of unfolding events because republicans had not believed it until this point. Sceptics would counter that such matters of fact were too lightly discarded as the republicans searched for a new narrative with which, ultimately, to justify the end of their terrorist campaign. In any event, Hume's argument appeared to be given added validity in November 1990 when Margaret Thatcher's then Secretary of State Peter Brooke found utility in declaring that Britain had 'no selfish strategic or economic interest' in remaining in Northern Ireland. In fairness, Brooke's words were also apparently intended to signal an emotional allegiance to the Union that only a majority for Irish unity could displace. However, and inevitably perhaps, the focus remained on the argument that it was primarily republican violence that gave the British reason to stay – and that London would present no obstacle if only nationalists and republicans could persuade unionists that their future lay outside the United Kingdom in some form of 'New' and 'Agreed' Ireland.

It later emerged that from at least 1982 Adams had also been engaged in secret diplomacy with Redemptorist priest Father Alec Reid, a largely unsung inspiration of what was known in the first instance as the 'Irish' peace process. Adams had also opened indirect contact the previous year with Charles Haughey, as the then Taoiseach sought to negotiate a resolution of the 1981 IRA hunger strikes with Prime Minister Thatcher. In August 1986, some months before Haughey was again elected Taoiseach, Father Reid travelled to see him at his Georgian estate at Kinsealy outside Dublin. According to one authoritative account, this crucial discussion resulted in the first offer of an IRA ceasefire just nine months later and the subsequent creation of the strategy that would see the end of the IRA's long war against the British state in Northern Ireland.[3]

Others, too, helped shape and direct it, not least Irish diplomat Sean O hUiginn, regarded by many as the single most formidable exponent of Irish nationalism. Much attention focused for a time on proposals thought to have resulted from the famous 'Hume/Adams' dialogue. But O hUiginn was the intellectual driving force in the Irish Department of Foreign Affairs where Labour leader Dick Spring served as Foreign Minister in the 1992/4 Fianna Fail/Labour coalition led by Taoiseach Albert Reynolds.

[3] Ed Moloney, *A Secret History of the IRA* (Harmondsworth: Penguin/Allen Lane, 2002), pp. 261–2.

It is also necessary to record that the much-vaunted 'pan-nationalist front' in this period was hardly a seamless robe. The effort to bring the IRA and Sinn Fein into politics saw profound pressures brought to bear within the SDLP and upon successive coalition governments in Dublin. It could hardly have been otherwise as the 'constitutional' parties debated how far they would be prepared to go to accommodate republicans who continued to kill and bomb, and purported to do so 'in the name of the Irish people'.

This internal nationalist debate was graphically illustrated at one point when Spring disagreed with a proposal by Reynolds to present, as the Irish government's own, a draft joint declaration sent to it by the Provisional IRA. The draft was in fact a response to one that had origi- nated from Reynolds' own emissary, the influential Martin Mansergh. At the core of this disagreement appears to have been Reynolds' plan to present the proposal to Major as a fait accompli. And it illuminated fun- damental questions which – while illustrating the significant advance already made in republican thinking – also revealed the extent to which they would still have to travel if ever there was to be a successful engage- ment with unionists. On the one hand, the republican draft indicated acceptance that 'self-determination by the people of Ireland' would have to be achieved 'with the agreement and consent of the people of Northern Ireland'. Against that, the republican expectation seemed to be that, in return, London would have to accept that this act of self-determination would result in 'agreed independent structures for the whole island within an agreed time-frame'.[4]

It was precisely such ambiguities that unionists detected in the Joint Declaration for Peace issued by Reynolds and Major in December 1993 and the Joint Framework Documents concluded by Major and then Taoiseach John Bruton in February 1995. The need for the 'consent' of the people of Northern Ireland for constitutional change was there. So too, however, were proposals for new North/South institutions with 'execu- tive, harmonising and consultative functions over a range of designated matters to be agreed'. Unionists regarded this as code for an embryonic all-Ireland parliament. Nor could it be said they were wrong, after Irish Foreign Minister David Andrews would declare the Irish intention was to see cross-border bodies operating with powers 'not unlike a government'.

Reynolds undoubtedly inspired his own officials and commanded the respect of Sinn Fein leaders. However, his apparent certainty about

    [4] Fergus Finlay, *Snakes and Ladders* (Dublin: New Island Books, 1998), pp. 188–9.

republican bona fides and his unshakeable 'can do' approach made life difficult for the Conservatives, not least by so discomfiting the unionists. Indeed, when Reynolds once famously asked 'Who's afraid of peace?' many unionists saw it as something of a threat.

Then Ulster Unionist leader James (Lord) Molyneaux would be widely ridiculed for suggesting that the emerging process had the capacity to 'destabilise' Northern Ireland. The point was not that unionists did not want peace – rather they feared 'the price' at which it was being offered, and that might be paid for it. Nationalists and republicans might have warmed to the spectacle of President Clinton overriding British concerns in granting Adams a visa to visit the US at a crucial juncture. And Clinton, along with leading figures in 'Irish America', would fairly claim their share in the credit for the events leading to the negotiation of the Belfast Agreement in 1998 and the DUP/Sinn Fein settlement subsequently brokered by Blair and Taoiseach Ahern in 2007. Back in 1995, however, unionists were easily psyched by a 'pan-nationalist consensus' stretching all the way from the office of the Taoiseach to the Clinton White House, and by the expectations it fostered.

The surprise was that unionists reacted as calmly as they did to the revelation of the Major government's own secret 'back channel' to the IRA. And some of them – including loyalist paramilitary spokesmen like Gusty Spence, Gary McMichael and the late David Ervine – attempted to make fairly sophisticated assessments of their own about the IRA's intentions. Major's Secretary of State Sir Patrick Mayhew, and his deputy Michael Ancram, also provided protection for unionists in the three-stranded talks process that would be the basis for the negotiation of the Belfast Agreement, and, above all, with the so-called 'triple lock' requiring that any outcome be acceptable to the parties and people of Northern Ireland and parliament at Westminster. However, it would be some time before it became clear that there was no 'secret deal' on an agreed outcome between the British and the Provisionals. Moreover, the Conservatives had 'form', most recently in the shape of the 1985 Anglo-Irish Agreement. It was perhaps not totally surprising then that Molyneaux's successor, David (Lord) Trimble, decided he could get a better deal from Blair – notwithstanding Labour's traditional policy of seeking Irish unity by consent.

New Labour, new policy

In one particularly memorable interview during the Iraq War, Blair defended his policy in respect of 'liberal interventionism' and the

American alliance, suggesting the situation was worse than the Labour left suspected – that he actually believed in these things.

As with Iraq, so in Northern Ireland, people would frequently ask whether the Prime Minister believed in anything much at all, and, more to the point, whether anything he said was to be trusted. The read-across from the international crisis – and the recurring question of 'trust' – would certainly inform thinking and reinforce prejudices across the Northern Ireland divide. For nationalists and republicans evidence that the Blair government and its security services manipulated the intelligence about Saddam Hussein's alleged weapons of mass destruction would be taken as proof of the unchanging character and nature of 'perfidious Albion'. Despite the support of their MPs for the war, meanwhile, many unionists were reminded of past American support for the IRA and thought Blair guilty of double standards – tough on terrorism abroad while accommodating its perpetrators and apologists at home.

Unacknowledged for the most part was what for some was the biggest paradox of all: the insistence of Anglo-Irish policy that Sinn Fein be included as of right in an Executive in Belfast, while the Ahern government maintained the party had not satisfied the democratic test, and therefore remained unfit for ministerial office in the Republic.

Blair finally addressed this issue in a speech in October 2002, admitting: 'To this blunt question: "how come the Irish Government won't allow Sinn Fein to be in government in the South until the IRA ceases its activity, but unionists must have them in government in the North?", there are many sophisticated answers. But no answer as simple, telling and direct as the question.'

Blair was speaking during the crisis sparked by the discovery of an alleged republican 'spy ring' at the heart of the Stormont administration, warning that he could not continue 'with the IRA half in, half out of the process'. Yet he obviously never thought to transform the situation by answering the 'blunt question' himself, and telling Dublin that he would no longer tolerate the paradox and that the question of devolution for the North would be put on hold until the South resolved its own republican problem.

In posing the question, the Prime Minister at least acknowledged its effect on unionist opinion. But did he actually share their sense of grievance? What was the merit in identifying a problem while doing nothing to seek its resolution? Was this not evidence rather of Blair's willingness to say what seemed to be required at any particular moment in time? As described above, much of the big thinking, and structural and administrative preparation, had preceded him. Did he have any strong views of his own about what would constitute a legitimate settlement on Northern Ireland? Or was the search for peace there simply one of those 'eye-catching initiatives' with which (courtesy of another embarrassing leaked email) we knew he liked to be associated?

Those irreconcilables who damn Blair and all his works would doubtless have him denied even his Irish peace prize and cheerfully answer this last question in the affirmative. However, the answer – at least in the 'big picture' terms that Blair himself liked to speak – must surely be 'no'.

Blair could certainly be inconsistent. His short-termism and lack of attention to detail would infuriate many. And he was indisputably capable of saying different things to different people. In this, however, he appeared to share a particular prime ministerial skill with his predecessor. On many occasions journalists had listened open-mouthed outside No. 10 as Northern Ireland's politicians left meetings with Major absolutely convinced that the Prime Minister was on their side. Downing Street seemed to have that effect on players from all sides.

However, from his earliest days as Opposition leader, Blair was telling anyone who would listen that he would be firmly on the side of those seeking an accommodation and an end to the conflict. Rather like in that Iraq interview, he also gave notice that he would be in it for the long haul. And, vitally, he made the policy adjustment that would give him the prospect of succeeding where so many others had failed.

Few were paying much attention in September 1995 when Blair told the *Irish Times* he expected Northern Ireland would prove 'as important an issue' as any that would confront him in British politics.[5] On the eve of a trip to Dublin, Londonderry and Belfast he was hardly going to admit that the British public were monumentally bored with the subject – or that he would have 'bigger fish to fry' as an incoming Prime Minister following Labour's eighteen years in opposition.

Yet that had been precisely the fear harboured in Dublin. Mo Mowlam, the Opposition spokesperson who would become his first Secretary of State for Northern Ireland, performed an important role in maintaining Irish faith. During one encounter in the Travellers Club in London Blair likewise assured senior NIO officials that he would be 'free to act' on Northern Ireland and would not be 'tied by party issues' of the kind perceived to have inhibited Major.

[5] Tony Blair interview, *Irish Times*, 4 September 1995.

This might have appeared to be a reference to the 'High Tory Unionist' tradition that found expression from time to time through people like Viscount (Robert) Cranborne, then Conservative leader in the House of Lords. It did not, however, portend a Labour lurch in an anti-unionist direction. On the contrary, while Mowlam schmoozed nationalists and republicans – and set the scene for the restoration of the IRA ceasefire and Sinn Fein's speedy admission to talks – Blair had already embarked on his own charm offensive with the unionists.

Not yet reconciled to the principle of 'consent' – and thus Northern Ireland's right to say 'No' – republicans wanted Blair to assume the role Major had declined, and act as a 'persuader' for Irish unity. In his *Irish Times* interview Blair made clear he would be doing nothing of the sort. Confirming his change in Labour's 'unity by consent' policy, Blair said: 'I believe the most sensible role for us is to be facilitators, not persuaders in this, not trying to pressure or push people towards a particular objective.' Declaring himself 'easy either way' as to whether Northern Ireland stayed in the United Kingdom or joined a united Ireland, he replied: 'What I personally want to see is the wishes of the people there adhered to . . . If it is their consent that matters, and their wishes that are uppermost, then that is what I want to see implemented.' He was also clear: 'If I was to sit here and say "well, I want to give effect to the wishes of the people of Northern Ireland but I'm going to be in there trying to tell them they've got to unite with the South", the only result of that would be to incapacitate my government from playing a proper role.'

This was painful for supporters of Labour's traditional Irish policy. But, as with Iraq, so in respect of Northern Ireland it might prove even worse than they thought. Some may have comforted themselves that Blair's policy shift was about presentation, the compulsion to tack to the Tory position, the desperate need not to be seen or cast as 'soft on terrorism'. Others doubtless hoped there was 'New Labour' artifice here, designed to lure unionists into negotiations in which they would inevitably lose ground. In fact, Blair had set Labour on a path beyond ostensible 'neutrality' on Northern Ireland's constitutional position to one of effective support for maintaining the Union.

In observing this, it is not necessary to contend that Blair started out from a position of high principle, or with a carefully considered plan. He never planned his relationship with President George W. Bush, and obviously could not have known how the events of 9/11 would recast his entire foreign policy. But few would doubt that he became a believer. In one respect, indeed, it is possible that Blair's war experiences reinforced his

sense of 'the United Kingdom'. Even if for purely pragmatic and presentational reasons, Blair would also be able to argue that Northern Ireland
could not exclude itself from his government's UK-wide devolution
project. And by the time the rising nationalist tide overwhelmed Labour
in Scotland in 2007, Blair, like Gordon Brown, was ever more insistent that
the Kingdom was greater than the sum of its parts.

Whatever his original motivation, Blair made Belfast the port of call
for his first official trip outside London following the 1997 general election. Fresh from electoral triumph, and plainly feeling anything but inca-
pacitated, he assured his audience this was no accident: 'I said before the
election that Northern Ireland was every bit as important to me as for my
predecessor. I will honour that pledge in full.' Their destination was clear,
said Blair: 'To see a fair political settlement in Northern Ireland – one that
lasts, because it is based on the will and consent of the people here.' But so
too was the context. Assuring them that his agenda was 'not a united
Ireland', the young Prime Minister ventured to say that none in his audience were likely to see it in their lifetime. Then he declared: 'Northern
Ireland is part of the United Kingdom, alongside England, Scotland and
Wales. The Union binds the four parts of the United Kingdom together.
I believe in the United Kingdom. I value the Union.'

This was music to the ears of Trimble, who had already decided Blair
was a man with whom he would do business. However, their subsequent
successful enterprise would rely heavily on a third 'moderniser'. In June
1997 Bertie Ahern became Taoiseach for the first time. And it would be
Ahern's ground-breaking engagement with Trimble – and, in particular,
his subsequent willingness to withdraw the Irish constitutional claim to
Northern Ireland in face of fierce resistance within the Irish system – that
would finally enable Blair to put the Union on a secure footing.

It would be a very different Union, with compulsory power-sharing
between unionists and nationalists and republicans, an effective dual premiership at Stormont, checks, balances and mutual vetoes in an unprecedented system of devolved government bound to the principles of
equality and 'parity of esteem', and tied to an over-arching North/South
and East/West British–Irish framework. In strict constitutional terms,
however, Blair's eventual bequest would give unionism the best deal
available from any British Prime Minister in fifty years.

As the original civil rights crisis erupted in the late 1960s, Prime
Minister Harold Wilson actively pursued a fifteen-year plan for Irish
unification. Heath's government was seen as instinctively anti-unionist
and abolished the discredited Stormont Parliament in 1972. And the

'most unionist' of them all, Thatcher, had excluded unionists from the process leading to the 1985 Anglo-Irish Agreement that for the first time formally recognised Dublin's interest in, and right to be consulted about, Northern Ireland.

The subsequent Belfast Agreement secured by Blair and Ahern on Good Friday, 10 April 1998, would trigger the biggest crisis within union-ism since the early 1970s, and eventually see Paisley's Democratic Unionists supplant the once hegemonic Ulster Unionist Party. Yet by May 2007 DUP ministers in Belfast would be echoing Trimble, loudly trum-peting that Northern Ireland's constitutional position was secure, and likely to grow even more so following the restoration of devolved govern-ment (though this would seem at least questionable).

Perhaps British policy would have naturally evolved in this way after the IRA abandoned its violent campaign. Ironically, too, the IRA's vio-lence had forced a fundamental Irish rethink of what Garret FitzGerald describes as 'the counter-productive and provocative anti-Partition policy' to which the parties in the Republic had committed themselves between 1949 and 1969: 'It also forced a recognition that the security interests of the Irish State required a stabilisation of the Northern Irish polity within the UK.'[6] The fact, however, is that it only finally happened on Blair's watch.

The hand of history

The Prime Minister would be mocked mercilessly after first feeling the 'hand of history' during an emergency dash to the province in April 1998. His task then was to save the inter-party talks chaired by former US Senator George Mitchell. With only days left to what would prove the first of many British–Irish 'deadlines', the Ulster Unionists and the moderate Alliance Party had reacted angrily to the first draft of an agreement pre-sented by the independent international chairman. 'If Tony Blair wants an agreement he'd better get over here fast' was the terse message from then Alliance leader John (Lord) Alderdice. Trimble's private communi-cation to Blair's Chief of Staff Jonathan Powell, meanwhile, ensured the Downing Street cavalry were already on their way. And of course Powell himself was a vital member of the elite troop. Acting as Blair's 'shock absorber' and 'early warning system', as well as 'interface' for Blair's Northern Ireland strategy across other departments of government, this

---

[6] Garret FitzGerald article, *Irish Times*, 19 May 2007.

unusual 'civil servant' would also at times be expected to go to places and talk to people when and where prevailing political conditions decreed that a Prime Minister or Secretary of State could not.

Ironically, given what was to pass in 2007, a crowd of Paisleyites were on hand to jeer Blair's arrival at Hillsborough Castle and, they hoped, to witness his failure. There was seemingly no guarantee that he would succeed.

Senator Mitchell would later suggest that Paisley's decision to boycott the original inter-party talks actually cut Trimble the necessary slack with which to make the first landmark Agreement from which all else would subsequently flow. However, there was little sign of it on 7 April as Mowlam welcomed her Prime Minister to the Queen's official residence in Northern Ireland. Blair was pessimistic, his communications director Alastair Campbell apparently even more so.[7] Yet in an episode that might have made even the legendary spin-doctor blush, Blair appeared to experience one of his 'Princess Diana' moments. Just in time for the early evening news and with no hint of embarrassment, the Prime Minister solemnly declared: 'Now is not the time for soundbites, we can leave those at home. I feel the hand of history upon our shoulders.'

This was classic Blair, oblivious to ridicule, commanding attention to that 'big picture'. And 'history' would indeed be made just three days later, and less than twenty-four hours beyond the original deadline. A full quarter of a century after the then Ulster Unionist and SDLP leaders Brian Faulkner and Gerry Fitt had attempted it in the Sunningdale Agreement, here was a power-sharing settlement to be driven by the constitutional 'centre parties' in what Seamus Mallon – Hume's subsequent nominee for Deputy First Minister in the first Executive – would characterise as 'Sunningdale for slow learners'.

In spite of Hume's pre-eminence – and that he and Trimble would subsequently share the Nobel Peace Prize – Mallon was the acclaimed SDLP star of this negotiation. Like many others he wept tears of joy on the final morning after what he described as 'the greatest night' in a long political career.

The tears were, of course, fuelled in part by the sheer exhaustion of some of the principals. The conflicting briefings of the rival parties also pointed to what Adams correctly predicted would be 'trench warfare' still to come. Yes, it was possible that day to anticipate the light after Northern Ireland's long darkness. Yet, as a triumphant and finally vindicated Hume

---

[7] Andrew Rawnsley, *Servants of the People* (Harmondsworth: Penguin, 2000), p. 131.

reminded, this was not so much the end, or even the beginning of the end, more the end of the beginning.

From the outset controversy attached to a 'sidebar letter' given by Blair to Trimble even as Mitchell prepared to unveil the final Agreement. In it the Prime Minister assured the UUP leader that if the Agreement's provisions for excluding ministers who failed to honour the commitment to exclusively peaceful means proved ineffective he (Blair) would change them. This spoke directly to continuing unionist concerns about the 'conditional' nature of the republican movement's participation in the political process and, of course, to the issue of republican weapons that had dogged the process since the first IRA ceasefire.

It would become a commonplace that the question of 'decommissioning' had been a particularly unhelpful invention by the Major government. In fact, Tanaiste Spring had been among the first to suggest that ceasefires would have to be followed by 'a handing up of arms'. Echoing this, Major and Mayhew argued that disarmament was rendered necessary by the IRA's refusal to confirm that its cessation was 'permanent' and intended to hold in all circumstances.

In what would become a familiar theme explaining many subsequent controversies from the republican perspective, Adams and McGuinness characterised the decommissioning demand as evidence of an agenda devised by British 'securocrats' (MI5 and other servants of the secret state) intent on republican humiliation and defeat. However, the response from Sir John Chilcot, former Permanent Secretary at the NIO, is compelling and accords with the objective political realities. According to him, decommissioning was 'the snake coiled at the heart of the peace process' and 'an inescapable physical and political problem which had to be addressed in the full knowledge of all the republican history, sentiment and resistance surrounding it'. For Trimble, certainly, it became the litmus test of the republican commitment to the Mitchell Principles of exclusively peaceful and democratic means.[8] This translated into a UUP policy proclaiming the simple message, 'no guns, no government'.

Unfortunately for Trimble, it would never be so simple. Secretary of State Mowlam eventually finessed the issue, declaring IRA and loyalist paramilitary disarmament 'an obligation' under the Agreement. However,

---

[8] Senator Mitchell was originally asked to head an international body to report on the decommissioning issue. On 22 January 1996 it said that prior decommissioning would not happen but suggested that decommissioning could take place in parallel with political negotiations. It also set out a list of anti-violence statements – the 'Mitchell Principles' – that parties in the negotiations should accept.

she and Blair sided with Sinn Fein, the SDLP and the Irish against Trimble –
upholding their view that the Agreement did not stipulate decommissioning as a 'pre-condition' for Sinn Fein's entry into government.

They were right, and the seeds were sown of Trimble's eventual down-
fall. The Agreement placed an obligation on the parties to use such influence as they had to secure decommissioning by May 2000. And Mallon at
one point – in an initiative conspicuously not taken up by the rest of his
party or the Irish government – expressed a willingness to see Sinn Fein
ministers expelled from office if the IRA did not meet the May 2000 target
date. Trimble, moreover, would contend that he never abandoned the 'no
guns, no government' policy – continuing his effort to disarm the IRA
through the suspensions of the Executive forced by him in 2000 and 2002.
However, his failure to make it a condition of the Agreement foretold the
scenario in November 1999 when he was finally forced to 'jump first' into
government with Sinn Fein, albeit with a post-dated letter of resignation
that would oblige Mowlam's successor Peter Mandelson to impose the
first suspension just six weeks later.

In taking the power to do so, Mandelson faced stern opposition from
Sinn Fein and the SDLP, as well as the Irish government and the Clinton
administration. They viewed this exercise of British sovereign power as a
clear breach of the international treaty that was the Belfast Agreement. The
calculation in Downing Street and the NIO, however, was that they had no
choice, since there was no guarantee that Trimble, if allowed to resign,
would secure a unionist majority in the Assembly for his re-election as
First Minister.

The Belfast Agreement had won a spectacularly fair wind by way of
popular endorsement in the dual referendums held simultaneously in
May 1998 in Northern Ireland and the Republic. Private polling ordered
by Tom Kelly – then Mowlam's communications director, later to become
Blair's official spokesman and a significant player in relation to Northern
Ireland policy – suggested the vote in Northern Ireland could be lost.
Senior SDLP and Irish figures would complain bitterly that Blair took terrible liberties with the Agreement in order to assuage unionist doubts
about decommissioning and the proposed release of paramilitary prisoners. But they would at least acknowledge that it was Blair's campaigning
zeal – and the solemn 'pledges' written in his own hand, albeit broken at
great cost to Trimble – that saved the day.

Blair, however, could not return to the fray for the 'internal' Northern
Ireland elections to the new Assembly the following month. And it
was at this point – beset by critics in his own party led by MP Jeffrey

Donaldson – that Trimble fell short of a secure majority and found himself effectively 'holed below the water line'.

True to form, Paisley, then still the minority unionist leader, had characterised the Agreement as another 'sell out' on the road to a united Ireland. In this, and his subsequently successful effort to destroy Trimble's majority leadership, he would be greatly assisted by Adams' repeated assertion that the Agreement provided for a 'transition' to Irish unity.

Trimble's counter-argument was that the IRA and Sinn Fein had in fact been fought to a standstill by the British state and brought to accept a 'partitionist' settlement. To his mind, Adams' talk of transition to unity was strictly for the birds – necessary rhetoric to keep the republican troops on board as the republican movement made the all-important 'transition' from terror to democracy. In this, crucially, Trimble was bolstered by the acceptance of the principle of 'consent' for any future change in the constitutional position – and Ahern's final amendment of Articles 2 and 3 of the Irish Constitution withdrawing the Republic's formal claim to the territory of Northern Ireland.

After the high-water mark of the referendums, however, unionists showed an increasing tendency to believe Adams and Paisley over any assurance by Trimble and Blair. First Minister Trimble would also be further undone both by the explicit provisions of the Agreement and – more corrosive still – by his failure to have secured on decommissioning that which he said was necessary to sustain unionist confidence.

The release of loyalist and republican prisoners and the reform of the Royal Ulster Constabulary – complete with the removal of its royal title – strengthened and emboldened Trimble's internal enemies and DUP rivals. To which might be added that Trimble himself often appeared conflicted about the Agreement he had signed. Something of the intense pressure on the man was certainly reflected by his initial welcome for the legislation effecting the prisoner releases, and his subsequent decision to vote against it in the Commons. Policing reform was likewise always going to be neuralgic from the unionist perspective. Yet Trimble and his party appeared in denial about the really quite predictable proposals of the international commission led by former Conservative Party chairman Chris (Lord) Patten.

The Patten Commission was specifically tasked to advise on the culture and ethos of the policing service, and it was widely expected, at minimum, that Patten would propose the removal of titles and emblems exclusively identifying the police with the symbolism of the British state. Long after it was credible to do so, Ulster Unionists maintained that since

Northern Ireland's constitutional position had been accepted the symbols of its Britishness could hardly be in dispute. Nationalists and republicans countered that they had not made the Agreement in order themselves to become unionists, and that the Agreement established their right to regard themselves as Irish while promising 'parity of esteem' for their tradition. For all the furore, critics of Trimble's handling of this issue would also note that, while denouncing Patten, his party (and Paisley's DUP) took their positions on the new Policing Board and cooperated enthusiastically with the new dispensation. Indeed Trimble would subsequently venture that its ultimate success would see the recruitment of officers to the 'new' Police Service of Northern Ireland (PSNI) from within the republican community.[9]

In the final event, however, it was the admitted opacity[10] over decommissioning – and the inevitable requirement that Trimble 'jump first' into government with Sinn Fein, having said that he would not – that marked the beginning of the loss of trust that would contribute to Paisley's triumph in the second Assembly elections held in November 2003.

Trimble refuses to concede that he might have been 'suckered' by Blair and suggests that – even as it was being hailed around the world – he regarded the Belfast Agreement as a work-in-progress. 'I knew there were battles still to come, that there was going to be a battle over putting the IRA out of business', he would say later: 'But for me on 10 April 1998 having an agreement – yes, with that battle still to fight – was much better than having no agreement, and the world blaming me for there not being one.'[11]

The price of international approbation, however, was disillusionment and increasing vulnerability on the home front. In failing to resolve the issue with Blair in the week of the Good Friday negotiation, Trimble left an enormous hostage to Paisley's subsequent electoral good fortune. Unbelievably, too, in neglecting to stipulate republican support for the PSNI as the price of participation in government, Trimble also left Paisley a trump card to play in the 2006 St Andrews negotiations leading to the 2007 settlement between the DUP and Sinn Fein.

Reg Empey, who succeeded Trimble after the party's rout in the 2005 general election, would frequently complain that they had done all the 'heavy lifting', making the task easier in turn for Paisley's DUP. And as the

---

[9] Frank Millar, *David Trimble: The Price of Peace* (Dublin: Liffey Press, 2004), pp. 101–4.
[10] *Ibid.*, ch. 3, 'Guns and Government'.   [11] *Ibid.*, p. 76.

so-called 'extremes' themselves began converging on the centre ground, some veterans of the process would reflect that there had perhaps been something almost inevitable about the eclipse of the moderate Ulster Unionists and the SDLP.

However, Blair could see no inevitably happy outcome in November 2003 when he realised, too late, that he had trusted to Trimble's luck holding once too often. Trimble would subsequently admit that 'hubris' led him to think he could negotiate a better deal with Adams in the late summer of 2003 than Blair and Ahern had managed.[12] And he would compound his internal difficulties with an extraordinarily ill-considered attempt to expel Donaldson and two other dissident MPs from his parliamentary party. In such circumstances the UUP leader did astoundingly well to trail Paisley's DUP by just three seats when the 2003 Assembly election count was completed. However Donaldson's prompt defection to the DUP along with two colleagues instantly transformed Paisley's margin of advantage – one that would see the DUP take nine Westminster seats in the ensuing general election while Trimble lost his own and saw his party reduced to one seat in the new House of Commons.

Blair was downcast, and took time to convince that there was the remotest possibility of rebuilding the essential architecture of the Belfast Agreement during Paisley's reign as undisputed leader of Ulster's unionists. In invoking 'history', the Prime Minister had risked its cruel rebuke. After all, equally great if not greater men and women than him had sought to end centuries of conflict in and about Ireland. It would also be entirely in character that Paisley – the self-styled 'Dr No' of unionist politics – might think to see Blair off, as he had done Wilson, Heath, Callaghan, Thatcher and Major before him.

'History', its hand and its challenge, would be invoked again and again through the tortuous and interminable negotiations that followed in Downing Street, Lancaster House and Leeds Castle. However, when the putative 'Comprehensive Agreement' failed in December 2004 – again on the issue of verifiable IRA decommissioning, and after Paisley demanded republicans wear 'sackcloth and ashes' in token of their repentance – that call to history came to be regarded as devalued currency in a process that began to look like an end in itself. Within days of that attempt, police in both states were blaming the IRA for the £26.5 million Northern Bank robbery. And by the time President Bush snubbed Adams in favour of the sisters of murdered Belfast man Robert McCartney at the annual

---

[12] *Ibid.*, p. 172.

St Patrick's Day festivities in Washington the following March, the wheels looked finally to have come off the peace train.

Amazingly, though, Blair's own luck was to hold, and suddenly it seemed he would not be denied the prize after all. It would not be until January 2007 that it became clear that Paisley had overruled the strong instinct of some of his closest colleagues to deny Blair and 'wait for Gordon' Brown before concluding a settlement. By that stage, however, a most unlikely relationship had developed between the two men. There would be suggestions that they liked to discuss theology, although – with Blair reportedly contemplating conversion to Rome – it would seem likely that speculation along these lines was overheated. Yet the famous Blair 'empathy' was undoubtedly once more in play. And the Prime Minister grew convinced that Paisley sensed the time right for a settlement provided Sinn Fein met his terms on decommissioning, and, crucially, agreed to 'cross the Rubicon' and finally accept the legitimacy of the Northern Ireland state by fully endorsing the police. Blair was lucky also in that, while fast approaching his own 'sell by' date, he found himself dealing with an ageing DUP leader also in something of a hurry to secure a more satisfactory 'legacy'.

So the world watched in disbelief as television beamed the remarkable images of Paisley and Adams sitting down together at Stormont on 26 March 2007 to seal their very own DUP/Sinn Fein agreement. And there would be tears again too, this time in the Republic a week later, as Dr Paisley shook hands with Taoiseach Ahern and declared a new era in relations between Northern Ireland and the Republic.

Thus Blair's Irish 'legacy' was secured at the last gasp. And many of those who played their part along the way would testify to the Prime Minister's heroic role, time and again citing his extraordinary tenacity and commitment. Yet, about a man never knowingly undersold by the Downing Street spin-doctors, such descriptions themselves suddenly appeared to err on the side of historic understatement.

Introducing the honoured guest to address both Houses of Parliament in the Royal Gallery at Westminster on 15 May 2007, Blair was equally clear that he could not have done it without Taoiseach Ahern. And rightly so. Various 'solutions' had been tried before, each assuring unionists that the principle of 'consent' was sacrosanct, and all of them invalidated in unionist eyes by the Republic's territorial claim to Northern Ireland. Had Ahern not amended Articles 2 and 3 of his country's Constitution, there would have been no engagement with Trimble, no Belfast Agreement, and certainly no Paisley goodwill trip to Dublin.

During the final stages of the 2007 negotiations Peter Hain, who had
succeeded John Reid at the Northern Ireland Office, specifically warned
the DUP they could not count on anything like the same level of commitment or interest from any alternative Labour Prime Minister. With Blair's
departure and Labour's leadership election hovering into view, the specific message was that Prime Minister Gordon Brown would have more
compelling priorities before attempting to win a fourth term in office.
Some close to Paisley suspected an element of bluff. Interestingly,
however, they decided not to call it, and they were probably wise. Of
course, Brown would not have rejected a peace deal early on his watch.
However, the ever present risk, frequently cited by Ahern in particular,
was of 'events' – whether planned by 'dissident' republicans or others –
that might see the process derailed. Mandelson might strike a chord when
he complained that for Blair at times the 'process' was indeed everything,
its maintenance if not forward movement necessary if only to ensure
things did not slip back.[13] Yet after the extraordinary events of May 2007,
who would say that Blair had been wrong?

Right and wrong

Was there a moral dimension to making peace? And did Blair – 'a guy
with a moral dimension to everything' – observe it? The Prime Minister
would retire to worldwide acclaim for bringing people and parties not
always famed for being on the side of 'good' to a new, common and peaceful purpose. So many would find it surprising that, by this writing,
former Deputy First Minister Mallon should have emerged as Blair's
sharpest critic – openly suggesting that the Prime Minister was 'amoral'
in his political dealings and 'didn't know the meaning of the word
"honesty"'.[14]

Downing Street was dismissive when Mandelson accused Blair of at
times 'conceding and capitulating' to republicans. But they were surely
stung when Mallon, in the same newspaper series, described Blair as a
man who would 'buy' and 'sell' anyone, while accusing London and
Dublin of deliberately disposing of the 'centre parties' in favour of 'the
extremes' represented by the DUP and Sinn Fein. 'It was strategy',
Mallon would insist: 'You had people like Jonathan Powell and others in
Dublin who had decided that to make this work you had to dispense with

---

[13] Peter Mandelson interview, *The Guardian*, 13 March 2007.
[14] Seamus Mallon interview, *The Guardian*, 14 March 2007.

middle unionism and middle nationalism. I think it was as calculated as that.'

The inevitable retort would be 'sour grapes' on the part of Mallon, who had failed, after all, along with First Minister Trimble, to 'make it work' and thus preserve the moderate centre. While admitting the question also in his own mind, the impact of Mallon's charge would be lessened by Trimble's belief that 'Blair was probably the last one to buy into the NIO view that this [DUP/Sinn Fein ascendancy] had to happen'.[15]

Mallon's contention is that Blair betrayed Trimble by allowing the fateful 2003 Assembly election to proceed despite the failure of General John De Chastelain, head of the Independent International Decommissioning Commission, to report on IRA disarmament with the detail and transparency demanded by Trimble and deemed necessary for his political survival.

In fairness to Blair, Trimble recalls that SDLP leader Mark Durkan was with the Irish and the Americans in pressing Blair that the election, already twice postponed by London, must proceed. Trimble's natural temptation to conclude that perhaps he was 'sold short' by Blair is also tempered by his experience that – on the issue of decommissioning – the SDLP had invariably sided with Sinn Fein against him.

That said, Trimble would share the underlying concern reflected by Mallon, and by Durkan, before the 2007 Assembly elections, when he asked: 'Can the parties that gave us the worst of our past [Sinn Fein and the DUP] give us the best of our future?'

Admirers of 'realpolitik' would rightly dismiss complaints about the verdict ultimately delivered by the electorate. And they would draw comforting signs from the early days of the new Stormont administration that the DUP and Sinn Fein might actually make a better job of working the partnership arrangement than the Ulster Unionists and the SDLP had managed.

However, the Durkan question would find a resonance among many people who genuinely wished to see the new power-sharing venture succeed. It would be attended by continuing and legitimate questioning as to whether it had been necessary for Blair to lose the two parties – the UUP and SDLP – seen to protect and defend politics through more than thirty years of assault by republican violence and DUP sectarianism and intransigence. Many close observers would remain convinced that Sinn Fein had played a deliberately 'long peace' in pursuit of its goal to

15 David Trimble, interview by author, 22 May 2007.

supplant the SDLP in preparation for a bid for power in the Irish Republic, which failed badly in the May 2007 Irish election. Had Prime Minister Blair been too indulgent of a republican leadership plainly seeking a way out of violence while maximising its leverage through continual internal 'management' problems? And specifically – following the '9/11' outrages in America, said by Blair and Bush to have changed the global climate in relation to terrorism and its toleration – should Blair have demanded better, tougher terms, and earlier, from a republican leadership for whom there really was now no going 'back to war'?

Looking forward rather than back, there will be uneasy, still-to-be-answered questions too about the 'character' of Northern Ireland's new political elite. Having seized power, will the DUP and Sinn Fein prove capable of genuinely 'sharing' it for the common good? Can commitments to justice and equality have meaning without a shared commitment to reconciliation between communities still living a segregated, 'apartheid' existence behind the so-called 'peace walls'? Will declared republican support for the police be reflected in the cultivation of a culture of lawfulness and the breaking of paramilitary control on both sides? Crucially, will devolution provide a settlement finally permitting the development – never before experienced – of a common commitment to a place called 'Northern Ireland'? And, while plainly desired by unionists, how would that sit with Sinn Fein's insistence still on 'process' and 'transition' leading to Irish unity?

Questions. Blair's great promise to the people of Northern Ireland was that, henceforth, they would be explored and addressed in conditions of peace and with a commitment on all sides to purely peaceful and democratic means. In delivering that transformation, this British Prime Minister really did make history in Ireland. Even he, of course, could not have thought to end it.

24

Europe

IAN BACHE AND NEILL NUGENT

Introduction

Labour assumed office in May 1997 amidst expectations that there would be significant improvements in Britain's relations with the European Union (EU). These expectations were based on the Conservatives' record on the one hand and Labour's promises on the other. Expectations that Britain's relations with the EU would change under Labour were held as strongly on the Continent as they were at home.

This chapter evaluates Labour's record on Europe under Blair and argues that the net effect of government policy on British–EU relations was more substantive than is often credited.[1] A key reason why the record has been underestimated is that throughout Blair's premiership the loudest voices came from, on the one hand, that (very considerable) part of the media which disapproved of Blair's EU policies because he was too pro-European for their tastes and, on the other hand, a relatively small band of strong pro-Europeans who believed that Blair had betrayed them – most particularly by not attempting to join the single currency. A second important reason for the underestimation of the record is that from 2003 'Europe', along with most other policy issues, was crowded out by the overwhelming focus on Iraq.[2]

Generally, Europe is only to the fore when sovereignty concerns are at stake and/or when Britain is seen to be engaged in confrontational,

---

[1] Strictly speaking, 'Europe' is not, of course, completely synonymous with 'the EU'. However, in common parlance, and so in this chapter too, they are treated as if they were interchangeable.

[2] The scale of the dominance of the Iraq issue is indicated by a BPIX online survey of 2304 adults, conducted between 16–19 March 2007, the results of which were published in *The Observer*, on 8 April. 58% identified 'The war in Iraq' as Blair's biggest failure. The next largest perceived failure was the widening gap between rich and poor, which was identified by 10%. Only 1% identified 'Failure to encourage greater integration in the European Union' as Blair's biggest failure.

high-level, and high-profile exchanges with other member states. These conditions applied on several occasions during the Blair years – most notably in respect of the single currency, EU treaty reform rounds, and EU budgetary reform. Yet though public attention is focused on the EU only periodically, enduring processes of change in Britain's relations with Europe are continually under way beneath the surface. This being so, the lens in this chapter is focused not just on the elite level but also on the more routine domains of politics and policy-making – where European and domestic affairs have in some respects become almost indistinguishable.

Further to this, when thinking about Britain and Europe it is necessary to consider the relevant domestic changes which, while not necessarily directly connected to policy on Europe, have influenced the nature of Britain's relations with the EU. These changes too have been a relatively neglected part of the narrative of the Blair governments' relations with the EU. Of particular importance here have been institutional and constitutional changes – in particular those promoting devolution – which have increased the degree of 'fit' between the British and the EU systems of governance.

As we write, the dust has yet to settle on the Blair years, Iraq remains prominent and the country has just undergone a change of leadership. In developing our analysis we have tried to stand back from this immediate context, difficult though it is. We begin by considering the legacy of Britain's relations with the EU that was inherited by the Blair government in 1997.

The Conservative legacy

During the years of Conservative government after 1979 Britain came to be seen as Europe's most 'awkward' partner.[3] This conception was based on essentially Eurosceptic governments adopting either oppositionalist or minimalist positions on virtually all significant European issues other than those that were designed to open up and liberalise the internal market. Underlying this stance was a dilemma in Conservative attitudes to Europe that continued throughout the Blair years: on the one hand a recognition and acceptance of the benefits accruing to Britain from the Single European Market; on the other hand strongly held beliefs, going to

---

[3] See Stephen George, *An Awkward Partner: Britain in the European Community*, 3rd edn (Oxford: Oxford University Press, 1998).

the very heart of the political identity of most Conservatives, that European integration involves a loss of national sovereignty in a zero-sum manner: what Britain loses 'Brussels' gains.

In policy terms, Thatcher's antipathy to the EU was most strongly signalled in relation to the UK budgetary rebate and in opposition to the Common Agricultural Policy (CAP) and to the redistributive accompaniments to the single market programme. Major stamped his own brand of awkwardness through opting out of the single currency, rejecting the Social Chapter at Maastricht, and for a short time in 1996 obstructing decision-making in the Council of Ministers in response to the EU's ban on the export of British beef following the BSE outbreak.

Major's position in the 1996–7 Intergovernmental Conference (IGC), which was established to prepare the EU for the anticipated accession of former Soviet bloc states, was to block it unless there were changes to the Common Fisheries Policy and a reversal of a European Court of Justice (ECJ) decision that the directive on a 48-hour maximum working week should apply to Britain.[4] Largely because of his government's obstructionist stand, very little progress was made in the IGC in 1996 or early 1997 on such difficult issues as extensions to qualified majority voting (QMV) in the Council and revisions to law-making procedures. This was despite the IGC being scheduled to be concluded by the European Council in June 1997. However, this lack of progress was viewed with general equanimity in EU circles because the Major government was the main hindrance to decisions being made and it was known that a UK election would have to be held before June 1997, with all the indications being that a more amenable Labour government would be returned to power.

Things can only get better? The Blair years

In line with the words of Labour's 1997 adopted campaign anthem,[5] it seemed the new government could barely fail to alter the perceived negative and dismal British record on Europe under the Conservatives. The promise in May 1997 was of a positive approach to Europe, a 'step change' in the relationship, with Britain taking advantage of the opportunities offered by the EU rather than concentrating on the threats that the Conservatives had emphasised. However, many of the dilemmas that the

---

[4] Ian Bache and Stephen George, *Politics in the European Union* 2nd edn (Oxford: Oxford University Press, 2006), p. 185.　　[5] 'Things Can Only Get Better', by D:Ream.

Labour government was to face over Europe turned out to be those that had hamstrung the Conservatives. Moreover, the response was sometimes similar, both in style and substance.

But there was an essential difference between the approach of New Labour and that of the Conservatives, which rested on a different world-view. Blairism was built on reconciling paradoxes – economic excellence and social justice, better relations with both the US and the EU, a stronger Britain and a stronger EU. On the latter, Blair sought to advance a different conception of sovereignty in Britain's relations with the EU: a shift from the Conservatives' zero-sum view of what Europe gains, Britain must lose, to a positive-sum view that both Britain and the EU would win by closer integration. As Blair put it in 2001:

> I see sovereignty not merely as the ability of a single country to say no, but as the power to maximise our national strength and capacity in business, trade, foreign policy, defence and the fight against crime. Sovereignty has to be employed for national advantage. When we isolated ourselves in the past, we squandered our sovereignty – leaving us sole masters of a shrinking sphere of influence.[6]

Labour's aims

Labour approached office in 1997 with relatively modest European policy aims. The 1997 election manifesto identified six specific goals: the rapid completion of the single market; a high priority to be given to EU enlargement; urgent reform of the CAP; the pursuit of greater openness and democracy in EU institutions; the retention of the national veto over key matters of national interest; and the signing of the Social Chapter.[7] Of these six goals, only the last was different from Conservative policy. On the thorny issue of the single currency, Labour was non-committal, with membership not being excluded (as it was by the Conservatives) but with any decision to be determined by 'a hard-headed assessment of Britain's economic interests' and to require the approval of the British people in a referendum.[8]

Labour's specific policy goals in 1997 were, therefore, much like those of the Thatcher and Major governments. What was intended to be

---

[6] Tony Blair, Speech to the European Research Institute, University of Birmingham, 23 November 2001, http://politics.guardian.co.uk/euro/story/0,,604413,00.html (accessed 3 April 2007).

[7] Labour Party Manifesto, 1997, accessible at http://www.labour-party.org.uk/manifestos/1997/1997-labour-manifesto.shtml.   [8] Labour Party Manifesto, 1997.

significantly different, however, was the tone. Unlike the claimed negativity and suspiciousness that Labour (with cause) claimed had characterised Conservative policy in the EU, a much more positive and cooperative approach was to be taken. As Blair stated in April 1995, and in so many words repeated frequently in the period up to and beyond May 1997: 'My belief is that the drift towards isolation in Europe must stop and be replaced by a policy of constructive engagement.'[9]

Such an approach would be allied with a resolve that Britain should seek to exercise a leadership role in the EU. Before being elected Blair frequently emphasised that Britain had traditionally played a leading role on the world stage and under Labour would continue to do so. But, such a role could now only be exercised from a firm and positively participating European base: 'The fact is that Europe is today the only route through which Britain can exercise power and influence. If it is to maintain its historic role as a global player, Britain has to be a central part of the politics of Europe.'[10] At the same time, Blair was keen to stress that Britain's Atlanticism would be a strength rather than a weakness in relations with Europe: 'we have deluded ourselves for too long with the false choice between the US and Europe'.[11] The Labour government would provide a bridge between the two.

Labour in government

Following the Tories, it was not difficult early on for Blair to score high and score easily on Europe.[12] The signing of the Social Chapter shortly after taking office was seen as an 'important symbol of positive intent'.[13] Moreover, the new government instigated changes in Whitehall to improve the internal coordination of policy-making to enhance Britain's capacity to project its preferences onto the EU: before 1997 Whitehall had been much more geared to the task of processing EU policies than trying to influence them. The overall effect of these changes within Whitehall though was to centralise European policy-making, in particular by closer

[9] This quote is taken from a speech delivered at the Royal Institute of International Affairs, reproduced in Tony Blair, *New Britain: My Vision of a Young Country* (London: Fourth Estate, 1996), p. 280. [10] Tony Blair, *New Britain*, p. 283.
[11] See Anne Deighton, 'European Union Policy', in A. Seldon (ed.), *The Blair Effect: The Blair Government 1997–2001* (London: Little, Brown and Company), p. 310.
[12] Deighton, 'European Union Policy', p. 312.
[13] Ian Bache and Andrew Jordan, 'Britain in Europe and Europe in Britain', in I. Bache and A. Jordan (eds.), *The Europeanization of British Politics* (Basingstoke: Palgrave Macmillan, 2006), p. 8.

integration of work of the Cabinet Office European Secretariat and No. 10 and by augmenting the staffing and resourcing of both. [14]

Yet while it became increasingly popular to characterise Blair's style generally as presidential and to equate government policy on Europe with the position of the Prime Minister, there were early indications of the limits to this authority: particularly in relation to the economy. Chancellor of the Exchequer Gordon Brown's announcement in November 1997 that membership of the single currency would depend on five economic tests disappointed Blairites, even if it was not a major surprise. Moreover, as the Treasury made it clear that there was no immediate prospect of these tests being met, the position was effectively understood as an indefinite opt-out.

This decision was a defining moment for UK–EU relations in the early years of Blair's premiership. For to provide the leadership role in Europe that Blair had talked about would have meant to end Britain's opt-outs on key issues. In opposition, Labour had promised a referendum on entry to the single currency and, while it was uncertain whether the government could have secured a vote in favour even in its honeymoon period, it seemed clear to most in government (though in Blair's case not as early as in that of most others) that once the honeymoon period was over, it probably could not. Moreover, this episode demonstrated above all others that government policy on Europe was not being determined exclusively by the Prime Minister.

In the later Blair years, absence from the Eurozone continued to damage Blair's EU leadership aspirations, though less so than initially, as the merits of the British case for not adopting the euro became more widely recognised and as the number of non-Eurozone states grew with enlargement in 2004. In any event, from late 2002 Britain's non-membership of the euro became overshadowed by Iraq: an issue that distanced the UK from some other key EU member states. For though more EU states initially sympathised with the US–UK position on Iraq than opposed it, Blair's position on the war drove a deep policy division between himself and several very important EU leaders, not least the French President and German Chancellor. And, unlike the single currency, Britain's position on the war clearly had Blair's personal imprint.

Blair's European polices have been described by Peter Riddell as being a failure overall.[15] But though, as the following sections will show, they

[14] Simon Bulmer and Martin Burch, 'Central Government', in I. Bache and A. Jordan (eds.), *The Europeanization of British Politics*, pp. 37–51.

[15] See, for example, Peter Riddell, 'Europe', in A. Seldon and D. Kavanagh (eds.), *The Blair Effect*, 2001–5 (Cambridge: Cambridge University Press), pp. 362–83.

certainly did fail in important respects, the case should not be overstated. In important areas and in important respects there were clear policy successes.

Labour's successes

Policy orientation successes

One general policy aim that was achieved was that the UK came to be seen much more as a 'normal' EU member state rather than as an awkward partner. To be sure, under Blair the British government remained towards the Eurosceptic end of the integrationist/Eurosceptic spectrum of opinion amongst the governments of the member states, but it was not seen to be as anything like as difficult as its Conservative predecessors. Indeed, by the time Blair left office the Czech Republic, Poland and Sweden were arguably more sceptical EU members than the UK.

This changed position of the UK was partly accounted for by some softening of the UK's stance in certain key policy areas, such as aspects of social policy and internal security policy, but was also a consequence of 'mood change'. The Major government had at times seemed almost to want to raise confrontational stakes so as to satisfy domestic audiences – not least hard-line backbench Conservative MPs – that it was defending Britain's corner. Under Blair a more open and positive approach was adopted by British ministers from the outset. Certainly they sought to defend national interests in Council forums, but the tone was less defensive than under the Conservatives and generally was more one of 'we have come here to be helpful and to do a deal'.

Specific policy successes

As for specific policy successes, three in particular stand out. The first is EU enlargement, which has long been supported by British governments of both political persuasions. The main reason for this support is the economic benefits likely to accrue to the UK, as a major trading country, from a European market that is as wide as possible. Associated with this reason is the fact that both Labour and Conservative governments have subscribed to a European vision that starts with a focus on market integration and tends not, especially in the case of the Conservatives, to stray too far beyond this.[16] One way of trying to ensure that integration does

---

[16] Some exceptions to this focus under Labour have included the government's leadership on tobacco advertising, food labelling and some environmental policies. On the latter, the

indeed not proceed too far is to have a larger and more heterogeneous EU, in which decision-making becomes increasingly difficult and in which it becomes almost impossible for the hopes of those who dream of some sort of European federal state to be realised.[17] During Blair's premiership the UK government was a consistent champion of the enlargement process, both as regards the enlargement round that in 2004 and 2007 saw ten former Central and Eastern European countries (CEECs) plus Cyprus and Malta join, and the enlargement round that was launched in 2005 with the opening of accession negotiations with Croatia and Turkey. Both of these enlargement rounds have been controversial, with several member state governments believing the accession of the CEECs was being over-rushed and some governments – notably the Austrian, French and Cypriot – being opposed to the opening of accession negotiations with Turkey. As it is charged to do, the Commission provided much of the policy lead in respect of both enlargement rounds – notably through the compiling of detailed annual reports on the preparedness of applicants for accession, coupled with recommendations on action to be taken by the EU – but the UK government was the strongest advocate in the European Council and Council of Ministers for moving forward at a rapid pace.

A particular problem that arose in respect of enlargement was the government's decision to grant free access to the UK to CEEC workers on their countries' EU accession in May 2004. Most other EU member states erected transitional restrictions of various kinds (permanent restrictions were not permitted) but Blair, though subject to pressures from some Cabinet colleagues and hostile tabloids to adopt exclusionist measures, insisted that 'open not closed' was the right approach. He appears to have done so partly on principled grounds, but partly also because as a leading advocate of enlargement he would not have been well placed to be seen to be acting in a restrictive manner. When, two years later, the accessions of Bulgaria and Romania approached – they joined the EU in January 2007 – Blair flirted with granting free movement to their workers too. However, on this occasion, in the knowledge that the earlier 'let them come' decision had resulted in the arrival of far more CEEC workers than had been anticipated, and faced with overwhelming opposition in Cabinet, especially

Footnote 16 (*cont.*)
    Stern Report on climate change commissioned by the Blair government has been seen as influential on EU policy in this area.
[17] Although, the issue is less than straightforward, in that enlargement is also generally supported by federalists.

from the Home Secretary, John Reid, Blair conceded that temporary restrictions should indeed be put in place.[18]

The second specific policy success was in playing a leading role in advancing the prominence on the EU's agenda of the further opening and liberalising of the Single European Market (SEM). Although in theory the SEM was supposed to have been 'completed' in 1992, the fact was that by the late 1990s all sorts of internal market barriers were still in place – including major impediments in respect of services (which account for almost 70% of EU gross domestic product), public procurement (which account for about 15%), and movement of labour. Blair was active, both in the European Council and in bilateral meetings with other EU leaders, in promoting the need for remaining market barriers to be removed. In so doing, he contributed significantly to the impetus that led in March 2000 to the so-called Lisbon Agenda, under which the EU leaders committed themselves to adopting measures designed to make the EU economy the most competitive economy in the world by 2010. In the event, this ambition proved to be over-ambitious and was subsequently scaled back during the Lisbon Agenda's mid-term review in 2004–05. Nonetheless, although not as much progress as Blair would have liked to have seen had been made by the time he left office, significant advances had occurred in respect, for example, of the opening up of competition in certain key services areas – including the crucial area of public utilities.

The third specific policy success concerns reform of the EU's treaties. Since the mid-1980s there has been a pattern of treaty reform rounds being held every five years or so. During Blair's premiership there were three such rounds: the end of the 1996–7 round that resulted in agreement in June 1997 on the Treaty of Amsterdam; the 1999–2000 round that produced the Treaty of Nice; and the round that started in 2002 (if the convening of the Constitutional Convention is taken as marking the starting point) that resulted in the 2004 Constitutional Treaty and the June 2007 European Council agreement on the guidelines for the IGC that would draft the Constitutional Treaty's successor – the so-called Reform Treaty. British government policy in each of these rounds was consistent: to be willing to accept certain limited reforms that were deemed to be necessary for the smooth operation of the EU – including some extensions to the availability of QMV in the Council – but to be resistant to the extension of supranational EU powers and operating practices in such sensitive areas

---

[18] This account of Blair's position on CEEC workers is based largely on information provided to us by a senior Downing Street official.

as taxation, social welfare, and foreign and defence policy. For the most part, these policy goals were achieved, with nothing of major significance in any of the three treaties or in the June 2007 agreement to which the government was deeply resistant. Indeed, there was much in the treaties and the agreement that was welcomed, not least the marginal shift in the Constitutional Treaty, which was confirmed in the June 2007 agreement, away from supranationalism towards intergovernmentalism.

The highly controversial Constitutional Treaty was, indeed, widely portrayed in the European press as a famous victory for Blair. In France, the view developed that British influence had resulted in a treaty that was so neo-liberal in spirit as to actually pose a threat to the French social model. In fact, the Treaty was no more neo-liberal, no more Anglo, than any previous EU treaty, but that this view was widely held was testimony to perceptions of Blair's stance and influence. Certainly the perception was a factor in the French rejection of the Treaty by referendum in May 2005. The irony of this was that, together with the Dutch rejection a week later, it saved Blair from having to honour his promise to hold a referendum on the Treaty: a referendum that he almost certainly would have lost.

Labour's failures

Policy orientation failures

At a general level, Blair's policy ambitions towards Europe were not fulfilled in three major respects. The first two of these concerned the influence and position of the British government in the EU and the other concerned the place of Europe in British politics.

Regarding the influence and position of the British government in the EU, Blair was not, of course, the first Prime Minister who wanted to see Britain being a lead player. In their different ways, all prime ministers since Britain joined the EC have harboured such hopes, rhetorically at least. Even John Major, for all his internal party problems with Eurosceptics, expressed his desire to put Britain 'at the heart of Europe'. But, since the establishment of the European Communities in the 1950s the so-called Franco-German axis had been central to the driving of the European integration process. Founded on well-established structural working relationships between the two governments, and for many years also close personal relationships between the French and German leaders, many of the EU's major initiatives over the years have owed much to close Franco-German conciliation. Blair recognised that he could hardly hope to break into this alliance on a full and consistent basis, not least because of Britain's continuing non-participation in the single currency system, but he did see leadership opportunities being presented by establishing close relations with the French and German leaders. To this end, in his early years in office he strongly courted both President Chirac and Chancellor Schroeder. With Chirac, this courting was successful early on and played an important role in easing the way to the 1998 Saint-Malo Agreement, which saw the British and French governments lay foundations for what was to become the fledgling European Security and Defence Policy (ESDP) by sinking some of their long-held differences about defence and agreeing that the EU should develop a (limited) defence policy dimension. However, the initially warm relationship between the two gradually cooled, to the extent that in October 2002 during difficult European Council negotiations on reform of the CAP Chirac reportedly told Mr Blair: 'You have been very rude and I have never been spoken to like this before.'[19] With Schroeder, there was some initial joint thinking on social democracy/Third Way ideas, but this did not in the event produce much and the two men never established cordial personal relations.

But in seeking to establish a leadership role for himself and Britain, and more broadly to advance Britain's interests in the EU, Blair never over-relied on France and Germany. He recognised that different member states could be allies on different issues. Accordingly, he pressed ministers, Labour MPs and MEPs, and civil servants to establish bilateral relations with their counterparts in other member states wherever possible.[20] As Julie Smith has put it, under Blair Britain practised a 'promiscuous bilateralism'.[21] This practice resulted in several of Blair's closest working relationships with other heads of EU governments being with centre-right rather than centre-left politicians: with Chirac on defence policy in the early years; with José Maria Aznar, the Spanish Prime Minister, in helping to set the agenda for the March 2000 European Council meeting that launched the Lisbon Process; and with Aznar again and also the Italian Prime Minister, Silvio Berlusconi, on Iraq.

---

[19] 'Chirac and Blair Trade Insults over Farm Reform' by Toby Helm and Philip Delves Broughton, 29 October 2002, www.telegraph.co.uk/news/main.jhtml?xml=/news/2002/10/29/neu29.xml (accessed 10.04.07).

[20] See Julie Smith and Mariana Tsatsa, *The New Bilateralism: The UK's Bilateral Relations Within the EU*, (London: Royal Institute of International Affairs. 2002).

[21] Julie Smith, 'A Missed Opportunity? New Labour's European Policy 1997–2005', *International Affairs*, 81(4), 2005: pp. 703–21.

The other policy orientation policy regarding Britain's influence and position in the EU that must be judged to have been a failure was the non-realisation of Blair's hopes to be able to take advantage of Britain's position as the most Atlanticist of the EU-15 (pre-May 2004) member states. He believed that privileged relations with the US could be used to further Britain's standing in the EU, especially in the foreign and security policy areas. Yet rather than Britain's special relationship with the US helping matters, the evidence suggests that if anything the close personal ties Blair cultivated with Presidents Clinton and Bush made some EU leaders, especially Chirac and Schroeder, very wary of British government intentions. It is true that towards the end of his premiership this became less of a problem – with most of the new member states being strongly Atlanticist and with new leaders coming to office in several EU-15 states, including Germany – but in the early 2000s it certainly damaged Blair's standing with some key heads of EU governments. The close relations with Bush were viewed with particular suspicion given that, on assuming office in 2001, Bush quickly showed – by, for example, announcing that he would not be seeking to ratify the Kyoto Protocol or to support the International Criminal Court – that he was not prepared to consult in a meaningful way with European allies and was willing to be isolationist in pursuit of US policy goals.

Blair appears to have believed that by staying close to Bush he could restrain the US from over-aggressive unilateralism, but there is little evidence that he succeeded in doing so – or, indeed, given Bush's policy orientations and Blair's limited policy delivery capacities, that there was ever any realistic prospect of it being possible.[22] Riddell probably overstates the case when he alleges that by late 2001 Blair was 'trying to be both a messenger between Europe and the United States and a missionary around the world on part of President Bush',[23] but there is no doubt that this is how he was widely perceived. When, in 2002–03, the prospect of a US-led invasion of Iraq, with or without explicit UN authorisation, began to loom, the EU-15 governments divided into two camps, with Blair the most active EU leader in the pro-invasion camp. With this policy, Blair destroyed any hope of providing a bridge between Europe and America.

Regarding the place of Europe in British politics, Blair had hoped to defuse it as a divisive political issue and to make the nation more com-

---

[22] This view that Blair was unrealistic in his hopes of being able to influence Bush is forcibly argued by William Wallace, 'The Collapse of British Foreign Policy', *International Affairs*, 82(1), 2005: pp. 53–68.   [23] Riddell, 'Europe', p. 368.

fortable with Britain's EU membership. The issue was indeed sufficiently defused not to feature as much of a vote-shaping issue in either the 2001 or 2005 general elections, despite Conservative attempts – especially in 2001 – to make it so, but this was not because the issue of British membership did not continue to divide British opinion. Rather it was because on the one hand none of the major parties actually advocated withdrawal from the EU, and on the other hand the edge was taken off the two European issues that could have been electorally salient – British membership of the euro (in both elections), and British ratification of the EU's Constitutional Treaty (in the 2005 election) – by Labour promises of referendums.

But though Europe was largely defused as a significant electoral issue in the 2001 and 2005 general elections, it was not so in the 2004 European Parliament (EP) elections when, with the use of proportional representation removing much of the 'wasted vote' concern that is such a problem for smaller political parties in general elections, the United Kingdom Independence Party (UKIP) won 16.8% of the national votes cast (2.7 million votes) and 12 of the UK's 78 seats in the EP.

The UKIP vote has to be seen in the context of the fact that by the time Blair left office Britain was no more reconciled to EU membership and the British people were no more recognising the benefits of EU membership than had been the case when Blair was elected. This is clearly demonstrated in the twice-yearly public opinion surveys that are conducted on behalf of the European Commission in the member states: in response to the standard question that appears in all of the surveys – 'Generally speaking, do you think that the United Kingdom's membership of the European Union is . . .' – in the spring of 1997 36 % said 'a good thing', 26% said 'a bad thing', and 27% said 'neither a good nor bad thing'; in the autumn of 2006, 34% said 'a good thing', 31% said 'a bad thing', and 27% said 'neither a good nor bad thing'.[24] The 'good thing' figures were higher for a while in late 1997 and in 1998, which led Blair and some commentators to think a referendum on the euro might have been winnable had one been held then, but they were not sustained. Although Blair himself continued into 2003 to take an optimistic view on the possibility of being able to win a vote on the euro, from around 2000 most commentators thought this was nigh impossible, as later they thought similarly in respect of a referendum on the ratification of the Constitutional Treaty.

---

[24] *Eurobarometer*, numbers 47 (published November 1997) and 66 (published December 2006) respectively. Accessible at: http://ec.europa.eu/public_opinion/standard_en.htm.

Given the persistent and seemingly deep-seated nature of Euroscepticism in the UK, which most of the media helps to maintain and promote, it is questionable whether a Blair-led government could have done much to turn public opinion around. But, there was only a modest attempt on Blair's part to try to do so. It is true that in his public statements on Europe he would assert his Europeanism and his commitment to a Europe that went beyond a mere trade area, and he would also emphasise the opportunities provided by Europe. So, for example, in perhaps his most celebrated speech on Europe, which was delivered to the European Parliament in June 2005 at the beginning of the UK Presidency, he stated:

> I am a passionate pro-European. I always have been. . .
> This is a union of values, of solidarity between nations and people, of not just a common market in which we trade but a common political space in which we live as citizens. . .
>   I believe in Europe as a political project. I believe in Europe with a strong and caring social dimension. I would never accept a Europe that was simply an economic market.[25]

But the problem was that if there was to be any chance of moving public opinion, the positive European message needed driving home in a more consistent and remorseless manner than it was. Moreover, at crunch times, Blair sometimes preferred to avoid taking risks with the British people on Europe and to adopt somewhat defensive positions. This was no more clearly demonstrated than in his domestic stance towards the Constitutional Treaty when, though he certainly made the case for the need of treaty reform post-enlargement, the dominant theme of many of his and his ministers pronouncements was the defence of British 'red lines' on issues such as defence, taxation and social security.

Specific policy failures

There were two main specific EU policy failures for Blair: on the euro and on the linked issues of CAP and budgetary reform.

In 1997 Labour adopted a cautious position on the euro. Unlike the Conservatives, who rejected euro entry in principle (the principle being preservation of national sovereignty), Labour stated that it would be prepared to enter if it was shown to be clearly in the country's economic

---

[25] PM speech to the European Parliament. Accessed on 10 May 2007 from the No. 10 website at: www. number-10.gov.uk/output/Page7714.asp.

interests. However, as was noted above, so as to deflect possible political damage arising from this open stance, Labour's 1997 election manifesto promised a referendum if a Labour government recommended entry to the new single currency system. In his early years of office Blair certainly favoured Britain adopting the single currency and entering the Eurozone. The absence of any referendum on the issue therefore can be counted as a personal failure for him, although not necessarily for the government as a whole. Three factors explain the absence of a referendum on the euro, each one of which was probably powerful enough in its own right.

The first factor arose from the conceding in the early months of office of the control of economic policy to Gordon Brown and the Treasury. Brown himself was initially open-minded on the issue, but quickly moved to oppose British membership – seemingly persuaded by long-standing Treasury doubts and the firm scepticism of his main personal economic adviser, Ed Balls. What amounted to virtually a compromise between the 'pro' and 'anti' camps was reached when a major Treasury enquiry into the implications of euro membership for Britain was launched in the autumn of 1997, but long before the results of the enquiry were announced it was clear that the 'antis' had gained the upper hand and that no recommendation to join the currency would be forthcoming. When the results of the enquiry were published, in the summer of 2003, Britain was deemed to have clearly 'passed' just one of the five (very generally couched and open to different interpretations) economic tests of membership. Britain's performance in relation to these tests was to be kept under review, but in practice the Treasury had lain down its sceptical position.

The second factor was that, quite simply, in most key respects the British economy performed better than the Eurozone throughout the Blair period, and therefore the economic case for entry was weakened. The expressed concerns of euro membership supporters that Britain would be economically disadvantaged by non-membership – with the likelihood of lower growth, higher unemployment, higher inflation, and diversion of inward investment – proved to be unfounded. For example, growth in Britain averaged just under 3%, as compared with under 2% in the Eurozone, whilst unemployment levels were much lower than the 10% averaged by the most comparable with Britain Eurozone economies, France and Germany.

The third factor was political calculations of the implications for future electoral success of holding a referendum. A failed referendum, which was seen by most observers from an early stage as being the most likely outcome, could have been electorally damaging in that it could have been interpreted as a government not in control of events, it would show that the government could be defeated, and it would have buoyed the Conservatives.

On CAP and budgetary reform, Britain maintained its long-standing strategy of keeping the issues linked. This was partly because of the continuing prominent position of CAP spending in the EU's budget – it has accounted for around 45% in recent years – and partly because EU budgetary debates habitually result in other member states calling for the abolition of the UK rebate which Mrs Thatcher secured in 1984. Domestically, Blair could not be seen to concede on the demands that Britain give up its rebate without securing agreement to the reform of CAP.

During the Blair years, the key times during which these issues were most prominently on the agenda were in the two periods during which financial perspectives – the medium-term financial planning instruments within which all of the EU's annual budgets are framed – were being considered and negotiated. The first of these financial perspectives, covering the years 2000–06, did not result in too much disputation between the member states, with Britain not over-pressing the need for cuts in CAP expenditure and the other member states not over-focusing on the UK rebate. The contents of the second financial perspective, however, covering 2007–13, were much more strongly contested, not least because of the financial support that would have to be given to the new member states. On the CAP content of the budget, Blair, at a time when he was anxious not to alienate other EU governments because of the looming war in Iraq, was outflanked by Chirac and Schroeder in late 2002 when they pushed an agreement through the European Council that stipulated that CAP spending in the EU-15 states would not be cut during the next financial perspective. As for the UK rebate, Blair was highly desirous – for political prestige reasons – to reach a final agreement on the financial perspective during the British presidency in the second half of 2005, so to help achieve this he agreed to a modest cut in the rebate at the December 2005 European Council meeting. The final agreement on the 2006–13 financial perspective meant that Blair agreed to give up approximately 20% of the British rebate without securing a commitment to the reform of CAP or without a reduction in CAP spending. He did secure an agreement to a Commission review of all EU spending, including on CAP and the British rebate, that would be completed by 2008/9, but that gave no guarantees of either proposed CAP reform or the implementation by the member states of Commission proposals for reform.

Europeanisation and Constitutional Change

Most of the focus on Britain's relationship with the EU under Blair understandably is concerned with high-level and direct EU–UK matters. Our discussion above reflects this focus. But many other, lower-level and less direct, policy, institutional, and process-related changes occurred in Britain under Blair with implications for Britain's relations with the EU. In this section we consider some of the changes that have occurred as a result of 'Europeanisation' and constitutional change.

Europeanisation

Recent research highlights a trend of deepening relations between Britain and the EU in relation to policy, institutions and political processes. The trend, which is commonly described as constituting a process of Europeanisation, did not begin in 1997, but it continued and in many respects was accelerated under Blair.

In relation to policy, three examples may be taken to briefly illustrate how after 1997 the Europeanisation of policy content, structures and style was advanced. In the case of environmental policy, the advancement was located within a greater, partly EU-driven, environmental awareness in which, amongst other things, there was a shift towards more source-based emission controls and a more explicit acceptance by the UK government of EU-specified guiding principles and objectives, such as precaution, prevention and sustainability. Paralleling this greater acceptance of EU-level initiatives, Britain became more active in promoting its own ideas at the EU level, to such an extent that it is now 'found exporting domestic environmental ideas to Brussels with a passion that would have been unimaginable even 15 years ago. Britain is no longer perceived as *the* Dirty Man of Europe.'[26] In the case of competition policy, under the Conservatives British policy had generally been viewed in EU circles as being incompatible with the EU model. The Conservative governments had, however, resisted any significant changes.[27] The Labour government's 1988 Competition Act, though partly based on US designs, brought British practices much more into line with those of the EU. The Act signalled a shift away from

[26] Jordan, 'Environmental Policy', in Bache and Jordan (eds), *The Europeanization of British Politics*, p. 237.
[27] Michelle Cini, 'Competition Policy', in Bache and Jordan (eds), *The Europeanization of British Politics*, pp. 216–30.

pragmatism and a case-by-case approach to competition issues to an outright banning of all cartels and abuses by monopolies. In the case of regional policy, there was a greater acceptance after 1997 of some of the EU-level guiding principles. In particular, the EU's partnership requirement was embraced by Labour and some of the EU's experiments with bottom-up decision-making influenced domestic regeneration and neighbourhood programmes.[28] In short as regards the Europeanisation of policies, in a number of areas the 'fit' between domestic and EU policies improved after 1997 – partly as a result of changes to domestic practices, but also through Britain projecting its preferences more effectively onto the EU.

In terms of institutional change, the changes in Whitehall that took place in how EU affairs were handled under the Blair government have been described as a 'quiet revolution'.[29] The changes included the centralising thrust described above, but also took the form of attempts to shift organisational culture. So, there was a 'mainstreaming' of Europe within every department and a Blair-instigated networking offensive by ministers and officials aimed at developing better bilateral relations with counterparts in other member states. Beyond Whitehall, there were also ongoing Europeanisation effects at the subnational level with, for example, Regional Development Agencies (RDAs) created in England that were built on policy networks and administrative boundaries that were either instigated or strengthened by the requirements of the EU's structural funds.

As for processes, the post-1997 years saw a consolidation, and in some respects a gathering of pace, of informal processes of exchange between a wide range of interest groups on the one hand and EU-level institutions on the other – a process stimulated in part by the European Commission having become an increasingly active promoter of the third sector, both transnationally and domestically.[30] UK environmental and business interests, for example, reoriented an increasing amount of their representational effort towards the EU and restructured internally to facilitate more differentiated approaches to lobbying.[31] And despite there being a

---

[28] Ian Bache, *Europeanization and Multi-level Governance: Cohesion Policy in the European Union and Britain* (New York: Rowman and Littlefield, forthcoming).

[29] Bulmer and Burch, 'Central Government', p. 37.

[30] Rachael Chapman, 'The Third Sector', in Bache and Jordan, *The Europeanization of British Politics*, pp. 168–86.

[31] Jenny Fairbrass, 'Organized Interests', in Bache and Jordan , *The Europeanization of British Politics*, pp. 135–51.

Labour government in power, trade unions and local authorities continued treading the path to Brussels first worn in the face of restrictive Thatcherite policies of the 1980s.[32]

In short, after 1997 Britain's politicians, officials and organised interests became more deeply enmeshed in a wide range of territorially overarching policy networks, which resulted in Britain's relationship with the EU becoming increasingly interdependent and the boundaries between domestic and international politics becoming increasingly blurred.

The impact of constitutional change

A number of constitutional changes introduced under the Blair governments have brought Britain closer to continental systems of governance and, more specifically, to the multi-level governance system that characterises the EU itself. These changes most obviously relate to devolution, but there were also many other changes: independence for the Bank of England (which, in passing, meant the UK fulfilled a requirement for joining the euro); the adoption of proportional representation for elections to devolved authorities and the European Parliament; the incorporation of the European Convention on Human Rights (ECHR) – even though this is a Council of Europe rather than an EU construct; the introduction of a Freedom of Information Act; reform of the House of Lords; and modernisation of the House of Commons.[33]

EU membership was not, and is not, critical in promoting the devolution process in the UK, though it has had a contributory effect – mainly through the way it creates space for the articulation of regional and substate national interests and identities. But though devolution is not because of the EU, the fact of devolution has instigated a much closer fit between the British and EU systems of governance that may make accommodation to future EU policies easier and promote domestic preferences in the European arena more effectively. Devolution has already necessitated a culture shift in the formulation of Britain's EU policy, particularly where the devolved institutions have a responsibility for implementation.

[32] Erin Van der Maas, 'Trade Unions', in Bache and Jordan , *The Europeanization of British Politics*, pp. 152–167.

[33] Simon Bulmer and Martin Burch, 'The Europeanization of UK Government: From Quiet Revolution to Explicit Step-Change?' Paper presented at the ESRC/UACES conference on 'Britain in Europe and Europe in Britain: The Europeanisation of British Politics?' Sheffield Town Hall, July 16, 2004, p. 2.

In effect, 'the basic structure of the state has been changed creating a potentially more varied interpretation of 'national' European interests and objectives'[34]. Moreover, it is difficult to see how even under a less sympathetic government Britain's emerging multi-level governance might be reversed: the main features of Labour's constitutional reforms are now accepted by all of the major parties and to reject them would be electorally unpalatable.

Overall evaluation

At the end of Blair's premiership, the nature of the EU was in important respects more to the government's liking than it had been in 1997: economic policies and priorities had become more liberal in tone and focus; membership had increased to 27 member states, and with more would-be members, including Turkey, in line; and – in no small part because of the increased membership – the prospect of the EU drifting in a federal direction was remote. At the same time, Britain's position as an EU member state had improved: it had come to be more of a mainstream policy actor and was not viewed by other member states with the almost innate suspicion that had so characterised the years of Conservative governments; when it did adopt Eurosceptic positions in policy deliberations it was more likely than formerly to find allies – not just from the two previous main possibilities, Denmark and Sweden, but also from some of the new member states, notably the Czech Republic and Poland; and with the accession of the CEECs, it had more potential allies for its Atlanticist position on external security policy matters.

So, the record of British policy in Europe during the Blair years is strong in very important respects. It is true that Blair cannot be said to have succeeded in his aim of elevating Britain into a consistent leadership position in the EU, but then the nature of the EU is such that in so far as leadership is provided by member states it is inevitably diffused and has to be shared. To talk of providing leadership in the EU context can only mean providing it in partnership with others. And under Blair Britain was a leading player in several core EU policy areas: starting with the Saint-Malo Declaration, in respect of security and defence policy; most prominently with the leading role in helping to launch the Lisbon Process, in respect of internal market, and especially competitiveness, policy; most particularly in the discussions and negotiations that led

---

[34] Burch and Bulmer, 'Central Government', pp. 47–8.

to the Constitutional Treaty, in respect of treaty reform policy; and consistently in respect of EU enlargement policy. It has been further argued that the EU's monetary policy is actually being 'Anglicized', although not through any conscious effort by the Treasury to upload British ideas.[35]

Beyond specific policies, there was a growing British influence under Blair in the broader realm of ideas, particularly in relation to the economy. In facing economic pressures and the attendant policy dilemmas that Britain has largely confronted, EU states have been increasingly attracted to what has been described as the 'Anglo-Social' model in which a robust emphasis on economic competitiveness is accompanied by a minimum wage, tax credits, and other 'safety net' measures to ensure some protection for weaker social groups.

The broad contours of Britain's relationship with the EU under Blair were shaped by a policy of constructive engagement, albeit an engagement that stopped short of participation in the major EU project of the Blair years: the single currency. As part of giving effect to this policy, Blair expended considerable time and effort in cultivating relations with his European counterparts. However, the Iraq War made the policy of constructive engagement more difficult, for it then became an almost impossible challenge to reconcile the simultaneous deepening of relations with both the US and key EU allies. The fact is that although Blair came to office in the guise of apparently the most European-inclined British Prime Minister since Edward Heath, he was also a very strong Atlanticist and never wavered from sticking close to the White House on the most important foreign policy issue of his watch.

This observation takes us to what was perhaps the biggest failing of the Blair governments on Europe: their failure to make headway in changing public opinion on the merits of European integration. This was, of course, a very tall challenge, but the fact is that whilst there was an attempt to 'go beyond the traditional perception of the EU as a threat',[36] at several key moments Blair and other prominent Labour figures tended to set out the government's position in defensive terms rather than presenting a positive case for integration.[37] Yet if Blair wanted to persuade people of his view of sovereignty in which the British–EU relationship

[35] Jim Buller, 'Monetary Policy', in Bache and Jordan (eds.), *The Europeanization of British Politics*, pp. 201–15.
[36] Simon Bulmer, 'Britain and European Integration', in Bill Jones *et al.*, *Politics UK*, 6th edn (Harlow: Longman, 2006), p. 810.
[37] Riddell, 'Europe', p. 379.

could be win-win, it was essential that the argument be taken to the public more forcefully and less equivocally.

But, overall, when the dust has settled, the record of the Blair governments on Europe is likely to be seen as being more positive than negative. There were significant achievements in terms of both style and substance, which related not only to the oft-reported big issues but also to less obvious developments and to domestic reforms that may prove to be of enduring significance for Britain's relationship with Europe.

25

Development

RICHARD MANNING

What was the state of Britain's contribution to international development when Labour took office in May 1997?

No British government can ignore issues of international development. The United Kingdom's history, the Commonwealth connection, the reality of trade, migration and personal links, and the concern of many citizens for humanitarian action see to that. But in the run-up to the 1997 election, the Conservative government, while maintaining its tradition-ally open attitude to international trade and indeed claiming in its elec-tion manifesto[1] a leadership role on addressing issues of debt, was not seen as a powerful force in international support for development.

A significant reason for that was an aid programme that was declining in real terms. Also, the government had been found to have acted illegally in the case of a high-profile project in Malaysia, the Pergau Dam, a project which ministers had been advised was uneconomic. Indeed, the govern-ment had made a point of asserting that the political and commercial interests of the UK would be given particular weight in decisions on aid. But, more broadly, neither the UK nor many other OECD countries had found it easy to generate strong domestic support for more than human-itarian aid, or for giving development issues a high political profile. This had already in 1996 stimulated the Development Assistance Committee of the OECD to set out, in a landmark document, *Shaping the Twenty-first Century: The Role of Development Cooperation*,[2] a new approach to aid, linking it strongly to specific development results. But in 1997, while both the main parties genuflected in their manifestos[3] to the UN target for aid

---

[1] Conservative Party manifesto for the 1997 general election, p. 35.

[2] OECD, *Shaping the Twenty-First Century: The Role of Development Co-operation* (Paris: OECD, 1996).

[3] 1997 Labour Party election manifesto, p. 36: 'We reaffirm the UK's commitment to the 0.7 percent UN aid target and in government Labour will start to reverse the decline in aid spending'; Conservative Party manifesto, p. 27: 'We will continue to maintain a significant

to reach 0.7% of gross national income (GNI), neither committed themselves to any particular level of funding.

What was the state of Britain's contribution to international development when Tony Blair left office?

Ten years later, issues of international development are much harder to ignore, international aid from the UK and from most other donor countries has risen sharply, and the developing world – and even, in the past few years, sub-Saharan Africa – is routinely growing faster in terms of income per head than the countries of the OECD.

As far as aid is concerned, a revealing comment on the domestic debate is that the Conservative manifesto for the 2005 election,[4] far from distancing itself from the Labour government's approach, said 'We believe that British aid programmes are among the best in the world', and matched the government's pledge to reach the 0.7% target by 2013. The OECD Development Assistance Committee (DAC), in its review of the UK's development programme in 2006,[5] started with the headline 'UK offers a powerful model for development cooperation', and said that the Department for International Development had gone through a 'golden age' of growth and achievement since 1997. And at the Gleneagles Summit in 2005, Tony Blair persuaded his colleagues to sign up to a $50 billion increase in aid worldwide,[6] and a doubling of aid to Africa between 2004 and 2010. In 2006, for the first time in the history of international aid, the UK was surpassed in its aid levels only by the United States.

But the concerns pressed by the British government, and not least by Tony Blair himself, went well beyond aid. As noted below, Tony Blair became convinced that in some cases 'hard' power had to be deployed to achieve durable change, and he developed a strong interest in issues around peacekeeping and governance. The government backed treaties on both landmines and the trade in small arms. It became more and more assertive on issues around climate change (discussed in chapter 26). And it continued Britain's longstanding support for freer trade and for tackling the problem of unsustainable debt.

Footnote 3 (*cont.*)
    bilateral and multilateral aid programme reflecting the aspiration of meeting the UN's target of 0.7% of GDP as a long-term objective.'
[4] Government election manifesto 2005, p. 27.
[5] 'Peer Review of the United Kingdom', *OECD Journal on Development*, 7, 2006: 11.
[6] The Gleneagles Communiqué, Africa, paras. 28 and 27.

Overall, although necessarily affected by Britain's involvement in Iraq, the UK's international profile on development issues has probably not been higher since John Maynard Keynes was negotiating the establishment of the World Bank in 1944.

What changed and why?

The change has been driven in part by genuine changes in articulate public opinion. The public support for the Jubilee 2000 campaign, the willingness to contribute on an unprecedented scale to relief and rehabilitation after the Indian Ocean tsunami, the success of the 'Make Poverty History' and 'Live 8' campaigns, and the rise of the Fair Trade movement all showed heightened public concern about the well-being of poor people worldwide. In the world of realpolitik, the implications of 9/11, and the rapid rise of China and India and their impact on raw material supplies were all significant reasons for politicians to reassess the priority of international development. Many countries as well as the UK gave development issues more weight (as witness the increase in US aid under George W. Bush after its decline under Bill Clinton). But there was something special about what happened in the UK, and public policy must be allowed considerable weight in assessing the reasons for the change.

The story starts with the Foreign Policy Review, carried out by the Labour Party in Opposition in 1994–6, under the leadership of Robin Cook, with Joan Lestor as the shadow spokesperson on aid matters. This review – itself a very normal Labour Party procedure – included a proposal to establish a new department under a cabinet minister with a brief to promote international development. Similar proposals, designed essentially to reduce the use of aid for political and commercial ends, had been included in Labour's three previous manifestos in opposition, no doubt influenced by the setting-up by Harold Wilson in 1964 of the Ministry of Overseas Development under Barbara Castle. The legacy of the Ministry of Overseas Development, which had in practice quickly lost influence after Barbara Castle's departure, remained in the form of the Overseas Development Administration (ODA), which ran Britain's international aid programmes as a separate unit within the Foreign and Commonwealth Office.

As the 1997 election approached, Clare Short, who was by now the shadow International Development spokesperson, was asked by Tony Blair to look again at whether a separate department of state was justified.

Her conclusion, after reviewing the practice of other countries, consulting leading development think-tanks and taking advice from the Permanent Secretary of the ODA, Sir John Vereker, was that the proposal for a new department headed by a cabinet minister should stand. Tony Blair's first important decision in this area was to accept her advice. The party manifesto[7] stated: 'In Government we will strengthen and restructure the British aid programme and bring development issues back into the mainstream of government decision-making. A Cabinet Minister will lead a new department of international development.' The presence of a cabinet-level Secretary of State and a separate department was to prove a powerful signal both internally in Whitehall and externally.

Clare Short herself had had no particular background in the field of development before her appointment. As she read herself into her brief before the election, a particularly significant encounter was with the distinguished academic and former deputy head of UNICEF, Sir Richard Jolly. Jolly brought to her attention the DAC report mentioned above, which had been agreed earlier in 1996 and which set out a limited number of quantitative goals for achievement by specific dates (usually 2015) in fields such as poverty reduction, education, health and the environment. Clare Short determined that working to achieve these measurable results would be the core of the mission of the new department. Thanks in no small measure to her advocacy, the International Development Goals set by the DAC were taken up by the United Nations at the Millennium Assembly in the form of the Millennium Development Goals, which set an agreed framework for the results to be achieved by international development efforts over the period to 2015.[8] Together with the successful UN Conference on Financing for Development in Monterrey in March 2002,[9] which emphasised the responsibilities of both recipients and donors for real progress, and which was the focus for important aid commitments by both the United States and the European Union, this gave the international development effort a much clearer frame of reference than it had had before.

The handling of the Goals was characteristic of a strong feature of the UK's approach under successive Labour Secretaries of State: the attempt to influence the international system. Whether in the World Bank, the UN system, the EU or the OECD, DFID and its Secretary of State worked

[7] 1997 Labour Party election manifesto, p. 36.
[8] UN General Assembly Resolution 55, of 8 September 2000, United Nations.
[9] Monterrey Consensus of the International Conference on Financing for Development, United Nations Department of Public Information, October 2003.

to encourage other actors to join it to make changes in accordance with its development philosophy. The policy was clearly stated in the government's first White Paper on International Development in November 1997:[10] 'We should not over-estimate what we can do by ourselves. We should not under-estimate what we can do with others . . . Helping to lead the world in a commitment to poverty elimination and sustainable development is an international role in which all the people of Britain could take pride.' Nine years later, the 2006 DAC Review[11] observed: 'As DFID proactively seeks to influence international donors towards common approaches, it needs to strike a balance between its objective of leadership in aid reform and being perceived as promoting its own model' – in a way, a backhanded testament to the strength and determination of DFID's advocacy. Clare Short had quickly found allies in the president of the World Bank, Jim Wolfensohn, and in her fellow ministers from Norway, the Netherlands and Germany, with whom she formed the 'Utstein Group', later to develop into a wider 'Nordic Plus' group of like-minded donors.

However, the influencing of Britain's partners was not just a matter for DFID and its Secretary of State. Both Gordon Brown as Chancellor and Tony Blair as Prime Minister used their own networks with increasing effect to promote Britain's aims for international development and specific initiatives. In the Chancellor's case, these included the International Monetary and Finance Committee, of which Gordon Brown was chair from 1999, the G7 Finance Ministers' meetings (crucial entities for promoting solutions to the debt problems of poor countries), and the European Council of Ministers of Economy and Finance (ECOFIN), which played a particularly important role in setting the aid commitments for European Union members that were adopted by the Barcelona Summit in 2002. For the Prime Minister, the main formal stage was the succession of G7/G8 Summits. But his personal links with developing-country leaders, particularly those of the Commonwealth, were also used to good effect, for example in the Commission for Africa. More is said on the role of the Prime Minister and Chancellor below.

The attempt to spread influence was backed up by a conscious policy of publishing policy papers to develop and promote new ideas. Already in 1997, the first White Paper set out a clear message that elimination of poverty was to be the headline goal of the policy. A further White Paper in

---

[10] DFID, *Eliminating World Poverty: A Challenge for the 21st Century*, Cm. 3789 (London: HMSO, 1997), para. 1.23.   [11] 'Peer Review of the United Kingdom', p. 6.

2000,[12] the product of Clare Short's experience of the anti-globalisation backlash at the failed WTO meeting in Seattle the previous year, set out how development policies could make globalisation work for the poor. And this tradition was maintained in a third White Paper in 2006[13] that looked similarly at governance. These White Papers, and the stream of more detailed policy documents that were published, contrasted starkly with the absence of any such high-level government-wide policy papers under the Conservatives. DFID also invested heavily in development education, in collaboration with the Department for Education and Employment, and began a series of regional events around the UK to build support at local level.

The clear – almost relentless – focus on the reduction and eventual elimination of poverty as the raison d'être of the British aid programme was locked in by the International Development and Cooperation Act of 2002.[14] By this measure, parliament made it illegal for the aid programme to be used for any purpose other than poverty reduction and humanitarian relief (there is a modest exception that recognises the government's particular responsibilities for the Dependent Territories, where other objectives are also permitted). This is a thoroughgoing measure: for example, it makes the tying of aid to British goods and services illegal. One response was the establishment in 2002 of a 'Global Opportunities Fund' at the FCO, which provides some £60 million a year for activities that assist the UK's overseas objectives but which fall outside the purpose of reducing poverty.

A further change was in the resources devoted to Britain's aid programme. Here, as elsewhere, the retention of the previous government's spending ceilings for 1997/8 and 1998/9 meant that aid increases only showed up gradually. Indeed, the UK's aid reached its lowest ever level as a percentage of GNI as late as 1999. But each public spending round saw DFID at or near the top of the table of percentage increases. Figure 25.1 shows how this translated into a notable rise in the UK's official development assistance as a percentage of GNI. This climbed steadily above the average for the major Western donors of the OECD's Development Assistance Committee (which is pulled down by low US performance on this measure) and in 2006 also, for the first time, exceeded the level of the mid-point member of the DAC.

[12] DFID, *Eliminating World Poverty: Making Globalisation Work for the Poor*, Cm. 5006 (London: HMSO, 2000).
[13] DFID, *Eliminating World Poverty: Making Governance Work for the Poor*, Cm. 6876 (London: TSO, 2006).
[14] *International Development and Cooperation Act* (London: HMSO, 2002).

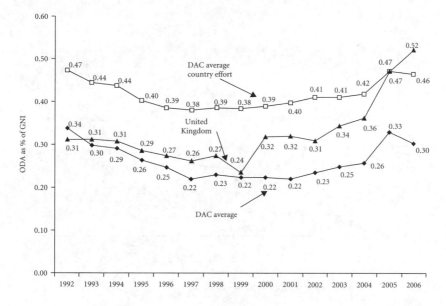

Figure 25.1. UK official development assistance (ODA) compared to the average of
OECD/DAC (as percentage of GNI, 1992–2006)
Source: OECD/DAC

Figure 25.2 compares the UK's aid with the levels of the other 'top five'
OECD donors. The UK's total aid rose from 2000 onwards to levels comparable to those of France or Germany, from a position of little more than
half their weight when the Labour government assumed office. In 2005,
the UK's aid, for the first time, exceeded that of both France and
Germany, and in 2006 it rose even above that of Japan.

One more change was that DFID increasingly played a role in the promotion of more coherent policies towards developing countries, something noted, for example, in successive reports by the DAC. Key areas
of collaboration included debt (with the Treasury), the new Doha
'Development' Round of trade talks (with the DTI), security and development (with the FCO, the MOD and indeed No. 10), and environment
(with DEFRA and its predecessors). The Secretary of State was consulted
on arms export licensing decisions, the first time that a development
agency in the UK had been given such a role. The successive White Papers
cemented these cross-government policies. In contrast to the arguments
that had taken place over the first White Paper, DFID's proposal for the
second one, on globalisation, won swift support from across Whitehall.

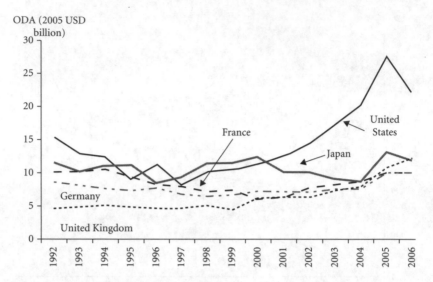

Figure 25.2. Net ODA from 'top five' DAC donors, 1992–2006
Source: OECD/DAC.

This more 'joined-up' approach was backed up by some interesting innovations at the administrative level. Joint targets with departments such as the Treasury and the FCO were agreed in the Public Service Agreements that accompanied each spending round.[15] Based on experience in the Sierra Leone crisis of 1998–2000 in particular, which had underlined the need for closely coordinated policies, 'conflict pools' were set up for Africa and for the rest of the world, under which DFID, FCO and MOD had to sit together with the Cabinet Office and the Treasury to agree on strategies toward conflict-prone states, following which each department received back money from the 'pool' to finance its part in the strategy. A joint FCO/DFID unit was set up to handle the difficult situation in the Sudan. And in 2004 a special cross-departmental unit comprising staff from the Ministry of Defence, the Foreign and Commonwealth Office and DFID was set up to promote joint working in specific conflict situations.

How successful and effective have the changes been?

Where development problems were susceptible to additional resources, sensibly applied, the Blair years saw some very positive results for British

---

[15] See, for example, DFID, *Public Service Agreement 2005–2008* (London: Department for International Development, 2005).

aid. Countries such as Ghana, Mozambique, Rwanda, Tanzania and Uganda, in all of which the UK was a major donor, experienced rapid growth and poverty reduction during the Blair government. While in some cases these countries were building on a longer track record of progress, it seems reasonable to suppose that increased British aid was one element in the progress that they recorded. It also seems clear that DFID's role as a major funder of both Rwanda and Uganda enabled its Secretaries of State to be effective in defusing some potentially serious disputes between the two countries. And clearly, Britain's deployment of military, political and development assets in Sierra Leone went far in transforming the prospects of that tragic country.

The readiness of the UK to underwrite the development programmes of these and other countries with more flexible forms of finance, notably general support for their budgets, and to encourage other donors to do likewise, gave the central agencies in such countries the ability to shape their own development path to a greater extent than would have been the case with a more traditional project-by-project approach. This approach involved some risks: a donor offering such support is very vulnerable to any poor decision that the leaders of the country in question may take. Successive ministers were ready to take such risks for the wider benefits, though pulling back where problems arose (as in Uganda in 2005 when President Museveni re-wrote the Constitution to enable him to secure a third term, or in Ethiopia in 2006 when the government cracked down harshly on the Opposition: in each case Hilary Benn reacted by reallocating unrestricted budget support to more closely defined ends, while maintaining the overall flow of resources).

Internationally, the UK was effective in promoting its development agenda in the various groups and institutions of which it was a member. A particularly good example in the later part of the period was the European Union. From a traditionally sceptical position on the quality of EC aid and on the value of the Brussels process, the UK began to appreciate the value of European Commission pressure on EU laggards (well illustrated by the Commission's role in encouraging major commitments in the context of the Monterrey Conference) and found the EC a very significant ally in promoting the concept of general budget support.

In 2004, the new EC Development Commissioner, Louis Michel, began to argue for an EU-wide development policy. One might have predicted that this would have either proved hopelessly ambitious (previous strategies had in practice merely bound the Commission itself) or ended up as a verbose and ineffective document of little significance or interest to

Britain. In fact, the UK Presidency managed to get agreement in November 2005 to a policy statement[16] that did bind member states as well as the Commission, and seems to be regarded as a very influential point of reference, not least for the many new member states now developing programmes of their own. A separate policy paper on Africa[17] was endorsed a month later, also under the UK Presidency. Taken together with the unexpected success of the EU in agreeing in May of the same year on aid targets for all its members for 2010 and indeed 2015,[18] this showed that the UK could work effectively with an EU-wide agenda in the development arena.

One element in the new European Union Strategy is renewed commitment to coherent policies towards developing countries, a legal requirement since the Maastricht Treaty of 1991 but one often overlooked. DFID, in contrast to the Ministry of Overseas Development and the Overseas Development Administration, seems to have had some influence on the wider set of policies in both the UK and in the EU. This has been in part because it has invested more heavily in policy-relevant research and in staff who were seen as credible interlocutors by their Whitehall colleagues. But it is also significantly because other departments can increasingly see that many of their agendas, from trade negotiations to climate change, require the active support of developing countries. DFID has therefore managed to position itself as in many cases assisting the achievement of the objectives of other departments. Clear examples include a positive stance on 'aid for trade', in other words for using aid to meet developing-country concerns about lack of competitiveness, a willingness to put substantial resources into conflict-prone states such as Sierra Leone or the Democratic Republic of Congo, and market-friendly interventions in the health sector, such as an Advance Market Commitment[19] to stimulate research into treatment of diseases of the poor. In each of these cases – trade, conflict and global health – DFID can claim to have had some influence on the policy approach of the UK government as a whole.

DFID can also claim some genuine success in its own departmental management, drawing on the exceptional degree of commitment of its staff at all levels. Year in and year out, it is, with the Treasury, at the top of the departments of choice in the home civil service for fast-stream

---

[16] 'European Union Development Policy: The "European Consensus"', *Official Journal C* 46/0, 24 February 2006.   [17] European Union Strategy for Africa, 24 May 2005.
[18] Council of the European Union, 24 May 2005.   [19] *The Independent*, 10 February 2007.

entrants. Under Sir John Vereker's successor, Sir Suma Chakrabarti, it has pushed the boundaries in recruiting top-level staff from outside, not least from the World Bank, and significantly improved the gender balance of its senior staff. Staff surveys show that it has developed an enviable reputation in Whitehall as a department with well-respected top management and in particular a strong sense of direction. This is due not least to a well-thought-out system of objective-setting at all levels, drawing on Public Service Agreements with the Treasury that have linked the purpose of the department closely to progress against the Millennium Development Goals, and cascading down into the 'Delivery Plans' of each director, and so to the objectives of departments and individual members of staff. And in 2007 DFID was the top-rated department in the series of 'Capability Reviews'[20] of Government Departments carried out under the leadership of the Cabinet Secretary, Sir Gus O'Donnell.

Where relevant, why was more not achieved?

Not everything worked smoothly, however. Within the aid programme itself, the implications of 9/11 posed some very difficult issues, both of country priorities and of how DFID could work in areas where security was a major issue. The invasions of Afghanistan and Iraq put these problems into stark relief.

The public expenditure round of 2002 had set DFID an objective of providing 90% of all its aid by the year 2006 for countries classified by the World Bank as 'low-income'. While Afghanistan fell into this category, Iraq did not, and hence the build-up of a large programme in Iraq set a major problem for the department. Rather than sacrifice the 90% target, a brave decision was made to cut bilateral aid to some eight other middle-income countries to accommodate the rising expenditure on Iraq. This had the benefit of reducing the UK's extremely numerous set of programmes (important, as civil service numbers were to be cut back by Treasury decree), but at the cost of cutting relationships and activities at short notice.

Within both Iraq and Afghanistan, DFID found itself operating in a very taxing environment, where traditional approaches (for example, an incremental and participatory approach to development activities, maximum use of host-country systems) were either impossible or

[20] Capability Review of the Department for International Development, Cabinet Office, March 2007.

severely constrained by security problems on the one hand and very
weak institutions on the other. Although some positive experience
had been gained in such environments as Bosnia and Kosovo, it proved
very difficult to manage effective programmes or to find an easy relationship with the military, who were of course anxious to see very fast
results.

Other areas where DFID found it difficult to influence other government departments effectively included migration policy, although the
National Health Service did agree guidelines in 2001 against hiring staff
from developing countries with a critical scarcity of health professionals, and later encouraged similar action by private agencies; the
problem of narcotic drugs, where simplistic attempts to address supply-
side issues continued in defiance of much development experience; and
anti-corruption, where the Home Office was poorly resourced to cope
with international dimensions of the issue.

And of course, there were severe limits to the broader UK ability to
influence key international events, as the tortured history of the Doha
Round negotiations showed, despite the many positive references in G8
communiqués (notably in 2006 at St Petersburg) to the need for early
progress.

To what extent was change driven by the Prime Minister himself, or from No. 10 in general, by Gordon Brown, by other ministers, departments, think-tanks or any other factors?

It is very clear that the successes described above would have been impossible without support and leadership from the Prime Minister and the
Chancellor, as well as the personal contribution of the Secretaries of State
for International Development and the motivation and effectiveness of
their department. However, this played out in different ways at different
times.

Both Tony Blair and Gordon Brown have strong convictions about the
need to promote better lives for poor people across the world. Both
became aware early on in the first Labour term of the political strength
of both faith-based and secular campaigns for development. The Jubilee
2000 'Drop the Debt' campaign was particularly significant, and its
demonstration at the 1998 G8 Summit in Birmingham particularly
effective. The handling of the debt issue at the Köln Summit the following
year was a good example of how the government worked in a coordinated
way between Gordon Brown, who had to make the detailed case to his

G7 Finance Minister colleagues, and the Prime Minister, who had to persuade the leaders themselves.[21]

It would, however, be true to say that in Labour's first term, with the exception of the debt issue, DFID had reasonable scope to develop its policies and systems in the knowledge that it was seen as making a positive contribution to the government's overall objectives. Pressure for short-term 'initiatives' could usually be handled in a way coherent with longer-term objectives, such as when the Prime Minister was able to commit the UK at the Denver Summit of 1997 to raising by 50% Britain's bilateral support for basic healthcare, basic education and clean water in Africa, or when Gordon Brown announced at the Commonwealth Finance Ministers' Meeting that same year the writing-off of much of Britain's remaining aid loans. Clare Short made the maximum use of the policy space thus created, and the 2001 Labour manifesto[22] declared that 'with strong UK leadership, the international development effort is now increasingly focused on poverty reduction'.

The second and third terms, by contrast, saw a considerable increase in interest from No. 10, now with a full-time policy adviser on development and climate change, and the launching of new high-profile proposals from the Treasury.

Tony Blair had had longstanding links with Thabo Mbeki, who succeeded Nelson Mandela as President of South Africa. He and Mbeki worked together increasingly from 2001 to promote a new approach to development in Africa, which was to be more African-'owned' and less dependent on donors. They wrote a joint article for The Guardian in the summer of 2001 on what was then called the 'New Africa Initiative'. These ideas were the subject of special mention at the G8 Summit in Genoa in June, where leaders agreed to appoint high-level personal representatives to work with African leaders on a plan to be presented to the Kananaskis Summit of 2002, and were further developed in the run-up to the Labour Party conference of 2001. Tony Blair held an already planned meeting with key African leaders just a week after the 9/11 atrocities in New York. At that year's conference he made a powerful statement[23] about the need to give much more attention to Africa.

Tony Blair's view of what was needed in Africa rightly went well beyond issues of aid. He had taken a decisive line (supported by

[21] Report of G7 Finance Ministers on the Köln Economic Summit, 18–20 June 1999; G8 Communiqué, Köln, 20 June 1999, paras. 29–30.
[22] Labour Party election manifesto 2001, p. 60.
[23] Speech by Tony Blair at the Labour Party conference, Brighton, September 2001.

Clare Short) in using UK military weight to end the rebel threat in Sierra Leone. As a result, he had developed a strong interest in better arrangements for peacekeeping, using a mix of rich countries' logistic assets and African 'boots on the ground'. He also saw the significance of progress on access for African agriculture to Northern markets, and indeed crossed swords with President Chirac over it at an EU Summit in 2002. Tony Blair strongly supported the Canadian government in per-suading the Kananaskis Summit in the same year to agree a wide-ranging 'G8 Africa Action Plan' in support of Africa's own 'New Partnership for Africa's Development'.[24] G8 African Personal Representatives (Baroness Amos being the UK representative) presented comprehensive proposals to the Evian Summit in 2003,[25] following which President Chirac pushed through plans for a more permanent 'Africa Partnership Forum', includ-ing non-G8 aid donors and African countries and institutions.

This might have been thought sufficient G8 attention to Africa. Tony Blair, however, decided in 2003 on two further initiatives: that Africa would be one of the two major themes of the Gleneagles Summit of 2005, and that in preparation for this a 'Brandt-style' international Commission would be created to assess what progress was being made and what more needed to be done. The decision to establish the Commission owed a good deal to the concerns expressed to the Prime Minister by Bob Geldof fol-lowing a visit to Africa that far too little was being done despite wide agreement on what was needed to improve local conditions.

The Africa Commission brought together a mix of African leaders and policymakers – who between them constituted a numerical majority within the Commission – and senior figures from a wide range of non-African countries. Bob Geldof himself was a member. Its crucial meeting was hosted in Addis Ababa by Ethiopian Prime Minister Meles Zenawi and attended by Tony Blair. The degree of consensus was remarkable and, working against a tight deadline, a report (*Our Common Interest*) was issued in March 2005.[26] What made it different was its comprehensive approach and recognition that different clusters of issues could not be approached in isolation from each other; its intellectual rigour with which those linkages were demonstrated; the strong degree of African participation in and ownership of its recommendations (which were endorsed in full by the African Union Summit just days before

[24] G8 Africa Action Plan, Kananaskis Summit Communiqué, 27 June 2002.
[25] Implementation Report by Africa Personal Representatives to Leaders on the G8 Africa Action Plan, June 2003.
[26] Commission for Africa, *Our Common Interest* (London: Penguin, 2005).

Gleneagles); and the thorough consultation process across Africa, within the G8, with the international organisations and elsewhere which took place before and during the writing of the report.

The report was used effectively by the UK as the intellectual driver for the Gleneagles Summit conclusions. These do indeed amount to a fairly comprehensive and linked set of commitments: on peace and stability; on governance; on investing in people; on growth; on development finance; and on mutual accountability. The Gleneagles communiqué captures very much what Tony Blair was aiming at in relation to Africa over several years.

Gordon Brown also took a strong and increasing role in the area of development. While Tony Blair concentrated on the 'big picture', with Africa as a particular focus of concern, Gordon Brown worked in several areas where Finance Ministers were key to progress, and tenaciously pursued a limited number of major themes which had relevance for poor countries as a whole. Probably the one with the highest profile was debt, where his chairmanship of the International Monetary and Finance Committee (in essence, the IMF Board meeting at ministerial level) gave him an excellent position to influence the international financial institutions. Crucial advances were made at the Köln Summit in 1999[27] and then in 2005,[28] where the UK secured the writing off of IFI loans and credits to countries covered by the Heavily Indebted Poor Countries initiative (HIPC). The Labour government was at the forefront of proposing ways of addressing the debt problems of poor countries – as indeed was its Conservative predecessor – and could fairly claim that by 2005 it had achieved pretty well all its objectives, including a very significant settlement of the international official debts of Nigeria.

Gordon Brown, however, appreciated that debt relief alone was not an adequate or in isolation a sustainable response to the problems faced by poor countries. He saw both trade and aid as important contributors to development. The international trade agenda was set essentially by the Doha Round, but Brown had a more direct stake in the issue of aid volume.

Gordon Brown played a central role in the extent of increases allowed for DFID in the various public spending rounds during his chancellorship. It seems unlikely that Tony Blair put the Chancellor under pressure to be particularly favourable to DFID, though of course he accepted the figures put down by the Chancellor. Figure 25.3 shows the percentage

[27] Report of G7 Finance Ministers on the Köln Debt Initiative, June 1999.
[28] Report of G7 Finance Ministers, 11 June 2005.

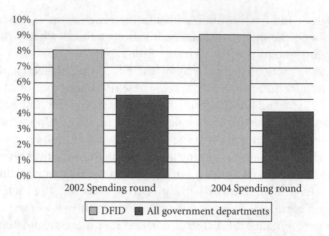

Figure 25.3. Annual increase in department expenditure limits (source: DFID).

increases provided to DFID in each spending round compared to the average across all government departments.

This degree of consistent increase was certainly fundamental to the UK's ability to influence its international peers, and translated into large increases in the aid receipts of countries where UK bilateral aid was significant. But Gordon Brown's approach was not limited to action by the UK alone.

Brown was impressed, in the run-up to the Monterrey Conference of 2002, by the report of an international team led by former Mexican President Zedillo,[29] which suggested that international aid would have to rise by some $50 billion a year from its then level (also of the order of $50 billion) if the Millennium Development Goals were to be reached. He was therefore sympathetic to an attempt, put in motion by Koos Richelle, the Director-General of the Development Directorate of the European Commission in late 2001, to find a formula which would enable EU member states to go to Monterrey with a common approach to increasing the volume of their aid. Brown backed the formula (a commitment of 0.39% of GNI at EU level and a minimum of 0.33% in any one member state by 2006), and played a key role in getting ECOFIN agreement to it in time for the Barcelona Summit of 2002 that endorsed this ambitious proposal.

The increases agreed by the EU at Barcelona and the parallel initiatives by the Bush administration were quite impressive in a context of static or

[29] Report of the High-Level Panel on Financing for Development, 28 June 2001, www.un. org/reports/financing.

declining international aid. However, they fell far short of the doubling of aid called for by Zedillo in order to achieve the Millennium Development Goals. Brown and his advisers therefore looked, even before the EU discussions, at the scope for innovative measures to boost aid in the short to medium term.

In November 2001 Gordon Brown launched in his annual autumn statement[30] a proposal for a new way of financing a major increase in aid – the 'International Finance Facility'. This concept, originally developed with his advisers and Goldman Sachs, was to float bonds on the market whose proceeds would be used to 'front-load' aid spending, and which would be redeemed from the aid programme at some future date. Because the bonds would not be redeemable if certain specified events were to take place, the 'mortgaging' of future aid budgets would not be treated as a Budget liability. At the same time, the specified events – for example, a breach with the IMF – were designed to be sufficiently unusual to give some comfort to the bondholders, and thus minimise the interest charge on the bonds.

Gordon Brown's announcement was met with some surprise by his G7 colleagues, although they could see the theoretical attractions of achieving extra aid spending without having to write it into their own immediate public spending plans. Many of them argued that their systems would not permit what some regarded as budgetary legerdemain. However, Gordon Brown continued to press the idea in bilateral and multilateral forums. He secured French backing at a meeting with the then French Finance Minister, Nicolas Sarkozy, in the spring of 2004. From subsequent technical work emerged the idea of a pilot scheme for doubling the rate of vaccinations financed by the Global Alliance on Vaccinations and Immunisation, and this became a reality in the autumn of 2006, with the Pope symbolically purchasing the first bond. Although there still seems little likelihood that the much more substantial scheme originally proposed will generate a critical mass of support, Gordon Brown's determination was central to achieving the 'International Financing Facility for Vaccines and Immunisation',[31] which is resulting in a doubling of the rate of vaccinations for a series of life-threatening childhood diseases and is predicted to save the lives of five million children by 2015. It also enabled him to be in a position to encourage his G7 colleagues to come up with alternative possibilities for increasing aid.

---

[30] Statement by the Chancellor of the Exchequer on the Pre-Budget Report, 27 November 2001.   [31] See www.iff-immunisation.org.

In February 2004, Gordon Brown called a meeting, chaired by Lord Carey, the former Archbishop of Canterbury and involving non-governmental organisations, the president of the World Bank and public figures such as Bono and Bob Geldof, to assess what sort of options should be considered in the context of the UK's Presidency of the G8 in 2005. At this meeting, the Chancellor made a speech[32] in which he emphasised a triple strategy of further debt relief, progress on trade and a further push on more aid. In the light of NGO pressure, he also concluded that the UK should, for the first time, aim to achieve the UN 0.7% target for aid as a percentage of GNI by a set date (2013), a very radical change in the UK's traditional position of supporting the target in principle while avoiding any set date for reaching it. This decision, announced in the 2004 public expenditure round, gave the UK useful moral high ground in arguing the case for its G7 and EU partners to do more.

In February 2005, Gordon Brown persuaded his G7 colleagues to put work in hand so that decisions could be made at the summit on a 'financing package to achieve the Millennium Development Goals'.[33] By June 2005, the G7 Finance Ministers were able to talk in terms of a possible increase in ODA between 2004 and 2010 of $42 billion,[34] with decisions still awaited from Canada and the US. This was a key building block on the road to the Gleneagles conclusion of a planned $50 billion increase in aid between the two dates.

As far as the EU was concerned, a formula based on that of 2002 was proposed by the Commission for 2010 and strongly backed by the UK: an aid/GNI ratio of 0.56% at EU level, with a minimum of 0.51% for the EU15 and best endeavours to reach 0.17% by the same date for the new member states. This time, the key meeting was between Development Ministers on the eve of a General Affairs Council meeting in May 2005. Again, success was (just) achieved, and endorsed at the Gleneagles Summit – a tribute to teamwork both within the UK system between Tony Blair, Gordon Brown and Hilary Benn, and between the UK and the Commission, whose attempts to encourage public spending by member states are normally opposed by the UK.

[32] Speech by the Chancellor of the Exchequer at Conference on 'Making Globalisation Work for All – The Challenge of Delivering the Monterrey Consensus', hm-treasury.gov.uk.
[33] G7 Finance Ministers' Conclusions on Development, London, 4–5 February 2005, hm-treasury.gov.uk.
[34] G8 Finance Ministers' Conclusions on Development, London, 10–11 June 2005, hm-treasury.gov.uk.

With the headline commitments now agreed, but clearly representing a huge and difficult increase from several key donors, Gordon Brown began a stronger focus on the need for delivery in key sectors. He had long been interested in better financing for education in developing countries. In May 2006, he floated at a meeting in Nigeria the establishment of ten-year plans by African governments for basic education, which would then receive equally long-term commitments from donor governments. By May 2007, some twenty-five such plans were at various stages of readiness, and Gordon Brown was promoting long-term support for such plans among the donor community at a meeting in Brussels co-hosted by the European Commission and the World Bank.

It is therefore clear that in this area both Tony Blair and Gordon Brown were influential, and over time increasingly so, on what was seen as a set of issues of increasing international significance and public resonance. However, Clare Short's unusually long tenure of six years as Secretary of State and her own forceful personality enabled her to do much to set the main directions of UK development policy, at least until the approach of the Iraq conflict. Her consistency of message, readiness to engage in policy debate, willingness to stand up to outside pressures and to leave her civil servants to manage the department, all made her a highly effective departmental minister. Much of the shape and ethos of the UK development effort bears her stamp.

Her immediate successor, Baroness Amos, had less impact, having less than a year in the post, and having to deal with the difficulties inherent in the immediate aftermath of the fall of Saddam Hussein. She was in turn replaced in October 2003 by Hilary Benn, who had already had some experience as a junior minister under Clare Short and as Minister of State since May 2003. Hilary Benn made it his business to improve relations with colleagues in other parts of government, while still using the protection of the 2002 Act to avoid the aid programme being pressured into activity of marginal developmental benefit. He worked very effectively with the Prime Minister and Chancellor in the joint effort to achieve the results set out in the Gleneagles communiqué.

What has been the net Blair effect between 1994/7 and 2007?

As indicated above, Tony Blair left behind a radically strengthened UK voice in international development, backed by a very significant increase in public resources, and by institutional arrangements (notably energetic cabinet-level leadership of the development agenda) that underpin that voice.

The willingness of the Chancellor and the Prime Minister to press the development agenda with their peers was very significant to the outcome. As his speeches to the World Economic Forum in Davos in 2005[35] and 2007 make plain, Tony Blair consistently urged that the problems of Africa should be given higher priority than narrowly conceived realpolitik might suggest. This reflected his view, set out in the 2007 Davos[36] speech, that 'power over global issues can only be effectively wielded today by global alliances, based on global values'.

In support of this approach, both he and the Chancellor were unusually open to involving civil society in their policy discussions, to the point where the 'Make Poverty History' and 'Live 8' campaigns of 2005 came near to being a 'UK Inc.' approach to exerting effective international pressure on less positive members of the G8, linked to major international events. It is fair to say that this was qualitatively different from policies under previous governments of either main party. Indeed it can be seen as quite a sophisticated form of 'new diplomacy' in which international civil society networks were encouraged to press a range of governments to move in directions that the British government was ready to support. In particular, the strength of popular support in the UK, combined with the forceful arguments of the Commission for Africa – and Bob Geldof always saw one of his key roles as being to galvanise public opinion behind the Commission's findings – proved to be a formidable combination in the run-up to the Gleneagles Summit.

To what extent did policy mark a departure from traditional Labour (and Tory) policy?

In terms of policy, the changes that have taken place may be regarded as less than radical. Many strands of UK development policy, such as free trade, readiness to work with the grain of a globalising world, an aid programme largely directed to poor countries, a pragmatic attitude to debt problems, and a positive attitude to competent international organisations, are in the blood stream of policymakers across the political spectrum and strongly reflected in the attitudes of the civil service. And the concept of a development agency that combined virtually all forms of British bilateral and multilateral aid (including contributions to the Multilateral Development Banks) in one institution has been a reality since 1964.

[35] Prime Minister's speech at World Economic Forum in Davos, 26 January 2005.
[36] Prime Minister's speech at World Economic Forum in Davos, 27 January 2007.

What has been new has been the top-level commitment to international development as a matter of real significance, the willingness to resource it much more seriously, and the readiness to broaden alliances (e.g. to the European Commission and to the civil society campaigners) to support it.

How enduring might those changes prove?

Many things could change. It is not axiomatic that future prime ministers and chancellors will be as personally interested in development issues as Tony Blair and Gordon Brown; that the UK's aid programme will continue to rise beyond the period set in the 2007 public expenditure round; or even that the structure of a specialist department under a cabinet minister will prove enduring.

But the continuous pressure from the poorer members of the ever more populous but ever more present 'global village' is surely a fact of life that any British government is going to want to take seriously. Secondly, progress towards 'global public goods', from climate change to dealing with risks of infections such as avian flu, and avoidance of 'bads' such as terrorism or failed states, will increasingly require rich countries to find constructive ways of working with middle-income and low-income countries. Thirdly, the UK is in a vastly better economic state to play a forward role than when the Wilson government sought in the 1960s to give a coherent push to the UK's role in international development. For these three reasons, the changes brought about by Tony Blair, Gordon Brown, and successive Secretaries of State for International Development in the direction of whole-of-government attention to issues affecting developing countries, backed by an effective aid programme and a strong UK voice within the international system, seem likely to set the tone – whatever the political leanings of future governments – for a significant period ahead.

26

Climate change

KUNAL KHATRI

Introduction

Over the last decade climate change has developed into the most pressing environmental issue facing policymakers in the UK today. It remains, however, one of the most difficult problems to tackle.

Firstly, the production of greenhouse gases (GHGs) is deeply embedded in the way that modern society has developed and operated since the industrial revolution. Breaking humankind's addiction to fossil fuels without harming our aspirations for growth necessitates seismic socio-economic and political shifts in order to develop radically new concepts and models of sustainable development. Tony Blair himself even talks of the need for a new 'green, industrial revolution'.[1] Without this change there will never be the popular ambition to tackle climate change, and governments will forever be paralysed by electoral constraints.

Secondly, even with such a colossal change in the zeitgeist, controlling GHG emissions requires coherent and collective action across society, the entire machinery of government and the international system. Citizens, consumers, businesses and governments all produce emissions through their own activities, and thus have a responsibility to bear in tackling climate change. As such, the issue impinges on an array of major policy areas including transport, housing, energy, business and international relations. Tackling climate change therefore requires an unprecedented level of coordinated action, and 'joined-up thinking' within and between societies and governments across the world.

This chapter assesses the extent to which Blair and New Labour have led and developed the climate change agenda in light of these challenges.

[1] Tony Blair, 'International Action Needed on Global Warming', speech at the Banqueting House, 14 September 2004; available at: www.number-10.gov.uk/output/page6333.asp (accessed 20 May 2007).

The climate change agenda in 1997

In the late 1980s and early 1990s, climate politics was not high on the political agendas of any of the main three parties. Indeed the UK was still being branded the 'dirty man' of Europe due to its reluctance to reduce the high levels of sulphur emissions from its power stations in the 1980s. Nonetheless, a speech by Thatcher in 1988 on the importance of environmental protection marked a watershed, with climate change and damage to the ozone layer being the chief beneficiaries of this newfound focus. Behind the scenes, Sir Crispin Tickell was widely acclaimed as the man responsible for the 'greening of Thatcher'.

Internationally, concerns over global warming and carbon dioxide emissions were gaining ground, leading to the creation of the Inter-Governmental Panel on Climate Change (IPCC) in 1988. The IPCC is primarily responsible for assessing the available scientific information on climate change, assessing the likely environmental and socio-economic impacts of it, and formulating responses to the problem. Further to this, the UN Framework Convention on Climate Change (UNFCCC) was devised and signed at the Rio Earth Summit in 1992, with the express aim of 'the stabilisation of greenhouse gas concentrations in the atmosphere at a level that would prevent dangerous anthropogenic interference with the climate system'.[2]

In responding to this new dynamic, the Conservative government set the UK the target of returning CO_2 emissions back to 1990 levels by 2000, and in 1994 produced the UK's first Climate Change Programme. Key policies developed in this period included the introduction of the fuel duty escalator in 1993 at a rate of 3% (later 5%) per year, the imposition of VAT on domestic fuel in 1994 (though not to the full 15% rate), the creation of the Energy Saving Trust (EST) in 1992, and the introduction of a Non-Fossil Fuel Obligation on electricity generators to supply a proportion of their electricity from renewable sources.

However, environmental concerns were often compromised by other policy priorities. As such the Climate Change Programme itself remained heavily focused on voluntary measures, in what it termed its 'partnership approach'. This was most clearly the case in the energy sector, where the primary focus of policy had not been to reduce CO_2 emissions, but instead, to secure energy supply at the lowest possible cost through the privatisation of the oil, gas, coal and electricity industries. For instance,

---

[2] *United Nations Framework Convention on Climate Change* (Bonn: UN, 1992), p. 5.

in 1995 the government rejected the Gas Bill and its call to place an environmental duty on the regulator, arguing that competitive markets would suffice to encourage energy efficiency measures.[3] Other policies and initiatives focusing on increasing energy efficiency, such as the EST and the Home Energy Efficiency Scheme, were undermined by chronic shortages of funding in a political climate urging the retreat of the state and cuts in public spending.

Nonetheless, the fuel duty escalator tying future Chancellors to annual increases in the price of petrol, was a bold initiative that would reap significant carbon savings whilst also encouraging more fuel-efficient cars. Yet, typical of much 'environmental' policy at the time, these decisions were made with rather more concern for the budget and macro-economic strategy than the environment. For instance, there was no change to the fuel duty escalator as falling petrol prices buffered its impact, despite the Royal Commission on Environmental Pollution (RCEP) insisting that a 9% escalator was necessary to meet the UNFCCC objective.[4]

What success the Conservative administrations had in reducing the country's CO_2 emissions between 1990 and 1995 was more through chance than intent. The Department of Environment itself acknowledged at the time that the drop was due to the economic recession in 1992, and then the shift from coal to the less CO_2-polluting gas in the supply of electricity, with nuclear power also making a greater contribution than expected.

Clearly, by 1997 climate change had neither registered as a fundamental threat nor become a lens through which economic, transport, and energy policy were to be directed. Rather, the Department of Environment remained relatively weak in the ministerial hierarchy and environmental measures were moulded to fit the Treasury's priorities, which under the Conservative administrations inevitably meant budget cuts. However, one could argue that, at this time, neither were the British public of the mind to accept that such core policies should be 'compromised' by climate change concerns.

The climate change agenda in 2007

In contrast, ten years on, the climate change agenda has developed an irresistible momentum within the UK and internationally. The threat

---

[3] Ute Collier, '"Windfall" Emission Reductions in the UK', in Ute Collier and Ragnar Löfstedt (eds.), *Cases in Climate Change Policy: Political Reality in the European Union* (London: Earthscan, 1997), p. 93.

[4] RCEP, *Transport and the Environment, 18th Report* (London: HMSO, 1994).

that climate change poses has been absorbed by politicians, businessmen and women and individual consumers alike, to the extent that it is appreciated as being much more than just a marginal environmental issue.

In terms of popular opinion and attitude, climate change has leapt up the league table of people's concerns, with a 2006 MORI poll indicating that many see climate change as the most significant threat to the world's well-being, over and above global terrorism.[5] The groundswell of popular support over the climate change agenda mirrors the way in which anti-poverty campaigns successfully promoted issues of international development on national and international agendas. Climate change has also managed to infiltrate popular culture, as exemplified by films such as *The Day After Tomorrow* (2004), and the Academy Award for Al Gore's seminal documentary, *An Inconvenient Truth* (2006).

Business has also seized the initiative, with companies seeking to outdo each other in terms of environmentally friendly policies. The growing public concern for ethical and environmental consumerism, as demonstrated most aptly by the Fair Trade movement, has created an entirely new market that companies have been keen to capitalise on. For instance, Tesco announced this year that it would carbon footprint its entire inventory, partly in response to Marks and Spencer's announcement that it would make the company carbon neutral within five years.[6]

Coupled with this, climate change has cemented its position on the international agenda, starting with the Kyoto Protocol in 1997, and to a greater extent through Blair's presidency of the G8 Summit in Gleneagles in 2005. The Stern Review, commissioned by the British government at Gleneagles, has been crucial to this changing international atmosphere and has managed to take climate change out of the exclusive and marginalised domain of environmentalism. Whereas ecological arguments have often been stigmatised as condemning society to lower rates of economic growth, Stern allied the climate change agenda with aspirations for growth and prosperity, immediately granting the cause a wider audience and legitimacy.

New Labour has undoubtedly stolen a march on the climate change agenda, and Britain has clearly worked itself to a level of unprecedented international influence within this movement. This success has not been lost on the main opposition parties, with David Cameron striving to rebrand the Conservative Party as the green choice, even adopting a tree as the party's new symbol.

---

5 'A New Dawn', *The Guardian*, 31 October 2006.
6 David Derbyshire, 'Tesco's Carbon "Footprints" ', *The Telegraph*, 21 January 2007.

New Labour in power

A fundamental challenge in tackling climate change has been the need to rearticulate the climate change threat and its solutions in new and constructive terms. Indeed, New Labour has proved extremely successful and flexible in the manner in which it has capitalised on the growing climate change movement, yet simultaneously adapted and rearticulated it for mainstream consumption.

Climate change had originally been propelled up national and international agendas as a result of a number of environmental movements, in much the same way as international development had been through campaigns such as Drop the Debt, the Jubilee campaign, and Make Poverty History. The growth of NGOs such as Greenpeace, and the success of various 'Green' parties in elections across Europe, have proved testimony to the growing strength of the environmental movement from the 1990s. Yet environmentalism was never in and of itself the primary concern of Labour party policy. Rather it has been constructed within the ideological narratives of the party's economic and social agendas, as the government tried to redefine the entire climate change agenda away from a 'green movement' that was increasingly associated with its minority and radical extremes. 'By exaggerating the trade off between economic dynamism and environmental protection, between human welfare and nature, the politics of the environment failed to gain the legitimacy needed to make it a governing idea for a majority party.'[7] Environmental policies for New Labour were to be combined with economic and social progress, with the challenges of climate change and economic growth framed in terms of sustainable development and ecological modernisation. For New Labour and for Blair, 'the very act of solving [climate change] can unleash a new and benign commercial force to take the action forward, providing jobs, technology spin-offs and new business opportunities as well as protecting the world we live in'.[8]

The attempt to mainstream the climate change agenda was further buoyed by the growing scientific consensus on anthropogenic climate change. Across the environmental sector, given the very nature of the subject, the scientific community has a unique role to play in setting the political agenda. It is only through scientific and authoritative assessment that issues such as climate change can be demonstrated to be real, threat-

---

[7] David Miliband, 'Red-Green Labour in Power', *Fabian Review*, 119(1), 2007: 16.
[8] Blair, 'International Action Needed on Global Warming'.

ening, and worthy of political attention. Without this catalyst, environmental issues are typically marginal concerns for politicians preoccupied with the immediate threats and priorities of health, crime, the economy and security.

As such, the scientific developments over the last ten years have helped propel the climate change agenda, regardless of individual politicking. In 1995, the IPCC produced its Second Assessment Report in which it stated that 'the balance of evidence suggests a discernible human influence on the global climate'.[9] Though extremely cautious in its conclusion, this was the first time that the IPCC had ever made such a link between climate extremes and theories of human-caused climate change. Further to this, the RCEP in its 2000 report *Energy: The Changing Climate*, stated as its basic premise that anthropogenic climate change is already happening, with negative consequences for the UK.

Pushing for a scientific consensus was central to the government's, and in particular Blair's, strategy to promote the climate change agenda in the run-up to the G8 Summit in 2005. A key event in this was the scientific conference held at the Hadley Centre in Exeter in February 2005, entitled 'Avoiding Dangerous Climate Change'. Given the gap since the last IPCC report in 2001, the conference served as Blair's way of updating the world community on the science of climate change. Indeed, with the Hadley Centre recognised as one of the world's leading places for modelling the environment, the conference served 'as a milestone in building an international consensus on climate change'.[10]

A second challenge to confronting climate change is the need for collective and coherent policy action, and Labour's 1997 manifesto did indeed indicate an appreciation of the need to develop consistent policy across the entire machinery of government. The 1997 manifesto stated that 'The foundation of Labour's environmental approach is that protection of the environment cannot be the sole responsibility of any one department of state. All departments must promote policies to sustain the environment.'[11] To this end the government created a super-ministry in the form of the Department for Environment, Transport and the Regions, along with the Sustainable Development Unit. In addition, the

[9] IPCC Second Assessment, *Climate Change, A Report of the Intergovernmental Panel on Climate Change* (Geneva: IPCC, 1995), p. 5.
[10] 'Towards a Consensus on Climate Change', Met Office, Hadley Centre, Exeter, 3 February 2005.
[11] Labour Party Manifesto, 1997, available at: www.labour-party.org.uk/manifestos/1997/1997-labour-manifesto.shtml.

Environmental Audit Committee was established to strengthen parliamentary scrutiny of the government's environmental policy.

The government has also sought to take the policy lead through emission targets and policy innovations that were much more stringent than those of the UK's European and more distant neighbours. The 1997 manifesto committed the government to a target of a 20% reduction in CO_2 levels by 2010 based on 1990 levels, which was above the Kyoto target negotiated internationally that year to reduce emissions of GHGs by 12.5% over a similar period. Despite this, the RCEP 2000 report challenged the government to cut CO_2 emissions by 60% from their 2000 levels by 2050, which at the time the Cabinet Office's Performance and Innovation Unit declared too ambitious a long-term target, especially when no other state in the world was yet emphatically committed to addressing climate change. Nonetheless, the 2003 Energy White Paper, *Our Energy Future – Creating a Low Carbon Economy*, did indeed commit the UK to reducing its CO_2 emissions by 60% in accordance with the RCEP's recommendations.

The 2000 UK Climate Change Programme set out a raft of policy measures that the government intended to pursue in order to achieve these targets. Given that much of the input to this document came from the former president of the Confederation of British Industries, Lord Marshall, it is unsurprising that New Labour's most significant policy innovations have been in the business sector. One such example is the Climate Change Levy (CCL), imposed on businesses as a means of encouraging energy efficiency. Those companies that successfully increased energy efficiency had their revenue reimbursed through lower National Insurance contributions. Indeed, successful cooperation with business in tackling climate change has been a key feature of Labour's approach to the problem, as exemplified by the formation of the Carbon Trust, with the express aims of reducing carbon emissions in business, and encouraging change in business attitude and behaviour towards climate change. In addition, the top CEOs from the UK's leading companies were brought together under the banner of the Climate Group in April 2004, with the task of leading the UK business sector in tackling climate change.

As for the transport sector, the 1997 manifesto promised to develop an integrated transport policy to fight congestion and pollution. This was echoed by the DETR's 1998 White Paper, *A New Deal for Transport – Better for Everyone*, expressing a commitment to a 'sustainable' transport system. Indeed, the road fuel duty escalator, introduced by the Conservatives in 1993, had been most effective to this end, and in 1997 Gordon Brown raised the escalator from 5% to 6%. The UK Climate

Change Programme itself stated that the duty had 'sent a clear signal to manufacturers to design more fuel-efficient vehicles, and to motorists to avoid unnecessary journeys and to consider alternatives to the car'.[12]

However, rising oil prices towards the end of the 1990s led to intense criticism of the UK's relatively high levels of fuel taxation, and to subsequent fuel protests in September 2000. Terrified that the blockades could cripple the government, the escalator was abandoned in Brown's pre-Budget report in November 2000, with fuel duties in the future decided on a Budget-by-Budget basis. Since 2000 the main transport sector initiative has thus been voluntary agreements on car fuel efficiency, and a Europe-wide 1996 Community Strategy to improve the average fuel efficiency of new cars sold in the EU by 35% by 2010 against a 1995 baseline.[13] As a further mechanism to encourage changes in consumer attitudes, the Vehicle Excise Duty was introduced in 1998, with a top rate of £400 for the most polluting cars as of the 2007 Budget. Finally, as of November 2005, transport fuel suppliers were required by the Renewables Transport Obligation to ensure that 5% of their sales are from renewable sources by 2010–11.

In the housing sector, Labour has most successfully balanced its social, economic and environmental goals through the Warm Front scheme and the Energy Efficiency Commitment (EEC). Through the EEC, gas and electricity suppliers are required to achieve certain targets for the promotion of energy efficiency, with the extra stipulation that half the savings must be in households on low income-related benefits or tax credits. Nonetheless, the EEC aside, it is already apparent that, compared to the business sector, Labour has found it difficult to tackle domestic or indeed transport emissions. Whereas taxation in the business sector through the CCL has been successful and grudgingly accepted, there are paralysing concerns that taxation in the domestic and transport sectors is highly regressive, hitting the poorest hardest and thus heavily undermining the party's social and economic agendas.

In terms of addressing the UK energy sector, successive Labour governments have failed to develop a coherent strategy to meet the country's future energy needs and mix. Since coming to office, Labour has completed three energy reviews, none of which have come close to resolving the problem. Blair himself has pushed the case for nuclear energy, in the face of stiff opposition from a number of senior cabinet ministers, as

[12] DETR, *Climate Change: The UK Programme* (London: TSO, 2000), p. 92.
[13] Friends of the Earth, 'EU Targets for Greener Cars too Weak', press release, 7 February 2007.

the only way for the UK to meet its energy security and environmental needs. However, the 2006 energy review arguing the economic case for new nuclear build has since been subject to successful legal action by Greenpeace for the flaws in the review process. In terms of renewable energy there remains the government's 1997 manifesto commitment to meet 10% of UK energy needs from renewable resources by 2010. To this end the Renewable Obligation was launched in 2002, replacing the Conservative's Non-Fossil Fuel Obligation, tying energy suppliers to producing 10.4% of their energy from renewable sources by 2010/11. More recently, the incorporation of the UK energy sector and other energy-intensive industries into the European Emissions Trading Scheme as of 2005 seeks to further boost energy efficiency and renewable energy through market-driven competition.

Yet, as the UK only accounts for approximately 2% of global CO_2 emissions, tackling climate change also necessitates overcoming the key challenges discussed above at the international level. In this respect, Blair's governments have not only signalled their dedication to the climate change agenda domestically, but also managed to drag other countries and institutions into binding commitments and targets. This was most clearly the case with the UK's presidency of the G8 at Gleneagles where climate change figured alongside Africa as a key theme for the summit. As a result of this summit, the G8 leaders for the first time reached an agreement on the role of human activity in global warming and the need for urgent action, including substantial cuts in their own emissions. Further to this, and reinforcing the message that this was not a temporary fad for the G8 to concern itself with, the G8 leaders committed themselves, along with the leaders of India, Brazil, China, Mexico and South Africa, to continue a dialogue on climate change, clean energy and sustainable development to lay the foundations for a successor to the Kyoto Treaty.

Critically, just as Blair's governments were redefining climate change domestically as more than just a niche environmental concern, this rearticulation proved vital on the international stage. Crucial to this change was the publication of the Stern Review in October 2006, originally commissioned at the G8 in Gleneagles.

The Stern Review categorically states that 'Tackling climate change is the pro-growth strategy for the longer term, and it can be done in a way that does not cap the aspirations for growth of rich or poor countries. The earlier effective action is taken, the less costly it will be.'[14] Though

---

[14]   Stern Review, *The Economics of Climate Change* (London: HM Treasury, 2006), p. ii.

Stern's message echoed much of what was reported elsewhere in the climate change literature at the time, the fact that the message came from an entirely different messenger – that is, from a world-renowned economist with the endorsement of the UK Treasury and Prime Minister (rather than just the 'environment ministry', DEFRA) – meant that the national and international audience was immediately more attuned to what the Review had to say. The Stern Review completely reshaped the political atmosphere with respect to the climate change agenda and created the political space and opportunity which Blair has capitalised on both nationally and internationally. However, as the following section details, it has proved extremely difficult to translate intent, ambition and desire into quantifiable achievements.

The green industrial revolution?

The UK has had some marked success in reducing emissions of GHGs, and is on course to surpass its Kyoto targets. DEFRA's 2006 review of the UK's Climate Change Programme (figure 26.1) stated that annual emissions of the six GHGs covered by the Kyoto Treaty fell by 14.6% between 1990 and 2004, with the expectation that emissions of these GHGs will be 20% below 1990 levels by 2010. Yet the report admits that CO_2 emissions specifically had only fallen by 5.6% since 1990, and the review admitted that the UK was unlikely to meet its self-imposed domestic goal of a 20% reduction in CO_2 emissions (from the 1990 baseline) by 2010.

Indeed, table 26.1 demonstrates that whilst CO_2 emissions have fallen over the entire period 1990 to 2006, from a 1997 baseline they have actually increased by approximately 2.2%. Whilst emissions fell in the commercial, agriculture and public sectors from 1997, they rose in both the energy supply and transport sectors, with little change in the domestic sector.

In reality, the government's CO_2 record is considerably worse than these figures suggest. Despite its dramatic growth in emissions in the last decade, the aviation sector is not incorporated into either the Kyoto or domestic CO_2 targets, and as such is not included in these statistics on the UK's carbon emissions. Indeed the issue of aviation has been ominously absent in the discussion thus far, largely because New Labour has failed almost entirely to tackle the staggering growth in emissions from this sector. Between 1990 and 2004 emissions from aviation doubled, and are expected to double again by 2030 if no

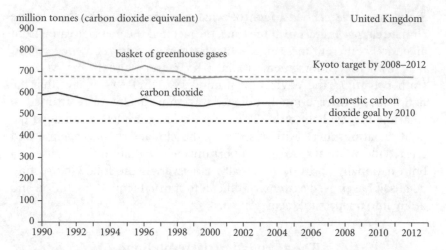

Figure 26.1. Emissions of greenhouse gases, 1990–2005 (DEFRA, available at: http://www.defra.gov.uk/environment/statistics/globatmos/gagccukem.htm).
Source: AEA Energy & Environment

further action is taken.[15] Despite raising the Air Passenger Duty again in February 2007, the DfT has acknowledged that current rates of progress on aviation taxation will not stop the massive predicted growth in flights. Indeed the DfT's aviation White Paper, *The Future of Air Transport*, sanctioned new runways at Birmingham, Edinburgh, Stansted and Heathrow, plus new terminals throughout the UK. The Tyndall Centre warns that, on current trends, by 2030 aviation will be consuming some 60% of the UK's 2050 CO_2 target, and that it is inconceivable that reductions in other sectors would be able to accommodate this.[16]

With respect to land transport, emissions were approximately 7% above 1990 levels by 2006. With the scrapping of the fuel duty escalator, and a further cut in 2001, the fuel duty has fallen in real terms at almost every Budget since then, and as a result driving in Britain in 2004 was 7% cheaper in real terms than in 1997.[17] According to Chris Huhne, the Liberal Democrat spokesperson for the Environment, 'The steady rise in

[15] Friends of the Earth, 'How Green Was Gordon? The Environmental Record of Gordon Brown's Budgets 1997–2007', briefing, March 2007, available at: www.foe.co.uk.
[16] 'Climate Change and the UK Aviation White Paper', Tyndall Centre, University of East Anglia, Norwich, December 2003.
[17] 'Climate Change: Hot Under the Collar', *The Economist*, 1 April 2006.

Table 26.1. CO$_2$ emissions by source (million tonnes of carbon, MtC) (DTI, available at: www.dtistats.net/energystats/et_mar07.pdf)

	1990	1991	1992	1993	1994	1995	1996	1997	1998	1999	2000	2001	2002	2003	2004	2005	2006
Power stations	55.6	55.3	52.1	46.8	45.5	44.6	44.6	40.7	41.9	39.4	42.4	45.2	44.0	46.5	46.4	47.0	49.2
Other energy industry	8.7	8.8	9.1	9.5	9.6	9.6	10.0	10.4	10.2	9.9	9.7	9.6	10.3	10.1	9.9	9.9	9.1
Other industrial	31.2	30.7	29.7	29.4	29.9	29.2	29.7	29.9	29.4	29.7	29.6	29.2	26.8	27.3	26.7	26.9	26.9
Domestic	21.4	23.8	23.1	24.1	22.9	21.8	24.8	22.9	23.4	23.3	23.4	24.0	23.2	23.4	23.8	23.7	22.2
Commercial and public services	7.0	7.7	7.6	7.5	7.3	7.3	7.9	7.3	7.4	7.5	7.3	7.4	6.3	6.3	6.5	6.4	6.5
Agriculture and forestry fuel use	1.4	1.4	1.4	1.4	1.4	1.4	1.5	1.4	1.4	1.4	1.3	1.3	1.3	1.3	1.3	1.2	1.2
Transport	31.8	31.6	32.0	32.3	32.3	32.1	33.4	33.8	33.6	33.8	33.6	33.5	34.1	34.4	34.8	35.2	35.9
Other sectors[1]	3.6	3.2	3.2	3.3	3.3	3.7	3.8	3.0	2.8	2.7	2.5	2.5	2.5	2.4	2.4	2.5	2.5
Total (excluding net LULUCF[2])	160.7	162.6	158.1	154.3	152.3	149.6	155.6	149.4	150.0	147.6	149.8	152.8	148.5	151.7	151.8	151.7	153.5
Net LULUCF[2]	0.8	0.8	0.6	0.3	0.2	0.3	0.2	0.1	−0.0	−0.1	−0.1	−0.2	−0.3	−0.3	−0.5	−0.6	−0.6
Total (including net LULUCF[2])	161.5	163.3	158.7	154.6	152.5	149.9	155.8	149.6	150.0	147.5	149.7	152.6	148.2	151.4	151.3	151.1	152.9

[1] Includes waste, fugitive emissions from fuels.
[2] Land Use, Land Use Change and Forestry.

carbon emissions since 2000, when the government capitulated to the fuel protestors, is now coming home to roost.'[18]

As for the energy sector, part of the explanation for the rise in emissions was related to the higher than expected economic growth of the country, and the rise in global energy prices which led to the increased use in coal at the expense of gas. For instance, in 2006 alone the shifting balance from gas to coal-intensive means of electricity generation led to an increase in emissions from power stations of 6%.[19] What emissions reductions were achieved in the early Blair years from the energy sector were a result of a prolonged windfall from the 'dash for gas' that occurred under the previous Conservative administration, and were a temporary and transitional effect. In addition, the Renewables Obligation on electricity generators has had limited success given the huge obstacles presented by the UK planning process. It is clear that living off the windfall effect from the 'dash for gas' will become increasingly difficult for the UK's energy sector, especially as its ageing nuclear power stations come to the end of their lives. As such the question of the UK's future energy mix will become ever more pressing.

In tackling housing sector emissions, programmes such as the EEC and Warm Front are set to deliver emissions savings of 1MtC annually by 2010. However, if the domestic sector is to reduce its emissions by 60% by 2050, savings of up to 24MtC per year are required.[20] Though the thought of taxing domestic energy use has been anathema to New Labour, there has also been a reluctance to implement less radical measures. These include policies such as council tax rebates on cavity wall and loft insulation and a reduction in VAT on high-quality environmental refurbishments, both of which have been recommended by the EST and the Sustainable Development Commission. Similarly, the government has remained rather conservative in implementing the CCL on businesses. With only two in-line-with-inflation rises of the levy since its introduction, the CCL was in fact 13% lower in real terms in 2006 than when it was introduced.[21]

Yet, on the other hand, it is clear that the UK has had remarkable success in steering international priorities towards tackling climate change. For instance, building on the UK's lead, in 2007 the EU set its member states the target of a 20% reduction of CO_2 emissions by 2020, with the will to increase this to 30% if other states such as the US sign up

---

[18] Hilary Osborne, 'Coal Comeback Pushes up UK Emissions', *The Guardian*, 29 March 2007.
[19] *Ibid.*   [20] Friends of the Earth, 'How Green Was Gordon?'
[21] Institute for Fiscal Studies, *The UK Tax System and the Environment* (London: IFS, 2006).

too. There is now also a binding renewable energy target of 20% by 2020. In addition, the UK was the first country to introduce a market-based emissions trading scheme, which the EU has developed, launching the largest carbon trading scheme in the world in 2002 (the European Trading Scheme, ETS). Preliminary data suggest, however, that almost 93% of the industrial plants covered in the EU's trading scheme emitted less than their quota of free permits in 2006, effectively handing them a sizeable cash windfall from the scheme. Though the UK's allocations were tighter than many of their European counterparts, British generators are still estimated to have pocketed around £1 billion. Nevertheless, this failure has created an appreciation of the need to tighten allocations for the 2008 ETS to a much greater extent than previously anticipated.[22]

Beyond the EU, one of the most significant achievements has been the about-turn exhibited by the US and President G. W. Bush on the climate change agenda. From a position of outright climate change denial, Bush has since signed the Gleneagles Declaration, and also recognised in his State of the Union address in 2007 that climate change was a serious challenge, and that he would commit the US to reduce its dependency on oil and increase the use of bio-fuels in its transport sector.

Why was more not achieved?

That is, tackling climate change is fraught with an enormous complexity of administration, management and integrated thinking both domestically and internationally, with various mitigation policies inevitably undermined by scientific doubt. Stern aptly described the climate change problem as 'a multi-disciplinary collective action problem under uncertainty'.[23] These factors go some way to explaining why it has been so difficult for the UK government to achieve more in terms of reducing emissions in the last ten years.

In addition, The Economist argues that the government has failed to achieve more because 'In the end . . . climate change is not yet a vote winner.'[24] Despite the attempts of New Labour to rearticulate and impress the importance of climate change on UK society, tackling it seems to offer little electoral gain compared to issues of employment, crime, health and education.

[22] David Gow, 'Smoke Alarm: EU Shows Carbon Trading Is Not Cutting Emissions', The Guardian, 3 April 2007.
[23] Michael Roux, 'Complacent Inaction Is just Not an Option', The Australian, 26 April 2007.
[24] 'Climate Change: Hot Under the Collar'.

However, a number of polls indicate that there may in fact be a growing public willingness to take the necessary political measures to tackle climate change, and a growing appreciation that this is a real and dangerous threat. A *Guardian*/ICM poll in 2007 revealed that 63% of respondents would approve of green taxes to discourage behaviour that harms the environment, whereas 34% would not.[25] More significant, however, is a poll in *The Observer* that revealed that only 11% of respondents were satisfied with the government's record on climate change,[26] suggesting that the government may have become a victim of its own success in raising climate change concern and the expectation of radical action. Nonetheless, as the furore over proposals for road pricing has demonstrated, there are still vast swathes of British society that are unwilling to make the link between their own behaviour and climate change, or alter their behaviour because of it.

Leading from this, a fundamental problem has been that when it has come to the tough choices, such as the UK's energy mix, or tackling aviation and transport emissions, successive Labour governments have found it hard to maintain the environmental imperative in face of tough opposition from business or voters. Though Labour has advanced the rhetoric of sustainable development and ecological modernisation, neither of these offer a panacea to tackling climate change nor absolve the government of its duty to make the tough decisions, even where these risk jeopardising short-term electoral goals.

This has been clearest in the transport sector, where concerns over alienating 'Middle England', or the 'Mondeo Man'[27] have seen the government back-pedal or abstain on policies to tackle growing emissions. For instance, though low-cost air travel has been heralded as the great class equaliser, the Civil Aviation Authority's 2005 report shows that approximately 70% of all UK leisure flights are taken by people in the top half of the income distribution, the very electoral base that New Labour is loathe to offend.

The environment has not traditionally been at the heart of New Labour policymaking and its climate change policies have typically been most successful only when environmental, social and economic goals

[25] David Adam and Patrick Wintour, 'Most Britons Willing to Pay Green Taxes to Save the Environment', *The Guardian*, 22 February 2006.

[26] 'The Blair Years 1997–2007; Blair: The Poll', *The Observer*, 8 April 2007.

[27] Andrew Jordan, 'Environmental Policy', in Patrick Dunleavy, Andrew Gamble, Ian Holliday and Richard Heffernan (eds.), *Developments in British Politics*, vol. VI (Basingstoke: Macmillan, 2000), p. 270.

have simply coincided. To seriously tackle climate change, however, 'The UK cannot afford to bask in speculative forecasts of energy consumption reduction and chance connections of policy agendas.'[28]

New Labour's agenda-setters

Blair, and later Brown, only began to steal a march on the climate change agenda towards the latter years of the Blair decade. Prior to this, much of the UK's work (internationally at least) was under the stewardship of Margaret Beckett and John Prescott. Both Beckett and Prescott had been heavily involved in the negotiations at the UN Conference at The Hague and Bonn over the new Kyoto Protocol, with Prescott keen to be credited as personally responsible for promoting the climate change agenda on the UK's behalf. Beckett likewise had developed a strong interest in climate change, and indeed the decision to promote her to Foreign Minister in May 2006 was partly out of Blair's desire to send a signal that climate change was a key foreign policy issue, and also galvanise the Foreign and Commonwealth Office (FCO) into following his international lead on the issue.

Gordon Brown, on the other hand, has been much derided by the environmental NGOs given his apparent lack of enthusiasm, certainly before the G8, for environmental and climate change issues. In addition, the fact that his Budgets resulted in a steady decline in 'green' taxes as a proportion of total tax revenue (from 9.4% to 7.7% from 1997 to 2005[29]) made the Chancellor an easy target.

Nonetheless, it was Gordon Brown who introduced the successful CCL and he who commissioned the Stern Review, largely without the prior knowledge of, or consultation with, Blair and No. 10. Nevertheless the Stern Review fitted neatly into a milieu of which Blair had been the chief architect. It had always been part of the government's political strategy to incorporate an economic analysis of climate change, as it was clear that it would be impossible to have a breakthrough on the issue unless it was understood as more than an environmental issue. To this end, Brown and Stern brought the hard-nosed high-level economic analysis that propelled the agenda to a new level.

By the time the Stern Review had been published, Brown had also taken a leading role in publicly reinforcing the threat and challenge posed

[28] Tim O'Riordan and Elizabeth J. Rowbotham, 'Struggling for Credibility: The United Kingdom's Response', in T. O'Riordan and J. Jäger (eds.), *Politics of Climate Change, A European Perspective* (London: Routledge, 1996), p. 263.
[29] Friends of the Earth, 'How Green was Gordon?'

by climate change. In his speech at the launch of the Stern Review, Brown referred to climate change as 'the world's largest market failure' and 'not just an environmental and economic imperative, but a moral one'.[30] To some extent, the climate change agenda reinforced his development agenda, given that the poorest countries and people would suffer the earliest and the most from the impacts of climate change.[31] For instance, the 2006 Budget contained a commitment to £10 billion World Bank fund to help developing countries invest in renewable energy. By demonstrating and presenting issues of development and climate change as so closely interconnected through the Stern Review and the G8, the government has managed to propel both issues to a much higher level than may have been originally anticipated.

Blair, on the other hand, developed a much earlier interest in climate change and most vividly demonstrated his commitment to the cause with his speech on the environment at the Banqueting House on 14 September 2004. The speech came in response to criticism from the Conservative leader Michael Howard in a talk at the Green Alliance, lamenting the government's record on climate change. Blair's speech itself was a bolt out of the blue for the audience of intellectuals and business people, as he promised to give climate change his own personal attention and elevate it to one of two key issues at the Gleneagles Summit in 2005. Indeed, the decision to make climate change a priority at Gleneagles was taken a long time before the run-up to the summit, with suggestions that Blair had decided upon this as early as January 2002 at the Earth Summit in Johannesburg.

It is also clear that Blair had pushed the climate change agenda on to the international stage at the G8 despite senior advice to the contrary from the people in No. 10 and also from the FCO. There was a concern that there was little opportunity in 2005 for Blair to make any material difference on the issue, as Kyoto was not an active global treaty, the US had already withdrawn from it, and the FCO thought it extremely unlikely that Russia would ratify it. In particular, with the Bush administration unwilling to undertake action on domestic emissions trading, or any other measures to reduce the carbon intensity of the US economy, it was assumed that there was no hope that any of the rapidly developing economies (particularly China and India) would accept the case for doing anything more. Nonetheless, Blair took personal control over the climate

---

[30] James Sturcke, 'We Must Pay Now to Avoid Climate Disaster, Says Blair', *The Guardian*, 30 October 2006.   [31] Stern Review, *The Economics of Climate Change*, p. vii.

change strategy that the government adopted on the international stage in the run-up and aftermath of the G8 Summit, including his own article in *The Economist* on 29 December 2004.

In terms of those that acted as significant influences on the Prime Minister, Sir David King, the government's chief scientific adviser, had been extremely important. Indeed, King had been working with Blair when the foot-and-mouth crisis broke out, and risked escalating into a national crisis right at the time of the 2001 general election. The successful management of the epidemic played a pivotal role in shaping Blair's outlook to a realisation that science could actually deliver for government. King himself had taken the initiative to organise the Hadley Centre conference to this end, and had also stirred greater public engagement on climate change through his article in the journal *Science* in 2004, where he referred to climate change as a more serious threat to humans than the threat of international terrorism.[32]

There was also a strong symbiotic relationship between the government and UK business in driving and addressing the climate change agenda. This is in contrast to meetings held with NGOs and pressure groups which were often considered negative and unconstructive. Indeed at the end of his speech at the Banqueting House in 2004, Blair made a personal, unscripted plea calling for business input to feed into the concepts and policies required to encourage climate-responsible business. Focusing efforts to tackle climate change through business and high-powered groups such as the Climate Group, Blair was keen to emphasise that climate change would not be resolved exclusively through environmental policy. Rather it was an environmental problem that necessitated wholesale societal shifts, in which business could take the lead.

Blair's leadership

It is clear from what has already been discussed that through Blair's own leadership climate change has achieved an unprecedented position of prominence on the national and international agenda. In addition, through Blair's efforts, the UK finds itself in a position of unparalleled international influence within that movement. The Gleneagles Summit was fundamental to this success and marked a rare occasion when any G8 leader has managed to use the grouping to gain leverage on specific issues, as opposed to general international economic concerns. This

[32] David A. King, 'Climate Change Science: Adapt, Mitigate, or Ignore?', *Science*, 9, 2004: 176–7.

achievement was even more significant given Putin's failure to do the same with energy at the summit the following year.

Much that was achieved at the G8 in 2005 was through Blair's personal endeavour. His insistence that the G8 must develop a climate change dialogue that incorporated the world's most rapidly developing countries was initially met with derision. Yet it has been through his persistence, and the work of Sir Michael Jay (former head of the diplomatic services), that the Gleneagles Dialogue was eventually agreed to, leading to the G8 Energy and Environment ministerial meetings in London in November 2005 and in Mexico in October 2006. Further to this, Blair himself was critical in convincing the Japanese Prime Minister Junichiro Koizumi to make time for a report back from the Gleneagles Dialogue at the G8 meeting in 2008.

Arguably, Blair's most significant achievement on the climate change agenda has been convincing the Bush administration to come on board. It is only through Blair's personal relationship with Bush that such change had been affected, and is indicative of the influence that Blair alone has over the internal debates of the American administration. Though it would have been easy and tempting for Blair to play the environmentalist and anti-American card and shame the US over its inaction over climate change, it is testimony to Blair's restraint, or at least his affinity for the Bush administration, that he refrained from indulging in such an opportunity. Nonetheless, it would be naïve to dismiss the notion that, as a secondary motive, international leadership on climate change was seized upon by Blair as the ideal way to pander to a Labour Party increasingly disaffected by the war in Iraq. Nor is it possible to dismiss Blair's personal motives, in that the climate change agenda offered an opportunity to outdo Brown on the development agenda and also secure a personal legacy that was not so mired in Iraq.

Conclusion

The change in discourse achieved over the last ten years, has cemented the threat from climate change as a priority on political agendas across the world. It is clear that there have been significant political shifts, with new concepts of sustainable development and low CO_2 trajectories widely accepted.

Internationally, there are now EU binding targets on emissions and regulations across a variety of industrial sectors in order to meet these goals, and the G8 leaders have also committed themselves to a climate change Plan of Action. In the case of the US, despite the antipathy of the

Bush administration which continued to reject any specific commitment to cut carbon emissions at the June 2007 G8 Summit in Germany,[33] individual states such as California have taken measures to tackle the threat through their own emissions trading schemes. Though Blair has played a critical role in this change, the issue will not subside in his absence. The climate change movement has developed too strong a momentum to be ignored. This is even more so with the IPCC's 2007 Report making its strongest statement to date that the warming of the climate is unequivocal and 90% likely to be due to human activity.[34]

More importantly, the vast majority of developed and developing nations now see it as in their economic interests to act to tackle climate change, with the Stern Review laying the foundations for this approach. Whereas issues such as international development and fair trade are forever constrained in as much as they rely heavily on conscience and principle, the issue of climate change has crossed this divide and has been brought to marry with states' own egoistic interests and priorities.

Indeed most recently, at the behest of the UK, the climate change debate has attempted to take another leap forward into the realm of national and international security. In October 2006, Margaret Beckett delivered a speech at the British embassy in Berlin warning that the failure to tackle climate change will lead to mass migrations of an unprecedented scale and a succession of failed states unable to cope with the consequences. Indeed, in April 2007, the UK pursued this agenda further when climate change was raised for the first time at the UN Security Council in the face of stiff opposition from the US, Russia and China who refuse to see it as an appropriate Security Council issue. Though the government has refrained from citing specific examples of global-warming-related conflicts, this nevertheless marks a continued attempt to shift climate change into the realms of high politics. Whether such an attempt to transform climate change into a security issue is legitimised by citizens, politicians, media outlets and other opinion-formers within the UK, let alone in other countries, remains to be seen. It is clear, however, that any attempt to do so will inevitably be much the weaker in the absence of Blair.

The politics of climate change has also left an indelible mark on British politics. There are already emerging signs that all the main parties see the issue as a key vote winner and as such are attempting to outdo each other at

[33] Andrew Grice, 'Bush dashes Blair Hopes of Breakthrough on Climate Change Deal', *The Independent*, 7 June 2007.
[34] Peter Walker, 'World "Must Act to Avoid Devastating Global Warming"', *The Guardian*, 4 May 2004.

every turn. For instance, in September 2006, David Cameron wrote a letter to the Prime Minister, backed by the Liberal Democrats and Friends of the Earth, calling for the new Climate Change Bill to incorporate annual CO_2 reduction targets, which Labour has so far been reluctant to do. More superficially, concerns over climate change have come to shape a media agenda that the main parties are constrained to tally with. In this way, climate change and the environment have become fully fledged weapons in the Conservative Party's media arsenal, with some of Cameron's most iconic moments to date involving him cycling to work and sledging across the Arctic ice sheets.

Yet, on the other hand, New Labour has been less successful in institutionalising coherent and coordinated strategies across domestic policy and Whitehall. Whereas the Prime Minister has been prominent in terms of international leadership, there has been a vacuum in terms of domestic leadership. The lack of a strong central body driving climate change concerns through all aspects of government policy has meant that the UK is likely to fail to meet its self-imposed emission targets. With this, Britain risks whittling away its international credibility and influence on the climate change agenda.

Whilst climate change is commonly understood to be a real and dangerous threat, there is still little appreciation of the sacrifices, nor consensus on the policies, that the threat necessitates. Much of Blair's time has been spent arguing that tackling climate change is the pro-growth strategy, and to all extents and purposes it is. However, difficult decisions will have to be made, as even Stern recognises that stabilising CO_2 levels to sustainable levels by 2050 would cost at least 1% of GDP. Where Blair has failed is in making the bold decisions to sacrifice economic growth or populist measures, for instance in aviation and road transport, for the sake of tackling climate change.

It remains to be seen whether there is the public will to see bold climate change policies through, or whether there are leaders strong enough to push them through. The following decade may indeed prove testimony to a new era where the long-term challenge of climate change suppresses and overcomes the short-term pressures of modern democratic politics, eliciting the sustained inter-governmental and inter-generational response it necessitates. Alternatively, the 'mismatch in timing between the environmental and electoral impact of climate change'[35] may continue to paralyse British and international politics, leaving the progress achieved from 1997 as little more than a false dawn.

[35] Blair, 'International Action Needed on Global Warming'.

27

Foreign policy

MICHAEL CLARKE

Tony Blair made a big difference to British foreign policy during his decade in Downing Street. He rose rapidly to the status of a key world leader, taking to foreign affairs more quickly and naturally than most Prime Ministers. His policies partly defined the turbulent international decade of his premiership and it was in foreign policy that he hoped his legacy might be most lasting. It was not that he had a well-worked design for foreign policy when he became Prime Minister; or that he was particularly well-informed on international affairs. He was said to travel light into global politics. But he had clear instincts, he had luck on his side in the early years, and he was determined in this, as in other fields, to find new ways of achieving old objectives. He both honoured the erstwhile continuity of British foreign policy and traduced it by effectively reinterpreting its goals. Part of that reinterpretation was driven by his perception of what he was inheriting. There seemed to be some easy, early gains to be made.

The legacy of Conservative foreign policy

The Conservative foreign policy that Tony Blair inherited was characterised by a realist orthodoxy based on a strong, Thatcherite, conception of nationhood and sovereignty. Foreign policy was fundamentally orientated to the politics and economics of European, Mediterranean, and Transatlantic spheres, with a hard-nosed concentration on trade and commerce elsewhere. This was logical enough in the circumstances of the Thatcher era, but was clearly under pressure in the circumstances of the mid-1990s. The realist orthodoxy had become a default position – and a purely reactive one at that – in the difficult years of the Major governments. The end of the Cold War had not just defused the central antagonism of the age; it had affected politics and economics in every sphere of Britain's external interests. The influence of the Asian economies and the

593

changes they wrought in the nature of overseas economic competition were clearly evident by 1997, if not fully appreciated within government. The politics of Europe had become the politics of an enlarging Europe, as the locus of influence shifted away from the Franco–German–British triangle. The collapse of Yugoslavia had already indicated that European security was a quite different game, and other crises around the world between 1991 and 1997 – in Somalia, Haiti, Rwanda, Chechnya, and Albania – had all indicated that weak and failing states created the instabilities that most severely tested the major powers' foreign and security policies.

Not least, the United States itself was uncertain how it should play its role as the sole remaining superpower. The victorious war to liberate Kuwait in 1991 had not consolidated George H.W. Bush at home, nor augmented the US position abroad. The Clinton presidency was marked by liberal internationalist ideas but vacillation in the way they were implemented. It was characterised by some as 'the crisis of liberal internationalism'.[1] Partly out of sheer exasperation, the 1994–97 period marked the beginnings of a decisive shift in the US towards unilateralist approaches to global politics.[2]

So rapid a process of global change in this environment of foreign policy would have taxed the ingenuity of any British government, let alone a fourth term administration struggling to maintain its unity. As it was, it left the government with a foreign policy that was by no means unsuccessful, but which looked increasingly out of kilter, and out of step, with the times. The government took a strong line in backing the results of the 1991 war to liberate Kuwait. It could hardly do otherwise. The operation of the 'No-Fly Zones' over northern and southern Iraq had to be maintained, though their purpose had clearly altered after the first two years. Another crisis in 1996 resulted in a concerted allied bombing campaign in Iraq, and France withdrew from the operation in the most public breakdown of the transatlantic consensus on Iraq. In Conservative thinking, the war and subsequent air operations – even including later bombing raids around Baghdad – had taken on a Falklands-style commitment to international law and the authority of the

[1] Stanley Hoffman, *World Disorders: Troubled Peace in the Post-Cold War Era* (New York: Rowman & Littlefield, 1998), pp. 70–86.
[2] Michael Cox, 'American Power before and after September 11', in R. Singh (ed.), *Governing America: The Politics of a Divided Democracy* (Oxford: Oxford University Press, 2003), pp. 467–79. Andrew Bacevich, *American Empire* (Cambridge, Mass.: Harvard University Press, 2002).

United Nations.[3] In parallel, Britain welcomed all efforts the US could make to address the Israel/Palestinian problem and warmly welcomed US (and Russian) guarantees behind the Oslo Peace Accords of 1993. There was relief, and support, too for the eventual efforts the US made effectively to impose a peace agreement on Bosnia in 1995 and begin a long-term commitment to make it stick.[4] In 1997 the Conservatives faced the election campaign with a strong statement that argued, with some consistency, that foreign policy was based on a conception that 'the nation state is a rock of security . . . a precious source of stability' and that maintenance of our efforts to promote peace in former Yugoslavia, Kashmir, Cyprus and the Middle East, to reform the UN and to help enlarge NATO and the European Union, constituted a pragmatic and realist international policy.[5]

But this realist consistency was not, by then, based on strong international foundations. There was a reluctance to engage with the uncomfortable realities of modern interdependence and to recognise the effects of this on conceptions of sovereignty. Some Conservatives lamented this failure but, in truth, there was no enthusiasm for a reorientation towards less tangible sources of power and stability, nor a Whitehall structure that would promote it.[6] The concentration on a 'partnership of nations' conception of Europe's future was an understandable reaction to a vigorous intra-party debate on Europe that had only really impacted on the Conservative parliamentary party during the 1990s.[7] It was also consistent with the Thatcherite legacy and then the numbing effects of being forced out of the Exchange Rate Mechanism in 1992. Whilst understandable, the approach nevertheless served to distract the government from embracing the bigger changes taking place in Europe. The startling effects of the commitment to enlargement after 1994 at once reinforced a 'partnership of nations' image of a much larger 'Europe' but also initiated major shifts in the transatlantic relationship that were later to be characterised, accurately enough, as a dichotomy between 'old' and 'new'

---

[3] William Hague, 'Blair's Lack of Leadership on Atlantic Alliance', Speech 20 February 2001, Conservative Central Office, www.conservatives.com/tile.do?def=news.story.page&obj_id=674&speeches=1.

[4] Ivo H. Daalder, *Getting to Dayton: The Making of America's Bosnia Policy* (Washington, DC., Brookings Institution Press, 2000), pp. 15–27.

[5] Conservative Party Manifesto 1997, *Our Vision for Britain* (London: Conservative Central Office, 1997), Chapter 9.

[6] David Howell, 'Britannia's Business', *Prospect*, 15, 15 January 1997.

[7] Nicholas J. Crowson, *The Conservative Party and European Integration since 1945: At the Heart of Europe?* (London: Routledge, 2006), p. 45.

Europe. The transatlantic bridge between the US and Europe that most Conservative leaders felt they naturally represented was becoming more difficult to manage. The effort to contain Saddam Hussein's Iraq seemed to be drifting towards an aimless antagonism from which most European states wanted to disengage. The Oslo peace process was running out of credibility even as President Clinton's own political authority slipped away in repeated scandal after 1995. The Europeans remained resentful, too, at the divisions the Balkan crises had opened up in transatlantic relations. The Dayton Peace Accord of 1995 was holding, but there remained great doubts about its long-term viability and anger at the way the Europeans had been brushed aside in its conclusion. On all these fronts the Conservative government was locked into reactive mode. At one side of the transatlantic bridge there was growing awareness, certainly in Paris, Berlin and Rome, of a gap in the shared international interests that had united the Western allies so well in the past.[8]

At the other end of the transatlantic bridge the government was unable to invigorate its relations with Washington in a way that suggested real influence. The Bush and Clinton administrations instinctively leant towards Germany as the keystone decision-maker in Europe and preferred a bilateral relationship with Chancellor Kohl rather than some mediated position via London. And while the British had been the most critical of Clinton's 'lift and strike' recipe for dealing with Bosnia at arm's length, it was France, nevertheless, that finally pressured Washington into meaningful involvement in the summer of 1995. Even on Iraq, the British privately felt they were in a cul de sac simply to support the US. Britain was a loyal, but not influential, ally in these critical transition years at the end of the Cold War.

Nor had John Major been able to make a personal success of his relations with George H.W. Bush or with Bill Clinton. The decision of the White House to receive Gerry Adams in March 1995 caused great irritation in Downing Street. For several days John Major reportedly refused to take calls from the President.[9] In 1996 there were allegations in Washington that the British government was involved in efforts to discredit the Clinton election campaign with material from Clinton's days as a Rhodes Scholar. There was little in these years of traditional

---

[8] Philip H.Gordon and Jeremy Shapiro, *Allies at War: America, Europe and the Crisis over Iraq* (New York: McGraw-Hill, 2004), pp. 34–6.

[9] Reported in an interview with Bill Clinton, 'Mandela helped me survive Monicagate, Arafat could not make the leap to peace – and for days John Major wouldn't take my calls', *The Guardian*, 21 June 2004.

Anglo-American summitry or assertions of political kinship. British policy seemed increasingly to offer little more than highly constrained reaction to vacillating US behaviour; a far cry from the Reagan-Thatcher era when so many ambitious things had seemed possible.

Such a reactive policy of realist orthodoxy left a good deal of room for a Labour challenge. Continuity from one administration to the next is a characteristic of British foreign policy, but by 1997 New Labour could claim not only that policy was not being implemented competently enough – a typical charge – but also that it was predicated on an out-dated view of the global environment – a much more challenging contention. Conservative policy had been duly conservative. Security and defence policy was altering piecemeal in a series of quite large, ad hoc steps that were justified carefully enough in the Ministry of Defence but never derived from a governmental overview of the totality of Britain's new external relations.[10] Foreign policy was struggling to cope with the strains in transatlantic relations, a concentration on Europe and the Mediterranean that was replete with nothing but crises and dislocation, and a failure either to extricate itself from Middle East entanglements or to affect the US's ability to deal with them. It was not clear what the government felt about foreign involvements in this global hiatus. On the one hand it had been pulled into Bosnian operations without clear political objectives – for which it was roundly criticised by all sides. On the other hand it shared the international determination to stand out of any Rwandan involvement – for which it was guiltily criticised by all sides. Realist orthodoxy was proving difficult to apply in the world of the 1990s. It was based on an implicit faith in the value of Britain, as an independent state, doing what it could to uphold the institutions, alliances and diplomatic norms that had stood the test of time and were now in the process of rapid transition. But there was no consistent philosophy behind all this; no overview of the world and Britain's place within it, beyond a recognition of the need to 'cope' in increasingly new and difficult circumstances. It was an approach that New Labour could cast in very negative terms.

A decade of Labour's foreign policy

In fact, Tony Blair characterised the foreign policy approach he inherited as 'a doctrine of benign inactivity . . . the product of the conventional view of foreign policy since the fall of the Berlin Wall. This view holds

---

[10] See, Andrew Dorman, *Defence Under Thatcher* (London: Palgrave, 2002), pp. 156–63.

that there is no longer a defining issue in foreign policy.'[11] For the Prime Minister and his new government, the world of foreign policy was full of defining issues. Ideas evolved, inevitably, over the course of the decade and were made to appear more consistent in 2007 than they were in 1997. The controversies over the Iraq War drove Blair's government to 'define' its foreign policy challenges much more stridently after 2003. Nevertheless there was, from the beginning, a distinct world view at the root of Labour's foreign policy, embodied in both a style and a substance that marked it out from what had gone before. It was characterised by three interconnected sets of principles that shaped the way the government looked at the conflicting trends the changing international environment threw up at it. These principles were reportedly articulated in a 2006 cabinet paper discussing the decade of Labour's foreign policy.[12]

The first set of principles was embodied in the headline that British foreign policy should fundamentally concern values. This was no mere assertion of virtue or pious idealism. It certainly went a good deal further than reorientations at the Foreign Office that aimed to emphasise the 'ethical dimensions' of British foreign policy. It was based more broadly on a particular analysis of the way globalised interdependence was thought to operate. 'It is by furthering our values that we further our interests in the modern era of globalisation and interdependence', said Blair in 2007.[13] 'Idealism becomes realpolitik'.[14] In such a world 'soft' power – the power of information, of culture, of economic magnetism, of persuasion and imitation, of norms and rules – all comes down to an ability to project certain values into other societies. In the case of Western powers such values can be simply stated as 'liberty, democracy, tolerance and justice'.[15] This values/interests nexus was backed up by a belief in further liberalisation within the world economy. Only economic liberalism would allow societies to cope with globalisation and benefit from it; for the poor as well as the rich, disruptive as that may be for both. The constraints that globalisation places on all state actors – the openness it irresistibly promotes – gives them a bigger stake in shared rules and agreed procedures.[16] Nor was the 'national interest as values' approach

---

[11] Tony Blair, *A Global Alliance for Global Values* (London: The Foreign Policy Centre, 2006), p. 10.
[12] Reported in, Tony Blair, 'Our Nation's Future', Lecture delivered 12 January 2007, 10 Downing Street, Press Office, Text.   [13] *Ibid.*
[14] Tony Blair, 'A Battle for Global Values', *Foreign Affairs*, 86.1, 2007: 90.
[15] Blair, *A Global Alliance for Global Values*, p. 7.
[16] Tony Blair, 'What I've Learned', *The Economist*, 31 May 2007, pp. 29–31.

confined to soft power. There were any number of challenges to these values in hard-edged political and military terms; from Russia and other post-communist societies who were becoming disillusioned with their transition, from rogue leaderships around the world, from radicalised Islamic groups – which, to his credit, Blair recognised as a challenge almost from the beginning. Values may have to be fought for with military power.[17] The world, in this view, is not an essentially benign environment for the major powers, who could choose to exercise their consciences and get involved, or not, in the Bosnias or the Rwandas. It is a world in which there is a clash, not *between* civilisations, but rather *about* civilisation; about the willingness to embrace a liberal democratic capitalist world order on a globalised scale. From this perspective, non-involvement in this struggle is not an exercise in 'realist orthodoxy' that safeguards the national interest. It is, rather, a simple failure to recognise genuine national interests.

A second set of related principles involved a holistic conception of how power should be exercised in the pursuit of values. Traditional foreign policy had tended to make a clear distinction between elements of 'hard' and 'soft' power. It was administratively easier to do that. But it was more effective, though more difficult, to integrate them into a single approach. Over the decade this went from the rhetoric of more 'joined up government' to the articulation of a 'comprehensive approach' and the creation of a number of agencies to try to promote it. The Strategic Defence Review of 1998 was based on a major Foreign and Commonwealth Office paper which sought to unite all the instrumentalities of power. And the FCO's first ever official strategy White Paper in 2003 tried to do much the same.[18] It was published simultaneously with a 2003 Defence White Paper, and was intended to be read 'in conjunction' with it.[19] The use of hard power was intrinsically more controversial than soft power, but that should not be allowed to deter states from using it, or confine them to impotent displays of soft power only.[20] Thus British use of its military forces, for fighting, policing, training and diplomacy could be as much a policy instrument in the developing world as foreign aid, which became

[17] *Ibid.*
[18] *The Strategic Defence Review: Supporting Essays* (London: TSO, 1998), pp. 2.1–2.2. *United Kingdom International Priorities: A Strategy for the Foreign and Commonwealth Office,* Cm. 6052 (London: TSO, 2003).
[19] *Defence White Paper: Delivering Security in a Changing World,* Cm. 6041–I (London: TSO, 2003). Statement by Secretary of State for Defence, *Hansard,* House of Commons, 11 December 2003, col.1209.   [20] Blair, 'Our Nation's Future'.

increasingly conditional on economic liberalisation, transparency and governance milestones. It was all part of the same thing.

A third set of principles revolved round the perception of just what was at stake in these foreign policy choices that must be made. In November 1997 Tony Blair outlined a vision for a proactive Britain that would use its power and influence to make an impression on the world on the basis of the key values we shared with the United States and the Commonwealth.[21] International institutions had not proved adaptable enough to cope with the new challenges. Collective national power needed to be harnessed to drive the necessary adaptation. Ten years later the message remained consistent though in a more refined and assertive form. 'Our values', Blair wrote, 'represent humanity's progress throughout the ages. At each point we have had to fight for them . . . As a new age beckons, it is time to fight for them again.'[22] This was echoed in his last message to British troops in Iraq, who were doing something that was, 'of importance to the future of not just Iraq but the rest of the world.'[23] In Blairite foreign policy the stakes of this battle for values could not be higher. It went further than any traditional attempt to affect the international environment in ways favourable to one's own society. Instead, he perceived a genuine and deepening struggle in the post-Cold War environment between progressive forces and those of reaction and autocracy. The *jihadi* terrorist threat to Western societies was only the most evident facet of it.[24]

The mechanisms by which these various principles should be enacted were no less assertive. An activist policy of 'liberal interventionism' was built in from the beginning and articulated eloquently in Blair's Chicago Speech of April 1999.[25] It was a more reflective version of the soundbite that had accompanied the Strategic Defence Review, that 'we must be prepared to go to the crisis, rather than have the crisis come to us'.[26] By 2007 this had even become an aspiration to define an agenda for 'progressive pre-emption', based on a need 'to think sooner and act quicker'.[27] It was heady stuff and relied on a willingness, and an ability, to deploy forces, diplomacy, aid and training around the world, possibly well away

---

[21] John Kampfner, *Blair's Wars* (London: The Free Press, 2003), pp. 16–17.
[22] Blair, *A Global Alliance for Global Values*, p. 6.   [23] BBC News Reports, 19 May 2007.
[24] Tony Blair, 'What I've Learned'.
[25] Prime Minister's Speech: 'Doctrine of the International Community', at the Economic Club, Chicago, 24 April 1999, 10 Downing Street, Press Office, Text.
[26] *The Strategic Defence Review*, Cm. 3999 (London, The Stationery Office, 1998), p. 2.
[27] Blair, *A Global Alliance for Global Values*, p. 34.

from Britain's old Cold War 'area of concentration' in Europe, the Mediterranean and parts of the Middle East.

Above all, these principles could only be enacted through explicit leadership and through positioning. Leadership in world politics came with the political strength of substantial domestic majorities and growing experience in foreign affairs. It came, too, with success in the Kosovo and Sierra Leone operations and in the forums provided by the G8 summits, the United Nations and through more intensive bilateral diplomacy than the Western world had seen for some years. 'Positioning', for the Blair government, was the concomitant to leadership and was a more subtle affair. It was more fundamental than 'grand strategy' and was based on a long-term perspective of world politics, in which Britain should be positioned in such a way as to help mobilise the Western world's resources to meet the challenge. In practice this meant staying intrinsically close to the United States whilst also shaping a new European agenda. The Blair government felt well able to do this by simply rising above the reactive constraints that had hobbled its predecessor. It began immediately with Downing Street meetings with President Bill Clinton at the end of May, and then at the Amsterdam EU Summit in June 1997.

It could rise above erstwhile domestic suspicions over the destination of the 'European project' by embracing them in the service of the greater issues at stake across the continent. Of course, entry into the Eurozone and the movement to conclude a European constitution would have to be handled carefully. But these were seen essentially as issues of timing rather than of principle. The Conservatives had claimed – implausibly – to put themselves 'at the heart of Europe'. New Labour aimed to make that a reality by concentrating on the bigger issues; enthusiasm for enlargement, wholehearted support for a common foreign and security policy, new initiatives in European defence, and a renewed push for greater trade liberalisation across the whole continent. A great deal of faith was invested by Downing Street in Gerhard Schroeder's assumption of power in 1998, and in a new European defence relationship with President Chirac around the Saint-Malo summit of the same year. By these means Britain could achieve that integration between Atlanticism and Europeanism which had been repeatedly asserted since 1960 but never attained; leadership among Europeans in more equal and collective partnership with the United States. If Blair's Britain was to be a transatlantic bridge, it could be so in a way that was ever-shortening, as Europe and America became more united in values, means, and responses to globalisation.

There was no hesitation in putting relations with the United States at the top of the immediate positioning agenda. President Clinton had already articulated the old Kennedy maxim that British influence in Washington would largely depend on its influence across Europe, and Tony Blair instinctively agreed.[28] But Clinton was also persuasively aspirational, in the same way that Kennedy had been, and that sense during his final years in office of a mission for the Western alliance chimed exactly with what Blair increasingly believed. 'Positioning' meant that the US was fundamental to anything the Western powers wanted to achieve. Non-engagement with the US, almost regardless of its policy direction, was simply not a feasible political option for the Europeans. When the going became really tough in the aftermath of the Iraq War in 2003, the line of argument was consistently repeated. The US will remain the global leader, Jack Straw told Parliament – how ever 'US domestic policies evolve', he added euphemistically.[29] But the job was becoming harder. In a speech to FCO diplomats the Prime Minister only thinly veiled the reality: 'We should remain the closest ally of the US, and as allies influence them to continue broadening their agenda.'[30] The Foreign Office strategy paper was explicit to the point of unaccustomed gloom: 'Building a shared agenda' between the US and Europe remained vital to both parties in an interdependent world, despite 'the emergence of new US strategic priorities outside Europe' and 'the erosion, since the Cold War, of a clearly understood sense of common purpose', or 'divergence between US and European attitudes towards the use of power'.[31] 'Positioning', it was clear, was for the long term. And during the neo-conservative ascendancy in Washington, it was certainly not for the faint-hearted.

Nevertheless, the Labour government took on during the decade a powerful series of old and new 'isms': a new transatlanticism, humanitarian interventionism, foreign policy idealism, and a holistic response to globalism. And it confronted with them growing instability across the Middle East, new security and economic problems in Africa, failing states in central and southern Asia, a terrorist offensive against Western powers and an increasingly politicised environmental agenda. The 'ism'

---

[28] Kampfner, *Blair's Wars*, pp. 12–13.
[29] Jack Straw, Written Statement to Parliament, in 'United Kingdom International Priorities: A Strategy for the Foreign and Commonwealth Office', p. 2.
[30] Tony Blair, 'Britain's Place in the World', Prime Minister's Speech to FCO Leadership Conference, 7 January 2003, 10 Downing Street, Press Office, Text.
[31] *United Kingdom International Priorities: A Strategy for the Foreign and Commonwealth Office*, p. 26.

that was least articulated but increasingly relevant over the period was – inevitably – pragmatism.

The perception of success

It is unusual for the general reputation of a government, or a prime minister, to rest so much on a matter of foreign policy, still more one that involved a military operation that was initially so successful. But all assessments of the foreign policy of the Blair government must be predicated on the distinction between pre- and post-Iraq; effectively the five years before and the five years after the fateful decisions of summer 2002. The very principles on which Blairite foreign policy was founded make it impossible to divorce this one crucial foreign policy issue from all the others. Tony Blair himself repeatedly insisted they were all of a piece, all derived from a coherent view of global politics.

In the first five years a foreign policy of new 'isms' was seen to have some effect, at least in initiating fresh approaches. A concentration on the politics of Europe was the most immediately evident. The emphasis was on results and outputs, not on institutions. In EU negotiations Blair displayed a greater sense of give-and-take than his predecessors. He was playing for bigger stakes than detailed negotiating points, in seeking to reconcile social protection with dynamic market economies, in building a credible defence capability for the Europeans – whether through NATO or the EU, really did not matter too much – and in pressing for enlargement. The idea of Turkish membership of the EU was relaunched, largely thanks to Britain, at the Helsinki summit in 1999. Certainly, there was some sense of momentum after the disappointments at the way the Bosnia crisis had been handled. That momentum was tested, but maintained, in the Kosovo crisis of 1999, ironically by the very controversy that surrounded it.[32] Lacking a sufficient UN resolution, NATO's own resolutions, backed up by the EU, were deemed appropriate to legitimise tough, indeed coercive, military action against Serbian behaviour in its most sensitive province. From both a political and military point of view it was a close call. But it worked, pragmatically and messily, creating a dynamic that saw the fall of Milosevic in Serbia, his delivery to the International Criminal Tribunal in the Hague, and Kosovo to the brink of independence. Humanitarian interventionism looked like

---

[32] Benjamin S. Lambeth, *NATO's Air War for Kosovo* (Santa Monica, Calif.: RAND, 2001), pp. 219–47.

a muscular and moral response to the problem of tyranny. As genuine partners to the US – despite the evident strains – the Europeans proved that Kosovo was within their competence, deploying a range of 'soft power' assets, with enough 'hard power' muscle to make them count. It was a good demonstration to incoming Russian President Putin that involvement with the American/European partnership was worth having. Above all, it offered an indication – equivocal to be sure – to the US that a rejuvenated and muscular partnership could solve the 'crisis of liberal internationalism' that so worried US analysts and policymakers. This was what the new transatlanticism should be all about. True, the Desert Fox bombing campaign against Iraq the previous year had been more controversial for the relationship; Washington and London had again gone ahead without explicit UN authorisation, and the results were not then judged a success, but at that time the Middle East entanglement could be confined to a discrete area of US-led policy. It had met with tepid support from Germany, nothing from Italy, and outright hostility from France. If anything, it had proved that proper European leadership was required.

Kosovo had offered all the participants both hard lessons and realistic hopes. In Sierra Leone in 2000 Britain undertook another humanitarian intervention that might have been a textbook demonstration of the art form. A limited and effective military operation restored the authority of the legitimate government, tyrannical rebels were put to flight, and a relatively 'joined-up' aid and assistance operation swung into action that restored stability. No matter that official assistance to the Sandline private security company operating in Sierra Leone had already embarrassed the FCO in 1998. That was ignored as a pragmatic reaction to try to restore the legitimate government in Freetown – the same government that had to be rescued in 2000. No matter, too, that the humanitarian intervention hardly had the effect of transforming Sierra Leone's dislocated economy. The pragmatic result was better than all the likely alternatives had the intervention not occurred.[33]

It was on this general wave of optimism and opportunity that the government confronted the implications of the 9/11 terrorist attack in 2001 and the subsequent war in Afghanistan. Most commentators felt that 9/11 would be a world-changing event on the basis of the likely US reaction to it.[34] Tony Blair, however, seems instinctively to have felt that

[33] Bruce Baker, 'The African Post-conflict Policing Agenda in Sierra Leone', *Conflict, Security and Development*, 6.1, 2006: 25–49.
[34] Caroline Kennedy-Pipe and Nicholas Rengger, 'Apocalypse Now? Continuity or disjunctions in world politics after 9/11', *International Affairs*, 82.3, 2006: 540.

it was world-changing in itself; an intrinsic challenge to the democratic free-market global order. His personal shock at the attacks was at least as great as that of President Bush and he was determined to offer both partnership and leadership in responding to it. 'We are in this for the long haul', he told MPs at the beginning of the joint bombing campaign in Afghanistan. 'Even when al-Qaeda is dealt with, the job is not done.'[35] In fact, he had some difficulty maintaining a meaningful partnership with the US in the operations in Afghanistan. Despite a significant British force on manoeuvres in Oman the US moved quickly, and unilaterally, to conduct largely its own campaign in removing the Taliban from Kabul. British cruise missiles were fired in the opening salvo of the air campaign and up to 1,000 British special forces were sent to work with the Americans on the ground. But the US had no real need of any European military support and little time to discuss it. Insofar as this stage of the Afghanistan operation was a coalition effort, it was for the sake of appearances rather than effectiveness. But the operation was not particularly controversial in a foreign policy sense. Though there was some domestic disquiet in public opinion throughout Europe at the implications of the campaign, there was a general consensus, on which London traded heavily, that this was a justifiable US reaction to the 9/11 atrocities. Post-conflict reconstruction and 'nation-building' would be another matter altogether,[36] but this did not dim the sense of momentum in Downing Street that events were demonstrating the value of the activist approach to foreign policy. The trick was how to keep the US engaged in the nation-building aftermath of military operations.

The Iraq War and its implications

The US wanted to move quickly on from Afghanistan, however, and was clearly determined to address ways of breaking out of the blind alley that had consumed the Iraq policy. This proved to be the crucible for the Blair approach to foreign policy and the turning point between a growing momentum of success and a policy failure that compelled revaluation. The Iraq War of 2003, by common consent, has been the most evident US foreign policy blunder since Vietnam, and may ultimately prove to have

---

[35] Quoted in Kampfner, *Blair's Wars*, pp. 130–1.
[36] Amalendu Misra, 'Afghanistan: The Politics of Post-war Reconstruction', *Conflict, Security and Development*, 2.3, 2002: 5–27.

even greater consequences for the US role in the world. *Fiasco*, the seminal insider study by Thomas Ricks, has been widely acknowledged by middle-range policymakers in the US as an accurate summary of the whole sorry affair.[37] Bob Woodward's trilogy of books on the dynamics of the administration dealing with the war also tells the story of an unfolding – perhaps inevitable – tragedy for the Americans, the Iraqis and the Middle East as a whole.[38]

For the Blair government, concerned with 'positioning' for long-term global objectives, two crucial decisions determined the British share in this blunder; both taken before the war began. The first was in April 2002 when Tony Blair returned from a private meeting with President Bush convinced that the US was determined, come what may, to act against Iraq. There was no question in his own mind that Britain must back US policy, but it did so with a complex and ambitious diplomatic agenda. It would deliver united European support for Washington that would build on the Kosovo experience. It could achieve this because it would simultaneously deliver the US to the United Nations for a legitimising resolution. It would leverage such a resolution on the basis of a renewal of the 'road map' for peace between Israel and the Palestinians. Putin would huff and puff about the use of coercion but would follow his best interests and fall in behind a united front. And 'dealing with Iraq' would be presented in the Middle East as a prerequisite to a bigger new deal for the region as a whole. If this diplomatic coup could be pulled off, coercive diplomacy might serve to prevent a war at all. The British diplomatic machine went into high gear to try to manufacture these outcomes, Tony Blair himself confident that they were within reach. In the event, they all failed.[39]

The second key decision was to commit large British forces to the war that ensued – some 40,000 service personnel – sufficient to command a divisional sector of the battlefield and then the arena of reconstruction. This was both a demonstration of commitment to Washington and to the

---

[37] Thomas Ricks, *Fiasco: The American Military Adventure in Iraq* (New York: Penguin Press, 2006). 'From Planning to Warfare to Occupation, How Iraq Went Wrong', *New York Times*, 25 July 2006. Michael O'Hanlon, 'Taking it to the Streets', *Slate Magazine*, 28 July 2006.

[38] Bob Woodward, *Bush at War* (New York: Simon and Schuster, 2002). Bob Woodward, *Plan of Attack* (New York: Simon and Schuster, 2004). Bob Woodward, *State of Denial: Bush at War, Part III* (New York: Simon and Schuster, 2006). See also, Michael Gordon and Bernard Trainor, *Cobra II: The Inside Story of the Invasion and Occupation of Iraq* (London: Atlantic Books, 2006).

[39] Michael Clarke, 'The Diplomacy that Led to War in Iraq', in Paul Cornish (ed.), *The War in Iraq, 2003* (London: Macmillan, 2004), pp. 40–6.

enterprise, as well as another case where a British approach to the integration of hard and soft power could contribute to a favourable outcome. It was a further demonstration of the practical partnership between the US and Britain. This too, went wrong, chiefly because the British had very little influence on the overall political picture of which south-eastern Iraq and Basra were a part. Ultimately Blair and Bush were fighting different wars. For Blair, Iraq was about upholding values and the will of the international community; for Bush it was a demonstration of raw power to achieve a national purpose. As reconstruction and efforts at nation-building foundered across Iraq the British position became increasingly untenable. Far from offering leadership to the Europeans and partnership to the Americans, the Iraq commitment left Britain isolated and lacking influence in Washington – lauded for its loyalty but identified with a disastrous lame-duck presidency. The failure of the enterprise undermined British influence throughout the Middle East at least as much as the Suez debacle had done 40 years previously. In his various valedictory addresses, Tony Blair acknowledged that many mistakes had been made, that the situation in Iraq was deeply unsatisfactory, but that time would show it was the right thing to do.[40] If it was a US blunder, key officials have opined, then Washington could not be allowed to make it alone.[41] Positioning again.

Not the least significant consequence of the Iraq failure was the effect it had on other areas of policy. It absorbed British diplomatic and prime ministerial attention so that the imaginative approach to European politics foundered after 2002, despite a high energy level from a prime minister keen to mend bilateral fences.[42] But his run of good luck was over. The subtleties of the British approach to European defence questions were an immediate casualty of the Iraq War and relations with France and Germany deteriorated on a range of issues. Downing Street even felt that Chirac, Schroeder and Putin effectively formed a diplomatic front against Blair. Nor was this much ameliorated by the desire of the major European powers to get back on better terms with the Bush Administration at the end of 2004. Britain was keen to push for a renewed commitment to nation-building in Afghanistan. It would be a way for the Europeans in

---

[40] Blair, *A Global Alliance for Global Values*, pp. 8–9.
[41] On blundering, see Barnett R.Rubin, 'Saving Afghanistan', *Foreign Affairs*, 86.1, 2007: 66. On positioning, see Alex Daachev, '"I'm with You": Tony Blair and the Obligations of Alliance', in C. Lloyd *et al.* (eds.), *Iraq and the Lessons of Vietnam* (New York: The New Press, 2007), pp. 46–8.
[42] Julie Smith, 'A Missed Opportunity? New Labour's European Policy 1997–2005', *International Affairs*, 81.4, 2005: 715–21.

NATO to make a tangible contribution to US policy objectives but still keep them out of Iraq. And Afghanistan needed more determined nation-building in the face of a lacklustre US performance that had concentrated almost exclusively on counter-terrorist operations. NATO, however, was issuing a blank cheque in taking over a potentially massive commitment at a time when it appeared just about feasible. By the time of deployment in the spring of 2006, however, the situation had deteriorated considerably. The arrival of NATO forces led the Taliban and al-Qaeda to open a more active front in the country and the Europeans fell into public arguments over their willingness to meet the challenges and reinforce their troops. Britain again found itself positioned squarely with the US – and Canada – in taking on most of the fighting, but unable to 'lead' its European partners into a more positive, let alone holistic, response. Unlike Iraq, Afghanistan seemed to British officials to offer some hope of at least interim success. But by the time Tony Blair had left Downing Street it had become another anvil on which European unity, and its relationship to US global policy, was being regularly hammered.

It was understandable that the commitment to the principles behind New Labour's foreign policy should find other outlets after the failure of Iraq and its immediate consequences. Tony Blair returned heavily to the themes of interdependence and the necessary responses to globalisation. His increasing concentration on anti-terrorism following the 2005 bomb attacks in London was all couched in terms of the failure of the jihadis and their supporters to grasp what was at stake in a globalised world and their visceral fear of the onward march of real democracy. He returned, too, to the instrumentalities of effecting change – the need to design comprehensive, multinational policies and to understand the sheer interrelatedness of policy challenges. Africa emerged as a new focus for long-term thinking. It seemed an appropriate moment given Britain's presidency of the G8 during 2005 and the Gleneagles Summit, the UN climate change conference and the World Trade Organisation ministerial meeting that would follow.[43] The government had shown a renewed interest in African affairs during its second term, but the particular challenges of Zimbabwe, Somalia, the Democratic Republic of Congo and latterly Darfur were not readily accessible to external influences acting independently.[44] Nevertheless, the more structural aspects of Africa's foreign policy problems offered scope for

---

[43] Tony Blair, 'A Year of Huge Challenges', *The Economist*, 1 January 2005, p. 25.
[44] Tom Porteous, 'British Government Policy in Sub-Saharan Africa under New Labour', *International Affairs*, 81.2, 2005:292–4.

some imaginative initiatives on development aid, debt relief, trade liberalisation, HIV/AIDS, environment, capacity-building, support for the African
Union, and so on.[45] The Gleneagles agenda formed the centrepiece of a new
emphasis in Britain's activist foreign policy and raised new hopes in diplomats and pop stars alike.[46] The results were more than cynics had suggested
would be possible. There was agreement to double international aid to
Africa, create financial mechanisms to put more money into public health,
cancel all of Africa's multilateral debts and help beef up the AU's capacity to
deploy peacekeepers. There were climate change initiatives, too, though the
unspoken goal remained to find a way of bringing the US into a follow-on to
the Kyoto protocol after 2012.[47] Such headlines normally disguise an aggre-
gation of existing trends and policies, however, and there has been a vigorous debate about the fungibility of the promises made at Gleneagles.[48]
Gleneagles was, however, an undoubted personal triumph for Tony Blair. In
his farewell tour round Africa he made a big pitch for the worth of the initiatives undertaken in 2005. In reality, the locus of British policymaking on
Africa had shifted from the FCO to the Department for International
Development and the Treasury. Gordon Brown talked about aid and debt:
Tony Blair talked about security and intervention. By the end of his premiership it was not clear that British policy was appropriately 'comprehensive' nor that international efforts were close to any step-change. But the
agenda was very much his.

The scorecard

The decade of Blairite foreign policy was turbulent and distinctive. Much of
it ended in failure, but certainly not all. And out of the remains of immediate policy wreckage always emerges a legacy that may be more lasting. It was
an approach to foreign policy that was based around Tony Blair's own self-
belief and commitment. It drew both upon an older conservative tradition
that Margaret Thatcher and Winston Churchill would certainly have recognised, and on a social democratic internationalism that was close to the

---

[45] Commission for Africa, *Our Common Interest* (London: Penguin Books, 2005).

[46] Alex Ramsbotham, Alhaji M.S.Bah and Fanny Calder, 'Enhancing African Peace and
     Security Capacity: A Useful Role for the UK and the G8?' *International Affairs*, 81.2, 2005:
     325–39.

[47] Tony Blair, 'A Year After Gleneagles', Speech, 26 June 2006, 10 Downing Street, Press
     Office, Text.

[48] Anthony Payne, 'Blair, Brown and the Gleneagles Agenda', *International Affairs*, 82.5,
     2006: 934–5.

traditional Labour heart. The key difference between old and new Labour interpretations of this internationalism was in the Churchillian determination to carry it through – with or without legal institutional backing, with or without a solid domestic consensus. Internationalism, in Blair's view, could not be shackled by the constraints and vetoes of an old system in the face of such new and urgent challenges. The approach boasted a coherent view of the world, but in truth that view was characterised more by vigour in action than rigour in analysis. Key concepts – such as these new and urgent challenges – were never carefully defined. Action was thought through, more than principles closely interrogated, by officials and advisers at the top who had little time for reflection and who were serving a hyperactive, instinctive, Prime Minister with youth on his side.

Blairite foreign policy is irrevocably identified with the principles of liberal – or humanitarian – interventionism and with the empirical reality of Iraq as its exemplar. For some, like Simon Jenkins, it is already time to consign the notion to the history of a vainglorious showman: 'Liberal interventionism talks the talk but can barely walk the length of a red carpet. It has failed the most crucial test of any policy in being neither morally even-handed nor effective in action.'[49] For others, it is a necessary response to modern instability whose failures – and successes – leave Britain with something that any country with international interests and aspirations will seek to refine.[50] Conservative policy in Bosnia, after all, began precisely as a humanitarian intervention, but in a world where all such interventions are bound to be morally ambiguous and inconsistently applied, no one had the cheek to elevate it out of the realm of the merely pragmatic. The British military still retain great respect throughout the world, if only for their sheer tactical acumen, and for a mixture of good and bad reasons all the major Western allies have committed themselves to seek success in the Afghanistan operation. It is reasonable to suppose that future leaders will be more cautious in committing themselves to interventions in the future. But it is unlikely that the demand for them will decrease. Many good lessons were drawn from the messy interventions of the 1990s, but then not learned, or wilfully ignored, in those interventions that were deemed part of the 'war on terror' a few years later.

The central question will persist, whether Iraq demonstrated fatal flaws in the very concept of liberal intervention, or whether that parti-

[49] Simon Jenkins, 'Blair Reinvented the Middle Ages and Called It Liberal Intervention', *The Sunday Times*, 3 June 2007, p. 16.
[50] Robert Cooper, *The Breaking of Nations* (London, Atlantic Books, 2004), pp. 182–7.

cular operation was so badly conceived and executed by the Bush Administration that no generic conclusions can be drawn from it. Perhaps it stands as a singular, egregious tragedy in a more nuanced land-scape. It seems likely, however, that Tony Blair might be judged less harshly by history than by his contemporary critics in his decision to back US actions in the way that he did. It seems inconceivable that after the 1991 Gulf War, after the No-Fly-Zones, after all the pressure London had absorbed in backing US policy through the 1990s, and after 9/11 itself, that Britain could have let the US go it alone in 2002. For Tony Blair it was barely a decision to make. He had set out his stall in 1997 on the assump-tion that he was able to run an Atlanticist and a European policy in genuine synergy; without having to make a strategic choice between them. But 9/11 and the war on terror – unluckily for him – forced Blair to make a choice. There was no question how he would jump when it was finally forced on him. It was simple positioning. And it offered him a tempting personal diplomatic opportunity of global importance.

Could he have stopped the war by refusing Washington his support? Opinion remains sharply divided.[51] The key point, however, is that while he may have hoped he could achieve some sort of success without a war, he was never motivated by a desire to stop the Bush Administration from acting altogether. He too wanted to escape from the stalemate that the Iraq policy had become. More telling is the charge that Blair's positioning actually made US policy drift under Bush worse than it might otherwise have been. Zbigniew Brzezinski and former members of the Bush team credit Tony Blair with giving a finesse and persuasive power to policies that did not deserve it; helping to shield the President in some key moments from domestic and international criticism that was his due.[52] Whether this is an over-estimate, there is no doubt that Blair's personal commitment to the Bush Administration cost Britain dearly, at least in the short term. Its position on a number of arms control issues changed to accommodate US shifts, and the reluctance of the Prime Minister to air any disagreements with Bush in public contributed to a growing image of 'poodleism' which considerably diminished domestic support in Britain for foreign operations. In April 2007 a YouGov survey indicated a scepti-cal low point in the public's appetite for any more foreign involvements.[53]

[51] On the view that he could, see, Ted Widmer, 'A Legacy That Is Very Mixed, Even in America', *Financial Times*, 11 May 2007, p. 15. On the view that he could not, see Strobe Talbot, quoted in Edward Luce, 'Articulate Premier Who Gave Tongue-tied President an Easier Ride', *Financial Times*, 11 May 2007, p. 3.   [52] *Ibid.*
[53] YouGov Poll, 26–28 March 2007, reported in *The Daily Telegraph*, 3 April 2007, p. 16.

In the Middle East Tony Blair was forced to suppress some under-standable exasperation at the failure of the 'road map' for an Israel/Palestinian settlement to gain any momentum. He had staked a good deal of personal capital on pushing the vision of a new start in regional relations within and between the key players. There was a modicum of success with the announcement in December 2003 that Libya would give up its nuclear programme. That was a step in the right direction for a new deal. But it paled beside the growing instabilities across the region and the continuing failure to gain any diplomatic pur-chase on nuclear proliferation, or any other matters, with Iran. Britain's own position in the region had been fatally undermined by Iraq and there was little it could do but fall back into reactive mode. The short Lebanon war in summer 2006 left the government under international pressure for, in effect, supporting an Israeli folly against Hizbollah in Lebanon and a US policy that made it worse. A Downing Street insider described those weeks as the 'lowest point' in Britain's Middle East odyssey. It was another short-term cost of long-term positioning.

European relations needed the impetus of new leadership, which it had by 2007 as Blair left Downing Street. This was not only provided by Paris and Berlin. The Bush Administration had made copious efforts to repair some of the damage after 2003. It had not reversed any of its fundamental positions and Bush himself was so damaged that it hardly mattered. But officials and technocrats on both sides of the Atlantic worked hard to reconnect on policy details and provided some of the diplomatic infra-structure for a new start. In this there was some evidence of a new realism on both sides that the transatlantic relationship would never be the same again.[54] Tony Blair was marginal to this process. His failure to achieve membership of the Eurozone and the collapse of the constitutional treaty only weakened his ability to be an initiator. The grand project that would again raise European politics out of the realm of the institutional – and the constitutional – to make an independent impact on world politics would have to be driven by a new generation of leaders. Outside Iraq and Afghanistan, there was little he could tilt at that engaged most of the Europeans directly. The investment that Tony Blair had made in President Putin was dwarfed by Russia's deteriorating relations with the US and Britain had little scope to do anything more than react to the pro-gressive chill.

[54] Daniel Dombey, 'Transatlantic Climate Shift', *Financial Times*, 4 June 2007, Supplement, p. 2.

The legacy

The empirical balance of the scorecard is only part of an assessment. Intentions also matter and Tony Blair argued strongly after 2003 that his intentions, throughout the decade, ought to have been better understood. He bequeathed to foreign policy a deep commitment that globalisation had to be embraced, politically, economically and morally. It followed that a narrow view of national interests was self-defeating. It also followed that his much vaunted, but little analysed, 'values' in world politics represented a genuine innovation compared with previous approaches. In a world where power is so disbursed, and where individuals and dynamic social organisations are so empowered, where the very nature of the state is changing, only a consensus on values can create the mechanisms for meaningful political action.[55] If prevailing Western values are under challenge they may simply lose their power to mobilise people. Promoting them is therefore not an act of idealism but a hard-nosed investment in political survival. This constituted a claim to internationalism that retains considerable resonance, though how it is enacted from era to era will naturally vary, and opinions continue to differ over how vulnerable our values presently are to challenge.

Like Bill Clinton, Tony Blair also succeeded in putting some global political issues – Africa, development, climate change – on the contemporary agenda. He contributed a determination to try to translate global aspirations into practical policy initiatives. He probably under-estimated the power of international constraints on action and over-estimated his own power to persuade. He was constantly frustrated that the breakneck pace of review and action in the first term could not be maintained thereafter. Nevertheless, a determination to try to unite the genuinely aspirational with the politically practical is an honourable legacy. Indeed some of the 'spin and hype' that surrounded all Tony Blair's initiatives was partly driven by a desire to create momentum, to build and direct a consensus, using all means possible.

The underlying question of Blair's legacy was something he raised himself in his final months as Prime Minister. Having, as he felt, set the aspirational course for the twenty-first century, he posed the question that Britain, as a society, has to decide whether it is prepared to take on

---

[55] See, Michael Mandelbaum, *The Ideas That Conquered the World: Peace, Democracy and Free Markets in the Twenty-first Century* (New York: Public Affairs, 2002).

the task; rise to the challenge.[56] The Western world, he had decided, is divided into those states that are able and prepared to take the initiative and act on behalf of freedom, tolerance and democracy, and those who are not. In a sense it is the old distinction between 'producers' and 'consumers' of security, but in this case on a much wider, foreign policy stage of the twenty-first century. To critics, such a stance seemed to be tantamount to asking whether, as he departed, the nation was really worthy of him. To supporters, it was merely an honest assessment of the choices all European states now face. Few Prime Ministers would have expressed the matter so clearly or with such conviction.

[56] Oral Evidence to the House of Commons Liaison Committee, 6 February 2007. Blair, 'Our Nation's Future'.

28

Defence

LAWRENCE FREEDMAN

Speaking in Plymouth in January 2007, Tony Blair argued that there were two types of nations among Britain's allies: 'Those who do war-fighting and peacekeeping and those who have, effectively, except in the most exceptional circumstances, retreated to the peacekeeping alone.'[1] The sharpness of the distinction drawn here, in addition to the description of abandoning a war-fighting role as a 'retreat', is revealing. When Blair had become Prime Minister almost a decade earlier the distinction would have followed American lines, with war-fighting about great power confrontations involving the full range of military capabilities. Everything else, including peacekeeping, came into the lesser category of 'operations other than war' – possibly altruistic in motive, invariably limited in scope and rarely an appropriate use of proper war-fighting forces. During the 1990s this sharp distinction became questionable. The peacekeeping category became stretched in the post-Cold War world. From the original concept of policing cease-fire lines, with the consent of the belligerents and using minimum force, it expanded into helping conflicts wind down and, more difficult still, acting on behalf of civilians caught up in vicious civil wars, by which point peacekeepers were in effect taking sides. By then these missions were hazardous, albeit on a small scale, and hard to distinguish at a tactical level from war-fighting. The language tried to keep up, as they came to be described as an extension or variation of the traditional peacekeeping model – a 'third-generation' or 'wider' type, or about 'peace support' or 'peace enforcement'.

By the time Labour came to office, prompted by the activity surrounding the implosion of Yugoslavia, the talk was increasingly of 'humanitarian interventions', which contained elements of both war-fighting and peacekeeping. The new Labour government had embraced

---

[1] Rt Hon. Tony Blair, 'Our Nation's Future – Defence', Speech on board HMS *Albion*, Plymouth, 17 January 2007, www.pm.gov.uk/output/Page10735.asp.

this development more enthusiastically than its Conservative predecessor. The frequency with which Blair sent Britain's armed forces into battle became one of the defining features of his premiership. The first set of interventions with which he was associated – air strikes against Iraq in 1998, the campaign over Kosovo in 1999 and the intervention in Sierra Leone in 2000 were not without critics but gained considerable domestic and international support. The two of the 2000s – Afghanistan and Iraq – were far more controversial, and Iraq in particular cast a large cloud. They were justified using the more altruistic rationales developed during the 1990s – to fight against repression, promote democracy and support economic reconstruction – but a national security purpose was also acquired– to eliminate terrorist bases and weapons of mass destruction. As a result the question of when it is right and proper to resort to armed force dominated debate about foreign policy. Blair was always happy to contribute, even more so when the criticisms reached a crescendo as the situation in Iraq turned out so badly.

This was the purpose of the Plymouth speech. As was so often the case Blair's argument depended on his conviction that Britain was a country that could combine opposites and reconcile the contradictory. Rather than pose values against interests, he argued that it was 'by furthering our values that we further our interests in the modern era of globalisation and interdependence'. Nor was there any need to choose between America and Europe as alternative allies, or even between different types of power. Uniquely, he insisted, Britain could bring 'hard' and 'soft' power together, using armed force where necessary while at the same time acting to the fore in addressing the big questions of poverty and climate change. And when it used hard power this required seeing the purpose of both warfighting and peacekeeping. After the bruising experience of the previous few years of combat, Blair was arguing against a retreat away from warfighting as if this would be tantamount to a retreat from Britain's world role.

This was at heart a debate about this role and, as Blair would have it, about whether Britain should be activist and internationalist or passive and insular. The larger questions of foreign policy and the diplomatic origins of the various interventions that reflected this policy are dealt with elsewhere in this book. My focus is on how Blair's ambitious views on the contemporary value of a war-fighting capability developed and, as a result of their vigorous application, whether such missions will be embraced so readily in the future.

The legacy

Defence for Labour prior to Blair had been an electoral disaster zone. Historically, 'Labour's stance on security issues' had been 'much less assured than the Conservatives'.[2] As a result of its preoccupation with grandiose schemes for disarmament and an apparent squeamishness when it came to applying force, it was regularly castigated as naïve, bordering on unpatriotic, and far too ready to discount external threats. During the Thatcher decade of the1980s, caught out by the successful prosecution of a popular war over the Falkland Islands in 1982, and then by deep divisions over nuclear policy, defence had become a key vulnerability. By the start of the 1990s the Labour leadership had begun to reposition the party as pro-military and the nuclear issue had already lost its salience as a result of the end of the Cold War. During John Major's administration, the *Vanguard*-class submarines with their US Trident D-5 missiles, entered service, but short-range systems were abandoned. Labour sought to keep the focus on domestic issues, and in particular the economy and the future of the welfare state, where the Major government was seen to be most vulnerable. Under Blair this continued. The brief of the Shadow Defence Secretary, David Clark, was assumed to be to keep defence as low a profile issue as possible, and avoid attracting any fire. In this he succeeded.

The 1997 manifesto promised retention of Trident and strength in 'defence through NATO'. It mentioned the new threats of proliferating 'weapons of mass destruction, the growth of ethnic nationalism and extremism, international terrorism, and crime and drug trafficking'. After paying tribute to the 'professionalism and courage' of the armed forces, it promised to 'conduct a strategic defence and security review to reassess our essential security interests and defence needs'.[3] Demanding a defence review was an alternative to developing clear and unequivocal policies, avoiding controversial stances while hinting at something radical to come. Yet even talk of a defence review carried dangers, for it implied cuts. During the 1970s, as the economy deteriorated, Labour had constantly raided the defence budget for expenditure savings. In the 1997 manifesto Labour promised that this time the review would be 'foreign policy led'. The lack of a Treasury role was greeted with considerable scepticism. Labour was still associated with expansionary plans for the

[2] Dan Keohane, *Security in British Politics, 1945–99*, (London: Macmillan, 2000).
[3] *New Labour because Britain Deserves Better*, Labour Party manifesto, May 1997.

welfare state, and in this context it was questioned whether the Treasury could help itself.

Yet there was no particular budgetary reason for a defence review in May 1997. The peace dividend following the end of the Cold War had been taken; there was not much fat left to cut; many of the organisational upheavals set in motion under the Conservatives had yet to be fully digested and implemented; service morale was fragile and there was only limited room for manoeuvre in force structure. By contrast there was a case for a foreign policy-led review. Under an exercise called 'options for change', set in motion by Defence Secretary Tom King in 1990, the impression was gained that a peace dividend could be taken without any reshaping of the forces. The focus was still on Europe and a possible, resurgent Russian threat. The aim seemed to be 'smaller but better', although the forces grumbled that the emphasis was on the smaller. Over the 1990s defence spending was cut by over 20%, moving from over 4% of GDP to under 3%. Because the 1991 Gulf War involved exactly the sort of forces – armed divisions and air power – intended for the Warsaw Pact it obscured the possibilities that quite different types of adversary might have to be faced in the coming years.

The Americans seemed even more prepared to ignore these possibilities and continued to prepare for big wars, stressing the imminence of a 'revolution in military affairs' based on intrusive sensors, precisions munitions and fast communications. The crises within the former Yugoslavia, and in particular Bosnia, soon demonstrated the alternative possibilities and notably the need for troops on the ground. Some of the cuts in army manpower were reinstated to cope with the new demands. Unlike Margaret Thatcher, who, out of office, was an early proponent of humanitarian intervention (with the Kurds in 1991) John Major was unenthusiastic. It had taken time to recognise the severity of the Bosnia situation.[4] So the Conservative government's attitude towards the developing agenda of humanitarian interventions was equivocal. This provided a reason for Labour's review: to explain the importance of new missions connected with humanitarian intervention, and how the forces could be configured to meet the demands they posed. It would be about the use of armed force as much as the more traditional questions of budgets, procurement and the distribution of resource between the three services.

[4] For a critique see Brendan Simms, *Unfinest Hour: Britain and the Destruction of Bosnia*, (London: Penguin Books, 2001).

Labour's Strategic Defence Review

This was the backdrop to the arrival of the new ministerial team to the Ministry of Defence in May 1997. Unlike many of his cabinet colleagues, George Robertson as Secretary of State had taken a pro-defence line during the opposition years, even when it was unfashionable in the party to do so. John Reid, who had developed good defence contacts in opposition, came in as Minister of State. Yet there was still a credibility issue because of past policies and practice. The new intake of MPs was drawn from the liberal professions. A decade earlier and they would have been assumed to be hostile to defence. Now they could be assumed to be ignorant. Few were left of the generation that had served in the Second World War or could remember national service. Even those who had entered politics during the Vietnam period were among the veterans. None of the Labour front bench had any military experience or even much background in foreign policy. The two top players – Tony Blair and Gordon Brown – had made their names on domestic policy. Robin Cook was best known in defence circles as one of the most articulate exponents of unilateralism during the 1970s and 1980s.

Robertson used the defence review process to ensure that defence issues were pushed to the fore and some sort of national consensus on a way forward was developed. He was helped by the fact that officials had assumed both a new government and a defence review, so thoughts inside the MoD were well advanced and this ensured that the review process could be structured quite quickly. The process was unusually open, with a range of industrialists and academics as well as the services themselves being consulted, and an independent panel of experts was established.[5] This had the effect of creating a reasonably supportive constituency and also ensuring that the main messages of the review came as no surprise.

The idea of a reconstituted Russian threat, especially as its forces struggled against rebels in Chechnya, seemed more remote than ever. Anxieties here were more to do with Russia's somewhat chaotic internal state following the loss of its European empire, and in particular what this might mean for the management of its substantial nuclear assets. If

[5] Including the author. The demands placed on this panel were not onerous. In the United States a comparable panel set up to advise and comment on the 1997 Quadrennial Defense Review produced its own report. In contrast to the American practice, the British panel did not get a chance to form a corporate view, let alone travel extensively at government expense (although it did eat quite well).

there was no need to worry about a revived conventional Russian threat, then – more than ever before – defence of the realm was not very difficult. Britain was unusually secure, even amongst its allies, far away from most trouble spots and not needing to worry about balancing a would-be hegemonic power in Europe. Yet absent the Cold War, the world was not necessarily peaceful and harmonious. Many regions, notably Africa and parts of post-communist Europe, were suffering from severe disorder. Though geography allowed Britain to avoid the most direct consequences of upheavals elsewhere, the consensus view in London was that the country could not stand aside. As one of the five permanent members of the Security Council it had a responsibility to support UN operations, while as the leading European member of NATO it could not easily decide to opt out. If Britain were unprepared to act then in most cases the rest of Europe would not be able to pick up the slack. More seriously all the arguments that might persuade Britain that it had no reason to get involved, would apply to the United States. Any effort to encourage Washington to remain engaged with the rest of the world would falter if Britain began to disengage as well. When introducing the Strategic Defence Review (SDR) in July 1998, Robertson argued that armed forces should be geared not only to defending rights but also to discharging international responsibilities.[6]

Although the 'ethical dimension' to foreign policy, proclaimed by Foreign Secretary Robin Cook soon after taking office, was normally judged as if it was all about arms sales, at its core was a commitment to human rights.[7] Thus 'doing good' was about helping the weak and vulnerable in distress, but that also implied getting involved in distant civil wars and regional squabbles. This raised issues which cut across party boundaries. Bosnia led many on the left to argue for the use of armed force in good causes, just as many on the right were highly dubious about dabbling in other peoples' problems when British national interests were not at stake.[8] At the same time those on the left who assumed that no good could ever come from Western military action opposed it instinctively, even when directed against oppressive regimes, while those on the right who strained for Britain to be a major player on the world stage were uncomfortable with the idea that Britain could fail to join any major military expedition.

[6] Secretary of State for Defence, *The Strategic Defence Review*, Cm. 3999 (London: TSO, 1998).   [7] Robin Cook, 'British Foreign Policy', 12 May 1997, www.fco.gov.uk.

[8] This is well brought out in Michael Ignatieff's exchange with Robert Skidelsky in *Prospect*, reproduced in *Virtual War: Kosovo and Beyond* (London: Chatto & Windus, 2000).

The government demonstrated from early on that it was inclined to an activist stance. In the summer of 1997, British troops were involved in the seizure of alleged war criminals in Bosnia. Then the aircraft carrier HMS *Invincible* was despatched to the Gulf to put pressure on Saddam Hussein not to impede UN weapons inspectors. In this case Secretary-General Kofi Annan's diplomatic efforts eased the immediate crisis, although only in practice postponed the eventual confrontation. Annan's statement at the time – 'You can do a lot with diplomacy but, of course, you can do a lot more with diplomacy backed by firmness and force' – appeared in Robertson's introduction to the SDR.

An activist foreign policy required some reconfiguration of the forces to become more organised for expeditionary warfare. So despite its privileged geographical position and limited resources, Britain would be improving its ability to operate overseas. Forces would be geared to active operations rather than passive deterrence. This required a capacity to move units to where they would be needed through improved air- and sea-lift capabilities, proper training, adequate stocks, extra troops and reserves able to provide specialist capabilities rather than just make up the numbers. In addition, joint commands were to become a norm rather than ad hoc arrangements to prevent the three services each fighting their own separate wars, with a joint staff college, doctrine centre, command headquarters and rapid reaction force. The latter became operational in April 1999, two years earlier than originally planned. The modest savings required to make room for all of this were largely the result of either one-off asset sales or promises of greater efficiency in equipment procurement and the management of stores. With the risk of a traditional military threat low, the insurance premium could be correspondingly reduced. This was reflected in reduced numbers of combat aircraft, frigates and nuclear warheads.

The most significant indication of this shift in focus was the consensus within the defence establishment behind the need for new, large aircraft carriers. The old requirement for carrier battle groups to wrest control of the Atlantic from another major sea power would be both prohibitively expensive as well as strategically obsolescent. In the post-Cold War world carriers could serve as mobile air bases able to project power to wherever trouble was brewing. They would not require favours from local governments if they did not wish to be publicly associated with a military action. Few important cities and military facilities were so far inland that they could not be struck from the sea. They could also serve as command and control posts for the conduct of any large-scale rescue or humanitarian operation, whether or not lethal force was involved. This would require ships twice the size of the *Invincible*-class carriers.

The SDR was never intended to reappraise the Trident programme, although it did provide the fullest account of UK nuclear capabilities yet published. Each of the four Trident submarines carried no more than 48 warheads, with a total operational stockpile of less than 200 warheads, 100 down from the planned numbers inherited from the Conservatives. The idea appeared to be to explore to the full the possible meaning of a 'minimum' deterrent, by not running the submarines intensively, with only one on patrol at any time, and only one crew per boat (compared with two during the Cold War). The missiles would not be on quick reaction alert but kept days away from operational readiness and not targeted against anyone in particular. Yet despite this, and the fact that Trident was just entering service as Labour entered office, by the third term the government argued that unless early preparations were made to prepare for replacement submarines, the system could become obsolescent by the 2020s.[9] This led to a debate that previous generations of Labour leaders would have avoided at all costs, but it was surprisingly muted. The best argument for was future uncertainty, and with the background noise of Iran's nuclear exertions, it was not clear why this was the moment for Britain, alone among the nuclear powers, to abandon the status. The best argument against appeared to be that the £20 billion expenditure would be wasteful and meet no evident security purpose. As both sets of arguments were speculative, the debate was conducted with little passion and scant public interest. Labour dissidence was not as high as with the 2003 Iraq vote, although Conservatives were still necessary for a majority.[10]

The impact of Kosovo

The first main test of the underlying approach came in the Serbian province of Kosovo. In the summer of 1998 Blair was among the first Western leaders to urge that a strong stand be taken against Yugoslav President Milosevic whose forces were turning on the Muslim majority in Kosovo in response to an outbreak of violence led by the Kosovo

[9] Secretary of State for Defence and the Secretary of State for Foreign and Commonwealth Affairs, *The Future of the United Kingdom's Nuclear Deterrent*, Cmnd 6994 (December 2006).

[10] There were 409 MPs supporting the proposals, and 161 against, including 88 Labour backbenchers, a majority of 248. In 2003, 138 Labour MPs voted against the Iraq War. http://news.bbc.co.uk/go/pr/fr/-/1/hi/uk_politics/6448173.stm.

Liberation Army (KLA). Beginning on 26 March 1999, allied air forces attacked targets in Serbia. It took until June for the campaign to conclude with Milosevic effectively conceding on all of NATO's demands. The intervening weeks were extremely difficult for NATO. Its initial coercive threat failed as Milosevic called the bluff. The air strikes had little impact on the Serb campaign on the ground in Kosovo. Instead there was a massive outflow of refugees across the province's borders into Macedonia and Albania. The very process that NATO was supposed to be preventing was accelerating. Yet this ruthlessness also sealed the Serbs' fate, for it gave new purpose to the KLA's campaign, and provided it with opportunities to acquire and train new recruits. In addition, whatever the misgivings expressed during the first days of the NATO campaign, outrage at Serb behaviour created a bedrock of popular support that saw the alliance through many difficult days.[11] The big question was whether public opinion would tolerate a shift from a strategy that relied on air power alone. The United States in particular (though not uniquely) was reluctant to commit ground forces in combat. Yugoslav forces were considered to be tough and capable of imposing severe casualties on Western forces. Kosovo was also a logistical nightmare. Gradually it dawned on NATO leaders that explicitly ruling out land operations was mistaken, and planning began. Air power was problematic: the Serbs were largely using small paramilitary units, not easily disrupted by aircraft flying at high altitude. It was more effective when directed against the Serb political and economic system, but this was morally awkward for an alliance that claimed to be attacking military targets and seeking to avoid civilian casualties. In the event bridges, railway lines, power supplies and some factories could be described as militarily relevant, although the main consequences were felt by the Serb population.

For Blair Kosovo was a turning point. This was not the first time he had demonstrated his readiness to take a robust stance on armed force. He had already taken a tough line on Iraq. The continuing arguments over Iraq's refusal to cooperate with UN inspectors led to a sharp series of air strikes in December 1998, known as Desert Fox. These were inconclusive in their effects, and led to niggling activity over the following years as Iraq unsuccessfully attempted to control its air space. It was therefore not surprising to find Blair to the fore in making the case for NATO action over Kosovo. As the issue of ground operations was debated there was no

---

[11] See Lawrence Freedman, 'Victims and Victors: Reflections on the Kosovo War', *Review of International Studies*, 26:3, 2000.

doubt which country was pushing hardest for a bold and decisive move. Yet for most of the time Britain's actual military contribution was modest, in line with other European countries. It was better prepared than others for ground operations, which had given Blair's offers of a substantial contribution for a new strategy added force, and when the capitulation took place and NATO peacekeepers streamed into Kosovo British units were to the fore and led by a British general.[12]

It was during the Kosovo war that Blair made the case for Western states to take on those responsible for genocide, ethnic cleansing and repression. In April 1999, during one of the more difficult periods for NATO, Blair set out his stall in a major speech in Chicago.[13] This was part of an itinerary that also involved a 50th anniversary NATO summit in Washington and an argument with Clinton over the use of ground forces in Kosovo. This speech challenged the norm of non-interference in the internal affairs of others, including by forceful means, while setting stringent tests against which any military intervention would be judged. This picked up on a well-developed debate among the commentariat. In this regard it was significant not so much for the originality of its content but because here was a European leader challenging the traditional right of states to non-interference in internal affairs when it was being used as a cover for genocide and oppression and making the case for the use of force in pursuit of objectives that were described in altruistic terms. Another reading of the speech was that at the same time it answered critics who argued that this line of argument created for NATO a right to intervene wherever and whenever it chose. Five tests were set down: a strong case, exhausted diplomacy, realistic military options, a readiness to accept a long-term commitment and a link to national interests. These were potentially restrictive, and in late 1999 could be used to explain why there was little that could be done in response to the Russian campaign in

---

[12] The government's analysis of Kosovo is found in Ministry of Defence, *Kosovo: Lessons from the Crisis*, Cmnd 4724 (June 2000). A more critical, although still generally supportive analysis is found in the Fourteenth Report of the House of Commons Defence Committee, *Lessons of Kosovo*, 24 October 2000.

[13] Speech to the Economic Club of Chicago, Thursday 22 April 1999, www.fco.gov.uk. I was later 'outed' as the author of the first draft of the relevant section of the Chicago speech. Those interested in how this came about are referred to John Kampfner's *Blair's Wars* (London: Free Press, 2004). This remains Blair's speech. This is not only because the final draft was not an exact copy of my first draft, but because once the words had been used by the Prime Minister it was the meaning that he attached to the words that was important rather than the meaning I attached to them. The same thoughts could have been expressed in different ways.

Chechnya. Yet Chicago did provide a rationale for later interventions, and was used in this form with East Timor (where Britain played a minor role in an Australian-led UN operation) and, in the middle of 2000, in Sierra Leone. In Sierra Leone, contrary to expectations, British forces acted without allies, initially to provide a rescue operation for personnel caught up in a nasty civil war and then to shore up a separate UN mission that was falling apart at the seams.

A further consequence of Kosovo, although this goes back to the October 1998 crisis, was the determination of Blair to press ahead with a European Strategic Defence Initiative. The American reluctance to put forces at risk was becoming a critical strategic weakness for an alliance dependent upon American support. Blair took the view that it was rather pathetic for a rich and populous group of European nations, with substantial numbers apparently under arms, to consistently fail to muster significant forces for actual operations. If European pretensions to a coherent foreign policy were to have any substance then something had to be done about the ineffectuality of its collective military response to crises. The Blair– Chirac summit of December 1998 at Saint-Malo that launched the project to create a new European security and defence initiative was presented in Europe as something of a U-turn for Britain, and perhaps a way of engaging with the European project that posed fewer domestic political difficulties than joining the euro. Blair however was not trying to create a European defence entity as an alternative to the US or NATO but more to insure against the US failing to meet its obligations to European security. Blair also needed to be able to argue that this effort would give Washington the European support that it claimed to crave. Furthermore, the objective, as stated at Saint-Malo, was quite demanding, pointing towards a war-fighting capability: 'the Union must have the capacity for autonomous action, backed up by credible military forces, the means to decide to use them, and a readiness to do so, in order to respond to international crises'.[14] In Britain the Eurosceptics took the French aspiration more seriously and claimed this to be an inflammatory policy change. This – rather than actual military interventions – was potentially the most controversial aspect of defence policy in the run-up to the 2001 election. Opinion poll evidence was mildly supportive of the Euro-force, although this was very much an elite issue. Blair was able to get the language he wanted stressing the importance of the Atlantic

---

[14] Joint Declaration on European Defence, issued at the British-French summit, Saint-Malo, France, 3–4 December 1998.

relationship, avoiding any suggestion that a definitive choice had to be made between NATO and the EU. The EU would still depend on NATO infrastructure and would not aspire to be able to cope with major wars. Nonetheless, ambiguities in language, and suspicions between the two organisations (despite their largely overlapping membership) meant that this issue was never quite resolved. All the talk of a Euro-force displacing NATO and providing the foundation for a superstate missed the point that the real risk was that, as with a number of other European initiatives in the area of foreign and security policy, the whole would be far less than the sum of individual parts. In the event the concept moved forward into relatively productive areas, although more in the peacekeeping than the war-fighting arenas.

The impact of 9/11

Al-Qaeda's attacks on the United States of 11 September 2001 changed the terms of the relationship with the United States and the wider defence debate. A furious US was bound to respond and try to take the fight (quickly labelled a 'global war on terror') to this new and unexpected enemy. Humanitarian interventions appeared as discretionary wars of choice, with which the Bush Administration had appeared reluctant to get involved. Islamist terrorism had created a new strategic imperative which potentially drew Western countries into any part of the world where such groups had acquired a foothold. Defences that could deal with rival great powers appeared inadequate against terrorism, creating new requirements for what became known as 'homeland security'. The British also accepted that they were entering a new and more dangerous period of international affairs. It was now not safe to assume that armed forces would no longer be needed for local defence, while the sort of operations required to eliminate the sources of terrorist attack might be quite different to those engaged in humanitarian missions. For these reasons the government commissioned a 'new chapter' to the SDR. Defence Secretary Geoff Hoon (Robertson had left to run NATO) observed in the introduction how much better it would be to engage the enemy overseas – 'in their backyard than in ours, at a time and place of our choosing and not theirs'. 'But', he added, 'opportunities to engage terrorist groups may be only fleeting, so we need the kind of rapidly deployable intervention forces which were the key feature of the SDR.'[15]

[15] Ministry of Defence, *The Strategic Defence Review: A New Chapter*, Cm. 5566, July 2002.

Blair also had a quite different sort of ally to deal with. Previously he had been concerned about the US's somewhat narrow definition of its strategic interests and disinterest in global problems. Now he saw an opportunity to get it engaged in his broader international agenda. By standing 'shoulder to shoulder' as the closest ally,[16] Blair hoped to gain Washington's attention as he argued for acquiring the greatest possible international support for its endeavours, and to address the economic, social and political roots of terrorism. Bush listened politely and responded where he could, but to the extent he moved in Blair's direction, for example by working with the UN or addressing the Palestinian issue, it was out of expediency as much as conviction. The conviction politicians closest to him, Vice-President Richard Cheney and Secretary of Defence Donald Rumsfeld, retained a narrower, nationalist, unilateralist perspective.[17] So when it came to dealing with the Taliban in Afghanistan, it was Blair who published the dossier demonstrating the role of al-Qaeda in 9/11,[18] and as Taliban resistance crumbled he was pushing to get substantial ground forces into Afghanistan in order to help shape the inevitable struggle for power on the ground. The British were regularly frustrated with the lack of effort the Americans were putting into Afghan reconstruction, as opposed to chasing remnants of al-Qaeda in and around the borders with Pakistan, and when it was apparent that the Taliban was starting to make a come-back in Helmand province in 2005 the British accepted the leadership of a NATO force designed to help the Afghan government regain control.

The most important and fateful consequence of 9/11 was the occupation of Iraq in 2003. Unlike Bush, Blair was always careful not to argue that Iraq was linked to al-Qaeda, but the 9/11 attacks had shifted the balance of power within the US administration towards those who argued that the country dare not wait for big threats to develop but instead must nip them in the bud. While Blair might not have chosen this moment to go after Saddam Hussein, it is a caricature to suggest that he only did so because he was in thrall to Bush. He had already demonstrated his willingness to take on Iraq with Desert Fox in December

---

[16] On 21 September 2001. See http://news.bbc.co.uk/1/hi/uk_politics/1555590.stm.
[17] With the exception of Paul Wolfowitz at the Pentagon, the role of 'neo-conservatives' has been exaggerated. In some ways if they had been more influential it would have suited Blair as at least they had an ambitious international agenda. In the end it was the indifference to the broader context, despite Bush's rhetorical flourishes, that created the most severe problems.
[18] Office of the Prime Minister, 'Responsibility for the Terrorist Atrocities in the United States', 11 September 2001, 4 October 2001.

1998. The official reports on the management of intelligence information in the period leading up to Iraq demonstrate many failings, but there has been no suggestion that the government ever doubted the existence of weapons of mass destruction or that there was a real problem to be solved.[19] During 2002 Blair accepted the likelihood of military action but also believed that it was more likely to be effective if it could be sanctioned by the UN. His strategy went awry as Bush decided to authorise an American military build-up ostensibly designed to coerce Iraq but in practice creating an artificial deadline for military action, while President Chirac decided to campaign against the American push for war. The conviction with which he had campaigned on the issue gave Blair little room for manoeuvre despite the opposition in his own party and among public opinion. Initially the speed of the coalition victory and the overthrow of an undoubtedly obnoxious regime provided a degree of vindication. This was short-lived. The failure to find weapons of mass destruction, and claims that the pre-war intelligence had been 'sexed-up' to justify a war undertaken for other reasons, were damaging enough. Most damaging was the continuation of resistance to the coalition occupation and the failure to translate undoubted support for democracy into a stable government that could bring together Iraq's divided communities. The security situation in Iraq deteriorated catastrophically.[20]

For the armed forces the Iraq campaign was frustrating but not calamitous. During the initial operations American mistakes put forces more at risk than Iraqi resistance. The British task was to take Basra, where they showed patience and tactical skill, although they were as taken aback as the Americans were in Baghdad by the looting and anarchy that followed the collapse of the old regime. As the insurgency gathered pace they were critical of American strategy and tactics,[21] and could argue that they had coped somewhat better in southern Iraq than the Americans had in Baghdad. Yet the south was largely Shi'ite and so less challenging than the American sector and the British did little to confront the militias or shape local politics. Evidence of the unpopularity of the Iraq War in the senior ranks of the Army came in an October 2006 interview given by General

---

[19] *Report of the Inquiry into the Circumstances Surrounding the Death of Dr David Kelly C.M.G. by Lord Hutton*, HC 247, 28 January 1984; Chairman Lord Butler of Brockwell, *Review of Intelligence on Weapons of Mass Destruction*, 14 July 2004.

[20] On what went wrong two of the best books are George Packer, *The Assassin's Gate: America in Iraq* (New York: Farrar, Straus and Giroux, 2005); Thomas E. Ricks, *Fiasco: The American Military Adventure in Iraq* (New York: The Penguin Press, 2006).

[21] Brigadier Nigel Aylwin-Foster, 'Changing the Army for Counterinsurgency Operations', *Military Review*, November–December 2005.

Richard Dannatt, Chief of the General Staff, when he observed that the war 'exacerbates the security problems for the UK', and that 'planning for what happened after the initial successful war fighting phase was poor, probably based more on optimism than sound planning'.[22] By 2007 plans were in place to reduce forces and hand over responsibility of security to Iraqi forces.

One reason that the Army was keen to get out of Iraq was the increasing demands of Afghanistan to push back a resurgent Taliban in the south. This was in some ways a more challenging but also more satisfactory campaign. The commitment was made without anything like the fuss surrounding Iraq, which meant that public opinion was not prepared for a tough campaign that soon involved casualties at the same rate as Iraq. By the end of May 2007, after over five years, 150 military personnel had died in Iraq, of which 115 were killed after hostile action. In Afghanistan, 57 died, of which 34 were the result of enemy action, the bulk after the spring of 2006. The political case however was stronger: UN resolutions, a NATO operation, and a legitimate government. The enemy was fortunately strategically inept, and although tactically brave and resourceful it did not adapt well. If anything the Taliban were more geared to regular warfare, albeit of a rather crude sort, rather than insurgency operations. Their boasts about the ease with which they would see off NATO forces did not survive 2006. After initially being spread too thin, and with never enough troops to hold on to areas retaken from the Taliban, NATO command developed tactics for taking the war to the enemy. During the first months of 2007 the Taliban suffered a number of reverses, including the disruption of their command structure. Military campaigns of counter-insurgency can only create the conditions for political, economic and social action, without which they become much more difficult, and success here was less easy to realise. Moreover, there was an apparently inexhaustible supply of recruits for the Taliban, many training in the inaccessible parts of an increasingly fragile Pakistan. The indications therefore were that this was a long-term commitment, without any guarantee of victory though somewhat more promising than Iraq.

Pressures on armed forces

While all this was going on the pressures were building up on the armed forces. In part this was because of demands that the forces become in

---

[22] Sarah Sands, 'Sir Richard Dannatt: A very Honest General', *Daily Mail*, 12 October 2006.

some way more socially inclusive, by tackling racism and homophobia. These issues were managed with little fuss. More difficult was the role of women. In terms of recruitment they were of growing importance, and studies suggested that there was no inherent bar to effective battlefield performance. The issue was more one of whether men and women could work together professionally in the unusual and highly charged conditions of military operations and exercises. This was not a new issue – the Royal Navy had both sexes serving on warships for some time – and the experience suggested the importance of clear rules if a series of scandals were not to result. In an unfortunate incident in April 2007, a female member of an RN boarding party abducted by the Iranians was picked upon and coerced into writing embarrassing letters denouncing the British role in Iraq. As she was released a report came through of two women, along with two men, killed in Iraq, where the insurgency did not acknowledge a front line.

The complexities of irregular and asymmetrical warfare were producing their own stresses and strains. Instant communications and a global media meant that any lapses in discipline, such as mistreatment of prisoners, or just the harsher aspects of modern soldiering were soon likely to be shared and exposed. During his brief period as Defence Secretary, John Reid made a challenging speech at King's College London on the role of the media as a 'virtual battleground'. The microscopic analysis of behaviour this made possible was combined with a real though often exaggerated role being played by human rights legislation in assessing the conduct of troops. Add an enemy happy to exploit this while 'systematically rejecting any previously accepted constraints, conventions or standards in combat', and the result was what Reid called an 'uneven playing field of scrutiny'.[23]

A further pressure resulted from Labour's difficulty in finding any better ways than its predecessors to prevent the delays and cost overruns that had long disfigured the equipment procurement process. When forces were being used more actively this mattered more than might have been the case in earlier times. The sheer length of these programmes meant that even after a decade many problems were still being caused by the procurement decisions of the Conservative years. The most obvious example of this was the farce of the Bowman radio, which had failed to materialise as commercial systems went through a number of technological generations.

---

[23] Speech by John Reid MP, Secretary of State for Defence, to King's College London on 20 February 2006.

The new Typhoon aircraft were both expensive (232 aircraft at a total bill of around £20 billion) but of uncertain value in supporting counter-insurgency operations. After a decade of discussion, by the time Blair left office the proposed aircraft carriers had still not been ordered and their fate would depend on the forthcoming comprehensive spending review. The carriers were costed at £3.6 billion; the 150 Joint Strike Fighters that would fly from them some £8 billion.

It was not until the 2000 Comprehensive Spending Review (CSR) that some increases in forces were agreed.[24] After 9/11 there were more arguments for additional funding. In the 2002 CSR and the new chapter of the Strategic Defence Review, agreement was given to the largest increase in defence expenditure for two decades, with a projected increase of £3.5 billion by 2005/6. At a time of substantial increases elsewhere, real terms annual increases of an average 1.2% per year were hardly spectacular. Including the extra funding for Iraq and Afghanistan, spending has remained constant at roughly around 2.5% of GDP and at around £32 billion a year plus some £1.5 billion for Iraq and Afghanistan. By 2007 however there were regular complaints about substantial underfunding, and a lack of kit appropriate to the operations being undertaken. ' For ordinary soldiers', observed the *Economist*, 'the strains are visible from the moment they leave Britain in clapped-out Tristar jets to the moment they reach the valleys of Afghanistan with little or no American-style computer networking.'[25]

The decline of the Northern Ireland commitment brought some relief, and other forms of support to the civil power, such as acting as stand-in firemen or organising the cull of livestock to beat foot-and-mouth disease, were only occasional. But with Iraq and Afghanistan turning into demanding missions of long duration, the question of the stretch on forces became more acute. To some extent this was a matter of elasticity. It was one thing to stretch capabilities at times of particular stress if they could ease back to a form of normality when the stress was over. The risk was that the stretch would cause the capabilities to snap, with it becoming progressively more difficult to recruit and retain personnel, and give those in service proper training or time with their families. The stress was felt particularly in the army, which tried to cope by restructuring battalions and increased development of special forces and reserves in operational

---

[24] *Spending Review 2000*, Cm 4807 (London: TSO, 2000). CSR 2000 added almost £400 million to the previous budget for 2001/2, a 0.1% real increase rise to £23.75 billion, growing to 0.7% in 2003/4.   [25] 'The Battle of the Budget', *The Economist*, 3 May 2007.

roles. By and large it coped, although some areas that had been hit by past cuts, for example medical services, remained problematic.

Conclusion

In his Plymouth speech Blair professed himself struck by the contrast between the front line and the home front. At the front the troops were professional, with high morale and a sense of mission. Yet at home there was anxiety. This was in part because of the pain caused by each casualty but also because of questions of logistics, inadequate equipment or sub-standard accommodation. 'Any grievances, any issues to do with military life, will be more raw, more sensitive, more prone to cause resentment.' The absence of a victory as previously understood and the 'propaganda of the enemy, often quite sympathetically treated by their own media', would encourage the view that it's really the West's fault. In turn that risked demoralising the forces, who wanted the full support of public opinion, and not just admiration for their courage. If politicians on both sides of the Atlantic would not so much slip into the caricature of ill-judged adventurism but instead decide that it was 'all too difficult and default to an unstated, passive disengagement, that doing the right thing slips almost unconsciously into doing the easy thing' and the armed forces would no longer be 'warfighters as well as peacekeepers', the enemy would be emboldened and the country's 'reach, effect and influence qual-itatively reduced'. The tragedy for Blair was that Iraq in particular had reduced the country's appetite for such a role. Polling at the end of March 2007 found majorities seeking immediate withdrawal from Iraq and Afghanistan (barely differentiating between the missions), two thirds of voters believing that Britain was over-extended and that it should not 'become involved in any foreign conflict unless it is absolutely clear that it is in Britain's own interests to do so'.[26] Events could change these percep-tions again, but for the moment, despite Blair's best efforts, the military were seen as a force for national security but not a force for good.

[26] Anthony King, 'Voters Want Britain to Scale Down World Role', *Daily Telegraph*, 5 April 2007.

Commentary

TIMOTHY GARTON ASH

'What is the essence of Blairism in foreign policy?' I asked Tony Blair, at the end of his decade in power. 'It is liberal interventionism', he replied.[1] His foreign policy, he explained, was about combining soft and hard power, and about strengthening Britain's key alliances – with the United States and with our partners in the European Union. Britain, a country of sixty million people 'in a relatively small geographical space', can only 'make its weight and influence count through its alliances'. Yes, relations with other democracies are important, but 'you build out from the European–American alliance'.

Only thus can you confront the big, supranational problems which, over his ten years as Prime Minister, had come increasingly to dominate his agenda. This produced an acute dilemma: 'your country expects you to be focused on the domestic and yet the truth is [that] the challenges you're facing are often global'. Sometimes, he said, it was almost ridiculous. Consider climate change, for example. Of course a country like Britain should take domestic action on climate change, but all the time you know that 'the purpose of it is to give yourself traction on international leadership'. In this respect, something fundamental has changed since 1997. Today, 'foreign policy is no longer foreign policy'.

Minerva's owl flies at dusk. When Tony Blair became Prime Minister in May 1997, he did so on a manifesto that was almost entirely domestic. Only one of the ten promises in the New Labour manifesto was about foreign policy: 'We will give Britain the leadership in Europe which Britain and Europe need.' (A characteristically vague New Labour formula: did it mean that Britain would lead Europe or simply that Britain would ensure that Europe had good leadership?) The one thing that was clear was that he wanted to improve Britain's relations with the European Union, after the *froideur* of the Thatcher–Major years.

[1] All quotations are from a conversation with him in London on 23 April 2007.

Otherwise, Blair's foreign policy was an unwritten book. He had given a few speeches on the subject, long on British patriotism and vague pro-Europeanism, short on detail. No one could have predicted from them that he would end up sending Britain's armed forces to fight in Sierra Leone, Kosovo, Afghanistan and Iraq. He learned on the job and he made it up as he went along. The intervention in Kosovo in 1999 was a forma-tive moment, prompting as it did his Chicago speech, in which he enun-ciated his neo-Gladstonian 'doctrine of international community'. Only at the end, looking back with the advantages of retrospective rationalisa-tion, could he sum it up so clearly.

There are two ways of responding to Blair's own retrospective summary. One is to disagree with the agenda itself. Liberal intervention-ism, you could say, is a lousy idea. What business is it of ours to stop for-eigners killing each other if they want to? Our morally superior, pacific European attitude is demonstrated by not intervening anywhere. We keep our hands clean by not lifting a finger. And we do not want to be close to the US in any case (Blairophobes of the left), or to Europe (Blairophobes of the right).

The other response is to examine his record in the light of his own pro-claimed goals. If you believe, as I do, in genuine liberal intervention – that is, intervention to prevent genocide or other massively inhumane or life-threatening behaviour within the borders of another state – then high on the credit side of the balance sheet must be Kosovo. There, Blair led the way in forging an international action to reverse a genocide being perpe-trated by Slobodan Milosevic against the mainly Muslim Kosovar Albanians. And we did not make a complete bloody mess of the occupa-tion afterwards. Kosovo in 2007 was hardly Switzerland, but it was begin-ning the journey to being a European democracy. And both Serbian and Kosovan warlords were being prosecuted in The Hague. For a liberal interventionist, Kosovo was Blair's finest hour. In Sierra Leone, too, Blair is remembered with gratitude as someone who rescued the country from terrible civil strife.

Britain's relations with both the US and our partners in the European Union were better when he left No. 10 Downing Street than when he entered it. In the European context, devolution to Scotland and Wales, and the amazing spectacle of Ian Paisley and Martin McGuinness starting to govern together in Northern Ireland, must be counted to his credit. Britain was also better placed in Europe and the world because it had a relatively strong economy, mixed with a partly reformed welfare state. That success – Blairism building on the foundations of Thatcherism – is part of Britain's soft power, a concept defined by Joseph Nye as the power to attract. For all the problems that remained, you must ask yourself this question: who was better off? Britain after ten years of Blair, France after twelve years of Jacques Chirac, Germany following eight years of Gerhard Schröder, or the US in the seventh year of George Bush?

On the debit side, there was one overwhelming red figure – Iraq. Blair kept insisting that history would give the final verdict on Iraq but, writing in summer 2007, I believe we can already say with confidence that the invasion and occupation of Iraq has proved to be a disaster. To describe it as a case of liberal interventionism is the greatest disservice anyone could do to the cause of liberal interventionism. Britain and the United States went to war on a false prospectus about weapons of mass destruction and without proper authority, either legal or political. The failure to prepare for the likely consequences was a disgrace. It would be difficult for things to be worse than they were under Saddam Hussein, but in 2007 they were. Hundreds of thousands of people had been killed or maimed, and there was no good end in sight. US intelligence agencies said Iraq had become a breeding ground for a new generation of terrorists. The hundreds of billions of dollars squandered on the war and occupation could have bettered the lives of many of the world's poor.

Drawing away troops from Afghanistan when the job there was only half done, we created two failures instead of one possible success. The Shia–Sunni rift had been inflamed across the Muslim world. The theocratic dictatorship of Iran was greatly strengthened. The moral authority of the US was in tatters, and that of the United Kingdom dragged down with it. Iraq alienated Muslims everywhere, including our own fellow citizens in Britain. Need I go on? This was the most comprehensive British foreign policy disaster since the Suez crisis of 1956.

Iraq also exposed the weakness of another strand of Blairite foreign policy – the attempt to influence American policy by working privately through the corridors of power in Washington, while avoiding all public disagreement. This is what I call the Jeeves school of diplomacy. To America's Bertie Wooster the British government plays Jeeves – the impeccably loyal gentleman's gentleman in public, but privately whispering 'Is that wise, sir?' Although Bush administration officials insisted that the President actively sought Blair's advice, it is hard to point to a single issue on which Britain actually changed or decisively shaped American policy. Britain alone was no longer big enough to sway the hyperpower, especially when Washington assumed that British support could always be taken for granted.

What the US needed was a friend big enough that Washington had to listen to him. That friend could only be a strong EU, speaking with a single voice. Here is the third key failing of Blair's foreign policy. To achieve that European voice would require the full commitment of Germany, France and Britain; but for more than fifteen years Britain's European policy has been drastically constrained, if not actually dictated, by our Eurosceptic media. Blair saw the problem clearly. When I reminded him of the 1997 manifesto promise he said, somewhat defensively, that Britain had been 'a leader in Europe', but went on immediately to acknowledge that 'on the surface British attitudes remain stolidly Eurosceptic'. A lot of this was due to the media. 'Europe is the area, above all others, where I'm urged by even quite sensible areas of the media to do things that are completely daft and that anyone sitting in my chair would think is completely daft.' This is true, and an important structural truth about British European policy; but the truth is also that Blair himself never dared to face down the unelected newspaper proprietors and editors on whom New Labour had depended so heavily throughout. He left that to his successors – who will probably also duck the challenge.

This sketch of Blair's world would not be complete without dwelling for a moment on its other side: the world's Blair. For Blair is one of relatively few world leaders who has had a major resonance in the political imagination of other countries. This is not just a matter of those directly affected by his interventions, like the people in Pristina, Kosovo, who expressed their gratitude with a graffito proclaiming 'Thank you Tony Bler', or the people in Sierra Leone who said they owed their lives to him, or those in Iraq, many of whom were initially grateful to him, but with time came to regard him as an author of their current misery.

Well beyond these places, whether in the United States, Germany, France or Italy, there was a strong image of Blair and of something they called Blairism, *Blairisme* or *Blairismo*. (No one, to my knowledge, ever talked of *Majorisme* or *Callaghanismo*.) Sometimes these images were at a considerable remove from the real personality and policies of Tony Blair. Often they were projections of local hopes and preoccupations. Many Americans, for example, saw him as a more articulate and moderate exponent of tough-minded views on combating terrorism. For them, Blairism was, so to speak, Bushism with a human face – or at least, with unmangled syntax. Some Democrats could never forgive him for siding with George W. Bush, but others remained admiring. Many Republicans adored him precisely because he sided with Bush. Both Democrats and Republicans remembered his swift and unwavering solidarity after the 11 September 2001 attacks.

In continental Europe, Iraq and his closeness to Bush cost his reputation dear. Many concluded that Britain had not changed as much as they had initially hoped in 1997. When push comes to shove, they sighed, the Brits will always side with the Americans. Yet even then, some admiration remained. As Blair approached the end of his decade in power, I asked the Italian Foreign Minister and left-wing reformist Massimo d'Alema for his verdict. Blair, he said, was 'the greatest moderniser of the Left'.[2] Iraq had been a big mistake, to be sure. On Europe, he thought Blair was genuinely a very pro-European leader in his thinking and speaking, but 'less so in his actions'. A very balanced judgement.

What many Europeans continued to see as the greatest success of Blairism was the ability to combine a dynamic market economy with a strong welfare state. It was in this sense that both the leading candidates in the French presidential elections of 2007, Ségolène Royale and Nicolas Sarkozy, could be described as Blairist – although the candidate of the right was much happier to wear that label than the candidate of the left. Most historians would argue that this domestic, socio-economic achievement cannot be ascribed solely to Tony Blair. It owed at least as much to Margaret Thatcher and Gordon Brown. It was, in substance, Thatcher-Brown-Blairism. But he was in the happy position of being identified with it. In politics, such perceptions are also realities. And these positive images of Blair and Blairism were themselves also part and parcel of Britain's soft power.

Tony Blair was therefore, amongst other things, a rather successful British cultural export, and like many cultural exports, he acquired new meanings abroad. In other countries, people saw in him what they wanted to see, made of him what they wanted to make. Beside Blair's world, there was the world's Blair.

This leads me to one final reflection. As he prepared to leave office, Blair professed himself happy for the historians to write the verdict on his record. When I invited him to list his three greatest successes and failures, he replied: 'I don't do the successes/failures thing . . . I leave that to you guys.' But, even if that was his basic attitude, it could not be the reality. For a start, unless all the rumours were incorrect, he would surely give his own version of this history in his memoirs. And then, as a relatively young ex-leader, there would be a whole life after No. 10, as there was for Bill Clinton after the White House. How he used the opportunity of his

---

[2] Remarks following the annual European Studies Centre lecture at St Antony's College, Oxford, on 8 May 2007.

worldwide fame, what broad international themes he chose to promote and how he went about promoting them – this would also shape the way the world looked back on his years in power. What Clinton did after he left office undoubtedly changed, and probably improved, many people's views of him, his period in office and his legacy.

The same might be true of Blair. He had every qualification for being a most adept elder statesman, and a skilled teller of his own tale. His place in history would be determined partly by the emergence of new documents, the longer-term consequences of his actions while in office, and the judgements of 'you guys' on those documents and consequences. But it would also be determined, in no small measure, by what he himself said and did for the rest of his life. The Blair premiership might be over, but the history of the Blair effect had only just begun.

Commentary

PHILIP STEPHENS

Tony Blair was the most accomplished politician of his generation. A gifted communicator with an intuitive grasp of the national mood, he was the dominant figure in British politics for more than a decade. Three consecutive election victories assure him a place in the history books as Labour's most successful leader. Margaret Thatcher apart, no other prime minister since the Napoleonic Wars can claim an uninterrupted ten years in 10 Downing Street. Like Thatcher, Blair changed the political weather.

The rest, if we are to believe the angry epitaphs that mostly accompanied his departure in the summer of 2007, was disappointment and deceit. Brilliant performance was not the same as solid achievement. A capacity to articulate the nation's fears and aspirations was one thing, the ability to shape them another. Above all, though, the story of Blair's premiership was of political genius squandered to a disastrous and deeply unpopular war in Iraq.

Few politicians have so enraged the metropolitan intelligentsia who penned these first drafts of history. A decade earlier many had flocked to Blair as the politician who would return power and prestige to the drawing-rooms of the thinking centre-left. The talk was of social democracy reinvented, third ways discovered, political ideas reclaimed for liberalism. That, of course, was before Blair made common cause with a hick Republican in the White House.

There is an element of exaggeration here, but only an element. In the latter years of his premiership to defend Blair in the company of London's self-selecting political classes was often to feel one was talking about an entirely different politician. It was obvious, wasn't it, that he was a neo-liberal Thatcherite – never mind all those tens of billions spent on health and education. Clearly he had lied over Iraq's weapons of mass destruction – forget the copious evidence otherwise provided by the numerous independent inquiries. Of course, he had sold honours for cash – *pace* the failure of the intrepid Inspector Yates of the Yard to provide the evidence.

The BBC never did get over the scorching indictment of its journalism provided by an honest judge from Northern Ireland.

None of the above is to say that Blair was a politician without flaws. He had many, some of them grave. It was not enough, as he sought to imply in a parting self-justification, that he had believed deposing Saddam Hussein had been 'the right thing to do'. Politicians do not absolve themselves of responsibility for errors of policy by protesting the honesty of their intentions. But history will produce a more balanced, nuanced judgement than the recent spluttering of those mourning their own loss of intellectual relevance.

Britain, it must be said, fell out of love with the youthful forty-four-year-old who stood on the steps of Downing Street in May 1997. In the afterglow of that first famous general election victory of May 1997, Blair shattered every record for prime-ministerial popularity. By the end, his ratings touched the low points on the pollsters' graphs. Elected in the euphoria of expectation, he departed, as had most others who have survived so long in office, in the shadow of experience.

Such is the familiar narrative of politics: exaggerated expectations prefigure predictable disillusion. Longevity runs against the reputation of political leaders. As time passes, the soaring rhetoric of their trade grinds ever more painfully against the immutable realities of the modern world. Trust – and Blair had bucketfuls when he first entered Downing Street – is sacrificed to the grubby compromises of office. Hard now to think of a European, let alone a British, leader in modern times who has departed in the warmth of popular approval.

Yet this tells only half the story. Angry as many were – about Iraq especially – the people of Britain seemed otherwise content. Even as they cheered his leaving, more than half thought that, all in all, the Prime Minister had done a good job. The same voters who repudiated Blair seemed to be saying they wanted to hold on to Blairism. The organising idea on which he built his extraordinary political success – that in an age of globalisation the role of government is to link strong economic performance with a fairer society – seems as prescient in 2007 as it was at the birth of New Labour. Strange though it is to say in these jaded times, things did get better in the decade from 1997. The Britain Blair left behind felt a more modern, progressive nation. Much of what was deemed radical at the outset had been quietly absorbed into a more open, and yes, liberal national consensus.

The images in the summer of 2007 of the Democratic Unionist Party's Ian Paisley and Sinn Fein's Martin McGuinness – the firebrand unionist and the IRA commander – side by side at Stormont were the most vivid demonstration of how the exceptional can become almost the unremarkable. A decade ago to suggest such a reconciliation between the extremes in Northern Ireland would have been to invite guffaws. Now the province's decision to exchange violence for politics is all but taken for granted. Northern Ireland saw Blair at his best – the patience, the resilience and the genius for persuasion. But – or perhaps it was because – Blair knew all along that there were no votes in this extraordinary enterprise to build peace.

Elsewhere, a national minimum wage, a parliament in Scotland, an assembly in Wales, incorporation into British law of the European Convention on Human Rights, the defenestration of most of the hereditary peers from the House of Lords, a step change in spending on health and education, the introduction of same-sex civil partnerships, equality in the workplace: all were effortlessly absorbed into the national mindset. The Britain of the Blair years made its peace with the cultural liberalism that respects the growing diversity of modern societies. It adjusted better than most of its European neighbours to the competitive winds of globalisation. The tensions remained, and in places sharpened: the disruptions, economic and social, of large-scale immigration, the economic insecurities and widening income inequalities flowing from borderless trade and capital flows. But the government showed broadly the right instincts, combining openness to global change with help for those left behind by the outgoing economic tides.

Blair's domestic record was far from unblemished. Missed opportunities jostled with achievements. The Prime Minister had more than his share of good fortune in a relatively benign economic environment, and in Gordon Brown's stewardship of the Treasury. For all the energy with which he latterly gripped the notions of choice, competition and diversity, the initial approach to public service reform was painfully timid. Many of the extra billions poured into modernising schools and hospitals were wasted. Elsewhere, good intentions went unmatched by practice. Blair never mastered the mysteries of management: the ability to turn political intention into administrative achievement. Intuition is not a substitute for careful deliberation. He can claim that he introduced unprecedented transparency into the conduct of government and the funding of politics. Yet he did not properly respect the spirit of his own rules. Ten years on, that first promise that his administration would be 'purer than pure' left a bitter taste.

Blair did remake the landscape of politics. The shallow, if fashionable, reflection on the past decade is that Blair's redefinition of politics' boundaries did little more than soften the edges of Thatcherism. That judgement was belied by unprecedented investment in health and education, by a discretionary increase in taxes and by a determined, albeit only partially successful, effort to reduce poverty. The central political insight was to separate the enduring 'ends' of a left-of-centre government – a fairer society with a wider spread of opportunity – from his party's century-long addiction to the socialist 'means' of an ever more mighty state. What-works pragmatism elbowed aside outdated ideology.

Here, the leader's distance from his own party – he never respected Labour's rituals nor was comfortable in its tribalism – was a strength and a weakness. A strength because it reassured the middle classes within the New Labour coalition that compassion need not elbow aside aspiration; a weakness because it amplified the accusations of betrayal from those in his party who would always prefer the purity of opposition to the necessary compromises of government. For all that he dazzled them, the Prime Minister was never much loved by the Labour MPs who rose on his political coat-tails. Some simply never forgave him for winning.

The better gauge of his political legacy comes from David Cameron's Conservatives. During three general elections – the last fought in the dark shadow of Iraq – the Prime Minister forced the Conservatives on to the arid margins of the far right. Only after a decade did a young Tory leader begin to rescue his party from threatened electoral oblivion. Cameron, reclaiming the political centre ground, has broadly accepted the New Labour settlement. He presents himself as much as an heir to Blair than his ideological adversary.

The complexities of this record held up a mirror to the many strands of Blair's character. Criticised at the outset as a flimsy product of New Labour's image-makers, mesmerised by the ebb and flow of public opinion, he was latterly condemned as one too messianic in his convictions. His charm and persuasiveness co-existed with a ruthlessness that saw him more than once dispense with the services of close friends and allies. The low politics of sofa government in 10 Downing Street sat uneasily with his profession of a devout Christian faith. The Gladstonian interventionist willing to gamble his political future on rescuing Kosovo later became a prisoner to belief in his own righteousness.

Abroad, for all the furore about Iraq, Blair mostly beguiled. In the select club of world political leaders, electoral success is the most important measure of peer-group prestige. Winning three times earned Blair special status among fellow presidents and prime ministers. Iraq soured some relationships – notably with France's Jacques Chirac and Germany's

Gerhard Schröder – but for the most part Blair remained at the centre of the international argument. A strong relationship with Ireland's Bertie Ahern was a key to securing a settlement in Northern Ireland. His closeness to George W. Bush never dented an enduring friendship with Bill Clinton. Angela Merkel lamented the impending departure of 'my friend Tony', a sentiment shared by the newly elected Nicolas Sarkozy in France. Vladimir Putin, it is fair to say, was glad to see him go, but then Blair would not have wanted it otherwise. What surprised even those close to the Prime Minister was how, after all the disappointments, Blair remained loyal to Bush.

The world stage was the place where he escaped the bitter rivalry with Gordon Brown that so often scarred the government. Summitry, with its mix of negotiation, strategic judgement and badinage, entirely suited Blair's temperament. Abroad was the opportunity to deploy his persuasive charm and display his thespian skills. The bargains at the Gleneagles Summit between the world's leading industrial nations on debt relief for Africa and on action against climate change were personal as well as political triumphs.

The doctrine of humanitarian interventionism that Blair espoused at the time of the Kosovo crisis was tarnished in the minds of some by the experience of Iraq. Yet his 1999 Chicago speech remains one of the best analyses of the implications of global interdependence and of the case for liberal interventionism in defence of civilised standards. The United Nations has reaffirmed that citizens must be afforded basic human rights that transcend the sovereignty of nation states. The experience of Iraq may well tempt politicians, in the US as well as Europe, to retreat into the comfort zone of isolationism. The realities of global interdependence, understood by Blair better than most of his peers, will force them to act otherwise. The West can no longer ignore chaos and inhumanity beyond its borders.

The bitter debate about the decision to join George W. Bush in removing Saddam Hussein, of course, will rage for many years yet. That the subsequent conflict inflicted terrible bloodshed on Iraq was self-evident. So too was the startling incompetence of the Bush administration in the conduct of what was supposed to be the peace. Yet the commonplace charge that the Prime Minister lied and cheated Britain into an illegal war by falsifying evidence of Iraq's weapons of mass destruction failed the test of myriad independent inquiries.

Blair's mistake was rather to invest too much in the significance of NATO's success in Kosovo. The victory against Slobodan Milosevic, he concluded, could be repeated in Iraq. But his war to topple Saddam was not the same as Bush's war. Blair saw in the removal of Saddam an extension of the doctrine he had enunciated at the time of Kosovo: a determination to uphold the will of the international community. The US President had something quite different in mind – a raw demonstration of American power that defied the spirit of the same international rules Blair had wanted to strengthen. The British Prime Minister never resolved this contradiction. Nor did he properly understand that in joining the US in a war of choice, he assumed responsibility without power. From the beginning his own reputation was thus a hostage to US hubris.

The central assumption of Blair's foreign policy – that Britain serves as a natural bridge between Europe and North America – buckled under the weight of the divisions in Europe about Iraq. Forced to choose, Blair sided with Washington. Yet in other respects he could claim some progress. Britain no longer sits on the margins of influence of the European Union. It is now something approaching a 'normal' member of the club, even if Brown denied Blair his wish to join the single currency. As far as Europe goes, the big failure was at home: the Prime Minister never properly confronted voters with the necessary compromises demanded by engagement, and influence, in Europe.

Historians will argue too about his attitude to the extreme Islamism that brought the destruction of New York's Twin Towers and subsequent attacks in London and cities across three continents. Faster than most to grasp the geopolitical consequences of 9/11, there has been too much of the clash of civilisations in his response to radical Islamism. Right to insist this will be a long struggle, waged both at home and at a distance, he was too ready to see the many difficult conflicts in the Muslim world as part of a single ideological confrontation between political Islam and the West.

What stands above all the reckonings – positive and negative – of Blair's premiership is the extent to which he became the reference point for the nation's politics. Like Margaret Thatcher, he filled almost all the available political space. For all the troubles that beset his many cabinets, his colleagues were essentially supporting characters, and quite often bystanders, in the drama. Even Brown, a formidable politician, and quite often Blair's only real opponent, spent much of the decade in the shadows. Blair, in other words, can blame no one else for the judgement of history. Iraq will always cast its shadow, but that judgement will be a great deal kinder than most of the first drafts that now confront him.

Conclusion

The net Blair effect, 1994–2007

ANTHONY SELDON

This short concluding chapter will attempt to answer just two questions: what did Blair achieve and why did his achievement come so late in his premiership? Tony Blair's first three years as party leader while in opposition (1994–97) had been principally directed to sweeping the party clear of unpopular and outdated 'Old' Labour policies, on the economy, tax, trade unions, defence and Northern Ireland, and then embedding the 'New' Labour style and policies. The hard thinking on policy was put in not by him, but by Gordon Brown. For this was to be a very different kind of premiership to anything previously known in British history: to a significant extent it would be shared, with Brown being primarily responsible for economic and welfare policy and Blair responsible for the rest. The 'rest' did not initially amount to much. But Blair did benefit from four legacies from John Major: a strong economy to provide surpluses to fund increases in spending, embryonic work taking Thatcher's reforms into the public services, Northern Ireland moving in the direction of peace, and the Maastricht opt-out, which made his European policy viable.

In his first term, (1997–2001), Blair's principal achievement, shared with Brown and Peter Mandelson, came at its very outset: the electoral victory with a majority of 179. The remarkable fact for Blair personally was quite how bare the first term was of personal domestic success, beyond providing the stable platform for others to achieve. Constitutional reform (including devolution to Scotland and Wales), economic vitality and welfare reform were the achievements principally of others, with the legacy of John Smith and the work of Derry Irvine primarily responsible for the first, and Brown for the latter. The Good Friday Agreement in 1998 was Blair's main domestic achievement, while his bold decisions to deploy British troops in Kosovo in 1999 and Sierra Leone in 2000 were his chief foreign achievements. In Chicago in April 1999, he outlined his philosophy justifying military intervention in sovereign countries on humanitarian grounds, which later underpinned the invasions of Afghanistan and Iraq. It was the most important speech of his premiership. Towards the end of the first term, No. 10 developed a narrative which was that the first term was merely 'laying the foundations' for radical reform to follow after a 'historic' second election victory. But as I stated at the end of *The Blair Effect* in 2001: 'The edifice may prove more difficult to erect than the foundations to lay.'

The second term (2001–5) began in June with a 167 majority for Labour, with honours shared equally between Blair and Brown. At home, Blair achieved more himself in the second term, despite his authority being weaker, and Brown more obstructive, than in his first term. He extended choice and competitiveness unevenly into education and health. The two most controversial pieces of legislation which passed with wafer-thin majorities were to introduce variable top-up fees for universities and foundation hospitals, which was much watered down by the Treasury. He invested great personal energy in law and order, and particularly in immigration and asylum, with some positive results. After the cap on spending came off after 1999, huge investment began to be pumped into the public services, especially the NHS, and he insisted that extra money should be matched by reform. Abroad, his first term successes were not matched. His decisive leadership on the world stage in the days following 9/11 appeared vindicated by initial military success in Afghanistan. Convinced of the threat to world peace from WMD and that Saddam could not continue to flout the UN, and in order to stand with the US, he went to war willingly against Iraq, but the war soon turned sour. He invested considerable capital and time in establishing a relationship with the Bush administration every bit as close as he had with Clinton before January 2001. But for what? Despite Bush committing himself to a 'two-state' solution in June 2002 and the 'road map' in April 2003, he was unable to persuade the Bush administration on the Middle East Peace Process, which he saw as critical to winning the 'ideas war' in Iraq. By the end of the second term, his relationship with Bush and the lack of apparent gain to Britain damaged him greatly.

The second term stands out as a period of disappointment in many areas: little was achieved on transport after Brown made his opposition clear to road pricing and to increasing expenditure. Constitutional reform, including to the House of Lords, local government and regionalism, all failed to make headway, while his proposals in mid-2003 to reform the Lord Chancellor's department and create a Supreme Court, were damaged by his chronic ineffectiveness at managing reshuffles. Northern Ireland stood still. In Europe he agreed an unfavourable CAP budget deal in 2002, and he failed in 2003 for a second time (the first was in late 1997) to convince Brown of the case for Britain joining the euro (Brown was right: Britain did better by not joining). His principal second-term achievement came in mid-2004 when he prevented the federalist Guy Verhofstadt from becoming President of the EU Commission, and secured in his place the free-market José Manuel Barroso, and his push on 'enlargement' to Eastern Europe.

The gains from reforms to public services were far from evident, and many questioned whether they were right. I concluded the volume on the second Blair government by saying that Blairism had yet to establish itself, and consisted to date of a 'crazy salad', mixing traditional Labourite beliefs in high spending with a Harold Wilson belief in managerialism and a neo-Thatcherite antenna to markets. The book was nearly sub-titled *A Failed Government?* It was a fair question to pose.

Blair's third term (2005–7) was his most successful. This is paradoxical, given that his authority was at its weakest of the three terms and he had to cope with Brown at his most rampant. It began with a general election victory that delivered a majority of sixty-six, which he tried to win on his own, although he was forced to bring Brown in as joint leader in the final three weeks of the campaign. The unpopularity of Iraq and the related issue of trust damaged the party badly. Yet, in the space of just two years, Blair achieved far more than in his earlier two terms, with reform extended across the public services: pushing further competition and choice in the NHS and schools, with academies reaching a critical mass and a post-comprehensive system established in secondary schools; reforming pensions in the teeth of implacable opposition from the Treasury; welfare reform, notably to incapacity benefit; pushing ahead on nuclear energy and modernising Britain's nuclear deterrent; and reform in criminal justice. The historic accord between Sinn Fein's Gerry Adams and the DUP's Ian Paisley in May 2007 saw the completion of the Northern Ireland Peace Process heralded nine years before with the Good Friday Agreement. Over that time, Northern Ireland became less of a 'problem' for Britain, with peace and prosperity slowly returning to the streets of Ulster. In this term, Blair took the Thatcherite project forward as far as it was politically possible to push it. Overall he had not repudiated any of Thatcher's policies (bar the first-term rowing back on foundation schools and GP fund-holding): her privatisations remained and were even added to; no ground of any significance was given on trade union reform; and PFI was extended.

In Europe, the third term saw Blair making decisive progress, aided by the disappearance of his arch-rivals Jacques Chirac and Gerhard

Schroeder, and their replacement by Angela Merkel in 2005 and Nicolas Sarkozy in early 2007, with whom he was far more in tune personally and politically. Blair's defining moment was his speech to the European Parliament in June 2005 which set out a new agenda for the EU: less obsessed by its inner workings and more committed to economic and energy reform. Skilfully using the accession of the Eastern European countries which boosted the EU's membership from fifteen to twenty-five, Blair oversaw a shifting of gravity away from the traditional power-base of France, Germany and the three 'Benelux' countries. At the Gleneagles G8 in July 2005, he successfully pushed his chosen topics of Africa and climate change; a measure of his success was how much of the agenda Merkel continued with at her G8 summit at Heiligendamm in his final days as Prime Minister. Blair's achievements at Gleneagles and during the EU Presidency in 2005 contrasted starkly with his leadership of the G8 and EU during the British Presidencies at Birmingham and Cardiff in 1998. He achieved an acceptable deal for Britain at his final EU Council on 2 June 2007. Iraq and Afghanistan never came right for Blair, however, and the former cast a dark cloud over his entire premiership.

Blair's ten years saw an economic resurgence. The policies were Brown's but Blair was the guarantor of the political and social climate which permitted his social democratic government to function without deterring wealth creation and financial investment in Britain. Credit too is due to Blair for his assurance as a national leader, after Princess Diana's death, 9/11 or the 7/7 bomb attacks on London, or in helping win the Olympics for London in 2012. Central government was modernised and geared towards delivering policy, often in the face of strong opposition from the traditional civil service. However, taken together, Blair fell short of leading the 'great radical reforming government' which he had. Few prime ministers, and none from Labour, were blessed with such unrivalled opportunities, electoral, political and economic. Only in 2006–7 did Blair's agenda begin to crystallise as a coherent body of reform. But will his achievements endure?

Great prime ministers need to establish legacies that live on. This is where contemporary judgements are at their most provisional. It is not only Blair's Iraq legacy that is still wide open. So too is his 'war on terrorism', Afghanistan, climate change policy, and his handling of the Muslim question. It is yet to be shown whether his reforms to public services will endure and produce lasting benefits, and whether the extra money pumped in since 2000 will have proved of little lasting benefit. Britain is certainly a more economically competitive country in 2007 than it was in

1997, and in some ways it is more socially just and tolerant too. But longer-term analysis will be needed before one can fully measure the impact of Blair on Britain. It is thus not fully clear how he will look in twenty-five years.

What of his mistakes? His greatest weakness was his reluctance to stand up to powerful figures. Essentially a kind and courteous man, he had neither the toughness nor the ruthlessness required for a truly great leader. His reshuffles were often shambolic and he was not always a good judge of character. He was at his weakest in standing up to President Bush, to the exasperation of many in his entourage. He was deeply imbued with the notion that Britain's interests dictated that it worked closely with Washington at all costs, and refrain from criticising in public. Blair made some headway with Bush on climate change and Africa, but little on the conduct of the Iraq War, or the Middle East Peace Process. He did not bargain or suggest his support was conditional. Too often, he was thus taken for granted.

Why did he not achieve more earlier on? Blair was still young when he became Prime Minister, aged only forty-three, and he had never served as a government minister. Neither had his most senior colleagues. He had no idea how to run a government, and thought he could run it as he had the Labour Party from 1994 to 1997: heavy on communication, light on policy and process. He was forced to appoint a number of Labour Party figures, such as Frank Dobson to Health, whose politics were anathema to him. When from 1999 he was able to promote his own figures more, he was restricted by the lack of able Blairites. Shortly after the 2001 general election, he told the four Secretaries of State appointed to his four top priority departments, Alan Milburn at Health, Stephen Byers at Transport, David Blunkett at the Home Office and Estelle Morris at Education, that he wanted to keep them there for the full second term. None survived. Mandelson proved unsteady, as did another Blairite, Stephen Byers. It was indicative that as his government ended in June 2007, there were only three 'Blairite' reforming ministers in major departments: John Reid at the Home Office, John Hutton at Work and Pensions and Andrew Adonis at Education, and the last was only a junior minister.

Blair's first significant appointment after he was elected party leader in July 1994 was hugely indicative. It was not a policy chief, as most leaders would have chosen, but a media chief, Alastair Campbell. He did not appoint a policy supremo until after he arrived in No. 10, and then selected a young lightweight in terms of understanding Whitehall, David

Miliband, who was never a full Blairite. His economic adviser, Derek Scott, was not a figure to match the heavy artillery around Brown and in the Treasury.

Domestically, Blair's premiership only began to take off in 2001, after a critical mass of like-minded figures coalesced in No. 10: Adonis on education, Simon Stevens on health, Jeremy Heywood as principal private secretary and John Birt as his 'blue skies' thinker operating across domestic policy. Adonis, Miliband's successor as policy chief, was to become the most influential figure on Blair domestically (as Jonathan Powell was to be on foreign and Northern Ireland policy). More than anyone, Adonis was responsible for helping Blair define his 'choice and diversity' agenda. But the second term was handicapped by a weak manifesto in 2001 and a lack of thinking beforehand in the run-up to the election. It was hard for Adonis, Stevens and Heywood to devise policy on the hoof, especially when only three months into his second term came 9/11. Dealing with Afghanistan and the build-up of the Iraq War took much of Blair's attention from late 2001 to early 2003, and the war and its aftermath took much of his political capital subsequently. Determined to avoid the mistakes of his first and second terms, in 2004 he appointed Milburn and Birt separately to help devise the third-term strategy, a fissiparous process which nevertheless resulted in the 2005 manifesto being the most detailed and 'programmatic' of the three. With his mind at last clear about what he wanted, with a strong No. 10 and some effective ministers running departments, he was able to drive policy through in 2005–7, despite repeated attempts from the Brown camp to destabilise him.

Blair should be seen in history as Labour's most successful party leader. The fact that in his last few months in power both Gordon Brown and David Cameron came to embrace much of his public service reform agenda is highly significant But for the Iraq War, he might have been considered one of the great prime ministers, on a par with Attlee and Thatcher. The irony is that Iraq saw him at his most courageous (some thought intransigent) and principled. To the end he maintained that his decisions were in Britain's interests. Given his character and beliefs, the Iraq War had a certain inevitability about it. Had he not taken those decisions, he would not have been the man that he was. One can only judge Blair as he was, and Iraq was the authentic Blair.

BIBLIOGRAPHY

Abreu, D. and Pearce, D., 'Bargaining, Reputation and Equilibrium Selection in Repeated Games with Contracts', *Econometrica*, 75, 2007: 653–710.

Aghion, P. and Howitt, P., *Endogenous Growth Theory* (Cambridge, MA: MIT Press, 1998).

Anderson, Bridget, Ruhs, Martin, Rogaly, Ben and Spencer, Sarah, *Fair Enough? Central and Eastern European Migrants in Low Wage Employment in the UK* (York: Joseph Rowntree Foundation, 2006).

Atkinson, A. B., *Public Economics in Action: The Basic Income/Flat Tax Proposal* (Oxford: Oxford University Press, 1995).

Aylwin-Foster, Brigadier Nigel, 'Changing the Army for Counterinsurgency Operations', *Military Review*, November–December 2005.

Bacevich, Andrew, *American Empire* (Cambridge MA: Harvard University Press, 2002).

Bache, Ian, *Europeanization and Multi-level Governance: Cohesion Policy in the European Union and Britain* (New York: Rowman and Littlefield, forthcoming).

Bache, Ian and George, Stephen, *Politics in the European Union*, 2nd edn (Oxford: Oxford University Press, 2006).

Bache, Ian and Jordan, Andrew (eds.), *The Europeanization of British Politics* (Basingstoke: Palgrave Macmillan, 2006).

Baker, Bruce, 'The African Post-Conflict Policing Agenda in Sierra Leone', *Conflict, Security and Development*, 6(1), 2006: 25–49.

Barber, Michael, *The Learning Game* (London: Victor Gollancz, 1996).

    Instruction to Deliver: Tony Blair, the Public Services and the Challenge of Delivery (London: Politico's, 2007).

Barnett, Steven and Gaber, Ivor, *Westminster Tales: The Twenty-first-century Crisis in Political Journalism* (London: Continuum, 2001).

Bartle, John, 'The Labour Government and the Media', in J. Bartle and A. King (eds.), *Britain at the Polls 2005* (Washington DC: CQ Press, 2006).

Beckett, Francis and Henke, David, *The Blairs and their Court* (London: Aurum, 2004).

Beecham, J., 'Heading Back to the Silo', *Public Finance*, 21–27 March 2003.

Behrendt, Christina, *At the Margins of the Welfare State: Social Assistance and the Alleviation of Poverty in Germany, Sweden and the United Kingdom* (Aldershot: Ashgate, 2002).

Berkeley, Nigel, Donnelly, Tom, Morris, David and Donnelly, Martin, 'Industrial Restructuring and the State: The Case of MG Rover', *Local Economy*, 20, 2005: 360–71.

Berman, Sheri, *The Primacy of Politics: Social Democracy and the Making of Europe's Twentieth Century* (Cambridge: Cambridge University Press, 2006).

Bevir, Mark and Rhodes, R. A. W., 'Prime Ministers, Presidentialism and Westminster Smokescreens', *Political Studies*, 54, 2006: 671–90.

Bird, Karen, 'Gendering Parliamentary Questions', *British Journal of Politics and International Relations*, 7, 2005: 353–70.

Blair, Tony, *Socialism* (London: Fabian Society, 1994).

   New Britain: My Vision of a Young Country (London: Fourth Estate, 1996).

   Leading the Way: A New Vision for Local Government (London: IPPR, 1998).

   The Third Way: New Politics for the New Century (London: Fabian Society, 1998).

   'Beveridge Revisited: A Welfare State for the 21st Century', in Robert Walker (ed.), *Ending Child Poverty: Popular Welfare for the 21st Century* (Bristol: Policy Press, 1999).

   The Courage of our Convictions: Why Reform of the Public Services Is the Route to Social Justice (London: Fabian Society, 2002).

   A Global Alliance for Global Values (London: Foreign Policy Centre, 2006).

   'A Battle for Global Values', *Foreign Affairs*, 86(1), 2007: 90.

Bosanquet, Nick, *A Successful National Health Service* (London: Adam Smith Institute, 1999).

Bottoms, Anthony, 'Empirical Research Relevant to Sentencing Frameworks', in A. Bottoms, S. Rex and G. Robinson (eds.), *Alternatives to Prison* (Cullompton: Willan, 2004).

Bourles, Renaud and Cette, Gilbert, 'Les évolutions de la productivité "structurelle" du travail dans les principaux pays industrialisés', *Bulletin de la Banque de France*, 150, 2006: 23–30.

Bovaird, Tony and Russell, Ken, 'Civil Service Reform in the UK , 1999–2005: Revolutionary Failure of Evolutionary Success?' *Public Administration*, 85, 2007: 301–28.

Brazier, Alex, Flinders, Matthew and McHugh, Declan, *New Politics, New Parliament? A Review of Parliamentary Modernisation since 1997* (London: Hansard Society, 2005).

Brealey, R., Goodhart, C., Healey, J., Hoggarth, G., Shu, C. and Sinclair, P., *Financial Stability and Central Banks* (London: Routledge, 2001).

Bresnahan, Timothy, Brynjolfsson, Erik and Hitt, Lorin, 'Information Technology, Workplace Organization and the Demand for Skilled Labor: Firm-level Evidence', *Quarterly Journal of Economics*, 117, 2002: 339–76.

Brewer, Mike, Goodman, Alissa, Muriel, Alistair and Sibieta, Luke, *Poverty and Inequality in the UK: 2007* (London: Institute for Fiscal Studies, 2007).

Burch, Martin and Holliday, Ian, 'The Blair Government and the Core Executive', *Government and Opposition*, 39, 2004: 1–21.

Butler, David and Kavanagh, Dennis, *The British General Election of 1997* (Basingstoke: Macmillan, 1997).

The British General Election of 2001 (Basingstoke: Palgrave, 2002).

Butler, David, Adonis, Andrew and Travers, Tony, *Failure in British Government: The Politics of the Poll Tax* (Oxford: Oxford University Press, 1994).

Campbell, Alistair, *The Blair Years: Extracts from the Alastair Campbell Diaries* (London: Hutchinson, 2007).

Card, D. and Krueger, A., *Myth and Measurement: The New Economics of the Minimum Wage* (Princeton, NJ: Princeton University Press, 1997).

Castles, Stephen, 'Why Migration Policies Fail', *Ethnic and Racial Studies*, 27(2), 2004.

Chakrabati, Shami, 'Rights and Rhetoric: The Politics of Asylum and Human Rights Culture in the United Kingdom', *Journal of Law and Society*, 32(1), 2005.

Childs, Sarah, *New Labour's Women MPs: Women Representing Women* (London: Routledge, 2004).

Childs, Sarah and Withey, Julie, 'Do Women Sign for Women? Sex and the Signing of Early Day Motions in the 1997 Parliament', *Political Studies*, 52, 2004: 552–64.

Childs, Sarah, Lovenduski, Joni and Campbell, Rosie, *Women at the Top 2005: Changing Numbers, Changing Politics* (London: Hansard Society, 2005).

Clarke, Harold D., Sanders, David, Stewart, Marianne C. and Whiteley, Paul, *Political Choice in Britain* (Oxford: Oxford University Press, 2004).

Clarke, Michael, 'The Diplomacy that Led to War in Iraq', in Paul Cornish (ed.), *The War in Iraq, 2003* (London: Macmillan, 2004).

Collier, Ute, '"Windfall" Emissions Reductions in the UK', in Ute Collier and Ragnar Löfstedt (eds.), *Cases in Climate Change Policy, Political Reality in the European Union* (London: Earthscan Publications, 1997).

Commission for Africa, *Our Common Interest* (London: Penguin, 2005).

Cooper, Robert, *The Breaking of Nations* (London: Atlantic Books, 2004).

Cowley, Philip, *Revolts and Rebellions: Parliamentary Voting under Blair* (London: Politico's, 2002).

The Rebels: How Blair Mislaid his Majority (London: Politico's, 2005).

Cowley, Philip and Childs, Sarah, 'Too Spineless to Rebel? New Labour's Women MPs', *British Journal of Political Science*, 33, 2003: 345–65.

Cox, Michael, 'American Power before and after September 11', in R. Singh (ed.), *Governing America: The Politics of a Divided Democracy* (Oxford: Oxford University Press, 2003).

Crafts, Nicholas, 'Regulation and Productivity Performance', *Oxford Review of Economic Policy*, 22, 2006: 186–202.

Crafts, Nicholas and O'Mahony, Mary, 'A Perspective on UK Productivity Performance', *Fiscal Studies*, 22, 2001: 271–306.

Crawford, Adam, *Crime Prevention and Community Safety* (Harlow: Longman, 1998).

Crowson, Nicholas J., *The Conservative Party and European Integration since 1945: At the Heart of Europe?* (London: Routledge, 2006).

Curran, James, Gaber, Ivor and Petley, Julian, *Culture Wars: The Media and the British Left* (Edinburgh: Edinburgh University Press, 2005).

Curtice, J., 'The Electoral System: Biased to Blair?', *Parliamentary Affairs*, 54, 2001: 803–14.

'New Labour, New Protest? How the Liberal Democrats Profited from Blair's Mistakes', *Political Quarterly*, 78, 2007: 117–27.

Curtice, J. and Fisher, S., 'The Power to Persuade? A Tale of Two Prime Ministers', in A. Park, J. Curtice, K. Thomson, L. Jarvis and C. Bromley (eds.), *British Social Attitudes, The 20th Report: Continuity and Change over Two Decades* (London: Sage, 2003).

Curtice, J. and Park, A., 'Region: New Labour, New Geography?', in G. Evans and P. Norris (eds.), *Critical Election: British Parties and Voters in Long-Term Perspective* (London: Sage, 1999).

Daalder, Ivo H., *Getting to Dayton: The Making of America's Bosnia Policy* (Washington DC: Brookings Institution Press, 2000).

Daachev, Alex, '"I'm with You": Tony Blair and the Obligations of Alliance', in C. Lloyd *et al.* (eds.), *Iraq and the Lessons of Vietnam* (New York: The New Press, 2007).

Darcy, M. and Mclean, R., *Nightmayor* (London: Politico's, 2000).

Darkin, Beverley, 'Pledges, Politics and Performance: An Assessment of UK Climate Policy', *Climate Policy*, 6(3), 2006: 257–74.

Davies, Paul and Freedland, Mark, *Towards A Flexible Labour Market – Labour Legislation and Regulation since the 1990s* (Oxford: Oxford University Press, 2007).

Davis, Aeron, *Public Relations Democracy: Public Relations, Politics and the Mass Media in Britain* (Manchester: Manchester University Press, 2002).

Deacon, David, Golding, Peter and Billig, Michael, 'Press and Broadcasting: "Real Issues" and Real Coverage', *Parliamentary Affairs*, 54, 2001: 666–78.

Dell, Edmund, *A Strange Eventful History: Democratic Socialism in Britain* (London: HarperCollins, 2000).

Dickens, Linda and Hall, Mark, 'Fairness – Up to a Point. Assessing the Impact of New Labour's Employment Legislation', *Human Resource Management Journal*, 16(4), 2006.

Dickens, Richard, Gregg, Paul and Wadsworth, Jonathan, *The Labour Market under New Labour* (London: Palgrave 2003).

Donohue, John and Siegelman, Peter, 'Allocating Resources among Prisons and Social Programs in the Battle against Crime', *Journal of Legal Studies*, 27(1), 1998: 1–43.

Doob, Anthony and Webster, Cheryl, 'Countering Punitiveness: Understanding Stability in Canada's Imprisonment Rate', *Law and Society Review*, 40(2), 2006.

Doppelhofer, G., Miller, R. and Sala-i-Martin, X., 'Determinants of Long-Term Growth: A Bayesian Averaging of Classical Estimates (Bace) Approach', *American Economic Review*, 94, 2004: 813–35.

Dorman, Andrew, *Defence under Thatcher* (London: Palgrave, 2002).

Draper, Derek, *Blair's Hundred Days* (London: Faber and Faber, 1997).

Driver, R. and Westaway, P., 'Concepts of Equilibrium Exchange Rates', in R. Driver, P. Sinclair and C. Thoenissen (eds.), *Exchange Rates, Capital Flows and Policy* (London: Routledge, 2005).

Driver, Sean and Martell, Luke, *New Labour* (Cambridge: Polity, 2006).

Dunleavy, Patrick, 'Facing up to Multi-party Politics', *Parliamentary Affairs*, 58, 2005: 503–32.

Evans, Andrew. A., 'Rail Safety and Rail Privatisation', *Significance*, 4(1), 2007.

Evans, G. and Heath, A., 'The Measurement of Left–Right and Libertarian–Authoritarian Scales: Comparing Balanced and Unbalanced Scales', *Quality and Quantity*, 29, 1995: 191–206.

Evans, G., Heath, A. and Payne, C., 'Labour as a Catch-All Party?', in G. Evans and P. Norris (eds.), *Critical Election: British Parties and Voters in Long-Term Perspective* (London: Sage, 1999).

Fairclough, Norman, *New Labour, New Language* (London: Routledge, 2000).

Fielding, Steven, *The Labour Party: Continuity and Change in the Making of New Labour* (London: Palgrave, 2002).

Finlay, Fergus, *Snakes and Ladders* (Dublin: New Island Books, 1998).

Finlayson, Alan, 'Elements of the Blairite Image of Leadership', *Parliamentary Affairs*, 55, 2002: 586–99.

Fitzgerald, Marian, Stockdale, Jan and Hale, Chris, *Young People and Street Crime* (London: Youth Justice Board, 2003).

Foley, Michael, *The British Presidency* (Manchester: Manchester University Press, 2000).

 John Major, Tony Blair and a Conflict of Leadership (Manchester: Manchester University Press, 2002).

Foster, Christopher D., *British Government in Crisis* (Oxford: Hart Publishing, 2005).

Franklin, Bob, 'The Hand of History: New Labour, News Management and Governance', in S. Ludlam and M. J. Smith (eds.), *New Labour in Government* (Basingstoke: Macmillan, 2001).

Freedman, Lawrence, 'Victims and Victors: Reflections on the Kosovo War', *Review of International Studies*, 26(3), 2000.

Gaber, Ivor, 'Lies, Damn Lies . . . and Political Spin', *British Journalism Review*, 11(1), 2000: 60–70.

Garland, David, *The Culture of Control* (New York: Oxford University Press, 2001).

George, Stephen, *An Awkward Partner: Britain in the European Community*, 3rd edn (Oxford: Oxford University Press, 1998).

Georgi, Giacomo, 'The New Deal for Young People Five Years On', *Fiscal Studies*, 26(3), 2005: 371–83.

Glaister, Stephen, 'British Rail Privatisation – Competition Destroyed by Politics', Occasional Paper 23 (Bath: Centre for Regulated Industries, 2005).

Glaister, Stephen and Graham, Dan, *National Road Pricing: Is it Fair and Practical?* (London: Social Market Foundation, 2006).

Glaister, Stephen and Travers, Tony, *Governing the Underground: Funding, Management and Democracy for London's Tube* (Bath: Centre for Regulated Industries, 1997).

Glaister, Stephen, Scanlon, Rosemary and Travers, Tony, *Getting Partnerships Going: Public Private Partnerships in Transport* (London: Institute for Public Policy Research, 2000).

Goodman, Alissa and Webb, Steve, *For Richer, For Poorer: The Changing Distribution of Income in the United Kingdom 1961–1991* (London: Institute for Fiscal Studies, 1994).

Gordon, Michael and Trainor, Bernard, *Cobra II: The Inside Story of the Invasion and Occupation of Iraq* (London: Atlantic Books, 2006).

Gordon, Philip H. and Shapiro, Jeremy, *Allies at War: America, Europe and the Crisis over Iraq* (New York: McGraw-Hill, 2004).

Gould, Philip, *The Unfinished Revolution: How the Modernisers Saved the Labour Party* (London: Little, Brown, 1998).

Gray, John, *After Social Democracy: Politics, Capitalism and the Common Life* (London: Demos, 1996).

Greer, Scott L., *Territorial Politics and Health Policy: UK Health Policy in Comparative Perspective* (Manchester: Manchester University Press 2004).

Griffith, Rachel, Redding, Stephen and van Reenen, John, 'Measuring the Cost-effectiveness of an R & D Tax Credit for the UK', *Fiscal Studies*, 22, 2001: 375–99.

Gust, C. and Marquez, J., 'International Comparisons of Productivity Growth: The Role of Information Technology and Regulatory Practices', *Labour Economics*, 11, 2004: 33–58.

Hagerty, Bill, 'Cap'n Spin *Does* Lose his Rag', *British Journalism Review*, 11(2), 2000: 7–20.

Hall, R. and Jones, C., 'The Value of Life and the Rise in Health Spending', *Quarterly Journal of Economics*, 122, 2007: 39–72.

Harfield, Clive, 'SOCA: A Paradigm Shift in British Policing', *British Journal of Criminology*, 46(4), 2006.

Hay, Colin, *The Political Economy of New Labour: Labouring under False Pretences* (Manchester: Manchester University Press, 1999).

Hazell, Robert (ed.), *The State of the Nations 2003: The Third Year of Devolution in the United Kingdom* (Exeter: Imprint Academic, 2003).

Healey, Denis, 'Why the Treasury is so Difficult', in H. Davies (ed.), *The Chancellors' Tales: Managing the British Economy* (Cambridge: Polity, 2006).

Heath, A., Jowell, R. and Curtice, J., *The Rise of New Labour: Party Policies and Voter Choices* (Oxford: Oxford University Press, 2001).

Heffernan, Richard, *New Labour and Thatcherism: Political Change in Britain* (London: Palgrave, 2001).

'Why the Prime Minister Cannot Be a President: Comparing Institutional Imperatives in Britain and America', *Parliamentary Affairs*, 58, 2005: 53–70.

Hennessy, Peter, *The Prime Minister* (London: Penguin, 2001).

Whitehall, rev. edn (London: Secker and Warburg, 2001).

'Rulers and Servants of the State: The Blair Style of Government 1997–2004', *Parliamentary Affairs*, 58, 2005: 6–16.

Hill, Richard, *The Labour Party and Economic Strategy, 1979–97* (Basingstoke: Palgrave, 2001).

Hills, John, *Inequality and the State* (Oxford: Oxford University Press, 2004).

Hills, John and Stewart, Kitty (eds.), *A More Equal Society? New Labour, Poverty, Inequality and Exclusion* (Bristol: Policy Press, 2005).

Hirsch, Donald, 'Welfare In Work: The Missing Link in Welfare Reform', in Kate Bell (ed.), *Staying On, Stepping Up: How Can Employment Retention and Advancement Policies be Made to Work for Lone Parents?* (London: One Parent Families, 2006).

What Will it Take to End Child Poverty? Firing on all Cylinders (York: Joseph Rowntree Foundation, 2006).

Hoffman, Stanley, *World Disorders: Troubled Peace in the Post-Cold War Era* (New York: Rowman and Littlefield, 1998).

Hough, Mike, Jacobson, Jessica and Millie, Andrew, *The Decision to Imprison: Sentencing and the Prison Population* (London: Prison Reform Trust, 2003).

Hyman, Peter, *1 out of 10: From Downing Street Vision to Classroom Reality* (London: Vintage, 2005).

Inklaar, Robert, O'Mahony, Mary and Timmer, Marcel, 'ICT and Europe's Productivity Performance: Industry-level Growth Account Comparisons with the United States', *Review of Income and Wealth*, 51, 2005: 505–36.

Jenkins, S., *Big Bang Localism – A Rescue Plan for British Democracy* (London: Policy Exchange, 2004).

Johnson, Joy, 'Rupert's Grip?', *British Journalism Review*, 9(1), 1998: 13–19.

Johnston, R., Pattie, C., Dorling, D. and Rossiter, D., *From Votes to Seats: The Operation of the UK Electoral System since 1945* (Manchester: Manchester University Press, 2001).

Johnston, Ron, Cowley, Philip, Pattie, Charles and Stuart, Mark, 'Voting in the House or Wooing the Voters at Home: Labour MPs and the 2001 General Election Campaign', *Journal of Legislative Studies*, 8, 2002: 9–22.

Jones, Janet, *Labour of Love* (London: Politico's, 1999).

Jones, Bill, Kavanagh, Dennis, Moran, Michael and Norton, Philip, *Politics UK*, 6th edn (Harlow: Pearson, 2006).

Jones, Nicholas, *Soundbites and Spin Doctors* (London: Cassell, 1995).

    Sultans of Spin (London: Victor Gollancz, 1999).

    The Control Freaks (London: Politico's, 2001).

Jordan, Andrew, 'Environmental Policy', in P. Dunleavy, A. Gamble, I. Holliday and G. Peele (eds.), *Developments in British Politics 6* (Basingstoke: Macmillan, 2000).

    'Is There a Climate for Policy Change? The Contested Politics of a Low Carbon Economy', *Political Quarterly*, 72(2), 2001: 249–54.

    'Decarbonising the UK: A "Radical Agenda" from the Cabinet Office?', *Political Quarterly*, 73(3), 2002: 344–52.

Kampfner, John, *Blair's Wars* (London: The Free Press, 2004).

Karmen, Andrew, *New York Murder Mystery* (New York: New York University Press, 2000).

Katz, Richard and Mair, Peter, 'The Ascendancy of the Party in Public Office: Party Organisational Change in Twentieth Century Democracies', in R. Gunther, J. R. Montero and J. Linz (eds.), *Political Parties: Old Concepts and New Challenges* (Oxford: Oxford University Press, 2002).

Kavanagh, Dennis and Butler, David, *The British General Election of 2005* (Basingstoke: Palgrave, 2005).

Kelso, Alexandra, ' "Where Were the Massed Ranks of Parliamentary Reformers?" – "Attitudinal" and "Contextual" Approaches to Parliamentary Reform', *Journal of Legislative Studies*, 9, 2003: 57–76.

Kennedy-Pipe, Caroline and Rengger, Nicholas, 'Apocalypse Now? Continuity or Disjunctions in World Politics after 9/11', *International Affairs*, 82(3), 2006: 540.

Keohane, Dan, *Security in British Politics, 1945–99* (London: Macmillan, 2000).

King, Anthony, 'Conclusions and Implications', in A. King (ed.), *Leaders' Personalities and the Outcomes of Democratic Elections* (Oxford: Oxford University Press, 2002).

King, David A., 'Climate Change Science: Adapt, Mitigate, or Ignore?', *Science*, 9, 2004: 176–7.

Kneller, Richard, Bleaney, Michael and Gemmell, Norman, 'Fiscal Policy and Growth: Evidence from OECD Countries', *Journal of Public Economics*, 74, 1999: 171–90.

Laffan, Martin and Shaw, Eric, 'British Devolution and the Labour Party: How a National Party Adapts to Devolution', *British Journal of Politics and International Relations*, 9, 2007: 55–72.

Lagos, R. and Wright, R., 'A Unified Framework for Monetary Theory and Policy Analysis', *Journal of Political Economy*, 113, 2005: 463–84.

Lambeth, Benjamin S., *NATO's Air War for Kosovo* (Santa Monica, CA: RAND, 2001).

Laws, David and Marshall, Paul (eds.), *The Orange Book – Reclaiming Liberalism* (London: Profile Books, 2004).

Lees-Marchment, Jennifer, *Political Marketing and British Political Parties: The Party's Just Begun* (Manchester: Manchester University Press, 2001).

Lloyd, John, *What the Media Are Doing to our Politics* (London: Constable, 2004).

Loader, Ian, 'Fall of the "Platonic Guardians": Liberalism, Criminology and Political Responses to Crime in England and Wales', *British Journal of Criminology*, 46(4), 2006.

Loader, Ian and Mulcahy, Aoghan, *Policing and the Condition of England* (Oxford: Oxford University Press, 2003).

Loader, Ian and Walker, Neil, *Civilizing Security* (Cambridge: Cambridge University Press, 2007).

Lovenduski, Joni, *Feminizing Politics* (Cambridge: Polity, 2005).

Ludlam, Steve and Smith, Martin J. (eds.), *Governing as New Labour: Policy and Politics under Blair* (London: Palgrave, 2004).

Maguire, M., Morgan, R. and Reiner, R. (eds.), *The Oxford Handbook of Criminology*, 4th edn (Oxford: Oxford University Press, 2007).

Mandelbaum, Michael, *The Ideas that Conquered the World: Peace, Democracy and Free Markets in the Twenty-first Century* (New York: Public Affairs, 2002).

Mandelson, Peter and Liddle, Roger, *The Blair Revolution: Can New Labour Deliver?* (London: Faber and Faber, 1996).

Mansell, Warwick, *Education by Numbers: The Tyranny of Testing* (London: Politico's, 2007).

Marshall, A. and Finch, D., *City Leadership Giving City-Regions the Power to Grow*, Centre for Cities (London: IPPR, 2006).

Massey, Andrew and Pyper, Robert, *Public Management and Modernisation in Britain* (Houndmills, Basingstoke: Palgrave Macmillan, 2005).

McCallum, J., 'National Borders Matter: Canada–US Regional Trade Patterns', *American Economic Review*, 85, 1995: 615–23.

McLean, Iain, 'Scotland: Towards Quebec or Slovakia?', *Regional Studies*, 35, 2001: 637–44.

   The Fiscal Crisis of the United Kingdom (Basingstoke: Palgrave, 2005).

McLean, Iain and McMillan, Alistair, *State of the Union* (Oxford: Oxford University Press, 2005).

McNair, Brian, *Journalism and Democracy* (London: Routledge, 2000).

Micklewright, John and Stewart, Kitty, *The Welfare of Europe's Children: Are EU Member States Converging?* (Bristol: Policy Press, 2000).

Miliband, David, 'Red-Green Labour in Power', *Fabian Review*, 119(1), 2007: 16–17.

Millar, Frank, *David Trimble: The Price of Peace* (Dublin: Liffey Press, 2004).

Mishkin, F. S., *The Next Great Globalization: How Disadvantaged Countries Can Harness their Financial Systems to Get Rich* (Princeton, NJ: Princeton University Press, 2006).

Misra, Amalendu, 'Afghanistan: The Politics of Post-war Reconstruction', *Conflict, Security and Development*, 2(3), 2002: 5–27.

Moloney, Ed, *A Secret History of the IRA* (Harmondsworth: Penguin/Allen Lane, 2002).

Morgan, Rod, 'With Respect to Order, the Rules of the Game Have Changed: New Labour's Dominance of the "Law and Order" Agenda', in Tim Newburn and Paul Rock (eds.), *The Politics of Crime Control: Essays in Honour of David Downes* (Oxford: Clarendon Press, 2006).

Mulgan, Geoff, and Bury, Fran, *Double Devolution: The Renewal of Local Government* (London: Smith Institute, 2006).

Naughtie, James, *The Rivals* (London: Fourth Estate, 2001).

Neil, Andrew, *Full Disclosure* (London: Pan, 1997).

Newburn, Tim, ' "Tough on Crime": Penal Policy in England and Wales', in M. Tonry and A. Doob (eds.), *Crime and Justice 36* (Chicago: University of Chicago Press, 2007).

Newburn, Tim and Jones, Trevor, 'Symbolising Crime Control: Reflections on Zero Tolerance', *Theoretical Criminology*, 11(2), 2007.

Nickell, Stephen, 'Competition and Corporate Performance', *Journal of Political Economy*, 104, 1996: 724–46.

Norrbin, Stefan and Yigit, Pinar, 'The Robustness of the Link Between Volatility and Growth of Output', *Review of World Economics*, 144, 2005: 343–56.

Norton, Philip, 'Cohesion without Discipline: Party Voting in the House of Lords', *Journal of Legislative Studies*, 9, 2003: 57–72.

'Governing Alone', *Parliamentary Affairs*, 56(4), 2003: 543–59.

O'Mahony, Mary and Robinson, Catherine, 'UK Growth and Productivity in International Perspective: Evidence from EU KLEMS', *National Institute Economic Review*, 200, 2007: 79–86.

O'Riordan, Tim and Rowbotham, Elizabeth J., 'Struggling for Credibility: The United Kingdom's Response', in T. O'Riordan and J. Jäger (eds.), *Politics of Climate Change, A European Perspective* (London: Routledge, 1996).

O'Shaughnessy, James (ed.), *The Leadership Effect: Can Headteachers Make a Difference?* (London: Policy Exchange, 2007).

O'Shaughnessy, Nicholas Jackson, *Politics and Propaganda* (Manchester: Manchester University Press, 2004).

Oborne, Peter, *Alastair Campbell: New Labour and the Rise of the Media Class* (London: Aurum, 1999).

Oborne, Peter and Walters, Simon, *Alastair Campbell* (London: Aurum, 2004).

Osmond, John (ed.), *Labour's Majority in Doubt: Monitoring the National Assembly December 2004 to April 2005* (Cardiff: IWA and London: Constitution Unit 2005).

Packer, George, *The Assassin's Gate: America in Iraq* (New York: Farrar, Straus and Giroux, 2005).

Park, A., Curtice, J., Thomson, K., Phillips, M. and Johnson, M. (eds.), *British Social Attitudes, The 23rd Report: Perspectives on a Changing Society* (London: Sage, 2007).

Payne, Anthony, 'Blair, Brown and the Gleneagles Agenda', *International Affairs* 82(5), 2006: 934–5.

Persson, Torsten and Tabellini, Guido, *The Economic Effects of Constitutions* (Cambridge, MA: MIT Press, 2005).

Pesaran, H., Smith, V. and Smith, R. (2007), 'What if the UK or Sweden had Joined the Euro in 1999? An Empirical Evaluation Using a Global VAR', *International Journal of Finance and Economics*, 12, 2007: 55–87.

Peston, Robert, *Brown's Britain* (London: Short Books, 2005).

Pimlott, B. and Rao, N., *Governing London* (Oxford: Oxford University Press, 2002).

Pittock, A. Barrie, *Climate Change, Turning up the Heat* (Collingwood, New South Wales: CSIRO Publishing, 2005).

Plant, Raymond, 'Crosland, Equality and New Labour', in Dick Leonard, *Crosland and New Labour* (London: Macmillan, 1999).

Porteous, Tom, 'British Government Policy in Sub-Saharan Africa under New Labour', *International Affairs* 81(2), 2005: 292–4.

Powell, A., 'The Argentine Crisis: Bad Luck, Bad Management, Bad Policies, Bad Advice', in *Brookings Trade Forum* (Washington DC: Brookings Institution Press, 2003).

Preston, Gabrielle (ed.), *A Route out of Poverty? Disabled People, Work and Welfare Reform* (London: Child Poverty Action Group, 2006).

Price, Lance, *The Spin Doctor's Diary* (London: Hodder and Stoughton, 2005).

Quinn, Thomas, 'Electing the Leader: The British Labour Party's Electoral College', *British Journal of Politics and International Relations*, 6, 2005: pp. 333–52.

Ramsbotham, Alex, Bah, Alhaji M. S. and Calder, Fanny, 'Enhancing African Peace and Security Capacity: A Useful Role for the UK and the G8?' *International Affairs* 81(2), 2005: 325–39.

Rawnsley, Andrew, *Servants of the People: The Inside Story of New Labour* (London: Penguin, 2000).

Reiner, Robert, *The Politics of the Police*, 3rd edn (Oxford: Oxford University Press, 2000).

  Law and Order: An Honest Citizen's Guide to Crime and Control (Cambridge: Polity, 2007).

Rhodes, Rod, *The Civil Service* in A. Seldon (ed.), *The Blair Effect* (London: Little, Brown, 2001), pp. 97–116.

Richards, David, *New Labour and the Civil Service: Reconstituting the Westminster Model* (Houndmills, Basingstoke: Palgrave Macmillan, 2007).

Ricks, Thomas E., *Fiasco: The American Military Adventure in Iraq* (New York: Penguin, 2006).

Rocheteau, G. and Wright, R., 'Money in Competitive Equilibrium, in Search Equilibrium, and in Competitive Search Equilibrium', *Econometrica*, 73, 2005: 175–202.

Rose, A., 'One Money, One Market: Estimating the Effect of Common Currencies on Trade', *Economic Policy*, 30, 2000: 7–45.

Rose, Richard, *The Prime Minister in a Shrinking World* (London: Polity, 2001).

Rosenblatt, Gemma, *A Year in the Life: From Member of Public to Member of Parliament* (London: Hansard Society, 2006).

Roth, Andrew, 'The Lobby's "Dying Gasps"?', *British Journalism Review*, 10(3), 1999: 21–5.

Rubin, Barnett R., 'Saving Afghanistan', *Foreign Affairs* 86(1), 2007: 66.

Russell, Meg, *Building New Labour: The Politics of Party Organization* (London: Palgrave, 2005).

Rush, M. and Giddings, P. (eds.), *The Palgrave Review of British Politics 2005* (London: Palgrave, 2006).

The Palgrave Review of British Politics 2006 (London: Palgrave, 2007).

Ryan, Mick, *Penal Policy and Political Culture in England and Wales* (Winchester: Waterside Press, 2003).

Scott, Derek, *Off Whitehall* (London: I. B. Taurus, 2004).

Seldon, Anthony (ed.), *The Blair Effect: The Blair Government 1997–2001* (London: Little, Brown, 2001).

Blair (London: The Free Press, 2004; 2nd edn 2005).

Seldon, Anthony and Kavanagh, Dennis (eds.), *The Blair Effect 2001–5* (Cambridge: Cambridge University Press, 2005).

Seymour-Ure, Colin, 'Newspapers: Editorial Opinion in the National Press', in P. Norris and N. Gavin (eds.), *Britain Votes 1997* (Oxford: Oxford University Press, 1997).

Prime Ministers and the Media (Oxford: Blackwell, 2003).

Shaw, Eric, *The Labour Party since 1979: Crisis and Transformation* (London: Routledge, 1994).

'New Labour in Britain: New Democratic Centralism?' *West European Politics*, 25, 2002: 147–70.

'The Control Freaks? New Labour and the Party', in Steve Ludlam and Martin J. Smith (eds.), *Governing as New Labour: Policy and Politics under Blair* (London: Palgrave, 2004).

Short, Clare, *An Honourable Deception* (London: The Free Press, 2004).

Simms, Brendan, *Unfinest Hour: Britain and the Destruction of Bosnia* (London: Penguin, 2001).

Simon, Jonathan, *Governing Through Crime* (New York: Oxford University Press, 2007).

Sinclair, P., 'On the Optimum Trend of Fossil Fuel Taxation', *Oxford Economic Papers*, 46, 1994: 869–77.

'The Optimum Rate of Inflation: An Academic Perspective', *Bank of England Quarterly Bulletin*, 43, 2003: 343–51.

Smith, Julie, 'A Missed Opportunity? New Labour's European Policy 1997–2005', *International Affairs*, 81(4), 2005: 703–21.

Smith, Julie and Tsatsa, Mariana, *The New Bilateralism: The UK's Bilateral Relations Within the EU* (London: Royal Institute of International Affairs, 2002).

Smithers, Alan, *England's Education: What Can Be Learned by Comparing Countries?* (London: The Sutton Trust, 2004).

Blair's Education: An International Perspective (London: The Sutton Trust, 2007).

Smithers, Alan and Robinson, Pamela, *Physics in Schools and Colleges: Teacher Deployment and Student Outcomes* (Buckingham: Carmichael Press, 2005).

School Headship: Present and Future (London: National Union of Teachers, 2005).

Smookler, Jennifer, 'Making a Difference? The Effectiveness of Pre-Legislative Scrutiny', *Parliamentary Affairs*, 59, 2006: 522–35.

Solomon, Enver, Eades, Chris, Garside, Richard and Rutherford, Max, *Ten Years of Criminal Justice under Labour: An Independent Audit* (London: Centre for Crime and Justice Studies, 2007).

Somerville, Will, *Immigration under New Labour* (Bristol: Policy Press, 2007, forthcoming).

Sones, Bonnie, Moran, Margaret and Lovenduski, Joni, *Women in Parliament: The New Suffragettes* (London: Politico's, 2005).

Spelman, William, 'The Limited Importance of Prison Expansion', in A. Blumstein and J. Wallman (eds.), *The Crime Drop in America* (New York: Cambridge University Press, 2000).

Spencer, Sarah, *Strangers and Citizens: A Positive Approach to Migrants and Refugees* (London: Rivers Oram, 1994).

The Politics of Migration: Managing Opportunity, Conflict and Change (Oxford: Blackwell, 2003).

Spencer, Sarah, Ruhs, Martin, Anderson and Bridget, Rogaly, Ben, *Migrants' Lives Beyond the Workplace: Central and East Europeans in the UK* (York: Joseph Rowntree Foundation, 2007).

Sriskandarajah, D., Cooley, L. and Reed, L., *Paying their Way: The Fiscal Contribution of Migrants in the UK* (London: IPPR, 2005).

Stern, Sir Nicholas, *The Economics of Climate Change* (Cambridge: Cambridge University Press, 2006).

Stevens, Robert, *The English Judges* (Oxford: Hart Publishing, 2002).

Strauss-Kahn, Dominique, 'What is a Just Society? For a Radical Reformism', in Peter Mandelson *et al.*, *Where Now for European Social Democracy?* (London: Policy Network, 2004).

Sutherland, Holly, *Poverty in Britain: The Impact of Government Policy since 1997. An Update to 2004–5 Using Microsimulation* (Cambridge: Microsimulation Unit, University of Cambridge, 2004).

Symeonidis, George, 'The Effect of Competition on Wages and Productivity', *Review of Economics and Statistics* (forthcoming).

Taylor, Cyril and Ryan, Conor, *Excellence in Education: The Making of Great Schools* (London: David Fulton Publishers, 2005).

Taylor, Miles, 'Labour and the Constitution', in Duncan Tanner, Pat Thane and Nick Tiratsoo (eds.), *Labour's First Century* (Cambridge University Press, 2000).

Taylor, Robert, *Britain's World of Work – Myths and Reality* (London: Economic and Social Research Council, 2002).

  'Margaret Thatcher's Conservative Party – Midwife of the New Labour Project', *Socialist History*, 27, 2005.

  The Delusion of the British Business Model (London: Renewal, 2006).

Tomlinson, Sally, *Education in a Post-Welfare Society* (Buckingham: Open University Press, 2001).

Tonry, Michael, *Punishment and Politics* (Cullompton: Willan, 2004).

  Thinking about Crime (New York: Oxford University Press, 2005).

Tonry, Michael and Farrington, David P., *Crime and Punishment in Western Countries, 1980–1999* (Chicago: University of Chicago Press, 2005).

Travers, T., *The Politics of London: Governing an Ungovernable City* (Basingstoke: Palgrave Macmillan, 2004).

Travers, T. and Glaister, S., *Local Transport: How Small Reforms Could Make a Big Difference* (London: Local Government Association, 2006).

Trench, Alan (ed.), *Has Devolution Made a Difference? The State of the Nations 2004* (Exeter: Imprint Academic, 2004).

Tsebelis, George, *Veto Players: How Political Institutions Work* (Princeton, NJ: Princeton University Press, 2002).

Tunney, Sean, *Labour and the Press: From New Left to New Labour* (Brighton: Sussex Academic Press, 2007).

Tymms, Peter, 'Are Standards Rising in English Primary Schools?' *British Educational Research Journal*, 30, 2004: 477–94.

Wallace, William, 'The Collapse of British Foreign Policy', *International Affairs*, 82(1), 2005: 53–68.

Webb, Paul, 'Party Responses to the Changing Electoral Market in Britain', in P. Mair, W. Muller and F. Plasser (eds.), *Political Parties and Electoral Change* (London: Sage, 2004).

Whitaker, Richard, 'Ping-Pong and Policy Influence: Relations Between the Lords and Commons, 2005–06', *Parliamentary Affairs*, 59, 2006: 536–45.

Woodward, Bob, *Bush at War* (New York: Simon and Schuster, 2002).

Plan of Attack (New York: Simon and Schuster, 2004).

State of Denial: Bush at War, Part III (New York: Simon and Schuster, 2006).

Wright, Tony, 'Prospects for Parliamentary Reform', *Parliamentary Affairs*, 57, 2004: 867–76.

Wring, Dominic, *The Politics of Marketing the Labour Party* (Basingstoke: Palgrave Macmillan, 2005).

Zedner, Lucia, 'Too Much Security?', *International Journal of the Sociology of Law*, 31(1), 2003.

Zimring, Franklin, *The Great American Crime Decline* (New York: Oxford University Press, 2007).

INDEX

climate change (*cont.*)
   tax instruments, 578–9, 582, 586, 587
Climbié, Victoria, 372
Clinton, Bill
   Blair and, 540, 601–2, 641
   development aid, 553
   European policy, 596
   Kosovo intervention, 624
   Major and, 596
   New Labour model, 324, 333
   Northern Ireland and, 513, 521
   welfare to work, 208
coalition governments, 497–9, 500
Cocker, Jarvis, 464
Cohen, Jane, 292
Coke, Edward, 313
Collins, Lawrence, 297–8
Colombia, 197
Communism, 167
competition
   EU and UK convergence, 545–6
   health service, 387, 388, 399, 402,
      452
   importance, 286
   policy, 278–9
Congo (DRC), 560, 608
Conservatives
   1950s, 172–3
   1997 legacy, 3, 182
   2005 elections, 445
   accepting New Labour agenda,
      14–15
   arts policy, 461
   backbench rebellions, 27
   Blair impact on, 163, 642
   climate change, 573–4, 575, 592
   Conference, 155
   constitutional status quo, 104, 105
   defence, 617–18, 622
   devolution, 489–90, 492, 503
   economic legacy, 171, 223
   economic reputation, 37, 47, 52
   education, 361, 362, 366, 369, 371,
      376, 377, 378, 380
   electoral record, 36, 38, 39–40
   energy policy, 580
   EU policy, 192, 530–1, 535, 542, 545,
      595, 601, 633

   foreign policy, 593–7, 610
   governance, 84
   health service, 5
   immigration, 341, 342
   industrial policy, 279, 285
   international aid, 551, 552, 556
   law and order, 318–19, 320, 329
   leaders, 144
   local government, 56, 57, 62
   Northern Ireland, 513, 516
   poll tax, 489
   press support, 129, 130, 131, 132
   public opinion, 39, 450
   public services, 436–8, 443
   rail privatisation, 247, 250, 252
   sleaze, 4, 11, 128, 445–6
   taxation, 201
   trade unions, 219
   transport policy, 242
   universities, 469–70, 477, 480, 481
constitutional reform
   2005 Act, 293–5
   assessment, 115–22
   Blair detachment, 121–2
   consensus, 4
   delivery, 107–14
   European Union and, 547–8
   Labour manifesto, 104–7
   lack of coherence, 119–20
   Smith's legacy, 105–6, 116, 121
   undelivered promises, 115–16
   unintended consequences, 116–19
consultants, 206, 251, 253, 254, 260,
      269, 270
control orders, 117–18
Conway, Paul, 463
Cook, Robin, 13, 18, 20, 21, 128, 155,
      160, 553, 619, 620
'Cool Britannia', 463
Corn Laws, 26
Corrigan, Paul, 9
Costello, Elvis, 463
Cotis, Jean-Philippe, 285, 286
Council of Europe, 547
council tax, 61, 70, 71, 73, 76, 201, 505
counter-terrorism. *See* war on terror
Cranborne, Lord, 109, 516
Cridland, John, 230, 233